# RIGOS PRIMER

## CPA EXAM REVIEW

## FINANCIAL ACCOUNTING

## QUESTIONS AND ANSWERS

## 2021 EDITION

### Table of Contents

Course 5292 Copyright 2021. The Rigos programs have educated over 100,000 professionals since 1980.

# INTRODUCTION TO FINANCIAL ACCOUNTING AND REPORTING

## 2021 Edition Contents

## INTRODUCTION TO FINANCIAL ACCOUNTING AND REPORTING

### I.    OVERVIEW:  PREPARING FOR AND TAKING THE CPA EXAMS

#### A.  <u>Welcome and Introduction</u>

Welcome to the 2021 Financial Accounting and Reporting section of the Rigos Primer Series® CPA Exam Review for the AICPA's current subject matter content outline.  The Rigos Primer Series® programs have over 150,000 alumni who successfully used our material in preparing for their professional entrance exams success.

#### B.  <u>Overview of Program</u>

This program contains everything you need to pass the American four CPA exam sections by taking our live affiliated classes or by preparing on your own using our inexpensive but effective home-learning program.  Please study the guidance in this preface in detail; the information contained herein is highly helpful to the success of your preparation program.

#### C.  <u>Our Former Students' Comments</u>

*"I cannot imagine attempting to take the rigorous entrance exam without a review course. ...I found your materials to be top notch.  The text was organized, well written, concise, up to date and comprehensive.  If provided sound advice...., and suggested strategies about how best to study.  There is no doubt in my mind that the Rigos Primer Series program was a large helpful factor in my Gold Medal award on the exam." – Mark Lyons, Sybase, Inc.*

*"The class material and instruction were excellent, and I have told many of my colleagues about the Rigos Primer Series Review Program.  It works well." – Marie K. O'Malley, Bard Cardiopulmonary.  Silver medal for second highest score on the exam*

*"Outstanding material!  I scored the #3 score in the U.S.A. on the exam.  A great course but it does take time and a serious study effort.  Tell your students this Primer Series program works well if they work at it.  Thanks." – Don Waddell, Willamette Industries.*

#### C.  <u>Positive Mental Attitude</u>

What the mind can conceive, hard work can achieve.  You must believe you can and you will pass the exam and become a successful CPA!  Your objective of passing the exam is very attainable simply by using our "seamless process".  We have over 100,000 professional alumni who have passed with us.  Exam confidence is simply the result of a well-organized and well-executed preparation program.  Candidates following our program are geared for exam success.

#### D.  <u>When to Take the Exam</u>

The exams test the knowledge and skill used by newly licensed CPAs primarily in public accounting firms.  The subjects tested are usually taught in the accounting program of quality business schools.  The exam is essentially an intellectual exercise similar to college examinations. Therefore, a candidate should ideally begin working through the exam sections during the fifth year of their university studies.  In most states you may sit within 120 days of graduation. However, if you have been out of school for years, don't be discouraged.  You have valuable experience applying the principles which are tested on the exam and covered in this text.

## II.    EXAM ORIENTATION

The 2021 CPA Exam contains questions requiring higher-order critical thinking skills such as "analysis, problem-solving, and expressions of professional skepticism and judgment". Data analytics is testable in 2021. Candidates should check https://www.aicpa.org/becomeacpa.html for the most current official information. All four parts of the CPA exam are computerized and are to be separately taken "on demand" at a Prometric Technology Testing Center

There are four two-month "windows" a year in which a candidate may take any of the four sections. Only one sitting for a section is allowed in a window. There is a one-month period in between each window for AICPA analysis when exams are not offered. A candidate is allowed six windows (18 months) to complete all four sections. The per part pass rate has risen to over 45% per part taken. Over 90% of candidates passed the section after one or two attempts.

### A   Exam Sections

| 2021 CBT-e Exam (16 Total Hours) |
| --- |
| Auditing & Attestation (4.0 hours) |
| Financial Accounting & Reporting (4.0 hours) |
| Regulation (4.0 hours) |
| Business Environment & Concepts (4.0 hours) |

### B.  Examination Blueprint

The 4-hour Financial Accounting and Reporting section is distributed in our review book as follows:

| Subject | Chapter | FAR Weight |
| --- | --- | --- |
| Theoretical Foundations and Balance Sheet Overview | FA-1 | 5-10% |
| Balance Sheet Assets | FA-2 | 8-12% |
| Receivables and Inventories | FA-3 | 8-12% |
| Balance Sheet Liabilities | FA-4 | 8-12% |
| Special Topics: Pensions; OPEB; Alternative Financial Accounting Models; Foreign Exchange; and Segment Reporting | FA-5 | 5-10% |
| Owners' Equity and Partnership Accounting | FA-6 | 8-12% |
| Income Statement | FA-7 | 10-15% |
| Statement of Cash Flows | FA-8 | 5-10% |
| Consolidations | FA-9 | 5-10% |
| Income Tax Accounting and Other Topics | FA-10 | 5-10% |
| Governmental Accounting | FA-11 | 8-12% |
| Not-for Profit Organizations | FA-12 | 8-12% |

The CBT-e contains:

**1.  IFRS Addition:** One of the most significant additions is that the International Financial Reporting Standards (IFRS) are now testable. CPAs may need to be bi-lingual because American GAAP is not required outside the U.S. We have updated our texts to include the significant differences.

**2. Ethics and Attest Independence:** The AICPA recodified Code of Professional Conduct is now testable on the Audit exam. A new set of ethical provisions apply to CPAs employed in business and industry. The professional ethical standards of conflicts of interest, and audit attestation independence impairment rules have substantially increased under the new AICPA "risk evaluation" procedures. The remainder of the AICPA's "recodification" of Professional Responsibility (ethics restraints) are tested in Regulation.

## CSOs – FAR

| AREA | Summary of CSOs |
|------|-----------------|
| I | Concepts and Standards for Financial Statements (17-23%) |
| II | Typical Items: Recognition, Measurement, Valuation, and Presentation in Financial Statements in Conformity with GAAP (27-33%) |
| III | Specific Types of Transactions and Events: Recognition, Measurement, Valuation, and Presentation in Financial Statements in Conformity with GAAP (27-33%) |
| IV | Accounting and Reporting for Governmental Entities (8-12%) |
| V | Accounting and Reporting for Non-Governmental Not-for-Profit Organizations (8-12%) |

## C. Schedule of Exams Availability to January 1, 2021

| Exam Window | January 1 – March 10 | April 1 – June 10 | July 1 – September 10 | October 1 – December 10 |
|-------------|----------------------|-------------------|-----------------------|-------------------------|
| Analysis Period | March 11 – March 31 | June 11 – June 30 | September 11 – September 30 | December 11 – December 31 |

## D. Exam Format

The exam (CBT-e) in 2021 consists of 4.0 hours for each section.

| Section | Multiple Choice | Task-Based Simulations | Written Communication |
|---------|-----------------|------------------------|-----------------------|
| AUD -Auditing & Attestation (4.0 hours) | 50% of Exam 2 Testlets 72 Questions Total | 50% of Exam 3 Testlets 8 Short Task-Based Simulations | n/a |
| FAR - Financial Accounting & Reporting (4.0 hours) | 50% of Exam 2 Testlets 66 Questions Total | 50% of Exam 3 Testlets 8 Short Task-Based Simulations | n/a |
| REG Regulation (4.0 hours) | 50% of Exam 2 Testlets 76 Questions Total | 50% of Exam 3 Testlets 8 Short Task-Based Simulations | n/a |
| BEC - Business Environment & Concepts (4.0 hours) | 50% of Exam 2 Testlets 62 Questions Total | 35% of Exam 2 Testlets 4 Short Task-Based Simulations | 15% of Exam 1 Testlet 3 Written Communication Tasks |

**1. Multiple-Choice:** Each multiple-choice testlet will include questions from all the subjects in the Examination Blueprint of the section. Recommendations for high performance on the multiple-choice questions are provided later in this preface. Adaptive multiple-choice testing allows the examiners to increase or decrease the difficulty level of the next testlet presented to the candidate. Thus, the difficulty of testing of the individual candidate is in part dependent upon their performance during the whole exam. If you "draw" a difficult testlet be happy, it probably means you did very well on the previous testlet.

**2. Task-Based Simulations:** Simulations are increased to 8 short tasks contained in three testlets. The short tasks are independent of each other and may not use a common set of facts. Thus, candidates should expect the tasks to cover a wider range of topics than in the prior exam format. Tutorials are now available on the AICPA CPA exam web site which we advise students to study for the most current application.

All of the tasks are designed to demonstrate application of the body of knowledge. Examples include: spreadsheet calculations, completion of sections of tax returns, matching lists, selecting multiple responses to a question, and conducting research in authoritative literature. Additional details are provided later in this preface.

**3. Written Communication Simulations:** In 2021 written communications simulations are tested only on the BEC section of the exam. Candidates will be required to type three task-based business communications. Candidates should practice using the AICPA word processing software, which includes a spell check function. To become proficient tutorials are now available on the CPA exam web site at https://www.aicpa.org/becomeacpa/cpaexam.html.

## III. GETTING STARTED

The CPA examination is administered at certain of the Prometric Technologies Testing Centers throughout the United States, American territories, and a growing number of foreign countries. Continuous testing will begin on January 1, 2021. You should make all your exam arrangements before you begin preparing for the section(s) you intend to pass in that particular window. It is recommended you begin the registration process at least 60 days before the week you want to take the exam. International site testing locations continue to grow.

### A. Register to Sit for Exam

Your first preparation step is to apply to sit for the exam with your state Board of Accountancy or their authorized representative. We suggest you go to the below website of your Board of choice and research their specific requirements and application forms.

| State | Website Address | Telephone Number |
|---|---|---|
| Alabama | http://www.asbpa.alabama.gov/ | 334-242-5700 |
| Alaska | https://www.commerce.alaska.gov/web/cbpl/professionallicensing/boardofpublicaccountancy.aspx | 907-4653811 |
| Arizona | https://www.azaccountancy.gov/ | 602-364-0900 |
| Arkansas | http://www.asbpa.arkansas.gov/ | 501-682-1520 |
| California | www.dca.ca.gov/cba | 916-263-3680 |
| Colorado | https://www.colorado.gov/pacific/dora/Accountancy | 303-894-7800 |
| Connecticut | http://www.ct.gov/sboa/guestaccount/login.asp | 860-509-6179 |
| Delaware | http://dpr.delaware.gov/boards/accountancy/ | 302-744-4500 |
| District of Columbia | http://www.pearsonvue.com/dc/accountancy/ | 202-442-4461 |
| Florida | http://www.myfloridalicense.com/DBPR/cpa/index.html | 352-333-2500 |
| Georgia | http://sao.georgia.gov/gsba | 478-207-1400 |
| Guam | http://www.guamboa.org/ | 671-477-1050 |
| Hawaii | http://cca.hawaii.gov/pvl/boards/accountancy/ | 808-586-2696 |
| Idaho | https://isba.idaho.gov/ | 208-334-2490 |
| Illinois | http://www.ilboe.org/ | 815-753-8900 |

| Indiana | http://www.in.gov/pla/accountancy.htm | 317-234-8800 |
|---|---|---|
| Iowa | https://plb.iowa.gov/board/accountants | 515-281-4126 |
| Kansas | www.ksboa.org | 785-296-2162 |
| Kentucky | http://cpa.ky.gov/Pages/default.aspx | 502-595-3037 |
| Louisiana | www.cpaboard.state.la.us | 504-566-1244 |
| Maine | http://www.maine.gov/pfr/professionallicensing/professions/accountants/ | 207-624-8603 |
| Maryland | http://www.dllr.state.md.us/license/cpa/ | 410-230-6258 |
| Massachusetts | http://www.mass.gov/ocabr/licensee/dpl-boards/pa/ | 617-727-1806 |
| Michigan | http://www.michigan.gov/lara/0,4601,7-154-72600_72602_72731_72855---,00.html | 517-241-9249 |
| Minnesota | www.boa.state.mn.us | 651-296-7938 |
| Mississippi | http://www.msbpa.ms.gov/Pages/Home.aspx | 601-354-7320 |
| Missouri | http://pr.mo.gov/accountancy.asp | 573-751-0012 |
| Montana | http://boards.bsd.dli.mt.gov/pac | 866-350-0017 |
| Nebraska | http://www.nbpa.ne.gov/ | 402-471-3595 |
| Nevada | www.nvaccountancy.com | 775-786-0231 |
| New Hampshire | http://www.oplc.nh.gov/accountancy/ | 603-271-2219 |
| New Jersey | http://www.njconsumeraffairs.gov/acc/Pages/default.aspx | 973-504-6380 |
| New Mexico | http://www.rld.state.nm.us/boards/accountancy.aspx | 505-222-9850 |
| New York | http://www.op.nysed.gov/prof/cpa/ | 518-474-3817 ext. 160 |
| North Carolina | https://nccpaboard.gov/ | 919-733-4224 |
| North Dakota | https://www.nd.gov/ndsba/ | 800-532-5904 |
| Ohio | www.acc.ohio.gov | 614-466-4135 |
| Oklahoma | https://www.ok.gov/oab_web/ | 405-521-2397 |
| Oregon | http://www.oregon.gov/BOA/Pages/index.aspx | 503-378-4181 |
| Pennsylvania | http://www.dos.pa.gov/ProfessionalLicensing/BoardsCommissions/Accountancy/Pages/default.aspx | 717-783-1404 |
| Puerto Rico | https://estado.pr.gov/en/authorized-public-accountants/ | 787-722-4816 |
| Rhode Island | http://www.dbr.state.ri.us/divisions/accountancy/ | 401-462-9500 |
| South Carolina | http://www.llr.state.sc.us/POL/Accountancy/ | 803-896-4770 |
| South Dakota | http://dlr.sd.gov/accountancy/default.aspx | 605-367-5770 |
| Tennessee | https://www.tn.gov/commerce/section/accountancy | 615-741-2550 |
| Texas | www.tsbpa.state.tx.us | 512-305-7800 |
| Utah | http://www.dopl.utah.gov/licensing/accountancy.html | 801-530-6628 |
| Vermont | https://www.sec.state.vt.us/professional-regulation/list-of-professions/accountancy.aspx | 802-828-2373 |
| Virgin Islands | http://dlca.vi.gov/businesslicense/steps/cparequirements/ | 340-718-6982 |
| Virginia | http://www.boa.virginia.gov/ | 804-367-8505 |
| Washington | www.cpaboard.wa.gov | 360-753-2586 |
| West Virginia | http://www.boa.wv.gov/Pages/default.aspx | 304-558-3557 |
| Wisconsin | http://dsps.wi.gov/Boards-Councils/Board-Pages/Accounting-Examining-Board-Main-Page/ | 608-266-5511 |
| Wyoming | https://sites.google.com/a/wyo.gov/wyoming-cpa/ | 307-777-7551 |

## B. Authorization Letter and NTS

Upon acceptance, the candidate will receive an authorization letter, payment coupon to be sent with the required fee, and instructions to schedule your sitting with Prometrics Testing Center. The Notice to Schedule (NTS) will designate a 120-day window period during which time you are eligible to take the exam. This period will cover two "windows." If you do not schedule to sit within this stipulated time period you will have to re-enroll.

Go to https://www.aicpa.org/membership/join.html?tab-1=5 after you receive the Notice to Schedule. Sign up on this website for the AICPA's discounted subscription to professional audit and accounting literature. Included are <u>AICPA Professional Standards</u> and <u>FASB Original Pronouncements</u>.

## C. Testing Centers Location List

Please contact Prometric Testing Centers at 1-800-479-6370 or visit their website at https://www.prometric.com/en-us/clients/cpa/Pages/landing.aspx to find the location with the necessary equipment nearest you. There is an online scheduler application available on the Prometric website. Prometric continues to add centers on an on-going basis as candidates grow – especially international locations. Try to register for the time of the day when you are normally the most mentally alert and focused. Schedule your exam place, date, and time as early as possible.

## IV.     YOUR PERSONAL PREPARATION PROGRAM

### A. Organized Approach

It is very important that your preparation program be well-organized. The better organized, the more effective and efficient your individual effort will be. To be competitive you must master every topic tested in the exam section you are taking. You should also study defensively by spending more time on your weak areas. Our exam section texts contain from 8 to 12 topical module chapters plus the preface for each section of the exam. Use the weekly calendars at the end of this preface to organize your daily routine so that your preparation time is given a priority. The goal is to prepare as efficiently and effectively as possible.

### B. Necessary Time Commitment

To be competitive, candidates must realize that a significant time commitment is necessary. The typical learning and question-answer review exercises effort expended by most successful first-time candidates is 80 to 100 hours per section. Recent top accounting graduates may find less time is adequate; candidates who have been away from academia for long periods will find more time is required. You must go beyond feeling comfortable with the subjects. As a result, a candidate must be ready to commit to a serious preparation effort.

### C. Part-By-Part Concentration

Under the new exam format, you should consider preparing for each section separately. If you concentrate on studying for only one section and pass it before starting on the next, your intensity and performance should increase.

### D. A Few Study Tips

**1. Preview Before the Main Learning Exposure:** Before the actual review session spend a little time going through the material to be covered. The more of a foundation you can build, the more productive the learning session will be for you.

**2. The Main Learning Exposure:** Pay careful attention in your subject-by-subject learning sessions. Use colored highlighters to underline key topics and make margin notes that will personalize the text. This involvement reinforces the key concepts while you read the text.

**3. Prepare Your Magic Memory Outlines®:** After completing the learning session exposure, the student should capture the essence of the text by using key words to complete their own Magic Memory Outlines®. This synthesis can be done on the paper at the beginning of every chapter, or by using the Rigos software templates. This technique allows the creation of your own small book to assist in memorizing the principles and processes. The objective is that the textual material becomes a part of your psyche so that exam recall is instantaneous.

**4. Work Old Questions:** You need practice to develop the ability to effectively master the CPA solution approach. This involves working thousands of old questions and answers under exam conditions. Our texts contain over 3,000 questions and answers at the same level or more difficult than the actual CPA Exam. Our question maps show you how the exam tests the rules. You need to gain experience working questions on a computer screen rather than on paper. Do not neglect this aspect of your preparation program. Prepare defensively by working more old exam questions from your weak topics. Put a red mark alongside all questions you answered wrong. Learn from your mistakes. The AICPA exam website has additional questions and answers which should also be worked through by candidates.

**5. Alternate Study Topics:** Studying different subjects within the prep class session may add variety to your schedule. After covering a quantitative subject such as the cash flow statement, change to a philosophical subject such as accounting principles. By varying the topics of study, most students find they can concentrate at high levels for longer periods of time.

**6. Your Own Study Place:** Some candidates find that learning concentration and efficiency are improved if they use a new study place. This is especially helpful if you normally study in your home where there are interruptions and/or distractions. Turn off cell phones and text messaging while you are studying. Use a bright light and a firm chair to aid concentration.

**7. Review Personal and Professional Commitments:** The most precious commodity a serious CPA candidate has is time. Commitments must be reviewed and priorities established. This is not the time to volunteer for new assignments. Optional professional and social activities should be deferred. Schedule your study time on the weekly calendar at the end of this preface. Short-term sacrifices now will lead to long-term benefits. Tell your friends and associates that between now and the next exam, they will see less of you. You will be busy preparing for the CPA exam. There is life after passing the CPA exam.

**8. Last Minute Cram:** While some recommend avoiding last minute cramming, most accounting students survived in college because of it. The last night (and morning of exam day if you pick an afternoon time) are very fertile time periods. Read over the Magic Memory Outlines® you have prepared and the hundreds of acronyms in the Primer Series text. Finally, look over all the questions you missed during your preparation.

## E. Motivational and Inspirational Tools

Candidates should be disciplined, motivated, and persistent in keeping their preparation program on schedule. You must approach your review with enthusiasm, sincerity and determination. Be the best you can be; go for the gusto. The CPA certificate is your stepping stone to professional accounting recognition. Your spouse, family, friends and other CPAs with whom you are associated should reinforce your sense of purpose.

## F. A Sound Mind in a Sound Body

Good health practices can assist you in efficiently studying and effectively writing the exam. Get plenty of sleep so you can concentrate at your highest level. Three square meals a day will keep your energy level high; avoid junk food which produces a letdown feeling and sluggish thinking. Regular exercise helps you think clearly and work harder.

## V.     EXAM PROCEDURES

### A. Be Punctual

Candidates should plan to arrive early at the designated Prometric center exam-site at least 30 minutes before the scheduled starting time. Avoid hurrying or arriving late because it is disconcerting and may adversely affect your composure. Check in at the registrar's desk. Look over the facilities and rest room locations. If you have transportation problems, consider a hotel near the exam location.

### B. Test Center Procedures

**1. Admission Card:** Candidates should bring to the exam site the written instructions from Prometric and the Notice to Schedule (NTS) admission card provided by the State Board. Also bring two pieces of backup identification with your signature, preferably a valid driver's license. One of the pieces must contain a current picture of you.

**a. NTS Reprint:** NASBA's National Candidate Database (NCD) has implemented an on-line service that allows you to download and reprint your Notice to Schedule (NTS). You will no longer need to contact NASBA to request a reprint of your NTS. The free service is available to candidates in all jurisdictions that have an open NTS. Previously attended or expired NTSs are not available for reprint.

**b. Other Helpful Instructions:** Additional instructions for reprinting your NTS include: the Jurisdiction ID numbers are on most score notices, and Texas, California and Virginia candidates' ID numbers contain both letters and numbers. Candidates can reprint their Notice to Schedule directly at https://ncd.nasba.org/gwprdv2/servlet/hgwcnr01.

**2. Comfort and Practicality:** Dress comfortably in whatever outfit makes you feel good and mentally sharp. You must place all your personal belongings, including cell phones, in a storage locker. Some locations allow you to bring a cushion to soften the chairs if you like. Some candidates who are easily distracted bring earplugs. The computer room may have 20 or more people operating at other screens. Prometric provides earplugs in some locations but they may be out of stock; the prudent action may be to bring your own.

**3. Technical Supplies:** You need to sign in and they will take your picture at the Center. The Prometric center staff will give you pencils and numbered scratch paper which must be turned in at the end of the exam.

**4. Snacks:** Food and beverages are not allowed in the exam room. Do not consume a large meal or massive liquids just before the exam. Unnecessary bathroom breaks waste time and break your concentration. Go for small amounts of light food that provide energy and is easy to digest (raisins, peanuts, energy bars), but that does not make you feel tired.

## C. Exam Procedures

**1. Relax and Contemplate:** Consciously attempt to relax; deep, slow breathing will facilitate this mental state. Don't talk or communicated with other candidates in the exam room. It is too late to add anything to your knowledge and any distraction will only confuse your objective. If other candidates near you are bothering you, complain to the testing room monitor and demand a different seat. Relax and loosen-up. Prepare yourself mentally to go for every grading point.

**2. Follow Instructions:** Read carefully the instructions on the computer program introduction screens. Go through the introductory exam tutorial drill at least once. Go through again, if you like, to be sure you understand the procedures and "look and feel" of the new exam. If you spend over 25 minutes on the 5 introductory screens you will "time out" and will not be allowed to go forward. The allowed maximum time period for each section starts only when you push "begin." Carefully budget your time and pace.

**3. Confidence and Poise:** Get psyched up to make the CPA exam your finest intellectual effort. Approach the exams with mental confidence and poise. Don't get discouraged. At least one-third of your competitors have not followed a thorough review program and are really in the exam "for practice." These people leave early because they don't recognize the issues.

**4. Preserve Your Mental Energy:** Get a full night's sleep before you take the exam. Fight to keep mentally sharp for the whole exam session.

**5. Focus on the Task:** During the exam session, the only thing in the world that matters is your performance on this exam. Personal problems should be left outside the exam room. The U.S. stock market may crash; stay focused on your task at hand.

**6. Exam Breaks:** You may, but are not required to, take breaks after each testlet is completed and leave the room. Half-way through the session there is an optional 15-minute break that stops the clock. If you so elect you must sign out on the test center log book when you leave the exam room. When you return from the break you must enter your examination password in order to continue. Keep any breaks short and don't communicate with your neighbors. This level of exam is not a casual social experience and the danger is that you may lose the intellectual competitive mental edge by taking a break.

**7. Time Management:** You need to monitor your time both within and across all the testlets. Don't leave any questions unanswered because you cannot go back to a prior testlet. It is important to work as quickly as possible without sacrificing thoroughness and accuracy.

## D. Score Reporting

Your exam results are compiled by the AICPA testing division and sent to NASBA one month after the last day of the two-month window. NASBA then sends the result to your State Board for distribution. Accelerated score reporting is possible for candidates sitting in the first month of the testing window. The AICPA continues to expedite the grades to the candidates in order to facilitate a quicker all-part completion period. Contact your State Board of Accountancy for their respective score release process and dates.

## E. Score Appeal

The AICPA has re-score and appeal procedures for candidates who do not pass. The AICPA cautions, however, that these procedures "very seldom result in score changes." Our experience is similar, particularly because the current exam objective format leaves little for discretion.

## VI. OBJECTIVE MULTIPLE-CHOICE QUESTIONS

50% of each exam testing is now four-stemmed multiple-choice questions. Questions are continually added to freshen up the question test base. Potential questions are contributed by practitioners, educators, students and the staff of the AICPA Examination Department. These are reviewed on a section-by-section basis by a specialized committee. The AICPA Examination Board of Regents approves the final questions and answer rationales. This process reduces or eliminates ambiguities or technical errors and ensures that the final CPA examination itself is high quality, well balanced, technically accurate, relevant, and fair.

### A. General Comments and Pitfalls

**1. Format and Time Management:** Every question in the testlet counts the same and there is no subtraction for wrong answers. All levels of testlet difficulty (A through C) are represented. The more difficult the testlet the higher the relative weight given for correct answers. Be careful to manage your time as you proceed through the testlets. Some of the most difficult C level questions may take a longer necessary time to work through. If a particular question is giving you difficulty, either skip it or make your best educated guess and mark it for later review if there is time left.

**2. Try a True-False Approach:** For some questions it may help to use a true-false analysis for each of the four alternatives. This is especially useful for negative call questions (see item 4 below). Ideally you will end up with a 3-1 split; the odd man is usually the right answer.

**3. Preferred Answer Objective:** Look for the best answer alternative. This may mean the most nearly correct or conversely, the least incorrect answer. There is often some truth in each alternative. The best alternative must be completely correct. Watch out for incomplete definitions. Appreciate the difference between the command adverbs "may" and "shall"/"must".

**4. Negatives:** A few questions may have negatives in the facts, the requirements, or the alternatives. This means that the correct best choice is the worst, least helpful, least likely, or most false alternative. The candidate must reason carefully through the alternatives and reverse their normal frame of reference. The "true-false" approach discussed in item 2 above is often very helpful here. If looking for the negative, the false or incorrect alternative is the best choice.

**5. Absolutes:** Be on the alert for sweeping exclusionary words such as "all," "always," "none," "never," "under no circumstances," or "solely." Such broad words are usually in the question's fact pattern for a reason. Ask yourself, "Is there any exception?" The more narrow statement is usually preferred to a broad abstract alternative choice.

**6. Nonsense Theory:** Occasionally the CPA exam will create answer alternatives to represent a nonsense principle, concept, or theory such as "consumer expectation theory." A good rule of thumb is that such an alternative is wrong unless you have seen it expressly in our CPA review textbooks.

**7. Be Selective:** More facts or theory may be given in the question than is necessary. Red herrings are often added to the basic question facts to support one of the wrong alternatives. Also look for seemingly meaningless detail because such a reference may provide a necessary fact required for the application of a controlling legal rule. If dates are given, they are usually important for the correct question conclusion.

**8. Analyze Modifiers in the Alternatives:** Many answer alternatives begin with the conclusion (e.g. "This statement is true," or "This is the best course of action.") The conclusion is then followed by a conditioned or limiting modifying word ("because," "since," "if," "only if," or "unless") and a statement of a supporting authoritative reasoning or rationale.

    **a. "Because," "Since," or "As":** These conditional requirement modifiers indicate the following rationale is usually the reasoning necessary to satisfy the right conclusion. The reasoning must be consistent with the facts given in the question. The reasoning must also resolve the central controlling issue in the question.

    **b. "If" and "Only If":** This limiting modifier indicates the following rationale presented need only be possible under the facts; it is not required to be totally consistent as in "because" or "since." As such, the "if" modifier can – and usually does – go beyond the question facts to create a more compelling factual argument to support the conclusion. "Only if" is similar except it creates an exclusive condition to be satisfied. An "if" or "only if" modifier also requires you to reason through the other three alternatives to be sure there is not a better "if" or "only if" argument.

    **c. "Unless":** This conditional modifier usually has a rationale following that directly addresses more of the required reasoning than the other modifiers. This "unless" factual reasoning must be necessary for the application of the controlling principles. If there is any other reason or way that the result can occur, an "unless" alternative is incorrect. Reason through all the other alternatives to be sure there is not a better "unless" argument.

    **9. Remember Your Default Rules:** Some topics on the CPA multiple-choice questions are tested at a very deep "C" level of difficulty. The time necessary to analyze and answer such questions may not be efficient since often there is still intellectual certainty even after the effort. Rather try eliminating wrong answers to reduce the choice to two alternatives; this is the time to consider the following default rules. They provide a logical basis for an educated guess.

    **a. Longest Alternative:** Everything else being equal, the longer alternative in a narrative question is more likely to be the correct answer than a shorter alternative. A correct answer must contain all required information and reasoning necessary for the best choice; a fragmented short alternative is less attractive. This concept favors the more detailed alternative; this is usually the one containing the most words.

    **b. Precision:** Everything else being equal, the more precise the alternative in a narrative question the better. Vagueness is never encouraged in accounting exercises. The three incorrect alternatives in such a question often contain distracters to create confusion.

    **c. Not Unrelated Subject:** An alternative that includes another subject in a narrative question is usually wrong on the CPA exam. Only infrequently do questions crossover between subjects and almost never is the alternative which refers to the other subject the correct answer.

    **10. Calculation Questions:** More data may be given than is necessary to make the calculation. Dates are very important. Apply current pronouncements and statutory rules unless the question expressly specifies to the contrary. Always watch for red herrings and extraneous numerical data. The correct numerical answer is rarely a number given in the fact pattern; some calculation is necessary. If guessing, avoid the high and low values; a middle value is the safest default rule. "None of the above" or "some other number" is almost never the best alternative because this would reward mistakes.

## B.  Approach to Multiple-Choice Questions

**1.  Interrelationships:**  Occasionally, different sequential questions may use the same fact pattern.  The computer program may thus appear to repeat the facts even though it is a new question.

**2.  "Mask" Down:**  In a pencil-and-paper testing format, a good rule of thumb is to lay a mask over the alternatives, read the facts carefully, and try to determine the correct answer before you look at the options.  This is more difficult to do in a computerized testing environment.  However, it is still a good mental practice to consider the facts and four answer choices separately because reading the alternatives may cause you to misinterpret some aspect of the factual story.  This intellectual "masking" technique will usually facilitate a more thorough understanding of the question-answer structure.

**3.  Adopt Writer's Position:**  It may help to put yourself in the shoes of the question's writer.  Concentrate on the question requirements and/or the fact pattern to determine what the answer should be.  Then search for that answer among the alternatives.  Even if you see the answer you guessed or calculated, you should still briefly consider the other alternatives to make sure none seem more correct.

**4.  Disagreement:**  If your favorite answer is not one of the alternatives, check your math and the logic of your approach.  If they both seem correct, pick what appears to be the most reasonable choice.  This is usually the alternative closest to your computation.

**5.  Test Tutorial:**  Before you start the actual exam questions, go through the tutorial at least once. The present value tables can be accessed by hitting the EXHIBIT key.

**6.  First Time Through:**  Go through every question in the testlet in order.  The first time through, every question should be put into one of three categories.

**a.  Sure of Answer:**  If you are reasonably certain, answer the question and move on.

**b.  No Clue:**  If you have no clue or if it would take too long to work, skip it.  Do not get frustrated by the skipped questions or spend more than one minute on the facts before finally deciding to skip it.  Hit the NEXT→ key at the bottom of the screen.

**c.  Unsure?  Mark It:**  If you have some idea, but are still unsure which alternative is correct, make your best educated guess.  Answer the question, but MARK it so you can come back and go over it again, if time permits.  Don't get "bogged down."

**7.  Second Time Through:**  After you have gone through the whole testlet, go back to the beginning.

**a.  Do Skipped Questions First:**  The second time through, work the skipped ones first. Do not get hung up, and remember your default rules (longest narrative answer or middle value in a calculation question).  Delete the SKIP command and then hit the NEXT→ key.

**b.  Do Marked Questions Last:**  After the skipped questions are completed, go through the marked questions to determine if you see anything new.  The questions you have completed may have jogged your memory or otherwise given you good reason to believe an answer change is warranted.

**c.  Remaining Uncertainty:**  If after the second read the uncertainty is still present after your final review don't change your first judgment.  It is probably your best shot at the correct answer.

Course 5292 Copyright 2021.  The Rigos programs have educated over 100,000 professionals since 1980.

## C. Testing Computer Screen Diagram

A depiction of a testlet multiple-choice testing screen is presented below.

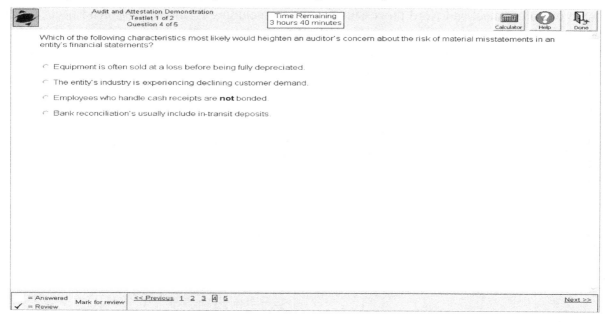

Prometric Technologies Testing Screen (Multiple Choice Questions)

## VII. TASK-BASED SIMULATIONS

In 2021, 50% of the AUD, FAR, and REG testlets of the exam use short task-based simulations focusing on work-related situations. Three testlets requiring the completion of a total of 8 tasks are required for each section except the BEC section that drops to 35% coverage and 4 tasks.

Relational case studies may require research, but the necessary research databases will be given on the screen. Many of these initial simulation questions are adaptations of the previous other-objective answer format (OOAF) questions involving pull-down screens. An example would be matching a list of items to another list or picking the best reason for a given outcome. Spreadsheets are likely to be used to test financial statement format.

### A. Sample Testing Screen

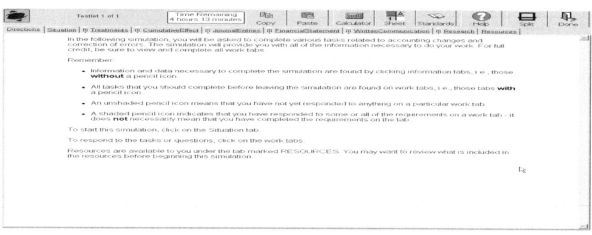

Prometric Technologies Testing Screen (Simulations)

## B. In General

**1. Basic Computer Skills:** CPA candidates are assumed to possess basic computer skills including the use of a mouse and keyboard. In addition they are expected to know how to use common spreadsheet and word processing functions, including formulae for spreadsheets. Note, however, that the word processor and spreadsheet applications in the examination are **not** identical to Microsoft Word™ or Excel™ features.

**2. Calculator and Spreadsheet:** Candidates must also have the ability to use a four-function calculator or a spreadsheet to perform standard financial calculations. During the exam, you can enter numbers on the online calculator by using the keyboard, or the keypad with the NumLock feature turned on. The calculator and spreadsheet features change periodically. Look for information about changes on the CPA exam web site (www.cpa-exam.org), and use the practice exams at to be sure you know how the features work.

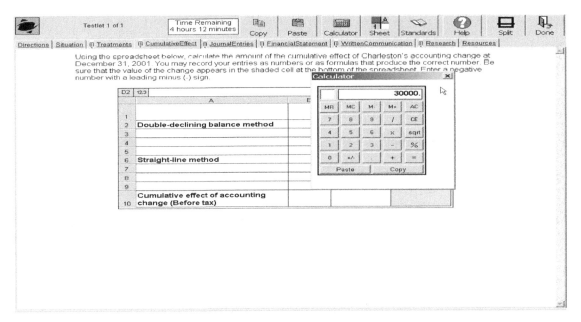

Prometric Technologies Testing Screen (Calculation Simulation)

| | Testlet Time Remaining 1 of 1  1 hours  20 minutes | Copy  Paste | Calculator Sheet | Standards |
|---|---|---|---|---|
| Help    Split    Done | | | | |

| Direction | Situation | ✎Cost Method | ✎Amt. to Rept. | ✎CO GS | ✎Invent Cost | ✎Form 1065 | ✎Co mm. | ✎Review Letter |
|---|---|---|---|---|---|---|---|---|
| | | | | | | | | |
| | | | | | | | | |
| | | | | | | | | |
| | | | | | | | | |
| | | | | | | | | |
| | | | | | | | | |
| | | | | | | | | |

Prometric Technologies Testing Screen (Spreadsheet Simulation)

**3. Best Resources:** Candidates will also be asked to use online authoritative literature in task-based simulations. The authoritative literature will be available for all tasks in a task-based simulation testlet. However, you should plan to use the literature only for tasks requiring research. There is insufficient time on the exam to conduct research for all tasks in a testlet.

The authoritative literature used in the CPA exam is updated periodically. For example, the FASB Accounting Standards Codification™ is now tested. This includes all the testable previous standards found in AICPA and FASB pronouncements. Check the exam website (https://www.aicpa.org/becomeacpa/cpaexam.html) for the most current information.

A tab on the simulation screen will allow you to access the authoritative literature.

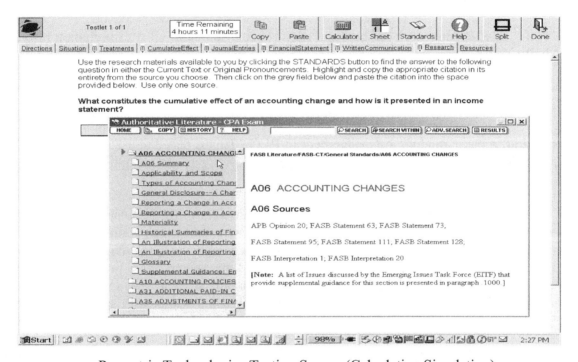

Prometric Technologies Testing Screen (Calculation Simulation)

**4. Research Task – New Format:** The candidate will first choose the authoritative source (e.g., "AU" for U.S. auditing standards). Then the computer will provide the candidate with input boxes that correspond with the selected authoritative source. Examples of this style of task are provided in the AUD, FAR, and REG sections of the Rigos textbooks. The most current tutorials are available on the CPA exam web site.

**5. Free 6-Month Subscription to Professional Literature:** When preparing for the CPA exam, candidates can obtain a free six-month online subscription to the AICPA Professional Standards releases. Substantial useful information is available on the AICPA exam web site. After registering and receiving the Notice to Schedule (NTS) approval, candidates may receive a discounted subscription to all FASB and AICPA professional literature at https://www.aicpa.org/becomeacpa.html. Practice using the literature is strongly recommended for all serious CPA candidates.

## C. AICPA Website Tutorial

The AICPA has created a hands-on tutorial to help candidates become familiar with new types of simulations to be used on the exam testing. Go to https://www.aicpa.org/search.html?source=AICPA&q=cpa+exam+tutorial. Another good source of information is at https://thiswaytocpa.com/. In addition to this review course, it is important that you use these AICPA resources. The AICPA will not license its software, so the CPA exam web site is your only source. The tutorial goes over such items as:

**1. Format:** A review of the exam's format is included. Also, a thorough demonstration of the navigation functions on the different screens which you must use will be covered.

**2. Sample Questions:** The AICPA tutorial will familiarize candidates with the multiple-choice, simulation, and written communication questions that will be included on the exam.

**3. Sample Test:** The AICPA has a sample test on its website. Candidates are strongly advised to go online and work through this exam at least once to become thoroughly familiar with the format. You can also find additional valuable resources by visiting NASBA at https://www.nasba.org/

**4. Best Resource:** Your best and most reliable source of CPA examination resources is the AICPA website.

## VIII. WRITTEN COMMUNICATIONS

**1. Description:** The candidate may be required to explain accounting or business matters or draft a memorandum to management in BEC. This is tested at a 15% weight of BEC. An example is a narrative memorandum to a client or CPA firm partner explaining the factors to be considered in a capital budgeting decision.

**2. Writing Skills:** Candidates should type answers in the simulations that are clear, concise, and well organized around an identifiable thesis statement which is directly responsive to the requirement of the question. Numerous paragraphs, each developing one major supporting idea, shows coherent organization. Start each paragraph with a topic sentence and favor short sentences with direct statements. Do not abbreviate or use jargon, and try to express as many clear technical terms as possible in your answer. Clarity is improved by using words with specific and precise meanings. Stay on point. Bullet points should NOT be used.

**3. Sample Testing Screen:**

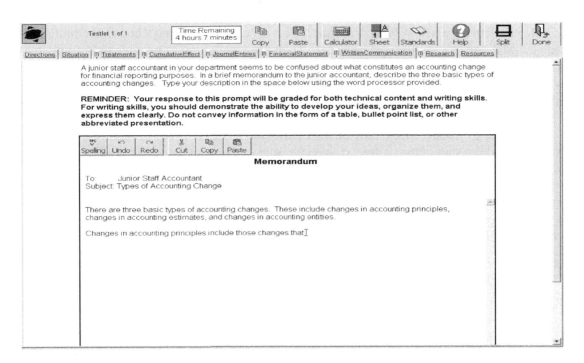

Prometric Technologies Testing Screen (Simulations)

# IX.    KEEP ALERT

The 2021 CPA exam continues to improve the testing as the CBT-e shortens the scoring timeline allowing for continual testing.  The exam continues to test a candidate's "higher level cognitive skills".

In our review course book, you will learn the substance of the rules that will be tested and gain expertise in working exam style questions.  50% of the Regulation exam is multiple-choice questions.  Data analytics and making decisions therefrom is a new topic somewhat likely to be tested (most likely in Audit and Attestation).

Simulation questions are found at the AICPA sites and this may involve computer knowledge.  The AICPA is not licensing this software, so it is your responsibility to continue monitoring https://thiswaytocpa.com/exam/articles/passing-exam/free-stuff/.  This is the best source for candidates to seek tutorial and sample tests that will familiarize you with the most current navigation functions.

Register now for the next window and order from us the book you need for the exam section you pick.  After the registration steps are all accomplished don't forget to sign up for the AICPA accounting standards database at https://www.aicpa.org/membership/join.html?tab-1=5.  Do this as soon as you receive your Notice to Sit (NTS).

Good luck in your preparation for the Financial Accounting portion of the uniform CPA exam.

James J. Rigos, CPA
Seattle, Washington
January 1, 2021

# RIGOS PRIMER SERIES® CPA REVIEW

## WEEKLY PLANNING SHEET

WEEK:  From Monday _____ to Sunday _____.

MY SCHEDULED DATE FOR _____ SECTION IS _____ WEEKS AWAY

## WEEKLY OBJECTIVES:

| <u>Subject</u> | <u>Topic Studied</u> | <u>Prepare MMO</u> | <u>Do Questions</u> | <u>Review Previous Chapters</u> |
|---|---|---|---|---|

_____

_____

_____

_____

_____

| Time | Monday | Tuesday | Wednesday | Thursday | Friday | Saturday | Sunday |
|---|---|---|---|---|---|---|---|
| 6-7:00am | | | | | | | |
| 7-8:00 | | | | | | | |
| 8-9:00 | | | | | | | |
| 9-10:00 | | | | | | | |
| 10-11:00 | | | | | | | |
| 11-12:00 | | | | | | | |
| 12-1:00pm | | | | | | | |
| 1-2:00 | | | | | | | |
| 2-3:00 | | | | | | | |
| 3-4:00 | | | | | | | |
| 4-5:00 | | | | | | | |
| 5-6:00 | | | | | | | |
| 6-7:00 | | | | | | | |
| 7-8:00 | | | | | | | |
| 8-9:00 | | | | | | | |
| 9-10:00 | | | | | | | |
| 10-11:00 | | | | | | | |
| 11-12:00 | | | | | | | |

# CHAPTER 1

## THEORETICAL FOUNDATIONS AND BALANCE SHEET OVERVIEW

### Question Map

I.  CONCEPTUAL FRAMEWORK
    A. Introduction
    B. House of GAAP -- 1, 2
    C. List of Abbreviations

II.  DEVELOPMENT OF FINANCIAL ACCOUNTING STANDARDS

III.  STATEMENTS OF FINANCIAL ACCOUNTING CONCEPTS
    A. SFAC No. 8 -- Objectives of Financial Reporting by Business Enterprises
    B. SFAC No. 8 -- Qualitative Characteristics of Accounting Information -- 5
    C. Definitions 3, 4, 6, 7, 8, 9
    D. SFAC No. 3 -- Elements of Financial Statements of Business Enterprises
    E. SFAC No. 4 -- Objectives of Financial Reporting by Nonbusiness Organizations
    F. SFAC No. 5 -- Recognition and Measurement In
       Financial Statements of Business Enterprises 13, 14, 16, 20, 76
    G. SFAC No. 6 -- Elements of Financial Statements
       1. Purpose
       2. Replacement Statement
       3. Definitions of Elements 10, 11, 12, 14, 15-18, 19
       4. Accrual Accounting and Related Concepts 13, 20, 21

IV.  OTHER BASIC CONCEPTS, ACCOUNTING PRINCIPLES, ASSUMPTIONS AND
    CONVENTIONS UNDERLYING FINANCIAL ACCOUNTING
    A. Accounting (Economic) Entity Concept
    B. Going Concern Assumption -- 23
    C. Periodicity Assumption
    D. Monetary Unit Assumption
    E. Approximation
    F. Judgments
    G. Substance Over Form
    H. Unit of Measure
    I. Historical Cost Principle
    J. Matching Principle
    K. Full Disclosure Principle -- 10
    L. Conservatism Convention -- 22, 34

V.  FAIR VALUE MEASUREMENTS

VI.  BALANCE SHEET OVERVIEW
    A. Operating Cycle
    B. Current Assets -- 25
    C. Long-Term Investments
    D. Property, Plant and Equipment
    E. Intangible Assets

# CHAPTER 1

## THEORETICAL FOUNDATIONS AND BALANCE SHEET OVERVIEW

### Multiple Choice Questions

**1.** FASB Interpretations of Statements of Financial Accounting Standards have the same authority as the FASB
  a. Statements of Financial Accounting Concepts.
  b. Emerging Issues Task Force Consensus.
  c. Technical Bulletins.
  d. Statements of Financial Accounting Standards.

**2.** Which of the following accounting pronouncements is the most authoritative?
  a. FASB Statement of Financial Accounting Concepts.
  b. FASB Technical Bulletin.
  c. AICPA Accounting Principles Board Opinion.
  d. AICPA Statement of Position.

**3.** According to Statement of Financial Accounting Concepts No. 8, relevance and reliability are the two primary qualities that make accounting information useful for decision making. Predictive value is an ingredient of

| | Relevance | Reliability |
|---|---|---|
| a. | No | No |
| b. | No | Yes |
| c. | Yes | Yes |
| d. | Yes | No |

**4.** According to the FASB conceptual framework, which of the following situations violates the concept of reliability?
  a. Financial statements were issued nine months late.
  b. Report data on segments having the same expected risks and growth rates to analysts estimating future profits.
  c. Financial statements included property with a carrying amount increased to management's estimate of market value.

  d. Management reports to stockholders regularly refer to new projects undertaken, but the financial statements never report project results.

**5.** Which of the following is considered a pervasive constraint by Statement of Financial Accounting Concepts No. 8?
  a. Benefits/costs.
  b. Conservatism.
  c. Timeliness.
  d. Verifiability.

**6.** According to Statement of Financial Accounting Concepts No. 8, an interim earnings report is expected to have which of the following?

| | Predictive value | Feedback value |
|---|---|---|
| a. | No | No |
| b. | Yes | Yes |
| c. | Yes | No |
| d. | No | Yes |

**7.** Under Statement of Financial Accounting Concepts No.2, feedback value is an ingredient of the primary quality of

| | Relevance | Reliability |
|---|---|---|
| a. | No | No |
| b. | No | Yes |
| c. | Yes | Yes |
| d. | Yes | No |

**8.** According to the FASB conceptual framework, which of the following relates to both relevance and reliability?
  a. Comparability.
  b. Feedback value.
  c. Verifiability.
  d. Timeliness.

**9.** The concept of consistency is sacrificed in the accounting for which of the following income statement items?
  a. Discontinued operations.
  b. Loss on disposal of a segment of a business.
  c. Extraordinary items.
  d. Cumulative effect of change in accounting principle.

**10.** Under Statement of Financial Accounting Concepts No. 6, interrelated elements that are directly related to measuring performance and status of an enterprise include

|  | Distribution to Owners | Notes to Financial Statements |
|---|---|---|
| **a.** | Yes | Yes |
| **b.** | Yes | No |
| **c.** | No | Yes |
| **d.** | No | No |

**11.** According to the FASB conceptual framework, which of the following is an essential characteristic of an asset?
    **a.** The claims to an asset's benefits are legally enforceable.
    **b.** An asset is tangible.
    **c.** An asset is obtained at a cost.
    **d.** An asset provides future benefits.

**12.** According to the FASB's conceptual framework, asset valuation accounts are
    **a.** Assets.
    **b.** Neither assets **nor** liabilities.
    **c.** Part of stockholders' equity.
    **d.** Liabilities.

**13.** Under Statement of Financial Accounting Concepts No. 6, gains on assets unsold are identified, in a precise sense, by the term
    **a.** Unrecorded.
    **b.** Unrealized.
    **c.** Unrecognized.
    **d.** Unallocated.

**14.** The FASB's conceptual framework classifies gains and losses based on whether they are related to an entity's major ongoing or central operations. These gains or losses may be classified as

|  | Nonoperating | Operating |
|---|---|---|
| **a.** | No | No |
| **b.** | Yes | No |
| **c.** | Yes | Yes |
| **d.** | No | Yes |

**15.** Under Statement of Financial Accounting Concepts No. 3, as superseded by SFAC No. 6, comprehensive income includes which of the following?

|  | Losses | Contribution Margin |
|---|---|---|
| **a.** | No | No |
| **b.** | No | Yes |
| **c.** | Yes | Yes |
| **d.** | Yes | No |

**16.** FASB's conceptual framework explains both financial and physical capital maintenance concepts. Which capital maintenance concept is applied to currently reported net income, and which is applied to comprehensive income?

|  | Currently reported net income | Comprehensive income |
|---|---|---|
| **a.** | Financial capital | Physical capital |
| **b.** | Physical capital | Physical capital |
| **c.** | Financial capital | Financial capital |
| **d.** | Physical capital | Financial capital |

**17.** Under FASB Statement of Financial Accounting Concepts No. 5, which of the following items would cause earnings to differ from comprehensive income for an enterprise in an industry **not** having specialized accounting principles?
    **a.** Unrealized loss on investments in available-for-sale securities.
    **b.** Unrealized loss on investments in trading securities.
    **c.** Loss on exchange of similar assets.
    **d.** Loss on exchange of dissimilar assets.

**18.** According to the FASB's conceptual framework, comprehensive income includes which of the following?

|  | Gross margin | Operating income |
|---|---|---|
| **a.** | No | Yes |
| **b.** | No | No |
| **c.** | Yes | No |
| **d.** | Yes | Yes |

**19.** According to the FASB conceptual framework, an entity's revenue may result from
   a. A decrease in an asset from primary operations.
   b. An increase in an asset from incidental transactions.
   c. An increase in a liability from incidental transactions.
   d. A decrease in a liability from primary operations.

**20.** According to the FASB's conceptual framework, the term recognized is synonymous with the term
   a. Recorded.
   b. Realized.
   c. Matched.
   d. Allocated.

**21.** When bad debt expense is estimated on the basis of the percentage of past actual losses from bad debts to past net credit sales, and this percentage is adjusted for anticipated conditions, the accounting concept of
   a. Matching is being followed.
   b. Matching is not being followed.
   c. Substance over form is being followed.
   d. Going concern is not being followed.

**22.** Uncertainty and risks inherent in business situations should be adequately considered in financial reporting. This statement is an example of the concept of
   a. Conservatism.
   b. Completeness.
   c. Neutrality.
   d. Representational faithfulness.

**23.** The valuation of a promise to receive cash in the future at present value on the financial statements of a business entity is valid because of the accounting concept of
   a. Entity.
   b. Materiality.
   c. Going concern.
   d. Neutrality.

**24.** Accruing net losses on firm purchase commitments for inventory is an example of the accounting concept of
   a. Conservatism.
   b. Realization.
   c. Consistency.
   d. Materiality.

**25.** The following is Gold Corp.'s June 30 trial balance:

| | | |
|---|---|---|
| Cash overdraft | | $ 10,000 |
| Accounts receivable (net) | $ 35,000 | |
| Inventory | 58,000 | |
| Prepaid expenses | 12,000 | |
| Land held for resale | 100,000 | |
| Property, plant, and equipment (net) | 95,000 | |
| Accounts payable and accrued expenses | | 32,000 |
| Common stock | | 25,000 |
| Additional paid-in capital | | 150,000 |
| Retained earnings | | 83,000 |
| | $300,000 | $300,000 |

Additional information:

• Checks amounting to $30,000 were written to vendors and recorded on June 29, resulting in a cash overdraft of $10,000. The checks were mailed on July 9.

• Land held for resale was sold for cash on July 15.

• Gold issued its financial statements on July 31.

In its June 30 balance sheet, what amount should Gold report as current assets?
   a. $225,000
   b. $205,000
   c. $195,000
   d. $125,000

**26.** Cook Co. had the following balances at December 31, 20x9:

| | |
|---|---|
| Cash in checking account | $350,000 |
| Cash in money-market account | 250,000 |
| U.S. Treasury bill, purchased 12/1/x8 maturing 2/28/x9 | 800,000 |
| U.S. Treasury bond, purchased 3/1/x8 maturing 2/28/x9 | 500,000 |

Cook's policy is to treat as cash equivalents all highly liquid investments with a maturity of three months or less when purchased. What amount should Cook report as cash and cash equivalents in its December 31, 20x9 balance sheet?
   **a.** $ 600,000
   **b.** $1,150,000
   **c.** $1,400,000
   **d.** $1,900,000

**27.** Jacob Corporation had the following account balances at December 31:

| | |
|---|---|
| Cash in banks | $1,250,000 |
| Cash on hand | 125,000 |
| Cash legally restricted for additions to plant (expected to be disbursed during the next year) | 1,600,000 |

Cash in banks includes $500,000 of compensating balances against short-term borrowing arrangements. The compensating balances are not legally restricted as to withdrawal by Jacob. In the current assets section of Jacob's December 31 balance sheet, total cash should be reported at
   **a.** $775,000
   **b.** $1,250,000
   **c.** $1,375,000
   **d.** $2,975,000

**28.** Greenfield Company had the following cash balances at December 31, 20x9:

| | |
|---|---|
| Cash in banks | $1,500,000 |
| Petty cash funds (all funds were reimbursed on December 31 20x1) | 20,000 |
| Cash legally restricted for additions to plant (expected to be disbursed in 20x3) | 2,000,000 |

Cash in banks includes $500,000 of compensating balances against short-term borrowing arrangements at December 31, 20x9. The compensating balances are not legally restricted as to withdrawal by Greenfield. In the current assets section of Greenfield's December 31, 20x9, balance sheet, what total amount should be reported as cash?
   **a.** $1,020,000
   **b.** $1,520,000
   **c.** $3,020,000
   **d.** $3,520,000

**29.** Lee Corporation's checkbook balance on December 31, 20x0, was $4,000. In addition, Lee held the following items in its safe on December 31:

- Check payable to Lee Corporation, dated January 2, 20x1, not included in December 31 checkbook balance $1,000

- Check payable to Lee Corporation, deposited December 20, and included in December 31 checkbook balance, but returned by bank on December 30, stamped "NSF." The check was redeposited January 2, 20x1, and cleared January 7. $200

- Postage stamps received from mail-order customers. $75

- Check drawn on Lee Corporation's account, payable to a vendor, dated and recorded December 31, but not mailed until January 15, 20x1. $500

The proper amount to be shown as Cash on Lee's balance sheet at December 31, 20x0, is
   **a.** $3,800
   **b.** $4,000
   **c.** $4,300
   **d.** $4,875

 Course 5292 Copyright 2021. The Rigos programs have educated over 100,000 professionals since 1980.

**30.** At October 31, Dingo. Inc. had cash accounts at three different banks. One account balance is segregated solely for a November 15 payment into a bond sinking fund. A second account, used for branch operations, is overdrawn. The third account, used for regular corporate operations, has a positive balance. How should these accounts be reported in Dingo's October 31 classified balance sheet?

    **a.** The segregated account should be reported as a noncurrent asset, the regular account should be reported as a current asset, and the overdraft should be reported as a current liability.

    **b.** The segregated and regular accounts should be reported as current assets, and the overdraft should be reported as a current liability.

    **c.** The segregated account should be reported as a noncurrent asset, and the regular account should be reported as a current asset net of the overdraft.

    **d.** The segregated and regular accounts should be reported as current assets net of the overdraft.

**31.** In preparing its August 31 bank reconciliation, Apex Corp. has available the following information:

| | |
|---|---|
| Balance per bank statement, 8/31 | $18,050 |
| Deposit in transit, 8/31 | 3,250 |
| Return of customer's check for insufficient funds, 8/31 | 600 |
| Outstanding checks, 8/31 | 2,750 |
| Bank service charges for August | 100 |

At August 31, Apex's correct cash balance is

    **a.** $18,550
    **b.** $17,950
    **c.** $17,850
    **d.** $17,500

**32.** The Jones Corporation presented the following bank reconciliation at 9/30:

| | |
|---|---|
| Balance per bank statement 9/30 | $21,000 |
| Plus: Deposit in transit | 2,000 |
| | $23,000 |
| Less: Outstanding Checks | 3,000 |
| Balance per cash account 9/30 | $20,000 |

Data included with the bank statement for the month of October listed the following:

| | |
|---|---|
| Total disbursements | $31,000 |
| Total deposits | 23,000 |

All reconciling items of 9/30 cleared through the bank in October. Outstanding checks at October 31 were $2,300. What is the balance in the cash account on 10/31?

    **a.** $13,700
    **b.** $14,000
    **c.** $12,000
    **d.** $10,700

**33.** Nola Co. has a portfolio of marketable equity securities which it does not intend to sell in the near term. How should Nola classify these securities, and how should it report unrealized gains and losses from these securities?

| | Classify as | Report as a |
|---|---|---|
| **a.** | Trading securities | Component of income from continuing operations |
| **b.** | Available-for-sale securities | Separate component of stockholders' equity |
| **c.** | Trading securities | Separate component of stockholders' equity |
| **d.** | Available-for-sale securities | Component of income from continuing operations |

**34.** Bicar Corporation owns 10% of the outstanding capital stock of Kopel, Inc. On December 31 when Kopel's retained earnings were $50,000, Bicar received a plot of land from Kopel in a nonreciprocal transfer. Kopel's cost of the land was $7,000 and its fair market value at December 31 was

$15,000. At what amount should this land be recorded on Bicar's books?

a. $0
b. $ 5,000
c. $ 7,000
d. $15,000

35. Dividends received relating to a portfolio of current marketable equities exceeded the investor's share of investee's undistributed earnings since the date of the investment. The amount of dividend revenue that should be reported in the investor's income statement for this year would be

a. The portion of the dividends received this year that were in excess of the investor's share of investee's undistributed earnings since the date of investment.
b. The portion of the dividends received this year that were **not** in excess of the investor's share of investee's undistributed earnings since the date of investment.
c. The total amount of dividends received this year.
d. Zero.

36. On July 1, Denver Corp. purchased 3,000 shares of Eagle Co.'s 10,000 outstanding shares of common stock for $20 per share. On December 15 of the same year, Eagle paid $40,000 in dividends to its common stockholders. Eagle's net income for the year ended December 31 was $120,000, earned evenly throughout the year. In its income statement for the year ended December 31, what amount of income from this investment should Denver report?

a. $36,000
b. $18,000
c. $12,000
d. $ 6,000

37. When the equity method is used to account for investments in common stock, which of the following affects the investor's reported investment income?

|  | Earnings From Investee | Cash dividends from investee |
|---|---|---|
| a. | Yes | Yes |
| b. | No | Yes |
| c. | No | No |
| d. | Yes | No |

**Items 38 through 40** are based on the following:

Lee, Inc. acquired 30% of Polk Corp.'s voting stock on January 1, 20x8, for $100,000. During 20x8, Polk earned $40,000 and paid dividends of $25,000. Lee's 30% interest in Polk gives Lee the ability to exercise significant influence over Polk's operating and financial policies. During 20x9, Polk earned $50,000 and paid dividends of $15,000 on April 1 and $15,000 on October 1. On July 1, 20x9, Lee sold half of its stock in Polk for $66,000 cash.

38. Before income taxes, what amount should Lee include in its 20x8 income statement as a result of the investment?

a. $40,000
b. $25,000
c. $12,000
d. $ 7,500

39. The carrying amount of this investment in Lee's December 31, 20x8 balance sheet should be

a. $100,000
b. $104,500
c. $112,000
d. $115,000

40. What should be the gain on sale of this investment in Lees' 20x9 income statement?

a. $16,000
b. $13,750
c. $12,250
d. $10,000

41. On January 1, 20x7, the Robohn Company purchased for cash 40% of the 300,000 shares of voting common stock of the Lowell Company for $1,800,000 when 40% of the underlying equity in the net assets of Lowell was $1,400,000. As a result of this transaction, Robohn has the ability to

exercise significant influence over the operating and financial policies of Lowell. Lowell's net income for the year ended December 31, 20x7, was $600,000. During 20x7, Lowell paid $325,000 in dividends to its stockholders. The income reported by Robohn for its investment in Lowell should be

a. $120,000.
b. $130,000.
c. $230,000.
d. $240,000.

**42.** A parent corporation which uses the equity method of accounting for its investment in a 40 percent owned subsidiary, which earned $20,000 and paid $5,000 in dividends, made the following entries:

Investment in subsidiary $8,000
  Equity in earnings of subsidiary     $8,000

Cash                2,000
  Dividend revenue            2,000

What effect will these entries have on the parent's statement of financial position?

a. Investment in subsidiary understated, retained earnings understated.
b. Investment in subsidiary overstated, retained earnings overstated.
c. Investment in subsidiary overstated, retained earnings understated.
d. Financial position will be fairly stated.

**43.** On January 1, 20x8, Mega Corp. acquired 10% of the outstanding voting stock of Penny, Inc. On January 2, 20x9, Mega gained the ability to exercise significant influence over financial and operating control of Penny by acquiring an additional 20% of Penny's outstanding stock. The two purchases were made at prices proportionate to the value assigned to Penny's net assets, which equaled their carrying amounts. For the years ended December 31, 20x8 and 20x9, Penny reported the following:

| | 20x8 | 20x9 |
|---|---|---|
| Dividends paid | $200,000 | $300,000 |
| Net income | 600,000 | 650,000 |

In 20x9, what amounts should Mega report as current year investment income and as an adjustment, before income taxes, to 20x8 income?

| | 20x9 investment income | Adjustment to 20x8 investment income |
|---|---|---|
| a. | $195,000 | $160,000 |
| b. | $195,000 | $100,000 |
| c. | $195,000 | $40,000 |
| d. | $105,000 | $40,000 |

**44.** Bort Co. purchased 2,000 shares of Crel Co. common stock on March 5, 20x8, for $72,000. Bort received a $1,000 cash dividend on the Crel stock on July 15, 20x8. Crel declared a 10% stock dividend on December 15, 20x8, to stockholders of record as of December 31, 20x8. The dividend was distributed on January 15, 20x9. The market price of the stock was $38 on December 15, 20x8, $40 on December 31, 20x8, and $42 on January 15, 20x9. What amount should Bort record as dividend revenue for the year ended December 31, 20x8?

a. $1,000
b. $8,600
c. $9,000
d. $9,400

**45.** Albert Co. acquired 4,000 shares of Nolan, Inc. common stock on October 20, 20x8, for $66,000. On November 30, 20x0, Nolan distributed a 10% common stock dividend when the market price of the stock was $25 per share. On December 10, 20x0, Albert sold 400 shares of its Nolan stock for $10,000. For the year ended December 31, 20x0, how much should Albert report as dividend revenue?

a. $10,600
b. $10,000
c. $ 4,600
d. $0

**46.** On January 3, 20x7, Falk Co. purchased 500 shares of Milo Corp. common stock for $36,000. On December 1, 20x9, Falk received 500 stock rights from Milo. Each right entitles the holder to acquire one share of stock for $85. The market price of Milo's stock was $100 a share immediately before the rights were issued, and $90 a share immediately after the rights were issued. Falk sold its rights on December 3, 20x9, for $10 a right. Falk's gain from the sale of the rights is

    a. $0
    b. $1,000
    c. $1,400
    d. $5,000

**47.** On July 1 Metaro Corporation purchased for $108,000, 2,000 shares of Jean Corporation's newly issued 6% cumulative $20 par value preferred stock. Each share also had one stock warrant attached, which entitled the holder to acquire, at $19, one share of Jean $10 par value common stock for each two warrants held. On July 2 the market price of the preferred stock (without warrants) was $50 per share and the market price of the stock warrants was $10 per warrant. On September 1 Metaro sold all the stock warrants for $19,800. What should be the gain on the sale of the stock warrants?

    a. $0
    b. $ 800
    c. $1,800
    d. $9,800

**48.** On April 1, 20x8, Saxe, Inc. purchased $200,000 face value, 9% U.S. Treasury Notes for $198,500, including accrued interest of $4,500. The notes mature July 1, 20x9, and pay interest semiannually on January 1 and July 1. They are classified as held-to-maturity securities. Saxe uses the straight-line method of amortization. The notes were sold on December 1, 20x8, for $206,500, including accrued interest of $7,500. In its October 31, 20x8, balance sheet, the carrying amount of this investment should be

    a. $194,000
    b. $196,800
    c. $197,200
    d. $199,000

**49.** On November 1, 20x1, Warrior Co. purchased Cosmo, Inc., 10-year, 7%, bonds with a face value of $50,000, for $48,000. An additional $1,167 was paid for the accrued interest. Interest is payable semiannually on January 1 and July 1. The bonds mature on July 1, 20x8, and are classified as held-to-maturity. Warrior uses the straight-line method of amortization. Ignoring income taxes, the amount reported in Warrior's 20x1 income statement as a result of Warrior's long-term bond investment in Cosmos was

    a. $533.
    b. $560.
    c. $583.
    d. $633.

**50.** On July 1, 20x0, Glenn Company purchased Dell Corporation 10-year, 9% bonds with a face value of $200,000, for $216,000, which included $6,000 of accrued interest. The bonds, which mature on March 1, 20x7, pay interest semiannually on March 1 and September 1. They will be held until they mature. Glenn uses the straight-line method of amortization. The amount of income Glenn should report for the calendar year 20x0 as a result of the above long-term investment would be

    a. $ 7,800
    b. $ 8,250
    c. $ 9,000
    d. $15,000

**51.** On January 1, 20x6, Darby Company purchased, at par, 500 of the $1,000 face value, ten-year, 8% bonds of Clark Corporation as a long-term investment. The bonds pay interest semiannually on July 1 and January 1. Darby classifies this investment as held-to-maturity. Clark incurred heavy losses from operations for several years and defaulted on the July 1, 20x0, and January 1, 20x1, interest payments. Because of the permanent decline in market value of Clark's bonds, Darby wrote down its investment to $400,000 at December 31, 20x0. Pursuant to Clark's plan of reorganization effected on July 1, 20x1, Darby received 5,000 shares of $100 par value, 8% cumulative preferred stock of Clark in exchange for the $500,000 face value bond investment. The quoted market value of the preferred stock was $70 per share on July 1, 20x1. What amount of loss should be included in the determination of Darby's net income for 20x1?

    a. $0
    b. $ 50,000
    c. $100,000
    d. $150,000

**52.** In 20x8, Lee Co. acquired, at a premium, Enfield, Inc. 10-year bonds as a long-term investment to be held to maturity. At December 31, 20x9, Enfield's bonds were quoted at a small discount. Which of the following situations is the most likely cause of the decline in the bonds' market value?

    a. Enfield issued a stock dividend.
    b. Enfield is expected to call the bonds at a premium, which is less than Lee's carrying amount.
    c. Interest rates have declined since Lee purchased the bonds.
    d. Interest rates have increased since Lee purchased the bonds.

**53.** An investor purchased a bond classified as a long-term investment between interest dates at a discount. It is the intent of the investor to hold the bond until it matures. At the purchase date, the carrying amount of the bond is more than the

| | Cash paid to seller | Face amount of bond |
|---|---|---|
| a. | No | Yes |
| b. | No | No |
| c. | Yes | No |
| d. | Yes | Yes |

**54.** An investor purchased a bond as a long-term investment on January 2. The bond will be held until it matures. The investor's carrying value at the end of the first year would be highest if the bond was purchased at a

    a. Discount and amortized by the straight-line method.
    b. Discount and amortized by the effective interest method.
    c. Premium and amortized by the straight-line method.
    d. Premium and amortized by the effective interest method.

**55.** On July 1, 20x9, York Co. purchased as a long-term investment $1,000,000 of Park, Inc.'s 8% bonds for $946,000, including accrued interest of $40,000. The bonds were purchased to yield 10% interest. The bonds mature on January 1, 20x6, will be held until they mature, and pay interest annually on January 1. York uses the effective interest method of amortization. In its December 31, 20x9, balance sheet, what amount should York report as investment in bonds?

    a. $911,300
    b. $916,600
    c. $953,300
    d. $960,600

**56.** The following information relates to noncurrent investments that Fall Corp. placed in trust as required by the underwriter of its bonds:

| | |
|---|---|
| Bond sinking fund balance, 12/31/x8 | $450,000 |
| 20x9 additional investment | 90,000 |
| Dividends on investments | 15,000 |
| Interest revenue | 30,000 |
| Administration costs | 5,000 |
| Carrying amount of bonds payable | 1,025,000 |

What amount should Fall report on its December 31, 20x9, balance sheet related to its noncurrent investment for bond sinking fund requirements?

    a. $585,000
    b. $580,000
    c. $575,000
    d. $540,000

**57.** An issuer of bonds uses a sinking fund for the retirement of the bonds. Cash was transferred to the sinking fund and subsequently used to purchase investments. The sinking fund

I. Increases by revenue earned on the investments.
II. Is **not** affected by revenue earned on the investments.
III. Decreases when the investments are purchased.

a. I only.
b. I and III.
c. II and III.
d. III only.

**58.** On January 2, 20x6, a company established a sinking fund in connection with an issue of bonds due in ten years. At December 31, 20x9, the independent trustee held cash in the sinking fund account representing the annual deposits to the fund and the interest earned on those deposits. How should the sinking fund be reported in the company's classified balance sheet at December 31, 20x9?

a. The entire balance in the sinking fund account should appear as a noncurrent asset.
b. The entire balance in the sinking fund account should appear as a current asset.
c. The cash in the sinking fund should appear as a current asset.
d. The accumulated deposits only should appear as a noncurrent asset.

**59.** In 20x4, Chain, Inc. purchased a $1,000,000 life insurance policy on its president, of which Chain is the beneficiary. Information regarding the policy for the year ended December 31, 20x9, follows:

| | |
|---|---|
| Cash surrender value, 1/1/x9 | $ 87,000 |
| Cash surrender value, 12/31/x9 | 108,000 |
| Annual advance premium | |
| paid 1/1/x9 | 40,000 |

During 20x9, dividends of $6,000 were applied to increase the cash surrender value of the policy. What amount should Chain report as life insurance expense for 20x9?

a. $40,000
b. $25,000
c. $19,000
d. $13,000

**60.** On January 2, 20x6, Beal, Inc. acquired a $70,000 whole-life insurance policy on its president. The annual premium is $2,000. The company is the owner and beneficiary. Beal charged officer's life insurance expense as follows:

| | |
|---|---|
| 20x6 | $2,000 |
| 20x7 | 1,800 |
| 20x8 | 1,500 |
| 20x9 | 1,100 |
| Total | $6,400 |

In Beal's December 31, 20x9 balance sheet, the investment in cash surrender value should be
a. $0
b. $1,600
c. $6,400
d. $8,000

**61.** Jent Corp. purchased bonds at a discount of $10,000. Subsequently, Jent sold these bonds at a premium of $14,000. During the period that Jent held this investment, amortization of the discount amounted to $2,000. What amount should Jent report as gain on the sale of bonds?
a. $12,000
b. $22,000
c. $24,000
d. $26,000

**62.** Kale Co. purchased bonds at a discount on the open market as an investment and intends to hold these bonds to maturity. Kale should account for these bonds at
a. Cost.
b. Amortized cost.
c. Fair value.
d. Lower of cost or market.

**63.** What are the Statements of Financial Accounting Concepts intended to establish?
a. Generally accepted accounting principles in financial reporting by business enterprises.
b. The meaning of "Present fairly in accordance with generally accepted accounting principles."

**c.** The objectives and concepts for use in developing standards of financial accounting and reporting.

**d.** The hierarchy of sources of generally accepted accounting principles.

**64.** Reporting inventory at the lower of cost or market is a departure from the accounting principle of
  **a.** Historical cost.
  **b.** Consistency.
  **c.** Conservatism.
  **d.** Full disclosure.

**65.** During a period when an enterprise is under the direction of a particular management, its financial statements will directly provide information about
  **a.** Both enterprise performance and management performances.
  **b.** Management performance but **not** directly provide information about enterprise performance.
  **c.** Enterprise performance but **not** directly provide information about management performance.
  **d.** Neither enterprise performance nor management performance.

**66.** What is the purpose of information presented in notes to the financial statements?
  **a.** To provide disclosures required by generally accepted accounting principles.
  **b.** To correct improper presentation in the financial statements.
  **c.** To provide recognition of amounts **not** included in the totals of the financial statements.
  **d.** To present management's response to auditor comments.

**67.** Brand Co. uses the equity method to account for its investment in Grand, Inc. common stock. How should Brand record a 2% stock dividend received from Grand?
  **a.** As dividend revenue at Grand's carrying value of the stock.
  **b.** As dividend revenue at the market value of the stock.

**c.** As a reduction in the total cost of Grand stock owned.

**d.** As a memorandum entry reducing the unit cost of all Grand stock owned.

**68.** One of the elements of a financial statement is comprehensive income. Comprehensive income excludes changes in equity resulting from which of the following?
  **a.** Loss from discontinued operations.
  **b.** Prior period error correction.
  **c.** Dividends paid to stockholders.
  **d.** Unrealized loss on investments in non-current marketable equity securities.

**69.** According to the FASB conceptual framework, the objectives of financial reporting for business enterprises are based on
  **a.** Generally accepted accounting principles.
  **b.** Reporting on management's stewardship.
  **c.** The need for conservatism.
  **d.** The needs of the users of the information.

**70.** At December 31, 20x8, Kale Co. had the following balances in the accounts it maintains at First State Bank:

| | |
|---|---|
| Checking account #101 | $175,000 |
| Checking account #202 | (10,000) |
| Money market account | 25,000 |
| 90-day certificate of deposit, due 2-28-x9 | 50,000 |
| 180-day certificate of deposit, due 3-15-x9 | 80,000 |

Kale classifies investments with original maturities of three months or less as cash equivalents. In its December 31, 20x8, balance sheet, what amount should Kale report as cash and cash equivalents?
  **a.** $190,000
  **b.** $200,000
  **c.** $240,000
  **d.** $320,000

**71.** In 20x9, Gar Corp. collected $300,000 as beneficiary of a keyman life insurance policy carried on the life of Gar's controller, who had died in 20x9. The life insurance proceeds are not subject to income tax. At the date of the controller's death, the policy's cash surrender value was $90,000. What amount should Gar report as revenue in its 20x9 income statement.

a. $0
b. $ 90,000
c. $210,000
d. $300,000

**72.** A company should report the marketable equity securities that it has classified as trading at

a. Lower of cost or market, with holding gains and losses included in earnings.
b. Lower of cost or market, with holding gains included in earnings only to the extent of previously recognized holding losses.
c. Fair value, with holding gains included in earnings only to the extent of previously recognized holding losses.
d. Fair value, with holding gains and losses included in earnings.

**73.** In its financial statements, Pare, Inc. uses the cost method of accounting for its 15% ownership of Sabe Co. At December 31, 20x9, Pare has a receivable from Sabe. How should the receivable be reported in Pare's December 31, 20x9, balance sheet?

a. The total receivable should be reported separately.
b. The total receivable should be included as part of the investment in Sabe, without separate disclosure.
c. Eighty-five percent of the receivable should be reported separately, with the balance offset against Sabe's payable to Pare.
d. The total receivable should be offset against Sabe's payable to Pare, without separate disclosure.

**74.** When the fair value of an investment in debt securities exceeds its amortized cost, how should each of the following debt securities be reported at the end of the year?

| Debt securities classified as | |
|---|---|
| Held-to-maturity | Available-for-sale |
| a. Amortized cost | Amortized cost |
| b. Amortized cost | Fair value |
| c. Fair value | Fair value |
| d. Fair value | Amortized cost |

**75.** When the equity method is used to account for investments in common stock, which of the following affect(s) the investor's reported invested income?

| | A change in market value of investees' common stock | Cash dividends from investee |
|---|---|---|
| a. | Yes | Yes |
| b. | Yes | No |
| c. | No | Yes |
| d. | No | No |

**76.** When a full set of general-purpose financial statements are presented, comprehensive income and its components should

a. Appear as a part of discontinued operations and cumulative effect of a change in accounting principle.
b. Be reported net of related income tax effect, in total and individually.
c. Appear in a supplemental schedule in the notes to the financial statements.
d. Be displayed in a financial statement that has the same prominence as other financial statements.

# CHAPTER 1

## THEORETICAL FOUNDATIONS AND BALANCE SHEET OVERVIEW

### Simulation Questions

**Number 1**                                          **(Estimated time - 15 to 25 minutes)**

**Question Number 1** consists of 10 items. Select the best answer for each item. Answer all items. Your grade will be based on the total number of correct answers.

**Items 1 through 4** are based on the following:

Camp Co. purchased various securities during 20x9 to be classified as held-to-maturity securities, trading securities, or available-for-sale securities.

**Required:**

    **Items 1 through 4** describe various securities purchased by Camp. For each item, select from the following list the appropriate category for each security. A category may be used once, more than once, or not at all.

### Categories

**H** -- Held-to-maturity         **T** -- Trading         **A** -- Available-for-sale

1. Debt securities bought and held for the purpose of selling in the near term.
2. U.S. Treasury bonds that Camp has both the positive intent and the ability to hold to maturity.
3. $3 million debt security bought and held for the purpose of selling in three years to finance payment of Camp's $2 million long-term note payable when it matures.
4. Convertible preferred stock that Camp does not intend to sell in the near term.

**Items 5 through 10** are based on the following:

The following information pertains to Dayle, Inc.'s portfolio of marketable investment securities for the year ended December 31, 20x9:

| | Cost | Fair value, 12/31/x8 | 20x9 activity Purchases | Sales | Fair value 12/31/x9 |
|---|---|---|---|---|---|
| **Held-to-maturity** | | | | | |
| Security ABC | | | $100,000 | | 95,000 |
| | | | | | |
| **Trading** | | | | | |
| Security DEF | $150,000 | $160,000 | | | 155,000 |
| | | | | | |
| **Available-for-sale** | | | | | |
| Security GHI | 190,000 | 165,000 | | $175,000 | |
| Security JKL | 170,000 | 175,000 | | | 160,000 |

Security ABC was purchased at par. All declines in fair value are considered temporary.

**Required:**

**Items 5 through 10** describe amounts to be reported in Dayle's 20x9 financial statements. For each item, select from the answer list below the correct numerical response. An amount may be selected once, more than once, or not at all. Ignore income tax considerations.

5. Carrying amount of security ABC at December 31, 20x9.

6. Carrying amount of security DEF at December 31, 20x9.

7. Carrying amount of security JKL at December 31, 20x9.

**Items 8 through 10** require a second response. For each item, indicate whether a gain (G) or loss (L) is to be reported.

8. Recognized gain or loss on sale of security GHI.

9. Unrealized gain or loss to be reported in 20x9 income statement.

10. Unrealized gain or loss to be reported at December 31, 20x9, as a separate component of stockholders' equity.

**Answer List**

| | |
|---|---|
| A | $0 |
| B | $5,000 |
| C | $10,000 |
| D | $15,000 |
| E | $25,000 |
| F | $95,000 |
| G | $100,000 |
| H | $150,000 |
| I | $155,000 |
| J | $160,000 |
| K | $170,000 |

# CHAPTER 1

## THEORETICAL FOUNDATIONS AND BALANCE SHEET OVERVIEW

### Multiple Choice Answers

1. /d/ According to SAS No. 69, FASB Statements and Interpretations have the same level of authority. See the GAAP hierarchy summarized in the "House of GAAP" in Figure 1-1.

2. /c/ The GAAP hierarchy summarized in SAS No. 69 assigns the highest level of authority to AICPA opinions. See Figure 1-1.

3. /d/ Based on the diagram provided in SFAC No. 8, predictive value is an ingredient of relevance only, not of reliability.

4. /c/ GAAP requires that property be carried at historical cost net of accumulated depreciation to date. Property that is carried at management's estimate of FMV lacks the necessary characteristic of neutrality - an essential component of reliability as depicted in the diagram provided in SFAC No. 8.

5. /a/ Based on the diagram provided in SFAC No. 8 (Figure 1-2 in the textbook), the pervasive constraint is the benefits/costs consideration. The other options are not considered by the FASB to be pervasive constraints.

6. /b/ Based on the provisions of SFAC No. 8, an interim earnings statement is useful in providing information which has both predictive value (concerning the future) and feedback value (concerning the past).

7. /d/ Based on the diagram provided in SFAC No. 8 (Figure 1-2 in the textbook), feedback value is an ingredient of relevance only, not of reliability.

8. /a/ Based on the diagram provided in SFAC No. 8 (Figure 1-2 in the textbook), comparability relates to both relevance and reliability. The other options are ingredients of either relevance or reliability.

9. /d/ When a change in accounting principles is made, the consistency principle is sacrificed. A firm must report the cumulative effect of the change in accounting principle in the financial statements to highlight the impact of the change.

10. /b/ According to SFAC No. 6, distribution to owners (dividends) are directly related to both measuring performance and the status of an enterprise, whereas notes to the financial statements are not related to both items.

11. /d/ According to SFAC No. 6, assets are probable future economic benefits obtained or controlled by a particular entity as a result of past transactions or events.

12. /b/ Asset valuation accounts do not meet the definitions of either assets or liabilities as set forth in SFAC No. 6. Furthermore, an asset valuation account would not be classified as a part of stockholders' equity.

13. /b/ A gain on an asset that is unsold is referred to as unrealized. A gain is realized only when it is caused by the actual sale of the asset.

**14.** /b/ According to SFAC No. 6, gains and losses arise from peripheral transactions, or events and circumstances which do not flow from major revenues, expenses, or investments by and distributions to owners. Therefore, gains and losses, by definition, are classified as nonoperating.

**15.** /c/ According to SFAC No. 6, comprehensive income is an all-inclusive definition of income which includes all items except investments by owners and distributions to owners.

**16.** /c/ SFAC No. 6 holds to the traditional capital concept view and emphasizes capital maintenance. Currently reported net income is a part of comprehensive income, and comprehensive income (as defined in SFAC No. 6) is a return on financial capital.

**17.** /a/ An unrealized loss on available-for-sale securities is not reported on the income statement and thus does not become a part of earnings. The loss would be reported as a separate component of the stockholders' equity section of the balance sheet. It would, therefore, contribute to a change in equity from nonowner sources, and as such, would be a component of comprehensive income for the period.

**18.** /d/ Comprehensive income, as defined in SFAC No. 6, includes all changes in owners' equity from transactions and other events and circumstances from nonowner sources. Both gross margin and operating income contribute to such a change.

**19.** /d/ SFAC No. 6 defines revenues as inflows or other enhancements of assets of an entity or settlement of its liabilities (emphasis added) from delivering or producing goods, rendering services, or other activities that constitute the entity's major or central operations.

**20.** /a/ The conceptual framework considers the terms recorded and recognized as interchangeable. The term recognized is not synonymous with realized, matched, or allocated.

**21.** /a/ The matching concept is being followed because the firm is attempting to record the appropriate amount of bad debt expense in the same accounting period as the related credit sales. Recording bad debt expense in this manner is unrelated to the concepts of substance over form or going concern.

**22.** /a/ The concept of conservatism requires that uncertainty and risk be adequately considered in financial reporting. It provides that when there is a doubt as to the accounting for a certain transaction, the preference for possible errors in measurement would be an understatement of net income and net assets. The other three options (B, C, and D) are unrelated to the issue of risk and uncertainty.

**23.** /c/ The going-concern concept assumes that the accounting entity will continue in operation indefinitely, in the absence of evidence to the contrary. Instead of recording a receivable at the total amount due, the firm would record a receivable at its present value. Any difference between the total amount and present value would be recorded over the life of the receivable. Options A, B, and D have nothing to do with the recording of receivables at present value.

**24.** /a/ Conservatism provides that when there is risk and uncertainty, the preference for possible errors in measurement would be an understatement of net income and net assets. Accruing a loss on firm purchase commitments when there are market declines is a conservative technique.

**25.** /a/

| $ 20,000 | Cash balance |
|---|---|
| 35,000 | Accounts receivable |
| 58,000 | Inventory |
| 12,000 | Prepaid expenses |
| 100,000 | Land held for resale |
| $225,000 | Total current assets |

- Cash overdraft did not exist on June 30 as checks were mailed July 9. Add back $30,000 in checks to $10,000 overdraft to arrive at June 30 balance.
- An asset (the land) held for resale qualifies for inclusion as a current asset.

**26.** /c/

| $ 350,000 | Checking account |
|---|---|
| 250,000 | Money-market account |
| 800,000 | U.S. Treasury bill |
| $1,400,000 | Total cash and cash equivalents |

- Treasury bond not included as did not have a maturity of 3 months or less when purchased.

**27.** /c/

| $1,250,000 | Cash in banks |
|---|---|
| 125,000 | Cash on hand |
| $1,375,000 | Total cash |

- $1,600,000 legally restricted cash not included in 12/31 balance sheet cash total. This would be segregated and reported separately within the current asset section.
- $500,000 of compensating balances included - are not legally restricted.

**28.** /b/

| $1,500,000 | Cash in banks |
|---|---|
| 20,000 | Petty cash funds |
| $1,520,000 | |

- $2,000,000 Not included because legally restricted for long-term use.
- $500,000 Compensatory balances included as are not legally restricted.

**29.** /c/

| $4,000 | Balance on 12/31 |
|---|---|
| +500 | Check not mailed until 1/15 -- leave in cash account |
| -200 | Deposit stamped NSF -- remove from cash account |
| $4,300 | |

- $1,000 Dated 1/2, should not be included in 12/31 cash
- $75 Postage stamps not considered cash

**30.** /a/ The segregated bond sinking fund payment account should be classified as a noncurrent asset. The overdrawn account is not netted against the positive cash balance because the accounts are at separate locations. It is reported as a current liability. Cash accounts used for regular operations are reported as current assets.

**31.** /a/ 

| | |
|---|---|
| $18,050 | Statement balance, 8/31 |
| +3,250 | Deposit in transit |
| -2,750 | Outstanding checks |
| $18,550 | Correct balance, 8/31 |

- Customer's insufficient funds check and the bank service charges are already included in the bank statement balance.

**32.** /d/ 

| | |
|---|---|
| $20,000 | Balance per cash account 9/30 |
| +23,000 | Bank deposits in October |
| - 2,000 | Deposit in transit from 9/30 |
| -31,000 | Bank disbursements in October |
| + 3,000 | Outstanding checks at 9/30 |
| - 2,300 | Outstanding checks at 10/31 |
| $10,700 | Cash balance at 10/31 |

**33.** /b/ The securities would not be classified as trading securities because there is no intent to sell them in the near term. ASC Topic 320 requires that these securities be classified as available-for-sale and that they be measured at fair market value in the statement of financial position. Unrealized gains and losses from holding available-for-sale securities are reported as a net amount in a separate component of the stockholders' equity section until realized. Unrealized gains and losses from holding both debt and equity securities classified as trading securities (held for the purpose of trading in the short term) are a component of income from continuing operations.

**34.** /d/ Report the asset received at its fair market value of $15,000. Since this is a receipt of an asset in a nonreciprocal transfer from a corporation to an investor, fair market value is the appropriate amount.

**35.** /b/ The dividend income that would be reported in the income statement relates to amounts received that were **not** liquidating dividends, i.e. amounts that were not in excess of the investor's share of undistributed earnings.

**36.** /b/ Equity method used because 30% of Eagle's shares purchased. Significant influence is to be assumed - even if not specifically stated.

| | |
|---|---|
| $36,000 | % of NI ($120,000 x .3) |
| x 1/2 | Purchase date 7/1 |
| $18,000 | Income from investment |

**37.** /d/ Under the equity method, earnings from the investee corporation increases the balances of both the equity in income of investee and the investment accounts. Receipt of cash dividends, however, affects only the investment account balance.

**38.** /c/ Equity method used because of significant influence. Investment income for 20x8 is 30% of the $40,000 net income reported by Polk Corp ($12,000). Under the equity method, dividends are not a component of investment income. Their receipt is recorded by a decrease in the investment account balance.

**39.** /b/ 

| | |
|---|---|
| $100,000 | Original cost 1/1/x8 |
| +12,000 | Investment income, x8 |
| - 7,500 | Dividends ($25,000 x .3) |
| $104,500 | Balance 12/31/x8 |

**40.** /c/ 

| | |
|---|---|
| $104,500 | Balance 12/31/x8 |
| + 7,500 | Investment income, x2 ($50,000 x 30% x 1/2 yr) |
| - 4,500 | Dividends 4/1/x9 ($15,000 x 30%) |
| $107,500 | Investment account balance, 7/1/x9 |
| x 1/2 | Half of shares sold |
| $ 53,750 | Cost of shares sold |
| 66,000 | Selling price |
| $ 12,250 | Gain on sale |

**41.** /d/ Equity method used because of significant influence

| | |
|---|---|
| $240,000 | % of NI (0.40 x $600,000) |
| - 0 | Amortization of Goodwill |
| $240,000 | Investment income |

Goodwill is no longer amortized and there is no impairment of goodwill given in the problem.

**42.** /b/ Should not have credited dividend revenue for $2,000, but should have credited investment in subsidiary for $2,000.

Result: Investment in subsidiary overstated -- because not credited.

Retained earnings overstated -- because revenue was overstated.

**43.** /c/ On 1/2/x9, a change in accounting method from cost to equity is required because Mega Corp. acquired significant influence over Penny, Inc. with its purchase on that date. A retroactive restatement in the investment account must be made equal to the difference between what the balance currently is and what it would have been had the equity method been used since the initial purchase on 1/1/x8.

Adjustment to 20x8 income:

| | |
|---|---|
| $60,000 | Equity method income ($600,000 x 10%) |
| -20,000 | Dividend income recorded ($200,000 x 10%) |
| $40,000 | Adjustment required |

20x9 investment income:

| | |
|---|---|
| $195,000 | 30% of $650,000 net income |

**44.** /a/ Dividend revenue recorded relates only to the cash dividends. No accounting entry is required for a stock dividend.

**45.** /d/ No dividend revenue is to be reported. Stock dividends do not require an accounting entry, and the sale of some of the shares is irrelevant to a discussion on dividend revenue.

**46.** /c/ The cost basis of the rights is allocated on relative fair value of rights and shares on date rights issued.

| | |
|---|---|
| $ 5,000 | Fair value of rights 12/1/x9 |
| 45,000 | Fair value of stock 12/1/x9 |
| $50,000 | Total fair value |
| $ 5,000 | Proceeds of sale, 12/3/x9 |
| - 3,600 | Cost assigned to rights ($5,000/$50,000 x $36,000) |
| $ 1,400 | Gain on sale of rights |

**47.** /c/

$$\frac{\$10}{\$10 + \$50} \times \$108,000$$

= $18,000 allocated to the warrants

$19,800 (proceeds) - $18,000 (cost)
= $1,800 gain on sale.

**48.** /b/

| | |
|---|---|
| $198,500 | Total paid 4/1/x8 |
| - 4,500 | Accrued interest paid |
| $194,000 | Carrying value 4/1/x8 |
| + 2,800 | Discount amortized ($200,000 face value - $194,000 carrying value = $6,000 total discount, divided by 15 months bonds to be held = $400 monthly amortization x 7 months = $2,800) |
| $196,800 | Carrying amount, 10/31/x8 |

**49.** /d/

| | |
|---|---|
| $583.33 | Gross interest earned ($50,000 x 0.07 x 2/12) |
| + 50.00 | Amortization of discount ($50,000 face value - $48,000 price paid = $2,000 divided by 80 months bonds to be held = $25 monthly amortization x 2 months = $50) |
| $633.33 | Interest income for the year |

**50.** /b/

| | |
|---|---|
| $9,000 | Gross interest income ($200,000 x 0.09 x 6/12) |
| - 750 | Amortization of premium [$216,000 (total) - $6,000 (accrued interest) = $210,000 (cost of bonds) - 200,000 (face) = $10,000 premium divided by 80 months bonds to be held = $125 monthly amortization x 6 months] |
| $8,250 | Interest income for year |

**51.** /b/

| | |
|---|---|
| $400,000 | Cost basis at 12/31/x0 (Significant & permanent decline in value; record loss & write down investment cost basis to $400,000) |
| 350,000 | FMV of PS received |
| $50,000 | Loss on settlement reported in 20x1 |

**52.** /d/ When the market rate < stated rate, bonds usually trade at a premium. When the market rate > stated rate, bonds sell at a discount. As the stated rate remains fixed, it follows that a change in market value from selling for a premium down to selling at a discount occurs when the market rate rises to a point where it exceeds the stated rate.

**53.** /b/ When bonds are purchased between interest dates, accrued interest is paid to the seller in addition to the purchase price of the bonds. This causes the cash paid to be greater than the carrying amount of the bonds on date of purchase. As bond discount is subtracted from face amount to arrive at carrying amount, it follows that the face value is greater than the carrying amount.

**54. /d/** Two factors contribute to the selection of the correct answer in this question. Firstly, since bond premium is added to the face value and bond discount is subtracted from it, the carrying value will be higher if the bond sells at a premium. Secondly, amortization of bond premium using the effective interest method yields periodic amortized amounts that start at their lowest point and increase during the life of bonds. This is because the difference between interest based on a decreasing carrying value at market rate gets progressively smaller compared with the interest actually received (face value x stated rate). As this difference grows wider each period, the amount of premium amortized each period increases. Thus, the premium will be reduced by a relatively small amount of amortization during the first year - causing the carrying value to remain relatively high. Note also that the amount of premium amortized using the straight-line method would be higher during the first half of the life of the bonds than the amortization under the effective method. See amortization schedules presented in Chapter 4 for reassurance on this point.

**55. /a/** The carrying value of the bonds increases by the amount of discount amortized since acquisition.

| | |
|---|---|
| $946,000 | Total paid 7/1/x9 |
| - 40,000 | Accrued interest |
| $906,000 | Carrying amount, 7/1/x9 |
| + 5,300 | Discount amortized, 12/31 |
| $911,300 | Investment in bonds, 12/31 |

| | |
|---|---|
| $ 45,300 | Effective interest ($906,000 x 10% x 6/12) |
| 40,000 | Stated interest ($1,000,000 x 8% x 6/12) |
| $ 5,300 | Discount amortization, 20x9 |

**56. /b/**

| | |
|---|---|
| $450,000 | Sinking fund 12/31/x8 |
| + 90,000 | Additional investment |
| + 15,000 | Dividends |
| + 30,000 | Interest revenue |
| - 5,000 | Administrative costs |
| $580,000 | Balance, 12/31/x9 |

**57. /a/** Revenue earned on the sinking fund investments becomes a part of the fund. The use of sinking fund cash for the purchase of sinking fund investments does not decrease the balance of the investment account.

**58. /a/** As the sinking fund was established for the specific, long-term purpose of meeting the bond obligation due in ten years, the entire balance of the fund should be classified as a noncurrent asset.

**59. /c/**

| | |
|---|---|
| $40,000 | Premium paid, 1/1/x9 |
| -21,000 | Increase in cash surrender value ($108,000 - $87,000) |
| $19,000 | Life insurance expense |

- The $108,000 cash surrender value as of 12/31 already includes the $6,000 increase from the application of the dividends.

**60. /b/** Since annual increases in cash surrender value reduce the related life insurance expense, the total cash surrender value as of 12/31/x9 must be equal to the difference between four years of premiums at $2,000 a year ($8,000) and the actual expense charged during the four-year period ($6,400).

**61. /b/** The gain is equal to the difference between maturity value and carrying value on date of sale (unamortized discount) plus the premium. Unamortized discount on date of sale is $8,000. That amount, added to the $14,000 premium indicates a gain of $22,000 on sale.

**62.** /b/ Bonds classified as held-to-maturity are accounted for at amortized cost.

**63.** /c/ The Statements of Financial Accounting Concepts are pronouncements which are intended by the FASB to set forth objectives and fundamentals that will be used as a basis for future development of financial accounting and reporting standards.

**64.** /a/ Generally accepted accounting principles (GAAP) currently require the use of historical cost when measuring transactions. The reporting of inventory at the lower of cost or market is a departure from this principle. Mark-down of inventories is appropriate when the utility of goods is impaired by damage, deterioration, obsolescence, changes in price levels, or other causes. (see Chapter 3)

**65.** /c/ Although certain conclusions can be drawn indirectly about some aspects of management's performance from the financial statements, the focus of the statements is to provide direct information about enterprise performance for a period of time and the financial position of the enterprise as of a point in time.

**66.** /a/ Generally accepted accounting principles require substantial disclosures with respect to financial statement reporting. While some disclosure is presented parenthetically on the face of the statements themselves, much of the disclosure is presented in the notes to the financial statements. As such, the notes are an integral part of those statements. They are not a vehicle for correction of improper presentation (that should be corrected before the statements are issued), recognition of amounts not included in financial statement totals, nor for presentation of management's response to auditor comments.

**67.** /d/ Whenever a stock dividend is received, the total number of shares owned increases with no corresponding change in total equity ownership. Therefore, the cost of the shares owned must be allocated over all shares owned, including those received in the stock dividend. The original cost is thus divided by the new number of shares owned to calculate the new cost per share figure. A and B are incorrect in that the stock dividends are not considered revenue to the recipient (nor an expense to the issuer.) Answer C is incorrect because there is no change in the **total** cost of the grand stock owned, just additional shares owned.

**68.** /c/ Comprehensive income includes all changes in equity over a period of time except for transactions involving inflows from or distributions to owners. Dividends paid to stockholders is a distribution to owners, and so would be excluded from comprehensive income. All other options listed would be included in comprehensive income.

**69.** /d/ According to SFAC No. 8, <u>Objectives of Financial Reporting by Business Enterprises</u>, the focus of the objectives of financial reporting is the needs of the users of the information presented in the external financial reports.

**70.** /c/ The cash balances in the checking accounts are netted because both accounts are at the same bank. The 90-day certificate of deposit falls within the company's guidelines for cash equivalents; however, the CD due 3/15/x9 does not because its original maturity period exceeds three months.

| | |
|---|---:|
| Cash accounts (netted) | $165,000 |
| Money market fund | 25,000 |
| 90-day CD, due 2/28/x9 | 50,000 |
| Total cash/cash equivalents | $240,000 |

**71.** /c/ Income to be reported as revenue from the life insurance is equal to the cash received ($300,000) less the cash surrender value of the policy at the time of the insured's death ($90,000).

**72.** /d/ Securities classified as "trading" are reported at fair value. Related holding gains and losses are included in earnings during the period incurred. Measurement at lower of cost or market is no longer allowed for such securities, and the reporting of holding gains is not restricted to the extent of previously recognized holding losses.

**73.** /a/ This is a related-party transaction between affiliated organizations, therefore, the receivable from Sabe Co. should be reported separately from trade and other non-trade receivables. Offsetting against a payable to the same organization is not appropriate, and no adjustment is made to the investment account.

**74.** /b/ Held-to-maturity debt securities are reported at amortized cost; available-for-sale, at fair value.

**75.** /d/ The investor's reported invested income is not affected by either a change in the fair value of the investee's stock or cash dividends received from the investee. The former has no effect on any of the investee's accounts. The latter is not treated as an element of invested income, rather it reduces the balance of the Investment in Investee account.

**76.** /d/ Comprehensive income and its components should be displayed as one of the required financial statements. It includes the effects of all changes in equity during a period from transactions and other events except those resulting from investments by owners and distributions to owners. Comprehensive income includes net income plus all the other non-owner changes in equity that do not go through the income statement. A and B are incorrect in that they represent only a part of comprehensive income (the income statement). C is incorrect because the statement is a part of a full set of financial statement, not supplemental information.

# CHAPTER 1

## THEORETICAL FOUNDATIONS AND BALANCE SHEET OVERVIEW

### Simulation Answers

**Number 1 Answer**

1.  /T/    Debt securities that are acquired for the purpose of resale in the near term with the objective of generating short-term profits are classified as trading securities.

2.  /H/    Since Camp has both the positive intent and the ability to hold these U.S. Treasury bonds to maturity, they will be classified as held-to-maturity securities.

3.  /A/    These debt securities are classified as available-for-sale because they do not meet the requirements for classification as either held-to-maturity (positive intent and ability to hold until they mature) or trading (held for the purpose of resale to generate profits in the near term). Plans to resell in three years are not near-term plans.

4.  /A/    Since these are equity securities, the only possible categories are trading (sell in the near term) and available-for-sale. They should be classified as available-for-sale because Camp does not plan to resell them in the near-term.

5.  /G/    Security ABC is classified as a held-to-maturity debt security. As such, it should be measured at amortized cost as of the balance sheet date, 12/31/x9. Since the security was purchased at par, the carrying value will be equal to its $100,000 cost throughout the life of the security. (See Chapter 4, Section III.)

6.  /I/    Security DEF is classified as a trading security. As such, it should be measured at its fair value of $155,000 in the statement of financial position at 12/31/x9.

7.  /J/    Security JKL is classified as an available-for-sale security. As such, it should be measured at its fair value of $160,000 in the statement of financial position at 12/31/x9.

8.  /D/L/    For available-for-sale securities, the net unrealized holding gain is reported as a separate component of stockholders' equity until realized. Since Security GHI is sold in 20x9, any related net holding gain/loss is realized at that time. By 12/31/x8, there was an unrealized holding loss of $25,000. From 1/1/x9 to the date of sale, $10,000 of this unrealized holding loss was recovered for a net unrealized holding loss to date of $15,000. On the sale of the security, this loss of $15,000 is realized.

9.  /B/L/    Unrealized gains or losses that are reported in the income statement are those which arise from holding trading securities. They are measured as the change in fair value over the period. The only trading security is item DEF. Its fair value as of 12/31/x8 was $160,000. Its fair value as of 12/31/x9 is $155,000. This represents an unrealized holding loss of $5,000.

10. /C/L/    The net unrealized gain or loss from holding available-for-sale securities is reported as a separate component of stockholders' equity. The only available-for-sale security still being held at 12/31/x9 is security JKL. The net unrealized gain or loss to be reported relating to this security is a net loss of $10,000, computed as follows:

Unrealized gain, 20x8 (fair value 12/31/x8 $175,000 less cost of $170,000)   $ 5,000
Unrealized loss, 20x9 (change in fair value from $175,000 to $160,000)       (15,000)
Net unrealized loss, 12/31/x9                                                ($10,000)

# CHAPTER 2

## BALANCE SHEET ASSETS

### Question Map

I.  DISCLOSURE OF INFORMATION ABOUT FINANCIAL
    INSTRUMENTS WITH OFF-BALANCE SHEET RISK
    A.  Definitions
        1.  Off-Balance-Sheet-Risk of Accounting Loss -- 2
        2.  Financial Instruments
        3.  Types of Risk
            a.  Credit Risk -- 1
            b.  Market Risk
    B.  Disclosures Required -- 3, 4, 5

II. DISCLOSURES ABOUT FAIR VALUE OF FINANCIAL
    INSTRUMENTS (ASC Topic 825) -- See essays
    A.  Estimate of Fair Value
    B.  Disclosures When Not Practicable to Estimate Fair Value

III. DISCLOSURE ABOUT DERIVATIVE FINANCIAL INSTRUMENTS
     AND FAIR VALUE OF FINANCIAL INSTRUMENTS (ASC Topic 815) -- See essays
     A.  Definition
     B.  Disclosures Required
         1.  Impact of ASC Topic 815
         2.  Held for Trading
         3.  Other than Traded
         4.  Hedging Anticipated Transactions
         5.  Disaggregation of Information
         6.  Fair Value Requirement

IV. PROPERTY, PLANT, AND EQUIPMENT
    A.  Acquisition Cost -- 8, 9
        1.  Cash Purchase -- 6, 7
        2.  Exchange for Stock -- 10
        3.  Exchange for a Note -- 12-16
        4.  Group Acquisition -- 17, 83
        5.  Exchanges
            a.  Definitions
                1)  Similar Assets
                2)  Dissimilar Assets
            b.  Accounting
                1)  Dissimilar -- 24-26
                2)  Similar -- 18
                    a)  No Cash Received -- 19, 22
                    b)  Cash (Boot) Received -- 20, 23, 31, 85
        6.  Donations -- 11

# CHAPTER 2

## BALANCE SHEET ASSETS

### Multiple Choice Questions

**1.** Disclosure of information about significant concentrations of credit risk is required for
   a. All financial instruments.
   b. Financial instruments with off-balance- sheet credit risk only.
   c. Financial instruments with off-balance-sheet market risk only.
   d. Financial instruments with off-balance-sheet risk of accounting loss only.

**2.** All of the following must be disclosed regarding financial instruments with off-balance-sheet risk of accounting loss **except** the
   a. accounting loss incurred if any party to the instrument failed completely to perform, and the collateral proved to be of no value.
   b. face or contract amount.
   c. instrument's nature and terms, including credit risk, market risk, cash requirements, and related accounting policies.
   d. amount by which earnings per share would change if the accounting loss were to occur.

**3.** As described in ASC Topic 815, disclosures are required for
   a. financial instruments with off-balance sheet risk, but **not** where there are concentrations of credit risk.
   b. financial instruments with market risk and credit risk, but not where there are concentrations of credit risk.
   c. financial instruments with off-balance sheet risk only.
   d. financial instruments with market risk, credit risk, and where there are concentrations of credit risk.

**4.** Dorothy Daly, controller of Bearing Manufacturing Company, is preparing Bearing's financial statements for the fiscal year ended November 30, 20x9. Below is an Investment Assets Report Daly received from the Investment Department. Daly needs to review each asset and determine the appropriate application of ASC Topic 815.

Bearing Manufacturing Company
Investment Assets
at November 30, 20x9
(in thousands)

| | |
|---|---:|
| Time deposits | $ 1,000 |
| Bonds carried at amortized cost | 5,500 |
| Convertible bonds | 3,500 |
| Common stock | 5,500 |
| Preferred stock | 2,000 |
| Variable coupon redeemable notes | 750 |
| Financial future contracts - hedged | 1,250 |
| Financial future contracts - nonhedged | 500 |
| Total investment assets | $20,000 |

Of the securities listed, disclosure is required for
   a. the time deposits, financial future contracts - hedged, and the variable coupon redeemable notes.
   b. the convertible bonds, preferred stock, and financial future contracts - unhedged.
   c. the financial future contracts, both hedged and unhedged, and the time deposits.
   d. the financial future contracts only, both hedged and unhedged.

**5.** All of the following must be disclosed with respect to financial instruments with off-balance sheet risk, **except**
   a. The face, contract, or principal amount.
   b. The nature and terms of the instrument and a discussion of the related credit and market risk.
   c. The accounting loss that would be incurred if any party to the instrument failed to perform.
   d. The present value of the future cash flows relating to any concentrations of credit risk.

**6.** On January 1, Dix Co. replaced its old boiler. The following information was available on that date:

| | |
|---|---|
| Carrying amount of old boiler | $ 8,000 |
| Fair value of old boiler | 2,000 |
| Purchase and installation price of new boiler | 100,000 |

The old boiler was sold for $2,000. What amount should Dix capitalize as the cost of the new boiler?

a. $ 92,000
b. $ 94,000
c. $ 98,000
d. $100,000

**7.** On October 1, Shaw Corp. purchased a machine for $126,000 that was placed in service on November 30. Shaw incurred additional costs for this machine as follows:

| | |
|---|---|
| Shipping | $3,000 |
| Installation | 4,000 |
| Testing | 5,000 |

In Shaw's December 31 balance sheet, the machine's cost should be reported as

a. $126,000
b. $129,000
c. $133,000
d. $138,000

**8.** During the year, Burr Co. had the following transactions pertaining to its new office building:

| | |
|---|---|
| Purchase of land | $ 60,000 |
| Legal fees for contracts to purchase land | 2,000 |
| Architect's fees | 8,000 |
| Demolition of old building on site | 5,000 |
| Sale of scrap from old building | 3,000 |
| Construction cost of new building (fully completed) | 350,000 |

In Burr's December 31 balance sheet, what amounts should be reported as the cost of land and cost of building?

| | Land | Building |
|---|---|---|
| a. | $60,000 | $360,000 |
| b. | $62,000 | $360,000 |
| c. | $64,000 | $358,000 |
| d. | $65,000 | $362,000 |

**9.** Land was purchased to be used as the site for the construction of a plant. A building on the property was sold and removed by the buyer so that construction on the plant could begin. The proceeds from the sale of the building should be

a. Classified as other income.
b. Deducted from the cost of the land.
c. Netted against the costs to clear the land and expensed as incurred.
d. Netted against the costs to clear the land and amortized over the life of the plant.

**10.** On December 1 Fontaine Corporation exchanged 1,000 shares of its $25 par value common stock held in treasury for a parcel of land to be held for a future plant site. The treasury shares were acquired by Fontaine at a cost of $50 per share, and on the exchange date the common shares of Fontaine had a fair market value of $60 per share. Fontaine received $7,500 for selling scrap when an existing building on the property was removed from the site. The land should be capitalized at

a. $42,500
b. $50,000
c. $52,500
d. $60,000

**11.** Bicar Corporation owns 10% of the outstanding capital stock of Kopel, Inc. On December 31 when Kopel's retained earnings was $50,000, Bicar received a plot of land from Kopel in a nonreciprocal transfer. Kopel's cost of the land was $7,000 and its fair market value at December 31 was $15,000. At what amount should this land be recorded on Bicar's books?

a. $0
b. $ 5,000
c. $ 7,000
d. $15,000

**12.** Glen, Inc., purchased certain plant assets under a deferred payment contract on December 31. The agreement was to pay $10,000 at the time of purchase and $10,000 at the end of each of the next five years. The plant assets should be valued at

    **a.** The present value of a $10,000 ordinary annuity for five years.
    **b.** $60,000.
    **c.** $60,000 plus imputed interest.
    **d.** $60,000 less imputed interest.

**13.** Electro Corporation bought a new machine and agreed to pay for it in equal annual installments of $5,000 at the end of each of the next five years. Assume a prevailing interest rate of 15%. The present value of an ordinary annuity of $1 at 15% for five periods is 3.35. The future amount of an ordinary annuity of $1 at 15% for five periods is 6.74. The present value of $1 at 15% for five periods is 0.5. How much should Electro record as the cost of the machine?

    **a.** $12,500
    **b.** $16,750
    **c.** $25,000
    **d.** $33,700

**14.** On August 1 Bamco Corporation purchased a new machine on a deferred payment basis. A down payment of $1,000 was made and 4 monthly installments of $2,500 each are to be made beginning on September 1. The cash equivalent price of the machine was $9,500. Bamco incurred and paid installation costs amounting to $300. The amount to be capitalized as the cost of the machine is

    **a.** $ 9,500
    **b.** $ 9,800
    **c.** $11,000
    **d.** $11,300

**15.** On January 1 Liberty Company sold a machine to Bell Corporation in an "arm's length" transaction. Bell signed a noninterest-bearing note requiring payment of $20,000 annually for ten years. The first payment was made on January 1. The prevailing rate of interest for this type of note at date of issuance was 12%. Information on present value factors is as follows:

| Period | Present value of $1 at 12% | Present value of an ordinary annuity of $1 at 12% |
|---|---|---|
| 9 | 0.361 | 5.328 |
| 10 | 0.322 | 5.650 |

Liberty should record the above sale in January at

    **a.** $64,400
    **b.** $84,980
    **c.** $113,000
    **d.** $126,560

**16.** On January 1, 20x9, Gray Company sold a building which cost $190,000 and had accumulated depreciation of $80,000 on the date of sale. Gray received as consideration a $200,000 noninterest-bearing note due on January 1, 20x2. There was no established exchange price for the building, and the note had no ready market. The prevailing rate of interest for a note of this type at January 1, 20x9, was 10%. The present value of $1 at 10% for three periods is 0.75. What amount of interest income should be included in Gray's 20x9 income statement?

    **a.** $6,750
    **b.** $15,000
    **c.** $16,667
    **d.** $20,000

**17.** During the year the Commander Corporation acquired 3 pieces of machinery at an auction for a lump sum price of $240,000. In addition, Commander paid $12,000 to have the machines installed. An appraisal disclosed the following values:

| | |
|---|---|
| Machine A | $50,000 |
| Machine B | $150,000 |
| Machine C | $100,000 |

What costs should be assigned to Machines A, B, and C, respectively?

    **a.** $40,000, $120,000, and $80,000
    **b.** $42,000, $126,000, and $84,000
    **c.** $50,000, $150,000, and $100,000
    **d.** $84,000, $84,000, and $84,000

**18.** Minor Baseball Company had a player contract with Doe that was recorded in its accounting records at $145,000. Better Baseball Company had a player contract with Smith that was recorded in its accounting records at $140,000. Minor traded Doe to Better for Smith by exchanging each player's contract. The fair value of each contract was $150,000. What amount should be shown in the accounting records after the exchange of player contracts?

|     | Minor | Better |
| --- | --- | --- |
| a. | $140,000 | $140,000 |
| b. | $140,000 | $145,000 |
| c. | $145,000 | $140,000 |
| d. | $150,000 | $150,000 |

**19.** On December 1 Leonard Company exchanged a delivery truck (that was acquired four years previously) for a new delivery truck. The old truck was purchased for $14,000 and had a book value of $5,600. On the date of the exchange the old truck had a market value of $6,000. In addition, Leonard paid $7,000 cash for the new truck, which had a list price of $16,000. At what amount should Leonard record the new truck for financial accounting purposes?
- **a.** $10,000
- **b.** $12,600
- **c.** $13,000
- **d.** $16,000

**20.** May Co. and Sty Co. exchanged nonmonetary assets. The exchange did not culminate an earnings process for either May or Sty. May paid cash to Sty in connection with the exchange. To the extent that the amount of cash exceeds a proportionate share of the carrying amount of the asset surrendered, a realized gain on the exchange should be recognized by

|     | May | Sty |
| --- | --- | --- |
| a. | Yes | Yes |
| b. | Yes | No |
| c. | No | Yes |
| d. | No | No |

**21.** In an exchange of similar assets, Transit Co. received equipment with a fair value equal to the carrying amount of equipment given up.

Transit also contributed cash. As a result of the exchange, Transit recognized
- **a.** A loss equal to the cash given up.
- **b.** A loss determined by the proportion of cash paid to the total transaction value.
- **c.** A gain determined by the proportion of cash paid to the total transaction value.
- **d.** Neither a gain nor a loss.

**22.** Dahl Co. traded a delivery van and $5,000 cash for a newer van owned by West Corp. The following information relates to the values of the vans on the exchange date:

|         | Carrying value | Fair value |
| --- | --- | --- |
| Old van | $30,000 | $45,000 |
| New van | $40,000 | $50,000 |

Dahl's income tax rate is 30%. What amounts should Dahl report as gain on exchange of the vans?
- **a.** $15,000
- **b.** $1,000
- **c.** $700
- **d.** $0

**23.** Amble, Inc. exchanged a truck with a carrying amount of $12,000 and a fair value of $20,000 for a truck and $5,000 cash. The fair value of the truck received was $15,000. At what amount should Amble record the truck received in the exchange?
- **a.** $7,000
- **b.** $9,000
- **c.** $12,000
- **d.** $15,000

**24.** On September 1, 20x9, Bertz, Inc., exchanged a delivery truck for a parcel of land. Bertz bought this truck in 20x7 for $10,000. At September 1, 20x9, the truck had a book value of $6,500 and a fair market value of $5,000. Bertz gave $6,000 in cash in addition to the truck as part of this transaction. The previous owner of the land had listed the land for sale at $12,000. At what amount should Bertz record the land?
- **a.** $11,000
- **b.** $11,500
- **c.** $12,000
- **d.** $12,500

**25.** In January Kemper Construction Company exchanged an old truck, which cost $54,000 and was one-third depreciated, and paid $35,000 cash for a used crane having a current fair value of $65,000. At what amount should the crane be recorded on the books of Kemper?

- a. $54,000
- b. $65,000
- c. $71,000
- d. $89,000

**26.** In October Ewing Company exchanged an old packaging machine, which cost $120,000 and was 50% depreciated, for a dissimilar used machine and paid a cash difference of $16,000. The market value of the old packaging machine was determined to be $70,000. For the year ended December 31 what amount of gain or loss should Ewing recognize on this exchange?

- a. $0.
- b. $6,000 loss.
- c. $10,000 loss.
- d. $10,000 gain.

**27.** During the year, Bay Co. constructed machinery for its own use and for sale to customers. Bank loans financed these assets both during construction and after construction was complete. How much of the interest incurred should be reported as interest expense in the income statement for the year?

| | Interest incurred for machinery for own use | Interest incurred for machinery held for sale |
|---|---|---|
| a. | All interest incurred | All interest incurred |
| b. | All interest incurred | Interest incurred after completion |
| c. | Interest incurred after completion | Interest incurred after completion |
| d. | Interest incurred after completion | All interest incurred |

**28.** On January 1, 20x0, Richmond, Inc., signed a fixed-price contract to have Builder Associates construct a major plant facility at a cost of $4,000,000. It was estimated that it would take three years to complete the project. Also on January 1, 20x0, to finance the construction cost, Richmond borrowed $4,000,000 payable in 10 annual installments of $400,000, plus interest at the rate of 11%. During 20x0 Richmond made deposit and progress payments totaling $1,500,000 under the contract; the average amount of accumulated expenditures was $650,000 for the year. The excess borrowed funds were invested in short-term securities, from which Richmond realized investment income of $250,000. What amount should Richmond report as capitalized interest at December 31, 20x0?

- a. $71,500
- b. $165,000
- c. $190,000
- d. $440,000

**29.** Herr, Inc., has a fiscal year ending April 30. On May 1, 20x8, Herr borrowed $10,000,000 at 15% to finance construction of its own building. Repayments of the loan are to commence the month following completion of the building. During the year ended April 30, 20x9, expenditures for the partially completed structure totaled $6,000,000. These expenditures were incurred evenly throughout the year. Interest earned on the unexpended portion of the loan amounted to $400,000 for the year. How much should be shown as capitalized interest on Herr's financial statements as of April 30, 20x9?

- a. $0
- b. $50,000
- c. $450,000
- d. $1,100,000

**30.** Star Co. leases a building for its product showroom. The ten-year non-renewable lease will expire on December 31, 20x5. In January 20x0, Star redecorated its showroom and made leasehold improvements of $48,000. The estimated useful life of the improvements is 8 years. Star used the straight-line method of amortization. What amount of leasehold improvements, net of amortization, should Star report in its June 30, 20x0, balance sheet?

- a. $45,600
- b. $45,000
- c. $44,000
- d. $43,200

**31.** On January 4 Hadley Company signed a 10-year nonrenewable lease for a building to be used in its manufacturing operations. During January Hadley incurred the following costs:

- $64,000 for general improvements to the leased premises with an estimated useful life of eight years.

- $32,000 for a movable assembly line equipment installation with an estimated useful life of eight years.

A full year's amortization is taken for the calendar year. What amount should Hadley record as amortization of leasehold improvements for the year?
- **a.** $6,400
- **b.** $8,000
- **c.** $9,600
- **d.** $12,000

**32.** On January 1, 20x8, Bay Co. acquired a land lease for a 21-year period with no option to renew. The lease required Bay to construct a building in lieu of rent. The building, completed on January 1, 20x9, at a cost of $840,000, will be depreciated using the straight-line method. At the end of the lease, the building's estimated market value will be $420,000. What is the building's carrying amount in Bay's December 31, 20x9, balance sheet?
- **a.** $798,000
- **b.** $800,000
- **c.** $819,000
- **d.** $820,000

**33.** On June 18, Paul Printing Company incurred the following costs for one of its printing presses:

| | |
|---|---|
| Purchase of collating and stapling | |
| Attachment | $42,000 |
| Installation of attachment | 18,000 |
| Replacement parts for overhaul of press | 13,000 |
| Labor and overhead in connection with | |
| Overhaul | 7,000 |
| Total | $80,000 |

The overhaul resulted in a significant increase in production. Neither the attachment nor the overhaul increased the estimated useful

life of the press. How much of the above costs should be capitalized?
- **a.** $42,000
- **b.** $55,000
- **c.** $60,000
- **d.** $80,000

**34.** During 20x8, Yvo Corp. installed a production assembly line to manufacture furniture. In 20x9, Yvo purchased a new machine and rearranged the assembly line to install this machine. The rearrangement did not increase the estimated useful life of the assembly line, but it did result in significantly more efficient production. The following expenditures were incurred in connection with this project:

| | |
|---|---|
| Machine- | $75,000 |
| Labor to install machine- | 14,000 |
| Parts added in rearranging the assembly line to provide future benefits | 40,000 |
| Labor and overhead to rearrange the assembly line | 18,000 |

What amount of the above expenditures should be capitalized in 20x9?
- **a.** $147,000
- **b.** $107,000
- **c.** $ 89,000
- **d.** $ 75,000

**35.** On January 1, 20x8, Kent Corporation purchased a machine for $50,000. Kent paid shipping expenses of $500 as well as installation costs of $1,200. The machine was estimated to have a useful life of ten years and an estimated salvage value of $3,000. In January 20x9 additions costing $3,600 were made to the machine in order to comply with pollution control ordinances. These additions neither prolonged the life of the machine nor did they have any salvage value. If Kent records depreciation under the straight-line method, depreciation expense for 20x9 is
- **a.** $4,870
- **b.** $5,170
- **c.** $5,270
- **d.** $5,570

**36.** On July 1, one of Rudd Co.'s delivery vans was destroyed in an accident. On that date, the van's carrying value was $2,500. On July 15, Rudd received and recorded a $700 invoice for a new engine that had been installed in the van in May, and another $500 invoice for various repairs. In August, Rudd received $3,500 under its insurance policy on the van, which it plans to use to replace the van. What amount should Rudd report as gain (loss) on disposal of the van in its income statement for the year?

    **a.** $1,000
    **b.** $300
    **c.** $0
    **d.** $(200)

**37.** A building suffered uninsured fire damage. The damaged portion of the building was refurbished with higher quality materials. The cost and related accumulated depreciation of the damaged portion are identifiable. To account for these events, the owner should

    **a.** Reduce accumulated depreciation equal to the cost of refurbishing.
    **b.** Record a loss in the current period equal to the sum of the cost of refurbishing and the carrying amount of the damaged portion of the building.
    **c.** Capitalize the cost of refurbishing and record a loss in the current period equal to the carrying amount of the damaged portion of the building.
    **d.** Capitalize the cost of refurbishing by adding the cost to the carrying amount of the building.

**38.** On July 1, Stone Corporation received a condemnation award of $300,000 as compensation for the forced sale of a plant located on company property which stood in the path of a new highway. On this date the plant building had a depreciated cost of $150,000 and the land cost was $50,000. On October 1 Stone purchased a parcel of land for a new plant site at a cost of $125,000. Ignoring income taxes, Stone should report on its income statement for the year ended December 31 a gain of

    **a.** $0
    **b.** $25,000
    **c.** $75,000
    **d.** $100,000

**39.** On June 30, 20x9, a fire in Ruffing Company's plant caused a total loss to a production machine. The machine had a book value of $80,000 at December 31, 20x8, and was being depreciated at an annual rate of $10,000. The machine had a fair value of $110,000 at the date of the fire, and Ruffing received insurance proceeds of $100,000 in October 20x9. The same month Ruffing purchased a replacement machine for $130,000. Ignoring income taxes, what amount should Ruffing report on its 20x9 income statement as involuntary conversion gain or loss?

    **a.** $0.
    **b.** $10,000 loss.
    **c.** $20,000 gain.
    **d.** $25,000 gain.

**40.** Lano Corp's forest land was condemned for use as a national park. Compensation for the condemnation exceeded the forest land's carrying amount. Lano purchased similar, but larger, replacement forest land for an amount greater than the condemnation award. As a result of the condemnation and replacement, what is the net effect on the carrying amount of forest land reported in Lano's balance sheet?

    **a.** The amount is increased by the excess of the replacement forest land's cost over the condemned forest land's carrying amount.
    **b.** The amount is increased by the excess of the replacement forest land's cost over the condemnation award.
    **c.** The amount is increased by the excess of the condemnation award over the condemned forest land's carrying amount.
    **d.** No effect, because the condemned forest land's carrying amount is used as the replacement forest land's carrying amount.

**41.** On January 1, 20x5, Walton Company purchased a machine for $200,000 and established an annual straight-line depreciation rate of 10%, with no salvage value. During 20x9 Walton determined that the machine will not be economically useful in its production process after December 31, 20x9. Walton estimated that the machine had no scrap value at December 31, 20x9, and would be disposed of in early 20x0 at a cost of $5,000. In its income statement for the year ended December 31, 20x9, what amount(s) and type of charge(s) should Walton report for the machine?

|    | Depreciation Expense | Loss on abandonment |
|----|----------|----------|
| a. | $0 | $125,000 |
| b. | $20,000 | $100,000 |
| c. | $20,000 | $105,000 |
| d. | $120,000 | $ 5,000 |

**42.** On December 27 Holden Company sold a building, receiving as consideration a $400,000 noninterest-bearing note due in three years. The building cost $380,000 and the accumulated depreciation was $ 160,000 at the date of sale. The prevailing rate of interest for a note of this type was 12%. The present value of $1 for three periods at 12% is 0.71. In its income statement for the year, how much gain or loss should Holden report on the sale?
- a. $20,000 gain.
- b. $64,000 gain.
- c. $96,000 loss.
- d. $180,000 gain.

**43.** On January 1, Jambon purchased equipment for use in developing a new product. Jambon uses the straight-line depreciation method. The equipment could provide benefits over a 10-year period. However, the new product development is expected to take five years, and the equipment can be used only for this project. Jambon's expense for the year equals
- a. The total cost of the equipment.
- b. One-fifth of the cost of the equipment.
- c. One-tenth of the cost of the equipment.
- d. Zero.

**44.** In January Action Corporation entered into a contract to acquire a new machine for its factory. The machine, which had a cash price of $150,000, was paid for as follows:

| | |
|---|---|
| Down payment | $15,000 |
| Notes payable in 10 equal monthly installments | 120,000 |
| 500 shares of Action common stock with an agreed value of $50 per share | 25,000 |
| Total | $160,000 |

Prior to the machine's use, installation costs of $4,000 were incurred. The machine has an estimated useful life of 10 years and an estimated salvage value of $5,000. What should Action record as depreciation expense for the year under the straight-line method?
- a. $15,900
- b. $15,500
- c. $15,000
- d. $14,900

**45.** On January 2, 20x6, Reed Co. purchased a machine for $800,000 and established an annual depreciation charge of $100,000 over an eight-year life. During 20x9, after issuing its 20x8 financial statements, Reed concluded that: (1) the machine suffered permanent impairment of its operational value, and (2) $200,000 is a reasonable estimate of the amount expected to be recovered through use of the machine for the period January 1, 20x9, through December 31, 20x3. In Reed's December 31, 20x9, balance sheet, the machine should be reported at a carrying amount of
- a. $0
- b. $100,000
- c. $160,000
- d. $400,000

**46.** Which of the following depreciation methods is computed in the same way as depletion is computed?
- a. Straight-line.
- b. Sum-of-the-years'-digits.
- c. Double-declining-balance.
- d. Productive-output.

**47.** Net income is understated if, in the first year, estimated salvage value is excluded from the depreciation computation when using the

| | Straight-line Method | Production or Use method |
|---|---|---|
| a. | Yes | No |
| b. | Yes | Yes |
| c. | No | No |
| d. | No | Yes |

**48.** When a fixed asset with a five-year estimated useful life is sold during the second year, how would the use of the sum-of-the-years'-digits method of depreciation instead of the straight-line method of depreciation affect the gain or loss on the sale of the fixed asset?

| | Gain | Loss |
|---|---|---|
| a. | Decrease | Increase |
| b. | Increase | Decrease |
| c. | No effect | No effect |
| d. | No effect | Decrease |

**49.** Flex Company owns a machine that was bought on January 2, 20x6, for $94,000. The machine was estimated to have a useful life of five years and a salvage value of $6,000. Flex uses the sum-of-the-years'-digits method of depreciation. At the beginning of 20x9, Flex determined that the useful life of the machine should have been four years and the salvage value $8,800. For the year 20x9, Flex should record depreciation expense on this machine of
a. $11,100
b. $14,800
c. $17,600
d. $21,300

**50.** On January 2, 20x7, Mogul Company acquired equipment to be used in its manufacturing operations. The equipment has an estimated useful life of 10 years and an estimated salvage value of $5,000. The depreciation applicable to this equipment was $24,000 for 20x9, computed under the sum-of-the-years' digits method. What was the acquisition cost of the equipment?
a. $165,000
b. $170,000
c. $240,000
d. $245,000

**51.** A machine with a 5-year estimated useful life and an estimated 10% salvage value was acquired on January 1, 20x6. On December 31, 20x9, accumulated depreciation, using sum-of-the-years' digits method, would be
a. (Original cost less salvage value) multiplied by 1/15.
b. (Original cost less salvage value) multiplied by 14/15.
c. Original cost multiplied by 14/15
d. Original cost multiplied by 1/15

**52.** In January 20x8, Colonial Company purchased equipment for $120,000, to be used in its manufacturing operations. The equipment was estimated to have a useful life of 8 years, with salvage value estimated at $12,000. Colonial considered various methods of depreciation and selected the sum-of-the-years'-digits method. On December 31, 20x9, the related allowance for accumulated depreciation should have a balance
a. $15,000 less than under the straight-line method.
b. $15,000 less than under the double declining balance method.
c. $18,000 greater than under the straight-line method.
d. $18,000 greater than under the double declining balance method.

**53.** At the end of the expected useful life of a depreciable asset with an estimated 15% salvage value, the accumulated depreciation would equal the original cost of the asset under which of the following depreciation methods?

| | Straight-line | Sum-of-the-years'-digits |
|---|---|---|
| a. | Yes | Yes |
| b. | No | No |
| c. | Yes | No |
| d. | No | Yes |

**54.** South Co. purchased a machine that was installed and placed in service on January 1, 20x8, at a cost of $240,000. Salvage value was estimated at $40,000. The machine is being depreciated over 10 years by the double-declining balance method. For the year ended December 31, 20x9, what amount should South report as depreciation expense?
a. $48,000
b. $38,400

c. $32,000
d. $21,600

**55.** On July 1 Carol Corporation purchased factory equipment for $25,000. Salvage value was estimated to be $1,000. The equipment will be depreciated over ten years using the double-declining balance method. Counting the year of acquisition as one-half year, Carol should record depreciation expense for the next year on this equipment of
a. $3,840
b. $4,500
c. $4,800
d. $5,000

**56.** Shaw Company purchased a machine on January 1, 20x8, for $350,000. The machine has an estimated useful life of five years and a salvage value of $50,000. The machine is being depreciated using the double-declining balance method. The asset balance net of accumulated depreciation at December 31, 20x9, should be
a. $126,000
b. $158,000
c. $170,000
d. $224,000

**57.** Essex Company purchased a machine on July 1 for $300,000. The machine has an estimated useful life of five years and a salvage value of $40,000. The machine is being depreciated from the date of acquisition by the 150% declining balance method. For the year ended December 31 Essex should record depreciation on this machine of
a. $39,000
b. $45,000
c. $60,000
d. $90,000

**58.** Which of the following utilizes the straight-line depreciation method?

| | Composite Depreciation | Group Depreciation |
|---|---|---|
| a. | No | No |
| b. | No | Yes |
| c. | Yes | No |
| d. | Yes | Yes |

**59.** A company using the composite depreciation method for its fleet of trucks, cars, and campers retired one of its trucks and received cash from a salvage company. The net carrying amount of these composite asset accounts would be decreased by
a. Cash proceeds received and original cost of the truck.
b. Cash proceeds received.
c. Original cost of the truck less the cash proceeds.
d. Original cost of the truck.

**60.** When one machine is retired, the accumulated depreciation account is debited for the original cost of that machine less any residual recovery under which of the following depreciation methods?

| | Composite | Group |
|---|---|---|
| a. | No | No |
| b. | No | Yes |
| c. | Yes | No |
| d. | Yes | Yes |

**61.** On January 1, 20x5, Crater Inc. purchased equipment having an estimated salvage value equal to 20% of its original cost at the end of a 10-year life. The equipment was sold December 31, 20x9, for 50% of its original cost. If the equipment's disposition resulted in a reported loss, which of the following depreciation methods did Crater use?
a. Double-declining balance.
b. Sum-of-the-years' digits.
c. Straight-line.
d. Composite.

**62.** On June 30, Union, Inc. purchased goodwill of $125,000 when it acquired the net assets of Apex Corp. During the year, Union incurred additional costs of developing goodwill by training Apex employees ($50,000) and hiring additional Apex employees ($25,000). Union's December 31 balance sheet should report goodwill of
a. $200,000
b. $175,000
c. $150,000
d. $125,000

Course 5292 Copyright 2021. The Rigos programs have educated over 100,000 professionals since 1980.

**63.** Which of the following costs of goodwill should be capitalized?

| | Developing goodwill | Restoring goodwill |
|---|---|---|
| a. | Yes | Yes |
| b. | Yes | No |
| c. | No | Yes |
| d. | No | No |

**64.** The owners of the Zoot Suit Clothing store are contemplating selling the business to new interests. The cumulative earnings for the past 5 years amounted to $450,000. The annual earnings based on an average rate of return on investment for this industry would have been $76,000. If excess earnings are to be capitalized at 10%, then implied goodwill should be
a. $120,000
b. $140,000
c. $440,000
d. $450,000

**65.** On June 30, 20x9 Finn, Inc. exchanged 2,000 shares of Edlow Corp. $30 par value common stock for a patent owned by Bisk Co. The Edlow stock was acquired in 20x7 at a cost of $50,000. At the exchange date, Edlow common stock had a fair value of $40 per share, and the patent had a net carrying amount of $100,000 on Bisk's books. Finn should record the patent at
a. $50,000
b. $60,000
c. $80,000
d. $100,000

**66.** On January 1, 20x8, Robert Harrison signed an agreement to operate as a franchisee of Perfect Pizza, Inc., for an initial franchise fee of $40,000. Of this amount, $15,000 was paid when the agreement was signed and the balance is payable in five annual payments of $5,000 each beginning January 1, 20x9. The agreement provides that the down payment is not refundable and no future services are required of the franchisor. Harrison's credit rating indicates that he can borrow money at 12% for a loan of this type. Information on present and future value factors is as follows:

Present value of $1 at 12% for 5 periods 0.567

Future amount of $1 at 12% for 5 periods 1.762

Present value of an ordinary annuity of $1
at 12% for 5 periods                          3.605

Harrison should record the acquisition cost of the franchise on January 1, 20x8, at
a. $29,175
b. $33,025
c. $40,000
d. $44,050

**67.** Hull Co. bought a trademark from Roe Corp. on January 1, 20x9, for $224,000. Hull retained an independent consultant who estimated the trademark's remaining finite useful life to be 50 years. Its book value on Roe's accounting records was $112,000. Hull decided to amortize the trademark over the maximum period allowed. In Hull's December 31, 20x9, balance sheet, what amount should be reported as accumulated amortization?
a. $5,600
b. $4,480
c. $2,800
d. $2,240

**68.** Say Co. purchased Ivy Co. at a cost that resulted in recognition of goodwill having an expected 10-year benefit period. However, Say plans to make additional expenditures to maintain goodwill for a total of 40 years. What costs should be capitalized and over how many years should they be amortized?

| | Costs capitalized | Amortization period |
|---|---|---|
| a. | Acquisition costs only | -0- years |
| b. | Acquisition costs only | 40 years |
| c. | Acquisition costs only | 10 years |
| d. | Acquisition and maintenance costs | 10 years |

**69.** On January 1, 20x6, Taft Co. purchased a patent for $714,000. The patent is being amortized over its remaining legal life of 15 years. During 20x9, Taft determined that the economic benefits of the patent would not last longer than ten years from the date of acquisition. What amount should be reported in the balance sheet for the patent, net of accumulated amortization, at December 31, 20x9?

    **a.** $428,000
    **b.** $489,600
    **c.** $504,000
    **d.** $523,600

**70.** A consideration in determining the useful life of an intangible asset is not the

    **a.** Legal, regulatory, or contractual provisions.
    **b.** Provisions for renewal or extension.
    **c.** Expected actions of competitors.
    **d.** Initial cost.

**71.** On January 1, 20x4, an intangible asset with a thirty-five-year estimated useful life was acquired. On January 1, 20x9, a review was made of the estimated useful life, and it was determined that the intangible asset had an estimated useful life of forty-five more years. As a result of the review

    **a.** The original cost at January 1, 20x4, should be amortized over a fifty-year life.
    **b.** The original cost at January 1, 20x4, should be amortized over the remaining thirty-year life.
    **c.** The unamortized cost at January 1, 20x9, should be amortized over a forty-five-year life.
    **d.** The unamortized cost at January 1, 20x9, should be amortized over a thirty-five-year life.

**72.** Howe Corporation bought a cola franchise from Pennington, Inc., on January 2, 20x9, for $100,000. A highly regarded independent research company estimated that the remaining useful life of the franchise was a finite 50 years. Its unamortized cost on Pennington's books at January 1, 20x9, was $15,000. Howe has decided to write off the franchise over the longest possible period. How much should be amortized for the year ended December 31, 20x9?

    **a.** $375
    **b.** $2,000

    **c.** $2,500
    **d.** $15,000

**73.** During 20x9, Lyle Co. incurred $400,000 of research and development costs in its laboratory to develop a product for which a patent was granted on July 1, 20x9. Legal fees and other costs associated with the patent totaled $82,000. The estimated economic life of the patent is 10 years. What amount should Lyle capitalize for the patent on July 1, 20x9?

    **a.** $0
    **b.** $82,000
    **c.** $400,000
    **d.** $482,000

**74.** On January 2, 20x5, Hermes Corporation acquired a patent for $192,000. The patent had a remaining legal life of twelve years and an estimated useful life of eight years. In January 20x9 Hermes paid $12,000 in legal fees in a successful defense of the patent. What should Hermes record as patent amortization for 20x9?

    **a.** $16,000
    **b.** $24,000
    **c.** $25,500
    **d.** $27,000

**75.** Which of the following statements concerning patents is correct?

    **a.** Legal costs incurred to successfully defend an internally developed patent should be capitalized and amortized over the patent's remaining economic life.
    **b.** Legal fees and other direct costs incurred in registering a patent should be capitalized and amortized on a straight-line basis over a five-year period.
    **c.** Research and development contract services purchased from others and used to develop a patented manufacturing process should be capitalized and amortized over the patent's economic life.
    **d.** Research and development costs incurred to develop a patented item should be capitalized and amortized on a straight-line basis over 17 years.

 Course 5292 Copyright 2021. The Rigos programs have educated over 100,000 professionals since 1980.

**76.** Malden, Inc. has two patents that have allegedly been infringed by competitors. After investigation, legal counsel informed Malden that it had a weak case on Patent A34 and a strong case in regard to patent B19. Malden incurred additional legal fees to stop infringement on B19. Both patents have a remaining legal life of 8 years. How should Malden account for these legal costs incurred relating to the two patents?

   **a.** Expense costs for A34 and capitalize costs for B19.
   **b.** Expense costs for both A34 and B19.
   **c.** Capitalize costs for both A34 and B19.
   **d.** Capitalize costs for A34 and expense costs for B19.

**77.** On December 31, 20x8, the New Bite Company had capitalized costs for a new computer software product with an economic life of four years. Sales for 20x9 were ten percent of expected total sales of the software. At December 31, 20x9, the software had a net realizable value equal to eighty percent of the capitalized cost. The unamortized cost reported on the December 31, 20x9, balance sheet should be

   **a.** Net realizable value.
   **b.** Ninety percent of net realizable value.
   **c** Seventy-five percent of capitalized cost.
   **d.** Ninety percent of capitalized cost.

**Items 78 and 79 are based on the following information:**

During 20x8, Pitt Corp. incurred costs to develop and produce a routine, low-risk computer software product, as follows:

| | |
|---|---|
| Completion of detail program design | $13,000 |
| Costs incurred for coding and testing to establish technological feasibility | 10,000 |
| Other coding costs after establishment of technological feasibility | 24,000 |
| Other testing costs after establishment of technological feasibility | 20,000 |
| Costs of producing product masters for training materials | 15,000 |
| Duplication of computer software and training materials from product masters (1,000 units) | 25,000 |
| Packaging product (500 units) | 9,000 |

**78.** In Pitt's December 31, 20x9, balance sheet, what amount should be reported in inventory?
   **a.** $25,000
   **b.** $34,000
   **c.** $40,000
   **d.** $49,000

**79.** In Pitt's December 31, 20x9, balance sheet, what amount should be capitalized as software cost, subject to amortization?
   **a.** $54,000
   **b.** $57,000
   **c.** $59,000
   **d.** $69,000

**80.** On December 31, 20x8, Bit Co. had capitalized costs for a new computer software product with an economic life of five years. Sales for 20x9 were 30 percent of expected total sales of the software. At December 31, 20x9, the software had a net realizable value equal to 90 percent of the capitalized cost. What percentage of the original capitalized cost should be reported as the net amount on Bit's December 31, 20x9, balance sheet?
   **a.** 70%
   **b.** 72%
   **c.** 80%
   **d.** 90%

**81.** The Gunther Company acquired a tract of land containing an extractable natural resource. Gunther is required by its purchase contract to restore the land to a condition suitable for recreational use after it has extracted the natural resource. Geological surveys estimate that the recoverable reserves will be 4,000,000 tons, and that the land will have a value of $1,000,000 after restoration. Relevant cost information follows:

| | |
|---|---|
| Land | $9,000,000 |
| Estimated restoration costs | 1,200,000 |

If Gunther maintains no inventories of extracted material, what should be the charge to depletion expense per ton of extracted material?
   **a.** $2.00
   **b.** $2.25
   **c.** $2.30
   **d.** $2.55

**82.** Suris Corporation acquired a mineral mine for $900,000 of which $150,000 was ascribed to land value after the mineral has been removed. Geological surveys have indicated that 15 million units of the mineral could be extracted. During the year 1,200,000 units were extracted and 800,000 units were sold. What is the amount of depletion for the year?

    a. $40,000
    b. $48,000
    c. $60,000
    d. $72,000

**83.** On July 1, 20x9, Casa Development Co. purchased a tract of land for $1,200,000. Casa incurred additional costs of $300,000 during the remainder of 20x9 in preparing the land for sale. The tract was subdivided into residential lots as follows:

| Lot Class | Number of lots | Sales price per lot |
|---|---|---|
| A | 100 | $24,000 |
| B | 100 | $16,000 |
| C | 200 | $10,000 |

Using the relative sales value method, what amount of costs should be allocated to the Class A lots?

    a. $300,000
    b. $375,000
    c. $600,000
    d. $720,000

**84.** Cole Co. began constructing a building for its own use in January 20x9. During 20x9, Cole incurred interest of $50,000 on specific construction debt, and $20,000 on other borrowings. Interest computed on the weighted-average amount of accumulated expenditures for the building during 20x9 was $40,000. What amount of interest cost should Cole capitalize?

    a. $20,000
    b. $40,000
    c. $50,000
    d. $70,000

**85.** Slate Co. and Talse Co. exchanged similar plots of land with fair values in excess of carrying amounts. In addition, Slate received cash from Talse to compensate for the difference in land values. As a result of the exchange, Slate should recognize

    a. A gain equal to the difference between the fair value and the carrying amount of the land given up.
    b. A gain in an amount determined by the ratio of cash received to total consideration.
    c. A loss in an amount determined by the ratio of cash received to total consideration.
    d. Neither a gain nor a loss.

**86.** Turtle Co. purchased equipment on January 2, 20x7, for $50,000. The equipment had an estimated five-year service life. Turtle's policy for five-year assets is to use the 200% double-declining depreciation method for the first two years of the asset's life, and then switch to the straight-line depreciation method. In its December 31, 20x9, balance sheet, what amount should Turtle report as accumulated depreciation for equipment?

    a. $30,000
    b. $38,000
    c. $39,200
    d. $42,000

**87.** On January 2, 20x9, Rafa Co. purchased a franchise with a useful life of ten years for $50,000. An additional franchise fee of 3% of franchise operation revenues must be paid each year to the franchisor. Revenues from franchise operations amounted to $400,000 during 20x9. In its December 31, 20x9, balance sheet, what amount should Rafa report as an intangible asset - franchise?

    a. $33,000
    b. $43,800
    c. $45,000
    d. $50,000

 Course 5292 Copyright 2021. The Rigos programs have educated over 100,000 professionals since 1980.

# CHAPTER 2

## BALANCE SHEET ASSETS

### Simulation Questions

**Number 1    (Estimated time - 25 minutes)**

**Question Number 1** consists of 8 items. Select the **best** answer for each item. **Answer all items.**

During 20x9, Sloan Inc. began a project to construct new corporate headquarters. Sloan purchased land with an existing building for $750,000. Sloan planned to demolish the building and construct a new office building on the site. Items 1 through 8 represent various expenditures by Sloan for this project.

**Required:**

For each expenditure in Items 1 through 8, select from the list below the appropriate accounting treatment.

    **L.** Classify as land and do not depreciate.
    **B.** Classify as building and depreciate.
    **E.** Expense.

**Items to be Answered:**

1.  Purchase of land for $700,000.
2.  Interest of $147,000 on construction financing incurred after completion of construction
3.  Interest of $186,000 on construction financing paid during construction.
4.  Purchase of building for $50,000.
5.  $18,500 payment of delinquent real estate taxes assumed by Sloan on purchase.
6.  $12,000 liability insurance premium during the construction period.
7.  $65,000 cost of razing existing building.
8.  Moving costs of $136,000.

**Number 2    (Estimated time - 25 minutes)**

**Question Number 2** consists of 14 items. Select the **best** answer for each item.

(Editor's comment:  Some of the items relate to topics presented in other chapters. Such chapters have been referenced.)

**Items 1 through 6** represent expenditures for goods held for resale and equipment.

**Required:** For each of the items 1 through 6, determine whether the expenditure should be capitalized **C** or expensed as a period costs **E**.

1.  Freight charges paid for goods held for resale. (Ch. 3)
2.  In-transit insurance on goods held for resale purchased F.O.B. shipping point. (Ch. 3)
3.  Interest on note payable for goods held for resale.
4.  Installation of equipment.
5.  Testing of newly-purchased equipment.
6.  Cost of current year service contract on equipment.

**Items 7 through 10** are based on the following 20x9 transactions:

- Link Co. purchased an office building and the land on which it is located by paying $800,000 cash and assuming an existing mortgage of $200,000. The property is assessed at $960,000 for realty tax purposes, of which 60% is allocated to the building.
- Link leased construction equipment under a 7-year capital lease requiring annual year-end payments of $100,000. Link's incremental borrowing rate is 9%, while the lessor's implicit rate, which is not known to Link, is 8%. Present value factors for an ordinary annuity for seven periods are 5.21 at 8% and 5.03 at 9%. Fair value of the equipment is $515,000. (Ch. 4)

- Link paid $50,000 and gave a plot of undeveloped land with a carrying amount of $320,000 and a fair value of $450,000 to Club Co. in exchange for a plot of undeveloped land with a fair value of $500,000. The land was carried on Club's books at $350,000.

**Required:** For each of the items 7 through 10, calculate the amount to be recorded for each item.

7. Building.
8. Leased equipment.
9. Land received from Club on Link's books.
10. Land received from Link on Club's books.

**Items 11 through 14** are based on the following information:

On January 2, 20x8, Half, Inc. purchased a manufacturing machine for $864,000. The machine has an 8-year estimated life and a $144,000 estimated salvage value. Half expects to manufacture 1,800,000 units over the life of the machine. During 20x9, Half manufactured 300,000 units.

**Required:** Items 11 through 14 represent various depreciation methods. For each item, calculate depreciation expense for 20x9 (the second year of ownership) for the machine described above under the method listed.

11. Straight-line.
12. Double-declining balance.
13. Sum-of-the-years'-digits.
14. Units of production.

# CHAPTER 2

## BALANCE SHEET ASSETS

### Multiple Choice Answers

1. /a/ This question focuses on the disclosures relating to financial instruments. Disclosure of information about significant concentrations of credit risk applies to all financial instruments.

2. /d/ The impact on earnings per share of the possible accounting loss is not required to be disclosed. All other options are specifically required to be disclosed.

3. /d/ Disclosures are required for all financial instruments where there is off-balance sheet risk (both credit and market risk), and where there are significant concentrations of credit risk. Answers A, B, and C are either not complete or incorrectly exclude a category of disclosure requirement.

4. /d/ Only the financial future contracts are financial instruments to which off-balance sheet risk would apply. For the hedged contracts, both market risk and credit risk would have to be considered. For the non-hedged contracts, just the credit risk would need to be considered.

5. /d/ The present value of future cash flows relating to financial instruments with concentrations of credit risk is not required to be disclosed. Each of the items A, B, and C is a required disclosure under the Standard.

6. /d/ The carrying value of the old boiler is not relevant to the acquisition cost of the new boiler because this was not an exchange transaction.

7. /d/ All costs given are ordinary and necessary costs of acquiring the asset and placing it in service.

8. /c/ Cost of land:

| | |
|---|---|
| $60,000 | Purchase price |
| + 2,000 | Legal fees |
| + 5,000 | Demolition of old building |
| - 3,000 | Proceeds of scrap sale |
| $64,000 | Cost of land |

Cost of building:

| | |
|---|---|
| $ 8,000 | Architect's fees |
| 350,000 | Construction costs |
| $358,000 | Cost of building |

9. /b/ The proceeds from the sale of an old building or of scrap from its demolition are recorded as a reduction in the cost of the land.

10. /c/

| | |
|---|---|
| $60,000 | Fair Market Value of Stock Given Up ($60 x 1,000) |
| - 7,500 | Scrap Proceeds |
| $52,500 | Capitalized Value of Land |

11. /d/ Nonreciprocal transfers are recorded at fair market value.

12. /d/ When assets are acquired under a deferred payment contract, the assets should be recorded at the present value of the cash payments, which equals the total payments of $60,000 less any imputed interest. Option A is incorrect because it ignores the $10,000 initial payment.

13. /b/ $5,000 (ordinary annuity) x 3.35 (present value factor) = $16,750

Record the asset at the present value of the cash payments.

**14.** /b/

| | |
|---|---|
| $9,500 | Cash Equivalent Price (Do not use total undiscounted cash payments.) |
| + 300 | Installation Costs Capitalized |
| $9,800 | Total Capitalized Cost |

**15.** /d/ $20,000 (annuity)

x 6.328 (PV of annuity due) =

$126,560

(Record at the present value of the cash payments. Present value of an annuity due is equal to the present value of an ordinary annuity for one less period, 5.328, plus 1.0.)

**16.** /b/ $200,000 x 0.75 = $150,000 Present Value of Note

Present value of $150,000 x 0.10 (imputed rate) = $15,000 interest

**17.** /b/ $240,000 + 12,000 = $252,000 Capitalized Amount

$$A = \frac{50,000}{300,000} \times \$252,000 = \$42,000$$

$$B = \frac{150,000}{300,000} \times 252,000 = \$126,000$$

$$C = \frac{100,000}{300,000} \times 252,000 = \$84,000$$

**18.** /d/

| | Minor | Better | |
|---|---|---|---|
| BV of Old | $145,000 | $140,000 | Similar |
| FMV of Old | 150,000 | 150,000 | Assets |
| Gain | $ 5,000 | $ 10,000 | Recognize |

The gain is recognized and both Minor and Better will record the new contract at fair value ($150,000).

**19.** /b/

| | |
|---|---|
| $ 6,000 | Fair Market Value of Old Truck |
| - 5,600 | Basis Value of Old Truck |
| $ 400 | Gain on Exchange of Assets |

**19.** (cont.)

| | |
|---|---|
| $ 6,000 | Fair Market Value of Old Truck Given Up |
| + 7,000 | Added Cash Paid |
| $13,000 | Assumed Fair Market Value of New Truck (Ignore $16,000 List Price) |

The gain would be recognized in the current year.

**20.** /c/ This is an exchange of a similar asset as it did not culminate an earnings process. The company that receives cash will recognize that portion of any gain realized based on the relative value of cash received to the total of cash and FMV of the asset received. The procedure described in the question will lead to the same result. May Co. did not receive any cash; Sty Co. did.

**21.** /a/ Exchange of similar assets.

· Carrying value of equipment given = FMV of asset received, AND
· FMV of equipment given + cash paid = FMV of asset received.

· Therefore, carrying value of equipment given must be greater than its FMV. This results in a loss equal to the amount of the cash paid to equalize the fair market values of the assets exchanged.

**22.** /d/ $45,000 (FMV of old van) - $30,000 (carrying value) = $15,000 gain. However, all the gain is deferred as this is an exchange of similar assets and no cash was received.

**23.** /b/ Exchange of assets.

| | |
|---|---|
| $20,000 | FMV of old truck |
| -12,000 | CV of old truck |
| $8,000 | Gain on exchange |
| -8,000 | Gain recognized |
| | All gains are recognized in the current year. |
| $0 | Gain deferred |
| $15,000 | Recorded amount of new truck. ($15,000 FMV) |

**24.** /a/ Dissimilar assets. Report the asset received at its fair market value of $11,000. This is equal to the $5,000 fair value of the asset given up plus the $6,000 cash given up. (Ignore the list price of $12,000.)

**25.** /b/ Dissimilar assets exchanged. Record any gain (or loss) on the exchange. The new asset (crane) is recorded on the books at its fair market value of $65,000.

**26.** /d/ 

| | |
|---|---|
| $60,000 | BV of Old ($120,000 x 0.50) |
| 70,000 | FMV of Old |
| $10,000 | Gain (All recorded because dissimilar assets.) |

**27.** d/ Interest incurred beyond the completion date of an asset constructed for a company's own use is not capitalized; it is expensed. Interest related to loans for construction of routinely manufactured inventories is expensed, not capitalized.

**28.** /a/ 

| | |
|---|---|
| $650,000 | Average Accumulated Expenditures |
| x 0.11 | Interest Rate on Specific Borrowing |
| $ 71,500 | Capitalized Interest |

**29.** /c/ 

| | |
|---|---|
| $3,000,000 | Average Accumulated Expenditures (6,000,000/2) |
| x 0.15 | Specific Interest Rate |
| $ 450,000 | Interest Capitalized |

Do not capitalize based on the total borrowing of $10,000,000 or the total accumulated expenditures of $6,000,000. Do not reduce capitalized interest for the $400,000 interest earned on investing unexpended portions of borrowings.

**30.** /c/ As of January 20x0, six years remain on the life of the lease. $48,000 -:- 6 years = $8,000 annual amortization.

$48,000 − ($8,000 x 1/2 year) = $44,000 net leasehold improvement, June 30.

**31.** /b/ $64,000/8 years = $8,000 Amortization

(The $32,000 installation costs are capitalized, but are not considered leasehold improvements as they are movable and therefore not restricted to use at the leased premises.)

**32.** /c/ $840,000 - $420,000 = $420,000 cost to be amortized in lieu of rent.

$420,000 -:- 20 years remaining on lease when building completed = $21,000 annual amortization. $840,000 - $21,000 (building been in use only 1 yr.) = $819,000

**33.** /d/ All costs should be capitalized. They are ordinary and necessary costs incurred in improving the assets.

**34.** /a/ All the costs should be capitalized. Rearrangement costs are capitalized if they have future benefits.

**35.** /c/ 

| | |
|---|---|
| $50,000 | Purchase Price |
| + 500 | Shipping Costs |
| + 1,200 | Installation Costs |
| $51,700 | Capitalized - 3,000 (SV) |
| | = $48,700/10 years |
| | = $4,870 |
| $ 3,600 | Capitalized Addition/9 years remaining = + 400 |
| | $5,270 |

**36.** /b/ 

| | |
|---|---|
| $2,500 | Carrying value, 7/1 |
| + 700 | Cost of new engine installed prior to accident |
| $3,200 | Total loss in accident |
| 3,500 | Insurance proceeds |
| $ 300 | Gain on disposal |

The cost of repairs is not capitalized. It is a period cost.

**37.** /c/ Although the events are related, each is accounted for separately. The uninsured damage is recorded as a loss, and the refurbishing is treated as the cost of an addition to be capitalized.

**38.** /d/

| | |
|---|---|
| $300,000 | Proceeds Received |
| -200,000 | Cost Basis ($150,000 + 50,000) |
| $100,000 | Gain (Not Deferred for Accounting Purposes) |

**39.** /d/

| | |
|---|---|
| $80,000 | BV 12/31/x8 |
| - 5,000 | Depreciation 1/1/x9 to 6/30/x9 ($10,000/2) |
| $75,000 | BV at 6/30/x9 |
| 100,000 | Insurance Proceeds Received |
| $25,000 | Gain Recorded for Accounting Purposes |

**40.** /a/ The cost of the condemned land is removed from the land account and the cost of newly acquired land is added to the land account. As the cost of the new is greater than the cost removed, the balance of the account will increase by the amount of the excess cost.

**41.** /c/ $20,000 Depreciation Expense -- The asset was used during 20x9.

Loss on Disposal: $100,000 (BV at 12/31/x9) + 5,000 Estimated Disposal Costs = $105,000

**42.** /b/

| | |
|---|---|
| $220,000 | (BV) = $380,000 Cost - $150,000 AD |
| 284,000 | PV of Note Received ($400,000 x 0.71) |
| $ 64,000 | Gain on Sale |

**43.** /a/ The equipment is being used solely for research and development purposes. Such costs are expensed in the period acquired.

**44.** /d/

| | |
|---|---|
| $150,000 | Cash Equivalent Price (Not $160,000) |
| + 4,000 | Installation Costs |
| $154,000 | Capitalized Amount |
| - 5,000 | Salvage Value |
| $149,000 | (depreciable value)/10 years = $14,900 Expense |

**45.** /c/

| | |
|---|---|
| $500,000 | Book value 1/1/x9 |
| -300,000 | Write-down for impairment ($500,000 book value - $200,000 recoverable) |
| $200,000 | To be depreciated over remaining years |
| -:- 5 | |
| $ 40,000 | Revised annual depreciation |

$500,000 book value 1/1/x9 - $300,000 write down- $40,000 depreciation 20x9 = $160,000 carrying amount 12/31/x9

**46.** /d/ The calculation of depletion is based on the productive output method (also called the units of production method). The other methods are not used to calculate depletion.

**47.** /b/ Salvage value is deducted from cost under both the straight-line and units-of-production methods. If it is excluded from the computations, the resulting depreciation expense amounts will be too high and net income will be understated.

**48.** /b/ Sum-of-the-years'-digits depreciation is initially higher than straight line depreciation, resulting in a lower book value than the straight-line method. method. Therefore, gains would be greater (increase) and losses would be lower (decrease) when sum-of-the-years-digits is used rather than straight line.

**49.** /b/ $94,000 - 6,000 = $88,000 (depreciable value) x (5/15 + 4/15 + 3/15) = $70,400 (AD)

$94,000 (cost) - 70,400 (AD) - 8,800 (SV) = $14,800 Expense in 4th Year

50. /b/ (Cost - 5,000) x 8/55 = $24,000
        (year 3 of 10-year life)
    $24,000 x 55/8 = $165,000
    $165,000 + $5,000 = $170,000 cost

51. /b/ Depreciation taken 20x6 through 20x9 = 5/15 + 4/15 + 3/15 + 2/15 = 14/15 of (cost less salvage value).

52. /c/ $\frac{(\$120,000 - 12,000)}{8}$ = $13,500

    $13,500/year x 2 years =  $27,000

    ($120,000 - 12,000) x
    (8/36 + 7/36) =          45,000

    SYD Greater Than
    SL Depreciation          $18,000

53. /b/ The accumulated depreciation should not equal the original cost under any depreciation method when a salvage value of 15 percent exists. Accumulated depreciation should be 85 percent of original cost.

54. /b/ 100% -:- 10 years x 2 = 20% a year
    $240,000 x 20% = $48,000 dep. Year 1
    $240,000 - $48,000 = $192,000 (book value 1/1/x9)
    $192,000 x 20% = $38,400 depreciation for 20x9.

55. /b/ 100% -:- 10yrs x 2 = 20%/year
    $25,000 (original cost) x 0.20 =
    5,000 x 1/2 =
    $2,500 (partial 1st year)

    $25,000 - 2,500 =
    $22,500 (BV) x 0.20 =
    $4,500 (2nd year)

56. /a/ 100% -:- 5yrs x 2 = 40% a year
    $350,000 x (0.40) = $140,000 (1st)
    $350,000 - 140,000 = $210,000
    $210,000 x 0.40 = $84,000 (2nd)

$350,000 - (140,000 + 84,000) = $126,000 (BV)

(Alternative method:  $350,00 x 60% x 60% = $126,000)

57. /b/ 100% -:- 5 yrs x 1.5 = 30% a year
    $300,000(original cost) x 0.30 =
    $90,000 x 6/12 =
    $45,000

58. /d/ Both the composite method (dissimilar assets) and the group method (similar assets) are based on the straight-line method of depreciation.

59. /b/ Under the composite method, no gain or loss on disposal is recorded. The cash proceeds received are equal to the net of the debits and credits to the asset and accumulated depreciation accounts. Therefore, the net carrying amount of the assets is reduced by an amount equal to the cash proceeds received.

60. /d/ Under both methods, the accumulated depreciation account is debited for the difference between the original cost and residual recovery. Therefore, no gain or loss is recorded on retirement.

61. /c/ The carrying amount of the equipment on 12/31/x9 must be greater than 50% of the original cost for the sale to generate a loss. Both the double-declining balance and sum-of-the-years' digits methods will yield book values equal to less than 50% of original cost after five years of depreciation. Under the composite method, no loss would be recognized. Therefore, the straight-line method must have been used.

62. /d/ Goodwill arises as a result of the purchase of a business. Costs relating to internally generated goodwill or to maintaining goodwill purchased are not capitalized.

63. /d/ Costs of developing or restoring goodwill are not capitalized and amortized.

64. /a/
| $88,000 | Average Annual Ordinary Earnings = ($450,000 - 10,000)/5 |
| -76,000 | Average Annual Industry Earnings |
| $12,000 | Excess Annual Earnings divided by 10% = |
| $120,000 | Implied Goodwill |

65. /c/ The patent is capitalized at the fair market value of the consideration (shares) given. 2,000 shares at $40/share = $80,000

66. /b/
| $15,000 | Payment at Signing of Agreement |
| +18,025 | PV of Future Payments ($5,000 x 3.605) |
| $33,025 | Acquisition Cost at 1/1/x8 |

67. /b/ There is no maximum period over which an intangible asset may be amortized. Therefore, Hull's cost of $224,000 ÷ 50 years = $4,480. Roe's unamortized cost is not relevant.

68. /a/ Capitalized goodwill costs arise only in a business acquisition situation. They are not to be amortized, but rather examined annually for any impairment loss. Costs to maintain goodwill are not capitalized.

69. /b/ Original amortization:
$714,000 cost / 15 years = $47,600/year
$714,000 - ($47,600 x 3 years) = $571,200 cost remaining.

Revised amortization:
$571,200/7 years = $81,600/year
Net patent cost, 12/31/x4:
$714,000 - ($47,600 x 3 years) - $81,600 (amortization 20x4) = $489,600

70. /d/ Initial cost has no bearing on the useful life of an asset. All other options are considered in determining the useful life of an intangible asset.

71. /c/ There is no maximum amortization period for an intangible asset. Therefore, the unamortized cost after the first five years of life can be spread over an additional 45 years (for a total amortization period of 50 years).

72. /b/
| $100,000 | Acquisition Cost to Howe |
| 50 Years | Amortization period allowed |
| = $2,000 | Annual Amortization |

There is no limit to the length of time to amortize an intangible asset.

73. /b/ Capitalize only the legal fees and costs associated with acquiring the patent. Research and development costs are expensed in the period incurred.

74. /d/
| $192,000/8 years | $24,000 |
| $12,000/4 years remaining | + 3,000 |
| Patent Amortization for Remaining Years | $27,000 |

75. /a/ Research and development costs are not capitalized. Legal costs incurred to successfully defend the rights related to an intangible asset should be added to the asset's cost and amortized over its remaining useful life.

76. /a/ Legal fees paid to successfully defend patent rights are capitalized. As the case for Patent A34 is weak, a successful defense is not likely. Therefore, expense legal costs related to Patent A34, but capitalize those for Patent B19 because the case is strong.

**77.** /c/ Cost amortized is the greater of the ratio of current revenue to current and future revenue (10%) or straight-line amortization over the remaining 4-year life (25%). 25% of straight-line will yield a greater amortization amount than the 10% revenue ratio. Furthermore, the balance sheet carrying amount should be the lower of unamortized cost (100% of cost less 25% amortization = 75% of cost), or net realizable value - 80% (given). 75% of cost is the lower amount.

**78.** /b/ Inventory costs include the $25,000 duplication costs and the $9,000 packaging = $34,000

**79.** /c/ Costs incurred after achieving technological feasibility through point of production for sales are capitalized. $24,000 + $20,000 + $15,000 to produce product masters = $59,000

**80.** /a/ Amortization for 20x9 is 30% of cost because the ratio of current revenue to current and future revenue (30%) is greater than straight-line amortization over the remaining economic life (25% - four years remaining). The balance sheet carrying amount should be the lower of unamortized cost (100% - 30% = 70% of cost) or net realizable value (90% of cost - given). 70% is lower.

**81.** /c/ $\dfrac{\$9,000,000 \quad + \quad \$1,200,000 \quad - \quad \$1,000,000}{4,000,000 \text{ tons}}$

= $2.30 per ton

**82.** /c/ $\dfrac{\$900,000 - \$150,000}{15,000,000 \text{ units}}$

= $0.05 per unit x 1,200,000 extracted = $60,000

**83.** /c/ $24,000/$60,000 X total costs of $1,500,000 = $600,000

**84.** /b/ Interest to be capitalized is the interest computed based on the weighted-average amount of accumulated expenditures for the building during the period, i.e. $40,000. Since this amount does not exceed total interest cost for the period ($70,000), no adjustment needs to be made.

**85.** /b/ Since the fair values exceed carrying values, there is the potential for a gain to be recorded. In an exchange of similar assets, gains are recorded only if cash is received. The amount of gain to be recorded is that portion of gain that is equal to the ratio of cash received to total consideration received (cash plus fair market value of land received).

**86.** /b/ DDB depreciation rate:

100%/5 years x 2 = 40% per year

Accumulated Depreciation, 12/31/x9:
Year 1, $50,000 x 40% =     $20,000
Year 2, $30,000 x 40% =     12,000
Year 3, switch to straight-line
Carrying value/years remaining.

$\dfrac{\$50,000 - \$20,000 - \$12,000}{3 \text{ years}}$    6,000

Accumulated depreciation,
12/31/x9     $38,000

**87.** /c/ The franchise is reported at cost less amortization to date. The franchise fee has no impact on the amortization process.

$50,000/10 years = $5,000 per year

$50,000 - $5,000 = $45,000

# CHAPTER 2

## BALANCE SHEET ASSETS

### Simulation Answers

**Number 1 Answer**

1. /L/     The cost of land is not depreciated.

2. /E/     Interest on construction financing related to self-constructed assets is not capitalized beyond the completion date of the asset.

3. /B/     Interest on construction financing is capitalized beginning with initial expenditures related to the building and continues until the asset is ready for its intended use.

4. /L/     When land is purchased as a building site, no part of the acquisition cost attributable to an existing building that is to be removed from the land is assigned to the building account. Such cost is considered part of the ordinary and necessary expenditures related to bringing the land to its intended use condition.

5. /L/     Delinquent taxes "run with the land." They are part of the necessary and ordinary costs of acquiring the land and are charged to the asset account.

6. /B/     The insurance costs are capitalized as part of the ordinary and necessary costs of construction (acquisition) of the building.

7. /L/     Any costs of razing an existing building are charged to the land account. They are ordinary and necessary costs of getting the land in the condition required for its intended use.

8. /E/     Moving costs are period costs. They are not capitalized

**Number 2 Answer**

1. /C/ Theoretically, freight charges paid for goods held for resale are costs that have been incurred to bring the inventories to their existing condition and location and, as such, should be capitalized. (See Ch. 3, "Inventory Costs.")

2. /C/ Goods shipped F.O.B. shipping point are included in the inventory of the buyer when they are transferred to the shipper. Thus, in-transit insurance charges are a part of the necessary and ordinary cost that the buyer incurs to bring the inventory to its existing condition and location. Theoretically, such charges should be capitalized. Note, however, that the practical difficulties and relatively high cost of tracking these costs on a unit or inventory batch basis lead these costs to be treated, usually, as period costs. The CPA exam, however, is looking for the answer that is theoretically correct. (See Ch. 3, Section II, "Inventory Costs.")

3. /E/ Except for capitalizing of some interest relating to the financing of certain self-constructed assets, interest costs are not generally capitalized. Rather, they are treated as an expense of the period for which the financing was secured, regardless of the underlying purpose for the borrowing.

4. /C/ Installation costs are part of the ordinary and necessary costs of acquiring an asset and bringing it to the location and condition required for its intended use.

5. /C/ Costs related to the testing of newly-purchased equipment are part of the ordinary and necessary costs of acquiring an asset and bringing it to the location and condition required for its intended use.

6. /E/ Service contracts on assets relate to maintenance charges for a period of time. Those costs that pertain to the current period are expensed.

7. /$600,000/ Total paid for building plus land is cash plus mortgage assumed, $1 million. However, since the building is allocated 60% of value for realty tax purposes, only 60% of the acquisition cost should be assigned to the building. The remaining $400,000 is assumed to be the cost of the land.

8. /$503,000/ The capital lease is to be recorded at the present value of the minimum lease payments. If the lessee knows the lessor's implicit interest rate, the present value is computed using the lower of the lessor's implicit rate or the lessee's incremental borrowing rate. However, since Link (the lessee) does not know the lessor's implicit rate, then Link's incremental borrowing rate of 9% must be used. $100,000 X present value factor of 5.03 (ordinary annuity for seven periods at 9%0) = $503,000. (See Chapter 4, Section VII.B.2.d.2 for full explanation.)

9. /$370,000/ This is an exchange of like assets. In each instance, the land is recorded at the FMV of the land received less any gain deferred. All gain is deferred if no cash is received. FMV of asset given up by Link, $450,000 less book value of $320,000 = total gain of $130,000. Since Link received no cash, all of this gain is deferred. The land received is recorded at its fair market value of $500,000 less the $130,000 gain deferred.

10. /$315,000/   Since Club received $50,000 cash, some amount of gain must be recognized. The amount to record is proportionate to the percentage of cash received when compared with the total market value of all assets received. $50,000 -:- ($50,000 cash + $450,000 FMV of land received) = 10%. FMV of asset given up by Club, $500,000 less book value of $350,000 = total gain of $150,000. $150,000 X 10% = $15,000 gain recognized. $150,000 less $15,000 recognized = $135,000 gain deferred.

$450,000 FMV of asset received less $135,000 gain deferred = $315,000.

11. /$90,000/   Straight-line depreciation is the same each year. Formula is (cost minus salvage value) divided by estimated life in years. ($864,000 - $144,000)/8 years = $90,000.

12. /$162,000/   Double-declining balance takes a fixed percentage of book value as of the beginning of the period each year. The rate to use is equal to twice the straight-line rate.
100% -:- 8 years = 12.5% x 2 = 25% a year.
Year 1.   Book value of $864,000 x 25% = $216,000 depreciation.
Year 2.   Book value ($864,000 - $216,000) = $648,000
$648,000 x 25% = $162,000

13. /$140,000/   Sum-of-the-years'-digits uses a fraction made up of the years in the life in reverse in the numerator and the sum of the digits in the life as the denominator. An eight-year life yields a denominator of 36. Year two would use 7 as the numerator. This fraction is applied to the cost minus salvage value of the asset. ($864,000 - $144,000) x (7/36) = $140,000

14. /$120,000/   Units of production allocates a fixed amount of depreciation per unit to the units produced by the asset during the period. Depreciation per unit is (cost minus salvage value) -:- total estimated units to be produced over the life of the asset. ($864,000 - $144,000)/1,800,000 units = $.40 per unit.
300,000 units x $.40 = $120,000

# CHAPTER 3

## RECEIVABLES AND INVENTORIES

### Question Map

V.   GENERAL GUIDELINES FOR VALUING INVENTORY
     A.  Lower of Cost or Market -- 43-48,57,87
     B.  Reporting Inventory Losses in Interim Financial Statements -- 49, 50
     C.  Treatment of Inventory Losses on Purchase Commitments
     D.  Valuing Inventory Above Cost

VI.  MAJOR INVENTORY ACCOUNTING METHODS -- 3-9
     A.  Perpetual -- 55-60, 65
     B.  Gross Profit -- 51-54
     C.  Periodic -- 57, 63, 65

VII. UNIT-BASED INVENTORY VALUATION METHODS
     A.  Specific Identification
     B.  Average Cost Methods
         1.  Perpetual Moving Average -- 55, 56, 58, 60
         2.  Periodic Weighted Average
     C.  Last In First Out (LIFO) -- 59, 61, 62, 66
     D.  First In First Out (FIFO) -- 62, 63, 65, 66, 67

VIII. AGGREGATE INVENTORY VALUATION METHODS
     A.  Dollar-value LIFO -- 64, 68
         1.  Basic Method -- 70, 71, 72, 88
         2.  Price Indexes
             a.  Double-extension Method – 69, 73
             b.  Link-chain Technique -- 69
     B.  Retail Methods
         2.  Six Varieties of the Retail Method
             a.  Conventional (Lower of Average Cost or Market) Retail -- 74, 75, 76
             b.  Average Cost Retail
             c.  Lower of FIFO Cost or Market Retail
             d.  FIFO Retail -- 77
             e.  Lower of LIFO Cost or Market Retail
             f.  LIFO Retail
     C.  Dollar-value LIFO Retail

IX.  CONSIGNMENTS -- 78-81, 89, 90

X.   COINSURANCE -- 82

XI.  DEPLETION COST OF INVENTORY -- 83, 91

# CHAPTER 3

# RECEIVABLES AND INVENTORIES

## Multiple Choice Questions

**1.** Steven Corporation began operations. For the year ended December 31, Steven made available the following information:

| | |
|---|---|
| Total merchandise purchases for the year | $350,000 |
| Merchandise inventory at December 31 | 70,000 |
| Collections from customers | 200,000 |

All merchandise was marked to sell at 40% above cost. Assuming that all sales are on a credit basis and all receivables are collectible, what should be the balance in accounts receivable at December 31?

a. $ 50,000
b. $192,000
c. $250,000
d. $290,000

**2.** The following information relates to Jay Co.'s accounts receivable for the year:

| | |
|---|---|
| Accounts receivable, 1/1 | $ 650,000 |
| Credit sales | 2,700,000 |
| Sales returns | 75,000 |
| Accounts written off | 40,000 |
| Collections from customers | 2,150,000 |
| Estimated future sales returns for next year | 50,000 |
| Estimated uncollectible accounts for next year | 110,000 |

What amount should Jay report for accounts receivable, before allowance for sales returns and uncollectible accounts, at December 31?

a. $1,200,000
b. $1,125,000
c. $1,085,000
d. $ 925,000

**3.** The Avec Company's account balances at December 31 for accounts receivable and the related allowance for uncollectible accounts were $800,000 and $40,000 respectively. An aging of accounts receivable indicated that $71,100 of the December 31 receivables may be uncollectible. The net realizable value of accounts receivable was

a. $688,900
b. $728,900
c. $760,000
d. $768,900

**4.** Based upon its past collection experience, Alden Company provides for bad debt expense at the rate of 2% of credit sales. On January 1, 20x9, the allowance for doubtful accounts balance was $10,000. During the year Alden wrote off $18,000 of uncollectible receivables and recovered $5,000 of bad debts written off in prior years. If credit sales for the year totaled $1,000,000, the allowance for doubtful accounts balance at December 31, 20x9, should be

a. $12,000
b. $17,000
c. $20,000
d. $30,000

**5.** The December 31 trial balance of the Mark Company before adjustments included the following accounts:

| | Debit | Credit |
|---|---|---|
| Allowance for doubtful accounts | $ 2,000 | |
| Sales | | $830,000 |
| Sales returns and allowances | 10,000 | |

Mark estimates its bad debts based upon 2% of net sales. What amount should Mark record as bad debt expense for the year?

a. $14,400
b. $14,600
c. $16,400
d. $16,600

**6.** The following information pertains to Tara Co.'s accounts receivable at December 31:

| Days outstanding | Amount | Estimated % uncollectible |
|---|---|---|
| 0 - 60 | $120,000 | 1% |
| 61 - 120 | 90,000 | 2% |
| Over 120 | 100,000 | 6% |
| | $310,000 | |

During the year, Tara wrote off $7,000 in receivables and recovered $4,000 that had been written off in prior years. Tara's December 31 allowance for uncollectible accounts was $22,000. Under the aging method, what amount of allowance for uncollectible accounts should Tara report at December 31?

    a. $ 9,000
    b. $10,000
    c. $13,000
    d. $19,000

**7.** Orr Co. prepared an aging of its accounts receivable at December 31 and determined that the net realizable value of the receivables was $250,000. Additional information is available as follows:

| | |
|---|---|
| Allowance for uncollectible accounts at January 1 – credit balance | $28,000 |
| Accounts written off during the year as uncollectible | 23,000 |
| Accounts receivable, December 31 | 270,000 |
| Uncollectible accounts recovery during the year | 5,000 |

For the year ended December 31, Orr's uncollectible accounts expense would be

    a. $23,000
    b. $20,000
    c. $15,000
    d. $10,000

**8.** Hall Co.'s allowance for uncollectible accounts had a credit balance of $24,000 at December 31, 20x8. During 20x9, Hall wrote off uncollectible accounts of $96,000. The aging of accounts receivable indicated that a $100,000 allowance for doubtful accounts was required at December 31, 20x9. What amount of uncollectible accounts expense should Hall report for 20x9?

    a. $172,000
    b. $120,000
    c. $100,000
    d. $ 96,000

**9.** A method of estimating uncollectible accounts that emphasizes asset valuation rather than income measurement is the allowance method based on

    a. Aging the receivables.
    b. Direct write off.
    c. Gross sales.
    d. Credit sales less returns and allowances.

**10.** Effective with the year ended December 31, 20x9, Grimm Company adopted a new accounting method for estimating the allowance for doubtful accounts at the amount indicated by the year-end aging of accounts receivable. The following data are available:

| | |
|---|---|
| Allowance for doubtful accounts, 1/1/x9 | $24,000 |
| Provision for doubtful accounts during 20x9 (2% on credit sales of $1,000,000) | 20,000 |
| Bad debts written off, 11/30/x9 | 19,500 |
| Estimated uncollectible accounts per aging, 12/31/x9 | 21,000 |

After year-end adjustment, the bad debt expense for 20x9 would be

    a. $16,500
    b. $19,500
    c. $20,000
    d. $21,000

**11.** When a specific customer's account receivable is written off as uncollectible, what will be the effect on net income under each of the following methods of recognizing bad debt expense?

| | Allowance | Direct Write Off |
|---|---|---|
| a. | None | Decreased |
| b. | Decreased | None |
| c. | Decreased | Decreased |
| d. | None | None |

**12.** Alden Corporation provides an allowance for its doubtful accounts receivable. At December 31, 20x8, the allowance account had a credit balance of $8,000. Each month Alden accrues bad debt expense in an amount equal to 2% of credit sales. Total credit sales during 20x9 amounted to $2,000,000. During 20x9 uncollectible accounts receivable totaling $22,000 were written off against the allowance account. An aging of accounts receivable at December 31, 20x9, indicates that an allowance of $42,000 should be provided for doubtful accounts as of that date. Accordingly, bad debt expense previously accrued during 20x9 should be increased by

    **a.** $62,000
    **b.** $42,000
    **c.** $26,000
    **d.** $16,000

**13.** When the allowance method of recognizing uncollectible accounts is used, the entries at the time of collection of a small account previously written off would

    **a.** Increase the allowance for uncollectible accounts.
    **b.** Increase net income.
    **c.** Decrease the allowance for uncollectible accounts.
    **d.** Have **no** effect on the allowance for uncollectible accounts.

**14.** Gibbs Co. uses the allowance method for recognizing uncollectible accounts. Ignoring deferred taxes, the entry to record the write-off of a specific uncollectible account

    **a.** Affects **neither** net income **nor** working capital
    **b.** Affects **neither** net income **nor** accounts receivable.
    **c.** Decreases both net income and accounts receivable.
    **d.** Decreases both net income and working capital

**15.** Wren Company had the following account balances at December 31:

| | |
|---|---|
| Accounts receivable | $ 900,000 |
| Allowance for doubtful accounts (before provision for doubtful accounts expense for the year) | 16,000 |
| Credit sales for the year | 1,750,000 |

Wren is considering the following methods of estimating doubtful accounts expense for the year:

- Based on credit sales at 2%
- Based on accounts receivable at 5%

What amount should Wren charge to doubtful accounts expense under each method?

| | Percentage of credit sales | Percentage of accounts receivable |
|---|---|---|
| **a.** | $51,000 | $45,000 |
| **b.** | $51,000 | $29,000 |
| **c.** | $35,000 | $45,000 |
| **d.** | $35,000 | $29,000 |

**16.** On July 1, 20x8, a company received a one-year note receivable bearing interest at the market rate. The face amount of the note receivable and the entire amount of the interest are due on June 30, 20x9. When the note receivable was recorded on July 1, 20x8, which of the following were debited?

| | Interest Receivable | Unearned Discount on Note Receivable |
|---|---|---|
| **a.** | Yes | No |
| **b.** | Yes | Yes |
| **c.** | No | No |
| **d.** | No | Yes |

**17.** Pie Co. uses the installment sales method to recognize revenue. Customers pay the installment notes in 24 equal monthly amounts, which include 12% interest. What is an installment note receivable's balance six months after the sale?

    **a.** 75% of the original sales price.
    **b.** Less than 75% of the original sales price.
    **c.** The present value of the remaining monthly payments discounted at 12%

**d.** Less than the present value of the remaining monthly payments discounted at 12%.

**18.** On August 15, 20x9, Benet Co. sold goods for which it received a note bearing the market rate of interest on that date. The four-month note was dated July 15, 20x9. Note principal, together with all the interest, is due November 15, 20x9. When the note was recorded on August 15, which of the following accounts increased?
   **a.** Unearned discount.
   **b.** Interest receivable.
   **c.** Prepaid interest.
   **d.** Interest revenue.

**19.** On December 31, Jet Co. received two $10,000 notes receivable from customers in exchange for services rendered. On both notes, interest is calculated on the outstanding principal balance at the annual rate of 3% and payable at maturity. The note from Hart Corp., made under customary trade terms is due in nine months, and the note from Maxx, Inc. is due in five years. The market interest rate for similar notes on December 31 was 8%. The compound interest factors to convert future values into present values at 8% follow:

Present value of $1 due in nine months: .944
Present value of $1 due in five years:   .680

At what amounts should these two notes receivable be reported in Jet's December 31 balance sheet?

|     | Hart     | Maxx    |
|-----|----------|---------|
| **a.** | $ 9,440 | $6,800 |
| **b.** | $ 9,652 | $7,820 |
| **c.** | $10,000 | $6,800 |
| **d.** | $10,000 | $7,820 |

**20.** Tallent Company received a $30,000, 6-month, 10% interest-bearing note from a customer. After holding the note for two months, Tallent was in need of cash and discounted the note at the United National Bank at a 12% discount rate. The amount of cash received by Tallent from the bank was

**a.** $31,260
**b.** $30,870
**c.** $30,300
**d.** $30,240

**21.** On July 1, 20x8, Kay Corp. sold equipment to Mando Co. for $100,000. Kay accepted a 10% note receivable for the entire sales price. This note is payable in two equal installments of $50,000 plus accrued interest on December 31, 20x8, and December 31, 20x9. On July 1, 20x9, Kay discounted the note at a bank at an interest rate of 12%. Kay's proceeds from the discounted note were
   **a.** $48,400
   **b.** $49,350
   **c.** $50,350
   **d.** $51,700

**22.** After being held for 40 days, a 120-day, 12%, interest-bearing note receivable was discounted at a bank at 15%. The proceeds received from the bank equal
   **a.** Maturity value less the discount at 12%.
   **b.** Maturity value less the discount at 15%.
   **c.** Face value less the discount at 12%.
   **d.** Face value less the discount at 15%.

**23.** Anderson Company accepted a $20,000, 90-day, 12% interest-bearing note dated September 15 from a customer. On October 15 Anderson discounted the note at Provident National Bank at a 15% discount rate. The customer paid the note at maturity. Based on a 360-day year, what amount should Anderson report as net interest revenue from the note transaction?
   **a.** $ 85
   **b.** $100
   **c.** $150
   **d.** $200

**24.** On December 1, 20x0, Tigg Mortgage Co. gave Pod Corp. a $200,000, 12% loan. Pod received proceeds of $194,000 after the deduction of a $6,000 nonrefundable loan origination fee. Principal and interest are due in 60 monthly installments of $4,450, beginning January 1, 20x1. The repayments yield an effective interest rate of 12% at a present value of $200,000 and 13.4% at a present value of $194,000. What amount of accrued interest receivable should Tigg include in its December 31, 20x0, balance sheet?

a. $4,450
b. $2,166
c. $2,000
d. $0

**25.** On June 1, 20x0, Yola Corp. loaned Dale $500,000 on a 12% note, payable in five annual installments of $100,000 beginning January 2, 20x1. In connection with this loan, Dale was required to deposit $5,000 in a noninterest-bearing escrow account. The amount held in escrow is to be returned to Dale after all the principal and interest payments have been made. Interest on the note is payable on the first day of each month beginning July 1, 20x0. Dale made timely payments through November 1. On January 2, 20x1, Yola received payment of the first principal installment plus all interest due. At December 31, 20x0, Yola's interest receivable on the loan to Dale should be

a. $0
b. $ 5,000
c. $10,000
d. $15,000

**26.** On Merf's April 30, 20x1, balance sheet a note receivable was reported as a noncurrent asset and its accrued interest for eight months was reported as a current asset. Which of the following terms would fit Merf's note receivable?

a. Both principal and interest amounts are payable on August 31, 20x1, and August 31, 20x2.
b. Principal and interest are due December 31, 20x1.
c. Both principal and interest amounts are payable on December 31, 20x1, and December 31, 20x2.
d. Principal is due August 31, 20x2, and interest is due August 31, 20x1, and August 31, 20x2.

**27.** Gar Co. factored its receivables without recourse with Ross Bank. Gar received cash as a result of this transaction, which is best described as a

a. Loan from Ross collateralized by Gar's accounts receivable.
b. Loan from Ross to be repaid by the proceeds from Gar's accounts receivable.
c. Sale of Gar's accounts receivable to Ross, with the risk of uncollectible accounts retained by Gar.
d. Sale of Gar's accounts receivable to Ross with the risk of uncollectible accounts transferred to Ross.

**28.** Inge Co. determined that the net value of its accounts receivable at December 31, 20x9, based on an aging of the receivables, was $325,000. Additional information is as follows:

| | |
|---|---|
| Allowance for uncollectible accounts -- 1/1/x9 | $ 30,000 |
| Uncollectible accounts written off during 20x9 | 18,000 |
| Uncollectible accounts recovered during 20x9 | 2,000 |
| Accounts receivable at 12/31/x9 | 350,000 |

For 20x9, what would be Inge's uncollectible accounts expense?

a. $ 5,000
b. $11,000
c. $15,000
d. $21,000

**29.** Delta, Inc. sells to wholesalers on terms of 2/15, net 30. Delta has no cash sales, but 50% of Delta's customers take advantage of the discount. Delta uses the gross method of recording sales and trade receivables. An analysis of Delta's trade receivables balances as of December 31, 20x9, revealed the following:

| Age | Amount | Collectible |
|---|---|---|
| 0 - 15 days | $100,000 | 100% |
| 16 - 30 days | 60,000 | 95% |
| 31 - 60 days | 5,000 | 90% |
| Over 60 days | 2,500 | $500 |
| | $167,500 | |

In its December 31, 20x9, balance sheet, what amount should Delta report for allowance for discounts?
- a. $1,000
- b. $1,620
- c. $1,675
- d. $2,000

**30.** Leaf Co. purchased from Oak Co. a $20,000, 8%, 5-year note that required five equal annual year-end payments of $5,009. The note was discounted to yield a 9% rate to Leaf. At the date of purchase, Leaf recorded the note at its present value of $19,485. What should be the total interest revenue earned by Leaf over the life of this note?
- a. $5,045
- b. $5,560
- c. $8,000
- d. $9,000

**31.** On December 1, 20x8, Money Co. gave Home Co. a $200,000, 11% loan. Money paid proceeds of $194,000 after the deduction of a $6,000 nonrefundable loan origination fee. Principal and interest are due in 60 monthly installments of $4,310, beginning January 1, 20x9. The repayments yield an effective interest rate of 11% at a present value of $200,000 and 12.4% at a present value of $194,000. What amount of income from this loan should Money report in its 20x8 income statement?
- a. $0
- b. $1,833
- c. $2,005
- d. $7,833

**32.** The criteria used to determine if control has been surrendered by the transferor in a transfer of financial assets include all of the following **except**
- a. Lack of repurchase or redemption agreement.
- b. Transfer of physical possession of asset to transferee.
- c. Transferee has pledging or exchange rights over the asset.
- d. Asset isolated from the transferor and its creditors.

**33.** After a trade of financial assets accounted for as a sale, the transferor should
- a. remove the asset from its books and measure assets and liabilities received at transferee's book value.
- b. recognize all assets and liabilities received at fair value, recognize any loss incurred in full, but defer and amortize any gain.
- c. recognize all assets and liabilities received at fair value, and recognize in earnings any gain or loss on the sale.
- d. recognize all assets received at fair value, liabilities incurred at present value, and recognize in earnings any gain or loss on the sale.

**34.** Ajax transferred a financial asset to Brown under conditions that did not meet ASC Topic 860 criteria for a sale. Accordingly, they each accounted for the transaction as a secured borrowing arrangement. The asset has been transferred to Brown, along with permission to sell or repledge it. Ajax does not have the right to redeem the asset on short notice. In this situation, the collateral will be
- a. retained on Ajax's books with no change in asset classification, and also included in Brown's assets at fair value.
- b. retained on Ajax's books, separately reported from unencumbered assets, and also included on Brown's books measured at Ajax's book value.
- c. retained on Ajax's books, separately reported from unencumbered assets, but only listed as collateral held in notes to Brown's financial statements.
- d. retained on Ajax's books, separately classified, and included with Brown's reported assets measured at fair value.

**35.** Paulson Company had inventories at the beginning and end of the year as follows:

|                 | Beginning | End      |
|-----------------|-----------|----------|
| Raw materials   | $55,000   | $65,000  |
| Work-in-process | 96,000    | 80,000   |
| Finished goods  | 50,000    | 85,000   |

During the year the following costs were incurred:

| | |
|---|---|
| Raw materials purchased | $400,000 |
| Direct labor payroll | 220,000 |
| Factory overhead | 330,000 |

Paulson's cost of goods sold for the year was
- **a.** $921,000
- **b.** $956,000
- **c.** $966,000
- **d.** $979,000

**36.** The following information is available for Cooke Company for the year:

| | |
|---|---|
| Net sales | $1,800,000 |
| Freight-in | 45,000 |
| Purchase discounts | 25,000 |
| Ending inventory | 120,000 |

The gross margin is 40% of net sales. What is the cost of goods available for sale?
- **a.** $ 840,000
- **b.** $ 960,000
- **c.** $1,200,000
- **d.** $1,220,000

**37.** Steven Corporation made the following information available for its first year of operations ending December 31:

| | |
|---|---|
| Total merchandise purchases for the year | $350,000 |
| Merchandise inventory at December 31 | 70,000 |
| Collections from customers | 200,000 |

All merchandise was marked to sell at 40% above cost. Assuming that all sales are on a credit basis and all receivables are collectible, what should be the balance in accounts receivable at December 31?
- **a.** $ 50,000
- **b.** $192,000
- **c.** $250,000
- **d.** $290,000

**38.** From a theoretical viewpoint, which of the following costs would be considered inventoriable?

| | Freight | Warehousing |
|---|---|---|
| **a.** | No | No |
| **b.** | No | Yes |
| **c.** | Yes | No |
| **d.** | Yes | Yes |

**39.** The following costs were among those incurred by Woodcroft Corporation during the year:

| | |
|---|---|
| Merchandise purchased for resale | $500,000 |
| Sales commissions | 40,000 |
| Interest on notes payable to vendors | 5,000 |

How much should be charged to the cost of the merchandise purchased?
- **a.** $500,000
- **b.** $505,000
- **c.** $540,000
- **d.** $545,000

**40.** On December 28, Kerr Manufacturing Co. purchased goods costing $50,000. The terms were F.O.B. destination. Some of the costs incurred in connection with the sale and delivery of the goods were as follows:

| | |
|---|---|
| Packaging for shipment | $1,000 |
| Shipping | 1,500 |
| Special handling charges | 2,000 |

These goods were received on December 31. In Kerr's December 31 balance sheet, what amount of cost for these goods should be included in inventory?
- **a.** $54,500
- **b.** $53,500
- **c.** $52,000
- **d.** $50,000

**41.** Dixon Menswear Shop regularly buys shirts from Colt Company and is allowed trade discounts of 20% and 10% from the list price. Dixon purchased shirts from Colt on May 27 and received an invoice with a list price amount of $5,000 and payment terms of 2/10, n/30. Dixon uses the net method to record purchases. Dixon should record the purchase at
- **a.** $3,600.
- **b.** $3,528.
- **c.** $3,500.
- **d.** $3,430.

**42.** West Retailers purchased merchandise with a list price of $20,000, subject to trade discounts of 20% and 10%, with no cash discounts allowable. West should record the cost of this merchandise as
  a. $14,000
  b. $14,400
  c. $15,600
  d. $20,000

**43.** The following information pertains to a flange that is carried in the inventory of Mills Wholesalers, Inc:

| | |
|---|---|
| Original cost (per unit) | $3.00 |
| Replacement cost | 1.20 |
| Net realizable value | 2.40 |
| Net realizable value less normal markup | 1.68 |

What should be the carrying value per unit on the basis of lower of cost or market?
  a. $1.20
  b. $1.68
  c. $2.40
  d. $3.00

**44.** Moore Company carries product A in inventory on December 31 at its unit cost of $7.50. Because of a sharp decline in demand for the product, the selling price was reduced to $8.00 per unit. Moore's normal profit margin on product A is $1.60, disposal costs are $1.00 per unit, and the replacement cost is $5.30. Under the rule of cost or market, whichever is lower, Moore's December 31 inventory of product A should be valued at a unit cost of
  a. $5.30.
  b. $5.40.
  c. $7.00.
  d. $7.50.

**45.** The replacement cost of an inventory item is below the net realizable value and above the net realizable value less the normal profit margin. The original cost of the inventory item is above the replacement cost and below the net realizable value. As a result, under the lower of cost or market method, the inventory item should be valued at the

  a. Replacement cost.
  b. Original cost.
  c. Net realizable value.
  d. Net realizable value less the normal profit margin.

**46.** The following information pertains to an item in Fort Co.'s inventory at year end:

| | |
|---|---|
| Cost | $1.45 |
| Replacement cost | $ .65 |
| Net realizable value | $1.15 |
| Net realizable value less normal profit | $ .78 |

Under the lower of cost or market approach, how much is the year-end inventory value of this item?
  a. $1.15
  b. $ .78
  c. $ .72
  d. $ .65

**47.** Moss Co. has determined its December 31 inventory on a FIFO basis to be $400,000. Information pertaining to that inventory follows:

| | |
|---|---|
| Estimated selling price | $408,000 |
| Estimated cost of disposal | 20,000 |
| Normal profit margin | 60,000 |
| Current replacement cost | 360,000 |

Moss records losses that result from applying the lower of cost or market rule. At December 31, what should be the net carrying value of Moss' inventory?
  a. $400,000
  b. $488,000
  c. $360,000
  d. $328,000

**48.** Kahn Co., in applying the lower of cost or market method, reports its inventory at replacement cost. Which of the following statements are correct?

|   | The original cost is greater than replacement cost | Net realizable value, less normal profit margin, is greater than replacement cost |
|---|---|---|
| a. | Yes | Yes |
| b. | Yes | No |
| c. | No | Yes |
| d. | No | No |

**49.** For interim financial reporting, an inventory loss from a market decline in the second quarter that is not expected to be restored in the fiscal year should be recognized as a loss

a. In the fourth quarter.
b. Proportionately in each of the second, third, and fourth quarters.
c. Proportionately in each of the first, second, third, and fourth quarters.
d. In the second quarter.

**50.** An inventory loss from a market price decline occurred in the first quarter, and the decline was not expected to reverse during the fiscal year. However, in the third quarter, the inventory's market price recovery exceeded the market decline that occurred in the first quarter. For interim financial reporting, the dollar amount of net inventory should

a. Decrease in the first quarter by the amount of the market price decline and increase in the third quarter by the amount of the decrease in the first quarter.
b. Decrease in the first quarter by the amount of the market price decline and increase in the third quarter by the amount of the market price recovery.
c. Decrease in the first quarter by the amount of the market price decline and **not** be affected in the third quarter.
d. Not be affected in either the first quarter or the third quarter.

**51.** Hestor Company's records indicate the following information:

| | |
|---|---|
| Merchandise inventory, January 1 | $ 550,000 |
| Purchases, January 1 through December 31 | 2,250,000 |
| Sales, January 1 through December 31 | 3,000,000 |

On December 31, a physical inventory determined that ending inventory of $600,000 was in the warehouse. Hestor's gross profit on sales has remained constant at 30%. Hestor suspects some of the inventory may have been taken by some new employees. At December 31, what is the estimated cost of missing inventory?

a. $100,000
b. $200,000
c. $300,000
d. $700,000

**52.** The following information is available for the Silver Company for the three months ended March 31:

| | |
|---|---|
| Merchandise inventory, January 1 | $ 900,000 |
| Purchases | 3,400,000 |
| Freight-in | 200,000 |
| Sales | 4,800,000 |

The gross margin recorded was 25% of sales. What should be the merchandise inventory at March 31?

a. $ 700,000
b. $ 900,000
c. $1,125,000
d. $1,200,000

**53.** Balan Co.'s pricing structure has been formulated to yield a gross margin of 40%. The following data pertain to the year ended December 31:

| | |
|---|---|
| Sales | $600,000 |
| Beginning inventory | 100,000 |
| Purchases | 400,000 |
| Physical inventory at year-end | 100,000 |

Balan is satisfied that all sales and purchases have been fully and properly recorded. How much might Balan reasonably estimate as missing inventory at December 31?

a. $0
b. $ 40,000
c. $140,000
d. $160,000

**54.** For external reporting purposes, it is appropriate to use estimated gross profit rates to determine the cost of goods sold for

| | Interim Financial Reporting | Year-end Financial Reporting |
|---|---|---|
| a. | Yes | Yes |
| b. | Yes | No |
| c. | No | Yes |
| d. | No | No |

**55.** Janis Manufacturing Company recorded the following data pertaining to raw material X:

| | Date | Units Rec'd | Cost | Issued | On hand |
|---|---|---|---|---|---|
| Inventory | 1/1 | | $1.00 | | 400 |
| Purchase | 1/8 | 600 | $1.10 | | 1,000 |
| Issue | 1/12 | | | 800 | 200 |

The weighted average unit cost of raw material X at January 12 is
a. $1.00
b. $1.05
c. $1.06
d. $1.10

**56.** Henley Company recorded the following data pertaining to raw material K during January:

| Date | Units Received | Unit Cost | Units Issued | Units On Hand |
|---|---|---|---|---|
| 1/1 | | | | |
| Inventory | | $2.20 | | 700 |
| 1/6 | | | | |
| Issue | | | 375 | 325 |
| 1/23 | | | | |
| Purchase | 1,300 | $2.60 | | 1625 |

The moving average unit cost of Y inventory at January 31 is:
a. $2.40.
b. $2.46.
c. $2.52.
d. $2.60.

**57.** Thread Co. is selecting its inventory system in preparation for its first year of operations. Thread intends to use either the periodic weighted average method or the perpetual moving average method, and to apply the lower of cost or market rule either to individual items or to the total inventory. Inventory prices are expected to generally increase throughout the year, although a few individual prices will decrease. What inventory system should Thread select if it wants to maximize the year-end inventory carrying amount at December 31?

| | Inventory method | Cost or Market application |
|---|---|---|
| a. | Perpetual | Total inventory |
| b. | Perpetual | Individual item |
| c. | Periodic | Total inventory |
| d. | Periodic | Individual item |

**Questions 58 and 59 are based on the following:**

During January, Metro Co., which maintains a perpetual inventory system, recorded the following information pertaining to its inventory:

| | Units | Unit Cost | Total Cost | Units on Hand |
|---|---|---|---|---|
| Balance 1/1 | 1,000 | $1 | $1,000 | 1,000 |
| Purchased 1/7 | 600 | 3 | 1,800 | 1,600 |
| Sold 1/20 | 900 | | | 700 |
| Purchased 1/25 | 400 | 5 | 2,000 | 1,100 |

**58.** Under the moving-average method, what amount should Metro report as inventory at January 31?
a. $2,640
b. $3,225
c. $3,300
d. $3,900

**59.** Under the LIFO method, what amount should Metro report as inventory at January 31?
a. $1,300
b. $2,700
c. $3,900
d. $4,100

**60.** Anders Co. uses the moving-average method to determine the cost of its inventory. During January, Anders recorded the following information pertaining to its inventory:

|  | Units | Unit Cost | Total Cost |
|---|---|---|---|
| Balance 1/1 | 40,000 | $5 | $200,000 |
| Sold 1/17 | 35,000 | | |
| Purchased 1/28 | 20,000 | 8 | 160,000 |

What amount of inventory should Anders report in its January balance sheet?
- **a.** $200,000
- **b.** $185,000
- **c.** $162,500
- **d.** $150,000

**61.** In a period of rising prices, the use of which of the following inventory cost flow methods would result in the highest cost of goods sold?
- **a.** FIFO.
- **b.** LIFO.
- **c.** Weighted average cost.
- **d.** Moving average cost.

**62.** The Hastings Company began operations on January 1, 20x8, and uses the FIFO method in costing its raw material inventory. Management is contemplating a change to the LIFO method and is interested in determining what effect such a change will have on net income. Accordingly, the following information has been developed:

| Final Inventory | 20x8 | 20x9 |
|---|---|---|
| FIFO | $240,000 | $270,000 |
| LIFO | 200,000 | 210,000 |

| Operating Income (computed under the FIFO method) | 120,000 | 170,000 |
|---|---|---|

Based upon the above information, a change to the LIFO method in 20x9 would result in operating income for 20x9 of
- **a.** $110,000.
- **b.** $150,000.
- **c.** $170,000.
- **d.** $230,000.

**63.** In a periodic inventory system which uses the FIFO cost flow method, the cost of goods available for sale is net purchases
- **a.** Plus the ending inventory.
- **b.** Plus the beginning inventory.
- **c.** Minus the ending inventory.
- **d.** Minus the beginning inventory.

**64.** Jones Wholesalers stocks a changing variety of products. Which inventory costing method will be most likely to give Jones the lowest ending inventory when its product lines are subject to specific price increases?
- **a.** Specific identification.
- **b.** Weighted average.
- **c.** Dollar-value LIFO.
- **d.** FIFO periodic.

**65.** During periods of rising prices, when the FIFO inventory method is used, a perpetual inventory system results in an ending inventory cost that is
- **a.** The same as in a periodic inventory system.
- **b.** Higher than in a periodic inventory system.
- **c.** Lower than in a periodic inventory system.
- **d.** Higher or lower than in a periodic inventory system, depending on whether physical quantities have increased or decreased.

**66.** Generally, which inventory costing method approximates most closely the current cost for each of the following?

|  | Cost of Goods Sold | Ending Inventory |
|---|---|---|
| **a.** | LIFO | FIFO |
| **b.** | LIFO | LIFO |
| **c.** | FIFO | FIFO |
| **d.** | FIFO | LIFO |

**67.** During 20x9, Olsen Company discovered that the ending inventories reported on its financial statements were understated as follows:

| Year | Understatement |
|---|---|
| 20x6 | $50,000 |
| 20x7 | $60,000 |
| 20x8 | $ -0- |

Olsen ascertains year-end quantities on a periodic inventory system. These quantities are converted to dollar amounts using the FIFO cost flow method. Assuming no other accounting errors, Olsen's retained earnings at December 31, 20x8, will be
   a. Correct.
   b. $ 60,000 understated.
   c. $ 60,000 overstated.
   d. $110,000 understated.

**68.** Which of the following inventory cost flow methods could use dollar-value pools?
   a. Conventional (lower of cost or market) retail.
   b. Weighted average.
   c. FIFO.
   d. LIFO.

**69.** The double-extension method and the link-chain method are two variations of which of the following inventory cost flow methods?
   a. Moving average.
   b. FIFO.
   c. Dollar-value LIFO.
   d. Conventional (lower of cost or market) retail.

**70.** On December 31, 20x0, Kern Company adopted the dollar-value LIFO inventory method. All of Kern's inventories constitute a single pool. The inventory on December 31, 20x0, using the dollar-value LIFO inventory method was $600,000. Inventory data for 20x1 are as follows:

| | |
|---|---|
| 12/31/x1 inventory at year-end prices | $780,000 |
| Relevant price index at year-end (base year 20x0) | 120 |

Under the dollar-value LIFO inventory method, Kern's inventory at December 31, 20x1, would be
   a. $650,000.
   b. $655,000.
   c. $660,000.
   d. $720,000.

**71.** The dollar-value LIFO inventory cost flow method uses which of the following?
   a. Specific goods (single item) pools.
   b. Specific cost identification method.
   c. Double-extension method.
   d. Moving-average method.

**72.** In 20x0, Cobb adopted the dollar-value LIFO inventory method. At that time, Cobb's ending inventory had a base-year cost and an end-of-year cost of $300,000. In 20x1, the ending inventory had a $400,000 base-year cost and a $440,000 end-of-year cost. What dollar-value LIFO inventory cost would be reported in Cobb's December 31, 20x1, balance sheet?
   a. $440,000
   b. $430,000
   c. $410,000
   d. $400,000

**73.** When the double-extension approach to the dollar-value LIFO inventory method is used, the inventory layer added in the current year is multiplied by an index number. Which of the following correctly states how components are used in the calculation of this index number?
   a. In the numerator, the average of the ending inventory at base year cost and at current year cost.
   b. In the numerator, the ending inventory at current year cost, and, in the denominator, the ending inventory at base year cost.
   c. In the numerator, the ending inventory at base year cost, and, in the denominator, the ending inventory at current year cost.
   d. In the denominator, the average of the ending inventory at base year cost and at current year cost.

**74.** The following data were available from the records of the Bricker Department Store for the year ended December 31:

|                        | At cost   | At retail  |
|------------------------|-----------|------------|
| Merchandise inventory, |           |            |
| January 1              | $180,000  | $260,000   |
| Purchases              | 660,000   | 920,000    |
| Markups                |           | 20,000     |
| Markdowns              |           | 80,000     |
| Sales                  |           | 960,000    |

Using the retail method, an estimate of the merchandise inventory at December 31, valued at the lower of average cost or market, would be

- a. $220,000.
- b. $160,000.
- c. $120,000.
- d. $112,000.

75. At December 31, the following information was available from Crisford Company's books for the year:

|                          | At Cost  | At Retail |
|--------------------------|----------|-----------|
| Inventory, January 1     | $14,700  | $20,300   |
| Purchases                | 83,300   | 115,500   |
| Additional markups       | _____ | 4,200     |
| Available for sale       | $98,000  | $140,000  |

Sales for the year totaled $110,600; markdowns amounted to $1,400. Under the approximate lower of average cost or market retail method, Crisford's inventory at December 31 was

- a. $19,600.
- b. $21,560.
- c. $28,000.
- d. $30,800.

76. Hutch, Inc. uses the conventional retail inventory method to account for inventory. The following information relates to operations for the year:

|                          | At Cost  | At Retail |
|--------------------------|----------|-----------|
| Beginning inventory      |          |           |
| and purchases            | $600,000 | $920,000  |
| Net markups              |          | 40,000    |
| Net markdowns            |          | 60,000    |
| Sales                    |          | 780,000   |

What amount should be reported as cost of sales for the year?

- a. $480,000
- b $487,500
- c. $520,000
- d. $525,000

77. Union Corp uses the first-in, first-out retail method of inventory valuation. The following yearly information is available:

|                          | At Cost  | At Retail  |
|--------------------------|----------|------------|
| Beginning inventory      | $12,000  | $ 30,000   |
| Purchases                | 60,000   | 110,000    |
| Net additional markups   |          | 10,000     |
| Net markdowns            |          | 20,000     |
| Sales revenue            |          | 90,000     |

If the lower of cost or market rule is disregarded, what would be the estimated cost of the ending inventory?

- a. $24,000
- b. $20,800
- c. $20,000
- d. $19,200

78. The inventory account of Benson Company at December 31 included the following items:

|                                                                          | Inventory Amount |
|--------------------------------------------------------------------------|------------------|
| Merchandise out on consignment at sales price (including markup of 40% on selling price) | $7,000 |
| Goods purchased, in transit (shipped f.o.b. shipping point)              | 6,000            |
| Goods held on consignment by Benson                                      | 4,000            |
| Goods out on approval (sales price $2,500, cost $2,000)                  | 2,500            |

Based on the above information, the inventory account at December 31 should be reduced by

- a. $ 7,300.
- b. $12,500.
- c. $13,500.
- d. $19,500.

**79.** Goods on consignment should be included in the inventory of
   a. The consignor but not the consignee.
   b. Both the consignor and the consignee.
   c. The consignee but not the consignor.
   d. Neither the consignor nor the consignee.

**80.** On December 1, Alt Department Store received 505 sweaters on consignment from Todd. Todd's cost for the sweaters was $80 each, and they were priced to sell at $100. Alt's commission on consigned goods is 10%. At December 31, 5 sweaters remained. In its December 31 balance sheet, what amount should Alt report as payable for consigned goods?
   a. $49,000
   b. $45,400
   c. $45,000
   d. $40,400

**81.** Stone Co. had the following consignment transactions during December of the current year:

| | |
|---|---|
| Inventory shipped on consignment to Beta Co. | $18,000 |
| Freight paid by Stone | 900 |
| Inventory received on consignment from Alpha Co. | 12,000 |
| Freight paid by Alpha Co. | 500 |

No sales of consigned goods were made through December 31. Stone's December 31 balance sheet should include consigned inventory at
   a. $12,000
   b. $12,500
   c. $18,000
   d. $18,900

**82.** On July 1 a fire destroyed $100,000 of Brody Company's $300,000 inventory (fair market values). Brody carried a $120,000 fire insurance policy with an 80% coinsurance clause. What is the maximum amount of insurance that Brody can collect as a result of this loss?

   a. $ 50,000
   b. $ 80,000
   c. $ 96,000
   d. $100,000

**83.** Canary Corp. based its depletion costs of coal properties on estimates of recoverable reserves using the units-of-production method. The unit rate for depletion is determined by dividing the total unrecovered carrying value of coal properties by the proved reserves. Canary's coal properties had proved reserves of 3,000,000 tons when they were acquired for $15,000,000. On January 1 of the current year, a revised estimate of the proved reserves showed 2,000,000 tons with an unrecovered carrying value of $11,000,000. During the year, Canary produced 350,000 tons of coal and sold 400,000 tons. What amount of depletion should Canary allocate to cost of goods sold for the year?
   a. $2,200,000
   b. $2,175,000
   c. $1,925,000
   d. $2,000,000

**84.** According to the FASB conceptual framework, which of the following attributes would **not** be used to measure inventory?
   a. Historical cost.
   b. Replacement cost.
   c. Net realizable value.
   d. Present value of future cash flows.

**85.** A company decided to change its inventory valuation method from FIFO to LIFO in a period of rising prices. What was the result of the change on ending inventory and net income in the year of change?

| | Ending Inventory | Net Income |
|---|---|---|
| a. | Increase | Increase |
| b. | Increase | Decrease |
| c. | Decrease | Decrease |
| d. | Decrease | Increase |

86. Bren Co.'s beginning inventory at January 1, 20x9, was understated by $26,000, and its ending inventory was overstated by $52,000. As a result, Bren's cost of goods sold for 20x9 was
   a. Understated by $26,000.
   b. Overstated by $26,000.
   c. Understated by $78,000.
   d. Overstated by $78,000.

87. Which of the following statements is/are correct when a company applying the lower of cost or market method reports its inventory at replacement cost?

I. The original cost is less than replacement cost.
II. The net realizable value is greater than replacement cost.

   a. I only.
   b. II only.
   c. Both I and II.
   d. Neither I nor II.

88. Walt Co. adopted the dollar-value LIFO inventory method as of January 1, 20x9, when its inventory was valued at $500,000. Walt's entire inventory constitutes a single pool. Using a relevant price index of 1.10, Walt determined that its December 31, 20x9, inventory was $577,500 at current year cost, and $525,000 at base year cost. What was Walt's dollar-value LIFO inventory at December 31, 20x9?
   a. $525,000
   b. $527,500
   c. $552,500
   d. $577,500

89. During 20x4, Kam Co. began offering its goods to selected retailers on a consignment basis. The following information was derived from Kam's 20x0 accounting records:

| | |
|---|---|
| Beginning inventory | $122,000 |
| Purchases | 540,000 |
| Freight in | 10,000 |
| Transportation to consignees | 5,000 |
| Freight out | 35,000 |
| Ending inventory: | |
| Held by Kam | 145,000 |
| Held by consignees | 20,000 |

In its 20x0 income statement, what amount should Kam report as cost of goods sold?
   a. $507,000
   b. $512,000
   c. $527,000
   d. $547,000

90. Mare Co.'s December 31, 20x9, balance sheet reported the following current assets:

| | |
|---|---|
| Cash | $ 70,000 |
| Accounts receivable | 120,000 |
| Inventories | 60,000 |
| Total | $250,000 |

An analysis of the accounts disclosed that accounts receivable consisted of the following:

| | |
|---|---|
| Trade accounts | $ 96,000 |
| Allowance for uncollectible accounts | ( 2,000) |
| Selling price of Mare's unsold goods out on consignment, at 130% of cost, **not** included in Mare's ending inventory | 26,000 |
| Total | $120,000 |

At December 31, 20x9, the total of Mare's current assets is
   a. $224,000
   b. $230,000
   c. $244,000
   d. $270,000

**91.** In January 20x0, Vorst Co. purchased a mineral mine for $2,640,000 with removable ore estimated at 1,200,000 tons. After it has extracted all the ore, Vorst will be required by law to restore the land to its original condition at an estimated cost of $180,000. Vorst believes it will be able to sell the property afterwards for $300,000. During 20x0, Vorst incurred $360,000 of development costs preparing the mine for production and removed and sold 60,000 tons of ore. In its 20x0 income statement, what amount should Vorst report as depletion?

    a. $135,000
    b. $144,000
    c. $150,000
    d. $159,000

**92.** Cap Corp. reported accrued investment interest receivable of $38,000 and $46,500 at January 1 and December 31 respectively. During the year, cash collections from investments included the following:

| | |
|---|---|
| Capital gains distribution | $145,000 |
| Interest | 152,000 |

What amount should Cap report as interest revenue from investments for the year?

    a. $160,500
    b. $153,500
    c. $152,000
    d. $143,500

# CHAPTER 3

## RECEIVABLES AND INVENTORIES

### Multiple Choice Answers

1. /b/

| | |
|---|---|
| $ -0- | Beginning Inventory |
| +350,000 | Purchases |
| - 70,000 | Ending Inventory |
| $280,000 | Cost of Goods Sold |

$280,000 x 1.40
= 392,000(sales) - 200,000(collections)
= $192,000 Accounts Receivable

2. /c/

| | |
|---|---|
| $ 650,000 | AR balance, 1/1 |
| +2,700,000 | Credit sales |
| -2,150,000 | Collections |
| - 75,000 | Sales returns |
| - 40,000 | Accounts written off |
| $1,085,000 | AR Balance, 12/31 |

3. /b/

| | |
|---|---|
| $800,000 | Gross Accounts Receivable |
| - 71,100 | Estimated Uncollectible Accounts -- Aging |
| $728,900 | Net Realizable Value of Accounts Receivable |

4. /b/

| | |
|---|---|
| $10,000 | Balance 1/1/x9 |
| + 20,000 | 20x1 Provision (0.02 x $1,000,000) |
| - 18,000 | 20x1 Write-offs |
| + 5,000 | 20x1 Recoveries |
| $17,000 | Balance 12/31/x9 |

5. /c/ Income statement focus. Basis is net credit sales. Ignore balance in allowance account.

$830,000 (sales) - $10,000 (sales R&A) = $820,000 (net sales)

$820,000 x 0.02 = $16,400 bad debt expense

6. /a/ Balance sheet focus. Desired balance 12/31 based on sum of products in aging schedule.

| | |
|---|---|
| $1,200 | ($120,000 x 1%) |
| 1,800 | ($90,000 x 2%) |
| 6,000 | ($100,000 x 6%) |
| $9,000 | Allowance balance needed. |

7. /d/ Balance sheet focus.

| | |
|---|---|
| $28,000 | Allowance, Jan. 1 |
| - 23,000 | Accounts written off |
| + 5,000 | Recoveries |
| $10,000 | Allowance, Dec. 31 |
| $270,000 | AR balance, 12/31 |
| -250,000 | Net realizable value |
| $ 20,000 | Allowance balance needed |
| - 10,000 | Unadjusted allowance balance |
| $10,000 | Uncollectible expense adjustment needed. |

8. /a/

| | |
|---|---|
| $100,000 | Allowance required |
| + 72,000 | Debit balance to be made up, 12/31 |
| $172,000 | Uncollectible expense |

9. /a/ The balance sheet focus using the aging of receivables schedule to determine the bad debts adjustment is an asset valuation approach.

10. /a/

| | |
|---|---|
| $24,000 | Allowance 1/1/x9 |
| +20,000 | Provision made during year |
| -19,500 | Annual Write-off |
| $24,500 | Allowance 12/31/x9 Before Adjustment |

| | |
|---|---|
| $21,000 | Required Allowance Based on Aging |

| | |
|---|---|
| $(3,500) | Reduction Required in Annual Provision |

| | |
|---|---|
| $20,000 | (annual provision) |
| - 3,500 | (reduction required) |
| = $16,500 | Adjusted Expense |

11. /a/ Under the allowance method, net income is not affected because the accounting entries only affect balance sheet accounts. Under the direct write-off method, net income is decreased because the accounting entry for the write-off is charged to bad debt expense.

12. /d/ 

| | |
|---|---|
| $ 42,000 | Desired balance 12/31/x9 -- based on aging schedule |
| | |
| $ 8,000 | Balance at 12/31/x8 |
| + 40,000 | Monthly accrual total (0.02 x $2,000,000) |
| - 22,000 | 20x9 write-offs |
| $ 26,000 | Balance 12/31/x9 before adjustment |
| | |
| $16,000 | Additional bad debt expense required |

13. /a/ Recovery of any account previously written off - large or small - requires an increase (debit) to accounts receivable and a corresponding increase (credit) to the allowance account.

14. /a/ Under the allowance method, the entry to record the write-off of a specific account does not affect net income because only balance sheet accounts are involved. Working capital (CA - CL) is not affected because the write-off does not change the net realizable value of accounts receivable. (The receivable and allowance accounts both decrease by the same amount.)

15. /d/ Percent of credit sales - income statement focus: $175,000 credit sales x 2% = $35,000 expense adjustment.

Percent of accounts receivable - balance sheet focus: $900,000 x 5% = $45,000 balance desired - $16,000 preadjusted balance = $29,000 adjustment needed.

16. /c/ The entry to record the accrual of interest on a note receivable that bears interest is made only when interest has been earned. On the date of the note receipt (7/1/x8), no entry is made for the interest element.

17. /c/ The note receivable balance is stated free of the interest element portion of the remaining installments. To arrive at this balance, the remaining monthly payments must be discounted at the interest rate of the note - 12%

18. /b/ Since the note was made on July 15, one month's interest has already been earned as of the date the note was received (August 15).

19. /d/ Both notes bear interest at an unrealistically low rate. The short-term note from Hart is recorded at face value. Per APB Opinion No. 21, the long-term note is recorded at its fair value using an imputed interest rate. Note that the maturity value of the note (its fair value) is the amount to be discounted.

| | |
|---|---|
| $ 1,500 | Stated interest ($10,000 x 3% x 5yrs) |
| 10,000 | Face value of note |
| $11,500 | Fair value to be discounted |
| x 0.680 | Present value factor |
| $ 7,820 | Reportable amount, 12/31 |

20. /d/ $30,000 x 0.10 x 6/12 = $1,500
$30,000 + $1,500 = $31,500 (maturity value)
$31,500 x 0.12 x 4/12 = $1,260 discount
$31,500 (maturity value) - 1,260 (discount) = $30,240 proceeds

**21.** /d/ Interest due on the note through 12/31/x8 was received. It is not a component of the maturity value due 12/31/x9.

| | |
|---|---|
| $50,000 | Principal balance, 1/1/x9 |
| 5,000 | Interest due 12/31/x9 |
| $55,000 | Maturity value due 12/31/x9 |
| - 3,300 | Discount ($55,000 x 12% x 6/12) |
| $51,700 | Proceeds 7/1/x9 |

**22.** /b/ Discount proceeds on interest-bearing notes are equal to the maturity value of the note less discount interest computed at the discount rate.

**23.** /a/ $20,000 x 0.12 x 90/360 = $600 interest

$20,000 + $600 = $20,600 (maturity value)

$20,600 x 0.15 x 60/360 = $515 (discount)

$20,600 (maturity value) - $515 (discount) = $20,085 (proceeds)

$20,085 (proceeds) - 20,000 (face) = $85 Net Interest Revenue

**24.** /c/ The present value of the loan on 12/1/x0 is the face value of $200,000. The $194,000 proceeds is not the present value of the loan because it does not represent the principal that has to be repaid. The interest rate to be used must be the rate which corresponds to the $200,000 present value - 12%.

$200,000 x .12 x 1/12 = $2,000 accrued interest receivable for December 20x0.

**25.** /c/ Interest due Dec. 1 and Jan. 1 is receivable as of December 31.

$500,000 x .12 x 2/12 = $10,000

**26.** /d/ Answer D is correct because it is the only alternative that would require the note to be classified as a long-term asset. Alternatives A, B, and C would all require that the note, or a portion of it, be classified as a current asset.

**27.** /d/ When accounts receivable are factored without recourse, the transaction is treated as a sale in which the purchaser assumes all risks.

**28.** /b/

| | |
|---|---|
| Accounts receivable at gross 12/31/x9 | $350,000 |
| Net value of accounts receivable, 12/31/x9 | $325,000 |
| Allowance needed | $ 25,000 |

| | |
|---|---|
| Allowance, 1/1/x9 | $30,000 |
| Less write-offs, x9 | (18,000) |
| Plus recoveries, x9 | 2,000 |
| Unadjusted balance | $14,000 |

Balance needed ($25,000) less unadjusted balance ($14,000) = $11,000 adjustment for bad debts expense.

**29.** /a/ The allowance for discounts should be 2% of 50% of those credit sales balances left which qualify for the discount. Since the terms are 2/15, net 30, balances relating to credit sales 16 days or older do not qualify.

$100,000 x 50% x 2% = $1,000

**30.** /b/ Total interest revenue is the difference between the total of all payments to be received and the present value of the note when issued.

| | |
|---|---|
| Total payments ($5,009 x 5 years) | $25,045 |
| Less present value | 19,485 |
| Total interest | $5,560 |

**31.** /c/ Interest income is computed as carrying value at the beginning of the month (equal to the proceeds issued of $194,000) times the effective interest rate that would yield a $194,000 present value, namely 12.4%

$194,000 x 12.4% = $2,005

**32.** /b/ Control has been surrendered only if (1) the assets have been isolated and are beyond the reach of the transferor and its creditors (Answer D), (2) the transferee has the right to pledge or exchange the asset (Answer C), and (3) the transferor has not retained an element of control through a repurchase or early redemption agreement (Answer A). Note that there is no specific requirement that the transferee have physical possession of the asset/s.

**33.** /c/ When a transfer of financial assets qualifies to be accounted for as a sale, the transferor must recognize, at fair value, all assets and liabilities over which it has control, and recognize in earnings any gain or loss on the sale. Answer A is not correct because assets and liabilities received as proceeds are not recognized at transferee's book value. Answer B is not correct because any gain realized is recognized; it is not deferred. Answer D is not correct because liabilities incurred are measured at fair value -- which may not be present value.

**34.** /d/ In a transfer of financial assets accounted for as a secured borrowing, and in which the transferor (Ajax) does not have a redemption right on short notice, the asset (i.e. collateral) will remain on the transferor's books, but it will be reclassified and reported in a separate classification from unencumbered assets. Since the asset has been transferred to Brown, along with right of sale and repledge, then Brown also will recognize the asset on its books, measured at fair value.

**35.** /a/

| | | |
|---|---|---|
| Beginning finished goods inventory | | $ 50,000 |
| Beginning work-in-progress inventory | | $ 96,000 |
| Beginning raw material inventory | $ 55,000 | |
| Raw material purchased | 400,000 | |
| Ending raw material inventory | (65,000) | |
| Raw material added | | 390,000 |
| Direct labor | | 220,000 |
| Factory overhead | | 330,000 |
| Ending work-in-progress inventory | | (80,000) |
| Work-in-progress added | | 956,000 |
| Ending finished goods inventory | | (85,000) |
| Cost of goods sold | | $921,000 |

**36.** /c/ Net Sales - Gross Margin = Cost of Goods Sold

Cost of Goods Sold + Ending Inventory = Goods Available for Sale

1,800,000 - 40% (1,800,000) = $1,080,000

1,080,000 + 120,000 = $1,200,000

**37.** /b/ Beginning Inventory + Purchases - Ending Inventory = COGS

Sales - Gross Margin = Cost of Goods Sold

Cost of Goods Sold + Gross Margin = Sales

Total Sales - Collections = Accounts Receivable

0 + 350,000 - 70,000 = $280,000

280,000 + [40% x (280,000)] = $392,000

392,000 - 200,000 = $192,000

**38.** /d/ Freight and warehousing are both part of the costs of acquiring and holding inventory; theoretically, therefore, they are properly included in inventory costs. Notice that this question asks for the theoretically correct response, not for the practical procedure usually followed.

**39.** /a/ Merchandise purchased for resale is obviously part of inventory. Sales commissions are part of the cost of selling and therefore are sales expenses not purchase costs. Interest on notes payable to vendors are correctly classified as interest expense and have nothing to do with purchase costs.

**40.** /d/ This question does not ask for a solution from the theoretical viewpoint. Although all costs presented are part of the cost of bringing the inventory items to their existing condition and location, as a practical matter, packaging, shipping, and special handling costs are treated as period expenses.

**41.** /b/

| | |
|---|---|
| List price of shirts | $5,000 |
| Less 20% trade discount | (1,000) |
| | $4,000 |
| Less 10% trade discount | (400) |
| | $3,600 |
| Less 2% payment discount | (72) |
| | $3,528 |

(Alternative, and faster method, is to use the complements of the rates given. Thus, $5,000 x 80% x 90% x 98% = $3,528.)

**42.** /b/

| | |
|---|---|
| List price | $20,000 |
| Less 20% trade discount | (4,000) |
| | 16,000 |
| Less 10% trade | (1,600) |
| Net price | $14,400 |

(Or: $20,000 x 80% x 90% = $14,400)

**43.** /b/

| | | |
|---|---|---|
| Cost | | $3.00 |
| Market figures: | | |
| Ceiling (NRV) | $2.40 | |
| Floor (NRV Less Markup) | 1.68 | |
| Replacement Cost | 1.20 | |
| Market | | 1.68 |
| LOCOM | | $1.68 |

**44.** /b/

| | | |
|---|---|---|
| Cost | | $7.50 |
| NRV Sales Price | $8.00 | |
| Disposal Cost | (1.00) | |
| NRV | | $7.00 |
| NRV Less Markup (7.00-1.60) | | 5.40 |
| Replacement | | 5.30 |
| Market | | 5.40 |
| LOCOM | | $5.40 |

**45.** /a/ Market is replacement cost with upper limit of net realizable value and lower limit of NRV less normal profit. Here replacement cost is between NRV and NRV less profit. LOCOM is lower of cost or market. In this case, the lower is market, i.e. replacement cost.

**46.** /b/

| Cost | | 1.45 |
|---|---|---|
| Replacement | $ .65 | |
| Ceiling (NRV) | $1.15 | |
| Floor (NRV-Normal markup) | $ .78 | |
| Market | | $ .78 |
| | | |
| LOCOM | | $ .78 |

**47.** /c/ Ceiling (NRV)
($408,000 - $20,000)     $388,000
Floor (NRV - normal markup)
($388,000 - $60,000)     $328,000
Current replacement cost   $360,000

Current replacement cost is the middle value in the comparison of NRV, NRV -MU, and CRC, so should be used as the market value. Furthermore, it will be the net carrying value of the inventory because it is lower than original cost, $400,000.

**48.** /b/ Since the inventory was reported at replacement cost, that figure must be lower than original cost. Additionally, the figure selected as "market" is the middle of three values: NRV (ceiling), NRV - normal markup (floor), and CRC. Since current replacement cost was the "market" selected, it follows that it must have been an amount greater than the floor figure of net realizable value less normal profit margin.

**49.** /d/ Under the conservatism convention, losses are reported in the period identified. Therefore, the loss should be recognized in the second quarter.

**50.** /a/ A loss due to decline in market price of inventory that is not expected to be recovered is recognized in the period in which the loss occurs. Recognition of subsequent recoveries, however, is limited to the amount of loss previously recorded. Recovery to an amount exceeding original cost is not permitted.

**51.** /a/ Sales - Gross Margin = Cost of Goods Sold

Beginning Inventory + Purchases - Ending Inventory = COGS

Beginning Inventory + Purchases - COGS = Ending Inventory

3,000,000 - 30%(3,000,000)  = $2,100,000

550,000 + 2,250,000 - 2,100,000  = 700,000

| Computed Inventory 12/31/x0 | $700,000 |
|---|---|
| Physical Inventory 12/31/x0 | (600,000) |
| Inventory Shrinkage | $100,000 |

**52.** /b/ Sales - Gross Margin = Cost of Goods Sold

Beginning Inventory + Purchases + Costs - COGS = Ending Inventory

$4,800,000 − (25% x $4,800,000) = $3,600,000

$900,000 + 3,400,000 + 200,000 - 3,600,000 = $900,000

**53.** /b/ Sales - Gross Margin = Cost of Goods Sold

Beginning Inventory + Purchases - COGS = Ending Inventory

600,000 - 40%(600,000)  =  $360,000
100,000 + 400,000 - 360,000 =  $140,000

| Computed Ending Inventory | $140,000 |
|---|---|
| Physical Inventory | (100,000) |
| Inventory Shrinkage | $ 40,000 |

**54.** /b/ Estimated gross profit rates are unacceptable for use in year-end external reporting. They are acceptable for internal reporting when physical inventories are not usually taken.

**55.** /c/

| | Quantity | Cost | Value | Unit Cost |
|---|---|---|---|---|
| 1/1 | 400 | $1.00 | $ 400.00 | $1.00 |
| | 600 | 1.10 | 660.00 | |
| 1/8 | 1000 | | $1060.00 | $1.06 |
| 1/12 | (800) | | = (848.00) | $1.06 |
| | 200 | | $ 212.00 | $1.06 |

**56.** /c/

$2.20 x 325 = $ 715.00
$2.60 x 1,300 = $3,380.00
$4,095.00

$4,095.00 -:- 1625 = $2.52

**57.** /a/ Since prices are generally rising, the perpetual moving average will increase during the year and the application of LOCOM to the total inventory will yield the higher ending inventory amounts.

**58.** /b/ A new moving average figure arises as the result of a purchase, not from a sale.

On hand, 1/7
| 1,000 units at $1 | $1,000 |
|---|---|
| 600 units at $3 | 1,800 |
| Total cost | $2,800 |
| Unit cost ($2,800/1,600 units) | $1.75 |

On hand, 1/25
| 700 units at $1.75 | $1,225 |
|---|---|
| 400 units at $5 | 2,000 |
| Inventory, 1/31 | $3,225 |

**59.** /b/ The sale on 1/20 will be accounted for using the costs related to the most recently acquired merchandise. Thus the sale of 900 units will be accounted for using the costs of all 600 units purchased 1/7 plus 300 units from the beginning inventory.

On hand, 1/31
Balance of 1/1 inventory
| 700 units at $1 | $ 700 |
|---|---|
| Units purchased 1/25 | 2,000 |
| Inventory, 1/31 | $2,700 |

**60.** /b/

Balance 1/17
| (5,000 units at $5) | $ 25,000 |
|---|---|
| Units purchased 1/28 | 160,000 |
| Inventory 1/31 | $185,000 |

**61.** /b/ In a period of rising prices, the most current costs are the highest. Since the LIFO inventory system places the most recent costs in cost of goods sold, its use would produce the highest cost of goods sold during an inflationary period. FIFO cost flow would produce a high ending inventory and low cost of goods sold. Weighted average and moving average would produce figures between LIFO and FIFO costs.

**62.** /b/ The change from FIFO to LIFO means a decrease in inventory costs in this case. This would increase cost of goods sold and reduce profit. The change is for 20x9, but the 20x8 inventory would also be retrospectively restated. The change for 20x9 ending inventory would be as follows:

| | |
|---|---|
| FIFO Inventory | $270,000 |
| LIFO Inventory | (210,000) |
| Difference (decrease in ending inventory) | ($60,000) |

The change in the beginning inventory (ending inventory for 20x8) would be:

| | |
|---|---|
| FIFO Inventory | $240,000 |
| LIFO Inventory | (200,000) |
| Difference (decrease in beginning inventory) | $40,000 |

| | |
|---|---|
| 20x9 Operating Income | $170,000 |
| Adjustment for Change in 20x8 | 40,000 |
| Adjustment for Change in 20x9 | (60,000) |
| Operating Income with LIFO | $150,000 |

**63.** /b/ Regardless of inventory valuation method (FIFO, LIFO, etc.), cost of goods available for sale is beginning inventory plus net purchases.

**64.** /c/ The LIFO method places most recent costs on the income statement, thereby placing older (and generally lower) costs in inventory. Furthermore, since Jones stocks a changing variety of goods, it would be preferable to use an aggregate valuation method (such as dollar-value) rather than a unit-based system.

**65.** /a/ Regardless of whether FIFO is used in a perpetual or periodic system, the cost in ending inventory will be the same amount. This is not the case, however, under the LIFO or weighted-average systems.

**66.** /a/ The most recent costs incurred for merchandise purchased will most closely approximate current cost as of the date of the financial statements. The LIFO system assumes a cost flow which places most recent costs on the income statement in COGS. The FIFO system, however, assumes a cost flow which places the earliest costs incurred in COGS and the most recent costs are accounted for in the ending inventory.

**67.** /a/ An inventory misstatement is self-correcting over a two-year period. This is because the ending inventory figure of the first period becomes the beginning inventory for the following period. Ending inventory errors impact net income in the same direction as the misstatement; i.e. under- or overstatement. However, in the next period, the error (now in the beginning inventory) has an equal but opposite effect, thus canceling out the previous year's misstatement. For the data given:

| | |
|---|---|
| 20x6, Net income understated | -$50,000 |
| 20x7, Beginning inventory effect | + 50,000 |
| Ending inventory effect | - 60,000 |
| 20x8, Beginning inventory | + 60,000 |
| Net effect of errors | $ 0 |

**68.** /d/ LIFO uses a layered approach of valuing inventory. The layers themselves are valued, rather than the particular content of a particular layer. The other methods use costs established at each purchase.

**69.** /c/ The double-extension method and link chain-method are ways of computing indexes which are used in dollar-value LIFO extensions.

**70.** /c/ Step 1:

| | |
|---|---|
| 12/31/x1 Inventory at 20x1 Prices | $780,000 |
| 20x1 Price Index Deflator Divide By | 1.20 |
| 20x1 Inventory at 20x0 Price | $650,000 |
| 20x0 Inventory | (600,000) |
| 20x1 Incremental Layer at 20x0 Price | $ 50,000 |

Step 2:

| | |
|---|---|
| 20x1 Layer | 50,000 |
| 20x1 Price Index Reinflator | x 1.20 |
| 20x1 Layer at 20x1 Price | $ 60,000 |

Step 3:

| | |
|---|---|
| 20x0 Layer | $600,000 |
| 20x1 Layer | 60,000 |
| Total Inventory | $660,000 |

**71.** /c/ The double extension method is used to compute a dollar value index for a particular year. The other answers refer to identifying costs based on regular LIFO computations.

**72.** /c/ The solution first requires computation of price indexes using the double-extension method. Index for 20x0 is $300,000/$300,000 = 1. Index for 20x1 is $440,000/$400,000 = 1.1

Step 1

| | |
|---|---|
| 20x1 inventory at x2 price | $440,000 |
| Deflate using 1.1 index ($440,000/1.1) | 400,000 |
| Less 20x0 inventory | (300,000) |
| 20x0 layer added | $100,000 |

Step 2

| | |
|---|---|
| 20x1 layer | $100,000 |
| Inflate using 20x1 index | x 1.1 |
| 20x1 layer added | $110,000 |

Step 3

| | |
|---|---|
| 20x0 Inventory | $300,000 |
| 20x1 Layer added | 110,000 |
| 20x1 Inventory | $410,000 |

**73.** /b/ To compute the index number under the double-extension method, ending inventory at year-end costs is divided by ending inventory at base-year costs.

**74.** /d/

| | Cost | Retail |
|---|---|---|
| Beginning Inv. | $180,000 | $ 260,000 |
| Purchases | 660,000 | 920,000 |
| Markups | | 20,000 |
| | $840,000 | $1,200,000 |

840/1,200 = 70%

| | Cost | Retail |
|---|---|---|
| | $840,000 | $1,200,000 |
| Markdowns | | $ (80,000) |
| Sales | | (960,000) |
| Ending Inventory | $112,000 | $ 160,000 |

70% x 160,000 = $112,000

Note that markdowns are not included in cost ratio computation in LOCOM average retail.

**75.** /a/

| | Cost | Retail |
|---|---|---|
| Beginning Inv. | $ 14,700 | $ 20,300 |
| Purchases | 83,300 | 115,500 |
| Markups | | 4,200 |
| | $ 98,000 | $ 140,000 |

98/140 = 70%

| | | |
|---|---|---|
| Markdowns | | $ (1,400) |
| Sales | | (110,600) |
| Ending Inv. | $ 19,600 | $ 28,000 |

$28,000 x 70% = $19,600

Note the exclusion of markdowns from the cost ratio computation in LOCOM average retail method.

**76.** /d/

| | Cost | Retail |
|---|---|---|
| BI & Purchases | $600,000 | $920,000 |
| Markups | | 40,000 |
| | $600,000 | $960,000 |

60 / 960 = 62.5%

| | | |
|---|---|---|
| Net markdowns | | $ 60,000) |
| Sales | | (780,000) |
| Ending Inventory | $ 75,000 | $120,000 |

62.5% x $120,000 = $75,000

| | |
|---|---|
| Cost of goods available | $600,000 |
| Less ending inventory | (75,000) |
| Cost of sales | $525,000 |

**77.** /a/ Lower of cost or market rule disregarded, so markdowns are included in the calculation of cost ratio. Under FIFO flow assumptions, ending inventory is assumed to come entirely from current purchases, so beginning inventory cost amounts are not included in the cost ratio calculation.

| | Cost | Retail |
|---|---|---|
| Purchases | $60,000 | $110,000 |
| Net markups | | 10,000 |
| Net markdowns | | (20,000) |
| | $60,000 | $100,000 |

60 / 100 = 60%

| | | |
|---|---|---|
| Beginning inventory | | 30,000 |
| Retail available for sale | | $130,000 |
| Sales | | (90,000) |
| Ending Inventory | $ 24,000 | $40,000 |

60% x $40,000 = $24,000

**78.** /a/

| | |
|---|---|
| Merchandise out on consignment overstated by 40% x 7000 | $2,800 |
| Goods held on consignment Should not be included | 4,000 |
| Goods out on approval overstated by 500 | 500 |
| Total Overstatement | $7,300 |

**79.** /a/ Goods on consignment belong to the consignor, not to the consignee. They should be in the inventory of the consignor only.

**80.** /c/ Alt owes Todd an amount equal to sales revenue (500 sweaters at $100 each) less 10% commission. $50,000 - 5,000 = $45,000

**81.** /d /Goods owned by Stone Co.:

| | |
|---|---|
| ·On consignment to Beta | $18,000 |
| ·Freight paid by Stone | 900 |
| Total consigned inventory | $18,900 |

**82.** /a/

Recovery = Face value of policy / (FMV of property x Coinsurance %) x Loss amount

$$\text{Recovery} = \frac{120{,}000}{300{,}000 \times 0.8} \times \$100{,}000$$

Recovery = $50,000

**83.** /b/ Cost of goods sold pertains to 50,000 tons produced in prior years and the 350,000 produced in the current year. $15,000,000 -:- 3,000,000 tons = $5/ton original depletion. $11,000,000 -:- 2,000,000 tons = $5.50/ton, revised depletion rate.

| | |
|---|---|
| 50,000 tons at $5/ton | $ 250,000 |
| 350,000 tons at $5.50/ton | 1,925,000 |
| Depletion in COGS | $2,175,000 |

**84.** /d/ Historical cost, replacement cost, and net realizable value are all attributes that could be used to measure inventory. However, since inventory is a current asset, it would not be appropriate to use a time-value of future cash flows approach.

**85.** /c/ LIFO valuation method places the most recent costs in cost of goods sold, and older costs in inventory. In a period of rising prices, inventory acquisition costs would rise during the year. As a result, a change from FIFO to LIFO would place the older (lower) costs in the inventory and the more recent (higher) costs in cost of goods sold.

**86.** /c/ Beginning inventory is an inclusion in cost of goods sold; therefore, the understated amount of $26,000 causes cost of goods sold to be understated. Ending inventory is a subtraction in the cost of goods sold computation. Since the ending inventory was overstated, not enough cost has been left in cost of goods sold -- another understatement error. Total understated is $78,000.

**87.** /b/ Since the inventory was reported at replacement cost, that cost must be lower than market, thus I is not correct. "Market" means current replacement cost (CRC) subject to an upper and lower limit. The higher limit is net realizable value (NRV). If NRV is higher than CRC, replacement cost is used as the market figure. The fact that replacement cost was used indicates that II is correct; i.e. the NRV is greater than replacement cost.

**88.** /b/ Steps in the dollar-value LIFO inventory method are
1. Deflate current year cost of ending inventory using current year index.
2. Separate resulting figure into layers.
3. Inflate each layer using the index appropriate for each layer.
4. Sum the layers.

In this problem, Step 1 does not need to be done, because the ending inventory at base year prices has been given -- $525,000.

| | |
|---|---|
| Base layer, 1/1/x9 | $500,000 |
| Additional layer | |
| $25,000 x 1.10 | 27,500 |
| Dollar-value inventory, 12/31/x9 | $527,500 |

**89.** /b/ 

| | |
|---|---|
| Beginning inventory | $122,000 |
| Plus: | |
| Purchases | 540,000 |
| Freight in | 10,000 |
| Transportation to consignees | 5,000 |
| Less: | |
| Total ending inventories owned by Kam | (165,000) |
| Cost of goods sold | $512,000 |

Freight out is a selling expense. Freight in is a cost of acquiring inventories. Transportation to consignees is properly includable in cost of goods sold.

**90.** /c/ The selling price of unsold goods out on consignment must be removed from Accounts Receivable, and the related cost of those goods ($26,000/130% = $20,000) must be added to the inventory figure.

| | |
|---|---|
| Cash | $70,000 |
| Accounts receivable ($120,000- $26,000) | 94,000 |
| Inventories ($60,000 + $20,000) | 80,000 |
| Total current assets | $244,000 |

**91.** /b/ Depletion per unit:
($2,640,000 cost + $180,000 estimated restoration costs - $300,000 residual value + $360,000 development costs to prepare mine for production) -:- 1,200,000 tons = $2.40 per ton

Depletion 20x0:
60,000 tons x $2.40/ton = $144,000

**92.** /a/

| | |
|---|---|
| $152,000 | Cash interest received |
| - 38,000 | Interest receivable 1/1 |
| + 46,500 | Interest receivable 12/31 |
| $160,500 | Investment interest revenue |

## TABLE 4-1

The following present and future value tables should be used in any calculations for the questions in Chapter 4.

### COMPOUND (FUTURE) VALUE OF $1.00

| N | 1% | 2% | 3% | 4% | 5% | 6% | 7% | 8% | 9% | 10% | 12% | 14% |
|---|-----|-----|-----|-----|-----|-----|-----|-----|-----|-----|-----|-----|
| 01 | 1.010 | 1.020 | 1.030 | 1.040 | 1.050 | 1.060 | 1.070 | 1.080 | 1.090 | 1.100 | 1.120 | 1.140 |
| 02 | 1.020 | 1.040 | 1.061 | 1.082 | 1.102 | 1.124 | 1.145 | 1.166 | 1.188 | 1.210 | 1.254 | 1.300 |
| 03 | 1.030 | 1.061 | 1.093 | 1.125 | 1.158 | 1.191 | 1.225 | 1.260 | 1.295 | 1.331 | 1.405 | 1.482 |
| 04 | 1.041 | 1.082 | 1.126 | 1.170 | 1.216 | 1.262 | 1.311 | 1.360 | 1.412 | 1.464 | 1.574 | 1.689 |
| 05 | 1.051 | 1.104 | 1.159 | 1.217 | 1.276 | 1.338 | 1.403 | 1.469 | 1.539 | 1.611 | 1.762 | 1.925 |
| 06 | 1.061 | 1.126 | 1.194 | 1.265 | 1.340 | 1.419 | 1.501 | 1.587 | 1.677 | 1.772 | 1.974 | 2.195 |
| 07 | 1.072 | 1.149 | 1.230 | 1.316 | 1.407 | 1.504 | 1.606 | 1.714 | 1.828 | 1.949 | 2.211 | 2.502 |
| 08 | 1.083 | 1.172 | 1.267 | 1.369 | 1.477 | 1.594 | 1.718 | 1.851 | 1.993 | 2.144 | 2.476 | 2.853 |
| 09 | 1.094 | 1.195 | 1.305 | 1.423 | 1.551 | 1.689 | 1.838 | 1.999 | 2.172 | 2.358 | 2.773 | 3.252 |
| 10 | 1.105 | 1.219 | 1.344 | 1.480 | 1.629 | 1.791 | 1.967 | 2.159 | 2.367 | 2.594 | 3.106 | 3.707 |
| 11 | 1.116 | 1.243 | 1.384 | 1.539 | 1.710 | 1.898 | 2.105 | 2.332 | 2.580 | 2.853 | 3.479 | 4.226 |
| 12 | 1.127 | 1.268 | 1.426 | 1.601 | 1.796 | 2.012 | 2.252 | 2.518 | 2.813 | 3.138 | 3.896 | 4.818 |
| 13 | 1.138 | 1.294 | 1.469 | 1.665 | 1.886 | 2.133 | 2.410 | 2.720 | 3.066 | 3.452 | 4.363 | 5.492 |
| 14 | 1.149 | 1.319 | 1.513 | 1.732 | 1.980 | 2.261 | 2.579 | 2.937 | 3.342 | 3.798 | 4.887 | 6.261 |
| 15 | 1.161 | 1.346 | 1.558 | 1.801 | 2.079 | 2.397 | 2.759 | 3.172 | 3.642 | 4.177 | 5.474 | 7.138 |

## TABLE 4-2
### COMPOUND (FUTURE) VALUE OF AN ANNUITY OF $1

| N | 1% | 2% | 3% | 4% | 5% | 6% | 7% | 8% | 9% | 10% | 12% | 14% |
|---|-----|-----|-----|-----|-----|-----|-----|-----|-----|-----|-----|-----|
| 01 | 1.000 | 1.000 | 1.000 | 1.000 | 1.000 | 1.000 | 1.000 | 1.000 | 1.000 | 1.000 | 1.000 | 1.000 |
| 02 | 2.010 | 2.020 | 2.030 | 2.040 | 2.050 | 2.060 | 2.070 | 2.080 | 2.090 | 2.100 | 2.120 | 2.140 |
| 03 | 3.030 | 3.060 | 3.091 | 3.122 | 3.153 | 3.184 | 3.215 | 3.246 | 3.278 | 3.310 | 3.374 | 3.440 |
| 04 | 4.060 | 4.122 | 4.184 | 4.246 | 4.310 | 4.375 | 4.440 | 4.506 | 4.573 | 4.641 | 4.779 | 4.921 |
| 05 | 5.101 | 5.204 | 5.309 | 5.416 | 5.526 | 5.637 | 5.751 | 5.867 | 5.985 | 6.105 | 6.353 | 6.610 |
| 06 | 6.152 | 6.308 | 6.468 | 6.633 | 6.802 | 6.975 | 7.153 | 7.336 | 7.523 | 7.716 | 8.115 | 8.536 |
| 07 | 7.214 | 7.434 | 7.662 | 7.898 | 8.142 | 8.394 | 8.654 | 8.923 | 9.200 | 9.487 | 10.089 | 10.731 |
| 08 | 8.286 | 8.583 | 8.892 | 9.214 | 9.549 | 9.897 | 10.250 | 10.637 | 11.029 | 11.436 | 12.300 | 13.233 |
| 09 | 9.369 | 9.755 | 10.159 | 10.583 | 11.027 | 11.491 | 11.978 | 12.488 | 13.021 | 13.580 | 14.776 | 16.085 |
| 10 | 10.462 | 10.950 | 11.464 | 12.006 | 12.578 | 13.181 | 13.816 | 14.487 | 15.193 | 15.937 | 17.549 | 19.337 |
| 11 | 11.567 | 12.169 | 12.808 | 13.486 | 14.207 | 14.972 | 15.784 | 16.646 | 17.560 | 18.531 | 20.655 | 23.045 |
| 12 | 12.683 | 13.412 | 14.192 | 15.026 | 15.917 | 16.870 | 17.889 | 18.977 | 20.141 | 21.384 | 24.133 | 27.271 |
| 13 | 13.809 | 14.680 | 15.618 | 16.628 | 17.713 | 18.882 | 20.141 | 21.495 | 22.953 | 24.523 | 28.029 | 32.089 |
| 14 | 14.947 | 15.974 | 17.086 | 18.292 | 19.599 | 21.015 | 22.551 | 24.215 | 26.019 | 27.975 | 32.393 | 37.581 |
| 15 | 16.097 | 17.293 | 18.599 | 20.024 | 21.279 | 23.276 | 25.129 | 27.152 | 29.361 | 31.773 | 37.280 | 43.842 |

## TABLE 4-3
## PRESENT VALUE OF $1.00

| N | 1% | 2% | 3% | 4% | 5% | 6% | 7% | 8% | 9% | 10% | 15% | 16% | 17% | 18% | 19% | 20% |
|---|---|---|---|---|---|---|---|---|---|---|---|---|---|---|---|---|
| 01 | .99010 | .98039 | .97087 | .96154 | .95238 | .94340 | .93458 | .92593 | .91743 | .90909 | .86957 | .86207 | .85470 | .84746 | .84034 | .83333 |
| 02 | .98030 | .96117 | .94260 | .92456 | .90703 | .89000 | .87344 | .85734 | .84168 | .82645 | .75614 | .74316 | .73051 | .71818 | .70616 | .69444 |
| 03 | .97059 | .94232 | .91514 | .88900 | .86384 | .83962 | .81630 | .79383 | .77218 | .75131 | .65752 | .64066 | .62437 | .60863 | .59342 | .57870 |
| 04 | .96098 | .92385 | .88849 | .85480 | .82270 | .79209 | .76290 | .73503 | .70843 | .68301 | .57175 | .55229 | .53365 | .51579 | .49867 | .48225 |
| 05 | .95147 | .90573 | .86261 | .82193 | .78353 | .74726 | .71299 | .68057 | .64993 | .62092 | .49718 | .47611 | .45611 | .43711 | .41905 | .40188 |
| 06 | .94204 | .88797 | .83748 | .79031 | .74622 | .70496 | .66634 | .63017 | .59627 | .56447 | .43233 | .41044 | .38984 | .37043 | .35214 | .33490 |
| 07 | .93272 | .87056 | .81309 | .75992 | .71068 | .66506 | .62275 | .58349 | .54703 | .51316 | .37594 | .35383 | .33320 | .31392 | .29592 | .27908 |
| 08 | .92348 | .85349 | .78941 | .73069 | .67684 | .62741 | .58201 | .54027 | .50187 | .46651 | .32690 | .30503 | .28478 | .26604 | .24867 | .23257 |
| 09 | .91434 | .83675 | .76642 | .70259 | .64461 | .59190 | .54393 | .50025 | .46043 | .42410 | .28426 | .26295 | .24340 | .22546 | .20897 | .19381 |
| 10 | .90529 | .82035 | .74409 | .67556 | .61391 | .55839 | .50835 | .46319 | .42241 | .38554 | .24718 | .22663 | .20804 | .19106 | .17560 | .16151 |
| 11 | .89632 | .80426 | .72242 | .64958 | .58468 | .52679 | .47509 | .42888 | .38753 | .35049 | .21494 | .19542 | .17781 | .16192 | .14756 | .13459 |
| 12 | .88745 | .78849 | .70138 | .62460 | .55684 | .49697 | .44401 | .39711 | .35553 | .31863 | .18691 | .16846 | .15197 | .13722 | .12400 | .11216 |
| 13 | .87866 | .77303 | .68095 | .60057 | .53032 | .46884 | .41496 | .36770 | .32618 | .28966 | .16253 | .14523 | .12989 | .11629 | .10420 | .09346 |
| 14 | .86996 | .75787 | .66112 | .57747 | .50507 | .44230 | .38782 | .34046 | .29925 | .26333 | .14133 | .12520 | .11102 | .09855 | .08757 | .07789 |
| 15 | .86135 | .74301 | .64186 | .55526 | .48102 | .41726 | .36245 | .31524 | .27454 | .23939 | .12289 | .10793 | .09489 | .08352 | .07359 | .06491 |

## TABLE 4-4
## PRESENT VALUE OF AN ORDINARY ANNUITY OF $1.00

| N | 1% | 2% | 3% | 4% | 5% | 6% | 7% | 8% | 9% | 10% | 15% | 16% | 17% | 18% | 19% | 20% |
|---|---|---|---|---|---|---|---|---|---|---|---|---|---|---|---|---|
| 01 | 0.9901 | 0.9804 | 0.9709 | 0.9615 | 0.9524 | 0.9434 | 0.9346 | 0.9259 | 0.9174 | 0.9091 | 0.8696 | 0.8621 | 0.8547 | 0.8475 | 0.8403 | 0.8333 |
| 02 | 1.9704 | 1.9416 | 1.9135 | 1.8861 | 1.8594 | 1.8334 | 1.8080 | 1.7833 | 1.7591 | 1.7355 | 1.6257 | 1.6052 | 1.5852 | 1.5656 | 1.5465 | 1.5278 |
| 03 | 2.9410 | 2.8839 | 2.8286 | 2.7751 | 2.7232 | 2.6730 | 2.6243 | 2.5771 | 2.5313 | 2.4868 | 2.2832 | 2.2459 | 2.2096 | 2.1743 | 2.1399 | 2.1065 |
| 04 | 3.9020 | 3.8077 | 3.7171 | 3.6299 | 3.5459 | 3.4651 | 3.3872 | 3.3121 | 3.2397 | 3.1699 | 2.8550 | 2.7982 | 2.7432 | 2.6901 | 2.6386 | 2.5887 |
| 05 | 4.8535 | 4.7134 | 4.5797 | 4.4518 | 4.3295 | 4.2123 | 4.1002 | 3.9927 | 3.8896 | 3.7908 | 3.3522 | 3.2743 | 3.1993 | 3.1272 | 3.0576 | 2.9906 |
| 06 | 5.7655 | 5.6014 | 5.4172 | 5.2421 | 5.0757 | 4.9173 | 4.7665 | 4.6229 | 4.4859 | 4.3553 | 3.7845 | 3.6847 | 3.5892 | 3.4976 | 3.4098 | 3.3255 |
| 07 | 6.7282 | 6.4720 | 6.2302 | 6.0020 | 5.7863 | 5.5824 | 5.3893 | 5.2064 | 5.0329 | 4.8684 | 4.1604 | 4.0386 | 3.9224 | 3.8115 | 3.7057 | 3.6046 |
| 08 | 7.6517 | 7.3254 | 7.0196 | 6.7327 | 6.4632 | 6.2098 | 5.9713 | 5.7466 | 5.5348 | 5.3349 | 4.4873 | 4.3436 | 4.2072 | 4.0776 | 3.9544 | 3.8372 |
| 09 | 8.5661 | 8.1622 | 7.7861 | 7.4353 | 7.1078 | 6.8017 | 6.5152 | 6.2469 | 5.9952 | 5.7590 | 4.7716 | 4.6065 | 4.4506 | 4.3030 | 4.1633 | 4.0310 |
| 10 | 9.4714 | 8.9825 | 8.5302 | 8.1109 | 7.7217 | 7.3601 | 7.0236 | 6.7101 | 6.4176 | 6.1446 | 5.0188 | 4.8332 | 4.6586 | 4.4941 | 4.3389 | 4.1925 |
| 11 | 10.3677 | 9.7868 | 9.2526 | 8.7604 | 8.3064 | 7.8868 | 7.4987 | 7.1389 | 6.8052 | 6.4951 | 5.2337 | 5.0286 | 4.8364 | 4.6560 | 4.4865 | 4.3271 |
| 12 | 11.2552 | 10.5753 | 9.9539 | 9.3850 | 8.8632 | 8.3838 | 7.9427 | 7.5361 | 7.1607 | 6.8137 | 5.4206 | 5.1971 | 4.9884 | 4.7932 | 4.6105 | 4.4392 |
| 13 | 12.1338 | 11.3483 | 10.6349 | 9.9856 | 9.3935 | 8.8527 | 8.3576 | 7.9038 | 7.4869 | 7.1034 | 5.5831 | 5.3423 | 5.1183 | 4.9095 | 4.7147 | 4.5327 |
| 14 | 13.0038 | 12.1062 | 11.2960 | 10.5631 | 9.8986 | 9.2950 | 8.7454 | 8.2442 | 7.7861 | 7.3667 | 5.7245 | 5.4675 | 5.2293 | 5.0081 | 4.8023 | 4.6106 |
| 15 | 13.8651 | 12.8492 | 11.9379 | 11.1183 | 10.3796 | 9.7122 | 9.1079 | 8.5595 | 8.0607 | 7.6061 | 5.8474 | 5.5755 | 5.3242 | 5.0916 | 4.8759 | 4.6755 |

# CHAPTER 4

## BALANCE SHEET LIABILITIES

### Question Map

# CHAPTER 4

## BALANCE SHEET LIABILITIES

### Multiple Choice Questions

**1.** On March 31, Dallas Co. received an advance payment of 60% of the sales price for special order goods to be manufactured and delivered within five months. At the same time, Dallas subcontracted for production of the special order goods at a price equal to 40% of the main contract price. What liabilities should be reported in Dallas' March 31 balance sheet?

|   | Deferred revenues | Payables to subcontractor |
|---|---|---|
| **a.** | None | None |
| **b.** | 60% of main contract price | 40% of main contract price |
| **c.** | 60% of main contract price | None |
| **d.** | None | 40% of main contract price |

**2.** How would the proceeds received from the advance sale of nonrefundable tickets for a theatrical performance be reported in the seller's financial statements before the performance?
   **a.** Revenue for the entire proceeds.
   **b.** Revenue to the extent of related costs expended.
   **c.** Unearned revenue to the extent of related costs expended.
   **d.** Unearned revenue for the entire proceeds.

**3.** Which of the following is an accrued liability?
   **a.** Cash dividends payable.
   **b.** Wages payable.
   **c.** Rent revenue collected one month in advance.
   **d.** Portion of long-term debt payable in current year.

**4.** Kemp Co. must determine the December 31, 20x1, year-end accruals for advertising and rent expenses. A $500 advertising bill was received January 7, 20x2, comprising costs of $375 for advertisements in December 20x1 issues, and $125 for advertisements in January 20x2 issues of the newspaper.

A store lease, effective December 16, 20x0, calls for fixed rents of $1,200 per month, payable one month from the effective date and monthly thereafter. In addition, rent equal to 5% of net sales over $300,000 per calendar year is payable on January 31 of the following year. net sales for 20x1 were $550,000.

In its December 31, 20x1, balance sheet, Kemp should report accrued liabilities of
   **a.** $12,875
   **b.** $13,000
   **c.** $13,100
   **d.** $13,475

**5.** Toddler Care Co. offers three payment plans on its 12-month contracts. Information on the three plans and the number of children enrolled in each plan for the September 1 through August 31 contract year follows:

| Plan | Initial payment per child | Monthly fees per child | Number of children |
|---|---|---|---|
| #1 | $500 | --- | 15 |
| #2 | 200 | 30 | 12 |
| #3 | --- | 50 | 9 |
|  |  |  | 36 |

Toddler received $9,900 of initial payments on September 1 and $3,240 of monthly fees during the period September 1 through December 31. In its December 31 balance sheet, what amount should Toddler report as deferred revenues?
   **a.** $3,300
   **b.** $4,380
   **c.** $6,600
   **d.** $9,900

**6.** Fell, Inc., operates a retail grocery store that is required by law to collect refundable deposits of $.05 on soda cans. Information for 20x1 follows:

Liability for returnable
deposits, 12/31/x0      $150,000
Cans of soda sold in 20x1      10,000,000
Soda cans returned in 20x1      11,000,000

On February 1, 20x1, Fell subleased space and received a $25,000 deposit to be applied towards rent at the expiration of the lease in 20x5. In Fell's December 31, 20x1, balance sheet, the current and noncurrent liabilities for deposits were

| | Current | Noncurrent |
|---|---|---|
| a. | $125,000 | $0 |
| b. | $100,000 | $ 25,000 |
| c. | $100,000 | $0 |
| d. | $ 25,000 | $100,000 |

**7.** Able, Inc. had the following amounts of long-term debt outstanding at December 31, 20x1:

| | |
|---|---|
| 14 1/2% term note, due 20x2 | $ 3,000 |
| 11 1/8% term note, due 20x5 | 107,000 |
| 8% note, due in 11 equal annual payments, plus interest, beginning December 31, 20x2 | 110,000 |
| 7% guaranteed debentures, due 20x6 | 100,000 |
| Total | $320,000 |

Able's annual sinking-fund requirement on the guaranteed debentures is $4,000 per year. What amount should Able report as current maturities of long-term debt in its December 31, 20x1, balance sheet?
     a.   $ 4,000
     b.   $ 7,000
     c.   $10,000
     d.   $13,000

**8.** Stark, Inc., has $1,000,000 of notes payable due June 15, 20x1. At the financial statement date of December 31, 20x0, Stark signed an agreement to borrow up to $1,000,000 to refinance the notes payable on a long-term basis. The financing agreement called for borrowings not to exceed 80% of the value of the collateral Stark was providing. At the date of issue of the December 31, 20x0, financial statements the value of the collateral was $1,200,000 and was not expected to fall below this amount

during 20x1. On the December 31, 20x0, balance sheet, Stark should classify
     a.   $40,000 of notes payable as short-term and $960,000 as long-term obligations.
     b.   $200,000 of notes payable as short-term and $800,000 as long-term obligations.
     c.   $1,000,000 of notes payable as short-term obligations.
     d.   $1,000,000 of notes payable as long-term obligations.

**9.** On December 31, 20x2, Largo, Inc. had a $750,000 note payable outstanding, due July 31, 20x3. Largo borrowed the money to finance construction of a new plant. Largo planned to refinance the note by issuing long-term bonds. Because Largo temporarily had excess cash, it prepaid $250,000 of the note on January 12, 20x3. In February 20x3, Largo completed a $1,500,000 bond offering. Largo will use the bond offering proceeds to repay the note payable at its maturity and to pay construction costs during 20x3. On March 3, 20x3, Largo issued its 20x2 financial statements. What amount of the note payable should Largo include in the current liabilities section of its December 31, 20x2, balance sheet?
     a.   $750,000
     b.   $500,000
     c.   $250,000
     d.   $0

**Questions 10 and 11** pertain to classification of short-term obligations expected to be refinanced and are based on the following data:

Royal Corporation's liabilities at December 31, 20x0, were as follows:

| | |
|---|---|
| Trade accounts payable | $100,000 |
| 16% notes payable issued 11/1/x0, maturing 7/1/x 1 | 30,000 |
| 14% debentures payable issued 2/1/x0; final installment due 2/1/x5; balance at 12/31/x0, including annual installment $50,000 due 2/1/x1 | 300,000 |
| | $430,000 |

Royal's December 31, 20x0, financial statements were issued on March 31, 20x1. On January 5, 20x1, the entire $300,000 balance of the 14% debentures was refinanced by issuance of a long-term obligation. In addition, on March 1, 20x1, Royal consummated a noncancelable agreement with the lender to refinance the 16% note payable on a long-term basis, on readily determinable terms that have not yet been implemented. Both parties are financially capable of honoring the agreement, and there have been no violations of any of the agreement's provisions.

**10.** The total amount of Royal's short-term obligations that may properly be excluded from current liabilities at December 31, 20x0, is
a. $0
b. $30,000
c. $50,000
d. $80,000

**11** Assume the same facts for Royal Corporation's liabilities, except that the agreement with the lender to refinance the 16% note payable on a long-term basis is cancellable at any time upon ten days' notice by the lender. The total amount of Royal's short-term obligations that may properly be excluded from current liabilities at December 31, 20x0, is
a. $0
b. $30,000
c. $50,000
d. $80,000

**12.** On August 1, Vann Corp.'s $500,000, one-year, noninterest-bearing note, due July 31 of the following year, was discounted at Homestead Bank at 10.8%. Vann uses the straight-line method of amortizing bond discount. What amount should Vann report for notes payable in its December 31 balance sheet?
a. $500,000
b. $477,500
c. $468,500
d. $446,000

**13.** A company issued a short-term note payable with a stated 12 percent rate of interest to a bank. The bank charged a 0.5% loan fee and remitted the balance to the company. The effective interest rate paid by the company in this transaction would be
a. Equal to 12.5%
b. More than 12.5%
c. Less than 12.5%
d. Independent of 12.5%

**14.** On January 1 Dorr Company borrowed $200,000 from its major customer, Pine Corporation, evidenced by a note payable in three years. The promissory note did not bear interest. Dorr agreed to supply Pine's inventory needs for the loan period at favorable prices. The going rate of interest for this type of loan is 14%. Assume that the present value (at the going rate of interest) of the $200,000 note is $135,000 at January 1. What amount of interest expense should be included in Dorr's income statement for the year?
a. $0
b. $18,900
c. $21,667
d. $28,000

**15.** Blue Corp.'s December 31, 20x1, balance sheet contained the following items in the long-term liabilities section:

| | |
|---|---|
| 9 3/4% registered debentures, callable in 20x1, due in 20x7 | $700,000 |
| 9 1/2% collateral trust bonds, convertible into common stock beginning in 20x0, due in 20y0 | 600,000 |
| 10% subordinated debentures ($30,000 maturing annually beginning in 20x7) | 300,000 |

What is the total amount of Blue's term bonds?
a. $ 600,000
b. $ 700,000
c. $1,000,000
d. $1,300,000

**16.** During the year, Lake Co. issued 3,000 of its 9%, $1,000 face value bonds at 101 1/2. In connection with the sale of the bonds, Lake paid the following expenses:

| | |
|---|---|
| Promotion costs | $ 20,000 |
| Engraving and printing | 25,000 |
| Underwriters' commissions | 200,000 |

What amount should Lake record as bond issue costs to be amortized over the term of the bonds?
a. $0
b. $220,000
c. $225,000
d. $245,000

**17.** Dixon Co. incurred costs of $3,300 when it issued, on August 31, 20x1, 5-year debenture bonds dated April 1, 20x1. What amount of bond issue expense should Dixon report in its income statement for the year ended December 31, 20x1?
a. $ 220
b. $ 240
c. $ 495
d. $3,300

**18.** On January 1, 20x1, Wolf Corp. issued its ten-year, 10% bonds in the face amount of $1,000,000. The bonds were issued for $1,135,000 to yield 8%, resulting in bond premium of $135,000. Wolf uses the interest method of amortizing bond premium. Interest is payable annually on December 31. At December 31, 20x1, Wolf's adjusted unamortized bond premium should be
a. $135,000
b. $125,800
c. $121,500
d. $101,500

**19.** How would the amortization of premium on bonds payable affect each of the following?

| | Carrying Value of Bond | Net Income |
|---|---|---|
| a. | Increase | Decrease |
| b. | Increase | Increase |
| c. | Decrease | Decrease |
| d. | Decrease | Increase |

**20.** On January 1, 20x5, Gilson Corporation issued for $ 1,030,000, one thousand of its 9%, $1,000 callable bonds. The bonds are dated January 1, 20x5, and mature on December 31, 20x9. Interest is payable semiannually on January 1 and July 1. The bonds can be called by the issuer at 102 on any interest payment date after December 31, 20x9. The unamortized bond premium was $14,000 at December 31, 20x2, and the market price of the bonds was 99 on this date. In its December 31, 20x2, balance sheet, at what amount should Gilson report the carrying value of the bonds?
a. $1,020,000
b. $1,016,000
c. $1,014,000
d. $ 990,000

**21.** On January 1, 20x1, when the market rate for bond interest was 14%, Luba Corporation issued bonds in the face amount of $500,000, with interest at 12% payable semiannually. The bonds mature on December 31, 20x0, and were issued at a discount of $53,180. How much of the discount should be amortized by the interest method at July 1, 20x1?
a. $1,277
b. $2,659
c. $3,191
d. $3,723

**22.** On January 1, 20x2, Hansen, Inc., issued for $939,000, one thousand of its 9%, $1,000 bonds. The bonds were issued to yield 10%. The bonds are dated January 1, 20x2, and mature on December 31 eleven years later. Interest is payable annually on December 31. Hansen uses the interest method of amortizing bond discount. In its December 31, 20x2, balance sheet, Hansen should report unamortized bond discount of
a. $57,100
b. $54,900
c. $51,610
d. $51,000

**23.** On January 1, 20x0, Korn Co. sold to Kay Corp. $400,000 of its 10% bonds for $354,118 to yield 12%. Interest is payable semiannually on January 1 and July 1.

What amount should Korn report as interest expense for the six months ended June 30, 20x0?

a. $17,706
b. $20,000
c. $21,247
d. $24,000

**24.** A 15-year bond was issued ten years ago at a discount. During the current year, a 10-year bond was issued at face amount with the proceeds used to retire the 15-year bond at its face amount. The net effect of the current year bond transactions was to increase long-term liabilities by the excess of the 10-year bond's face amount over the 15-year bond's

a. Face amount.
b. Carrying amount.
c. Face amount less the deferred loss on bond retirement.
d. Carrying amount less the deferred loss on bond retirement.

**25.** On January 1, 20x2, Jaffe Corporation issued at 95, five hundred of its 9%, $1,000 bonds. Interest is payable semiannually on July 1 and January 1, and the bonds mature on January 1 ten years later. Jaffe paid bond issue costs of $20,000 which are appropriately recorded as a deferred charge. Jaffe uses the straight-line method of amortizing bond discount and bond issue costs. On Jaffe's December 31, 20x2, balance sheet, the bonds payable should be reported at their carrying value of

a. $459,500
b. $477,500
c. $495,500
d. $522,500

**26.** For the issuer of a ten-year term bond, the amount of amortization using the interest method would increase each year if the bond was sold at a

|    | Discount | Premium |
|----|----------|---------|
| a. | No       | No      |
| b. | Yes      | Yes     |
| c. | No       | Yes     |
| d. | Yes      | No      |

**27.** On March 1, Clark Co. issued bonds at a discount. Clark incorrectly used the straight-line method instead of the effective interest method to amortize the discount. How were the following amounts, as of December 31 of the same year, affected by the error?

|    | Bond carrying amount | Retained earnings |
|----|----------------------|-------------------|
| a. | Overstated           | Overstated        |
| b. | Understated          | Understated       |
| c. | Overstated           | Understated       |
| d. | Understated          | Overstated        |

**28.** On January 1, 20x0, Battle Corporation sold at 97 plus accrued interest, two hundred of its 8%, $1,000 bonds. The bonds are dated October 1, 20x9, (the previous year) and mature on October 1, 20x9, (nine years in the future). Interest is payable semiannually on April 1 and October 1. Accrued interest for the period October 1, 20x9, to January 1, 20x0, amounted to $4,000. As a result, on, January 1, 20x0, Battle would record bonds payable, net of discount, at

a. $190,000
b. $194,000
c. $196,000
d. $198,000

**29.** On April 1, 20x2, Hill Corp. issued 200 of its $1,000 face value bonds at 101 plus accrued interest. The bonds were dated November 1, 20x1, and bear interest at an annual rate of 9% payable semiannually on November 1 and May 1. What amount did Hill receive from the bond issuance?

a. $194,500
b. $200,000
c. $202,000
d. $209,500

**30.** On November 1, Mason Corp. issued $800,000 of its 10-year, 8% term bonds dated October 1 of the same year. The bonds were sold to yield 10%, with total proceeds of $700,000 plus accrued interest. Interest is paid every April 1 and October 1. What amount should Mason report for interest payable in its balance sheet for the year ended December 31?

a. $17,500

b. $16,000
c. $11,667
d. $10,667

**31.** On July 1, 20x2, Chatham, Inc., called for redemption all of its $1,000,000 face amount bonds payable outstanding at the call price of 105. As of June 30, 20x2, the unamortized discount was $50,000 and the unamortized bond issue costs were $30,000. The market value of the bonds was $1,060,000 on July 1, 20x2. Chatham's effective income tax rate was 40% for 20x2. In its income statement for the year ended December 31, 20x2, what amount should Chatham report as gain or loss from bond redemption?

    a. $0.
    b. $30,000 gain.
    c. $60,000 loss.
    d. $78,000 loss.

**32.** Ray Finance, Inc. issued a 10-year, $100,000, 9% note on January 1, 20x0. The note was issued to yield 10% for proceeds of $93,770. Interest is payable semiannually. The note is callable after two years at a price of $96,000. Due to a decline in the market rate of 8%, Ray retired the note on December 31, 20x2. On that date, the carrying amount of the note was $94,582, and the discounted market rate was $105,280. What amount should Ray report as gain (loss) from retirement of the note for the year ended December 31, 20x2?

    a. $ 9,280
    b. $ 4,000
    c. $(2,230)
    d. $(1,418)

**33.** In open market transactions, Oak Corp. simultaneously sold its long-term investment in Maple Corp. bonds and purchased its own outstanding bonds. The broker remitted the net cash from the two transactions. Oak's gain on the purchase of its own bonds exceeded its loss on the sale of Maple's bonds. Oak should report the

    a. Net effect of the two transactions as a gain.
    b. Net effect of the two transactions in income before discontinued operations.
    c. Effect of its own bond transaction gain in income before extraordinary items, and report the Maple bond transaction as an extraordinary loss.
    d. Effect of its own bond transaction as a gain, and report the Maple bond transaction loss in income before discontinued operations.

**34.** On January 1, 20x0, Ben Corporation issued $600,000 of 5% ten-year bonds at 103. The bonds are callable at the option of Ben at 104. Ben has recorded amortization of the bond premium on the straight-line method (which was not materially different from the interest method). On December 31, 20x4, when the fair market value of the bonds was 97, Ben repurchased $300,000 of the bonds in the open market at 97. Ben has recorded interest and amortization for 20x4. Ignoring income taxes and assuming that the gain is material, Ben should report this reacquisition as

    a. A gain of $13,500.
    b. An extraordinary gain of $13,500.
    c. A gain of $21,000.
    d. An extraordinary gain of $21,000.

**35.** On June 30, 20x2, King Co. had outstanding 9%, $5,000,000 face value bonds maturing on June 30, 20x7. Interest was payable semiannually every June 30 and December 31. On June 30, 20x2, after amortization was recorded for the period, the unamortized bond premium and bond issue costs were $30,000 and $50,000 respectively. On that date, King acquired all its outstanding bonds on the open market at 98 and retired them. At June 30, 20x2, what amount should King recognize as gain before income taxes on redemption of bonds?

    a. $ 20,000
    b. $ 80,000
    c. $120,000
    d. $180,000

**36.** On January 1, 20x4, Provident Corporation issued for $1,040,000, one thousand of its 9%, $1,000 callable bonds. The bonds are dated January 1, 20x4, and mature on January 1 ten years in the future. Interest is payable semiannually on July 1 and January 1. The bonds can be called by the issuer at 101 at any time after December 31, 20x8. On July 1, 20x9, Provident called in all of the bonds and retired them. Assume that Provident uses the straight-line method of amortizing bond premium. Ignoring income taxes, what is the amount of gain or loss that Provident should record on this early extinguishment of debt in its income statement for the year ended December 31, 20x9?

    **a.** $ 8,000 gain.
    **b.** $10,000 loss.
    **c.** $12,000 gain.
    **d.** $30,000 gain.

**37.** Gains or losses from the early extinguishment of debt, if material, should be
    **a.** Recognized in income before taxes in the period of extinguishment.
    **b.** Recognized as an extraordinary item in the period of extinguishment.
    **c.** Amortized over the life of the new issue.
    **d.** Amortized over the remaining original life of the extinguished issue.

**38.** Which of the following material gains on refunding of bonds payable should be recognized separately as an extraordinary gain?

| | Issuance of New Bonds; Proceeds Used to Retire Old Bonds | Direct Exchange of Old Bonds for New Bonds |
|---|---|---|
| **a.** | Yes | No |
| **b.** | Yes | Yes |
| **c.** | No | Yes |
| **d.** | No | No |

**39.** How should the cash proceeds from convertible bonds sold at issue date at par be recorded?
    **a.** As additional paid-in capital for the portion of the proceeds attributable to the conversion feature and as a liability for the portion of the proceeds attributable to the debt.
    **b.** As retained earnings for the portion of the proceeds attributable to the conversion feature and as a liability for the portion of the proceeds attributable to the debt.
    **c.** As a liability for the entire proceeds.
    **d.** As additional paid-in capital for the portion of the proceeds attributable to the conversion feature and as retained earnings for the portion of the proceeds attributable to the debt.

**40.** Clay Corp. had $600,000 convertible, 8% bonds outstanding at June 30. Each $1,000 bond was convertible into 10 shares of Clay's $50 par value common stock. On July 1, the interest was paid to bondholders, and the bonds were converted into common stock, which had a fair market value of $75 per share. The unamortized premium on these bonds was $12,000 at the date of conversion. Under the book value method, this conversion increased the following elements of the stockholders' equity section by

| | Common stock | Additional paid-in capital |
|---|---|---|
| **a.** | $300,000 | $312,000 |
| **b.** | $306,000 | $306,000 |
| **c.** | $450,000 | $162,000 |
| **d.** | $600,000 | $ 12,000 |

**41.** At the time of conversion of bonds into common stock, the market value of the stock exceeds the net carrying amount of the bonds. A loss on conversion would be recognized when using the

| | Book value method | Market value method |
|---|---|---|
| **a.** | Yes | No |
| **b.** | Yes | Yes |
| **c.** | No | Yes |
| **d.** | Yes | No |

**42.** On December 1 the Simpson Company issued at 103, one hundred of its 5%, $1,000 bonds. Attached to each bond was one detachable stock purchase warrant entitling the holder to purchase 10 shares of Simpson's common stock. On December 1 the market value of the bonds, without the stock purchase warrants, was 94, and the market value of each stock purchase warrant was $60. The amount of the proceeds from the issuance that should be accounted for as the initial carrying value of the bonds payable would be

    a. $ 94,000.
    b. $ 96,820.
    c. $ 97,000.
    d. $103,000.

**43.** On March 1 Fence Corporation issued $500,000 of 8% nonconvertible bonds at 103, which are due on February 28 twenty years in the future. In addition each $1,000 bond was issued with 30 detachable stock warrants, each of which entitled the bondholder to purchase for $50 one share of Fence common stock, par value $25. On March 1 the fair market value of Fence's common stock was $40 per share and the fair market value of the warrants was $4. What amount should Fence record on March 1 as stock warrants outstanding?

    a. $ 15,000.
    b. $ 60,000.
    c. $375,000.
    d. $750,000.

**44.** When the cash proceeds from a bond issued with detachable stock purchase warrants exceeds the sum of the par value of the bonds and the fair value of the warrants, the excess should be credited to

    a. Additional paid-in capital.
    b. Retained earnings.
    c. Premium on bonds payable.
    d. Detachable stock warrants outstanding.

**45.** On July 1 Menzie Corporation sold a $1,000,000, 20-year, 10% bond issue for $1,060,000. Each $1,000 bond had a detachable warrant eligible for the purchase of one share of Menzie's $50 par value common stock for $60. Immediately after sale of the bonds, Menzie's securities had the following market values:

| | |
|---|---|
| 10% bond without warrants | $1,040 |
| Warrants | 20 |
| Common stock, $50 par value | 56 |

How much should Menzie credit to premium on bonds payable?
    a. $0
    b. $20,000
    c. $40,000
    d. 60,000

**46.** Bonds with detachable stock warrants were issued by Flack Co. Immediately after issue the aggregate market value of the bonds and the warrants exceeds the proceeds. Is the portion of the proceeds allocated to the warrants less than their market value, and is the amount recorded as contributed capital?

| | Less than warrants' market value | Contributed capital |
|---|---|---|
| a. | No | Yes |
| b. | Yes | No |
| c. | Yes | Yes |
| d. | No | No |

**47.** A portion of the proceeds should be allocated to paid-in capital for bonds issued with

| | Detachable Stock Purchase Warrants | Nondetachable Stock Purchase Warrants |
|---|---|---|
| a. | No | No |
| b. | No | Yes |
| c. | Yes | No |
| d. | Yes | Yes |

**48.** On June 4 Xmar Corporation sold $200,000 face amount of 12% bonds for $198,000, with interest payable semiannually beginning December 3. Each $1,000 bond had ten detachable warrants entitling the holder to buy one share of Xmar's common stock for each warrant surrendered, plus $20 cash. Shortly after the bonds were sold, each bond was selling for $1,000 without the warrants, while the warrants were selling for $10 each. What portion of the $198,000 proceeds should be credited to "Additional paid-in capital – warrants"?

a. $0
b. $ 2,000
c. $18,000
d. $20,000

**49.** During 20x2 Peterson Company experienced financial difficulties and is likely to default on a $500,000, 15%, three-year note dated January 1, 20x1, payable to Forest National Bank. On December 31, 20x2, the bank agreed to settle the note and unpaid interest of $75,000 for 20x2 for $50,000 cash and marketable securities having a current market value of $375,000. Peterson's acquisition cost of the securities is $385,000. Ignoring income taxes, what amount should Peterson report as a gain from the debt restructuring in its 20x2 income statement?

a. $ 65,000
b. $ 75,000
c. $140,000
d. $150,000

**50.** On October 15, 20x1, Kam Corp. informed Finn Co. that Kam would be unable to repay its $100,000 note due on October 31 to Finn. Finn agreed to accept title to Kam's computer equipment in full settlement of the note. The equipment's carrying value was $80,000 and its fair value was $75,000. Kam's tax rate is 30%. What amounts should Kam report as ordinary gain(loss) and ordinary gain for the year ended September 30, 20x2.

| | Ordinary gain(loss) | Extraordinary gain |
|---|---|---|
| a. | $(5,000) | $17,500 |
| b. | $0 | $20,000 |
| c. | $0 | $14,000 |
| d. | $20,000 | $0 |

**51.** On December 31, 20x1, Marsh Company entered into a debt restructuring agreement with Saxe Company, which was experiencing financial difficulties. Marsh restructured a $100,000 note receivable as follows:

- Reduced the principal obligation to $70,000.
- Forgave $12,000 of accrued interest.
- Extended the maturity date from December 31, 20x1, to December 31, 20x2.
- Reduced the interest rate from 12% to 8%. Interest was payable annually on December 31, 20x1, and 20x2.

In accordance with the agreement, Saxe made payments to Marsh on December 31, 20x1 and 20x2. How much interest income should Marsh report for the year ended December 31, 20x2?

a. $0
b. $ 5,600
c. $ 8,400
d. $11,200

**52.** Kent Co. filed a voluntary bankruptcy petition on August 15, and the statement of affairs reflects the following amounts:

| Assets: | Book value | Fair value |
|---|---|---|
| Assets pledged with fully secured creditors | $ 300,000 | $370,000 |
| Assets pledged with partially secured creditors | 180,000 | 120,000 |
| Free assets | 420,000 | 320,000 |
| | $ 900,000 | $810,000 |

| Liabilities: | |
|---|---|
| Liabilities with priority | $ 70,000 |
| Fully secured creditors | 260,000 |
| Partially secured creditors | 200,000 |
| Unsecured creditors | 540,000 |
| | $1,070,000 |

Assume that the assets are converted to cash at the estimated current values and the business is liquidated. What amount of cash will be available to pay unsecured nonpriority claims?

a. $240,000
b. $280,000
c. $320,000
d. $360,000

**53.** Seco Corp. was forced into bankruptcy and is in the process of liquidating assets and paying claims. Unsecured claims will be paid at the rate of forty cents on the dollar. Hale holds a $30,000 noninterest-bearing note receivable from Seco collateralized by an asset with a book value of $35,000 and a liquidation value of $5,000. The amount to be realized by Hale on this note is
   a. $ 5,000
   b. $12,000
   c. $15,000
   d. $17,000

**54.** On December 30, Hale Corp. paid $400,000 cash and issued 80,000 shares of its $1 par value common stock to its unsecured creditors on a pro rata basis pursuant to a reorganization plan under Chapter 11 of the bankruptcy statutes. Hale owed these unsecured creditors a total of $1,200,000. Hale's common stock was trading at $1.25 per share on December 30. As a result of this transaction, Hale's total stockholders' equity had a net increase of
   a. $1,200,000
   b. $ 800,000
   c. $ 100,000
   d. $ 80,000

**55.** How should a loss contingency that is reasonably possible and for which the amount can be reasonably estimated be reported?

|    | Accrued | Disclosed |
|----|---------|-----------|
| a. | Yes     | No        |
| b. | No      | Yes       |
| c. | Yes     | Yes       |
| d. | No      | No        |

**56.** During the year Volner Company's fire insurance premiums were increased from $60,000 to $200,000. To avoid paying such a substantial additional expense, Volner increased the deductible on its policy from $100,000 to $1,000,000. Volner's income tax rate is 40%. At December 31 how much of a contingent liability should Volner accrue to cover possible future fire losses?
   a. $0
   b. $ 540,000
   c. $ 600,000
   d. $1,000,000

**57.** Invern, Inc. has a self-insurance plan. Each year, retained earnings is appropriated for contingencies in an amount equal to insurance premiums saved less recognized losses from lawsuits and other claims. As a result of an accident in the current year, Invern is a defendant in a lawsuit in which it will probably have to pay damages of $190,000. What are the effects of this lawsuit's probable outcome on Invern's financial statements for the current year?
   a. An increase in expenses and no effect on liabilities.
   b. An increase in both expenses and liabilities.
   c. No effect on expenses and an increase in liabilities.
   d. No effect on either expenses or liabilities.

**58.** On January 17, 20x1, an explosion occurred at a Sims Co. plant causing extensive property damage to area buildings. Although no claims had yet been asserted against Sims by March 10, 20x1, Sims' management and counsel concluded that it is likely that claims will be asserted and that it is reasonably possible Sims will be responsible for damages. Sims' management believed that $1,250,000 would be a reasonable estimate of its liability. Sims' $5,000,000 comprehensive public liability policy has a $250,000 deductible clause. In Sims' December 31, 20x0, financial statements, which were issued on March 25, 20x1, how should this item be reported?
   a. As an accrued liability of $250,000.
   b. As a footnote disclosure indicating the possible loss of $250,000.
   c. As a footnote disclosure indicating the possible loss of $1,250,000.
   d. No footnote disclosure or accrual is necessary.

**59.** Taylor Company was involved in a tax dispute with the Internal Revenue Service at the close of its year ended December 31, 20x9. The company's tax counsel believes that an unfavorable outcome is probable. A reasonable estimate of additional tax payments is in the range between $300,000 and $800,000, but $500,000 is a better estimate than any other amount in that range. The situation was unchanged when the financial statements were issued on March 5, 20x0. What amount of additional taxes should be accrued and charged to income in 20x9?

a. $0
b. $300,000
c. $500,000
d. $800,000

**60.** A loss contingency for which the amount of loss can be reasonably estimated should be accrued when the occurrence of the loss is

|    | Reasonably Possible | Remote |
|----|---------------------|--------|
| a. | Yes                 | No     |
| b. | Yes                 | Yes    |
| c. | No                  | No     |
| d. | No                  | Yes    |

**61.** A particular warranty obligation is probable and the amount of the loss can be reasonably estimated. The particular parties that will make claims under the warranty are not identifiable. An estimated loss contingency should then be

a. Classified as an appropriation of retained earnings.
b. Neither accrued nor disclosed.
c. Disclosed but not accrued.
d. Accrued.

**62.** A truck owned and operated by Ward Company was involved in an accident with an auto driven by Stillman on January 12, 20x1. Ward received notice on April 24, 20x1, of a lawsuit for $800,000 damages for a personal injury suffered by Stillman. Ward's counsel believes it is reasonably possible that Stillman will be successful against the company for an estimated amount in the range between $100,000 and $400,000. No amount within this range is a better estimate of potential damages than any other amount. It is expected that the lawsuit will be adjudicated in the latter part of 20x2. What amount of loss should Ward accrue at December 31, 20x1?

a. $0
b. $100,000
c. $250,000
d. $400,000

**63.** On December 20, 20x2, an uninsured property damage loss was caused by a company car being driven on company business by a company salesman. The company did not become aware of the loss until January 25, 20x3. The amount of the loss was reasonably estimable before the company's 20x2 financial statements were issued. The company's December 31, 20x2, financial statements should report an estimated loss as

a. A disclosure, but not an accrual.
b. An accrual.
c. Neither an accrual nor a disclosure.
d. An appropriation of retained earnings.

**64.** Tackle Company sells football helmets. During the year Tackle discovered a defect in the helmets which has produced lawsuits that are reasonably estimated to result in losses of $900,000. Based on its own experience and the experience of other enterprises in the business, Tackle considers it probable that additional lawsuits that are reasonably estimated to result in losses of $1,600,000 will occur even though the particular parties that will bring suit are not identifiable at this time. What amount of loss, if any, should be accrued by a charge to income in for the year?

a. $0
b. $ 900,000
c. $1,600,000
d. $2,500,000

**65.** In 20x1, a personal injury lawsuit was brought against Halsey Co. Based on counsel's estimate, Halsey reported a $50,000 liability in its December 31, 20x1, balance sheet. In November 20x2, Halsey received a favorable judgment, requiring the plaintiff to reimburse Halsey for expenses of $30,000. The plaintiff has appealed the decision, and Halsey's counsel is unable to predict the outcome of the appeal. In its December 31, 20x2, balance sheet, Halsey should report what amounts of asset and liability related to these legal actions?

|    | Asset    | Liability |
|----|----------|-----------|
| a. | $30,000  | $50,000   |
| b. | $30,000  | $0        |
| c. | $0       | $20,000   |
| d. | $0       | $0        |

**66.** Gain contingencies are usually recognized in the income statement when
   a. Realized.
   b. Occurrence is reasonably possible and the amount can be reasonably estimated.
   c. Occurrence is probable and the amount can be reasonably estimated.
   d. The amount can be reasonably estimated.

**67.** In July 20x1 Simpson Company filed suit in federal court against White Corporation seeking to recover $750,000 for patent infringement. A court verdict was rendered in August 20x1 awarding Simpson $500,000 in damages. White has appealed the verdict but a final decision is not expected before October 20x2. Simpson's counsel believes it is probable that Simpson will be successful against White for an estimated amount of $400,000. What amount should Simpson accrue by a credit to income in the year ended December 31, 20x1?
   a. $0
   b. $400,000
   c. $500,000
   d. $750,000

**68.** In 20x1, a contract dispute between Dollis Co. and Brooks Co. was submitted to binding arbitration. In 20x1, each party's attorney indicated privately that the probable award in Dollis' favor could be reasonably estimated. In 20x2, the arbitrator decided in favor of Dollis. When should Dollis and Brooks recognize their respective gain and loss?

|    | Dollis' gain | Brooks' loss |
|----|-------------|--------------|
| a. | 20x1        | 20x1         |
| b. | 20x1        | 20x2         |
| c. | 20x2        | 20x1         |
| d. | 20x2        | 20x2         |

**69.** At December 31, Creole Co. was suing a competitor for patent infringement. The award from the probable favorable outcome could be reasonably estimated. Creole's financial statements for the year should report the expected award as a
   a. Receivable and revenue.
   b. Receivable and reduction of patent.
   c. Receivable and deferred revenue.
   d. Disclosure by footnote only.

**70.** Morgan Company determined that: (1) it has a material obligation relating to employees' rights to receive compensation for future absences attributable to employees' services already rendered, (2) the obligation relates to rights that vest, and (3) payment of the compensation is probable. The amount of Morgan's obligation as of December 31 is reasonably estimated for the following employee benefits:

| Vacation pay | $100,000 |
|--------------|----------|
| Holiday pay  | 25,000   |

What total amount should Morgan report as its liability for compensated absences in its December 31 balance sheet?
   a. $0
   b. $ 25,000
   c. $100,000
   d. $125,000

**71.** North Corp. has an employee benefit plan for compensated absences that gives employees 10 paid vacation days and 10 paid sick days. Both vacation and sick days can be carried over indefinitely. Employees can elect to receive payment in lieu of vacation days; however, no payment is given for sick days not taken. At December 31, North's unadjusted balance of liability for compensated absences was $21,000. North estimated that there were 150 vacation days and 75 sick days available at December 31.

North's employees earn an average of $100 per day. In its December 31 balance sheet, what amount of liability for compensated absences is North required to report?

a. $36,000
b. $22,500
c. $21,000
d. $15,000

**72.** An employer's obligation relating to employees' rights to receive compensation for future absences is attributable to employees' services already rendered. The payment of compensation is probable and the amount of compensation can be reasonably estimated. Employees' compensation should be

a. Accrued if the obligation relates to rights that vest or accumulate.
b. Accrued if the obligation relates to rights that do **not** vest or accumulate.
c. Expensed when paid.
d. Disclosed, but **not** accrued if the obligation relates to rights that vest or accumulate.

**73.** Case Cereal Co. frequently distributes coupons to promote new products. On October 1, 20x1, Case mailed 1,000,000 coupons for $.45 off each box of cereal purchased. Case expects 120,000 of these coupons to be redeemed before the December 31, 20x1, expiration date. It takes 30 days from the redemption date for Case to receive the coupons from the retailers. Case reimburses the retailers an additional $.05 for each coupon redeemed. As of December 31, 20x1, Case had paid retailers $25,000 related to these coupons and had 50,000 coupons on hand that had not been processed for payment. What amount should Case report as a liability for coupons in its December 31, 20x1, balance sheet?

a. $35,000
b. $29,000
c. $25,000
d. $22,500

**74.** Fulton Cereal Company inaugurated a new sales promotional program. For every 10 cereal box tops returned to the company, customers receive an attractive prize. Fulton estimates that only 30% of the cereal box tops reaching the consumer market will be redeemed.

Additional information is as follows:

| | Units | Amounts |
|---|---|---|
| Sales of cereal boxes | 2,000,000 | $1,400,000 |
| Purchase of prizes | 36,000 | 18,000 |
| Prizes distributed to customers | 28,000 | |

At the end of its year, Fulton recognized a liability equal to the estimated cost of potential prizes outstanding. What is the amount of this estimated liability?

a. $ 4,000
b. $16,000
c. $18,000
d. $42,000

**75.** In an effort to increase sales, Mills Company inaugurated a sales promotional campaign on June 30. Mills placed a coupon redeemable for a premium in each package of cereal sold. Each premium costs Mills $1 and five coupons must be presented by a customer to receive a premium. Mills estimated that only 60% of the coupons issued will be redeemed. For the six months ended December 31 the following information is available:

| Packages of Cereal Sold | Premiums Purchased | Coupons Redeemed |
|---|---|---|
| 1,600,000 | 120,000 | 400,000 |

What is the estimated liability for premium claims outstanding at December 31?

a. $ 80,000
b. $112,000
c. $144,000
d. $192,000

**76.** Dunn Trading Stamp Co. records stamp service revenue and provides for the cost of redemptions in the year stamps are sold to licensees. Dunn's past experience indicates that only 80% of the stamps sold to licensees will be redeemed. Dunn's liability for stamp redemptions was $6,000,000 at December 31, 20x1. Additional information for 20x2 is as follows:

| | |
|---|---|
| Stamp service revenue from stamps sold to licensees | $4,000,000 |
| Cost of redemptions (stamps sold prior to 1/1/x2) | 2,750,000 |

If all the stamps sold in 20x2 were presented for redemption in 20x3, the redemption cost would be $2,250,000. What amount should Dunn report as a liability for stamp redemptions at December 31, 20x2?

  a. $7,250,000
  b. $5,500,000
  c. $5,050,000
  d. $3,250,000

**77.** Bold Company estimates its annual warranty expense at 2% of annual net sales. The following data are available:

| | |
|---|---|
| Net sales for 20x0 | $4,000,000 |

Warranty liability account:

| | |
|---|---|
| December 31, 20x9 | $ 60,000 credit |
| Warranty payments during 20x0 | 50,000 debit |

After recording the 20x0 estimated warranty expense. The warranty liability account would show a December 31, 20x0, balance of

  a. $10,000
  b. $70,000
  c. $80,000
  d. $90,000

**78.** During 20x8 Lawton Company introduced a new line of machines that carry a three-year warranty against manufacturer's defects. Based on industry experience, warranty costs are estimated at 2% of sales in the year of sale, 4% in the year after sale, and 6% in the second year after sale. Sales and actual warranty expenditures for the first three-year period were as follows:

| | Sales | Actual Warranty Expenditures |
|---|---|---|
| 20x8 | $ 200,000 | $ 3,000 |
| 20x9 | 500,000 | 15,000 |
| 20x0 | 700,000 | 45,000 |
| | $1,400,000 | $63,000 |

What amount should Lawton report as a liability at December 31, 20x0?
  a. $0
  b. $5,000
  c. $68,000
  d. $105,000

**79.** In 20x1 Dubious Corporation began selling a new line of products that carry a two-year warranty against defects. Based upon past experience with other products, the estimated warranty costs related to dollar sales are as follows:

| | |
|---|---|
| First year of warranty | 2% |
| Second year of warranty | 5% |

Sales and actual warranty expenditures for 20x1 and 20x2 are presented below:

| | 20x1 | 20x2 |
|---|---|---|
| Sales | $500,000 | $700,000 |
| Actual warranty expenditures | 10,000 | 30,000 |

What is the estimated warranty liability at the end of 20x2?
  a. $39,000
  b. $44,000
  c. $49,000
  d. $84,000

**80.** Brower Corporation owns a manufacturing plant in the country of Oust. On December 31 the plant had a book value of $5,000,000 and an estimated fair market value of $8,000,000. The government of Oust has clearly indicated that it will expropriate the plant during the coming year and will reimburse Brower for 40% of the plant's estimated fair market value. What journal entry should Brower make on

December 31 to record the intended expropriation?

|  | Debit | Credit |
|---|---|---|
| **a.** Estimated loss on expropriation of foreign plant | $1,800,000 | |
|     Allowance for estimated loss on foreign plant | | $1,800,000 |
| **b.** Estimated loss on expropriation of foreign plant | 3,000,000 | |
|     Allowance for estimated loss on foreign plant | | 3,000,000 |
| **c.** Receivable due from foreign government | 3,200,000 | |
|     Investment in foreign plant | | 3,200,000 |
| **d.** Loss on expropriation of foreign plant | 1,800,000 | |
|     Receivable due from foreign government | 3,200,000 | |
|     Investment in foreign plant | | 5,000,000 |

**81.** On January 1, Card Corp. signed a three-year, noncancelable purchase contract, which allows Card to purchase up to 500,000 units of a computer part annually from Hart Supply Co. at $.10 per unit and guarantees a minimum annual purchase of 100,000 units. During the year, the part unexpectedly became obsolete. Card had 250,000 units of this inventory left at December 31, and believes these parts can be sold as scrap for $.02 per unit. What amount of probable loss from the purchase commitment should Card report in its income statement for the year ending December 31?

    **a.** $24,000
    **b.** $20,000
    **c.** $16,000
    **d.** $ 8,000

**82.** Brad Corp. has unconditional purchase obligations associated with product financing arrangements. These obligations are reported as liabilities on Brad's balance sheet, with the related assets also recognized. In the notes to Brad's financial statements, the aggregate amount of payments for these obligations should be disclosed for each of how many years following the date of the latest balance sheet?

    **a.** 0
    **b.** 1
    **c.** 5
    **d.** 10

**83.** Lease Y contains a bargain purchase option and the lease term is equal to 75 percent of the estimated economic life of the leased property. Lease Z contains a bargain purchase option and the lease term is equal to less than 75 percent of the estimated economic life of the leased property. How should the lessee classify these leases?

|  | Lease Y | Lease Z |
|---|---|---|
| **a.** | Operating lease | Operating lease |
| **b.** | Operating lease | Capital lease |
| **c.** | Capital lease | Capital lease |
| **d.** | Capital lease | Operating lease |

**84.** On January 1 of the current year, Mollat Co. signed a 7-year lease for equipment having a 10-year economic life. The present value of the monthly lease payments equaled 80% of the equipment's fair value. The lease agreement provides for neither a transfer of title to Mollat nor a bargain purchase option. In its income statement for the current year, Mollat should report

    **a.** Rent expense equal to the lease payments for the current year.
    **b.** Rent expense equal to the current year lease payments less interest expense.
    **c.** Lease amortization equal to one-tenth of the equipment's fair value.
    **d.** Lease amortization equal to one-seventh of 80% of the equipment's fair value.

**85.** Lease M does not contain a bargain purchase option, but the lease term is equal to 90% of the estimated economic life of the leased property. Lease P does not transfer ownership of the property to the lessee at the end of the lease term, but the lease term is equal to 75% of the estimated economic life of the leased property. How should the lessee classify these leases?

|   | Lease M | Lease P |
|---|---------|---------|
| a. | Capital lease | Operating lease |
| b. | Capital lease | Capital lease |
| c. | Operating lease | Capital lease |
| d. | Operating lease | Operating lease |

**86.** Kew Apparel, Inc. leases and operates a retail store. The following information relates to the lease for the current year ending December 31:

- The store lease, an operating lease, calls for a base monthly rent of $1,500 on the first day of each month.
- Additional rent is computed at 6% of net sales over $300,000 up to $600,000 and 5% of net sales over $600,000, per calendar year.
- Net sales for the year were $900,000.
- Kew paid executory costs to the lessor for property taxes of $12,000 and insurance of $5,000.

Kew's expenses relating to the store lease for the year are
- a. $71,000
- b. $68,000
- c. $54,000
- d. $35,000

**87.** Arro Company purchased a machine on January 1, 20x1, for $1,440,000 for the purpose of leasing it. The machine is expected to have an eight-year life from date of purchase, no residual value, and be depreciated on the straight-line basis. On February 1, 20x1, the machine was leased to Baxter Company for a three-year period ending January 31, 20x4, three years later, at a monthly rental of $30,000. Additionally, Baxter paid $72,000 to Arrow on February 1, 20x1 as a lease bonus. What is the amount of income before income taxes that Arrow should report on this leased asset December 31, 20x1?
- a. $172,000
- b. $187,000
- c. $222,000
- d. $237,000

**88.** On January 1, Wren Co. leased a building to Brill under an operating lease for ten years at $50,000 per year, payable the first day of each lease year. Wren paid $15,000 to a real estate broker as a finder's fee. The building is depreciated $12,000 per year. Wren incurred insurance and property tax expense totaling $9,000 for the year. Wren's rental income for the current year should be
- a. $27,500
- b. $29,000
- c. $35,000
- d. $36,500

**89.** On July 1, 20x1, Gee Inc. leased a delivery truck from Marr Corp. under a 3-year operating lease. Total rent for the term of the lease will be $36,000, payable as follows:

12 months at $ 500 = $ 6,000
12 months at $ 750 = $ 9,000
12 months at $1,750 = $21,000

All payments were made when due. In Marr's June 30, 20x3, balance sheet, the accrued rent receivable should be reported as
- a. $0
- b. $ 9,000
- c. $12,000
- d. $21,000

**90.** Conn Corp. owns an office building and normally charges tenants $30 per square foot per year for office space. Because the occupancy rate is low, Conn agreed to lease 10,000 square feet to Hanson Co. at $12 per square foot for the first year of a three-year operating lease. Rent for remaining years will be at the $30 rate. Hanson moved into the building on January 1, 20x1, and paid the first year's rent in advance. What amount of rental revenue should Conn report from Hanson in its income statement for the year ended September 30, 20x1?
- a. $ 90,000
- b. $120,000
- c. $180,000
- d. $240,000

Course 5292 Copyright 2021. The Rigos programs have educated over 100,000 professionals since 1980.

**91.** Rapp Co. leased a new machine to Lake Co. on January 1, 20x1. The lease expires on January 1, 20x6. The annual rental is $90,000. Additionally, on January 1, 20x1, Lake paid $50,000 to Rapp as a lease bonus and $25,000 as a security deposit to be refunded upon expiration of the lease. In Rapp's 20x1 income statement, the amount of rental revenue should be
   a. $140,000
   b. $125,000
   c. $100,000
   d. $ 90,000

**92.** Rent received in advance by the lessor for an operating lease should be recognized as revenue
   a. When received.
   b. At the lease's inception.
   c. In the period specified by the lease.
   d. At the lease's expiration.

**93.** For a capital lease, the amount recorded initially by the lessee as a liability should
   a. Exceed the present value at the beginning of the lease term of minimum lease payments during the lease term.
   b. Exceed the total of the minimum lease payments during the lease term.
   c. Not exceed the fair value of the leased property at the inception of the lease.
   d. Equal the total of the minimum lease payments during the lease term.

**94.** On January 1, 20x0, JCK Co. signed a contract for an eight-year lease of its equipment with a 10-year life. The present value of the 16 equal semiannual payments in advance equaled 85% of the equipment's fair value. The contract had no provision for JCK, the lessor, to give up legal ownership of the equipment. Should JCK recognize rent or interest revenue in 20x2, and should the revenue recognized in 20x2 be the same or smaller than the revenue recognized in 20x1?

| | 20x2 revenues recognized | 20x2 amount recognized compared to 20x1 |
|---|---|---|
| a. | Rent | The same |
| b. | Rent | Smaller |
| c. | Interest | The same |
| d. | Interest | Smaller |

**95.** A six-year capital lease entered into on December 31, 20x4, specified equal minimum annual lease payments due on December 31 of each year. The December 31, 20x5, minimum annual lease payment consists of which of the following?

| | Interest expense | Lease liability |
|---|---|---|
| a. | No | No |
| b. | No | Yes |
| c. | Yes | No |
| d. | Yes | Yes |

**96.** For a capital lease, an amount equal to the present value at the beginning of the lease term of minimum lease payments during the lease term, excluding that portion of the payments representing executory costs such as insurance, maintenance, and property taxes to be paid by the lessor, together with any profit thereon, should be recorded by the lessee as a (an)
   a. Expense.
   b. Liability but **not** an asset.
   c. Asset but **not** a liability.
   d. Asset and a liability.

**97.** An office equipment representative has a machine for sale or lease. If you buy the machine, the cost is $7,596. If you lease the machine, you will have to sign a noncancelable lease and make 5 payments of $2,000 each. The first payment will be paid on the first day of the lease. At the time of the last payment you will receive title to the machine. The present value of an ordinary annuity of $1 is as follows:

| Number of Periods | Present Value | | |
|---|---|---|---|
| | 10% | 12% | 16% |
| 1 | 0.909 | 0.893 | 0.862 |
| 2 | 1.736 | 1.690 | 1.605 |
| 3 | 2.487 | 2.402 | 2.246 |
| 4 | 3.170 | 3.037 | 2.798 |
| 5 | 3.791 | 3.605 | 3.274 |

The interest rate implicit in this lease is approximately
 a. 10%.
 b. 12%.
 c. Between 10% and 12%.
 d. 16%.

**98.** A six-year capital lease specifies equal minimum annual lease payments. Part of this payment represents interest and part represents a reduction in the net lease liability. The portion of the minimum lease payment in the fourth year applicable to the reduction of the net lease liability should be
 a. The same as in the third year.
 b. Less than in the third year.
 c. Less than in the fifth year.
 d. More than in the fifth year.

**99.** On January 1 Kerr Company signed a ten-year noncancelable lease for a new machine, requiring $20,000 annual payments at the beginning of each year. The machine has a useful life of 15 years, with no salvage value. Title passes to Kerr at the lease expiration date. Kerr uses straight-line depreciation for all of its plant assets. Aggregate lease payments have a present value on January 1 of $126,000, based on an appropriate rate of interest. For the year, Kerr should record depreciation (amortization) expense for the leased machine at
 a. $20,000
 b. $12,600
 c. $ 8,400
 d. $0

**100.** On January 2, Moul Mining Co. (lessee), entered into a 5-year lease for drilling equipment. Moul accounted for the acquisition as a capital lease for $120,000, which includes a $5,000 bargain purchase option. At the end of the lease, Moul expects to exercise the bargain purchase option. Moul estimates that the equipment's fair value will be $10,000 at the end of its 8-year life. Moul regularly uses straight-line depreciation on similar equipment. For the first year of the lease, what amount should Moul recognize as depreciation expense on the leased asset?

 a. $13,750
 b. $15,000
 c. $23,000
 d. $24,000

**101.** On January 1 Flip Corporation signed a ten-year noncancelable lease for certain machinery. The terms of the lease called for Flip to make annual payments of $30,000 for ten years with title to pass to Flip at the end of this period. The machinery has an estimated useful life of 15 years and no salvage value. Flip uses the straight-line method of depreciation for all of its fixed assets. Flip accordingly accounted for this lease transaction as an installment purchase of the machinery. The lease payments were determined to have a present value of $201,302 with an effective interest rate of 10%. With respect to this capitalized lease, Flip should record for the year
 a. Lease expense of $30,000.
 b. Interest expense of $16,580 and depreciation expense of $13,420.
 c. Interest expense of $20,130 and depreciation expense of $13,420.
 d. Interest expense of $13,420 and depreciation expense of $16,580.

**102.** On December 31 Ott Company leased a new machine from Wolf with the following pertinent information:

| | |
|---|---|
| Lease term | 12 years |
| Annual rental payable at beginning of each year | $100,000 |
| Useful life of machine | 15 years |
| Implicit interest rate | 12% |
| Present value of an annuity of 1 in advance for 12 periods at 12% | 6.94 |

The lease contains no renewal options and the machine reverts to Wolf at the termination of the lease. The cost of the machine on Wolf's accounting records is $750,000. At the inception of the lease, Ott should record a lease liability of
 a. $0
 b. $100,000
 c. $694,000
 d. $750,000

**103.** On January 2 Rice Company entered into a ten-year noncancelable lease, as lessee, requiring annual payments of $100,000 payable at the beginning of each year. Rice's incremental borrowing rate is 14%, while the lessor's implicit interest rate, known to Rice, is 12%. Present value factors of an annuity of 1 in advance for ten periods are 6.33 at 12%, and 5.95 at 14%. The leased property has an estimated useful life of 12 years. Ownership of the property remains with the lessor at expiration of the lease. At the inception of the lease, Rice should record a lease liability of

   a. $0
   b. $495,000
   c. $595,000
   d. $633,000

**104.** On December 31, Day Co. leased a new machine from Parr with the following pertinent information:

| | |
|---|---|
| Lease term | 6 years |
| Annual rental payable at beginning of each year | $50,000 |
| Useful life of machine | 8 years |
| Day's incremental borrowing rate | 15% |
| Implicit interest rate in lease (known by Day) | 12% |
| Present value of an annuity of 1 in advance for 6 periods at | |
| 12% | 4.61 |
| 15% | 4.35 |

The lease is not renewable, and the machine reverts to Parr at the termination of the lease. The cost of the machine on Parr's accounting records is $375,000. At the beginning of the lease term, Day should record a lease liability of

   a. $375,000
   b. $230,500
   c. $217,500
   d. $0

**105.** On December 29, 20x1, Action Corp. signed a 7-year capital lease for an airplane to transport its sports team around the country. The airplane's fair value was $841,500. Action made the first annual lease payment of $153,000 on December 31, 20x1. Action's incremental borrowing rate was 12%, and the interest rate implicit in the lease, which was known by Action, was 9%. The following are the rounded present value factors for an annuity due:

| | |
|---|---|
| 9% for 7 years | 5.5 |
| 12% for 7 years | 5.1 |

What amount should Action report as capital lease liability in its December 31, 20x1, balance sheet?

   a. $841,500
   b. $780,300
   c. $688,500
   d. $627,300

**106.** Robbins, Inc. leased a machine from Ready Leasing Co. The lease qualifies as a capital lease and requires 10 annual payments of $10,000 beginning immediately. The lease specifies an interest rate of 12% and a purchase option of $10,000 at the end of the tenth year, even though the machine's estimated value on that date is $20,000. Robbin's incremental borrowing rate is 14%.

The present value of an annuity due of 1 at:
| | |
|---|---|
| 12% for ten years is | 6.328 |
| 14% for ten years is | 5.946 |

The present value of 1 at:
| | |
|---|---|
| 12% for ten years is | 0.322 |
| 14% for ten years is | 0.270 |

What amount should Robbins record as lease liability at the beginning of the lease term?

   a. $62,160
   b. $64,860
   c. $66,500
   d. $69,720

**107.** On July 1, Glen Corp. leased a new machine from Ryan Corp. The lease contains the following information:

| | |
|---|---|
| Lease term | 10 years |
| Useful life of the machine | 12 years |
| Present value of the minimum lease payments | $120,000 |
| Fair value of the machine | 200,000 |
| Executory costs | 3,000 |

No bargain purchase option is provided, and the machine reverts to Ryan when the lease expires. What amount should Glen record as a capitalized leased asset at inception of the lease?

- a. $0
- b. $120,000
- c. $123,000
- d. $200,000

**108.** On January 1, 20x1, Day Corp. entered into a 10-year lease agreement with Ward, Inc. for industrial equipment. Annual lease payments of $10,000 are payable at the end of each year. Day knows that the lessor expects a 10% return on the lease. Day has a 12% incremental borrowing rate. The equipment is expected to have an estimated useful life of 10 years. In addition, a third party has guaranteed to pay Ward a residual value of $5,000 at the end of the lease.

The present value of an ordinary annuity of $1 for ten years is 5.6502 at 12% and 6.1446 at 10%. The present value of $1 for ten periods is 0.3220 at 12% and 0.3855 at 10%.

In Day's October 31, 20x1, balance sheet, the principal amount of the lease obligation was

- a. $63,374
- b. $61,446
- c. $58,112
- d. $56,502

**109.** On December 31, 20x1, Roe Company leased a machine under a capital lease for a period of ten years, contracting to pay $100,000 on signing the lease and $100,000 annually on December 31 of the next nine years. The present value at December 31, 20x1, of the ten lease payments over the lease term discounted at 10% was $676,000. At December 31, 20x2, Roe's total capital lease liability is

- a. $486,000
- b. $518,400
- c. $533,600
- d. $607,960

**110.** On January 1, 20x1, Babson, Inc. leased two automobiles for executive use. The lease requires Babson to make five annual payments of $13,000 beginning January 1, 20x1. At the end of the lease term, Babson guarantees the residual value of the automobiles will total $10,000. The lease qualifies as a capital lease. The interest rate implicit in the lease is 9%. Present value factors for the 9% rate implicit in the lease are as follows:

For an annuity due with 5 payments 4.240
For an ordinary annuity with 5 payments
3.890
Present value of $1 for 5 periods     0.650

Babson's recorded capital lease liability immediately after the first required payment should be

- a. $48,620
- b. $44,070
- c. $35,620
- d. $31,070

**111.** On December 31, 20x1, Roe Co. leased a machine from Colt for a five-year period. Equal annual payments under the lease are $105,000 (including $5,000 annual executory costs) and are due on December 31 of each year. The first payment was made on December 31, 20x1, and the second payment was made on December 31, 20x2. The five lease payments are discounted at 10% over the lease term. The present value of minimum lease payments at the inception of the lease and before the first annual payment was $417,000. The lease is appropriately accounted for as a capital lease by Roe. In its December 31, 20x2, balance sheet, Roe should report a lease liability of

- a. $317,000
- b. $315,000
- c. $285,300
- d. $248,700

**112.** On January 1, 20x1, Vick Company as lessee signed a ten-year noncancelable lease for a machine stipulating annual payments of $20,000. The first payment was made on January 1, 20x1. Vick appropriately treated this transaction as a capital lease. The ten lease payments have a present value of $135,000 at January 1, 20x1, based on implicit interest of 10%. For the year ended December 31, 20x1, Vick should record interest expense of

a. $0
b. $ 6,500
c. $11,500
d. $13,500

**113.** On December 31, 20x1, Ames Co. leased equipment under a capital lease for ten years. It contracted to pay $40,000 annual rent on December 31, 20x1, and by December 31 of each of the next nine years. The capital lease liability was recorded at $270,000 on December 31, 20x1, before the first payment. The equipment's useful life is 12 years, and the interest rate implicit in the lease is 10%. Ames uses the straight-line method to depreciate all equipment. In recording the December 31, 20x2, payment, by what amount should Ames reduce the capital lease liability?

a. $27,000
b. $23,000
c. $22,500
d. $17,000

**114.** A lessee had a ten-year capital lease requiring equal annual payments. The reduction of the lease liability in Year 2 should equal

a. The current liability shown for the lease at the end of Year 1.
b. The current liability shown for the lease at the end of Year 2.
c. The reduction of the lease obligation in Year 1.
d. One-tenth of the original lease liability.

**115.** On January 1, 20x1, Blaugh Co. signed a long-term lease for an office building. The terms of the lease required Blaugh to pay $10,000 annually, beginning December 30, 20x1, and continuing for each year for 30 years. The lease qualifies as a capital lease. On January 1, 20x1, the present value of the lease payments is $112,500 at the 8% interest rate implicit in the lease. In Blaugh's December 31, 20x1, balance sheet, the capital lease liability should be

a. $102,500
b. $111,500
c. $112,500
d. $290,000

**116.** On January 1, 20x1, Harrow Co., as lessee, signed a five-year noncancelable equipment lease with annual payments of $100,000 beginning December 31, 20x1. Harrow treated this transaction as a capital lease. The five lease payments have a present value of $379,000 at January 1, 20x1, based on interest of 10%  What amount should Harrow report as interest expense for the year ended December 31, 20x1?

a. $37,900
b. $27,900
c. $24,200
d. $0

**117.** On December 30, 20x1, Rafferty Corp. leased equipment under a capital lease. Annual lease payments of $20,000 are due December 31 for 10 years, and the interest rate implicit in the lease is 10%. The capital lease obligation was recorded on December 31, 20x1, at $135,000, and the first lease payment was made on that date. What amount should Rafferty include in current liabilities for this capital lease in its December 31, 20x1, balance sheet?

a. $ 6,500
b. $ 8,500
c. $11,500
d. $20,000

**118.** Benedict Company leased equipment to Mark, Inc., on January 1, 20x1. The lease is for an eight-year period expiring December 31, 20x9. The first of 8 equal annual payments of $600,000 was made on January 1, 20x1. Benedict had purchased the equipment on December 29, 20x0, for $3,200,000. The lease is appropriately accounted for as a sales-type lease by

Benedict. Assume that the present value at January 1, 20x1, of all rent payments over the lease term discounted at a 10% interest rate was $3,520,000. What amount of interest income should Benedict record in 20x2 (the second year of the lease period) as a result of the lease?

    a. $261,200
    b. $292,000
    c. $320,000
    d. $327,200

**119.** Winn Co. manufactures equipment that is sold or leased. On December 31, 20x1, Winn leased equipment to Bart for a five-year period. At the end of the lease, ownership of the leased asset will be transferred to Bart. Equal payments under the lease are $22,000 (including $2,000 executory costs) and are due on December 31 of each year. The first payment was made on December 31, 20x1. Collectability of the remaining lease payments is reasonably assured, and Winn has no material cost uncertainties. The normal sales price of the equipment if $77,000, and cost is $60,000. For the year ended December 31, 20x1, what amount of income should Winn realize from the lease transaction?

    a. $17,000
    b. $22,000
    c. $23,000
    d. $33,000

**120.** In a lease that is recorded as a sales-type lease by the lessor, unearned interest
    a. Does **not** arise.
    b. Should be recognized in full as income at the lease's inception.
    c. Should be amortized over the period of the lease using the interest method.
    d. Should be amortized over the period of the lease using the straight-line method.

**Questions 121 and 122** are based on the following information:

On January 2, 20x1, Doe Company leased a new crane from Leasement Corp. under the following terms:

- Noncancelable for eight years
- Annual lease payments of $10,000 beginning January 2, 20x1, through January 2, 20x8
- Nonrenewable
- Crane to be returned to Leasement on January 2, 20x9

Doe properly recorded the crane as a "Leased asset-crane" in the amount of $52,880, based on a 14% interest rate implicit in the lease. Leasement paid $56,000 for the crane on December 31, 20x0. The crane has an estimated useful life of ten years, with no salvage value. Both Doe and Leasement use the straight-line method of depreciation.

**121.** How much depreciation expense should Doe record in 20x1 for "Leased asset-crane?"
    a. $0
    b. $ 6,610
    c. $ 7,000
    d. $10,000

**122.** How much interest income should Leasement recognize in 20x1?
    a. $10,000
    b. $ 7,403
    c. $ 6,003
    d. $0

**123.** Rig Co. sold its factory at a gain, and simultaneously leased it back for 10 years. The factory's remaining economic life is 20 years. The lease was reported as an operating lease. At the time of the sale, Rig should report the gain as
    a. An ordinary gain net of income tax.
    b. An asset valuation allowance.
    c. A separate component of stockholders' equity.
    d. A deferred credit.

**124.** On December 31 Lane, Inc. sold equipment to Noll, and simultaneously leased it back for 12 years. Pertinent information at this date is as follows:

| | |
|---|---|
| Sales price | $480,000 |
| Carrying amount | 360,000 |
| Estimated remaining economic life | 15 years |

At December 31 how much should Lane report as deferred revenue from the sale of the equipment?
- a. $0
- b. $110,000
- c. $112,000
- d. $120,000

**125.** The following information pertains to a sale and leaseback of equipment by Mega Co. on December 31,

| | |
|---|---|
| Sales price | $400,000 |
| Carrying amount | 300,000 |
| Monthly lease payment | 3,250 |
| Present value of lease payments | 36,900 |
| Estimated remaining life | 25 years |
| Lease term | 1 year |
| Implicit rate | 12% |

What amount of deferred gain on the sale should Mega report at December 31?
- a. $0
- b. $ 36,900
- c. $ 63,100
- d. $100,000

**126.** On December 31, Dirk Corp. sold Smith Co. two airplanes and simultaneously leased them back. Additional information pertaining to the sale-leaseback follows

| | Plane #1 | Plane #2 |
|---|---|---|
| Sales price | $600,000 | $1,000,000 |
| Carrying amount | $100,000 | $ 550,000 |
| Remaining useful life | 10 years | 35 years |
| Lease term | 8 years | 3 years |
| Annual lease payments | $100,000 | $ 200,000 |

In its December 31 balance sheet, what amount should Dirk report as deferred gain on these transactions?

- a. $950,000
- b. $500,000
- c. $450,000
- d. $0

**127.** On January 1, 20x1, Hooks Oil Co. sold equipment with a carrying amount of $100,000, and a remaining useful life of 10 years to Maco Drilling for $150,000. Hooks immediately leased the equipment back under a 10-year capital lease with a present value of $150,000 and will depreciate the equipment using the straight-line method. Hooks made the first annual lease payment of $24,412 in December, 20x1. In Hook's balance sheet on December 31, 20x1, the unearned gain on equipment sale should be
- a. $50,000
- b. $45,000
- c. $25,588
- d. $0

**128.** On June 30 Gulch Corporation sold equipment to an unaffiliated company for $550,000. The equipment had a book value of $500,000 and a remaining useful life of 10 years. That same day, Gulch leased back the equipment at $1,500 per month for 5 years with no option to renew the lease or repurchase the equipment. Gulch's equipment rent expense for this equipment for the year ended December 31 should be
- a. $ 4,000.
- b. $ 5,000.
- c. $ 9,000.
- d. $11,000.

**129.** On June 30, Lang Co. sold equipment with an estimated useful life of eleven years and immediately leased it back for ten years. The equipment's carrying amount was $450,000; the sales price was $430,000; and the present value of the lease payments, which is equal to the fair value of the equipment, was $465,000. In its June 30 balance sheet, what amount should Lang report as deferred loss?
- a. $35,000
- b. $20,000
- c. $15,000
- d. $0

**130.** When equipment held under an operating lease is subleased by the original lessee, the original lessee would account for the sublease as a (an)

   **a.** Operating lease.
   **b.** Sales-type lease.
   **c.** Direct financing lease.
   **d.** Capital lease.

**131.** A lessee incurred landscaping costs to improve leased property. The estimated useful life of the landscaping costs is six years. The remaining term of the nonrenewable lease is five years. The landscaping costs should be

   **a.** Capitalized as leasehold improvements and depreciated over five years.
   **b.** Capitalized as leasehold improvements and depreciated over six years.
   **c.** Expensed as incurred and included with rent expense.
   **d.** Expensed as incurred but **not** included with rent expense.

**132.** On December 1, Clark Co. leased office space for five years at a monthly rental of $60,000. On the same date, Clark paid the lessor the following amounts:

| | |
|---|---:|
| First month's rent | $ 60,000 |
| Last month's rent | 60,000 |
| Security deposit (refundable at lease expiration date) | 80,000 |
| Installation of new walls and offices | 360,000 |

What should be Clark's expense for the year ending December 31 relating to utilization of the office space

   **a.** $ 60,000
   **b.** $ 66,000
   **c.** $120,000
   **d.** $140,000

**133.** Cali, Inc., had a $4,000,000 note payable due on March 15, 20x5. On January 28, 20x5, before the issuance of its 20x4 financial statements, Cali issued long-term bonds in the amount of $4,500,000. Proceeds from the bonds were used to repay the note when it came due. How should Cali classify the note in its December 31, 20x4, financial statements?

   **a.** As a current liability, with separate disclosure of the note refinancing.
   **b.** As a current liability, with no separate disclosure required.
   **c.** As a noncurrent liability, with separate disclosure of the note refinancing.
   **d.** As a noncurrent liability, with no separate disclosure required.

**134.** Black Co. requires advance payments with special orders for machinery constructed to customer specifications. These advances are nonrefundable. Information for 20x3 is as follows:

| | |
|---|---:|
| Customer advances balance 12/31/x2 | $118,000 |
| Advances received with orders in 20x3 | 184,000 |
| Advances applied to orders shipped in 20x3 | 164,000 |
| Advances applicable to orders cancelled in 20x3 | 50,000 |

In Black's December 31, 20x3, balance sheet, what amount should be reported as a current liability for advances from customers?

   **a.** $0
   **b.** $ 88,000
   **c.** $138,000
   **d.** $148,000

**135.** Hudson Hotel collects 15% in city sales taxes on room rentals, in addition to a $2 per room, per night, occupancy tax. Sales taxes for each month are due at the end of the following month, and occupancy taxes are due 15 days after the end of each calendar quarter. On January 3, 20x4, Hudson paid its November 20x3 sales taxes and its fourth quarter 20x3 occupancy taxes. Additional information pertaining to Hudson's operations is:

| 20x3 | Room rentals | Room nights |
|---|---|---|
| October | $100,000 | 1,100 |
| November | 110,000 | 1,200 |
| December | 150,000 | 1,800 |

What amounts should Hudson report as sales taxes payable and occupancy taxes payable in its December 31, 20x3, balance sheet?

| | Sales taxes | Occupancy taxes |
|---|---|---|
| a. | $39,000 | $6,000 |
| b. | $39,000 | $8,200 |
| c. | $54,000 | $6,000 |
| d. | $54,000 | $8,200 |

**136.** Under state law, Acme may pay 3% of eligible gross wages or it may reimburse the state directly for actual unemployment claims. Acme believes that actual unemployment claims will be 2% of eligible gross wages and has chosen to reimburse the state. Eligible gross wages are defined as the first $10,000 of gross wages paid to each employee. Acme had five employees each of whom earned $20,000 during 20x3. In its December 31, 20x3, balance sheet, what amount should Acme report as accrued liability for unemployment claims?

a. $1,000
b. $1,500
c. $2,000
d. $3,000

**137.** On July 1, 20x3, Ran County issued realty tax assessments for its fiscal year ended June 30, 20x4. On September 1, 20x3, Day co. purchased a warehouse in Ran County. The purchase price was reduced by a credit for accrued realty taxes. Day did not record the entire year's real estate tax obligation, but instead records tax expenses at the end of each month by adjusting prepaid real estate taxes or real estate taxes payable, as appropriate. On November 1, 20x3, Day paid the first of two equal installments of $12,000 for realty taxes. What amount of this payment should Day record as a debit to real estate taxes payable?

a. $ 4,000
b. $ 8,000
c. $10,000
d. $12,000

**138.** Lime Co.'s payroll for the month ended January 31, 20x5, is summarized as follows:

| Total wages | $10,000 |
|---|---|
| Federal income tax withheld | 1,200 |

All wages paid were subject to FICA. FICA tax rates were 7% each for employee and employer. Lime remits payroll taxes on the 15th of the following month. In its financial statements for the month ended January 31, 20x5, what amounts should Lime report as total payroll tax liability and as payroll tax expense?

| | Liability | Expense |
|---|---|---|
| a. | $1,200 | $1,400 |
| b. | $1,900 | $1,400 |
| c. | $1,900 | $ 700 |
| d. | $2,600 | $ 700 |

**139.** On July 1, 20x4, Eagle Corp. issued 600 of its 10%, $1,000 bonds at 99 plus accrued interest. The bonds are dated April 1, 20x4, and mature on April 1 ten years later. Interest is payable semiannually on April 1 and October 1. What amount did Eagle receive from the bond issuance?

a. $579,000
b. $594,000
c. $600,000
d. $609,000

**140.** On January 2, 20x4, Nast Co. issued 8% bonds with a face amount of $1,000,000 that mature on January 2 six years later. The bonds were issued to yield 12%, resulting in a discount of $150,000. Nast incorrectly used the straight-line method instead of the effective interest method to amortize the discount. How is the carrying amount of the bonds affected by the error?

| | At 12/31/x4 | At maturity date |
|---|---|---|
| a. | Overstated | Understated |
| b. | Overstated | No effect |
| c. | Understated | Overstated |
| d. | Understated | No effect |

**141.** Troop Co. frequently borrows from the bank to maintain sufficient operating cash. The following loans were at a 12% interest rate, with interest payable at maturity. Troop repaid each loan on its scheduled maturity date.

| Date of Loan | Amount | Maturity Date | Term of Loan |
|---|---|---|---|
| 11/1/x5 | $10,000 | 10/31/x6 | 1 year |
| 2/1/x6 | 30,000 | 7/31/x6 | 6 months |
| 5/1/x6 | 16,000 | 1/31/x7 | 9 months |

Troop records interest expense when the loans are repaid. Accordingly, interest expense of $3,000 was recorded in 20x6. If **no** correction is made, by what amount would 20x6 interest expense be understated?

- a. $1,080
- b. $1,240
- c. $1,280
- d. $1,440

**142.** On December 31, 20x3, Moss Co. issued $1,000,000 of 11% bonds at 109. Each $1,000 bond was issued with 50 detachable stock warrants, each of which entitled the bondholder to purchase one share of $5 par common stock for $35. Immediately after issuance, the market value of each warrant was $4. On December 31, 20x3, what amount should Moss record as discount or premium on issuance of bonds?

- a. $ 40,000 premium.
- b. $ 90,000 premium.
- c. $110,000 discount.
- d. $200,000 discount.

**143.** Eagle Co. has cosigned the mortgage note on the home of its president, guaranteeing the indebtedness in the event that the president should default. Eagle considers the likelihood of default to be remote. How should the guarantee be treated in Eagle's financial statements?

- a. Disclosed only.
- b. Accrued only.
- c. Accrued and disclosed.
- d. Neither accrued nor disclosed.

**144.** A six-year capital lease entered into on December 31, 20x4, specified equal minimum annual lease payments due on December 31 of each year. The first minimum annual lease payment, paid on December 31, 20x4, consists of which of the following?

| | Interest expense | Lease liability |
|---|---|---|
| a. | Yes | Yes |
| b. | Yes | No |
| c. | No | Yes |
| d. | No | No |

**145.** At the inception of a capital lease, the guaranteed residual value should be

- a. Included as part of minimum lease payments at present value.
- b. Included as part of minimum lease payments at future value.
- c. Included as part of minimum lease payments only to the extent that guaranteed residual value is expected to exceed estimated residual value.
- d. Excluded from minimum lease payments.

**146.** In a sale-leaseback transaction, a gain resulting from the sale should be deferred at the time of the leaseback and subsequently amortized when

I. The seller-lessee has transferred substantially all the risks of ownership.
II. The seller-lessee retains the right to substantially all of the remaining use of the property.

- a. I only.
- b. II only.
- c. Both I and II.
- d. Neither I nor II.

**147.** When a loan receivable is impaired but foreclosure is **not** probable, which of the following may the creditor use to measure the impairment?

I. The loan's observable market price.
II. The fair value of the collateral if the loan is collateral dependent.

    **a.** I only.
    **b.** II only.
    **c.** Either I or II.
    **d.** Neither I nor II.

**148.** Cott, Inc. prepared an interest amortization table for a five-year lease payable with a bargain purchase option of $2,000, exercisable at the end of the lease. At the end of the five years, the balance in the leases payable column of the spreadsheet was zero. Cott has asked Grant, CPA, to review the spreadsheet to determine the error. Only one error was made on the spreadsheet. Which of the following statements represents the best explanation for this error?

    **a.** The beginning present value of the lease did **not** include the present value of the bargain purchase option.
    **b.** Cott subtracted the annual interest amount from the lease payable balance instead of adding it.
    **c.** The present value of the bargain purchase option was subtracted from the present value of the annual payments.
    **d.** Cott discounted the annual payments as an ordinary annuity, when the payments actually occurred at the beginning of each period.

**149.** Park, Inc. issued $500,000, 10% bonds to yield 8%. Bond Issuance costs were $10,000. How should Park calculate the net proceeds to be received from the issuance?

    **a.** Discount the bonds at the stated rate of interest.
    **b.** Discount the bonds at the market rate of interest.
    **c.** Discount the bonds at the stated rate of interest and deduct bond issuance costs.
    **d.** Discount the bonds at the market rate of interest and deduct bond issuance costs.

**150.** Which of the following is not one of the four required criteria for a capital lease?

    **a.** Ownership of the lease property is transferred to the lessee by the end of the lease term.
    **b.** The present value of the minimum lease payments at the inception of the lease is 75% or more of the fair value of the leased property.
    **c.** The lease contains a bargain purchase option.
    **d.** The lease term is substantially (75% or more) equal to the remaining useful life of the leased property.

**151.** Which of the following is excluded in determining minimum lease payments?

    **a.** The lease payments called for during the lease term.
    **b.** An amount necessary to make up a deficiency from a specified minimum.
    **c.** A guarantee by the lessee to pay the lessor's debt on the leased asset.
    **d.** An amount stated to purchase the asset during the lease term.

**152.** Which of the following is a true statement pertaining to leases?

    **a.** The inception date of the lease is the date of the lease agreement or the date of a written commitment signed by the parties that sets the principal provisions of the lease.
    **b.** The inception date of the lease is always the date of a written commitment signed by the parties involved that sets the principal provisions of the lease.
    **c.** The inception of the lease can only be the date of the lease agreement.
    **d.** A written commitment that is missing some of the major provisions of the lease will still establish the inception date of the lease.

# CHAPTER 4

## BALANCE SHEET LIABILITIES

### Simulation Questions

**Number 1**                                                    **(Estimated time - 15 minutes**

Edge Co., a toy manufacturer, is in the process of preparing its financial statements for the year ended December 31, 20x3. Edge expects to issue its 20x3 financial statements on March 1, 20x4.

**Items 1 through 9** represent various information that has not been reflected in the financial statements. For each item, the following two responses are required:

   **a.** Determine if an adjustment is required and select the appropriate amount, if any, from the list below.

   **b.** Determine (Yes/No) if additional disclosure is **required**, either on the face of the financial statements or in the notes to the financial statements.

   Adjustment amounts
   A. No adjustment is required
   B. $100,000
   C. $150,000
   D. $250,000
   E. $400,000
   F. $500,000

**Items to be answered:**

1. Edge owns a small warehouse located on the banks of a river in which it stores inventory worth approximately $500,000. Edge is not insured against flood losses. The river last overflowed its banks twenty years ago.

2. Edge offers an unconditional warranty on its toys. Based on past experience, Edge estimates its warranty expense to be 1% of sales. Sales during 20x3 were $10,000,000.

3. On October 20, 20x3, a safety hazard related to one of Edge's toy products was discovered. It is considered probable that Edge will be liable for an amount in the range of $100,000 to $500,000.

4. On November 22, 20x3, Edge initiated a lawsuit seeking $250,000 in damages from patent infringement.

5. On December 17, 20x3, a former employee filed a lawsuit seeking $100,000 for unlawful dismissal. Edge's attorneys believe the suit is without merit. No court date has been set.

6. On December 15, 20x3, Edge guaranteed a bank loan of $100,000 for its president's personal use.

7. On January 24, 20x4, inventory purchased FOB shipping point from a foreign country was detained at that country's border because of political unrest. The shipment is valued at $150,000. Edge's attorneys have stated that it is probable that Edge will be able to obtain the shipment.

8. On January 30, 20x4, Edge issued $10,000,000 bonds at a premium of $500,000.

9. On February 4, 20x4, the IRS assessed Edge an additional $400,000 for the 20x2 tax year. Edge's tax attorneys and tax accountants have stated that it is likely that the IRS will agree to a $100,000 settlement.

## Number 2                                   (Estimated time – 15 to 25 minutes)

**Question Number 2** consists of 13 items. Select the **best** answer for each item. Answer all items. Your grade will be based on the total number of correct answers.

On January 2, 20x4, North Co. issued bonds payable with a face value of $480,000 at a discount. The bonds are due in 10 years and interest is payable semiannually every June 30 and December 31. On June 30, 20x4, and on December 31, 20x4, North made semiannual interest payments due, and recorded interest expense and amortization of bond discount.

**Required:**

**Items 1 through 7**, contained in the partially completed amortization table below, represent information needed to complete the table. For each item, select from the Rates and Amounts lists the correct numerical responses. A response may be selected once, more than once, or not at all.

| Date | Cash | Interest Expense | Amortization | Discount | Carrying Amount |
|------|------|------------------|--------------|----------|-----------------|
| 1/2/x4 | | | | | **(3)** |
| 6/30/x4 | **(2)** | 18,000 | 3,600 | **(1)** | |
| 12/31/x4 | $14,400 | **(6)** | **(7)** | | |

Annual Interest Rates:  Stated **(4)**
                        Effective **(5)**

| | Rates | | Amounts | | |
|---|-------|---|---------|---|---|
| A | 3.0% | G | $ 3,420 | P | $ 21,600 |
| B | 4.5% | H | $ 3,600 | Q | $116,400 |
| C | 5.0% | I | $ 3,780 | R | $120,000 |
| D | 6.0% | J | $ 3,960 | S | $123,600 |
| E | 9.0% | K | $ 14,400 | T | $360,000 |
| F | 10.0% | L | $ 17,820 | U | $363,600 |
| | | M | $ 18,000 | V | $367,200 |
| | | N | $ 18,180 | W | $467,400 |
| | | O | $ 18,360 | X | $480,000 |

**Items 8 through 13** are based on the following:

Town, Inc. is preparing its financial statements for the year ended December 31, 20x4.

**Required:**

**Items 8 through 13** represent various commitments and contingencies of Town at December 31, 20x4, and events subsequent to December 31, 20x4, but prior to the issuance of the 20x4 financial statements. For each item, select from the following list the appropriate reporting requirement. A reporting requirement may be selected once, more than once, or not at all.

### Reporting Requirement

**D** Disclosure only.
**A** Accrual only.
**B** Both accrual and disclosure.
**N** Neither accrual nor disclosure.

8. On December 1, 20x4, Town was awarded damages of $75,000 in a patent infringement suit it brought against a competitor. The defendant did not appeal the verdict, and payment was received by January 20x5.

9. A former employee of Town has brought a wrongful-dismissal suit against Town. Town's lawyers believe the suit to be without merit.

10. At December 31, 20x4, Town had outstanding purchase orders in the ordinary course of business for purchase of a raw material to be used in its manufacturing process. The market price is currently higher than the purchase price and is not anticipated to change within the next year.

11. A government contract completed during 20x4 is subject to renegotiation. Although Town estimates that it is reasonably possible that a refund of approximately $200,000 - $300,000 may be required by the government, it does not wish to publicize this possibility.

12. Town has been notified by a governmental agency that it will be held responsible for the cleanup of toxic materials at a site where Town formerly conducted operations. Town estimates that it is probable that its share of remedial action will be approximately $500,000.

13. On January 5, 20x5, Town redeemed its outstanding bonds and issued new bonds with a lower rate of interest. The reacquisition price was in excess of the carrying amount of the bonds.

# CHAPTER 4

## BALANCE SHEET LIABILITIES

### Multiple Choice Answers

1. /c/ Deferred revenues equal to 60% of the contract price are current liabilities because they represent Dallas Co.'s obligation to provide goods in the future. However, Dallas has no present economic obligation related to the production it has subcontracted out. The liability related to this production will arise when the goods are delivered to Dallas.

2. /d/ Advance ticket sales, even if nonrefundable, are not reported as revenues until they have been earned. The recognition event is the performance. The issue of related costs expended is not relevant to the timing of revenue recognition. The matching principle requires that expense recognition follow the revenue, not that the revenue be recognized because related expenses have been incurred.

3. /b/ Wages payable are accrued based on an estimate at period end. A, C, and D are incorrect because the exact amounts are known when booked.

4. /d/ 
| | |
|---|---:|
| Advertising, December | $ 375 |
| Rent, Dec. 10 - 31 | 600 |
| Additional rent based on sales ($250,000 x 5%) | 12,500 |
| Total accrued liabilities | $13,475 |

5. /c/ The deferred revenues are those portions of the initial payments that are to be earned in the eight months of the contract year after December 31.

| | |
|---|---:|
| Plan #1.  $500 x 15 x 8/12 | $5,000 |
| Plan #2.  $200 x 12 x 8/12 | 1,600 |
| Total deferred revenues | $6,600 |

6. /b/ Current - Refundable deposits, soda cans:

| | |
|---|---:|
| Balance 12/31/x0 | $150,000 |
| Cans sold (10M x $.05) | 500,000 |
| Cans returned (11M x $.05) | - 550,000 |
| Balance 12/31/x1 | $100,000 |

The $25,000 rent deposit is noncurrent deferred revenue because it will not be earned until the last month of the lease in 20x5.

7. /d/ 
| | |
|---|---:|
| 14 1/2% note due 20x2 | $ 3,000 |
| 8% installment note | 10,000 |
| Total current maturities | $13,000 |

Note that current portions refer to principal only, not to any related interest

8. /a/ 80% of $1,200,000 is $960,000 so that is the maximum that Stark could refinance on a long-term basis. The $40,000 balance of the loan is due by June 15, 20x1 and is short-term.

9. /c/ Current debt may not be reclassified to noncurrent to the extent that cash used to pay off the short-term debt is replaced with long-term debt. Largo must include $250,000 of the note in current liabilities - the amount of cash used then replaced with long-term funding.

10. /d/ The $30,000, 16% note is refinanced on a long-term basis. That removes the note from short-term to long-term status. $50,000 of the 14% debentures are reclassified because the remainder of the $300,000 balance is already long-term.

11. /c/ The fact that the $30,000, 16% note is callable on demand makes it short term. Only the $50,000 balance on the debentures remains long term.

**12.** /c/

| | |
|---|---:|
| Face value of note | $500,000 |
| Less discount ($500K x 10.8%) | - 54,000 |
| Carrying value 8/1 | $446,000 |
| Plus discount amortized: | |
| ($54,000/12) x 5 months | 22,500 |
| Carrying amount, 12/31 | $468,500 |

**13.** /b/ As the company did not receive the full face value of the note, the total interest paid (stated interest + loan fee) would lead to an effective rate greater than 12.5%. Had the full face value been received, the effective interest rate would have been equal to 12.5%.

**14.** /b/ The current year interest expense is 14% of $135,000. The carrying value of the note is its present value per ASC Topic 835.

**15.** /d/ The 10% subordinated debentures are serial bonds as they mature annually. Term bonds ($700,000 + $600,000) amount to $1,300,000.

**16.** /d/ Bond issue costs that are recorded as a deferred charge and amortized include printing, engraving, promotion, legal, and underwriting costs. All costs given qualify for deferred treatment.

**17.** /b/ Bond issue costs are amortized over the remaining life of the bond issue, generally using the straight-line method. Months remaining to maturity date of 4/1/x6 are 55. $3,300 -:- 55 months = $60/month x 4 months = $240

**18/** /b/

| | |
|---|---:|
| Bonds carrying value 1/1/x1 | $1,135,000 |
| Market interest rate | x 8% |
| Interest to be recorded | $ 90,800 |
| Interest to be paid: | |
| ($1,000,000 x 10%) | 100,000 |
| Premium to be amortized | $ 9,200 |

| | |
|---|---:|
| Premium balance 1/1/x1 | $135,000 |
| Less 20x1 amortization | 9,200 |
| Unamortized premium 12/31/x1 | $125,800 |

**19.** /d/ The amortization of a premium reduces the premium which reduces the carrying value of the bond. Interest expense is also reduced which increases net income.

**20.** /c/ The bonds are carried at par plus unamortized premium. Therefore, they are carried at $1,000,000 + 14,000 = $1,014,000.

**21.** /a/

| | |
|---|---:|
| Face value | $500,000 |
| Discount | (53,180) |
| Carrying value of bonds | $446,820 |
| | |
| Interest expense 7/1/x1 | |
| (7% x 446,820) | $31,277 |
| Cash to be paid | |
| (6% x 500,000) | (30,000) |
| Discount Amortized | $ 1,277 |

**22.** /a/

| | |
|---|---:|
| Face value (1000 x 1000) | $1,000,000 |
| Carrying value of bonds | (939,000) |
| Discount | $ 61,000 |
| | |
| Interest expense (10% x 939,000) | $ 93,900 |
| Cash to be paid (9% x 1,000,000) | 90,000 |
| Discount amortization | $ 3,900 |
| | |
| Original unamortized discount | $ 61,000 |
| 20x2 amortization | (3,900) |
| 20x2 unamortized discount balance | $ 57,100 |

**23.** /c/ Korn Co. should report interest expense computed at the market rate based on the carrying value of the bonds at the beginning of the period. $354,118 x 12% x 6/12 = $21,247.

**24.** /b/ The face values of the two bonds are equal. However, since the new, 10-year bond was issued at its face value, that will also be its carrying amount. The old, 15-year bond, on the other hand, was issued at a discount and, as it was retired before its maturity, its carrying amount on retirement would be less than its face value. The net effect of these transactions would be to increase long-term liabilities by the excess of the new bond's carrying amount (also its face amount) over the carrying amount of the old bond. Furthermore, any loss on extinguishment of the old debt is recognized as net of tax in the period incurred (options C and D).

**25.** /b/

| | |
|---|---:|
| Face value of bonds | $500,000 |
| Bond proceeds | |
|   (500,000 x 0.95) | (475,000) |
| Bond discount | $ 25,000 |

| | |
|---|---:|
| One year's discount | |
|   amortization (25,000/10) | $ 2,500 |
| Original bond proceeds | 475,000 |
| | $477,500 |

Only the amortization of the bond discount affects the carrying value. The amortization of the bond issue costs has no effect on the carrying value.

**26.** /b/ Regardless of whether the bonds are sold at a discount or premium, amortization increases annually using the interest method.

**27.** /c/ In the first period, discount amortized under the straight-line method would be higher than under the interest method. This would produce a lower unamortized discount balance, and lead to an overstated bond carrying amount. Interest expense would be overstated (stated interest + larger amount amortized), causing net income and retained earnings to be understated.

**28.** /b/ Battle should record bonds payable, net of discount, at $194,000 ($200,000 face value x 0.97). The accrued interest of $4,000, while part of the proceeds of the bond issue, does not affect the carrying value. It should be recorded as a liability

(bond interest payable) or as a credit to bond interest expense.

**29.** /d/

| | |
|---|---:|
| Proceeds at 101 | |
|   ($200,000 x 101%) | $202,000 |
| Accrued interest | |
| 11/1/x1 - 3/31/x2 | |
|   ($200,000 x 9% x 5/12) | 7,500 |
| Total received | $209,500 |

**30.** /b/ Interest payable is accrued at the stated rate, on the face value, from the last interest date to the end of the year. $800,000 x 8% x 3/12 = $16,000

**31.** /d/

| | | |
|---|---:|---:|
| Face value of bonds | | $1,000,000 |
| Less unamortized | | |
|   bond discount | 50,000 | |
| Less unamortized | | |
|   bond issue cost | 30,000 | (80,000) |
| Carrying value at retirement | | $ 920,000 |
| Cash paid (1,000,000 x 1.05) | | 1,050,000 |
| Total loss | | $ 130,000 |
| Tax (40% x 130,000) | | 52,000 |
| Extraordinary loss on early | | |
|   extinguishment of debt, | | |
|   net of tax | | $ 78,000 |

**32.** /d/

| | |
|---|---:|
| Callable amount | $96,000 |
| Less carrying amount | -94,582 |
| Loss on retirement | $ 1,418 |

**33.** /d/ The transactions should not be netted. The gain on the extinguishment of debt is reported, net of tax effect. The loss on sale of a long-term investment is reported as an "Other Gain or Loss" and is a component of income.

**34.** /a/

| | |
|---|---:|
| Bond proceeds | |
|   ($600,000 x 103) | $618,000 |
| Face value | (600,000) |
| Bond premium | $ 18,000 |
| Amortization to date | |
|   (18,000/10) x 5 | (9,000) |
| Unamortized premium | $ 9,000 |

Carrying value of all bonds
(600,000 + 9,000) — $609,000
Carrying value of 1/2 of
the bonds — 304,500
Cash paid (300,000 x 0.97) — (291,000)
Gain on redemption
of bonds — $ 13,500

The classification of income items as extraordinary has been eliminated.

**35.** /b/

| | |
|---|---|
| Face value 6/30 | $5,000,000 |
| Unamortized premium | 30,000 |
| Unamortized issue costs | - 50,000 |
| Carrying amount 6/30 | $4,980,000 |
| Cash paid ($5M x .98) | 4,900,000 |
| Gain before taxes | $ 80,000 |

**36.** /a/

| | |
|---|---|
| Original carrying value | $1,040,000 |
| Premium amortization to date (40,000/10) x 5.5 | (22,000) |
| Carrying value at retirement | $1,018,000 |
| Cash paid (1,000,000 x 1.01) | (1,010,000) |
| Gain on early extinguishment of debt | $ 8,000 |

As none of the alternatives was labeled "extraordinary," we must assume this gain is not material.

**37.** /a/ Recognition as an extraordinary item, net of tax effect, is no longer required.

**38.** /d/ The classification of income items as extraordinary has been eliminated.

**39.** /c/ No amount of the proceeds are allocated to the conversion feature.

**40.** /a/

| | |
|---|---|
| Bonds carrying value 7/1 | $612,000 |
| Par value of stock issued | |
| (600 bonds x 10 shares x $50/sh.) | 300,000 |
| Balance to APIC | $312,000 |

**41.** /c/ A gain or loss on conversion arises only under the market value method. Any difference between book value of bonds and par value of stock

issued is assigned to additional paid-in capital under the book value method.

**42.** /b/

$$\frac{\text{FMV of Warrants}}{\text{FMV of Warrants} + \text{FMV of Bonds}} \times \text{Total Proceeds}$$

= Amount Allocated to Warrants

$$\frac{\$60 \times 100}{(\$60 \times 100) + (\$100,000 \times 0.94)} \times \$103,000$$

$$\frac{6,000}{100,000} \times \$103,000$$

$6,180$, Amount allocated to warrants
$103,000 - $6,180
= $96,820 Initial carrying value of bonds

**43.** /b/ $\frac{\$4 \times 15,000}{515,000} \times 515,000 = \$60,000$

If the FMV of the bonds without the warrants is not given, assume the FMV of the warrants plus the FMV of the bonds equals the total proceeds. Then the value assigned to the warrants is their FMV.

**44.** /c/ Cash proceeds in excess of the sum of the par value of the bonds and the fair value of the warrants is attributable to the bonds and credited to premium on bonds payable, not additional paid in capital.

**45.** /c/ $\frac{\$20,000}{\$20,000 + \$1,040,000} \times \$1,060,000$

= $20,000 Allocated to warrants

| | | |
|---|---|---|
| $1,060,000 - 20,000 = $1,040,000 | Allocated to bonds |
| | (1,000,000) | Face value |
| | $ 40,000 | Premium |

**46.** /c/ Since allocation of the proceeds is based on relative market values, and since the aggregate market value exceeds the proceeds, the amount allocated to the warrants will be less than their actual market value.

Proceeds allocated to the warrants are recorded as "Additional paid-in capital - warrants."

**47.** /c/ A portion of the proceeds should be allocated only to detachable stock purchase warrants, and not to non-detachable stock purchase warrants.

**48.** /c/

$$\frac{\$20,000}{\$20,000 + \$200,000} \times \$198,000$$

$$\frac{\$20,000}{220,000} \times 198,000 = \underline{\$18,000}$$

**49.** /d/

| | |
|---|---:|
| Face value of note | $500,000 |
| Unpaid interest | 75,000 |
| Total carrying value | $575,000 |
| FMV of marketable securities and cash given up | 425,000 |
| Gain on debt restructuring | $150,000 |

FMV less book value of the securities is recorded separately as ordinary loss.

**50.** /a/

| | |
|---|---:|
| FV of computer equip. | $75,000 |
| CV of computer equip. | 80,000 |
| Ordinary loss | ($ 5000) |
| | |
| Debt balance owed | $100,000 |
| Less FV of equipment | 75,000 |
| Gain on restructuring | $ 25,000 |
| Less tax at 30% | - 7,500 |
| Ordinary gain, net of tax | $ 17,500 |

**51.** /a/

| | |
|---|---:|
| Carrying value of note | $100,000 |
| Future cash payments (70,000 + 5,600 + 5,600) | 81,200 |
| Loss on restructuring | $ 18,800 |

Since the future cash flows are less than the carrying value of the note, no interest revenue is recognized.

**52.** /d/ Amounts of fair value of collateral in excess of the related secured debt are available to pay unsecured, non-priority claims.

Cash available on liquidation:

| | |
|---|---:|
| After payment to fully secured ($370,000 - $260,000) | $110,000 |
| Free assets | 320,000 |
| Total cash | $430,000 |
| Less payment of priority liabilities | - 70,000 |
| Cash available to unsecured, non-priority claims | $360,000 |

Note that the deficiency in fair value of assets relating to partially secured creditor debt is not made up from excess cash after secured claims are paid. Such amounts are added to the unsecured, non-priority claims. The total of such claims would be $540,000 + $80,000 (from partially secured) = $620,000.

**53.** /c/ Hale receives an amount equal to the full liquidation value of the collateral plus a pro rata share of the cash available to unsecured creditors for the excess of the debt owed over collateral liquidation value. $5,000 (collateral) + ($25,000 x $.40 per dollar) = $15,000

**54.** /b/ Equities issued to creditors by debtors in Chapter 11 are valued at the dollar amount of the debt settled, regardless of the market value of the shares. Therefore, Hale's total stockholders' equity will increase by the excess of debt liquidated ($1,200,000) over the cash paid ($400,000) = $800,000

**55.** /b/ A loss contingency must be probable and the amount reasonably estimable before the loss should be accrued. If the loss contingency is reasonably possible and the amount can be reasonably estimated, the loss should be disclosed.

**56.** /a/ Potential losses from self-insured risks should not be accrued. The key phrase in the question is "to cover possible future fire losses?" A contingency depends upon a future event, but the event giving rise to the loss must have occurred by the balance sheet date.

57. /b/ If the outcome of an event that has already occurred is a probable loss that can be reasonably estimated, it should be accrued in the period in which the event that triggered the loss occurred.

58. /b/ Contingent liabilities that are reasonably possible require footnote disclosure. Accrual is required when likelihood of occurrence is probable. In this instance, the amount disclosed is limited to the deductible payable under the terms of the insurance policy.

59. /c/ Accrue the amount that is the best estimate when there is a range of dollar amounts for a loss contingency.

60. /c/ A loss contingency should be accrued only if the occurrence of the loss is probable, and the amount is reasonably estimable. No accrual should be made if the occurrence is only reasonably possible or remote.

61. /d/ By definition.

62. /a/ Since the loss is only reasonably possible, no loss is recognized. The loss contingency should be disclosed, however.

63. /b/ At the balance sheet date the loss was probable and the amount reasonably estimable; therefore, it should be accrued.

64. /d/ Since it is probable additional lawsuits will occur and the amount can be reasonably estimated, the $1,600,000 contingent losses should be included with the $900,000 contingent losses from current lawsuits.

65. /d/ No amount receivable should be recorded as gain contingencies are never recognized before they are realized. The liability previously recognized should be removed from the books, as the status of its payment obligation has changed from probable to less than remote.

66. /a/ A contingent gain is recognized only when realized, not before.

67. /a/ A contingent gain is only recognized upon realization.

68. /c/ Dollis' gain should be recognized in 20x2 when it will be realized. Brooks' loss should be accrued in 20x1 because its outcome is probable and the amount is reasonably estimable.

69. /d/ Only footnote disclosure is acceptable as gain contingencies are never recognized before they are realized.

70. /d/ Both the vacation pay and holiday pay should be included in Morgan's liability for compensated absences because all criteria for accrual have been met.

71. /d/ The right to payment vests for vacation days but not for sick days; therefore, the liability for compensated absences is computed at 150 vacation days x $100 per day = $15,000

72. /a/ By definition.

73. /a/

| | |
|---|---|
| Total coupons expected to be redeemed | 120,000 |
| Liability per coupon ($.45 + $.05) | x .50 |
| Total contingent liability | $60,000 |
| Less amounts already paid | -25,000 |
| Liability balance, 12/31 | $35,000 |

**74.** /b/

$$\frac{2,000,000 \text{ cereal boxes sold}}{10 \text{ box tops per prize}} = \frac{200,000 \text{ Potential}}{\text{prizes}}$$

| | |
|---|---|
| 200,000 | Potential Prizes |
| x 30% | Expected redemption rate |
| 60,000 | Prizes to be distributed |
| 28,000 | Prizes already distributed |
| 32,000 | Prizes still to be distributed |

Cost per Prize
36,000 Prizes purchased for $18,000 = $0.50

| | |
|---|---|
| 32,000 | Potential prizes outstanding |
| x $ 0.50 | Per prize |
| $16,000 | Liability |

**75.** /b/

1,600,000 -:- 5 coupons/premium = 320,000 potential premiums x 60% estimated will be redeemed = 192,000 estimated premiums to be issued.

400,000 coupons redeemed -:- 5 coupons/premium = 80,000 premiums issued.

192,000 - 80,000 = 112,000 premiums still to be issued x $1 per premium = $112,000

**76.** /c/

| | |
|---|---|
| Redemption liability | |
| 12/31/x1 | $6,000,000 |
| Liability for 20x2 stamps | |
| ($2,250,000 x 80%) | 1,800,000 |
| Less redemptions made | |
| in 20x2 | -2,750,000 |
| Balance 12/31/x2 | $5,050,000 |

**77.** /d/

| | |
|---|---|
| Beg. balance, warranty liability | $60,000 |
| Warranty payments during year | (50,000) |
| Warranty Expense for year | |
| (4,000,000 x 0.2) | 80,000 |
| Ending balance, warranty liability | $90,000 |

**78.** /d/ Because both tests are met for accruing a loss contingency (the warranty expenditures are probable and the amount reasonably estimable) and the event giving rise to the contingency has occurred at the balance sheet date (the sales) **all** the warranty liability should be recorded.

| | |
|---|---|
| 20x8 Sales | $ 200,000 |
| 20x9 Sales | 500,000 |
| 20x0 Sales | 700,000 |
| $1,400,000 | |
| 2% + 4% + 6% | x 0.12 |
| Accrued warranty liability | $ 168,000 |
| Actual warranty | |
| expenditures | 63,000 |
| Accrued warranty liability | |
| balance at 12/31/x0 | $ 105,000 |

**79.** /b/ $1,200,000 sales x 0.07

| | |
|---|---|
| estimated warranty liability | $84,000 |
| Less actual warranty | |
| expenditures | 40,000 |
| Liability at year end | $44,000 |

**80.** /a/

| | |
|---|---|
| Book value of plant | $5,000,000 |
| Amount reimbursed by | |
| Oust (0.40 x 8,000,000) | 3,200,000 |
| Estimated loss on | |
| expropriation | $1,800,000 |

**81.** /c/

| | |
|---|---|
| Obligated to purchase 100,000 units | |
| each of next two years | |
| at $.10 per unit | $20,000 |
| Less probable proceeds | |
| from scrap sale of future | |
| units (200,000 units | |
| x $.02/unit) | - 4,000 |
| Probable loss to report | $16,000 |

**82.** /c/ The amount should be disclosed for each of the five succeeding years from the latest balance sheet date.

**83.** /c/ To be classified as a capital lease, only one of the four tests need be satisfied. Both Lease Y and Lease Z contain a bargain purchase option. A bargain purchase option is a lease term which provides that the lessee may purchase the asset at a price that is expected to be sufficiently below the expected fair market value of the leased asset that exercise of the option is reasonably assured.

When a bargain purchase option is present, the lease is a capital lease, even if other of the four tests is not satisfied. Thus, Lease Z, which fails the economic life test (lease term equal to or greater than 75% of economic life), is a capital lease. Only one test need be satisfied, so Lease Y is a capital lease even though it also satisfies the economic life test.

84. /a/ Since the terms of the lease do not meet any of the criteria for a capital lease, this is an operating lease. Annual lease payments should be charged to rent expense in the period incurred.

85. /b/ Both leases qualify as capital leases because their terms meet the economic life test. Only one of the four capital lease tests need be satisfied to establish a capital lease.

86. /b/ All costs presented relate to the store lease.

87. /a/ This is a lessor operating lease. The lease bonus is a prepayment that is amortized over the life of the lease.

| | |
|---|---|
| Rental payments ($30,000 x 11 months) | $330,000 |
| Lease bonus earned ($72,000/3) x (11/12) | 22,000 |
| Less depreciation ($1,440,000/8) | -180,000 |
| Rental income, 20x1 | $172,000 |

88. /a/ The finder's fee must be amortized over the lease term.

| | |
|---|---|
| Rental revenue | $50,000 |
| Less: | |
| Depreciation | -12,000 |
| Amortization - finder's fee | - 1,500 |
| Taxes and insurance | -9,000 |
| Rental income | $27,500 |

89. /b/ As of 6/30/x3, two years' rent revenue has been earned.

| | |
|---|---|
| Rent earned | $24,000 |
| Payments received | -15,000 |
| Accrued rent receivable, 6/30 | $ 9,000 |

90. /c/

| | |
|---|---|
| Rent Year 1, 10,000 sq. ft, @ $12/sq. ft. | $120,000 |
| Rent Years 2 & 3, 10,000 sq. ft. @ $30/sq. ft. | 600,000 |
| Total rent on contract | $720,000 |

$720,000 -:- 36 months = $20,000 per month

$20,000 pcr month x 9 months = $180,000

91. /c/ Annual rental of $90,000 + $10,000 ($50,000/5 years) portion of bonus recognized for 20x1 = $100,000. The refundable security deposit is classified as a liability.

92. /c/ Prepayments made on operating leases are recognized according to the terms of the lease. If no particular periods are stated, such prepayments are amortized over the lease term.

93. /c/ The amount capitalized as the lease obligation by the lessee is generally the present value of the minimum lease payments. This amount, however, may not exceed the fair market value of the leased property at the inception of the lease.

94. /d/ Since the lease term is equal to 75% of the economic life of the equipment, this is a capital lease. Capital leases generate interest revenue, not rent revenue. Furthermore, the interest to be recognized decreases each year because it is computed using a constant, effective rate applied to the declining carrying amount of the lease receivable.

**95.** /d/ Each lease payment has two components: an interest component, calculated by multiplying the outstanding principal balance by the interest rate; and an amount which reduces principal which is also called the lease liability.

**96.** /d/ When a lease meets one or more of the requirements and is classified as a capital lease, both an asset and a liability are recorded. Executory costs (insurance, maintenance, taxes) are not included when the lessee reimburses them.

**97.** /d/ This is really a present value problem. PV = (rents) x (factor for n periods at i interest rate). Here the PV equals $7,596 and the rents equal $2,000. The factor thus is 3.798. But the table is for ordinary annuities and this payment schedule is an annuity in advance (annuity due). Convert an ordinary annuity factor to an annuity in advance: (factor (n-1 periods) + 1) = F(5-1)+1 = 2.798 + 1 = 3.798. Therefore, the interest rate is 16%.

**98.** /c/ The outstanding principal balance is multiplied by the applicable interest rate to determine the interest each year, with the remainder of the fixed payment applied to reduce the principal balance. Thus, each year relatively less of the payment will be interest cost and a greater amount will be applied to reduce the liability balance.

**99.** /c/ Although the lease term is less than 75 percent of the economic life of the asset (10/15), only one of the four tests must be satisfied. Here, we are told that title passes to the lessee at the expiration of the lease term, so this is a capital lease.

The lessee, therefore, should record a lease asset equal to the present value of the aggregate lease payments ($126,000). This asset will be depreciated using the same method the lessee uses for other similar assets, which we are told is straight line. The depreciation period is the economic life of the asset (15 years) since title passes to the lessee at the lease expiration date.

If this had been a capital lease because of the economic life test or because of the minimum lease payment test, the depreciation period would be the lease term if it was less than the expected economic life.

($126,000 / 15 years) = $8,400.

**100.** /a/ The cost of the leased asset properly includes an amount relating to the bargain purchase option. The asset will be depreciated over its economic life of 8 years because the determining criterion establishing this as a capital lease was the presence of the BPO. Depreciation is [$120,000 - $10,000 (salvage value)] -:- 8 years = $13,750.

**101.** /c/ This is a capital lease because title passes at the end of the lease term. Payments are made at the end of the year.

Interest expense: $201,302 x .10 = $20,130
Depreciation: $201,302/15 years = $13,420

When title passes to lessee at the end of the lease term, depreciate the asset over the life of the asset when this is longer than the lease term.

**102.** /c/ This is a capital lease because the lease term is equal to or greater than 75 percent of the economic life of the asset (lease term = 12 years; economic life = 15 years). There are no renewal options. However, if there was a bargain renewal option, the renewal period would be added to the lease term before determining the percentage test. A bargain renewal option is a lease term that permits the lessee to renew the lease at a price that is sufficiently below the expected market rate that exercise of the renewal option will be reasonably assured.

Since this is a capital lease, the lessee must record a lease asset together with a lease liability. The amount of the lease liability is the present value of the minimum lease payments. The first payment of an annuity in advance is built into the factor given and need not be further considered. Therefore, the lease liability is (6.94)($100,000) = $694,000.

103. /d/ This is a capital lease because the lease term is equal to or greater than 75 percent of the economic life of the asset (10 -:- 12). Only one test must be satisfied, so this is a capital lease even though the asset reverts to the lessor at the end of the lease term (title does not pass to the lessee).

The lessee will record a lease asset and lease liability equal to the present value of the minimum lease payments, discounted at either the lessee's incremental borrowing rate (here, 14 percent) or the lessor's interest rate implicit in the lease (here, 12 percent) if it is known to the lessee and less than the incremental borrowing rate.

The answer is:
(6.33)($100,000) = $633,000.

104. /b/ This is a capital lease because the lease term of 6 years is equal to 75% of the economic life of the machine (8 years). A lease liability equal to the present value of the minimum lease payments must be recorded using the implicit interest rate in the lease (12%) because it is known by Day and is lower than Day's incremental borrowing rate. $50,000 x 4.61 = $230,500.

105. /c/ The lease liability should be recorded on 12/29 at the present value of the minimum lease payments using the interest rate implicit in the lease because this rate is known by Action Corp. and is lower than the incremental borrowing rate. Balance 12/31; $153,000 x 5.15 = $841,500 (total PV of payments) less $153,000 payments 12/31 = $688,500.

106. /c/ The lease liability is recorded at the sum of the PV of the lease payments and the PV of the bargain purchase option. The rate used is the rate implicit in the lease because it is known by Robbins and is lower than Robbins' incremental borrowing rate.

| | |
|---|---|
| PV of lease payments | |
| ($10,000 x 6.328) | $63,280 |
| PV of BPO | |
| ($10,000 x 0.322) | 3,220 |
| Beginning lease liability | $66,500 |

107. /b/ The PV of the lease payments is less than 90% of the fair value of the machine, but this is a capital lease because its term is greater than 75% of the economic life of the asset. The asset is capitalized at the present value of the minimum lease payments. Executory costs of the lessee are not included in the determination of the asset's cost, and they are not considered a part of the minimum lease payments.

108. /b/ This is a capital lease because the lease term is equal to the economic life of the asset. A residual value guaranteed by the lessee would be included in the PV computation. However, this residual value is guaranteed by a third party and so is not included. The lease liability does not change until the payment date, 12/31/x1, therefore the balance is $10,000 x 6.1446 = $61,446.

**109.** /c/ This is an annuity in advance:

| | |
|---|---|
| Present value 12/31/x5 | $676,000 |
| less: payment made 12/31/x5 | -100,000 |
| | $576,000 |
| plus: interest for period | |
| 12/31/x5 - 12/31/x6 at 10% | + 57,600 |
| | $633,600 |
| less: payment made 12/31/x6 | -100,000 |
| Balance 12/31/x6 | $533,600 |

**110.** /a/ The residual value is included in the PV computation because it is guaranteed by the lessee.

| | |
|---|---|
| PV of lease payments | |
| ($13,000 x 4.24) | $55,120 |
| PV of guaranteed residual | |
| ($10,000 x 0.650) | 6,500 |
| Initial lease liability | $61,620 |
| Less payment 1/1/x1 | -13,000 |
| Balance after payment | $48,620 |

**111.** /d/ This is a capital lease in which the payments are made at the beginning of each period. Executory costs of the lessee are not a part of the lease payment.

| | |
|---|---|
| Beginning lease liability | $417,000 |
| Less payment 12/31/x1 | 100,000 |
| Balance | $317,000 |
| Payment 12/31/x2 $100,000 | |
| Less interest | |
| ($317,000 x 10%) 31,700 | |
| Reduction in principal | 68,300 |
| Lease liability 12/31/x2 | $248,700 |

**112.** /c/ For this capital lease, you are asked to determine the interest expense for the first year when the lease is an annuity in advance. The initial payment must be subtracted before the interest is computed.

| | |
|---|---|
| Lease liability 1/1/x1 | $135,000 |
| less: initial payment 1/1/x1 | 20,000 |
| Carrying value for | |
| year 20x1 | $115,000 |
| Interest calculated at 10% | |
| interest expense | $ 11,500 |

**113.** /d/ The lease liability will decrease by the balance of the $40,000 annual payment after interest based on the beginning lease balance has been computed.

| | |
|---|---|
| Lease liability 12/31/x1 | $270,000 |
| Less payment 12/31/x1 | ( 40,000) |
| Lease liability 1/1/x2 | $230,000 |
| | |
| Payment 12/31/x2 | $40,000 |
| Less interest on 1/1/x2 balance | |
| ($230,000 x 10%) | (23,000) |
| Reduction in lease liability | $17,000 |

**114.** /a/ The portion of long-term lease liability to be paid in 20x2 should have been reported as a current liability in the financial statements at the end of Year 1 in the current portion of long-term debt section.

**115.** /b/ As there was no initial payment on signing of the lease, the interest portion of the first payment is based on the present value of the lease payments on signing of the lease.

| | |
|---|---|
| Lease liability 1/1/x1 | $112,500 |
| Payment 12/31 $10,000 | |
| Less interest | |
| ($112,500 x 8%) 9,000 | |
| Reduction in liability | ( 1,000) |
| Lease liability 12/31/x1 | $111,500 |

**116.** /a/ Since there was no initial payment on signing of the lease, the interest expense in the first year is based on the present value of the five lease payments. $379,000 x 10% = $37,900

**117.** /b/ The current portion of the long-term lease liability as of 12/31/x1 is the portion of the lease payment to be made on 12/31/x2 that will be applied to the reduction of the lease liability on that date.

| | | |
|---|---|---|
| Lease liability 12/31/x1 | $135,000 | |
| Less payment 12/31/x1 | - 20,000 | |
| Lease liability 12/31/x1 | $115,000 | |
| | | |
| Lease payment due 12/31/x2 | $20,000 | |
| Less interest portion | | |
| ($115,000 x 10%) | 11,500 | |
| Payment portion to apply | | |
| to lease liability 12/31/x2 | $ 8,500 | |

**118.** /a/ 
| | |
|---|---|
| Lease obligations 1/1/x1 | $3,520,000 |
| Less payment 1/1/x1 | - 600,000 |
| | 2,920,000 |
| Plus interest for the year | + 292,000 |
| | 3,212,000 |
| Less payment 1/1/x2 | - 600,000 |
| Lease obligations 1/1/x2 | 2,612,000 |
| | x 10% |
| Interest income for year | $ 261,200 |

**119.** /a/ This is a lessor's capital lease. Any one of the same four tests applied by lessees must first be passed. Here, title passes to the lessee at the expiration of the lease term. Next, collectibility of the remaining lease payments must be reasonably assured. Further, there must be no material uncertainties with respect to the lessor's performance. Both of these two tests are stated to be satisfied. Therefore, this is a capital lease with respect to the lessor, Grey Company.

As to the lessor, a lease may be a sales-type lease if there is a dealer's profit or a direct financing lease if there is no dealer's profit. Here, there is a dealer's profit because the cost of the asset is less than its normal selling price. Any dealer's profit must be recognized as of the inception of the lease and not deferred. The first payment reduces principal balance does not include any interest income.

| | |
|---|---|
| The answer is: | |
| Normal sales price | $77,000 |
| Cost of manufacture | 60,000 |
| Income in 20x1 | $17,000 |

Note: If the question had required any computation using the minimum lease payments, the executory costs would not have been included as part of the payments.

**120.** /c/ For a capital lease, the lessor will record a receivable equal to the minimum lease payment times the number of payments to be made. This receivable will be reduced by a contra-asset account called "unearned interest." The unearned interest amount is the gross receivable less the net discounted present value of the minimum lease payments. The unearned interest is amortized using the effective interest method (the interest rate is multiplied times the principal amount outstanding). This procedure is followed on both sales-type and direct financing leases.

**121.** /b/ Lessee depreciates leased assets based on its usual methods over the lease term if the asset reverts to the lessor.

$52,880/8 = \underline{\$6,610}$.

**122.** /c/ 
| Lease payments receivable | |
|---|---|
| 1/2/x1 | $52,880 |
| Less payment 1/2/x1 | 10,000 |
| | 42,880 |
| x implicit interest rate | 14% |
| Interest income to lessor | $ 6,003 |

**123.** /d/ Assuming that Rig Co. leased all of the factory back, recognition of gain on its sale would be deferred and amortized. Amortization would be taken in proportion to the rental payments since this is an operating lease.

**124.** /d/ Sale and Leaseback: Gain realized in a sale and leaseback should be deferred and recognized over the lease term in proportion to the lease term since this is a capital lease. (Note that the lease term of 12 years is greater than 75 percent of the economic life of the asset, 15 years.)

| | |
|---|---|
| Sales price | $480,000 |
| Carrying amount | 360,000 |
| Gain realized | $120,000 |

This gain will be recognized over 12 years at $10,000 per year. Since the transaction date is the year end, all the gain will be deferred to future years, i.e. the answer is $120,000 gain deferred.

**125.** /a/ Since Mega Co. is leasing the equipment back for only 1 of the 25 remaining years of the life, and the present value of the lease payments ($36,900) is less than 10% of the fair value of the equipment sold ($400,000), then this is a "minor-portion" sale and leaseback. In such a situation, the sale and leaseback are treated as separate transactions and the entire gain of $100,000 ($400,000 - $300,000) is recognized immediately. No gain is deferred.

**126.** /b/ Gain realized on a sale in a sale-leaseback situation is deferred provided the seller-lessee enters into a lease for use of all (or substantially all) of the asset. In this situation, Dirk Corp. is leasing Plane #1 for substantially all of its remaining life, therefore the gain of $500,000 is reported as a deferred gain. However, Plan #2 is being leased for only a minor portion of its remaining life (3 of 35 years). In this instance, none of the gain of $450,000 is deferred.

**127.** /b/ This question requires the computation of the balance of the deferred gain after the first year's amortization. Since this is a capital lease, the gain is to be amortized in proportion to the amortization (depreciation) of the leased asset. The straight-line method is to be used over a 10--year lease term. Gain of $50,000 -:- 10 years = $5,000/year. $50,000 - $5,000 amortized = $45,000 balance.

**128.** /a/ For a sale and leaseback, the sale and lease are viewed together. The lease is classified following the same rules as for any other leases. Here this is an operating lease. Therefore, any gain on sale is amortized over the term of the lease as a reduction in rental expense.

Rents: $1,500 x 6 months = $9,000
Less gain amortization:
($550,000-500,000)/5 x 6/12 = $5,000
Rental expense $4,000

**129.** /b/ This is one of those special loss situations in a sale-leaseback transaction where the selling price ($430,000) is less than the carrying amount ($450,000), and the carrying amount is less than the fair value ($465,000). In this case, the loss of $20,000 (book value less selling price) is deferred.

**130.** /a/ For assets that are subleased, that is, leased to others by one who is a lessee, the sublease would be classified as an operating lease if the original lease was an operating lease.

If the original lease was a type (a) or (b) capital lease, the sublease will be classified using the same tests applied to lessors generally. Otherwise, it will be classified as an operating lease.

If the original lease was a type (c) or (d) lease, only test (c), (e) and (f) will be used otherwise the sublease will be an operating lease.

The original lease will continue to be accounted for as before.

**131.** /a/ Leasehold improvements are capitalized if the expected economic life of the asset is greater than one year. Capitalized leasehold improvements are amortized over the lower of the expected economic life or the lease term.

Here the economic life of the leasehold improvement is six years. The lease term is five years. Therefore, the amortization period is five years.

**132.** /b/ The items to be expensed include the first month's rent of $60,000 plus one month's amortization of the leasehold improvement cost. $360,000 -:- 60 months = $6,000 a month. Total expensed, $66,000.

**133.** /c/ This is a post-balance-sheet-date refinancing completed before the issuance of the financial statements. In such a situation, the current liability is reclassified to noncurrent, and the terms of the refinancing are separately disclosed.

**134.** /b/ The balance is the sum of the beginning balance and advances received in 20x3, less advances earned during the period. Note that advances are nonrefundable, therefore those applicable to orders canceled are deemed to be earned.

| | |
|---|---|
| Balance 12/31/x2 | $118,000 |
| Plus advances received, 20x3 | 184,000 |
| Less advances earned, 20x3 ($164,000 + $50,000) | (214,000) |
| Balance, 12/31/x3 | $ 88,000 |

**135.** /b/ October sales taxes will have been paid at the end of November. Therefore, as of December 31, sales taxes payable will include those owing for November and December -

- a total of $39,000. November taxes are $16,500 ($110,000 x 15%); December taxes are $22,500 ($150,000 x 15%). Occupancy taxes due for the quarter are for a total of 4,100 room-nights at $2 per room -- $8,200.

**136.** /a/ 5 employees x $10,000 eligible gross wages each x 2% = $1,000.

**137.** /b/ To solve this problem, it would be helpful to envision how the purchase of the warehouse would have been recorded.

| | |
|---|---|
| Building (warehouse) | Debit |
| Property taxes payable | $4,000* |
| Cash | Credit |

\* Accrued realty taxes at $2,000/month for each of the months July and August. (Total annual taxes are $24,000/12 months = $2,000 per month.)

At the end of each of the months of September and October, accruals of $2,000 each would have been additionally credited to Property taxes payable. Thus, when the $12,000 installment is paid on November 1, $8,000 of it would be a reduction of the liability account, with the remaining $4,000 recorded as prepaid real estate taxes.

**138.** /d/ Liability includes all taxes required to be deposited by the employer.

| | |
|---|---|
| Income taxes withheld | $1,200 |
| FICA taxes, employee portion ($10,000 x 7%) | 700 |
| FICA taxes, employer portion | 700 |
| Total liability | $2,600 |

Payroll tax expense pertains only to the employer portion of the FICA tax.

**139.** /d/ Proceeds include the issue price of the bonds, plus accrued interest for 3 months.

| | |
|---|---:|
| Issue price | $594,000 |
| (600 x $1,000 x 99% | |
| Accrued interest, April 1 - July 1 | |
| ($600,000 x 10% x 3/12) | 15,000 |
| Total proceeds | $609,000 |

**140.** /b/ The carrying value of bonds issued at a discount increases each period by the amount of discount amortized for that period. When amortizing a discount using the straight-line method, the discount amortized in the earlier years is higher than if the effective interest method is used. Thus, at the end of Year 1, the carrying value under the straight-line method will have risen to a higher amount than it would under the effective interest method. The following computations illustrate the difference (annual amortization periods are assumed for simplicity);

Straight-line Method:

| | |
|---|---:|
| Annual amortization amount | $ 25,000 |
| Beginning carrying value | 850,000 |
| Carrying value 12/31/x4 | $875,000 |

Effective Interest Method:

Amortization for 20x4

| | | |
|---|---:|---:|
| Interest recorded | | |
| ($850,000 x 12%) | $102,000 | |
| Interest paid | | |
| ($1,000,000 x 8%) | 80,000 | $ 22,000 |
| Beginning carrying value | | 850,000 |
| Carrying value 12/31/x4 | | $872,000 |

Regardless of the method used, the carrying value on maturity should be the same; i.e., the face (maturity) value of the bonds.

**141.** /a/ Interest expense should have been:

| | |
|---|---:|
| $10,000 x .12 x 10/12 | $1,000 |
| $30,000 x .12 x 6/12 | 1,800 |
| $16,000 x .12 x 8/12 | 1,280 |
| Total correct interest expense | 4,080 |

This exceeds the interest expense recorded by $1,080.

**142.** /c/ First: Compute the portion of proceeds allocated to the warrants based on the relative fair values of the bonds and bonds + warrants at time of issue (in this instance, fair value of bonds is not known).

$$\frac{1{,}000 \text{ bonds x 50 warrants x \$4 per warrant}}{1{,}000{,}000 \text{ x } 109\%}$$

$$\frac{\$200{,}000}{\$1{,}090{,}000} \text{ X } \$1{,}090{,}000$$

$$= \$200{,}000 \text{ (rounded)}$$

Second: Subtract value allocated to warrants from total proceeds to determine value allocated to bonds:

$1,090,000 - $200,000 = $890,000

Third: Compare proceeds allocated to bonds with face value of bonds to determine amount of premium or discount:

$1,000,000 - $890,000

$= \$110{,}000$ discount

**143.** /a/ If a loss is judged to be remote, no accrual or disclosure is ordinarily required. However, since this contingency relates to the guaranteed note of another (and, in this case, related) party, disclosure is required.

**144.** /c/ Since the first lease payment is to be made on the date the lease begins, no interest has yet been incurred. The entire payment consists of lease liability.

**145.** /a/ The amount of any residual value guaranteed by the lessee is included as part of minimum lease payments at discounted value.

**146.** /b/ If a seller retains only a minor portion of the asset and has given up substantially all use of the asset sold (i.e. has transferred substantially all the risks of ownership - Item I), then any gain resulting from the sale would be recognized immediately. Conversely, where retention of the right to substantially all of the remaining use of the property exists (Item II), any gain is deferred and amortized.

**147.** /c/ This question is dealt with under the text information on troubled-debt restructuring from the creditor's perspective. When a loan is impaired, but foreclosure is not probable, no loss is recorded, but footnote disclosure is required. Although the amount of such loss should, theoretically, be measured using the present value of future cash flows from the loan, for practical purposes, the fair value of the loan, or the fair value of underlying collateral may be used.

**148.** /a/ If the bargain purchase option is not included in a lease amortization, all lease liability amounts will be amortized by the end of the lease. This would yield a balance in the lease liability account of zero. If the bargain purchase option is included, the balance (at the end of the lease) in the leases payable account should be the initial present value of the bargain purchase option. B is incorrect in that if the interest is subtracted instead of added, the liability would most likely have a negative value (or at least not be zero). C and D are incorrect because these would also yield a negative amount at the end of the lease (not zero).

**149.** /d/ The proceeds of a bond issuance is calculated as the present value of the expected future cash flows (interest and principal repayment) less any bond issuance costs. The discount rate to use is the market rate in effect at the issue date. A, B, and C are incorrect in that they have either used the stated rate of interest to discount the bonds or have ignored bond issuance costs.

**150.** /b/ The present value of the minimum lease payments must be 90% or more than the fair value of the leased property. Answer A is incorrect because transfer of ownership to the lessee at some point during the lease term is one of the criteria for a capital lease. C is incorrect because a lease containing a bargain purchase option is a capital lease. D is incorrect because the lease term being substantially (75% or more) equal to the remaining useful life of the leased property is a capital lease criterion.

**151.** /c/ A guarantee made by the lessee to pay the lessor's debt on a leased property is excluded from the determination of minimum lease payments. Answers A, B, and D are all included in the calculation of minimum lease payments.

**152.** /a/ The inception of the lease agreement is either the date of the lease agreement or the date of a written commitment signed by the parties that sets the principal provisions of the lease. Answers B, C, and D all include incorrect responses as to the inception date of the lease agreement.

# CHAPTER 4

## BALANCE SHEET LIABILITIES

### Simulation Answers

**Number 1 Answer**

1. /A/N/ No accrual is made of loss contingencies related to self-insurance.

2. /B/N/ An amount equal to 1% of sales ($100,000) should be accrued to match the warranty expense with the period's sales. No additional disclosure is required.

3. /B/Y/ Since the loss is probable and the underlying event giving rise to the contingency has already occurred, then accrual in the minimum amount of the estimated range is required. Additional footnote disclosure of the nature of the contingency would also be appropriate.

4. /A/N/ No accrual is made for potential gain contingencies, regardless of the degree of probability of the outcome. No disclosure elsewhere

5. /A/N/ Since Edge's attorneys believe the suit is without merit, the probability of loss should be considered to be remote. No accrual for a contingency is necessary and no disclosure elsewhere is required.

6. /A/Y/ The guarantee of a bank loan for the company's president is a related- party transaction. When material, GAAP requires footnote disclosure of the nature of the related-party relationship, a description of the transaction, and the presentation of the dollar amount involved.

7. /A/N/ It is not clear whether the inventory was shipped before or after the end of the 20x3 fiscal period. However, the answer would be as indicated, regardless of the timing of the shipment, for the following reasons. (1) FOB shipping point would require recording the inventory on the shipment date. (2) If that occurred before the end of 20x3, the inventory records would already have been affected. (3) Since it is probable that the goods will actually arrive, then no adjustment to remove their cost from inventory is needed.

(4) If the goods were shipped after the end of 20x3, the inventory records prior to the end of the period would not have been affected. (5) Since the purchase cost would properly belong in 20x4 in this alternative view of the situation, an adjustment would be incorrect procedure for timing reasons.

8. /A/Y/ The issuance of bonds between the balance sheet date and the date of issuance of the report has no direct effect on the financial statements, but disclosure is advisable because the event has sufficient significance to the users of the statements. Accrual is not appropriate. Footnote disclosure is.

9. /B/Y/ Since the event underlying this situation (the assessment of 20x2 taxes) has already occurred, the occurrence is probable (likely), and an amount is reasonably estimable ($100,000), accrual and footnote disclosure giving supporting information would be appropriate.

**Number 2 Answer**

1. /Q/ Discount remaining is face value of bonds less carrying value after discount amortization 6/30/x4. $480,000 less $363,600 is $116,400.

2. /K/ Cash interest paid is constant each period because it is computed as par value times stated interest rate. Cash interest 6/30/x4 is therefore the same as that shown for 12/31/x4; namely, $14,400. Also, by computation,

remember that in a discount situation, interest expense recorded exceeds cash interest paid by the amount of discount amortized for the period. $18,000 interest expense less $3,600 discount amortized is $14,400.

**3.** /T/ Carrying amount on issuance is $480,000 less the total discount on issuance. Discount after the first period amortization is $116,400 (see Item 1 above). Therefore, original discount must have been $116,000 + $3,600 = $120,000. $480,000 less $120,000 = $360,000.

Alternatively, the carrying amount after amortization on 6/30/x4 increased by $3,600. Therefore, the original carrying amount must have been $363,600 - $3,600 = $360,000.

**4.** /D/ Stated rate is the rate indicated on the face of the bonds. It is used to compute the cash interest to be paid each semiannual period.

$$R = I/(P*T)$$
$$R = 14,400/(480,000*.5)$$
$$R = 14,400/240,000$$
$$R = 6\%$$

**5.** /F/ Effective rate is the rate implicit in the sale of the bonds. It is what is used to determine the interest expense to be recorded and is applied to the carrying amount of the bonds as of the beginning of the period.

$$R = I/(P*T)$$
$$R = 18,000/360,000*.5$$
$$R = 18,000/180,000$$
$$R = 10\%$$

**6.** /N/ Interest expense for the period ending 12/31/x4 is computed as the effective rate times the carrying amount for 6 months.

$$I = (P)(R)(T)$$
$$I = (\$363,600)(10\%)(.5year)$$
$$I = \$18,180$$

**7.** /I/ Amortization amount for the period is interest expense recorded less cash

interest paid. $18,180 (see Item 6 above) less $14,400 = $3,780.

**8.** /B/ This item is a completed event that requires accrual only. It is not a contingency because the court decision has been made, there is no appeal, and payment was received by January 20x5.

**9.** /N/ Since Town's attorneys believe that the suit is without merit, the likelihood of a loss occurring related to this pending lawsuit is remote. In such a situation, no contingent liability is recorded and no disclosure is required.

**10.** /N/ This situation is neither a purchase commitment nor an unconditional purchase obligation. It simply relates to outstanding purchase orders for routinely acquired items which, when filled, will likely result in incurring an obligation higher than was originally planned. The purchase price (and related obligation) will be recorded when the purchase orders are filled in the next period. No disclosure of possibly higher purchase prices is required.

**11.** /D/ Here a loss contingency exists. However, the likelihood of its occurrence is "reasonably possible" -- not probable. Therefore, only disclosure is required.

**12.** /B/ Here a loss contingency exists. Since the likelihood of incurrence is probable and the amount has been reasonably estimated, then accrual of the amount must be made in 20x4. Furthermore, the nature and circumstances of the obligation would also require accompanying disclosure information.

**13.** /D/ This event took place in 20x5 and will be recorded in that period as an ordinary loss (if material). Accrual in 20x4 is not appropriate. However, since this has occurred after the balance sheet date but prior to the issuance of the financial statements, and since it could have a significant impact on decisions to be made by users of those statements, it should be disclosed.

**SPECIAL TOPICS:**
**PENSIONS; OPEB; ALTERNATIVE FINANCIAL ACCOUNTING MODELS;**
**FOREIGN EXCHANGE; AND SEGMENT REPORTING**

### Question Map

B. Measuring Units
   1. Nominal Dollars
   2. Constant Dollars
C. Bases of Accounting - Definitions
D. Historical Cost/Nominal Dollars (HC/N$)
E. Historical Cost/Constant Dollars (HC/C$) -- 19, 21-24
   1. Attributes
   2. Definitions
      a. Monetary Items -- 27-33, 35
      b. Nonmonetary Items -- 25, 26
   3. Procedure
F. Current Cost/Nominal Dollars (CC/N$) -- 34, 36-43, 46, 93
G. Current Cost/Constant Dollars (CC/C$) -- 91
H. Financial Reporting and Changing Prices -- 44, 45

V.    FOREIGN EXCHANGE
Λ. Terminology
B. Foreign Currency Transactions -- 47-57, 92
C. Forward Exchange Contracts -- 58-61
D. Foreign Currency Financial Statement Translation
   1. Objectives
   2. Functional Currency
   3. Current Rate Method -- 62, 63, 66-68
   4. Remeasurement Method -- 64-67
   5. Exchange Rates Used

VI.    SEGMENT REPORTING -- ASC Topic 280
A. Operating Segments
   1. Management Approach
   2. Categories
   3. Reportable Industry Segments
      a. Revenue -- 69-74, 83, 85
      b. Operating Profit or Loss -- 75-82, 85
      c. Identifiable Assets -- 83-85
   4. Information Required for Reportable Industry Segments
   5. Other Considerations
B. Geographic Areas
   1. Reportable Foreign Operations -- 87
   2. Information Reported for Foreign Operations
C. Export Sales
D. Major Customers -- 86

# CHAPTER 5

## SPECIAL TOPICS: PENSIONS; OPEB; ALTERNATIVE FINANCIAL ACCOUNTING MODELS; FOREIGN EXCHANGE; AND SEGMENT REPORTING

### Multiple Choice Questions

**Items 1 and 2** are based on the following information:

The following information pertains to Jerry Corporation which provides a noncontributory defined benefit pension plan for its employees. The company's actuary has provided the following information for the year ended December 31, 20x1:

| | |
|---|---|
| Projected benefit obligation | $400,000 |
| Accumulated benefit obligation | 350,000 |
| Plan assets (fair value) | 410,000 |
| Service cost | 120,000 |
| Interest on PBO | 12,000 |
| Amortization of unrecognized prior service cost | 30,000 |
| Expected and actual return on plan assets | 41,000 |

The market-related asset value equals the fair value of the plan assets. Prior contributions to the defined benefit pension plan equaled the amount of net periodic pension cost accrued for the previous year end. No contributions have been made for 20x1 pension cost.

**1.** In its December 31, 20x1 balance sheet, Jerry should report a pension asset (liability) of
  a. $10,000
  b. ($10,000)
  c. $60,000
  d. ($60,000)

**2.** In its Income Statement for the year ended December 31, 20x1, Jerry should report a pension expense of

  a. $120,000
  b. $162,000
  c. $203,000
  d. $121,000

**3.** On January 2, 20x2, East Corporation adopted a defined benefit pension plan. The plan's service cost of $150,000 was fully funded at the end of 20x2. Prior service cost was fully funded by a contribution of $60,000 in 20x2. Amortization of prior service cost was $24,000 for 20x2. Interest cost and expected and actual return on assets was 7%. No pension payments were made in 20x2. What is the amount of East's pension asset (liability) at December 31, 20x2?
  a. $90,000
  b. $0
  c. $60,000
  d. $36,000

**4.** The following information pertains to the 20x0 activity of Ral Corp.'s defined benefit pension plan:

| | |
|---|---|
| Service cost | $300,000 |
| Return on plan assets (expected) | 80,000 |
| Interest cost on pension benefit obligation | 164,000 |
| Amortization of actuarial loss | 30,000 |
| Pension payments | 70,000 |

Ral's 20x0 pension cost was
  a. $316,000
  b. $494,000
  c. $414,000
  d. $644,000

**5.** On July 31, 20x1, Tern Co. amended its single employee defined benefit pension plan by granting increased benefits for services provided prior to 20x1. This prior service cost will be reflected in the financial statement(s) for
  a. Years before 20x1 only.
  b. Year 20x1 only.
  c. Year 20x1, and years before and following 20x1.
  d. Year 20x1, and following years only.

**6.** Waco amended its defined benefit pension plan, granting total credit of $200,000 to four employees for services rendered prior to the plan's adoption. Employees Arthur, Benjamin, Charles, and David, are expected to retire from the company as follows: Arthur will retire after three years, Benjamin and Charles after five, and David after seven years.

What is the amount of service cost amortization in the first year?

    **a.** $0
    **b.** $20,000
    **c.** $40,000
    **d.** $50,000

**7.** The following information pertains to Lee Corp.'s defined benefit pension plan for 20x1:

| | |
|---|---|
| Service cost | $160,000 |
| Actual and expected gain on plan assets | 35,000 |
| Unexpected loss on plan assets related to a 20x1 disposal of a subsidiary | 40,000 |
| Amortization of unrecognized prior service cost | 5,000 |
| Annual interest on pension obligation | 50,000 |

What amount should Lee report as pension expense in its 20x1 income statement?
    **a.** $250,000
    **b.** $220,000
    **c.** $210,000
    **d.** $180,000

**8.** Interest cost included in the net pension cost recognized by an employer sponsoring a defined benefit pension plan represents the
    **a.** Amortization of the discount on unrecognized prior service costs.
    **b.** Increase in the fair value of plan assets due to the passage of time.
    **c.** Increase in the projected benefit obligation due to the passage of time.
    **d.** Shortage between the expected and actual returns on plan assets.

**9.** The following information pertains to Seda Co.'s pension plan:

| | |
|---|---|
| Actuarial estimate of projected benefit obligation at 1/1/x1 | $72,000 |
| Assumed discount rate | 10% |
| Service costs for 20x1 | 18,000 |
| Pension benefits paid during 20x1 | 15,000 |

If no change in actuarial estimates occurred during 20x1, Seda's projected benefit obligation at December 31, 20x1 was
    **a.** $64,200
    **b.** $75,000
    **c.** $79,200
    **d.** $82,200

**10.** For a defined benefit pension plan, the discount rate used to calculate the projected benefit obligation is determined by the

| | Expected return on plan assets | Actual return on plan assets |
|---|---|---|
| **a.** | Yes | Yes |
| **b.** | No | No |
| **c.** | Yes | No |
| **d.** | No | Yes |

**11.** Barrett Co. maintains a defined benefit pension plan for its employees. At each balance sheet date, Barrett should report a liability or asset related to the pension plan at least equal to the
    **a.** Accumulated benefit obligation.
    **b.** Projected benefit obligation.
    **c.** Unfunded projected benefit obligation.
    **d.** Funded status of the plan.

**12.** Mercer, Inc. maintains a defined benefit pension plan for its employees. As of December 31, 20x1, the market value of the plan assets is less than the accumulated benefit obligation, and less than the projected benefit obligation. The projected benefit obligation exceeds the accumulated benefit obligation. In its balance sheet as of December 31, 20x1, Mercer should report a liability in the amount of the

    **a.** Excess of the projected benefit obligation over the value of the plan assets.
    b. Excess of the accumulated benefit obligation over the value of the plan assets.
    **c.** Projected benefit obligation.
    **d.** Accumulated benefit obligation.

**13.** At December 31, 20x2, the following information was provided by the Kerr Corporation pension plan administrator:

| | |
|---|---|
| Fair value of plan assets | $3,450,000 |
| Accumulated benefit obligation | 4,300,000 |
| Projected benefit obligation | 5,700,000 |

What is the amount of the pension liability that should be shown on Kerr's December 31, 20x2 balance sheet?

    **a.** $5,700,000
    **b.** $2,250,000
    **c.** $1,400,000
    **d.** $ 850,000

**14.** Which of the following amounts are reported as an asset or liability on the balance sheet?

    **a.** Fair value of plan assets.
    **b.** Accumulated benefits obligation.
    **c.** Projected benefits obligation.
    **d.** None of the above.

**15.** All of the following are components of pension expense except:

    **a.** Amortization of transition gains and losses.
    **b.** Amortization of unrecognized gains and losses.
    **c.** Interest on vested benefits.
    **d.** Interest on the projected benefits obligation

**16.** The funded status of a pension plan is the difference between the:

    **a.** Accumulated benefits obligation and the cost of plan assets.
    **b.** Accumulated benefits obligation and the fair value of plan assets.
    **c.** Projected benefits obligation and the fair value of plan assets.
    **d.** Projected accumulated benefits obligation and the sum of pension contributions.

**17.** Which of the following defined benefit pension plan disclosures should be made in a company's financial statements?

  I.    A description of the company's funding policies and types of assets held.
  II.    The amount of net periodic pension cost for the period.
  III.    The fair value of plan assets.

    **a.** I and II.
    **b.** I, II, and III.
    **c.** II and III.
    **d.** I only.

**18.** Which of the following information should be disclosed by a company providing health care benefits to its retirees?

  I.    The assumed health care cost trend rate used to measure the expected cost of benefits covered by the plan.
  II.    The accumulated postretirement benefit obligation.

    **a.** I and II.
    **b.** I only.
    **c.** II only.
    **d.** Neither I **nor** II.

**19.** During a period of inflation, the specific price of a parcel of land increased at a lower rate than the consumer price index. The accounting method that would measure the land at the highest price is

    **a.** Historical cost/nominal dollar.
    **b.** Current cost/nominal dollar.
    **c.** Current cost/constant dollar.
    **d.** Historical cost/constant dollar.

**20.** On December 31, Brooks Co. decided to end operations and dispose of its assets within three months. At December 31, the net realizable value of the equipment was below historic cost. What is the appropriate measurement basis for equipment included in Brooks' December 31 balance sheet?
   a. Historical cost.
   b. Current reproduction cost.
   c. Net realizable value.
   d. Current replacement cost.

**21.** In accordance with ASC Topic 255, the Consumer Price Index for All Urban Consumers is used to compute information on a
   a. Historical cost basis.
   b. Current cost basis.
   c. Nominal dollar basis.
   d. Constant dollar basis.

**22.** A method of accounting based on measures of historical prices in dollars, each of which has the same general purchasing power, is
   a. Current cost/constant dollar accounting.
   b. Current cost/nominal dollar accounting.
   c. Historical cost/constant dollar accounting.
   d. Historical cost/nominal dollar accounting.

**23.** Hadley Corporation purchased a machine in 20x0 when the average Consumer Price Index (CPI) was 180. The average CPI was 190 for 20x1, and 200 for 20x2. Hadley prepares supplementary constant dollar statements (adjusted for changing prices). Depreciation on this machine is $200,000 a year. In Hadley's supplementary constant dollar statement for 20x2, the amount of depreciation expense should be stated as
   a. $180,000.
   b. $190,000.
   c. $210,526.
   d. $222,222.

**24.** The following schedule lists the average consumer price index (all urban consumers) of the indicated year:

| | |
|---|---|
| 20x0 | 100 |
| 20x1 | 125 |
| 20x2 | 150 |

Carl Corporation's plant and equipment at December 31, 20x2, are as follows:

| Date Acquired | Percent Depreciated | Historical Cost |
|---|---|---|
| 20x0 | 30 | $30,000 |
| 20x1 | 20 | 20,000 |
| 20x2 | 10 | 10,000 |
| | | $60,000 |

Depreciation is calculated at 10% per annum, straight-line. A full year's depreciation is charged in the year of acquisition. There were no disposals in 20x2.

What amount of depreciation expense would be included in the income statement adjusted for general inflation (historical cost/constant dollar accounting)?
   a. $6,000.
   b. $7,200.
   c. $7,900.
   d. $9,000.

**25.** When computing information on a historical cost/constant dollar basis, which of the following is classified as nonmonetary?
   a. Obligations under warranties.
   b. Accrued expenses payable.
   c. Unamortized premium on bonds payable.
   d. Refundable deposits.

**26.** When computing information on a historical cost/constant dollar basis, which of the following is classified as nonmonetary?
   a. Allowance for doubtful accounts.
   b. Accumulated depreciation of equipment.
   c. Unamortized premium on bonds payable.
   d. Advances to unconsolidated subsidiaries.

**27.** When computing information on a historical cost/constant dollar basis, which of the following is classified as monetary?
- **a.** Equity investment in unconsolidated subsidiaries.
- **b.** Obligations under warranties.
- **c.** Unamortized discount on bonds payable.
- **d.** Deferred investment tax credits.

**28.** During a period of inflation, an account balance remains constant. When supplemental statements are being prepared, a purchasing power gain is reported if the account is a
- **a.** Monetary asset.
- **b.** Monetary liability.
- **c.** Nonmonetary asset.
- **d.** Nonmonetary liability.

**29.** The following assets were among those that appeared on Baird Co.'s books at the end of the year:

| | |
|---|---|
| Demand bank deposits | $650,000 |
| Net long-term receivables | 400,000 |
| Patents and trademarks | 150,000 |

In preparing constant dollar financial statements, how much should Baird classify as monetary assets?
- **a.** $1,200,000
- **b.** $1,050,000
- **c.** $ 800,000
- **d.** $ 650,000

**30.** During a period of inflation in which a liability account balance remains constant, which of the following occurs?
- **a.** A purchasing power gain, if the item is a nonmonetary liability.
- **b.** A purchasing power gain, if the item is a monetary liability.
- **c.** A purchasing power loss, if the item is a nonmonetary liability.
- **d.** A purchasing power loss, if the item is a monetary liability.

**31.** The following items were among those that appeared on Rubi Co.'s books at the end of the year:

| | |
|---|---|
| Merchandise inventory | $600,000 |
| Loans to employees | 20,000 |

What amount should Rubi classify as monetary assets in preparing constant dollar financial statements?
- **a.** $0
- **b.** $ 20,000
- **c.** $600,000
- **d.** $620,000

**32.** Level, Inc., was formed on January 1, 20x1, when common stock of $200,000 was issued for cash of $50,000 and land valued at $150,000. Level did not begin operations until 20x2, and no transactions occurred in 20x1 except the recording of the issuance of the common stock. If the general price-level index was 100 at December 31, 20x1, and 110 at December 31, 20x2, what would the general price-level gain or loss be in Level's 20x2 general price-level income statement?
- **a.** $0.
- **b.** $ 5,000 loss.
- **c.** $ 5,000 gain.
- **d.** $15,000 gain.

**33.** On January 1 Nutley Corporation had monetary assets of $2,000,000 and monetary liabilities of $1,000,000. During the year Nutley's monetary inflows and outflows were relatively constant and equal so that it ended the year with net monetary assets of $1,000,000. Assume that the Consumer Price Index was 200 on January 1 and 220 on December 31. In end-of-year constant dollars, what is Nutley's purchasing power gain or loss on net monetary items for the year?
- **a.** $0.
- **b.** $ 50,000 gain.
- **c.** $100,000 gain.
- **d.** $100,000 loss.

**Items 34 and 35 are based on the following:**

In a period of rising general price levels, Pollard Corp. disclosed income on a current cost basis in accordance with ASC Topic 255, Financial Reporting and Changing Prices.

**34.** Compared to historical cost income from continuing operations, which of the following conditions increases Pollard's current cost income from continuing operations?
  a. Current cost of equipment is greater than historical cost.
  b. Current cost of land is greater than historical cost.
  c. Current cost of goods sold is less than historical cost.
  d. Ending net monetary assets are less than beginning net monetary assets.

**35.** Which of the following contributes to Pollard's purchasing power loss on net monetary items?
  a. Refundable deposits with suppliers.
  b. Equity investments in unconsolidated subsidiaries.
  c. Warranty obligations.
  d. Wages payable.

**36.** At December 31, Jannis Corp. owned two assets as follows:

|  | Equipment | Inventory |
|---|---|---|
| Current cost | $100,000 | $80,000 |
| Recoverable amount | 95,000 | 90,000 |

Jannis voluntarily disclosed supplementary information about current cost at December 31. In such disclosure, at what amount would Jannis report total assets?
  a. $175,000
  b. $180,000
  c  $185,000
  d. $190,000

**37.** A method of accounting based on measures of current cost or lower recoverable amount, without restatement into units having the same general purchasing power, is
  a. Historical cost/constant dollar accounting.
  b. Historical cost/nominal dollar accounting.
  c. Current cost/constant dollar accounting.
  d. Current cost/nominal dollar accounting.

**38.** Could current cost financial statements report holding gains for goods sold during the period and holding gains on inventory at the end of the period?

|  | Goods Sold | Inventory |
|---|---|---|
| a. | Yes | Yes |
| b. | Yes | No |
| c. | No | Yes |
| d. | No | No |

**39.** The following information pertains to each unit of merchandise purchased for resale by Vend Co:

| March 1 | |
|---|---|
| Purchase price | $ 8 |
| Selling price | $12 |
| Price level index | 110 |

| December 31 | |
|---|---|
| Replacement cost | $10 |
| Selling price | $15 |
| Price level index | 121 |

Under current cost accounting, what is the amount of Vend's holding gain on each unit of this merchandise?
  a. $0
  b. $0.80
  c. $1.20
  d. $2.00

**40.** Fair Value, Inc., paid $1,200,000 in December 20x1 for certain of its inventory. In December 20x2, one half of the inventory was sold for $1,000,000 when the replacement cost of the original inventory was $1,400,000. Ignoring income taxes, what amount should be shown as the total gain resulting from the above facts in a current fair value accounting income statement for 20x2?

   **a.** $200,000.
   **b.** $300,000.
   **c.** $400,000.
   **d.** $500,000.

**41.** Essex Corporation bought a machine for $105,000 on January 3. The machine has an estimated useful life of ten years, with no salvage value. The current cost of this machine at December 31 was $135,000. Using straight-line depreciation on an average current cost basis, how much depreciation should be charged to current cost income from continuing operations for the year?

   **a.** $10,500.
   **b.** $12,000.
   **c.** $13,500.
   **d.** $24,000.

**42.** On December 30, 20x1, Future, Incorporated, paid $2,000,000 for land. At December 31, 20x2, the fair value of the land was $2,200,000. In January 20x3, the land was sold for $2,250,000. Ignoring income taxes, by what amount should stockholders' equity be increased for 20x2 and 20x3 as a result of the above facts in current fair value financial statements?

| | 20x2 | 20x3 |
|---|---|---|
| **a.** | $ 0 | $ 50,000 |
| **b.** | $ 0 | $250,000 |
| **c.** | $200,000 | $ 0 |
| **d.** | $200,000 | $ 50,000 |

**43.** Coleman, Incorporated, purchased a machine on January 1, 20x0, for $100,000. Coleman is depreciating the machine on a straight-line basis with no salvage value and a ten-year life. At December 31, 20x6, the replacement cost (current fair value) of the machine was $32,000. On January 1, 20x7, the machine was sold for $35,000. Ignoring income taxes, what amount should be shown as the gain or loss on the sale of the machine in a current fair value accounting income statement for 20x7?

   **a.** $2,000 gain.
   **b.** $3,000 loss.
   **c.** $3,000 gain.
   **d.** $5,000 gain.

**44.** Manhof Co. prepares supplementary reports on income from continuing operations on a current cost basis in accordance with ASC Topic 255, <u>Financial Reporting and Changing Prices</u>. How should Manhof compute cost of goods sold on a current cost basis?

   **a.** Number of units sold times average current cost of units during the year.
   **b.** Number of units sold times current cost of units at year end.
   **c.** Number of units sold times current cost of units at the beginning of the year.
   **d.** Beginning inventory at current cost plus cost of goods purchased less ending inventory at current cost.

**45.** Information with respect to Bruno Co.'s cost of goods sold for the year is as follows:

| | Historical cost | Units |
|---|---|---|
| Inventory, 1/1 | $1,060,000 | 20,000 |
| Production for year | 5,580,000 | 90,000 |
| | 6,640,000 | 110,000 |
| Inventory, 12/31 | 2,520,000 | 40,000 |
| Cost of goods sold | $4,120,000 | 70,000 |

The current cost per inventory unit was $58 at January 1 and $72 at December 31. In Bruno's voluntary supplementary information for the year, the cost of goods sold restated into average current cost would be

   **a.** $5,040,000
   **b.** $4,550,000
   **c.** $4,410,000
   **d.** $4,060,000

**46.** Generally, which inventory costing method approximates most closely the current cost for each of the following?

|     | Cost of goods sold | Ending inventory |
| --- | --- | --- |
| a. | LIFO | FIFO |
| b. | LIFO | LIFO |
| c. | FIFO | FIFO |
| d. | FIFO | LIFO |

**47.** On September 1, 20x0, Cano & Co., a U.S. corporation, sold merchandise to a foreign firm for 250,000 LCUs. Terms of the sale require payment in LCUs on February 1, 20x1. On September 1, 20x0, the spot exchange rate was $.20 per LCU. At December 31, 20x0, Cano's year end, the spot rate was $.19, but the rate increased to $.22 by February 1, 20x1, when payment was received. How much should Cano report as foreign exchange gain or loss in its 20x1 income statement?

- a. $0
- b. $2,500 loss
- c. $5,000 gain.
- d. $7,500 gain.

**48.** On April 8, 20x1, Day Corp. purchased merchandise from an unaffiliated foreign company for 10,000 units of the foreign company's local currency. Day paid the bill in full on March 1, 20x2, when the spot rate was $.45 per LCU. The spot rate was $.60 on April 8, 20x1 and was $.55 on December 31, 20x1. For the year ended December 31, 20x2, Day should report a transaction gain of

- a. $1,500
- b. $1,000
- c. $ 500
- d. $0

**49.** A December 15, 20x1, purchase of goods was denominated in a currency other than the entity's functional currency. The transaction resulted in a payable that was fixed in terms of the amount of foreign currency and was paid on the settlement date, January 20, 20x2. The exchange rates between the functional currency and the currency in which the transaction was denominated changed between the transaction date and December 31, 20x1, and again between December 31, 20x1, and January 20, 20x2. Both exchange rate changes resulted in gains. The amount of the gain that should be included in the 20x2 financial statements would be

- a. The gain from December 31, 20x1, to January 20, 20x2.
- b. The gain from December 15, 20x1, to January 20, 20x2.
- c. The gain from December 15, 20x1, to December 31, 20x1.
- d. Zero.

**50.** Ball Corp. had the following foreign currency transactions during the year:

- Merchandise was purchased from a foreign supplier on January 20 for the U.S. dollar equivalent of $90,000. The invoice was paid on March 20 at the U.S. dollar equivalent of $96,000.

- On July 1, Ball borrowed the U.S. dollar equivalent $500,000 evidenced by a note that was payable in the lender's local currency on July 1 two years later. On December 31, the U.S. dollar equivalents of the principal amount and accrued interest were $520,000 and $26,000 respectively. Interest on the note is 10% per annum.

In Ball's current-year income statement, what amount should be included as foreign exchange loss?

- a. $0
- b. $ 6,000
- c. $21,000
- d. $27,000

**51.** Shore Co. records its transactions in U.S. dollars. A sale of goods resulted in a receivable denominated in Japanese yen, and a purchase of goods resulted in a payable denominated in French francs. Shore recorded a foreign exchange gain on collection of the receivable and an exchange loss on settlement of the payable. The exchange rates are expressed as so many units of foreign currency to one dollar. Did the number of foreign currency units exchangeable for a dollar increase or decrease between the contract and settlement dates?

|    | Yen Exchangeable for $1 | Francs exchangeable for $1 |
|----|----|----|
| a. | Increase | Increase |
| b. | Decrease | Decrease |
| c. | Decrease | Increase |
| d. | Increase | Decrease |

**52.** On November 15, 20x1, Celt, Inc., a U.S. company, ordered merchandise FOB shipping point from an East German company for 200,000 marks. The merchandise was shipped and invoiced to Celt on December 10, 20x1. Celt paid the invoice on January 19, 20x2. The spot rates for marks on the respective dates are as follows:

| November 15, 20x1 | $.4955 |
| December 10, 20x1 | .4875 |
| December 31, 20x1 | .4675 |
| January 10, 20x2 | .4475 |

In Celt's December 31, 20x1, income statement, the foreign exchange gain is
a. $9,600
b. $8,000
c. $4,000
d. $1,600

**53.** On October 1, Velec Co., a U.S. company, contracted to purchase foreign goods requiring payment in LCUs one month after their receipt at Velec's factory. Title to the goods passed on December 15. The goods were still in transit on December 31, Velec's year end. Exchange rates were one dollar to 22 LCUs, 20 LCUs, and 21 LCUs on October 1, December 15, and December 31, respectively. Velec should account for the exchange rate fluctuation during the year as
a. A loss included in net income.
b. A gain included in net income.
c. A direct increase in retained earnings gain.
d. A direct decrease in retained earnings.

**54.** Dale, Inc., a U.S. corporation, bought machine parts from Kluger Company of West Germany on March 1, 20x1, for 30,000 LCUs, when the spot rate for LCUs was $.4895. Dale's year-end was March 31, 20x1, when the spot rate for LCUs was $.4845. Dale bought 30,000 LCUs and paid the invoice on April 20, 20x1, when the spot rate was $.4945. How much should be shown in Dale's income statements as foreign exchange gain or loss for the years ended March 31, 20x1 and 20x2?

|    | 20x1 | 20x2 |
|----|----|----|
| a. | $0 | $0 |
| b. | $0 | $150 loss |
| c. | $150 loss | $0 |
| d. | $150 gain | $300 loss |

**55.** On November 30, 20x0, Tyrola Publishing Company, located in Colorado, executed a contract with Ernest Blyton, an author from Canada, providing for payment of 10% royalties on Canadian sales of Blyton's book. Payment is to be made in Canadian dollars each January 10 for the previous year's sales. Canadian sales of the book for the year ended December 31, 20x1, totaled $50,000 Canadian. Tyrola paid Blyton his 20x1 royalties on January 10, 20x2. Tyrola's 20x1 financial statements were issued on February 1, 20x2. Spot rates for Canadian dollars were as follows:

| | |
|---|---|
| November 30, 20x0 | $.87 |
| January 1, 20x1 | $.88 |
| December 31, 20x1 | $.89 |
| January 10, 20x2 | $.90 |

How much should Tyrola accrue for royalties payable at December 31, 20x1?
- a. $4,350.
- b. $4,425.
- c. $4,450.
- d. $4,500.

**56.** On July 1, 20x1, Stone Company lent $120,000 to a foreign supplier, evidenced by an interest-bearing note due on July 1, 20x2. The note is denominated in the currency of the borrower and was equivalent to 840,000 local currency units (LCU) on the loan date. The note principal was appropriately included at $140,000 in the receivables section of Stone's December 31, 20x1, balance sheet. The note principal was repaid to Stone on the July 1, 20x2, due date when the exchange rate was 8 LCU to $1. In its income statement for the year ended December 31, 20x2, what amount should Stone include as a foreign currency transaction gain or loss?
- a. $0
- b. $15,000 loss.
- c. $15,000 gain.
- d. $35,000 loss.

**57.** Seed Company has a receivable from a foreign customer which is payable in the local currency of the foreign customer. On December 31, 20x1, this receivable was appropriately included in the accounts receivable section of Seed's balance sheet at $450,000. When the receivable was collected on January 4, 20x2, Seed converted the local currency of the foreign customer into $440,000. Seed also owns a foreign subsidiary in which exchange gains of $45,000 resulted as a consequence of translation in 20x2. What amount, if any, should be included as an exchange gain or loss in Seed's 20x2 consolidated income statement?
- a. $0.
- b. $10,000 exchange loss.
- c. $35,000 exchange gain.
- d. $45,000 exchange gain.

**Items 58 through 60** are based on the following information:

On December 12, 20x1, Imp. Co. entered into three forward exchange contracts, each to purchase 100,000 euros in 90 days. The relevant exchange rates are as follows:

| | Spot rate | Forward rate for 3/12/x2 |
|---|---|---|
| December 12, 20x1 | $.88 | $.90 |
| December 31, 20x1 | .98 | .93 |

**58.** Imp entered into the first forward contract to hedge the fair value of a payable resulting from a purchase of inventory in November 20x1, payable in March 20x2. At December 31, 20x1, what amount of foreign currency transaction gain should Imp include from this forward contract?
- a. $0
- b. $ 3,000
- c. $ 5,000
- d. $10,000

**59.** Imp entered into the second forward contract, designated as a cash flow hedge, to hedge a commitment to purchase equipment being manufactured to Imp's specifications. Delivery is expected in February 20x2 with settlement at that time. This is considered a fair value hedge. At December 31, 20x1, what amount of foreign currency transaction gain should Imp include in income from this forward contract?

    **a.** $ 0
    **b.** $ 3,000
    **c.** $ 5,000
    **d.** $10,000

**60.** Imp entered into the third forward contract for speculation. At December 31, 20x1, what amount of foreign currency transaction gain should Imp include in income from this forward contract?

    **a.** $ 0
    **b.** $ 3,000
    **c.** $ 5,000
    **d.** $10,000

**61.** On September 1, Brady Corp. entered into a foreign exchange contract for speculative purposes by purchasing 50,000 deutsche marks for delivery in 60 days. The rates to exchange $1 for 1 deutsche mark follow:

|  | 9/1 | 9/30 |
|---|---|---|
| Spot rate | .75 | .70 |
| 30-day forward rate | .73 | .72 |
| 60-day forward rate | .74 | .73 |

In its September 30 income statement, what amount should Brady report as foreign exchange loss?

    **a.** $2,500
    **b.** $1,500
    **c.** $1,000
    **d.** $ 500

**62.** Certain balance sheet accounts of a foreign subsidiary of Rowan, Inc. at December 31 have been translated into U.S. dollars as follows:

|  | Current rates | Historical rates |
|---|---|---|
| Note receivable, long-term | $240,000 | $200,000 |
| Prepaid rent | 85,000 | 80,000 |
| Patent | 150,000 | 170,000 |
|  | $475,000 | $450,000 |

The subsidiary's functional currency is the currency of the country in which it is located. What total amount should be included in Rowan's December 31 consolidated balance sheet for the above accounts?

    **a.** $450,000
    **b.** $455,000
    **c.** $475,000
    **d.** $495,000

**63.** Fay Corp. had a realized foreign exchange loss of $15,000 for the year ended December 31, 20x1, and must also determine whether the following items will require year-end adjustment:

- Fay had an $8,000 loss resulting from the translation of the accounts of its wholly owned foreign subsidiary for the year ended December 31, 20x1.

- Fay had an account payable to an unrelated foreign supplier payable in the supplier's local currency. The U.S. dollar equivalent of the payable was $64,000 on the October 31, 20x1 invoice date, and it was $60,000 on December 31, 20x1. The invoice is payable on January 30, 20x2.

In Fay's consolidated income statement, what amount should be included as a foreign exchange loss?

    **a.** $11,000
    **b.** $15,000
    **c.** $19,000
    **d.** $23,000

**64.** A balance arising from the translation or remeasuring of a subsidiary's foreign currency financial statements is reported in the consolidated income statement when the subsidiary's functional currency is the

|     | Foreign currency | U.S. Dollar |
|-----|------------------|-------------|
| a.  | No               | No          |
| b.  | No               | Yes         |
| c.  | Yes              | No          |
| d.  | Yes              | Yes         |

**65.** Certain balance sheet accounts in a foreign subsidiary, of the Brogan Company, at December 31 have been translated into United States dollars as follows:

|                                                              | Current rates | Historical rates |
|--------------------------------------------------------------|---------------|------------------|
| Marketable equity securities carried at cost                 | $100,000      | $110,000         |
| Marketable equity securities carried at current market price | 120,000       | 125,000          |
| Inventories carried at cost                                  | 130,000       | 132,000          |
| Inventories carried at net realizable value                  | 80,000        | 84,000           |
|                                                              | $430,000      | $451,000         |

What amount should be shown in Brogan's balance sheet at December 31 as a result of the above information?

- a. $430,000.
- b. $436,000.
- c. $442,000.
- d. $451,000.

**66.** The France Company owns a foreign-subsidiary with 2,400,000 local currency units (LCU) of property, plant, and equipment before accumulated depreciation at December 31 of the current year. Of this amount, 1,500,000 LCU were acquired two years ago when the rate of exchange was 1.5 LCU to $1, and 900,000 LCU were acquired one year ago when the rate of exchange was 1.6 LCU to $1. The rate of exchange in effect at December 31, of the current year was 1.9 LCU to $1. The weighted average of exchange rates which were in effect during the year was 1.8 LCU to $1. Assuming that the property, plant, and equipment are depreciated using the straight-line method over a ten-year period with no salvage value, how much depreciation expense relating to the foreign subsidiary's property, plant, and equipment should be charged in France's income statement for the current year?

- a. $126,316.
- b. $133,333.
- c. $150,000.
- d. $156,250.

**67.** A wholly owned foreign subsidiary of Union Corporation has certain expense accounts for the year ended December 31, 20x2, stated in local currency units (LCU) as follows:

|                                                                              | LCU     |
|------------------------------------------------------------------------------|---------|
| Amortization of patent (related patent was acquired January 1,20x0)          | 40,000  |
| Provision for doubtful accounts                                              | 60,000  |
| Rent                                                                         | 100,000 |

The exchange rates at various dates are as follows:

|                                         | Dollar equivalent of 1 LCU |
|-----------------------------------------|----------------------------|
| December 31, 20x2                       | $.20                       |
| Average for the year ended December 31, 20x2 | .22                   |
| January 1, 20x0                         | .25                        |

What total dollar amount should be included in Union's income statement to reflect the above expenses for the year ended December 31, 20x2?

- a. $40,000.
- b. $42,000.
- c. $44,000.
- d. $45,200.

**68.** On January 1, 20x2, Kiner Company formed a foreign branch. The branch purchased merchandise at a cost of 720,000 local currency units (LCU) on February 15, 20x2. The purchase price was equivalent to $180,000 on this date. The branch's inventory at December 31, 20x2, consisted solely of merchandise purchased on February 15, 20x2, and amounted to 240,000 LCU. The exchange rate was 6 LCU to $1 on December 31, 20x2, and the average rate of exchange was 5 LCU to $1 for 20x2. Assume that the LCU is the functional currency of the branch. In Kiner's December 31, 20x2, balance sheet, the branch inventory balance of 240,000 LCU should be translated into United States dollars at

    a. $40,000.
    b. $48,000.
    c. $60,000.
    d. $84,000.

**69.** Selected data for a segment of a business enterprise are to be separately reported in accordance with ASC Topic 280 when the revenues of the segment exceed 10 percent of the

    a. Combined net income of all segments reporting profits.
    b. Total revenues obtained in transactions with outsiders.
    c. Total revenues of all the enterprise's industry segments.
    d. Total combined revenues of all segments reporting profits.

**70.** In financial reporting for segments of a business enterprise, the revenue of a segment should include

    a. Intersegment billings for the cost of shared facilities.
    b. Intersegment sales of services similar to those sold to unaffiliated customers.
    c. Equity in income from unconsolidated subsidiaries.
    d. Income before income tax.

**71.** YIV Inc. is a multidivisional corporation which has both intersegment sales and sales to unaffiliated customers. YIV should report segment financial information for each division meeting which of the following criteria?

    a. Segment operating profit or loss is 10% or more of consolidated profit or loss.
    b. Segment operating profit or loss is 10% or more of combined operating profit or loss of all company segments.
    c. Segment revenue is 10% or more of combined revenue of all the company segments.
    d. Segment revenue is 10% or more of consolidated revenue.

**72.** Kaycee Corporation's revenues for the year ended December 31 were as follows:

| | |
|---|---|
| Consolidated revenue per income statement | $1,200,000 |
| Intersegment sales | 180,000 |
| Intersegment transfers | 60,000 |
| Combined revenues of all industry segments | $1,440,000 |

Kaycee has a reportable segment if that segment's revenues exceed

    a. $ 6,000
    b. $ 24,000
    c. $120,000
    d. $144,000

**73.** The following information pertains to Aria Corp. and its divisions for the year:

| | |
|---|---|
| Sale to unaffiliated customers | $2,000,000 |
| Intersegment sales of products similar to those sold to unaffiliated customers | 600,000 |
| Interest earned on loans to other industry segments | 40,000 |

Aria and all of its divisions are engaged solely in manufacturing in manufacturing operations. Aria has a reportable segment if that segment's revenue exceeds

    a. $264,000
    b. $260,000
    c. $204,000
    d. $200,000

**74.** The following information pertains to revenue earned by Timm Co.'s industry segments for the year:

| Segment | Sales to unaffiliated customers | Inter-segment sales | Total revenue |
|---|---|---|---|
| Alo | $ 5,000 | $ 3,000 | $ 8,000 |
| Bix | 8,000 | 4,000 | 12,000 |
| Cee | 4,000 | --- | 4,000 |
| Dil | 43,000 | 16,000 | 59,000 |
| Combined | $60,000 | $23,000 | $83,000 |
| Elimination | --- | (23,000) | (23,000) |
| Consolidated | $60,000 | $ --- | $60,000 |

In conformity with the revenue test, Timm's reportable segments were
  a. Only Dil.
  b. Only Bix and Dil.
  c. Only Alo, Bix, and Dil.
  d. Alo, Bix, Cee, and Dil

**75.** In financial reporting for segments of a business enterprise, the operating profit or loss of a segment should include among other items
  a. Traceable costs.
  b. Foreign income taxes.
  c. Administrative overhead.
  d. Loss on discontinued operations.

**76.** In financial reporting of segment data, which of the following items is used in determining a segment's operating income?
  a. Income tax expense.
  b. Sales to other segments.
  c. General corporate expense.
  d. Gain or loss on discontinued operations.

**77.** Plains, Inc., engages in three lines of business, each of which is considered to be a significant industry segment. Company sales aggregated $1,800,000 during the year of which Segment No. 3 contributed 60%. Traceable costs were $600,000 for Segment No. 3 out of a total of $1,200,000 for the company as a whole. In addition, $350,000 of common costs are allocated based on the ratio of a segment's income before common costs to the total income before common costs.

What should Plains report as operating profit for Segment No. 3 for the year?
  a. $200,000.
  b. $270,000.
  c. $280,000.
  d. $480,000.

**78.** Yola Corp., a diversified company, is required to report the operating profit or loss for each of its industry segments. For the year ended December 31, segment Wy's sales to segment Zee were $100,000. Segment Wy's share of Yola's allocated general corporate expenses was $20,000. In the computation of Wy's operating profit or loss for the year, the amount of the aforementioned items to be included is
  a. $120,000
  b. $100,000
  c. $ 80,000
  d. $ 20,000

**79.** In financial reporting for segments of a business enterprise, the operating profit or loss of a segment should include

| | Reasonably allocated common operating costs | Traceable operating costs |
|---|---|---|
| a. | No | No |
| b. | No | Yes |
| c. | Yes | No |
| d. | Yes | Yes |

**80.** In financial reporting for segments of a business enterprise, the operating profit or loss of a manufacturing segment includes

| | Interest expense | Portion of general corporate expense |
|---|---|---|
| a. | Yes | Yes |
| b. | Yes | No |
| c. | No | No |
| d. | No | Yes |

**81.** Hines Corporation reports operating profit as to industry segments in its supplementary financial information annually. The following information is available for the year:

| | Sales | Traceable costs |
|---|---|---|
| Segment A | $ 750,000 | $450,000 |
| Segment B | 500,000 | 225,000 |
| Segment C | 250,000 | 125,000 |
| | $1,500,000 | $800,000 |

Additional expenses not included above are as follows:

| | |
|---|---|
| Indirect operating expenses | $240,000 |
| General corporate expenses | 180,000 |
| Interest expense | 96,000 |

Hines allocates common costs based on the ratio of a segment's sales to total sales. What should be the operating profit for segment B for the year?
- **a.** $103,000.
- **b.** $135,000.
- **c.** $163,000.
- **d.** $195,000.

**82.** Kee Co. has five manufacturing divisions, each of which has been determined to be a reportable segment. Common costs are appropriately allocated on the basis of each division's sales in relation to Kee's aggregate sales. Kee's Sigma division comprised 40% or Kee's total sales during the year. For the year ended December 31 Sigma had sales of $1,000,000 and traceable costs of $600,000. During the year Kee incurred operating expenses of $100,000 that were not directly traceable to any of the five divisions. In addition, Kee incurred interest expense of $80,000 for the year. In reporting supplementary segment information, how much should be shown as Sigma's operating income for the year?
- **a.** $300,000.
- **b.** $328,000.
- **c.** $360,000.
- **d.** $400,000.

**83.** Cott Co.'s four business segments have revenues and identifiable assets expressed as percentages of Cott's total revenues and total assets as follows:

| | Revenues | Assets |
|---|---|---|
| Ebon | 64% | 66% |
| Fair | 14% | 18% |
| Gel | 14% | 4% |
| Hak | 8% | 12% |
| | 100% | 100% |

Which of these business segments are deemed to be reportable segments?
- **a.** Ebon only.
- **b.** Ebon and Fair only.
- **c.** Ebon, Fair, and Gel only.
- **d.** Ebon, Fair, Gel, and Hak.

**84.** In financial reporting for segments of a business enterprise, which of the following should be taken into account in computing the amount of an industry segment's identifiable assets?

| | Accumulated depreciation | Marketable securities valuation allowance |
|---|---|---|
| **a.** | No | No |
| **b.** | No | Yes |
| **c.** | Yes | Yes |
| **d.** | Yes | No |

**85.** Correy Corp. and its divisions are engaged solely in manufacturing operations. The following data (consistent with prior years' data) pertain to the industries in which operations were conducted for the year ended December 31:

| Industry | Total revenue | Operating profit | Identifiable assets at December 31 |
|---|---|---|---|
| A | $10,000,000 | $1,750,000 | $20,000,000 |
| B | 8,000,000 | 1,400,000 | 17,500,000 |
| C | 6,000,000 | 1,200,000 | 12,500,000 |
| D | 3,000,000 | 550,000 | 7,500,000 |
| E | 4,250,000 | 675,000 | 7,000,000 |
| F | 1,500,000 | 225,000 | 3,000,000 |
| | $32,750,000 | $5,800,000 | $67,500,000 |

In its segment information for the year, how many reportable segments does Correy have?
- **a.** Three
- **b.** Four
- **c.** Five
- **d.** Six

**Items 86 and 87** are based on the following information:

Grum Corp., a publicly-owned corporation, is subject to the requirements for segment reporting. In its income statement for the year ended December 31, Grum reported revenues of $50,000,000, operating expenses of $47,000,000, and net income of $3,000,000. Operating expenses include payroll costs of $15,000,000. Grum's combined identifiable assets of all industry segments at December 31 were $40,000,000.

**86.** In its financial statements for the year, Grum should disclose major customer data if sales to any single customer amount to at least
    a. $ 300,000
    b. $1,500,000
    c. $4,000,000
    d. $5,000,000

**87.** In its financial statements for the year, Grum should disclose foreign operations data if revenues from foreign operations are at least
    a. $5,000,000
    b. $4,700,000
    c. $4,000,000
    d. $1,500,000

**88.** The following information pertains to Gali Co.'s defined benefit pension plan for 20x4:

| | |
|---|---|
| Fair value of plan assets, beginning of year | $350,000 |
| Fair value of plan assets, end of year | 525,000 |
| Employer contributions | 110,000 |
| Benefits paid | 85,000 |

In computing pension expense, what amount should Gali use as actual return on plan assets?
    a. $ 65,000
    b. $150,000
    c. $175,000
    d. $260,000

**89.** An employer's obligation for postretirement health benefits that are expected to be provided to or for an employee must be fully accrued by the date the

    a. Employee is fully eligible for benefits.
    b. Employee retires.
    c. Benefits are utilized.
    d. Benefits are paid.

**90.** In its financial statements, Hila Co. discloses supplemental information on the effects of changing prices in accordance with Statement of Financial Accounting Standards No. 89, Financial Reporting and Changing Prices. Hila computed the increase in current cost of inventory as follows:

| | |
|---|---|
| Increase in current cost (nominal dollars) | $15,000 |
| Increase in current cost (constant dollars) | $12,000 |

What amount should Hila disclose as the inflation component of the increase in current cost of inventories?
    a. .$ 3,000
    b. $12,000
    c. $15,000
    d. $27,000

**91.** Financial statements prepared under which of the following methods include adjustments for both specific price changes and general price-level changes?
    a. Historical cost/nominal dollar.
    b. Current cost/nominal dollar.
    c. Current cost/constant dollar.
    d. Historical cost/constant dollar.

**92.** On September 22, 20x4, Yumi Corp. purchased merchandise from an unaffiliated foreign company for 10,000 units of the foreign company's local currency. On that date, the spot rate was $.55. Yumi paid the bill in full on march 20, 20x5, when the spot rate was $.65. The spot rate was $.70 on December 31, 20x4. What amount should Yumi report as a foreign currency transaction loss in its income statement for the year ended December 31, 20x4?
    a. $0
    b. $ 500
    c. $1,000
    d. $1,500

# CHAPTER 5

## SPECIAL TOPICS: PENSIONS; OPEB; ALTERNATIVE FINANCIAL ACCOUNTING MODELS; FOREIGN EXCHANGE; AND SEGMENT REPORTING

### Simulation Questions

**Number 1**        **(Estimated time - 20 to 25 minutes)**

Question Number 1 consists of 10 items. Select the **best** answer for each item. **Answer all items.** Your grade will be based on the total number of correct answers.

The following information pertains to Sparta Co.'s defined benefit pension plan.

| | |
|---|---|
| Discount rate | 8% |
| Expected rate of return | 10% |
| Average service life | 12 years |

At January 1, 20x1:

| | |
|---|---|
| Projected benefit obligation | $600,000 |
| Fair value of plan assets | 720,000 |
| Unrecognized prior service cost | 240,000 |
| Unamortized prior pension gain | 96,000 |

At December 31, 20x1:

| | |
|---|---|
| Projected benefit obligation | 910,000 |
| Fair value of pension plan assets | 825,000 |

Service cost for 20x1 was $90,000. There were no contributions made or benefits paid during the year. Sparta's unfunded accrued pension liability was $8,000 at January 1, 20x1. Sparta uses the straight-line method of amortization over the maximum period permitted.

**Required:**

**1. For items 1 through 5,** calculate the amounts to be recognized as components of Sparta's unfunded accrued pension liability at December 31, 20x1.

**Amounts to be calculated:**

1. Interest cost.
2. Expected return on plan assets.
3. Actual return on plan assets.
4. Amortization of prior service costs.
5. Minimum amortization of unrecognized pension gain.

**2. For Items 6 through 10,** determine whether the component increases (I) or decreases (D) Sparta's unfunded accrued pension liability and blacken the corresponding oval on the answer sheet.

**Items to be answered:**

6. Service cost.
7. Deferral of gain on pension plan assets.
8. Actual return on plan assets.
9. Amortization of prior service costs.
10. Amortization of unrecognized pension gain.

# CHAPTER 5

# SPECIAL TOPICS: PENSIONS; OPEB ALTERNATIVE FINANCIAL ACCOUNTING MODELS; FOREIGN EXCHANGE; AND SEGMENT REPORTING

## Multiple Choice Answers

**1.** /a/ The pension asset (liability) is the difference between pension asset fair value and the projected benefit obligation:

$410,000 - $400,000 = $10,000

**2.** /d/ Pension expense is the sum of service cost, interest on the PBO and amortization of prior service cost less the expected return on assets.

$120,000 + 12,000 + 30,000 – 41,000 = $121,000.

**3.** /b/ The pension asset (liability) is the difference between pension asset fair value and the projected benefit obligation. Contributions were made for prior service costs and current service cost, $210,000. These amounts also increased the PBO. Because the interest rate is the same for assets and liabilities, the ending balance for assets and PBO must be same; therefore, the pension asset/liability must be $0.

**4.** /c/

| | |
|---|---|
| Service cost | $300,000 |
| Return on plan assets | -80,000 |
| Interest cost on PBO | 164,000 |
| Amortization of actuarial loss | 30,000 |
| Pension cost, x0 | $414,000 |

**5.** /d/ Prior service cost will be amortized and become a component of pension cost in year 20x1 and forward.

**6.** /c/

| | |
|---|---|
| Total service years remaining | 20 |
| Number of employees | 4 |
| Average service years remaining per employee | 5 |

Amortization per year =
1/5 x ($200,000) = $40,000

**7.** /d/

| | |
|---|---|
| Service cost | $160,000 |
| Gain on plan assets | -35,000 |
| Amortization of unrecognized prior service cost | 5,000 |
| Annual interest on pension obligation | 50,000 |
| Pension expense, 20x1 | $180,000 |

**8.** /c/ The interest cost component of net pension cost represents the increase in the PBO over time.

**9.** /d/

| | |
|---|---|
| (1.10 x 72,000) | $79,200 |
| Service cost | +18,000 |
| Benefits paid | -15,000 |
| | $82,200 |

**10.** /b/ The discount rate used to calculate the PBO is neither the expected nor the actual return on plan assets. It is the "settlement interest rate," which is the rate applicable to settle the pension obligation currently such as the rate on high-quality fixed income investments.

**11.** /c/ The liability to be reported on the balance sheet is equal to at least the amount of the unfunded projected benefit obligation.

**12.** /a/ The liability to be reported in the balance sheet is the amount by which the projected benefit obligation exceeds the market value of the plan assets.

**13.** /b/ If the projected benefit obligation is greater than the fair value of the plan assets, the minimum pension liability is the excess of the PBO over the value of the plan assets.

| | |
|---|---|
| $5,700,000 | PBO |
| -3,450,000 | Value of plan assets |
| $2,250,000 | Liability to report |

**14.** /d/ Answers A, B, and C all relate to required disclosures to the Balance Sheet and would not be entered directly on the statement. the difference between the fair value of plan assets and the projected benefit obligation

**15.** /c/ The interest component of pension expense is based on the projected benefits obligation, not vested benefits. Therefore, answer C is the only item which is not a component of pension expense. Pension expense consists of six components – service cost, interest cost, return on plan assets, amortization of unrecognized prior service cost, amortization of unrecognized gains and losses, and amortization of the transition amount.

**16.** /c/ The funding status of a pension plan is the difference between the projected benefit obligation (PBO) and the fair value of the plan assets. If the fair value of plan assets exceed the PBO the plan is overfunded (an asset). On the other hand, if the fair value of the plan assets are less than the PBO the plan is underfunded (liability).

**17.** /b/ The extensive disclosure requirements identified in ASC Topic 715 include all the items presented in this question.

**18.** /a/ Both items presented are part of the extensive disclosure requirements identified in ASC Topic 715, Accounting for Postretirement Benefits Other than Pensions.

**19.** /d/ Since the general inflation increased at a rate higher than the specific increase in the price of the land, the historical cost/constant dollar model would measure the land at the highest price.

**20.** /c/ The appropriate measurement basis for equipment when a company is disposing of its assets and going out of business is the equipment's exit value (i.e. the net realizable value).

**21.** /d/ ASC Topic 255 encourages constant dollar supplemental information on a constant dollar basis using the CPI-U. Historical cost and nominal dollars do not require the use of the CPI-U. Current cost requires the consideration of specific (not general) price changes.

**22.** /c/ Historical cost/constant dollar accounting retains the attribute to be measured as historical cost, but changes the measuring unit (the dollar) to reflect dollars of the same general purchasing power. Current cost drops the historical cost attribute. Nominal dollars ignore general purchasing power changes.

**23.** /d/ $200,000 x 200/180 = $222,222

**24.** /c/

| | | |
|---|---|---|
| 30,000 x .10 = 3,000 x 150/100 = | $4,500 |
| 20,000 x .10 = 2,000 x 150/125 = | 2,400 |
| 10,000 x .10 = 1,000 x 150/150 = | 1,000 |
| Total | $7,900 |

**25.** /a/ Obligations under warranties are nonmonetary liabilities, because the amount to be paid is not fixed in terms of dollars by contract or otherwise. All other options are considered monetary.

**26.** /b/ Accumulated depreciation and the related asset are both considered nonmonetary items because the amount is not fixed in terms of dollars by contract or otherwise. All other options are considered monetary.

**27.** /c/ Unamortized discount on bonds payable is a valuation account and has the same classification as the related bonds payable, which is monetary. All other items are considered nonmonetary.

**28.** /b/ Holding a monetary liability during a period of inflation results in a purchasing power gain because the obligation can be paid using dollars which have less purchasing power than the original dollars financed.

**29.** /b/ Monetary assets are those items that represent fixed claims or amounts regardless of price level changes. The $150,000 of patents and trademarks represent historical cost, not a fixed amount that would be received were they to be sold. The bank deposits and receivable amounts, however, are fixed. $650,000 + $400,000 = $1,050,000

**30.** /b/ If the liability is monetary, the amount of dollars needed to satisfy the debt is fixed by contract and will not increase with inflation. As the debt can be liquidated using dollars which have less purchasing power than the original dollars borrowed or financed, the result is a purchasing power gain.

**31.** /b/ Monetary assets represent fixed claims to dollar amounts that do not change as price levels change. Loans to employees are the only fixed claims to monetary amounts presented.

**32.** /b/ $50,000    x 110/100 =
$55,000    needed to maintain same purchasing power
-50,000    actual cash on hand
$ 5,000    purchasing power loss

**33.** /d/ $2,000,000    M.A.
-1,000,000    M.L.
$1,000,000    N.M.A. - Beg. and end of year

$1,000,000
x 220/200
$1,100,000    needed to maintain purchasing power
-1,000,000    ending N.M.A. on hand
$ 100,000    purchasing power loss

**34.** /c/ If cost of goods sold, as reported on a current cost basis, is less than that on a historical cost basis, income from continuing operations on a current cost basis will be higher than historical cost income.

**35.** /a/ The only monetary items presented as choices are refundable deposits with suppliers and wages payable. The refundable deposits (an asset) would contribute to a purchasing power loss. Wages payable (a liability) would contribute to a purchasing power gain.

**36.** /a/ Use the lower of current cost or recoverable amount. $95,000 (recoverable amount for equipment) + $80,000 (current cost for inventory) = $175,000.

**37.** /d/ When there is no restatement into units having the same general purchasing power, a firm is using nominal dollar accounting. Historical cost accounting is not based on current costs, and constant dollar accounting does restate into units having the same general purchasing power.

**38.** /a/ Both the current cost/nominal dollar and current cost/constant dollar accounting models report holding gains related to cost of goods sold and goods held in inventory at the end of the period.

**39.** /d/ The holding gain is the increase in the current cost between March 1 and December 31. Current cost March 1 was purchase price of $8; current cost December 31 is lower of replacement cost ($10) or recoverable amount ($15). Holding gain is $2.

**40.** /d/
| | |
|---|---:|
| Sales revenue | $1,000,000 |
| Current cost COGS | - 700,000 |
| Current cost gross margin | $ 300,000 |
| Plus realized holding gain related to goods sold ($700K - $600K) | 100,000 |
| Income realized | $400,000 |
| Plus unrealized holding gain related to goods in inventory 12/31 (($700K - $600K) | + 100,000 |
| Total gain | $ 500,000 |

**41.** /b/
| | |
|---:|---|
| $105,000 | Beg. of year C.C. |
| 135,000 | End of year C.C. |
| $120,000 | Average C.C. for the year |
| ÷ 10 yrs | |
| $ 12,000 | C.C. depreciation expense |

**42.** /d/

1st year: 2,200,000 - 2,000,000 = $200,000

2nd year: 2,250,000 - 2,200,000 = $ 50,000

**43.** /c/
| | |
|---:|---|
| $35,000 | selling price |
| -32,000 | replacement cost at time of sale |
| $ 3,000 | gain on sale |

**44.** /a/ Cost of goods sold may be restated using an average current cost per unit approach.

**45.** /b/ Average current cost/unit x units sold.

($58 + $72)/2 x 70,000 units = $4,550,000.

**46.** /a/ Current cost is defined as replacement cost. The LIFO method places the most recent (i.e. replacement) costs in cost of goods sold. The FIFO method places these costs in ending inventory.

**47.** /d/ This is a receivable transaction. The transaction gain/(loss) for 20x1 is measured at the number of LCUs to be received times the change in the exchange rate from 12/31/x0 to 2/1/x1. As the value of the dollar depreciated during this time, Cano & Co. should report a gain equal to 250,000 LCUs x ($.22 - $.19) = $7,500.

**48.** /b/ This is a payable transaction. The transaction gain/(loss) for 20x2 is measured at the number of LCUs to be paid times the change in the exchange rate from 12/31/x1 to the date of payment on 3/1/x2. 10,000 LCUs x ($.55 - $.45) = $1,000 gain.

**49.** /a/ Gains resulting from exchange rate changes are recorded at the end of the fiscal year and at the settlement date if the settlement date falls after year-end. In such situations, the gain recorded on settlement date is measured using the change in the rate from the end of the previous fiscal year to date of settlement.

**50.** /d/ These transactions involve payable amounts.

| | | |
|---|---|---|
| Loss on merchandise transaction | | $ 6,000 |
| Loss on note principal | | 20,000 |
| Loss relating to interest: | | |
| $500,000 x 10% x 6/12 | $25,000 | |
| $520,000 x 10% x 6/12 | 26,000 | 1,000 |
| Total foreign exchange loss | | $27,000 |

**51.** /b/ In both instances, the number of foreign currency units per dollar must have decreased - i.e. the dollar depreciated against both currencies. When this happens, receivables are settled at a gain because the fixed number of foreign currency units to be received will be worth more dollars at settlement. Payables, however, are settled at a loss because more dollars are needed to acquire the fixed number of foreign currency units at which the liability is to be liquidated.

**52.** /c/ The gain is measured at the change in exchange rates between the transaction date and December 31. The transaction date is December 10, the date of shipment and invoicing. (Note the FOB shipping point terms.) 200,000 LCUs x ($.4875 - $.4675) = $4,000.

**53.** /b/ The transaction date of this contract is December 15. Since the number of francs to be exchanged for $1 increased from 20 to 21 between December 15 and December 31, it follows that Velec could have settled the liability on December 31 by using fewer dollars to purchase the same number of LCUs. This would be recorded as a foreign exchange gain.

**54.** /d/ 20x1: 30,000 LCUs x (.4895 - .4845) = $150 gain
20x2: 30,000 LCUs x (.4845 - .4945) = $300 loss
20x1: An account payable and U.S. dollar appreciated.
20x2: An account payable and U.S. dollar depreciated.

**55.** /c/

| | |
|---|---|
| $50,000 | CAN. |
| x .10 | |
| $ 5,000 | CAN. x .89 = $4,450 (U.S.) |

**56.** /d/

| | |
|---|---|
| $140,000 | A.R. Balance 12/31/x1 |
| -105,000 | Cash Collected (840,000 LCU/8) |
| $ 35,000 | loss in 20x2 |

**57.** /c/

| | |
|---|---|
| ($10,000) | exchange loss on collection of A.R. |
| 45,000 | exchange gain on translation |
| $35,000 | consolidated exchange gain |

**58.** /b/ This is a forward exchange contract to hedge a fair value position. Transaction gain is recognized on an accrual basis and measured using the difference between the forward rates from December 12 to December 31. 100,000 Euros x ($.93 - $.90) = $3,000.

**59.** /b/ Since this is a non-speculative forward exchange contract to hedge an identifiable commitment and is treated in the same manner as a forward exchange contract used to hedge an exposed liability. In this situation, ($.93 - $.90) x 100,000 Euros = $3,000 foreign currency transaction gain.

**60.** /b/ This is a forward exchange contract for speculation. Transaction gain is recognized on an accrual basis and is measured using the difference between the forward exchange rates over the contract life. 100,000 Euros x ($.93 - $.90) = $3,000.

**61.** /c/ Gains and losses connected with forward exchange contracts entered into for speculation are measured using the change in forward exchange rates over the life of the contract. The applicable forward rates are $.74 (60 days from 9/1) and $.72 (30 days from 9/30). 50,000 deutsche marks x ($.74 - $.72) = $1,000.

**62.** /c/ When a foreign subsidiary does business in the currency of its own country, the current rate method is used in translating the financial statements. Current amount figures would be used for all the items presented.

**63.** /a/ $15,000 realized exchange loss, less adjustment for foreign exchange transaction gain relating to the account payable = $11,000 loss. The $8,000 arising from the translation would not be reported on the income statement assuming the current rate method of translating. It would be reported in the equity section of the balance sheet.

**64.** /b/ When a subsidiary's functional currency is the U.S. dollar, the remeasurement method is used. This method includes a balance arising from translation in the income statement. However, when the functional currency is the foreign currency, the current rate method is used. This does not report a balance from translation in the income statement, rather an adjustment is made in the stockholders' equity section of the balance sheet.

**65.** /c/ Assuming that the remeasurement method is used (U.S. dollar is the functional currency), the following amounts would be used:

| | |
|---|---|
| $110,000 | M.S. at cost |
| 120,000 | M.S. at current market price |
| 132,000 | Inventory at cost |
| 80,000 | Inventory at N.R.V. |
| $442,000 | |

**66.** /d/ D is the correct answer if the remeasurement method is used (U.S. dollar is the functional currency).

$$\frac{\$1,500,000}{10 \text{ years}} = 150,000 \text{ LCU}/1.5 = \$100,000$$

$$\frac{9,000,000}{10 \text{ years}} = 90,000 \text{ LCU}/1.6 = \underline{56,250}$$

Total $156,250

B is the correct answer if the current rate method is used (foreign currency is the functional currency).

240,000 LCU/1.8 (Weighted Average rate for the current year) = $133,333

**67.** /d/ D is the correct answer if the remeasurement method is used (U.S. dollar is the functional currency).

| | | |
|---|---|---|
| 40,000 LCU x .25 | = | $10,000 |
| 60,000 LCU x .22 | = | 13,200 |
| 100,000 LCU x .22 | = | 22,000 |
| | | $45,200 |

C is the correct answer if the current rate method is used (foreign currency is the functional currency).

$200,000 LCU x .22 = $44,000

**68.** /a/ 240,000 LCU/6 (current rate at Balance Sheet date) = $40,000

(use the current rate to translate because the LCU is the functional currency).

**69.** /c/ Per ASC Topic 280, the criteria for a reportable industry segment must be more than 10% of the total revenues of all industry segments (including sales to outsiders and intersegment sales).

**70.** /b/ Intersegment sales are included in segment revenue. All other items presented are specifically excluded.

**71.** /c/ Segment information should be reported for segments whose revenue is 10% or more of the combined revenues of all industry segments. Options A, C, and D do not meet the specific criteria required to identify a segment.

**72.** /d/ Per ASC Topic 280, the criteria for reportable industry segment must be more than 10% of the total revenues of all industry segments (including sales to outsiders and intersegment sales/transfers).

$1,440,000 x .10 = $144,000

**73.** /b/ Ana Corp. has a reportable industry segment if revenue, including sales to unaffiliated customers and intersegment sales, is 10% or more of the combined revenue of all segments. Interest on intersegment loans is excluded from the 10% revenue determination.

(600,000 + 2,000,000) x 10%

= $260,000

**74.** /b/ Timm Co.'s reportable segments are those whose revenues are equal to or exceed 10% of the combined revenues of all industry segments ($83,000 x 10%). Sales to unaffiliated customers and intersegment sales are both included. Revenues of the Alo and Cee segments do not meet the required level of $8,300.

**75.** /a/ Traceable costs are included in the calculating segment operating profit or loss. All other items are specifically excluded from the calculation of segment's operating profit or loss.

**76.** /b/ Items A, C, and D are specifically excluded in the determination of a segment's operating income.

**77.** /a/

| | |
|---|---|
| $1,080,000 | Sales |
| - 600,000 | Traceable Costs |
| 480,000 | Segment Income Before Common Costs |
| - 280,000 | Allocated Common Costs (350,000 x .80) .80 = 480k/600k |
| $ 200,000 | Segment Operating Profit |

**78.** /b/ In the determination of segment profit or loss, intersegment sales are included, but allocation of general corporate expenses are excluded.

**79.** /d/ Reasonably allocated common costs and traceable operating costs are both deducted when calculating segment operating profit or loss.

**80.** /c/ Both interest expense and allocation of general corporate expenses are specifically excluded from the calculation of industry segment operating profit or loss.

**81.** /d/

| | |
|---|---|
| $500,000 | Sales |
| -225,000 | Traceable Costs |
| - 80,000 | Allocated Common Costs ($240,000 x 500,000/1,500,000) |
| _____ | Excludes general corporate expenses and interest expense |
| $195,000 | Segment B Operating Profit |

**82.** /c/

| | |
|---|---|
| $1,000,000 | Sales |
| - 600,000 | Traceable Costs |
| - 40,000 | Allocated Common Costs ($100,000 x .40)* |
| $ 360,000 | Segment Operating Income |

\* Excludes Interest Expense

**83.** /d/ All four business segments are reportable segments. Only one of the qualifying criteria needs to be met. Ebon and Fair meet both the 10% of combined revenues and 10% of identifiable assets test. Gel meets the 10% of revenues test, and Hak, the 10% of identifiable assets test.

**84.** /c/ Both items would be taken into account in computing an industry segment's identifiable assets.

**85.** /c/ Industry F is the only segment which does not meet one of the 10% or more of total combined revenues, operating profit, or identifiable assets tests.

**86.** /d/ A major customer is one to whom sales equal to 10% or more of total revenues are made.

**87.** /a/ Foreign operations data are disclosed if revenues from foreign sales to unaffiliated customers are equal to 10% or more of consolidated revenue.

**88.** /b/

| | |
|---|---|
| Fair market value of plan assets at end of year | $525,000 |
| Add back benefits paid | 85,000 |
| Less: | |
|   Employer contributions | (110,000) |
|   FMV, beginning of year | (350,000) |
| Actual return | $150,000 |

**89.** /a/ The attribution period to record the employer's obligation for postretirement health benefits extends from the date of hire (or some other date specified by the plan) to the date on which the employee is fully eligible to receive the benefits. Note that this is not necessarily retirement date.

**90.** /a/ The inflation component specifically relating to inventories is the amount by which the current cost of inventories exceeds the constant dollars amount, $15,000 less $12,000.

**91.** /c/ Only Option C allows for both specific price changes (current cost) and general price-level changes (constant dollar).

**92.** /d/ The amount of the loss is equal to the number of foreign currency units (10,000) X the change in spot rates from September 22 to December 31, ($.55 - $.70) = $1,500

# CHAPTER 5

## SPECIAL TOPICS: PENSIONS; OPEB; ALTERNATIVE FINANCIAL ACCOUNTING MODELS; FOREIGN EXCHANGE; AND SEGMENT REPORTING

### Simulation Answers

**Number 1 Answer**

1. /$48,000/ Beginning balance of projected benefit obligation x discount rate = interest cost.

   $600,000 x 8% = $48,000

2. /$72,000/ Beginning balance of fair value of plan assets x expected rate of return = expected return on plan assets.
   $720,000 x 10% = $72,000

3. /$105,000/ Ending fair value of plan assets - beginning balance - contributions added + benefits paid = actual return on plan assets.
   $825,000 - $720,000 - 0 + 0 = $105,000

4. /$20,000/ When prior service cost is amortized using the straight-line method, the average service life of existing employees is the maximum period permitted.

   $240,000 unrecognized cost 1/1/x1 ÷ average service life of 12 years = $20,000

5. /$2,000/ The computation of the amount to be amortized requires use of the "corridor" approach.

   - Step 1. Determine 10% of the greater of projected benefit obligation or fair value of plan assets as of 1/1/x1. Plan assets is greater. $720,000 x 10% = $72,000, (corridor amount).

   - Step 2. Determine the excess of unrecognized prior pension gain as of the beginning of the period over the corridor amount computed in Step 1. $96,000 - $72,000 = $24,000

   - Step 3. Calculate the amount to be amortized based on the average remaining service life of employees. $24,000 -:- 12 years = $2,000

6. /I/ Service cost represents the actuarial present value of the benefits earned relating to the current service period.

7. /I/ Any gain deferred is not available to reduce the current period's pension cost. Its amortization in later periods will reduce future pension costs. (See example in text.)

**8.** /D/    As described in ASC Topic 715, actual return on plan assets is a subtraction in the determination of periodic pension cost. However, any actual return in excess of expected return would be added back to the pension cost, and any actual return less than expected return would be additionally subtracted. The net effect of this adjustment results in the decrease in the pension cost for the period being equal to the expected return. Excess or deficient return amounts are deferred and amortized in future periods.

**9.** /I/    Prior service costs are additional costs incurred relating to prior service periods when an existing plan is amended. Amortization over the remaining service lives of existing employees increases pension cost.

**10.** /D/    Amortization of unrecognized pension gain reduces pension costs. Such gains arise as a result of actual returns on plan assets exceeding expected returns and also from changes in actuarial assumptions. Amortization amounts are based on the "corridor" approach method (see Answer No. 5 above).

## Question Map

# CHAPTER 6

## OWNERS' EQUITY AND PARTNERSHIP ACCOUNTING

### Multiple Choice Questions

**1.** Following is the condensed balance sheet of Fine Products, an individual proprietorship, at December 31:

| | |
|---|---|
| Current assets | $100,000 |
| Equipment | 200,000 |
| Accumulated depreciation | (120,000) |
| | $180,000 |
| | |
| Liabilities | $ 40,000 |
| Silvia Fine, Capital | 140,000 |
| | $180,000 |

Fair market values of assets at December 31 were as follows:

| | |
|---|---|
| Current assets | $110,000 |
| Equipment | 290,000 |

The liabilities were fairly stated at book values. On January 2 of the following year, the proprietorship was incorporated, with 2,000 shares of $20 par value common stock issued. How much should be credited to additional paid-in capital?

- **a.** $100,000
- **b.** $140,000
- **c.** $320,000
- **d.** $360,000

**2.** On March 1, Rya Corp. issued 1,000 shares of its $20 par value common stock and 2,000 shares of its $20 par value convertible preferred stock for a total of $80,000. At this date, Rya's common stock was selling for $36 per share, and the convertible preferred stock was selling for $27 per share. What amount of the proceeds should be allocated to Rya's convertible preferred stock?

- **a.** $60,000
- **b.** $54,000

- **c.** $48,000
- **d.** $44,000

**3.** Beck Corp. issued 200,000 shares of common stock when it began operations in 20x1 and issued an additional 100,000 shares in 20x2. Beck also issued preferred stock convertible to 100,000 shares of common stock. In 20x3, Beck purchased 75,000 shares of its common stock and held it in Treasury. At December 31, 20x3, how many shares of Beck's common stock were outstanding?

- **a.** 400,000
- **b.** 325,000
- **c.** 300,000
- **d.** 225,000

**4.** Earl was engaged by Farm Corp. to perform consulting services. Earl's compensation for these services consisted of 1,000 shares of Farm's $10 par value common stock, to be issued to Earl on completion of Earl's services. On the execution date of Earl's employment contract, Farm's stock had a market value of $40 per share. Six months later, when Earl's services were completed and the stock issued, the stock's market value was $50 per share. Farm's management estimated that Earl's services were worth $100,000 in cost savings to the company. As a result of this transaction, additional paid-in capital should increase by

- **a.** $100,000
- **b.** $ 90,000
- **c.** $ 40,000
- **d.** $ 30,000

**5.** How should the excess of the subscription price over the par value of common stock subscribed be recorded?

- **a.** As additional paid-in capital when the subscription is received.
- **b.** As additional paid-in capital when the subscription is collected.
- **c.** As retained earnings when the subscription is received.
- **d.** As additional paid-in capital when the capital stock is issued.

**6.** The Amlin Corporation was incorporated on January 1, 20x1, with the following authorized capitalization:

20,000 shares of common stock, no par value, stated value $40 per share.

5,000 shares of 5% cumulative preferred stock, par value $10 per share.

During 20x1 Amlin issued 12,000 shares of common stock for a total of $600,000 and 3,000 shares of preferred stock at $16 per share. In addition, on December 20, 20x1, subscriptions for 1,000 shares of preferred stock were taken at a purchase price of $17. These subscribed shares were paid for on January 2, 20x2. What should Amlin report as total contributed capital on its December 31, 20x1, balance sheet?
   a. $520,000
   b. $648,000
   c. $665,000
   d. $850,000

**7.** In 20x0, Fogg, Inc. issued $10 par value common stock for $25 per share. No other common stock transactions occurred until March 31, 20x2, when Fogg acquired some of the issued shares for $20 per share and retired them. Which of the following statements correctly states an effect of this acquisition and retirement?
   a. 20x2 net income is decreased.
   b. 20x2 net income is increased.
   c. Additional paid-in capital is decreased.
   d. Retained earnings is increased.

**8.** Cross Corp. had outstanding 2,000 shares of 11% preferred stock, $50 par. On August 8, Cross redeemed and retired 25% of these shares for $22,500. On that date, Cross' additional paid-in capital from preferred stock totaled $30,000. To record this transaction, Cross should debit (credit) its capital accounts as follows:

| | Preferred stock | Additional paid-in Capital | Retained Earnings |
|---|---|---|---|
| a. | $25,000 | $7,500 | ($10,000) |
| b. | $25,000 | ------ | (2,500) |
| c. | $25,000 | ($2,500) | ------ |
| D. | $22,500 | ------ | ------ |

**9.** The following accounts were among those reported on Luna Corp's balance sheet at December 31:

| | |
|---|---|
| Marketable securities (Market value $140,000) | $ 80,000 |
| Preferred stock, $20 par value 20,000 shares issued & outstanding | 400,000 |
| Additional paid-in capital on preferred stock | 30,000 |
| Retained earnings | 900,000 |

On January 20 of the following year, Luna exchanged all of the marketable securities for 5,000 shares of Luna's preferred stock. Market values at the date of the exchange were $150,000 for the marketable securities and $30 per share for the preferred stock. The 5,000 shares of preferred stock were retired immediately after the exchange. Which of the following journal entries should Luna record in connection with this transaction?

a.
| | |
|---|---|
| Preferred stock | 100,000 |
| APIC-Preferred | 7,500 |
| Retained earnings | 42,500 |
|    Marketable securities | 80,000 |
|    Gain on exchange of securities | 70,000 |

b.
| | |
|---|---|
| Preferred stock | 100,000 |
| APIC - preferred | 30,000 |
|    Marketable securities | 80,000 |
|    APIC from retirement of preferred stock | 50,000 |

c.
| | |
|---|---|
| Preferred stock | 150,000 |
|    Marketable securities | 80,000 |
|    APIC - preferred | 70,000 |

d.
| | |
|---|---|
| Preferred stock | 150,000 |
|    Marketable securities | 80,000 |
|    Gain on exchange of securities | 70,000 |

**10.** The stockholders' equity section of Peter Corporation's balance sheet at December 31 was as follows:

| | |
|---|---|
| Common stock ($10 par value, authorized 1,000,000 shares, issued and outstanding 900,000 shares) | $ 9,000,000 |
| Additional paid-in capital | 2,700,000 |
| Retained earnings | 1,300,000 |
| Total stockholders' equity | $13,000,000 |

On January 2 of the next year Peter purchased and retired 100,000 shares of its stock for $1,800,000. Immediately after retirement of these 100,000 shares, the balances in the additional paid-in capital and retained earnings accounts should be

| | Additional Paid-in Capital | Retained Earnings |
|---|---|---|
| **a.** | $ 900,000 | $1,300,000 |
| **b.** | $1,900,000 | $1,300,000 |
| **c.** | $1,400,000 | $ 800,000 |
| **d.** | $2,400,000 | $ 800,000 |

**11.** Georgia, Inc., has an authorized capital of 1,000 shares of $100 par, 8% cumulative preferred stock and 100,000 shares of $10 par common stock. The equity account balances at December 31 are as follows:

| | |
|---|---|
| Cumulative preferred stock | $ 50,000 |
| Common stock | 90,000 |
| Additional paid-in capital | 9,000 |
| Retained earnings | 13,000 |
| Treasury stock, common 100 shares at cost | (2,000) |
| | $160,000 |

Dividends on preferred stock are in arrears for the year. The book value of a share of common stock, at December 31 should be
- **a.** $11.78.
- **b.** $11.91.
- **c.** $12.22.
- **d.** $12.36.

**12.** Ventura Corporation was organized on January 1 with the following capital structure:

| | |
|---|---|
| 10% cumulative preferred stock, par and liquidation value $100; authorized, issued, and outstanding 1,000 shares | $100,000 |
| Common stock, par value $5; authorized 20,000 shares; issued and outstanding 10,000 shares | 50,000 |

Ventura's net income for the year ended December 31 was $450,000, but no dividends were declared. How much was Ventura's book value per common share at December 31?
- **a.** $44
- **b.** $45
- **c.** $49
- **d.** $50

**13.** Boe Corp,'s stockholders' equity at December 31 was as follows:

| | |
|---|---|
| 6% noncumulative preferred stock, $100 par (liquidation value $105 per share) | $100,000 |
| Common stock, $10 par | 300,000 |
| Retained earnings | 95,000 |

At December 31, Boe's book value per common share was
- **a.** $13.17
- **b.** $13.00
- **c.** $12.97
- **d.** $12.80

**14.** On December 1, Line Corp. received a donation of 2,000 shares of its $5 par value common stock from a stockholder. On that date, the stock's market value was $35 per share. The stock was originally issued for $25 per share. By what amount would this donation cause total stockholders' equity to decrease?
- **a.** $70,000
- **b.** $50,000
- **c.** $20,000
- **d.** $0

**15.** Pine City owned a vacant plot of land zoned for industrial use. Pine gave this land to Medi Corp. solely as an incentive for Medi to build a factory on the site. The land had a fair value of $300,000 at the date of the gift. This non-monetary transaction should be reported as
   a. Extraordinary income.
   b. Additional paid-in capital.
   c. A credit to retained earnings.
   d. A memorandum entry.

**16.** On March 31, Ashley, Inc.'s bondholders exchanged their convertible bonds for common stock. The carrying amount of these bonds on Ashley's books was less than the market value but greater than the par value of the common stock issued. If Ashley used the book value method of accounting for the conversion, which of the following statements correctly states an effect of this conversion?
   a. Stockholders' equity is increased.
   b. Additional paid-in capital is decreased.
   c. Retained earnings is increased.
   d. An extraordinary loss is recognized.

**17.** On December 31, 20x1, Dumont Corporation had outstanding 8%, $2,000,000 face value convertible bonds maturing on December 31, 20x5. Interest is payable annually on December 31. Each $1,000 bond is convertible into 60 shares of Dumont's $10 par value common stock. The unamortized balance on December 31, 20x2, in the premium on bonds payable account was $45,000. On December 31, 20x2, an individual holding 200 of the bonds exercised the conversion privilege when the market value of Dumont's common stock was $18 per share. Using the book value method, Dumont's entry to record the conversion should include a credit to additional paid-in capital of
   a. $ 80,000.
   b. $ 84,500.
   c. $ 96,000.
   d. $125,000.

**18.** In 20x1, Orlando, Inc., issued for $105 per share, 8,000 shares of $100 par value convertible preferred stock. One share of preferred stock can be converted into three shares of Orlando's $25 par value common stock at the option of the preferred shareholder. In August 20x2, all of the preferred stock was converted into common stock. The market value of the common stock at the date of the conversion was $30 per share. What total amount should be credited to additional paid-in capital as a result of the issuance of the preferred stock and its subsequent conversion into common stock?
   a. $ 80,000
   b. $120,000
   c. $200,000
   d. $240,000

**19.** During 20x0 Bradley Corporation issued for $110 per share, 5,000 shares of $100 par value convertible preferred stock. One share of preferred stock can be converted into three shares of Bradley's $25 par value common stock at the option of the preferred shareholder. On December 31, 20x1, all of the preferred stock was converted into common stock. The market value of the common stock at the conversion date was $40 per share. What amount should be credited to the common stock account on December 31, 20x1?
   a. $375,000
   b. $500,000
   c. $550,000
   d. $600,000

**20.** On January 2, 20x1, Air, Inc. agreed to pay its former president $300,000 under a deferred compensation arrangement. Air should have recorded this expense in 20x0 but did not do so. Air's reported income tax expense would have been $70,000 lower in 20x0 had it properly accrued this deferred compensation. In its December 31, 20x1, financial statements, Air should adjust the beginning balance of its retained earnings by a
   a. $230,000 credit.
   b. $230,000 debit.
   c. $300,000 credit.
   d. $370,000 debit.

**21.** On September 1, Hyde Corp., a newly formed company, had the following stock issued and outstanding:

- Common stock, no par, $1 stated value, 5,000 shares originally issued for $15 per share.
- Preferred stock, $10 par value, 1,500 shares originally issued for $25 per share.

Hyde's September 1 statement of stockholders' equity should report

|     | Common Stock | Preferred stock | Additional paid-in capital |
| --- | --- | --- | --- |
| a.  | $ 5,000 | $15,000 | $92,500 |
| b.  | $ 5,000 | $37,500 | $70,000 |
| c.  | $75,000 | $36,500 | $0 |
| d.  | $75,000 | $15,000 | $22,500 |

**22.** Zinc Co.'s adjusted trial balance at December 31 includes the following account balances:

| | |
| --- | --- |
| Common stock, $3 par | $600,000 |
| Additional paid-in capital | 800,000 |
| Treasury stock, at cost | 50,000 |
| Net unrealized loss on noncurrent marketable equity securities | 20,000 |
| Retained earnings: appropriated for uninsured earthquake losses | 150,000 |
| Retained earnings: unappropriated | 200,000 |

What amount should Zinc report as total stockholders' equity in its December 31 balance sheet?
   a. $1,680,000
   b. $1,720,000
   c. $1,780,000
   d. $1,820,000

**23.** At December 31, 20x1, Eagle Corp. reported $1,750,000 of appropriated retained earnings for the construction of a new office building, which was completed in 20x2 at a total cost of $1,500,000. In 20x2, Eagle appropriated $1,200,000 of retained earnings for the construction of a new plant. Also, $2,000,000 of cash was restricted for the retirement of bonds due in 20x3. In its 20x2

balance sheet, Eagle should report what amount of appropriated retained earnings?
   a. $1,200,000
   b. $1,450,000
   c. $2,950,000
   d. $3,200,000

**24.** The following information pertains to Meg Corp:

- Dividends on its 1,000 shares of 6%, $10 par value cumulative preferred stock have not been declared or paid for 3 years.
- Treasury stock that cost $15,000 was reissued for $8,000.

What amount of retained earnings should be appropriated as a result of these items?
   a. $0
   b. $1,800
   c. $7,000
   d. $8,800

**25.** Bal Corp. declared a $25,000 cash dividend on May 8 to stockholders of record on May 23, payable on June 3. As a result of this cash dividend, working capital
   a. Was not affected.
   b. Decreased on June 3.
   c. Decreased on May 23.
   d. Decreased on May 8.

**26.** At December 31, 20x1 and 20x2, Carr Corp. had outstanding 4,000 shares of $100 par value 6% cumulative preferred stock and 20,000 shares of $10 par value common stock. At December 31, 20x1, dividends in arrears on the preferred stock were $12,000. Cash dividends declared in 20x2 totaled $44,000. Of the $44,000, what amounts were payable on each class of stock?

|     | Preferred stock | Common stock |
| --- | --- | --- |
| a.  | $44,000 | $0 |
| b.  | $36,000 | $ 8,000 |
| c.  | $32,000 | $12,000 |
| d.  | $24,000 | $20,000 |

**27.** Arp Corp.'s outstanding capital stock at December 15 consisted of the following:

- 30,000 shares of 5% cumulative preferred stock, par value $10 per share, fully participating as to dividends. No dividends were in arrears.
- 200,000 shares of common stock, par value $1 per share.

On December 15, Arp declared dividends of $100,000. What was the amount of dividends payable to Arp's common stockholders?
- a. $10,000
- b. $34,000
- c. $40,000
- d. $47,500

**28.** Cash dividends on the $10 par value common stock of Ray Company were as follows:

| | |
|---|---|
| 1st quarter | $ 800,000 |
| 2nd quarter | 900,000 |
| 3rd quarter | 1,000,000 |
| 4th quarter | 1,100,000 |

The 4th quarter cash dividend was declared on December 20, to stockholders of record on December 31. Payment of the 4th quarter cash dividend was made on January 9 of the following year. In addition, Ray declared a 5% stock dividend on its $10 par value common stock on December 1, when there were 300,000 shares issued and outstanding and the market value of the common stock was $20 per share. The shares were issued on December 21. What was the effect on Ray's stockholders' equity accounts as a result of the above transactions?

| | Common Stock | Additional Paid-in Capital | Retained Earnings |
|---|---|---|---|
| a. | $ - 0 - | $ - 0 - | $3,800,000 dr |
| b. | $150,000 cr | $ - 0 - | $3,950,000 dr |
| c. | $150,000 cr | $150,000 cr | $4,100,000 dr |
| d. | $300,000 cr | $300,000 dr | $3,800,000 dr |

**29.** On June 27, Brite Co. distributed to its common stockholders 100,000 outstanding common shares of its investment in Quik, Inc., an unrelated party. The carrying amount on Brite's books of Quik's $1 par common stock was $2 per share. Immediately after the distribution, the market price of Quik's stock was $2.50 per share. In its income statement for the year ended June 30, what amount should Brite report as gain before income taxes on disposal of the stock?
- a. $250,000
- b. $200,000
- c. $ 50,000
- d. $0

**30.** On December 1, Nilo Corp. declared a property dividend of marketable securities to be distributed on December 31 to stockholders of record on December 15. On December 1, the marketable securities had a carrying amount of $60,000 and a fair value of $78,000. What is the effect of this property dividend on Nilo's retained earnings for the year, after all nominal accounts are closed?
- a. $0
- b. $18,000 increase
- c. $60,000 decrease
- d. $78,000 decrease

**31.** A property dividend should be debited to retained earnings at the property's
- a. Market value at date of declaration.
- b. Market value at date of issuance (payment).
- c. Book value at date of declaration.
- d. Book value at date of issuance (payment).

**32.** Ray Corp. declared a 5% stock dividend on its 10,000 issued and outstanding shares of $2 par value common stock, which had a fair value of $5 per share before the stock dividend was declared. This stock dividend was distributed 60 days after the declaration date. By what amount did Ray's current liabilities increase as a result of the stock dividend declaration?
- a. $0
- b. $ 500
- c. $1,000
- d. $2,500

**33.** On May 18, Sol Corp.'s board of directors declared a 10% stock dividend. The market price of Sol's 3,000 outstanding shares of $2 par value common stock was $9 per share on that date. The stock dividend was distributed on July 21, when the stock's market price was $10 per share. What amount should Sol credit to additional paid-in capital for this stock dividend?

    **a.** $2,100
    **b.** $2,400
    **c.** $2,700
    **d.** $3,000

**34.** The following stock dividends were declared and distributed by Sol. Corp:

| Percentage of shares outstanding at declaration date | Fair value | Par value |
|---|---|---|
| 10 | $15,000 | $10,000 |
| 28 | $40,000 | $30,800 |

What aggregate amount should be debited to retained earnings for these stock dividends?

    **a.** $40,800
    **b.** $45,800
    **c.** $50,000
    **d.** $55,000

**35.** The stockholders' equity of Slumber Company at July 31 is presented below:

| | |
|---|---|
| Common stock; par value $20; authorized 400,000 shares; issued and outstanding 150,000 shares | $3,000,000 |
| Capital in excess of par value | 140,000 |
| Retained earnings | 390,000 |
| | $3,530,000 |

On August 1 the board of directors of Slumber declared a 4% stock dividend on common stock, to be distributed on September 15th. The market price of Slumber's common stock was $35 on August 1 and $40 on September 15. What is the amount of the charge to retained earnings as a result of the declaration and distribution of this stock dividend?

    **a.** $0
    **b.** $120,000
    **c.** $210,000
    **d.** $240,000

**36.** Sprint Company has 1,000,000 shares of common stock authorized with a par value of $3 per share, of which 600,000 shares are outstanding. When the market value was $8 per share, Sprint issued a stock dividend whereby for each six shares held one share was issued as a stock dividend. The par value of the stock was not changed. What entry should Sprint make to record this transaction?

**a.** Retained earnings    300,000
    Common stock              300,000

**b.** Additional paid-in capital    300,000
    Common stock              300,000

**c.** Retained earnings    800,000
    Common stock              300,000
    Additional paid-in capital      500,000

**d.** Additional paid-in capital    800,000
    Common stock              300,000
    Retained earnings          500,000

**37.** The dollar amount of total stockholders' equity remains the same when there is a (an)

    **a.** Issuance of preferred stock in exchange for convertible debentures.
    **b.** Issuance of nonconvertible bonds with detachable stock purchase warrants.
    **c.** Declaration of a stock dividend.
    **d.** Declaration of a cash dividend.

**38.** The following information was abstracted from the accounts of the Oar Corporation at December 31:

| | |
|---|---|
| Total income since incorporation | $840,000 |
| Total cash dividends paid | 260,000 |
| Proceeds from sale of donated stock | $ 90,000 |
| Total value of stock dividends distributed | 60,000 |
| Excess of proceeds over cost of treasury stock sold | 140,000 |

What should be the current balance of retained earnings?
a. $520,000
b. $580,000
c. $610,000
d. $670,000

**39.** What is the most likely effect of a stock split on the par value per share and the number of shares outstanding?

| | Par Value per Share | Number of Shares Outstanding |
|---|---|---|
| a. | Decrease | Increase |
| b. | Decrease | No effect |
| c. | Increase | Increase |
| d. | No effect | No effect |

**40.** On July 1, Alto Corp. split its common stock 5 for 1 when the market value was $100 per share. Prior to the split, Alto had 10,000 shares of $10 par value common stock issued and outstanding. After the split the par value of the stock
a. Remained at $10
b. Was reduced to $8
c. Was reduced to $5
d. Was reduced to $2

**41.** How would a stock split in which the par value per share decreases in proportion to the number of additional shares issued affect each of the following?

| | Additional paid-in capital | Retained Earnings |
|---|---|---|
| a. | Increase | No effect |
| b. | No effect | No effect |
| c. | No effect | Decrease |
| d. | Increase | Decrease |

**42.** Ole Corp. declared and paid a liquidating dividend of $100,000. This distribution resulted in a decrease in Ole's

| | Paid-in capital | Retained earnings |
|---|---|---|
| a. | No | No |
| b. | Yes | Yes |
| c. | No | Yes |
| d. | Yes | No |

**43.** Assume the cost method of accounting for treasury stock transactions is used. Any excess of the amount received upon resale over the price paid for the treasury stock should be shown as an
a. Increase in additional paid-in capital.
b. Increase in retained earnings.
c. Element of operating income.
d. Extraordinary gain.

**44.** The stockholders' equity section of Sola Corporation as of December 31 was as follows:

| | |
|---|---|
| Common stock, $20 par value, authorized 150,000 shares, issued and outstanding 100,000 shares | $2,000,000 |
| Capital in excess of par value | 400,000 |
| Retained earnings | 200,000 |
| | $2,600,000 |

On March 1 Sola reacquired 10,000 shares for $240,000. The following transactions occurred during the year with respect to treasury stock acquired:

Jun 1  Sold 3,000 shares for $84,000.
Aug 1  Sold 2,000 shares for $42,000.
Sep 1  Retired remaining 5,000 shares.

Sola accounts for treasury stock on the cost method. As a result of these transactions
a. Stockholders' equity remained unchanged.
b. Common stock decreased $100,000 and retained earnings decreased $14,000.
c. Common stock decreased $100,000 and capital in excess of par decreased $14,000.
d. Common stock decreased $126,000.

**45.** Grid Corp. acquired some of its own common shares at a price greater than both their par value and original issue price but less than their book value. Grid uses the cost method of accounting for treasury stock. What is the impact of this acquisition on total stockholders' equity and the book value per common share?

| | Total stockholders' equity | Book value per share |
|---|---|---|
| a. | Increase | Increase |
| b. | Increase | Decrease |
| c. | Decrease | Increase |
| d. | Decrease | Decrease |

**46** On December 31, Pack Corp.'s board of directors canceled 50,000 shares of $2.50 par value common stock held in treasury at an average cost of $13 per share. Before recording the cancellation of the treasury stock, Pack had the following balances in its stockholders' equity accounts:

| | |
|---|---|
| Common stock | $540,000 |
| Additional paid-in capital | 750,000 |
| Retained earnings | 900,000 |
| Treasury stock, at cost | 650,000 |

In its December 31 balance sheet, Pack should report common stock outstanding of
a. $0
b. $250,000
c. $415,000
d. $540,000

**47.** At December 31, 20x1, Rama Corp. had 20,000 shares of $1 par value treasury stock that had been acquired during the year at $12 per share. In May of 20x2, Rama issued 15,000 of these treasury shares at $10 per share. The cost method is used to record treasury stock transactions. Rama is located in a state where laws relating to acquisition of treasury stock restrict the availability of retained earnings for declaration of dividends. At December 31, 20x2, what amount should Rama show in notes to financial statements as a restriction on retained earnings as a result of its treasury stock transactions?

a. $ 5,000
b. $10,000
c. $60,000
d. $90,000

**48.** Posy Corp. acquired treasury shares at an amount greater than their par value, but less than their original issue price. Compared to the cost method of accounting for treasury stock, does the par value method report a greater amount for additional paid-in capital and a greater amount of retained earnings?

| | Additional paid-in capital | Retained earnings |
|---|---|---|
| a. | Yes | Yes |
| b. | Yes | No |
| c. | No | No |
| d. | No | Yes |

**49.** Treasury stock was acquired for cash at a price in excess of its original issue price. The treasury stock was subsequently reissued for cash at a price in excess of its acquisition price. Assuming that the par value method of accounting for treasury stock transactions is used, what is the effect on total stockholders' equity of each of the following events?

| | Acquisition of treasury stock | Reissuance of treasury stock |
|---|---|---|
| a. | Decrease | No effect |
| b. | Decrease | Increase |
| c. | Increase | Decrease |
| d. | No effect | No effect |

**50.** On July 1 Round Company issued for $525,000 a total of 5,000 shares of $100 par value, 7% noncumulative preferred stock along with one detachable warrant for each share issued. Each warrant contains a right to purchase one share of Round's $10 par value common stock for $15 a share. The market price of the rights on July 1 was $2.25 per right. On October 31 when the market price of the common stock was $19 per share and the market value of the rights was $3.00 per right, 4,000 rights were exercised. As a result of the exercise of the 4,000 rights and the issuance of the related common stock, what journal entry would Round make?

| | | Debit | Credit |
|---|---|---|---|
| **a.** | Cash | $60,000 | |
| | Common stock | | $40,000 |
| | Additional paid-in capital | | 20,000 |
| **b.** | Cash | 60,000 | |
| | Common stock rights outstanding | 9,000 | |
| | Common stock | | 40,000 |
| | Additional paid-in capital | | 29,000 |
| **c.** | Cash | 60,000 | |
| | Common stock rights outstanding | 12,000 | |
| | Common stock | | 40,000 |
| | Additional paid-in capital | | 32,000 |
| **d.** | Cash | 60,000 | |
| | Common stock rights outstanding | 16,000 | |
| | Common stock | | 40,000 |
| | Additional paid-in capital | 36,000 |

**51.** Which of the following is issued to shareholders by a corporation as evidence of the ownership of rights to acquire its unissued or treasury stock?
 a. Stock options.
 b. Stock warrants.
 c. Stock dividends.
 d. Stock subscriptions.

**52.** On July 1, Vail Corp. issued rights to stockholders to subscribe to additional shares of its common stock. One right was issued for each share owned. A stockholder could purchase one additional share for 10 rights plus $15 cash. The rights expired on September 30 of the same year. On July 1, the market price of a share with the right attached was $40, while the market price of one right alone was $2. Vail's stockholders' equity on June 30 comprised the following:

| | |
|---|---|
| Common stock, $25 par value, 4,000 shares issued and outstanding | $100,000 |
| Additional paid-in capital | 60,000 |
| Retained earnings | 80,000 |

By what amount should Vail's retained earnings decrease as a result of issuance of the stock rights on July 1?
 a. $0
 b. $ 5,000
 c. $ 8,000
 d. $10,000

**53.** Tem Co. issued rights to its existing stockholders without consideration. A stockholder received a right to buy one share for each 20 shares held. The exercise price was in excess of par value, but less than the current market price. Retained earnings decreases when

| | Rights are issued | Rights are exercised |
|---|---|---|
| a. | Yes | Yes |
| b. | Yes | No |
| c. | No | Yes |
| d. | No | No |

**54.** A company issued rights to its existing shareholders to purchase, for $30 per share, 10,000 unissued shares of $15 par value common stock. When the rights are exercised
 a. Additional paid-in capital will be debited.
 b. Additional paid-in capital will be credited
 c. Stock rights outstanding will be debited.
 d. Retained earnings will be debited.

Course 5292 Copyright 2021. The Rigos programs have educated over 100,000 professionals since 1980.

**55.** Quoit, Inc. issued preferred stock with detachable common stock warrants. The issue price exceeded the sums of the warrants' fair value and the preferred stocks' par value. The preferred stocks' fair value was not determinable. What amount should be assigned to the warrants outstanding?

a. Total proceeds.
b. Excess of proceeds over the par value of the preferred stock.
c. The proportion of the proceeds that the warrants' fair value bears to the preferred stocks' par value.
d. The fair value of the warrants.

**56.** On January 1, Ward Corp. granted stock options to corporate executives for the purchase of 20,000 shares of the company's $20 par value common stock at 80% of the market price on the exercise date, December 28 of the same year. All stock options were exercised on December 28. The quoted market prices of Ward's $20 par value common stock were as follows:

| | |
|---|---|
| January 1 | $45 |
| December 28 | $60 |

As a result of the exercise of the stock options and the issuance of the common stock, Ward should record a credit to additional paid-in capital of

a. $800,000
b. $740,000
c. $560,000
d. $500,000

**Questions 57 and 58 are based on the following information:**

The Gaston Company has sustained heavy losses over a period of time and conditions warrant that Gaston undergo a quasi-reorganization at December 31. Selected balance sheet items prior to the quasi-reorganization are as follows:

• Inventory was recorded in the accounting records at December 31 at its market value of $6,000,000. Cost was $6,500,000.

• Property, plant and equipment was recorded in the accounting records at December 31 at $12,000,000, net of accumulated depreciation. The appraised value was $8,000,000.

• Stockholders' equity on December 31 was as follows:

| | |
|---|---|
| Common stock, par value $10 per share; authorized, issued and outstanding, 700,000 shares | $7,000,000 |
| Capital in excess of par | 1,600,000 |
| Retained earnings (deficit) | (900,000) |
| | $7,700,000 |

• Under the terms of the quasi-reorganization, the par value of the common stock is to be reduced from $10 per share to $5 per share.

**57.** Immediately after the quasi-reorganization has been accomplished, the total of stockholders' equity should be

a. $3,300,000.
b. $3,500,000.
c. $3,700,000.
d. $4,200,000.

**58.** Immediately after the quasi-reorganization has been accomplished, retained earnings (deficit) should be

a. $0.
b. $(200,000).
c. $(4,400,000).
d. $(4,900,000).

**59.** When a company goes through a quasi-reorganization, its balance sheet carrying amounts are stated at

a. Original cost.
b. Original book value.
c. Replacement value.
d. Fair value.

**60.** Roberts and Smith drafted a partnership agreement that lists the following assets contributed at the partnership formation:

|  | Contributed by | |
|---|---|---|
|  | Roberts | Smith |
| Cash | $20,000 | $30,000 |
| Inventory | – | 15,000 |
| Building | – | 40,000 |
| Furniture & Equipment | 15,000 | – |

The building is subject to a mortgage of $10,000, which the partnership has assumed. The partnership agreement also specifies that profits and losses are to be distributed evenly. What amounts should be recorded as capital for Roberts and Smith at the formation of the partnership?

|  | Roberts | Smith |
|---|---|---|
| a. | $35,000 | $85,000 |
| b. | $35,000 | $75,000 |
| c. | $55,000 | $55,000 |
| d. | $60,000 | $60,000 |

**61.** Algee, Belger, and Ceda formed a partnership by combining their separate business proprietorships. Algee contributed cash of $50,000. Belger contributed property with a $36,000 carrying amount, a $40,000 original cost, and $80,000 fair value. The partnership accepted responsibility for the $35,000 mortgage attached to the property. Ceda contributed equipment with a $30,000 carrying amount, a $75,000 original cost, and $55,000 fair value. The partnership agreement specifies that profits and losses are to be shared equally but is silent regarding capital contributions. Which partner has the largest capital balance upon formation of the partnership?
  a. Algee.
  b. Belger.
  c. Ceda.
  d. All capital account balances are equal.

**62.** Abel and Carr formed a partnership and agreed to divide capital equally, even though Abel contributed $100,000 and Carr contributed $84,000 in identifiable assets. Under the bonus approach to adjust the capital accounts, Carr's unidentifiable asset should be debited for
  a. $46,000
  b. $16,000
  c. $8,000
  d. $0

**63.** Four individuals who were previously sole proprietors form a partnership. Each partner contributes inventory and equipment for use by the partnership. What basis should the partnership use to record the contributed assets?
  a. Inventory at the lower of FIFO cost or market.
  b. Inventory at the lower of weighted average cost or market.
  c. Equipment at each proprietor's carrying amount.
  d. Equipment at fair value

**64.** Hayes and Jenkins formed a partnership, each contributing assets to the business. Hayes contributed inventory with a current market value in excess of its carrying amount. Jenkins contributed real estate with a carrying amount in excess of its current market value. At what amount should the partnership record each of the following assets?

|  | Inventory | Real estate |
|---|---|---|
| a. | Market value | Market value |
| b. | Market value | Carrying amount |
| c. | Carrying amount | Market value |
| d. | Carrying amount | Carrying amount |

**65.** On May 1, Cobb and Mott formed a partnership and agreed to share profits and losses in the ratio of 3:7, respectively. Cobb contributed a parcel of land that cost him $10,000. Mott contributed $40,000 cash. The land was sold for $18,000 on May 1, immediately after formation of the partnership. What amount should be recorded in Cobb's capital account on formation of the partnership?
  a. $18,000
  b. $17,400
  c. $15,000
  d. $10,000

**Questions 66 and 67 are based on the following information:**

Cor-Eng Partnership was formed on January 2. Under the partnership agreement, each partner has an equal initial capital balance accounted for under the goodwill method. Partnership net income or loss is allocated 60% to Cor and 40% to Eng. To form the partnership, Cor originally contributed assets costing $30,000 with a fair value of $60,000 on January 2, while Eng contributed $20,000 in cash. Drawings by the partners during the year totaled $3,000 by Cor and $9,000 by Eng. Cor-Eng's net income for the first year of operations was $25,000.

**66.** Eng's initial capital balance in Cor-Eng is
   **a.** $20,000
   **b.** $25,000
   **c.** $40,000
   **d.** $60,000

**67.** Cor's share of Cor-Eng's net income for the first year of operations is
   **a.** $15,000
   **b.** $12,500
   **c.** $12,000
   **d.** $ 7,800

**68.** The partnership agreement of Axel, Berg & Cobb provides for the year-end allocation of net income in the following order:

- First, Axel is to receive 10% of net income up to $100,000 and 20% over $100,000.
- Second, Berg and Cobb each are to receive 5% of the remaining income over $150,000.
- The balance of income is to be allocated equally among the three partners.

The partnership's net income for the year was $250,000 before any allocation to the partners. What amount should be allocated to Axel?

   **a.** $101,000
   **b.** $103,000
   **c.** $108,000
   **d.** $110,000

**69.** The partnership agreement of Reid and Simm provides that interest at 10% per year is to be credited to each partner on the basis of weighted-average capital balances. A summary of Simm's capital account for the year is as follows:

| | |
|---|---|
| Balance, January 1 | $140,000 |
| Additional investment, July 1 | 40,000 |
| Withdrawal, August 1 | (15,000) |
| Balance, December 31 | 165,000 |

What amount of interest should be credited to Simm's capital account for the year?

   **a.** $15,250
   **b.** $15,375
   **c.** $16,500
   **d.** $17,250

**70.** The partnership agreement of Donn, Eddy, and Farr provides for annual distribution of profits or loss in the following sequence:

- Donn, the managing partner, receives a bonus of 10% of profit.
- Each partner receives 6% interest on average capital investment.
- Residual profit or loss is divided equally.

Average capital balances for the year were:

| | |
|---|---|
| Donn | $80,000 |
| Eddy | 50,000 |
| Farr | 30,000 |

What portion of the $100,000 partnership profit for the year should be allocated to Farr?

   **a.** $28,600
   **b.** $29,800
   **c.** $35,133
   **d.** $41,600

**71.** The Flat and Iron partnership agreement provides for Flat to receive a 20% bonus on profits before the bonus. Remaining profits and losses are divided equally between Flat and Iron in the ratio of 2:3, respectively. Which partner has a greater advantage when the partnership has a profit or when it has a loss?

| | Profit | Loss |
|---|---|---|
| **a.** | Flat | Iron |
| **b.** | Flat | Flat |
| **c.** | Iron | Iron |
| **d.** | Iron | Flat |

**72.** The Low and Rhu partnership agreement provides special compensation to Low for managing the business. Low receives a bonus of 15% of partnership net income before salary and bonus, and also receives a salary of $45,000. Any remaining profit or loss is to be allocated equally. During the year, the partnership had net income of $50,000 before the bonus and salary allowance. As a result of these distributions, Rhu's equity in the partnership would

- **a.** Increase.
- **b.** Not change.
- **c.** Decrease the same as Low's.
- **d.** Decrease.

**73.** Beck, the active partner in Beck & Cris, receives an annual bonus of 25% of partnership net income after deducting the bonus. Partnership net income before the bonus amounted to $300,000 for the year ended December 31. Beck's bonus for the year should be

- **a.** $56,250
- **b.** $60,000
- **c.** $62,500
- **d.** $75,000

**74.** The capital accounts of the partnership of Newton, Sharman, and Jackson on June 1 are presented below, with their respective profit and loss ratios:

| | | |
|---|---|---|
| Newton | $139,200 | 1/2 |
| Sharman | 208,800 | 1/3 |
| Jackson | 96,000 | 1/6 |
| | $444,000 | |

On June 1 Sidney was admitted to the partnership when he purchased, for $132,000, a proportionate interest from Newton and Sharman in the net assets and profits of the partnership. As a result of this transaction, Sidney acquired a one-fifth interest in the net assets and profits of the firm. Assuming that implied goodwill is not to be recorded, what is the combined gain realized by Newton and Sharman upon the sale of a portion of their interests in the partnership to Sidney?

- **a.** $0
- **b.** $43,200
- **c.** $62,400
- **d.** $82,000

**75.** The following condensed balance sheet is presented for the partnership of Cooke, Dorry, and Evans who share profits and losses in the ratio of 4:3:3, respectively:

| | |
|---|---|
| Cash | $ 90,000 |
| Other assets | 820,000 |
| Cooke, loan | 30,000 |
| | $940,000 |
| | |
| Accounts payable | $210,000 |
| Evans, loan | 40,000 |
| Cooke, capital | 300,000 |
| Dorry, capital | 200,000 |
| Evans, capital | 190,000 |
| | $940,000 |

Assume that the assets and liabilities are fairly valued on the balance sheet and the partnership decides to admit Fisher as a new partner with a one-fourth interest. No goodwill or bonus is to be recorded. How much should Fisher contribute in cash or other assets?

- **a.** $172,500
- **b.** $175,000
- **c.** $230,000
- **d.** $233,333

**76.** In the Adel-Brick partnership, Adel and Brick had a capital ratio of 3:1 and a profit and loss ratio of 2:1, respectively. The bonus method was used to record Colter's admittance as a new partner. What ratio would be used to allocate, to Adel and Brick, the excess of Colter's contribution over the amount credited to Colter's capital account?

   **a.** Adel and Brick's new relative capital ratio.
   **b.** Adel and Brick's new relative profit and loss ratio.
   **c.** Adel and Brick's old capital ratio.
   **d.** Adel and Brick's old profit and loss ratio.

**77.** Kern and Pate are partners with capital balances of $60,000 and $20,000, respectively. Profits and losses are divided in the ratio of 60:40. Kern and Pate decided to form a new partnership with Grant, who invested land valued at $15,000 for a 20% capital interest. Grant's cost of the land was $12,000. The partnership elected to use the bonus method to record the admission of Grant into the partnership. Grant's capital account should be credited for

   **a.** $12,000
   **b.** $15,000
   **c.** $16,000
   **d.** $19,000

**78.** Blau and Rubi are partners who share profits and losses in the ratio of 6:4, respectively. On May 1, their respective capital accounts were as follows:

| | |
|---|---|
| Blau | $60,000 |
| Rubi | 50,000 |

On that date, Lind was admitted as a partner with a one-third interest in capital and profits for an investment of $40,000. The new partnership began with a total capital of $150,000. Immediately after Lind's admission, Blau's capital should be

   **a.** $50,000
   **b.** $54,000
   **c.** $56,667
   **d.** $60,000

**79.** Dunn and Grey are partners with capital account balances of $60,000 and $90,000, respectively. They agree to admit Zorn as a partner with a one-third interest in capital and profits, for an investment of $100,000, after revaluing the assets of Dunn and Grey. Goodwill to the original partners should be

   **a.** $0
   **b.** $33,333
   **c.** $50,000
   **d.** $66,667

**80.** On June 30, the condensed balance sheet for the partnership of Eddy, Fox, and Grimm, together with their respective profit and loss sharing percentages, was as follows:

| | |
|---|---|
| Assets, net of liabilities | $320,000 |
| | |
| Eddy, capital (50%) | $160,000 |
| Fox, capital (30%) | 96,000 |
| Grimm, capital (20%) | 64,000 |
| | $320,000 |

Hamm is admitted as a new partner with a 25% interest in the capital of the new partnership for a cash payment of $140,000. Total goodwill implicit in the transaction is to be recorded. Immediately after the admission of Hamm, Eddy's capital account balance should be

   **a.** $280,000
   **b.** $210,000
   **c.** $160,000
   **d.** $140,000

**81.** On June 30 the balance sheet for the partnership of Williams, Brown and Lowe together with their respective profit and loss ratios was as follows:

| | |
|---|---|
| Assets, at cost | $300,000 |
| Williams, loan | $ 15,000 |
| Williams, capital (20%) | 70,000 |
| Brown, capital (20%) | 65,000 |
| Lowe, capital (60%) | 150,000 |
| Total | $300,000 |

Williams has decided to retire from the partnership and by mutual agreement the assets are to be adjusted to their fair value of $360,000 at June 30. It was agreed that the partnership would pay Williams $102,000 cash for his partnership interest exclusive of his loan which is to be repaid in full. **No** goodwill is to be recorded in this transaction. After Williams retirement what are the capital account balances of Brown and Lowe, respectively?

a. $65,000 and $150,000
b. $72,000 and $171,000
c. $73,000 and $174,000
d. $77,000 and $186,000

**82.** The partnership of Metcalf, Petersen, and Russell shared profits and losses equally. When Metcalf withdrew from the partnership, the partners agreed that there was unrecorded goodwill in the partnership. Under the bonus method, the capital balances of Petersen and Russell were

a. Not affected.
b. Each reduced by one half of the total amount of the unrecorded goodwill.
c. Each reduced by one third of the total amount of the unrecorded goodwill.
d. Each reduced by one half of Metcalf's share of the total amount of the unrecorded goodwill.

**83.** Allen retired from the partnership of Allen, Beck, and Chale. Allen's cash settlement from the partnership was based on new goodwill determined at the date of retirement plus the carrying amount of the other assets. As a consequence of the settlement, the capital accounts of Beck and Chale were decreased. In accounting for Allen's withdrawal, the partnership could have used the

| | Bonus Method | Goodwill Method |
|---|---|---|
| a. | No | Yes |
| b. | No | No |
| c. | Yes | Yes |
| d. | Yes | No |

**84.** The condensed balance sheet for the partnership of Eddy, Fox, and Grimm, together with their respective profit and loss sharing percentages, was as follows:

| | |
|---|---|
| Assets net of liabilities | $320,000 |
| | |
| Eddy, capital (50%) | $160,000 |
| Fox, capital (30%) | 96,000 |
| Grimm, capital (20%) | 64,000 |
| | $320,000 |

Eddy decided to retire from the partnership and by mutual agreement is to be paid $180,000 out of partnership funds for his interest. Total goodwill implicit in the agreement is to be recorded. After Eddy's retirement, what are the capital balances of Fox and Grimm respectively?

a. $84,000 and $56,000
b. $102,000 and $68,000
c. $108,000 and $72,000
d. $120,000 and $80,000

**85.** The following balance sheet is presented for the partnership of Davis, Wright, and Dover who share profits and losses in the ratio of 5:3:2 respectively:

| | |
|---|---|
| Cash | $ 60,000 |
| Other assets | 540,000 |
| | $600,000 |
| | |
| Liabilities | $140,000 |
| Davis, capital | 280,000 |
| Wright, capital | 160,000 |
| Dover, capital | 20,000 |
| | $600,000 |

The partnership is liquidated and the other assets are sold for $400,000. How should the available cash be distributed to each partner?

a. Davis, $280,000; Wright, $160,000; Dover, $20,000.
b. Davis, $210,000; Wright, $118,000; Dover, $8,000.
c. Davis, $206,000; Wright, $114,000; Dover, $0.
d. Davis, $205,000; Wright, $115,000; Dover, $0.

**86.** The partnership of Jenson, Smith, and Hart share profits and losses in the ratio of 5:3:2, respectively. The partners voted to dissolve the partnership when its assets, liabilities, and capital were as follows:

| Assets | |
|---|---|
| Cash | $ 40,000 |
| Other assets | 210,000 |
| | $250,000 |
| Liabilities and Capital | |
| Liabilities | $ 60,000 |
| Jenson, Capital | 48,000 |
| Smith, Capital | 72,000 |
| Hart, Capital | 70,000 |
| | $250,000 |

The partnership will be liquidated over a prolonged period of time. As cash is available it will be distributed to the partners. The first sale of noncash assets having a book value of $120,000 realized $90,000. How much cash should be distributed to each partner after this sale?

a. Jenson $0; Smith $28,800; Hart $41,200

b. Jenson $0; Smith $30,000; Hart $40,000

c. Jenson $35,000; Smith $21,000; Hart $14,000

d. Jenson $45,000; Smith $27,000; Hart $18,000

**87.** The following condensed balance sheet is presented for the partnership of Bond, Whit, and Tell, who share profits and losses in the ratio of 5:3:2 respectively:

| | |
|---|---|
| Cash | $120,000 |
| Other assets | 600,000 |
| Total assets | $720,000 |
| | |
| Liabilities | $240,000 |
| Bond, Capital | 300,000 |
| Whit, Capital | 160,000 |
| Tell, Capital | 20,000 |
| Total liabilities and capital | $720,000 |

Assume that the partners decided to liquidate the partnership. If the other assets are sold for $460,000, how much of the available cash should be distributed to Bond?

a. $300,000
b. $230,000
c. $226,000
d. $225,000

**88.** The following condensed balance sheet is presented for the partnership of Fisher, Taylor, and Simon who share profits and losses in the ratio of 6:2:2, respectively:

| | |
|---|---|
| Cash | $ 40,000 |
| Other assets | 140,000 |
| | $180,000 |
| | |
| Liabilities | $ 70,000 |
| Fisher, capital | 50,000 |
| Taylor, capital | 50,000 |
| Simon, capital | 10,000 |
| | $180,000 |

The assets and liabilities are fairly valued on the above balance sheet, and it was agreed to by all the partners that the partnership would be liquidated after selling the other assets. What would each of the partners receive at this time if the other assets are sold for $80,000?

| | Fisher | Taylor | Simon |
|---|---|---|---|
| a. | $12,500 | $37,500 | $0 |
| b. | $13,000 | $37,000 | $0 |
| c. | $14,000 | $38,000 | $ 2,000 |
| d. | $50,000 | $50,000 | $10,000 |

**89.** The condensed balance sheet of Adams & Gray, a partnership, at December 31, is as follows:

| | |
|---|---|
| Current assets | $250,000 |
| Equipment (net) | 30,000 |
| Total assets | $280,000 |
| | |
| Liabilities | $ 20,000 |
| Adams, capital | 160,000 |
| Gray, capital | 100,000 |
| Total liabilities & capital | $280,000 |

On December 31, the fair values of the assets and liabilities were appraised at $240,000 and $20,000, respectively, by an independent appraiser. On January 2 of the following year, the partnership was incorporated and 1,000 shares of $5 par value common stock were issued. Immediately after the incorporation, what amount should the new corporation report as additional paid-in capital?

a. $275,000
b. $260,000
c. $215,000
d. $0

**90.** East Co. issued 1,000 shares of its $5 par common stock to Howe as compensation for 1,000 hours of legal services performed. Howe usually bills $160 per hour for legal services. On the date of issuance, the stock was trading on a public exchange at $140 per share. By what amount should the additional paid-in capital account increase as a result of this transaction?

   **a.** $135,000
   **b.** $140,000
   **c.** $155,000
   **d.** $160,000

**91.** During 20x2, Brad Co. issued 5,000 shares of $100 par convertible preferred stock for $110 per share. One share of preferred stock can be converted into three shares of Brad's $25 par common stock at the option of the preferred shareholder. On December 31, 20x3, when the market value of the common stock was $40 per share, all of the preferred stock was converted. What amount should Brad credit to Common Stock and to Additional Paid-in Capital - Common Stock as a result of the conversion?

| | Common Stock | Additional paid-in capital |
|---|---|---|
| **a.** | $375,000 | $175,000 |
| **b.** | $375,000 | $225,000 |
| **c.** | $500,000 | $ 50,000 |
| **d.** | $600,000 | $0 |

**92.** At December 31, 20x2, and 20x3, Apex Co. had 3,000 shares of $100 par, 5% cumulative preferred stock outstanding. No dividends were in arrears as of December 31, 20x1. Apex did not declare a dividend during 20x2. During 20x3, Apex paid a cash dividend of $10,000 on its preferred stock. Apex should report dividends in arrears in its 20x3 financial statements as a(an)

   **a.** Accrued liability of $15,000.
   **b.** Disclosure of $15,000.
   **c.** Accrued liability of $20,000.
   **d.** Disclosure of $20,000.

**93.** East Corp., a calendar-year company, had sufficient retained earnings in 20x3 as a basis for dividends, but was temporarily short of cash. East declared a dividend of $100,000 on April 1, 20x3, and issued promissory notes to its stockholders in lieu of cash. The notes, which were dated April 1, 20x3, had a maturity date of March 31, 20x4, and a 10% interest rate. How should East account for the scrip dividend and related interest?

   **a.** Debit retained earnings for $110,000 on April 1, 20x3.
   **b.** Debit retained earnings for $110,000 on March 31, 20x4.
   **c.** Debit retained earnings for $100,000 on April 1, 20x3, and debit interest expense for $10,000 on March 31, 20x4.
   **d.** Debit retained earnings for $100,000 on April 1, 20x3, and debit interest expense for $7,500 on December 31, 20x3.

**94.** On January 2, 20x4, Lake Mining Co.'s board of directors declared a cash dividend of $400,000 to stockholders of record on January 18, 20x4, payable on February 10, 20x4. The dividend is permissible under law in Lake's state of incorporation. Selected data from Lake's December 31, 20x3, balance sheet are as follows:

| | |
|---|---|
| Accumulated depletion | $100,000 |
| Capital stock | 500,000 |
| Additional paid-in capital | 150,000 |
| Retained earnings | 300,000 |

The $400,000 dividend includes a liquidating dividend of

   **a.** $0
   **b.** $100,000
   **c.** $150,000
   **d.** $300,000

   

**95.** Nest Co. issued 100,000 shares of common stock. Of these, 5,000 were held as treasury stock at December 31, 20x3. During 20x4, transactions involving Nest's common stock were as follows:

May 3        1,000 shares of treasury stock were sold.
August 6     10,000 shares of previously unissued stock were sold.
November 18  A 2-for-1 stock split took effect.

Laws in Nest's state of incorporation protect treasury stock from dilution. At December 31, 20x4, how many shares of Nest's common stock were issued and outstanding?

|     | Issued | Outstanding |
|-----|--------|-------------|
| a.  | 220,000 | 212,000 |
| b.  | 220,000 | 216,000 |
| c.  | 222,000 | 214,000 |
| d.  | 222,000 | 218,000 |

**96.** A company issued rights to its existing shareholders without consideration. The rights allowed the recipients to purchase unissued common stock for an amount in excess of par value. When the rights are issued, which of the following accounts will be increased?

|     | Common stock | Additional paid-in capital |
|-----|--------------|----------------------------|
| a.  | Yes | Yes |
| b.  | Yes | No |
| c.  | No | No |
| d.  | No | Yes |

**97.** In September 20x0, West Corp. made a dividend distribution of one right for each of its 120,000 shares of outstanding common stock. Each right was exercisable for the purchase of 1/100th of a share of West's $50 variable rate preferred stock at an exercise price of $80 per share. On March 20, 20x4, none of the rights had been exercised, and West redeemed them by paying each stockholder $0.10 per right. As a result of this redemption, West's stockholders' equity was reduced by

a. $ 120
b. $ 2,400
c. $12,000
d. $36,000

**98.** The primary purpose of a quasi-reorganization is to give a corporation the opportunity to
a. Obtain relief from its creditors.
b. Revalue understated assets to their fair values.
c. Eliminate a deficit in retained earnings.
d. Distribute the stock of a newly-created subsidiary to its stockholders in exchange for part of their stock in the corporation.

**99.** The stockholders' equity section of Brown Co.'s December 31, 20x4, balance sheet consisted of the following:

Common stock, $30 par, 10,000
  shares authorized & outstanding   $300,000
Additional paid-in capital          150,000
Retained earnings (deficit)        (210,000)

On January 2, 20x5, Brown put into effect a stockholder-approved quasi-reorganization by reducing the par value of the stock to $5 and eliminating the deficit against additional paid-in capital. Immediately after the quasi-reorganization, what amount should Brown report as additional paid-in capital?
a. $(60,000)
b. $150,000
c. $190,000
d. $400,000

**100.** When Mill retired from the partnership of Mill, Yale, and Lear, the final settlement of Mill's interest exceeded Mill's capital balance. Under the bonus method, the excess
a. Was recorded as goodwill.
b. Was recorded as an expense.
c. Reduced the capital balances of Yale and Lear.
d. Had **no** effect on the capital balances of Yale and Lear.

**101.** During 20x4, Young and Zinc maintained average capital balances in their partnerships of $160,000 and $100,000 respectively. The partners receive 10% interest on average capital balances, and residual profit or loss is divided equally. Partnership profit before interest was $4,000. By what amount should Zinc's capital account change for the year?

    **a.** $ 1,000 decrease.
    **b.** $ 2,000 increase.
    **c.** $11,000 decrease.
    **d.** $12,000 increase.

**102.** Which of the following statements is correct regarding the provision for income taxes in the financial statements of a sole proprietorship?

    **a.** The provision for income taxes should be based on business income using individual income tax rates.
    **b.** The provision for income taxes should be based on business income using corporate tax rates.
    **c.** The provision for income taxes should be based on the proprietor's total taxable income, allocated to the proprietorship at the percentage that business income bears to the proprietor's total income.
    **d.** No provision for income taxes is required.

**103.** On January 2, 20x3, Smith purchased the net assets of Jones' Cleaning, a sole proprietorship, for $350,000, and commenced operations of Spiffy Cleaning, a sole proprietorship. The assets had a carrying amount of $375,000 and a market value of $360,000. In Spiffy's cash-basis financial statements for the year ended December 31, 20x3, Spiffy reported revenues in excess of expenses of $60,000. Smith's drawings during 20x3 were $20,000. In Spiffy's financial statements, what amount should be reported as Capital-Smith?

    **a.** $390,000
    **b.** $400,000
    **c.** $410,000
    **d.** $415,000

**104.** On February 1, 20x5, Tory began a service proprietorship with an initial cash investment of $2,000. The proprietorship provided $5,000 of services in February and received full payment in March. The proprietorship incurred expenses of $3,000 in February, which were paid in April. During March, Tory drew $1,000 against the capital account. In the proprietorship's financial statements for the two months ended March 31, 20x5, prepared under the cash basis method of accounting, what amount should be reported as capital?

    **a.** $1,000
    **b.** $3,000
    **c.** $6,000
    **d.** $7,000

**105.** Selected information from the accounts of Row Co. at December 31, 20x5, follows:

| | |
|---|---|
| Total income since incorporation | $420,000 |
| Total cash dividends paid | 130,000 |
| Total value of property dividends distributed | 30,000 |
| Excess of proceeds over cost of treasury stock sold, accounted for using the cost method | 110,000 |

In its December 31, 20x5, financial statements, what amount should Row report as retained earnings?

    **a.** $260,000
    **b.** $290,000
    **c.** $370,000
    **d.** $400,000

# CHAPTER 6

## OWNERS' EQUITY
## AND PARTNERSHIP ACCOUNTING

### Simulation Questions

**Number 1     (Estimated time - 10 minutes)**

(Editorial note:  This question covers topics presented in Chapters 4 and 6.)

The following question consists of 5 items.  Select the **best** answer for each item.  Answer all items.  Your grade will be based on the total number of correct answers.

Hamnoff, Inc.'s $50 par value common stock has always traded above par.  During 20x2, Hamnoff had several transactions that affected the following balance sheet accounts:

I.      Bond discount
II.     Bond premium
III.    Bonds payable
IV.     Common stock
V.      Additional paid-in capital
VI.     Retained earnings

### Required:

For each item, determine whether the transaction increased (I), decreased (D), or had no effect (N) on each of the balances in the above accounts.

1.  Hamnoff issued bonds payable with a nominal rate of interest that was less than the market rate of interest.

2.  Hamnoff issued convertible bonds, which are common stock equivalents, for an amount in excess of the bonds' face amount.

3.  Hamnoff issued common stock when the convertible bonds described in Item 22 were submitted for conversion.  Each $1,000 bond was converted into 20 common shares.  The book value method was used for early conversion.

4.  Hamnoff issued bonds, with detachable stock warrants, for an amount equal to the face amount of the bonds.  The stock warrants have a determinable value.

5.  Hamnoff declared and issued a 2% stock dividend.

**Number 2   (Estimated time – 15 minutes)**

**Question number 2** consists of 8 items.  Select the **best** answer for each item.  Answer all items.  Your grade will be based on the total number of correct answers.

Min Co. is a publicly-held company whose shares are traded in the over-the-counter market.  The stockholders' equity accounts at December 31, 20x3, had the following balances:

| | |
|---|---|
| Preferred stock, $100 par value 6% cumulative; 5,000 shares authorized; 2,000 issued and outstanding | $ 200,000 |
| Common stock, $1 par value 150,000 shares authorized; 100,000 issued and outstanding | 100,000 |
| Additional paid-in capital | 800,000 |
| Retained earnings | 1,586,000 |
| Total stockholders' equity | $2,686,000 |

Transactions during 20x4 and other information relating to the stockholders' equity accounts were as follows:

- February 1, 20x4 -- Issued 13,000 shares of common stock to Ram Co. in exchange for land. On the date issued, the stock had a market price of $11 per share. The land had a carrying value on Ram's books of $135,000, and an assessed value for property taxes of $90,000.

- March 1, 20x4 -- Purchased 5,000 shares of its own common stock to be held as treasury stock for $14 per share. Min uses the cost method to account for treasury stock. Transactions in treasury stock are legal in Min's state of incorporation.

- May 10, 20x4 -- Declared a property dividend of marketable securities held by Min to common shareholders. The securities had a carrying value of $600,000; fair value on relevant dates were:

  | | |
  |---|---|
  | Date of declaration (May 10, 20x4) | $720,000 |
  | Date of record (May 25, 20x4) | 758,000 |
  | Date of distribution (June 1, 20x4) | 736,000 |

- October 1, 20x4 -- Reissued 2,000 shares of treasury stock for $16 per share.

- November 4, 20x4 -- Declared a cash dividend of $1.50 per share to all common shareholders of record November 15, 20x4. The dividend was paid on November 25, 20x4.

- December 20, 20x4 -- Declared the required annual cash dividend on preferred stock for 20x4. The dividend was paid on January 5, 20x5.

- January 16, 20x5 -- Before closing the accounting records for 20x4, Min became aware that no amortization had been recorded for 20x3 for a patent purchased on July 1, 20x3. The patent was properly capitalized at $320,000 and had an estimated life of eight years when purchased. Min's income tax rate is 30%. The appropriate correcting entry was recorded on the same day.

- Adjusted net income for 20x4 was $838,000.

**Required:**

Items 1 through 8 represent amounts to be reported in Min's financial statements. For all items, calculate the amounts requested and record your answer on the objective answer sheet.

**Items 1 through 4** represent amounts to be reported on Min's statement of retained earnings.

1. Prior period adjustment.

2. Preferred dividends.

3. Common dividends - cash.

4. Common dividends - property.

**Items 5 through 8** represent amounts to be reported on Min's statement of stockholders' equity at December 31, 20x4.

5. Number of common shares issued at December 31, 20x4.

6. Amount of common stock issued.

7. Additional paid-in capital, including treasury stock transactions.

8. Treasury stock.

# CHAPTER 6

## OWNERS' EQUITY
## AND PARTNERSHIP ACCOUNTING

### Multiple Choice Answers

1. /c/ At date of incorporation, the total fair value of assets - total fair value of liabilities is $400,000 - 40,000 = $360,000. Par value of shares issued = 40,000. Therefore, the credit to Paid-in Capital in Excess of Par is $320,000.

2. /c/ The lump-sum proceeds are allocated on the basis of the relative total market value of the shares.

   | | |
   |---|---|
   | Preferred market value (2,000 shares x $27) | $54,000 |
   | Common market value (1,000 shares x $36) | 36,000 |
   | Total market value | $90,000 |

   Allocated to preferred: ($54,000/$90,000) x $80,000 = $48,000

3. /d/ Total common shares outstanding are the common shares issued in 20x1 & x2 (300,000) less treasury shares purchased in 20x3, (75,000) = 225,000 shares. Preferred shares are not included as they have not yet been converted to common shares.

4. /d/ This transaction is measured using the market value of the stock on the date the contract was made. Management's estimate of cost savings generated by the services is a measure of the effect of the services being provided, not their cost. 1,000 shares. x $40/sh. = $40,000 - $10,000 par = $30,000 APIC.

5. /a/ The excess of the subscription price over the par value of common stock subscribed is correctly recorded as Additional Paid-in Capital when the subscription is received.

6. /c/ Total contributed capital is the sum of all amounts received or receivable from the sale of stock, i.e. $600,000 + 48,000 + 17,000 = $665,000

7. /c/ The entry to record retirement of shares removes the original amounts in the owners' equity accounts related to the shares being retired. Additional paid-in capital will decrease by $10 per share; i.e. the amount in excess of par that had to be paid to reacquire the stock.

8. /c/ Preferred stock is debited for the par value of the shares retired, 500 shares. x $50/sh. = $25,000. Since the shares were redeemed at less than par, APIC is increased by the excess of par over cash paid, $2,500. Options A and B are not correct because Retained Earnings would not be credited in a stock redemption. Option D is not correct because it does not account for the difference between cash paid and par value redeemed.

9. /a/ This transaction is measured using the fair value of the assets exchanged for the shares, $150,000. MES are removed from the books at cost and a $70,000 gain is recorded. The par value of 5,000 shares at $20/share is removed from Preferred Stock ($100,000). The $50,000 excess over par exchanged for the shares cannot all be debited to APIC, because only $7,500 of the $30,000 balance in APIC pertains to the 5,000 shares redeemed. [($30,000/20,000 shares) x 5,000 shares]. The difference of $42,500 is debited to Retained Earnings.

10. /d/ When shares are purchased for retirement, PIC in Excess of Par is debited for the average PIC in Excess of Par recorded when the shares were issued ($3 per share x 100,000 shares) and the excess of the purchase price over the price at which the shares were originally issued is debited to Retained Earnings ($500,000).

11. /b/ Book value of preferred = $50,000 + 4,000 = $54,000. Book value of common = $160,000 - 54,000 = $106,000. Book value per share = $106,000/8,900 shares = $11.91.

12. /c/ Total OE – $100,000 + 50,000 + 450,000 = $600,000. Book value of preferred = $100,000 + 10,000 = $110,000. Book value of common = $600,000 - 110,000 = $490,000. Book value per share = $490,000/10,000 shares = $49.

13. /b/ Total OE $495,000 - liquidation value of preferred (100 shares. x $105/sh.) = $390,000. $390,000/30,000 shares = $13 per share. Do not subtract preferred dividends because stock is not cumulative.

14. /d/ Donations of company shares by stockholders are treated as treasury stock. Under the cost method, only a memo entry is made to indicate the reduction in the number of shares outstanding. Under the par-value method, a debit to Treasury Stock is offset by an equal credit to Donated Capital. In either instance, total stockholders' equity will not change.

15. /b/ Since donations of property from parties other than stockholders can be recorded as a credit to Donated Capital or as a credit to Additional Paid-in Capital, Option B is the best answer. None of the other options presents an acceptable treatment.

16. /a/ Conversion of the bonds to equity will increase total stockholders' equity by the carrying amount of the bonds.

17. /b/ Total book value of bonds converted = $200,000 + 4,500 = $204,500. Par Value of new shares = 12,000 x $10 = $120,000. Therefore, PIC in Excess of Par = $84,500.

18. /d/ The book value method must be used for the conversion of preferred stock. The book value of the preferred is $840,000. The par value of the common is 8,000 x 3 x $25 = $600,000. Therefore, PIC in Excess of Par = $240,000.

19. /a/ The book value of the preferred is $550,000. The credit to Par Value-Common Stock is 5,000 x 3 x $25 = $375,000.

20. /b/ A prior period adjustment is needed to reduce the beginning balance of retained earnings by the amount of expense not taken in the previous year, net of tax. $300,000 - 70,000 = $230,000 debit.

21. /a/ Common:

| | |
|---|---|
| 5,000 shares. x $1 par | $ 5,000 |
| Preferred: | |
| 1,500 shares. x $10 par | $15,000 |
| APIC: | |
| Common, 5,000 x ($15 - $1) | 70,000 |
| Preferred, 1,500 x ($25 - $10) | 22,500 |
| Total APIC | $92,500 |

22. /a/

| | |
|---|---|
| Common stock | $ 600,000 |
| APIC | 800,000 |
| Retained Earnings: | |
| Appropriated | 150,000 |
| Unappropriated | 200,000 |
| Treasury Stock | (50,000) |
| Net unrealized loss on noncurrent MES | (20,000) |
| Total stockholders' equity | $1,680,000 |

Note that all retained earnings are included, not just the unappropriated.

23. /a/ The $1,750,000 appropriated in 20x1 would become unappropriated upon the completion of the building, leaving only the amount of $1,200,000 appropriated in 20x2 to be reported on the 12/31/x2 balance sheet. The cash restricted for retirement of bonds is not related to appropriations of retained earnings.

24. /a/ The board of directors may appropriate RE for a special purpose. Neither of the items presented, however, qualifies for such action.

25. /d/ Working capital = Current assets - Current liabilities. On May 8, the current liability account Dividends Payable was increased, thus decreasing working capital. Payment date has no effect on working capital because current assets (cash) and current liabilities (dividends payable) decrease by equal amounts. No measurable event occurs on the date of record.

26. /b/ Since the preferred stock is cumulative, the dividends in arrears must be included first in the calculation.

| | | |
|---|---|---|
| Cash available | | $44,000 |
| To Preferred: | | |
|   In arrears | $12,000 | |
|   Current year | 24,000 | |
|   ($40,000 x 6%) | | |
| Total to preferred | | 36,000 |
| Available to common | | $ 8,000 |

27. /c/ Since preferred stock is fully participating, dividends on each class must be equal to the same percent of par.

Step 1. Assign dividends at 5% of par to each class:

| | |
|---|---|
| Preferred: $300,000 x 5% | $15,000 |
| Common: $200,000 x 5% | 10,000 |
| Total Step 1 | $25,000 |

Step 2. Allocate balance ($100,000 - 25,000 = $75,000) available based on relative par values of stock.

Preferred: ($300,000/$500,000) x $75,000 = $45,000
Common: ($200,000/$500,000) x $75,000 = $30,000

Total to Preferred: $15,000 + $45,000 = $60,000. Total to Common: $10,000 + $30,000 = $40,000.

28. /c/ RE is debited for $3,800,000 because of the cash dividends. To record the stock dividend, RE is debited for $300,000 while Common Stock is increased by $150,000 and APIC by $150,000.

29. /c/ Property dividends are accounted for at FMV on the date declared. Any gain or loss on updating the property to fair value must be recorded. 100,000 shares x ($2.50 - $2) = $50,000 gain.

30. /c/ Retained earnings is affected in two ways: 1) Record the difference between book value and fair value of property to be distributed, $18,000 gain; 2) Record the dividend declaration at fair value of the property, $78,000. +$18,000 - $78,000 = $60,000 decrease in RE

31. /a/ The amount debited to RE for a property dividend is the fair value of property at the date of declaration.

**32.** /a/ No liability account is affected by a stock dividend declaration. An equity account "Stock Dividend Distributable" is credited for the par value of stock to be issued. APIC is credited for excess of market value over par, assuming that this 5% dividend is capitalized at the market value of the stock on the declaration date.

**33.** /a/ It is preferred that a 10% stock dividend be recorded at the stock's market price on declaration date. 3,000 shares x 10% = 300 shares at $9/share = $2,700. $2,700 - 600 par value = $2,100 APIC.

**34.** /b/ It is preferred that the stock dividend at less than 20%-25% of outstanding shares be capitalized at market value ($15,000), and that at greater than 20%-25% be capitalized at par ($30,800). Total debited to RE, $45,800.

**35.** /c/ 6,000 shares x $35 per share. The preferred method is to capitalize at market value when a stock dividend is less than 20%-25% of outstanding shares.

**36.** /c/ As the number of shares distributed (100,000) is less than 20% of the original shares outstanding (20% x 600,000 = 120,000), the preferred method of accounting for this distribution is as a stock dividend. Retained Earnings is debited for the market value of the shares; common stock is credited at par, and Additional Paid-in Capital is credited for the excess of market over par.

**37.** /c/ None of the methods of accounting for distributions of stock dividends affects total stockholders' equity.

**38.** /a/ $840,000 - 260,000 - 60,000 = $520,000. Note that the sale of donated stock and the sale of treasury stock above cost do not affect RE.

**39.** /a/ For most distributions accounted for as stock splits, the par value per share is decreased and the number of shares outstanding is increased.

**40.** /d/ Par value per share is recomputed in direct proportion to the split. $10 -:- 5 shares = $2 per share.

**41.** /b/ A stock split has no effect on APIC or on RE.

**42.** /d/ Liquidating dividends represent the distribution of contributed capital, not retained earnings, to the stockholders.

**43.** /a/ Under the cost method, the excess of the amount received on the sale over the cost of the treasury shares is credited to PIC in Excess of Par from Treasury Stock Transactions.

**44.** /c/ The June 1 sale of shares increases PIC from TST by $12,000. The August 1 sale decreases PIC from TST by $6,000. The September 1 retirement of shares decreases Common Stock by $100,000 and decreases PIC in Excess of Par-common by $4 x 5,000 shares = $20,000. Thus, the overall effect is to decrease common stock by $100,000 and decrease additional paid in capital by $14,000.

**45.** /c/ Total stockholders' equity decreases when treasury stock is acquired, regardless of the method used. However, since the shares were purchased at a price less than book value per share but more than original issue and par value, some of the book value of each share acquired is retained within common stockholders' equity (the numerator of the book value calculation). This "excess book value" is spread over fewer shares outstanding; therefore, book value per share will increase.

**46.** /c/ When treasury stock accounted for under the cost method is retired, par value of the shares is removed from the common stock account. 50,000 shares x $2.50/share = $125,000. $540,000 total par - $125,000 = $415,000.

**47.** /c/ The restriction amount should be equal to the cost of shares remaining in the treasury on 12/31/x2. 5,000 shares at $12/share = $60,000.

**48.** /c/ APIC would decrease under the par method, but it would not change under the cost method. Retained Earnings would not be affected under either method.

**49.** /b/ Total stockholders' equity would decrease by the acquisition cost and increase by the resale price.

**50.** /b/ The stock issued on exercise of the rights is recorded at the amount of cash received ($60,000) plus the value assigned to the rights (4,000 x $2.25 = $9,000).

**51.** /b/ Stock warrants are the physical evidence of rights to acquire unissued or treasury stock.

**52.** /a/ There is no change in the equity accounts when rights are issued to existing shareholders as evidence of their preemptive right to purchase additional shares.

**53.** /d/ Rights issued to existing shareholders do not generate an accounting effect until they are exercised. The entry to record their exercise, however, would not affect retained earnings.

**54.** /b/ Since the exercise price exceeds par value, APIC will be credited for the difference.

**55.** /d/ When the fair value of both securities is not known, the incremental method is used. In this case, the fair value of the warrants is assigned to the warrants and the balance of the proceeds is assigned to the stock.

**56.** /a/ This is a compensatory stock option plan. The value of the options becomes a part of the total price of the shares issued. Therefore, on exercise, each share is valued at $60. 20,000 shares x $40 excess over par = $800,000.

**57.** /c/ The write-down of Property, Plant, and Equipment will reduce total stockholders' equity by $4,000,000 to $3,700,000..

**58.** /a/ Immediately after a quasi-reorganization, the balance in RE should always be zero.

**59.** /d/ Assets and liabilities are adjusted to fair value when a quasi-reorganization occurs.

**60.** /b/ All assets contributed are identifiable assets. Each partner's capital account is credited for the fair value contributed net of related debt assumed by the partnership. Roberts: $20,000 + 15,000 = $35,000. Smith: $30,000 + 15,000 + 40,000 - 10,000 = $75,000.

**61.** /c/ Algee: $50,000 cash.

Belger: $80,000 (fair value of building) - 35,000 (mortgage assumed) = $45,000.

Ceda: $55,000 fair value of equipment.

**62.** /d/ Under the bonus approach, no unidentifiable asset is assumed to exist. Each partner would receive a capital balance of $92,000 ($184,000 identifiable assets divided equally).

**63.** /d/ Fair value is the basis used to record assets contributed to the partnership.

**64.** /a/ Assets are contributed at market (fair) value.

**65.** /a/ Cobb's capital account should be credited for the fair value of the land contributed. Its selling price immediately upon partnership formation indicates this value. Note that the partners' profit/loss sharing ratio has no bearing on the capital contributed.

**66.** /d/ Under the goodwill method, it is assumed that the partner contributing less identifiable assets is contributing "goodwill" equal to the difference. Since Cor contributed identifiable assets with a fair value of $60,000, Eng's capital will also be recorded at $60,000 ($20,000 cash + $40,000 goodwill).

**67.** /a/ $25,000 x 60% = $15,000

**68.** /c/

| Income to allocate | | $250,000 |
|---|---|---|
| Step 1. To Axel: | | |
| $100,000 x 10% | $10,000 | |
| $150,000 x 20% | 30,000 | (40,000) |
| Balance | | $210,000 |
| Step 2. To Berg & Cobb: | | |
| Each receives $60,000 x | | |
| 5% = $3,000 | | (6,000) |
| Balance to share equally | | $204,000 |
| Step 3. Each partner | | |
| receives $204,000/3 | | |
| = $68,000 | | (204,000) |
| Balance remaining | | $ 0 |

Axel receives: $40,000 (Step 1) + $68,000 (Step 3) = $108,000.

**69.** /b/

| 1/1 - 7/1 $140,000 x 6/12 | $ 70,000 |
|---|---|
| 7/1 - 8/1 $180,000 x 1/12 | 15,000 |
| 8/1 - 12/31 $165,000 x 5/12 | 68,750 |
| Weighted average bal. | $153,750 |
| Interest at 10% | $15,375 |

**70.** /a/

| Income to allocate | | $100,000 |
|---|---|---|
| Step 1. Bonus to Donn | | (10,000) |
| Balance | | $ 90,000 |
| Step 2. Interest at 6% | | |
| on capital balances: | | |
| Donn | $4,800 | |
| Eddy | 3,000 | |
| Farr | 1,800 | (9,600) |
| Balance | | $80,400 |
| Step 3. Each partner | | |
| receives $80,400 /3 | | |
| = $26,800 | | (80,400) |
| Balance | | $ 0 |

Farr receives: $1,800 (Step 2) + $26,800 (Step 3) = $28,600

**71.** /b/ Flat has the greater advantage in either situation. When there is a profit, Flat receives 20% of the income plus 40% of the remaining 80% of income (32%). This yields an effective rate of 52% of the income. When there is a loss, Flat is charged with only 40% of the loss.

**72.** /d/ Since the sum of Low's bonus and salary allowance exceeds the net income, the balance to be shared equally would be a negative amount. Rhu's share of net income is limited to the amount allocated when this negative balance is divided. Therefore, Rhu's equity will decrease and Low's will increase. (Actual figures for income of $50,000 are Low increase of $51,250, Rhu, decrease of $1,250.)

**73.** /b/
$$B = \text{Bonus}$$
$$B = .25(\$300,000 - B)$$
$$B = \$75,000 - .25B$$
$$1.25B = \$75,000$$
$$B = \underline{\$60,000}$$

**74.** /b/ 1/5 x $444,000 net assets = $88,800 book value of net assets acquired

| | |
|---|---:|
| Payment to Newton and Sharman | $132,000 |
| Less: Book value given up by Newton and Sharman | -88,800 |
| Gain realized by Newton and Sharman | $ 43,200 |

**75.** /c/ Total current capital represents 75% of new total capital balance. ($300,000 + $200,000 + $190,000) -:- 75% = $920,000 new total capital balance. Fisher must contribute $920,000 x 25% = $230,000 to ensure no goodwill or bonus.

**76.** /d/ The profit and loss ratio of continuing partners is used to allocate excess of contribution made over capital allocated to an incoming partner.

**77.** /d/ Total book value of new partnership, $60,000 + $20,000 + $15,000 (fair value of land contributed by Grant) = $95,000. $95,000 x 20% interest = $19,000.

**78.** /b/ Lind's capital on admission, $150,000 x 1/3 = $50,000. Bonus to Lind, $50,000 - 40,000 = $10,000. Share of bonus deducted from Blau's capital, $10,000 x 60% = $6,000. Blau's new capital balance, $60,000 - 6,000 = $54,000

**79.** /c/ $100,000 = 1/3 of implied total book value of the partnership. Therefore, $300,000 is the total implied book value. $300,000 - ($60,000 + 90,000 + 100,000) = $50,000 implied goodwill.

**80.** /b/ $140,000 contributed -:- 25% interest = $560,000 total implied book value. $560,000 - ($320,000 + 140,000) = $100,000 total implied goodwill. $100,000 x 50% = $50,000 goodwill allocated to Eddy. $160,000 + 50,000 = $210,000, Eddy's new capital balance.

**81.** /b/ Step 1. Increase to capital, asset write-up:

| | |
|---|---:|
| Williams, $60,000 x 20% | $12,000 |
| Brown, $60,000 x 20% | 12,000 |
| Lowe, $60,000 x 60% | 36,000 |
| Total write-up | $60,000 |

Step 2. Williams capital balance after asset write-up: $70,000 + 12,000 = $82,000. Additional amount needed to pay Williams, $102,000 - 82,000 = $20,000 bonus.

Step 3. Bonus to be paid to Williams shared between Brown and Lowe in their respective profit/loss sharing ratios (20:60)

| | |
|---|---:|
| Brown, $20,000 x (20/80) | $ 5,000 |
| Lowe, $20,000 x (60/80) | $15,000 |

Capital balances:

| | |
|---|---:|
| Brown: $65,000 + 12,000 (Step 1) - 5000 (Step 3) = | $72,000 |
| Lowe: $150,000 + 36,000 (Step 1) - 15,000 (Step 3) = | $171,000 |

**82.** /d/ Under the bonus method, excess amounts paid to a withdrawing partner are deducted from the remaining partners' capital balances in their respective profit/loss sharing ratio.

**83.** /d/ Since the remaining partners' capital accounts decreased, the bonus method must have been used. Had the goodwill method been used, each partner's capital balance would have been increased by a proportionate share of the goodwill and Allen would have received an amount equal to his/her capital balance on withdrawal.

**84.** /c/ $180,000 -:- 50% (Eddy's P/L sharing ratio) = $360,000 total implied book value. $360,000 - 320,000 = $40,000 implied goodwill.

Goodwill allocated:

| | |
|---|---|
| To Fox, $40,000 x 30% | $12,000 |
| To Grimm, $40,000 x 20% | $8,000 |

New capital balances:

| | |
|---|---|
| Fox, $96,000 + 12,000 = | $108,000 |
| Grimm, $64,000 + 8,000 = | $72,000 |

**85.** /d/

| | Davis (50%) | Wright (30%) | Dover (20%) |
|---|---|---|---|
| Balance | $280,000 | $160,000 | $20,000 |
| Loss of $140,000 | - 70,000 | - 42,000 | -28,000 |
| Balance | $210,000 | $118,000 | $(8,000) |
| Deficiency absorbed | - 5,000 | - 3,000 | + 8,000 |
| Distributed | $205,000 | $115,000 | $ 0 |

The loss on sale of other assets is $540,000 - 400,000 = $140,000. The deficiency is absorbed by Davis and Wright in their relative profit/loss sharing ratios: (50:30)

**86.** /a/

| | Jenson (50%) | Smith (30%) | Hart (20%) |
|---|---|---|---|
| Balance | $ 48,000 | $72,000 | $70,000 |
| Actual loss $30,000 | - 15,000 | - 9,000 | - 6,000 |
| Balance | $ 33,000 | $63,000 | $64,000 |
| Maximum potential loss of $90,000 | - 45,000 | -27,000 | -18,000 |
| Balance | $(12,000) | $36,000 | $46,000 |
| Deficiency absorbed | + 12,000 | - 7,200 | - 4,800 |
| Distributed | $ 0 | $28,800 | $41,200 |

Actual loss on sale of assets, $120,000 BV - $90,000 proceeds = $30,000. Maximum potential loss after sale is the book value of the assets not sold, $90,000. The deficiency is absorbed in the 30:20 ratio of Smith and Hart.

**87.** /d/

| | Bond (50%) | Witt (30%) | Tell (20%) |
|---|---|---|---|
| Balance | $300,000 | $160,000 | $20,000 |
| Loss of $140,000 | - 70,000 | - 42,000 | -28,000 |
| Balance | $210,000 | $118,000 | $(8,000) |
| Deficiency absorbed | - 5,000 | - 3,000 | + 8,000 |
| Distributed | $225,000 | $115,000 | $ 0 |

Loss on sale of other assets, $600,000 - 460,000 = $140,000. Deficiency absorbed in 5:3 ratio of Bond and Witt.

**88.** /a/

| | Fisher (60%) | Taylor (20%) | Simon (20%) |
|---|---|---|---|
| Balance | $50,000 | $50,000 | $10,000 |
| Loss of $60,000 | -36,000 | -12,000 | -12,000 |
| Balance | $14,000 | $38,000 | $(2,000) |
| Deficiency absorbed | - 1,500 | - 500 | + 2,000 |
| Distributed | $12,500 | $37,500 | $ 0 |

Loss on sale of other assets, $140,000 BV - 80,000 proceeds = $60,000. Deficiency absorbed in 60:20 ratio of Fisher and Taylor.

**89.** /c/ Total fair value of contributed assets ($240,000) - liabilities ($20,000) = $220,000 capital. $220,000 contributed capital - $5,000 par value of stock = $215,000 APIC.

**90.** /a/ The transaction is measured at the fair value of the shares on the date the contract was made. However, since that information is not provided, the fair value on the date of issuance - $140 per share - is used. Allowing for $5 par value per share leaves APIC per share of $135. 1,000 shares x $135 = $135,000.

**91.** /a/ The conversion will be accounted for at the book value of the preferred shares.

| | |
|---|---|
| Total book value converted (5,000 shares x $110) | $550,000 |
| Less par value of common shares (5,000 x 3 x $25) | (375,000) |
| Book value assigned to APIC | $175,000 |

**92.** /d/ Annual preferred dividends are $15,000 ($300,000 x 5%). Any dividends in arrears have a payment priority once dividends are declared. Since there was no dividend declaration in 20x1, the total $15,000 for that year was in arrears in 20x2. The dividend declaration in 20x2 must have been for only the $10,000 paid to the preferred stockholders because any additional amount would have also been paid to the preferred stockholders up to the $15,000 in arrears for 20x1. A dividend is not a liability until it is declared. Since $10,000 was declared and paid, no additional liability exists for accrual. However, the balance of dividends in arrears ($5,000 for 20x1 and the $15,000 accumulated for 20x2) must be disclosed in notes to the financial statements.

**93.** /d/ When scrip dividends are interest bearing, the portion of the payment that represents interest must be accounted for separately as interest expense. Retained earnings is debited for the $100,000 face value of the promissory note on the date of declaration. Interest for 9 months is recorded at the end of the year ($100,000 x 10% x 9/12 = $7,500.)

**94.** /b/ Dividends paid in excess of retained earnings available for dividends are, in substance, a liquidating dividend. $400,000 paid less $300,000 retained earnings = $100,000.

**95.** /a/ Issued:

| | |
|---|---|
| Original issue | 100,000 |
| Plus stock issued 8/6 | 10,000 |
| | 110,000 |
| 2-for-1 split | x 2 |
| Shares issued as of 12/31 | 220,000 |

Note that the treasury shares held at the time of the split are also included in the split because the fact pattern states that such shares are protected from dilution.

Outstanding:

| | |
|---|---|
| Shares issued (see above) | 220,000 |
| Less shares held in treasury (4,000 x 2-for-1 split) | 8,000 |
| Shares outstanding 12/31 | 212,000 |

**96.** /c/ When rights are issued without consideration, there is no change in the equity accounts upon issuance of the rights. When the rights are exercised, an entry is made to record the issuance of the shares and the cash received.

**97.** /c/ APIC is reduced by the amount of cash paid for the rights. 120,000 shares x $.10 = $12,000

**98.** /c/ The primary purpose of a quasi-reorganization is to eliminate a deficit in retained earnings so that a company can emerge from a situation in which it is legally not permitted to pay dividends.

**99.** /c/ The amount by which par value is reduced is added to APIC so that there is an adequate balance to eliminate the deficit.

| | |
|---|---|
| Original APIC | $150,000 |
| APIC created by reduction of par value (10,000 x $25) | 250,000 |
| Total APIC available | $400,000 |
| Less absorption of deficit | (210,000) |
| APIC balance after quasi-reorganization | $190,000 |

**100.** /c/ Under the bonus method, any settlement of a withdrawing partner's interest that exceeds that partner's actual capital balance is debited to the remaining partners' capital accounts in those partners' profit sharing ratio.

**101.** /a/

| | |
|---|---|
| Interest allocated to Young | $16,000 |
| Interest allocated to Zinc | 10,000 |
| Total allocated to interest | $26,000 |
| Less p/ship profit available | 4,000 |
| Excess of interest allocations over profit | 22,000 |
| Allocation to each partner | x 50% |
| Deficit to each partner's computation | $11,000 |

Zinc's capital account change:

| | |
|---|---|
| Increase for interest allocation | $10,000 |
| Decrease for deficit allocation | (11,000) |
| Net decrease | $(1,000) |

**102.** /d/ Sole proprietorships are not taxable entities. The owners are taxed for their business income arising from such ownership on their individual tax returns.

**103.** /a/ Smith's capital account is originally credited for the amount paid for the net assets of the business, $350,000. Neither the book value nor the market value are relevant in measuring the transaction.

| | |
|---|---|
| Original investment | $350,000 |
| Plus cash basis income | 60,000 |
| Less withdrawals | (20,000) |
| Capital balance, 12/31 | $390,000 |

**104.** /c/

| | |
|---|---|
| Original investment | $2,000 |
| Cash revenues received by 3/31 | 5,000 |
| Cash expenses paid by 3/31 | -0- |
| Withdrawals by 3/31 | (1,000) |
| Balance, 3/31 | $6,000 |

**105.** /a/ The balance of Retained Earnings is the $420,000 income since incorporation less amounts distributed relating to cash and property dividends. $420,000 -- ($130,000 + $30,000) = $260,000. Retained earnings is impacted by treasury stock transactions under the cost method only if (1) treasury shares are resold at a price less than cost, and (2) there is insufficient credit balance in PIC in Excess of Par -- Treasury Stock Transactions, to absorb all the "deficit." Since the proceeds from the sale of treasury shares exceeded their cost, there is no potential adjustment to Retained Earnings for this transaction.

# CHAPTER 6

# OWNERS' EQUITY
# AND PARTNERSHIP ACCOUNTING

## Simulation Answers

### Number 1.

1.  I and III increase. No effect on the other accounts. Bonds sell at a discount when their nominal rate is less than the market rate being sought by investors.

2.  II and III increase. No effect on the other accounts. No portion of the proceeds of a convertible bonds issue is allocated to the convertible feature. The common stock equivalent characteristic does not change this.

3.  II and III decrease to remove the carrying value of the bonds from the books. The stock is issued at the carrying value (book value) of the bonds, requiring an increase in both the Common stock account for the par value and the APIC account for excess above par amounts.

4.  I, III, and V increase. No effect on the other accounts. Since the warrants are detachable, the proceeds must be allocated between the bonds and the warrants. The proceeds were equal to the face value of the bonds, therefore the balance of the proceeds after deducting the allocation to the warrants will be less than face value, i.e. sale at a discount.

5.  IV and V will increase and VI will decrease. A small stock dividend is capitalized at the market value of the shares. The narrative indicates that Hamnoff's stock has always traded above par. Therefore, both the Common Stock and the APIC accounts will increase.

### Number 2

1.  $14,000. The amount of the prior period adjustment is that portion of amortization not recorded in 20x3, net of taxes.

    Amortization amount, 20x3:
    $320,000/8 years x 1/2 year = $20,000

    $20,000 less tax of $6,000 = $14,000

2.  $12,000. $200,000 par value of preferred stock X 6%

3.  $165,000. Number of shares outstanding as of November 15 (date of record) X $1.50 per share.

    | | |
    |---|---|
    | Shares outstanding 12/31/x3 | 100,000 |
    | Plus shares issued 2/1/x4 | 13,000 |
    | Less treasury stock purchased 3/1/x4 | (5,000) |
    | Plus treasury stock reissued 10/1/x4 | 2,000 |
    | Shares outstanding 11/15/x4 | 110,000 |

4.  $720,000. Property dividends are recorded using the fair value of the property dividend distributed as of the date of declaration.

5.  113,000. Do not confuse the number of shares issued with the number outstanding. The shares issued at 12/31/x4 are the 100,000 as of 12/31/x3 plus the 13,000 issued 2/1/x4. Shares outstanding 12/31/x4 (not required) are 110,000 (see Item 3 above).

**6.** $113,000. The amount to be reported on Min's statement of stockholders' equity as of 12/31/x4 for common stock is the total par value of stock issued to date. Since Min is using the cost method to account for treasury stock, the common stock par account is not affected by treasury stock transactions.

**7.** $934,000.

| | |
|---|---|
| APIC 12/31/x3 | $800,000 |
| APIC from issuance of | |
| 13,000 shares, 2/1/x4[1] | 130,000 |
| APIC from reiussuance of | |
| 2,000 shares of treasury | |
| stock, 10/1/x4[2] | 4,000 |
| Total APIC 12/31/x4 | $934,000 |

[1]When shares are issued in exchange for assets other than cash, they should be valued at the fair value of the assets received. If the fair value cannot be determined, the fair value (market value) of the stock can be used as the basis for valuation. Neither of the amounts given for the land is an acceptable fair value -- carrying value on Ram's books is not relevant and appraised value for tax purposes is not the same as fair value for trading purposes. Therefore, the market value of the stock on the date of issuance is used. Of the $11 per share market value, $1 represents par value, and $10 per share is additional paid-in capital.

[2] The treasury stock was acquired at a cost of $14 per share and reissued at $16 per share. Therefore, when 2,000 shares were reissued, 2,000 X $2 per share would have been credited to APIC from Treasury Stock Transactions. The cost of the shares (2,000 shares X $14 per share) would have been credited in the Treasury Stock account.

**8.** $42,000.

| | |
|---|---|
| 5,000 shares acquired at | |
| $14 per share, 3/1/x4 | $70,000 |
| Less the cost of 2,000 | |
| shares reissued 10/1/x4 | 28,000 |
| Treasury stock, 12/31/x4 | $42,000 |

# CHAPTER 7

## INCOME STATEMENT

### Question Map

3. Profit-Sharing Bonus -- 49, 69
   E. Royalties -- 70, 71
   F. Research and Development (ASC Topic 730) – 72, 73, 74, 75, 76

IV. DISCONTINUED OPERATIONS
   A. General
   B. Terminology
   C. Components of Discontinued Operations -- 79
      1. Income or Loss from Operation of the Discontinued Segment - 78, 80, 82, 83, 162
      2. Gain or Loss on Disposal of the Discontinued Segment -- 77, 81, 84, 85, 86, 87
   D. Additional Disclosures

V. UNUSUAL OR INFREQUENT ITEMS
   A. Unusual or Infrequent Items -- 98, 99, 100

VI. ACCOUNTING CHANGES
   A. Changes in Accounting Principle
      1. Definition
      2. Reporting Changes in Accounting Principle
         a. Cumulative Effect Changes – 58, 59, 101, 102, 103, 104, 105, 107, 108, 109, 110, 111, 115
         b. Retroactive Effect Changes -- 106, 112, 113, 114, 115, 116
         c. Change to the LIFO Method -- 117
         d. Changes in Amortization Methods
   B. Change in Accounting Estimate – 118, 119, 120, 167
   C. Change in Reporting Entity -- 121
   D. Correction of an Error – 122, 123, 124, 125, 126, 127, 164

VII. EARNINGS PER SHARE (ASC Topic 260)
   A. Objectives of ASC Topic 260-- 128, 141
   B. Requirements
      1. Simple Capital Structure
      2. Complex Capital Structure
      3. ASC Topic 505
   C. Basic Earnings Per Share -- 133, 134, 136, 143, 145, 146, 149, 152
      1. Earnings Available to Common Shareholders -- the Numerator -- 135
      2. Weighted Average Number of Shares Outstanding -- the Denominator -- 130
         a. Stock Splits and Stock Dividends -- 129, 131, 132
         b. New Shares Issued and Treasury Stock --132
   D. Diluted Earnings Per Share -- 137, 138, 142, 144, 147, 148, 150, 151
      1. Prescribed Procedure
      2. Convertible Securities -- 139, 140
         a. Convertible Preferred
         b. Convertible Bonds
      3. Stock Options, Warrants, and Rights
         a. Numerator Effect
         b. Denominator Effect -- Treasury Stock Method – 137, 138
   E. Calculating EPS -- Illustration
   F. Disclosures Required
      1. Reconciliation
      2. Preferred Dividends
      3. Excluded Securities
      4. Post Year-End Transactions

# CHAPTER 7

## INCOME STATEMENT

### Multiple Choice Questions

**1.** In Baer Foods Co.'s single-step income statement, the section titled "Revenues" consisted of the following:

| | |
|---|---|
| Net sales revenue | $187,000 |
| Results from discontinued operations: | |
| Loss from operations of segment (net of $1,200 tax effect) | $(2,400) |
| Gain on disposal of segment (net of $7,200 tax effect) 14,400 | 12,000 |
| Interest revenue | 10,200 |
| Gain on sale of equipment | 4,700 |
| Cumulative change in two previous years' income due to change in depreciation method (net of $750 tax effect) | 1,500 |
| Total revenues | $215,400 |

In the revenues section of the income statement for the year, Baer Food should have reported total revenues of
- a. $216,300
- b. $215,400
- c. $203,700
- d. $201,900

**2.** A loss from early extinguishment of debt, if material, should be reported as a component of income
- a. After cumulative effect of accounting changes and after discontinued operations of a segment of a business.
- b. After cumulative effect of accounting changes and before discontinued operations of a segment of a business.
- c. Before cumulative effect of accounting changes and after discontinued operations of a segment of a business.
- d. Before cumulative effect of accounting changes and before discontinued operations of a segment of a business.

**3.** According to the FASB conceptual framework, an entity's revenue may result from
- a. A decrease in an asset from primary operations.
- b. An increase in an asset from incidental transactions.
- c. An increase in a liability from incidental transactions.
- d. A decrease in a liability from primary operations.

**4.** On October 1, 20x1, Acme Fuel Co. sold 100,000 gallons of heating oil to Karn Oil at $3 per gallon. Fifty thousand gallons were delivered on December 15, and the remaining 50,000 gallons were delivered on January 15, 20x2. Payment terms were: 50% due on October 1, 25% due on first delivery, and the remaining 25% due on second delivery. What amount of revenue should Acme recognize from this sale during 20x1?
- a. $ 75,000
- b. $150,000
- c. $225,000
- d. $300,000

**5.** Fenn Stores, Inc. had sales of $1,000,000 during December. Experience has shown that merchandise equaling 7% of sales will be returned within 30 days and an additional 3% will be returned within 90 days. Returned merchandise is readily resalable. In addition, merchandise equaling 15% of sales will be exchanged for merchandise of equal or greater value. What amount should Fenn report for net sales in its income statement for the month of December?
- a. $900,000
- b. $850,000
- c. $780,000
- d. $750,000

**6.** Under a royalty agreement with another enterprise, a company will receive royalties from the assignment of a patent for four years. The royalties received in advance should be reported as revenue

a. In the period received.
b. In the period earned.
c. Evenly over the life of the royalty agreement.
d. At the date of the royalty agreement.

**7.** A company used the percentage-of-completion method of accounting for a 5-year construction contract. Which of the following items will the company use to calculate the income recognized in the third year?

| | Progress billings to date | Income previously recognized |
|---|---|---|
| a. | Yes | No |
| b. | No | Yes |
| c. | No | No |
| d. | Yes | Yes |

**8.** On April 1, 20x0, Pine Construction Company entered into a fixed-price contract to construct an apartment building for $6,000,000. Pine appropriately accounts for this contract under the percentage-of-completion method. Information relating to the contract is as follows:

| | At December 31, 20x0 | At December 31, 20x1 |
|---|---|---|
| Percentage of completion | 20% | 60% |
| Estimated costs at completion | $4,500,000 | $4,800,000 |
| Income recognized (cumulative) | 300,000 | 720,000 |

What is the amount of contract costs incurred during the year ended December 31, 20x1?
a. $1,200,000
b. $1,920,000
c. $1,980,000
d. $2,880,000

**9.** Haft Construction Co. has consistently used the percentage-of-completion method. On January 10, 20x1, Haft began work on a $3,000,000 construction contract. At the inception date, the estimated cost of construction was $2,250,000. The following data relate to the progress of the contract:

| | |
|---|---|
| Income recognized at 12/31/x1 | $ 300,000 |
| Costs incurred 1/10/x1 - 12/31/x2 | 1,800,000 |
| Estimated cost to complete at 12/31/x2 | 600,000 |

In its income statement for the year ended December 31, 20x2, what amount of gross profit should Haft report?
a. $450,000
b. $300,000
c. $262,500
d. $150,000

**10.** State Co. recognizes construction revenue and expenses using the percentage-of-completion method. During 20x1, a single long-term project was begun, which continued through 20x2. Information on the project follows:

| | 20x1 | 20x2 |
|---|---|---|
| Accounts receivable from construction contract | $100,000 | $300,000 |
| Construction expenses | 105,000 | 192,000 |
| Construction in progress | 122,000 | 364,000 |
| Partial billings on contract | 100,000 | 420,000 |

Profit recognized from the long-term construction contract in 20x2 should be
a. $ 50,000
b. $108,000
c. $128,000
d. $228,000

**11.** Gow Constructors, Inc. has consistently used the percentage-of-completion method of recognizing income. During one year, Gow started work on an $18,000,000 construction contract that was completed the following year. The following information was taken from Gow's accounting records for the first year of the contract:

| | |
|---|---|
| Progress billings | $6,600,000 |
| Costs incurred | 5,400,000 |
| Collections | 4,200,000 |
| Estimated costs to complete | 10,800,000 |

What amount of gross profit should Gow have recognized in the first year on this contract?

a. $1,400,000
b. $1,200,000
c. $ 900,000
d. $ 600,000

**12.** Tay Co. uses the percentage-of-completion method to account for a five-year construction contract. Third year progress billings collected in the fourth year would
   a. Be included in the calculation of third year income.
   b. Be included in the calculation of third year income insofar as they exceeded second year billings collected in the third year.
   c. Be included in the calculation of fourth year income.
   d. Not be included in the calculation of third, fourth, or fifth year income.

**13.** A company uses the completed-contract method to account for a long-term construction contract. Revenue is recognized when recorded progress billings

|     | Are collected | Exceed recorded costs |
| --- | --- | --- |
| a. | Yes | Yes |
| b. | No | No |
| c. | Yes | No |
| d. | No | Yes |

**14.** During 20x1, Mitchell Corp. started a construction job with a total contract price of $600,000. The job was completed on December 15, 20x2. Additional data are as follows:

|     | 20x1 | 20x2 |
| --- | --- | --- |
| Actual costs incurred | $225,000 | $255,000 |
| Estimated remaining costs | 225,000 | -- |
| Billed to customer | 240,000 | 360,000 |
| Received from customer | 200,000 | 400,000 |

Under the completed contract method, what amount should Mitchell recognize as gross profit for 20x2?
   a. $ 45,000
   b. $ 72,000
   c. $ 80,000
   d. $120,000

**Items 15 and 16** are based on the following data pertaining to Pell Co.'s construction jobs, which commenced during the year:

|     | Project 1 | Project 2 |
| --- | --- | --- |
| Contract price | $420,000 | $300,000 |
| Costs incurred during the year | 240,000 | 280,000 |
| Estimated costs to complete | 120,000 | 40,000 |
| Billed to customers during the year | 150,000 | 270,000 |
| Received from customers during the year | 90,000 | 250,000 |

**15.** If Pell used the completed contract method, what amount of gross profit (loss) would Pell report in its income statement for the year?
   a. $ (20,000)
   b. $ 0
   c. $ 340,000
   d. $ 420,000

**16.** If Pell used the percentage-of-completion method, what amount of gross profit (loss) would Pell report in its income statement for the year?
   a. $(20,000)
   b. $ 20,000
   c. $ 22,500
   d. $ 40,000

**17.** The completed contract method of accounting for long-term construction-type contracts is preferable when
   a. A contractor is involved in numerous projects.
   b. The contracts are of a relatively long duration.
   c. Estimates of costs to complete and extent of progress toward completion are reasonably dependable.
   d. Lack of dependable estimates or inherent hazards cause forecasts to be doubtful.

**18.** During the current year, Tidal Co. began construction on a project scheduled for completion two years later. At December 31 of the current year, an overall loss was anticipated at contract completion. What would be the effect of the project on current-year operating income under the percentage-of-completion method and the completed-contract method?

| | Percentage-of completion | Completed contract |
|---|---|---|
| a. | No effect | No effect |
| b. | No effect | Decrease |
| c. | Decrease | No effect |
| d. | Decrease | Decrease |

**19.** When progress billings are sent on a long-term contract, what type of account should be credited under the completed contract method and percentage-of-completion method?

| | Completed Contract | Percentage-of-Completion |
|---|---|---|
| a. | Revenue | Revenue |
| b. | Revenue | Contra asset |
| c. | Contra asset | Revenue |
| d. | Contra asset | Contra asset |

**20.** Dolce Co., which began operations on January 1, 20x1, appropriately uses the installment method of accounting to record revenues. The following information is available for the year ended December 31, 20x1 and 20x2:

| | 20x1 | 20x2 |
|---|---|---|
| Sales | $1,000,000 | $2,000,000 |
| Gross profit realized on sales made in: | | |
| 20x1 | 150,000 | 90,000 |
| 20x2 | --- | 200,000 |
| Gross profit percentages | 30% | 40% |

What amount of installment accounts receivable should Dolce report in its December 31, 20x2, balance sheet?

a. $1,225,000
b. $1,300,000
c. $1,700,000
d. $1,775,000

**Items 21 and 22 are based on the following information:**

Baker Co. is a real estate developer that began operations on January 2. 20x1. Baker appropriately uses the installment method of revenue recognition. Baker's sales are made on the basis of 10% down payment, with the balance payable over 30 years. Baker's gross profit percentage is 40%. Relevant information for Baker's first two years of operations is as follows:

| | 20x2 | 20x1 |
|---|---|---|
| Sales | $16,000,000 | $14,000,000 |
| Cash collections | 2,020,000 | 1,400,000 |

**21.** At December 31, 20x1, Baker's deferred gross profit was
a. $ 5,040,000
b. $ 5,600,000
c. $ 8,400,000
d. $12,600,000

**22.** Baker's realized gross profit for 20x2 was
a. $6,400,000
b. $2,020,000
c. $1,212,000
d. $808,000

**23.** Tillary Company, which began business on January 1, appropriately uses the installment sales method of accounting. The following data are available for the year:

| | |
|---|---|
| Installment accounts receivable, December 31 | $200,000 |
| Deferred gross profit, December 31 (before recognition of realized gross profit) | 140,000 |
| Gross profit on sales | 40% |

The cash collections and the realized gross profit on installment sales for the year ended December 31 should be

| | Cash Collections | Realized Gross Profit |
|---|---|---|
| a. | $100,000 | $80,000 |
| b. | $100,000 | $60,000 |
| c. | $150,000 | $80,000 |
| d. | $150,000 | $60,000 |

**24.** Taylor Corp. accounts for revenues using the installment method. Taylor's sales and collections for the year were $60,000 and $35,000 respectively. Uncollectible accounts receivable of $5,000 were written off during the year. Taylor's gross profit rate is 30%. In its December 31 balance sheet, what amount should Taylor report as deferred revenue?
- a. $10,500
- b. $ 9,000
- c. $ 7,500
- d. $ 6,000

**25.** On January 2 of the current year, Yardley Co. sold a plant to Ivory, Inc. for $1,500,000. On that date, the plant's carrying cost was $1,000,000. Ivory gave Yardley $300,000 in cash and a $1,200,000 note, payable in 4 annual installments of $300,000 plus interest. Ivory made the first principal and interest payment of $444,000 on December 31 of the current year. Yardley uses the installment method of revenue recognition. In its income statement for the year, what amount of realized gross profit should Yardley report?

- a. $344,000
- b. $200,000
- c. $148,000
- d. $100,000

**26.** For financial statement purposes, the installment method of accounting may be used if the
- a. Collection period extends over more than 12 months.
- b. Installments are due in different years.
- c. Ultimate amount collectible is indeterminate.
- d. Percentage-of-completion method is inappropriate.

**27.** Deb Co. records all sales using the installment method of accounting. Installment contracts call for 36 equal monthly cash payments. According to the FASB's conceptual framework, the amount of deferred gross profit relating to collections 12 months beyond the balance sheet date should be reported in the
- a. Current liability section as deferred revenue.
- b. Noncurrent liability section as a deferred revenue.
- c. Current section as a contra account.
- d. Noncurrent asset section as a contra account.

**28.** On December 31, 20x1, Mill Co. sold construction equipment to Drew Inc. for $1,800,000. The equipment had a carrying amount of $1,200,000. Drew paid $300,000 cash on December 31, 20x1, and signed a $1,500,000 note bearing interest at 10%, payable in five annual installments of $300,000. Mill appropriately accounts for the sale under the installment method. On December 31, 20x2, Drew paid $300,000 principal and $150,000 interest. For the year ended December 31, 20x2, what total amount of revenue should Mill recognize from the construction equipment sale and financing?
- a. $250,000
- b. $150,000
- c. $120,000
- d. $100,000

**29.** Several of Fox, Inc.'s customers are having cash flow problems. Information pertaining to these customers for the years ended March 31 20x1, and 20x2, follows:

|  | 3/31/x1 | 3/31/x2 |
|---|---|---|
| Sales | $10,000 | $15,000 |
| Cost of sales | 8,000 | 9,000 |
| Cash collections |  |  |
| on 20x1 sales | 7,000 | 3,000 |
| on 20x2 sales | – | 12,000 |

If the cost recovery method is used, what amount would Fox report as gross profit from sales to these customers for the year ended March 31, 20x2?
- a. $ 2,000
- b. $ 3,000
- c. $ 5,000
- d. $15,000

**30.** The following information pertains to a sale of real estate by Ryan Co. to Sud Co. on December 31, 20x1:

| Carrying amount |  | $2,000,000 |
|---|---|---|
| Sales price: |  |  |
| Cash | $ 300,000 |  |
| Purchase money |  |  |
| mortgage | 2,700,000 | 3,000,000 |

The mortgage is payable in nine annual installments of $300,000 beginning December 31, 20x2, plus interest of 10%. The December 20x2 installment was paid as scheduled, together with interest of $270,000. Ryan uses the cost recovery method to account for the sale. What amount of income should Ryan recognize in 20x2 from the real estate sale and its financing?
- a. $570,000
- b. $370,000
- c. $270,00
- d. $0

**31.** Amar Farms produced 300,000 pounds of cotton during the 20x1 season. Amar sells all of its cotton to Brye Co., which has agreed to purchase Amar's entire production at the prevailing market price. Recent legislation assures that the market price will not fall below $.70 per pound during the next two years. Amar's costs of selling and distributing the cotton are immaterial and can be reasonably estimated. Amar reports its inventory at expected exit value. During 20x1, Amar sold and delivered to Brye 200,000 pounds at a market price of $.70. Amar sold the remaining 100,000 pounds during 20x2 at the market price of $.72. What amount of revenue should Amar recognize in 20x1?
- a. $140,000
- b. $144,000
- c. $210,000
- d. $216,000

**32.** On January 1, Dell, Inc. contracted with the city of Little to provide custom built desks for the city schools. The contract made Dell the city's sole supplier and required Dell to supply no less than 4,000 desks and no more than 5,500 desks per year for two years. In turn, Little agreed to pay a fixed price of $110 per desk. During the year, Dell produced 5,000 desks for Little. At December 31, 500 of these desks were segregated from the regular inventory and were accepted and awaiting pickup by Little. Little paid Dell $450,000 during the year. What amount should Dell recognize as contract revenue for the year?
- a. $450,000
- b. $495,000
- c. $550,000
- d. $605,000

**33.** On December 31, Rice, Inc. authorized Graf to operate as a franchisee for an initial franchise fee of $150,000. Of this amount, $60,000 was received upon signing the agreement and the balance, represented by a note, is due in three annual payments of $30,000 each beginning December 31 of the following year. When the agreement was signed, the present value of the three annual payments appropriately discounted was $72,000. According to the agreement, the nonrefundable down payment represents a fair measure of the services already performed by Rice; however, substantial future services are required of Rice. Collectibility of the note is reasonably certain. In Rice's December 31 balance sheet, unearned franchise fees from Graf's franchise should be reported as
   a. $132,000
   b. $100,000
   c. $ 90,000
   d. $ 72,000

**34.** Seldin Co. owns a royalty interest in an oil well. The contract stipulates that Seldin will receive royalty payments semiannually on January 31 and July 31. The January 31 payment will be for 20% of the oil sold to jobbers between the previous June 1 and November 30, and the July 31 payment will be for oil sold between the previous December 1 and May 31. Royalty receipts for 20x1 amounted to $80,000 and $100,000 on January 31 and July 31, respectively. On December 31, 20x0, accrued royalty revenue receivable amounted to $15,000. Production reports show the following oil sales:

| | |
|---|---|
| June 1 - Nov. 30, 20x0 | $400,000 |
| Dec. 1, 20x0 - May 31, 20x1 | 500,000 |
| June 1 - Nov. 30, 20x1 | 425,000 |
| Dec. 1 - Dec 31, 20x1 | 70,000 |

What amount should Seldin report as royalty revenue for 20x1?
   a. $179,000
   b. $180,000
   c. $184,000
   d. $194,000

**35.** On January 2, Osborn Co. assigned its patent to Aile for royalties of 10% of related sales. On the same date, Osborn received a $40,000 advance to be applied against royalties for anticipated sales for the year. Royalties are payable every six months. Aile reported the following sales:

| Six months ended | Amount |
|---|---|
| June 30 | $150,000 |
| December 31 | 200,000 |

How much royalty revenue should Osborn report in its income statement for the year?
   a. $75,000
   b. $60,000
   c. $40,000
   d. $35,000

**Questions 36 through 38 are based on the following information:**

The general ledger of Rosson Corporation showed the following investments at January 1, 20x2:

| | |
|---|---|
| Common stock: | |
| Joyce Corp. (2,000 shares) | $ 100,000 |
| James Corp. (8,000 shares) | 400,000 |
| Real estate: | |
| Vacant lot No. 4 | |
| (leased to Whit Corp.) | 1,000,000 |
| Other: | |
| Textbook, Ancient Accounting | |
| (original preparation and | |
| printing costs) | 80,000 |
| Total investments | $1,580,000 |

Rosson owns 2% of Joyce and 30% of James. A majority of Rosson's directors are also directors of James. The Whit lease is for ten years, starting December 31, 20x0, at an annual rental of $60,000. In addition, Whit paid a nonrefundable rental deposit of $100,000 on December 31, 20x0, as well as a security deposit of $50,000 to be refunded upon expiration of the lease. Ancient Accounting, a textbook written by Rosson's personnel in 20x9, was sold to Endless Hall, Inc., for royalties of 20% of sales. Royalties are payable semiannually on April 30 (for sales in July through December of the previous year) and on October 31 (for sales in January through June of the same year).

During the year ended December 31, 20x2, Rosson received cash dividends of $2,000 from Joyce and $24,000 from James, whose 20x2 net incomes were $80,000 and $200,000 respectively. Rosson also received $60,000 of rent from Whit in 20x2, and the following royalty checks from Endless:

|        | April 30 | October 31 |
|--------|----------|------------|
| 20x1   | $12,000  | $15,000    |
| 20x2   | 10,000   | 13,000     |

Endless estimated that sales of Ancient Accounting would total $70,000 for the last half of 20x2.

**36.** How much dividend income should Rosson report in its 20x2 income statement?
   a. $0
   b. $ 2,000
   c. $26,000
   d. $61,600

**37.** How much rental revenue should Rosson report in its 20x2 income statement?
   a. $0
   b. $60,000
   c. $70,000
   d. $75,000

**38.** How much royalty revenue should Rosson report in its 20x2 income statement?
   a. $23,000
   b. $25,000
   c. $26,000
   d. $27,000

**39.** Empire Corporation owns an office building and leases the offices under a variety of rental agreements involving rent paid monthly in advance and rent paid annually in advance. Not all tenants make timely payments of their rent. Empire's balance sheets contained the following information:

|                   | 20x2   | 20x1   |
|-------------------|--------|--------|
| Rentals receivable | $3,100 | $2,400 |
| Unearned rentals   | 6,000  | 8,000  |

During 20x2, Empire received $20,000 cash from tenants. How much rental revenue should Empire record for 20x2?

   a. $17,300
   b. $18,700
   c. $21,300
   d. $22,700

**40.** The following balances were reported by Mall Co. at December 31, 20x1 and 20x0:

|                  | 12/31/x1  | 12/31/x0  |
|------------------|-----------|-----------|
| Inventory        | $260,000  | $290,000  |
| Accounts payable | 75,000    | 50,000    |

Mall paid suppliers $490,000 during the year ended December 31, 20x1. What amount should Mall report for cost of goods sold in 20x1?
   a. $545,000
   b. $495,000
   c. $485,000
   d. $435,000

**41.** Brock Corp. reports operating expenses in two categories: (1) selling expenses and (2) general and administrative. The adjusted trial balance at December 31 included the following expense and loss accounts:

| | |
|---|---|
| Accounting and legal fees | $120,000 |
| Advertising | 150,000 |
| Freight out | 80,000 |
| Interest | 70,000 |
| Loss on sale of long-term investment | 30,000 |
| Officers' salaries | 225,000 |
| Rent for office space | 220,000 |
| Sales salaries and commissions | 140,000 |

One-half of the rented premises is occupied by the sales department. Brock's selling expenses for the year are
   a. $480,000
   b. $400,000
   c. $370,000
   d. $360,000

**42.** Which of the following is an example of the expense recognition principle of associating cause and effect?
   a. Allocation of insurance cost.
   b. Sales commissions.
   c. Depreciation of fixed assets.
   d. Officers' salaries.

**43.** Which of the following is expensed under the principle of systematic and rational allocation?
    **a.** Salesmen's monthly salaries.
    **b.** Insurance premiums.
    **c.** Transportation to customers.
    **d.** Electricity to light office building.

**44.** Accruing net losses on firm purchase commitments for inventory is an example of the accounting concept of
    **a.** Conservatism.
    **b.** Realization.
    **c.** Consistency.
    **d.** Materiality.

**45.** Zach Corp. pays commissions to its sales staff at the rate of 3% of net sales. Sales staff are not paid salaries but are given monthly advances of $15,000. Advances are charged to commission expense, and reconciliations against commissions are prepared quarterly. Net sales for the year ended March 31 were $15,000,000. The unadjusted balance in the commissions expense account on March 31 was $400,000. March advances were paid the following April 3. In its income statement for the year ended March 31, what amount should Zach report as commission expense?
    **a.** $465,000
    **b.** $450,000
    **c.** $415,000
    **d.** $400,000

**46.** Fay Corp. pays its outside salespersons fixed monthly salaries and commissions on net sales. Sales commissions are computed and paid on a monthly basis (in the month following the month of sale), and the fixed salaries are treated as advances against commissions. However, if the fixed salaries for salespersons exceed their sales commissions earned for a month, such excess is not charged back to them. Pertinent data for the month of March for salespersons A, B, and C are as follows:

|   | Fixed salary | Net sales | Commission rate |
|---|---|---|---|
| A | $10,000 | $ 200,000 | 4% |
| B | 14,000 | 400,000 | 6% |
| C | 18,000 | 600,000 | 6% |
|   | $42,000 | $1,200,000 | |

What amount should Fay accrue for sales commissions payable at March 31?
    **a.** $70,000
    **b.** $68,000
    **c.** $28,000
    **d.** $26,000

**47.** An analysis of Thrift Corp.'s unadjusted prepaid expense account at December 31, 20x2, revealed the following:

- An opening balance of $1,500 for Thrift's comprehensive insurance policy. Thrift had paid an annual premium of $3,000 on July 1, 20x1.

- A $3,200 annual insurance premium payment made July 1, 20x2.

- A $2,000 advance rental payment for a warehouse Thrift leased for one year beginning January 1, 20x3.

In its December 31, 20x2, balance sheet, what amount should Thrift report as prepaid expenses?
    **a.** $5,200
    **b.** $3,600
    **c.** $2,000
    **d.** $1,600

**48.** On May 1, 20x0, Marno County issued property tax assessments for the fiscal year ended June 30, 20x1. The first of two equal installments was due on November 1, 20x0. On September 1, 20x0, Dyur Co. purchased a 4-year old factory in Marno subject to an allowance for accrued taxes. Dyur did not record the entire year's property tax obligation, but instead records tax expenses at the end of each month by adjusting prepaid property taxes or property tax payable, as appropriate. The recording of the November 1, 20x0, payment by Dyur should have been allocated between an increase in prepaid property taxes and a decrease in property taxes payable in which of the following percentages?

| | Percentage allocated to | |
|---|---|---|
| | Increase in prepaid property taxes | Decrease in property taxes payable |
| a. | 66 2/3% | 33 1/3% |
| b. | 0% | 100% |
| c. | 50% | 50% |
| d. | 33 1/3% | 66 2/3% |

**49.** Dana Co.'s officers' compensation expense account had a balance of $224,000 at December 31, before any appropriate year-end adjustment relating to the following:

- No salary accrual was made for December 30-31 salaries. Salaries for the two-day period totaled $3,500.

- Officers' bonuses of $62,500 for the year ending December 31 were paid on January 31 of the following year.

In its income statement for the current year ending December 31, what should Dana report as officers' compensation expense?
   a. $290,000
   b. $286,500
   c. $227,500
   d. $224,000

**50.** Pak Co.'s professional fees expense account had a balance of $82,000 at December 31 before considering year-end adjustments relating to the following:

- Consultants were hired for a special project at a total fee not to exceed $65,000. Pak has recorded $55,000 of this fee based on billings for work performed through December 31.

- The attorney's letter requested by the auditors dated January 28 of the next year indicated that legal fees of $6,000 were billed on January 15 for work which had been performed in November, and unbilled fees of $7,000 relating to work performed in December.

What amount should Pak report for professional fees expense for the year ending December 31?
   a. $105,000
   b. $ 95,000
   c. $ 88,000
   d. $ 82,000

**51.** Which of the following should be expensed as incurred by the franchisee for a franchise with an estimated useful life of ten years?
   a. Amount paid to the franchisor for the franchise.
   b. Periodic payments to a company, other than the franchisor, for that company's franchise.
   c. Legal fees paid to the franchisee's lawyers to obtain the franchise.
   d. Periodic payments to the franchisor based on the franchisee's revenues.

**52.** Compensatory stock options were granted to executives on May 1, 20x1, with a measurement date of October 31, 20x2, for services rendered during 20x1, 20x2, and 20x3. The excess of the market value over the option price at the measurement date was reasonably estimable at the date of the grant. The stock options were exercised on June 30, 20x4. Compensation expense should be recognized in which of the following years?

| | 20x1 | 20x3 |
|---|---|---|
| a. | Yes | No |
| b. | No | No |
| c. | Yes | Yes |
| d. | No | Yes |

**53.** On January 1, 20x1, Pall Corp. granted stock options to key employees for the purchase of 40,000 shares of the company's common stock at $25 per share. The fair market value of the options on that date was $5 per option. The options are intended to compensate employees for the next two years. The options are exercisable within a four-year period beginning January 1, 20x3 by grantees still in the employ of the company. The market price of Pall's common stock was $33 per share at the date of grant. No stock options were terminated during the year. What amount should Pall charge to compensation expense for the year ended December 31, 20x1?

   a. $320,000
   b. $160,000
   c. $100,000
   d. $200,000

**54.** In connection with a stock option plan for the benefit of key employees, Ward Corp. intends to distribute treasury shares when the options are exercised. These shares were bought one year ago at $42 per share. On January 1 of the current year, Ward granted stock options for 10,000 shares at $38 per share (the option price) as additional compensation for services to be rendered over the next three years. The value of each option was determined to be $9 each. The options are exercisable during a 4-year period beginning January 1, two years from the date of grant, by grantees still employed by Ward. Market price of Ward's stock was $47 per share at the grant date. No stock options were terminated during the year. In Ward's income statement for the current year ending December 31, what amount should be reported as compensation expense pertaining to the options?

   a. $90,000
   b. $40,000
   c. $30,000
   d. $0

**55.** In a compensatory stock option plan for which the grant, measurement, and exercise date are all different, the stock options outstanding account should be reduced at

   a. Date of grant.
   b. Measurement date.
   c. Beginning of the service period.
   d. Exercise date.

**56.** On June 1, 20x1, Oak Corp. granted stock options to certain key employees as additional compensation. The options were for 1,000 shares of Oak's $2 par value common stock at an option price of $15 per share. the value of one option at June 1 was $5 per option. Market price of this stock on June 1, 20x1, was $20 per share. The options were exercisable beginning January 2, 20x2, and expire on December 31, 20x3. On April 1, 20x2, when Oak's stock was trading at $21 per share, all the options were exercised. What amount of pretax compensation should Oak report in 20x1 in connection with the options?

   a. $6,000
   b. $5,000
   c. $2,500
   d. $2,000

**57.** For a compensatory stock option plan for which the date of grant and the measurement date are the same, compensation cost should be recognized in the income statement

   a. At the date of retirement.
   b. Of each period in which services are rendered.
   c. At the exercise date.
   d. At the adoption date of the plan.

**Questions 58 and 59 are based on the following information:**

During 20x4, Orca Corp. decided to change from the FIFO method of inventory valuation to the weighted-average method. Inventory balances under each method were as follows:

|  | FIFO | Weighted average |
|---|---|---|
| January 1, 20x4 | $71,000 | $77,000 |
| December 31, 20x4 | 79,000 | 83,000 |

Orca's income tax rate is 30%

**58.** In its 20x4 financial statements, what amount should Orca report as the cumulative effect of this accounting change?

   a. $2,800
   b. 4,000
   c. $4,200
   d. $6,000

**59.** Orca should report the cumulative effect of this accounting change as a(an)
  a. Prior period adjustment.
  b. Component of income from continuing operations.
  c. Extraordinary items
  d. Component of income.

**60.** Compensation cost should be recognized in the income statement of each period in which services are rendered for a compensatory stock option plan for which the date of grant and the measurement date are

|     | Different | Identical |
|-----|-----------|-----------|
| a.  | No        | No        |
| b.  | No        | Yes       |
| c.  | Yes       | Yes       |
| d.  | Yes       | No        |

**61.** Wolf Co.'s grant of 30,000 stock appreciation rights enables key employees to receive cash equal to the difference between $20 and the market price of the stock at the date each right is exercised. The service period is 20x0 through 20x2, and the rights are exercisable in 20x3 and 20x4. The market price of the stock was $25 and $28 at December 31, 20x0 and 20x1, respectively. What amount should Wolf report as the liability under the stock appreciation rights plan in its December 31, 20x1, balance sheet?
  a. $0
  b. $130,000
  c. $160,000
  d. $240,000

**62.** On January 2, Morey Corp. granted Dean, its president, 20,000 stock appreciation rights for past services. Those rights are exercisable immediately and expire on January 1, three years from the date of grant. On exercise, Dean is entitled to receive cash for the excess of the stock's market price on the exercise date over the market price on the grant date. Dean did not exercise any of the rights during the current year. The market price of Morey's stock was $30 on the grant date and $45 on December 31 of the same year. As a result of the stock appreciation rights, Morey should recognize compensation expense for the year of grant in the amount of

  a. $0
  b. $100,000
  c. $300,000
  d. $600,000

**63.** On January 1, Heath Corp. established an employee stock ownership plan (ESOP). Selected transactions relating to the ESOP during the year were as follows:

- On April 1, Heath contributed $45,000 cash and 3,000 shares of its $10 par value common stock to the ESOP. On this date, the market price of the stock was $18 a share.

- On October 1, the ESOP borrowed $100,000 from Union National Bank and acquired 6,000 shares of Heath's common stock in the open market at $17 a share. The note is for one year, bears interest at 10%, and is guaranteed by Heath.

- On December 15, the ESOP distributed 8,000 shares of Heath's common stock to employees of Heath in accordance with the plan formula. On this date, the market price of the stock was $20 a share.

In its income statement for the year, what amount should Heath report as compensation expense relating to the ESOP?
  a. $ 99,000
  b. $155,000
  c. $199,000
  d. $259,000

**64.** An employer's obligation relating to employees' rights to receive compensation for future absences is attributable to employees' services already rendered. The payment of compensation is probable and the amount of compensation can be reasonably estimated. Employees' compensation should be
  a. Accrued if the obligation relates to rights that vest or accumulate.
  b. Accrued if the obligation relates to rights that do **not** vest or accumulate.
  c. Expensed when paid.
  d. Disclosed, but **not** accrued if the obligation relates to rights that vest or accumulate.

**65.** The following information pertains to Rik Co.'s two employees:

- Ryan and Todd earn weekly salaries of $800 and $600 respectively. They both worked 52 weeks in the current year. Ryan's vacation rights vest or accumulate, but Todd's do not.

- Neither Ryan nor Todd took the usual two-week vacation during the year.

In the financial statements issued at the end of the year, what amount of vacation expense and liability should be reported?
  a. $2,800
  b. $1,600
  c. $1,400
  d. $0

**66.** Gavin Co. grants all employees two weeks of paid vacation for each full year of employment. Unused vacation time can be accumulated and carried forward to succeeding years and will be paid at the salaries in effect when vacations are taken or when employment is terminated. There was no employee turnover during the current year. Additional information relating to the current year ending December 31 is as follows:

| | |
|---|---|
| Liability for accumulated vacations at beginning of year | $35,000 |
| Pre-current year accrued vacations taken during the current year ending December 31 | 20,000 |
| Vacations earned for work during the current year (adjusted to current rates) | 30,000 |

Gavin granted a 10% salary increase to all employees on October 1, its annual salary increase date. For the current year ended December 31, Gavin should report vacation pay expense of
  a. $45,000
  b. $33,500
  c. $31,500
  d. $30,000

**67.** Cey, Inc. determined that it has an obligation relating to employees' rights to receive compensation for future absences attributable to employees' services already rendered. The obligation relates to rights that accumulate and vest. Payment of this compensation is probable. The amounts of Cey's obligations at the end of the current year on December 31 are reasonably estimated as follows:

| | |
|---|---|
| Vacation pay | $90,000 |
| Sick pay | 60,000 |

In Cey's income statement for the year, what mount should be reported as accrued expense for compensated absences?
  a. $0
  b. $ 60,000
  c. $ 90,000
  d. $150,000

**68.** Pine Corp. is required to contribute, to an employer' stock ownership plan (ESOP), 10% of its income after deduction for this contribution but before income tax. Pine's income before charges for the contribution and income tax was $75,000. The income tax rate is 30%. What amount should be accrued as a contribution to the ESOP?
  a. $7,500
  b. $6,818
  c. $5,250
  d. $4,773

**69.** Marsh, Inc., has an incentive compensation plan under which the president is paid a bonus of 10% of corporate income in excess of $100,000 before income tax but after deducting the bonus. The income for the year before income tax and bonus is $430,000. The bonus should be
    a. $39,091.
    b. $36,667.
    c. $33,000.
    d. $30,000.

**70.** On February 12, VIP Publishing, Inc. purchased the copyright to a book for $15,000 and agreed to pay royalties equal to 10% of book sales, with a guaranteed minimum royalty of $60,000. VIP had book sales of $800,000 during the year. In its income statement for the year, what amount should VIP report as royalty expense?
    a. $60,000
    b. $75,000
    c. $80,000
    d. $95,000

**71.** Based on the 20x0 sales of compact discs recorded by an artist under a contract with Bain Co., the artist earned $100,000 after an adjustment of $8,000 for anticipated returns. In addition, Bain paid the artist $75,000 in 20x0 as a reasonable estimate of the amount recoverable from future royalties to be earned by the artist. What amount should Bain report in its 20x0 income statement for royalty expense?
    a. $100,000
    b. $108,000
    c. $175,000
    d. $183,000

**72.** During the year Trencher, Inc., incurred research and development costs as follows:

| | |
|---|---|
| Experimental and development costs of a new process patented in December | $250,000 |
| Testing for evaluation of new products | 300,000 |
| Modification of the formulation of a chemical product | 150,000 |
| Research and development costs reimbursable under a contract with Quality Chemicals Corporation | 500,000 |

What amount should Trencher report as research and development expense in its income statement for the year ended December 31?
    a. $0
    b. $450,000
    c. $700,000
    d. $950,000

**73.** Heller Co. incurred the following costs during the year:

| | |
|---|---|
| Research and development services performed by Kay Corp. for Heller | $150,000 |
| Testing re. new product evaluation | 125,000 |
| Laboratory research aimed at discovery of new knowledge | 185,000 |

What amount should Heller report as research and development costs in its income statement for the year?
    a. $125,000
    b. $150,000
    c. $335,000
    d. $460,000

**74.** West, Inc. made the following expenditures relating to Product Y:

- Legal costs to file a patent on Product Y - $10,000. Production of the finished product would not have been undertaken without a patent.

- Special equipment to be used solely for development of Product Y - $60,000. The equipment has no other use and has an estimated useful life of four years.

- Labor and material costs incurred in producing a prototype model - $200,000.

- Cost of testing the prototype - $80,000.

What is the total amount of costs that will be expensed when incurred?
    a. $280,000
    b. $295,000
    c. $340,000
    d. $350,000

**75.** Which of the following costs is included in research and development expense?
  **a.** Ongoing efforts to improve existing products.
  **b.** Troubleshooting in connection with breakdowns during commercial production.
  **c.** Periodic design changes to existing products.
  **d.** Design, construction, and testing of preproduction prototypes and models.

**76.** An activity that would be expensed currently as research and development costs is the
  **a.** Adaptation of an existing capability to a particular requirement or customer's need as a part of continuing commercial activity.
  **b.** Legal work in connection with patent applications or litigation, and the sale or licensing of patents.
  **c.** Engineering follow-through in an early phase of commercial production.
  **d.** Testing in search for or evaluation of product or process alternatives.

**77.** How should the gain or loss from the disposal of a segment of a business enterprise be shown in the financial statements?
  **a.** An extraordinary item.
  **b.** A separate item after continuing operations.
  **c.** A separate item before income taxes.
  **d.** A retained earnings adjustment.

**78.** When reporting the loss on disposal of a segment of a business which is to be abandoned, an amount for operating losses during the phase-out period should
  **a.** Be included in the income statement as part of the loss on disposal of the discontinued segment.
  **b.** Be included in the income statement as part of the extraordinary items.
  **c.** Be included in the income statement as part of the income (loss) from continuing operations.
  **d.** Not be included in the income statement.

**79.** Gulliver Company is disposing of a segment of its business. At the measurement date the net loss from the disposal is estimated to be $475,000. Included in this $475,000 are severance pay of $50,000 and employee relocation costs of $25,000, both of which are directly associated with the decision to dispose of the segment, and estimated net operating losses of the segment from the measurement date to the disposal date of $100,000. Net losses of $75,000 from operations from the beginning of the year to the measurement date are not included in the $475,000 estimated disposal loss. Ignoring income taxes, how much should be reported on Gulliver's income statement as the total loss under the heading "Discontinued operations"?
  **a.** $175,000
  **b.** $425,000
  **c.** $450,000
  **d.** $550,000

**80.** On May 1, 20x2, the board of directors of Edgewood, Inc., approved a formal plan to sell its electronics division. The division is considered a segment of the business. It is expected that the actual sale will occur in the first three months of 20x3. During 20x2 the electronics division had a loss from operations of $1,200,000 which was incurred evenly during the year. Edgewood's effective tax rate for 20x2 is 40%. For the year ended December 31, 20x2, Edgewood should report a loss from operations of discontinued electronics division of
  **a.** $240,000.
  **b.** $400,000.
  **c.** $480,000.
  **d.** $720,000.

**81.** When a segment of a business has been discontinued during the year, the loss on disposal should
   a. Be an extraordinary item.
   b. Be an operating item.
   c. Include operating losses of the current period up to the measurement date.
   d. Exclude operating losses during the phase-out period.

**82.** On September 30, 20x0, a commitment was made to dispose of a business in early 20x1. The segment operating loss for the period October 1 to December 31, 20x0, should be included in the 20x0 income statement as part of
   a. Loss on disposal of the discontinued segment.
   a. Operating loss of the discontinued segment.
   c. Income or loss from continuing operations.
   d. Extraordinary gains or losses.

**Items 83 and 84 are based on the following information:**

On December 31, 20x1, the Board of Directors of Maxx Manufacturing, Inc. committed to a plan to discontinue the operations of its Alpha division in 20x2. Alpha's 20x2 operating loss was $500,000 and Alpha's facilities were sold for $300,000 less than their carrying amounts. Alpha's 20x1 operating loss was $1,400,000. Maxx's effective tax rate is 30%.

**83.** In its 20x1 income statement, what amount should Maxx report as a loss from discontinued operations?
   a. $ 980,000
   b. $1,330,000
   c. $1,400,000
   d. $1,900,000

**84.** In its 20x2 income statement, what amount should Maxx report as a loss from discontinued operations?
   a. $210,000
   b. $300,000
   c. $560,000
   d. $800,000

**85.** Munn Corp.'s income statement for the years ended December 31, 20x1 and 20x2, included the following:

|  | 20x2 | 20x1 |
|---|---|---|
| Operating income | $ 800,000 | $600,000 |
| Gain on sale of division | 450,000 | --- |
|  | 1,250,000 | 600,000 |
| Provision for income taxes | 375,000 | 180,000 |
| Net income | $ 875,000 | $420,000 |

On January 1, 20x2, Munn agreed to sell the assets and product line of one of its operating divisions for $1,600,000. The sale was consummated on December 31, 20x2, and resulted in a gain on disposition of $450,000. This division's net losses were $320,000 in 20x2, and $250,000 in 20x1. The income tax rate for both years was 30%. In preparing revised comparative income statements, Munn should report which of the following amounts of gain (loss) from discontinued operations?

|  | 20x2 | 20x1 |
|---|---|---|
| a. | $130,000 | $0 |
| b. | $130,000 | $(250,000) |
| c. | $ 91,000 | $0 |
| d. | $ 91,000 | $(175,000) |

**86.** On December 31, 20x0, Greer Co. entered into an agreement to sell its Hart segment's assets. On that date Greer estimated the gain from the disposition of the assets in 20x1 would be $700,000 and Hart's 20x1 operating losses would be $200,000. Hart's actual operating losses were $300,000 in both 20x0 and 20x1, and the actual gain on disposition of Hart's assets in 20x1 was $650,000. Disregarding income taxes, what net gain (loss) should be reported for discontinued operations in Greer's comparative 20x1 and 20x0 income statements?

|  | 20x1 | 20x0 |
|---|---|---|
| a. | $ 50,000 | $(300,000) |
| b. | $ 0 | $ 50,000 |
| c. | $ 350,000 | $(300,000) |
| d. | $(150,000) | $ 200,000 |

**87.** On May 15, 20x1, Munn, Inc. approved and put in motion a plan to dispose of a segment of its business. It is expected that the sale will occur on February 1, 20x2, at a selling price of $500,000. During 20x1, disposal costs incurred by Munn totaled $75,000. The segment had actual or estimated operating losses as follows:

| | |
|---|---|
| 1/1/x1 to 5/14/x1 | $130,000 |
| 5/15/x1 to 12/31/x1 | 50,000 |
| 1/1/x2 to 1/31/x2 | 15,000 |

The carrying amount of the segment at 12/31/x1 was expected to be $850,000. Before income taxes, what amount should Munn report as a loss on disposal of the segment in its 20x1 income statement?
- **a.** $490,000
- **b.** $475,000
- **c.** $605,000
- **d.** $255,000

**88.** An unusual item is one which
- **a.** Occurs infrequently and is uncontrollable in nature.
- **b.** Occurs infrequently or is unusual in nature.
- **c.** Is material and is unusual in nature.
- **d.** Is material and is uncontrollable in nature.

**89.** During the current year, hail damaged several of Toncan Co.'s vans. Hailstorms had frequently inflicted similar damage to Toncan's vans. Over the years, Toncan had saved money by not buying hail insurance and either paying for repairs, or selling damaged vans and then replacing them. During the current year, the damaged vans were sold for less than their carrying amount. How should the hail damage cost be reported in Toncan's financial statements for the current year?
- **a.** The actual hail damage loss for the year as an extraordinary item loss, net of income taxes.
- **b.** The actual hail damage loss for the year in continuing operations, with no separate disclosure.
- **c.** The expected average hail damage loss in continuing operations, with no separate disclosure.
- **d.** The expected average hail damage loss in continuing operations, with separate disclosure.

**90.** Midway Co. had the following transactions during the year:

- $1,200,000 pretax loss on foreign currency exchange due to a major unexpected devaluation by the foreign government.

- $500,000 pretax loss from discontinued operations.

- $800,000 pretax loss on equipment damaged by a hurricane. This was the first hurricane ever to strike in Midway's area. Midway also received $1,000,000 from its insurance company to replace a building, with a carrying value of $300,000, that had been destroyed by the hurricane.

What amount should Midway report in its income statement for the year as extraordinary loss before income taxes?
- **a.** $ 100,000
- **b.** $1,300,000
- **c.** $1,800,000
- **d.** $2,500,000

**91.** During the year, Peg Construction Co. recognized substantial gains from:

- An increase in value of a foreign customer's remittance caused by a major foreign currency revaluation.

- A court-ordered increase in a completed long-term construction contract's price due to design changes.

Should these gains be included in continuing operations or reported as an extraordinary item in Peg's income statement for the year?

| | Gain from major currency revaluation | Gain from increase in contract's price |
|---|---|---|
| **a.** | Continuing operations | Continuing operations |
| **b.** | Extraordinary item | Continuing operations |
| **c.** | Extraordinary item | Extraordinary item |
| **d.** | Continuing operations | Extraordinary item |

**92.** On January 1, 20x3, Ben Corporation issued $600,000 of 5% ten-year bonds at 103. The bonds are callable at the option of Ben at 104. Ben has recorded amortization of the bond premium on the straight-line method (which was not materially different from the interest method). On December 31, 20x7, when the fair market value of the bonds was 97, Ben repurchased $300,000 of the bonds in the open market at 97. Ben has recorded interest and amortization for 20x7. Ignoring income taxes and assuming that the gain is material, Ben should report this reacquisition as

   **a.** A gain of $13,500.
   **b.** An extraordinary gain of $13,500.
   **c.** A gain of $21,000.
   **d.** An extraordinary gain of $21,000.

**93.** Which of the following material gains on refunding of bonds payable should be recognized separately as an extraordinary gain?

|  | Direct exchange of old bonds for new bonds | Issuance of new bonds; proceeds used to retire old bonds |
|---|---|---|
| **a.** | Yes | No |
| **b.** | Yes | Yes |
| **c.** | No | Yes |
| **d.** | No | No |

**94.** Pierre Corp. had the following infrequent transactions during 20x1:

- A $210,000 gain from selling the only investment Pierre has ever owned.
- A $275,000 gain on the sale of equipment.
- A $70,000 loss on the write-down of inventories.

In its 20x1 income statement, what amount should Pierre report as total infrequent net gains (losses) that are not considered extraordinary?
   a. $415,000.
   b. $205,000.
   c. $485,000.
   d. $140,000.

**95.** During the year, Teller Co. incurred losses arising from its guilty plea in its first antitrust action, and from a substantial increase in production costs caused when a major supplier's workers went on strike. Which of these losses should be reported as an extraordinary item?

|  | Antitrust action | Production costs |
|---|---|---|
| **a.** | No | No |
| **b.** | No | Yes |
| **c.** | Yes | No |
| **d.** | Yes | Yes |

**96.** Wilma, Inc. incurred the following infrequent losses during 20x2:

- A $20,000 write-down of equipment leased to others.
- A $50,000 adjustment of accruals on long-term contracts.
- A $70,000 write-off of obsolete inventory.

In its 20x2 income statement, what amount should Wilma report as total infrequent losses that are not considered extraordinary?
   a. $90,000.
   b. $140,000.
   c. $70,000.
   d. $120,000.

**97.** Palo Corporation incurred the following losses, net of applicable taxes, for the year ended December 31:

| | |
|---|---|
| Loss on disposal of a segment of Palo's business | $400,000 |
| Loss on translation of foreign currency due to major devaluation | 500,000 |

How much should Palo report as extraordinary losses on its income statement for the year?
   a. $0
   b. 400,000
   c. $500,000
   d. $900,000

**98.** A transaction that is material in amount, unusual in nature, but not infrequent in occurrence, should be presented separately as a (an)

   **a.** Component of income from continuing operations, but not net of applicable income taxes.

   **b.** Component of income from continuing operations, net of applicable income taxes.

   **c.** Extraordinary item, net of applicable income taxes.

   **d.** Prior period adjustment, but not net of applicable income taxes.

**99.** Adam Corp. had the following infrequent transactions during the year:

- A $190,000 gain on reacquisition and retirement of bonds.

- A $260,000 gain on the disposal of a segment of a business. Adam continues similar operations at another location.

- A $90,000 loss on the abandonment of equipment.

In its income statement for the year, what amount should Adam report as total infrequent net gains that are not considered extraordinary?

   **a.** $100,000
   **b.** $170,000
   **c.** $360,000
   **d.** $450,000

**100.** Strand, Inc. incurred the following infrequent losses during the year:

- A $90,000 write-down of equipment leased to others.

- A $50,000 adjustment of accruals on long-term contracts.

- A $75,000 write-off of obsolete inventory.

In its income statement for the year, what amount should Strand report as total infrequent losses that are not considered extraordinary?

   **a.** $215,000
   **b.** $165,000
   **c.** $140,000
   **d.** $125,000

**101.** The retrospective application of changing to a new accounting principle should be recorded as an adjustment to previously issued financial statements presented except a change from the

   **a.** FIFO method of inventory pricing to the weighted average method.

   **b.** LIFO method of inventory pricing to the FIFO method.

   **c.** Percentage-of-completion method of accounting for long-term construction-type contracts to the completed-contract method.

   **d.** Cash basis of accounting for vacation pay to the accrual basis.

**102.** Shannon Company was formed on January 1, 20x8, and used an accelerated method of depreciation on its machinery until January 1, 20x0. At that time, Shannon adopted the straight-line method of depreciation for the machinery previously acquired as well as for any new machinery acquired in 20x0.

Information concerning depreciation amounts under each method is as follows:

| Year | Depreciation if accelerated method used | Depreciation if straight-line method used |
|------|------|------|
| 20x8 | $400,000 | $300,000 |
| 20x9 | 530,000 | 375,000 |
| 20x0 | 600,000 | 400,000 |

Assume that the direct effects of this change are limited to the effect on depreciation and the related tax provisions, and that the income tax rate was 40% in each of these years. What should be reported in Shannon's financial statements for the year ended December 31, 20x0, as the adjustment to Net Income because of changing to a different depreciation method?

   **a.** $0
   **b.** $153,000
   **c.** $255,000
   **d.** $273,000

**103.** On January 1, 20x0, Warren Co. purchased a $600,000 machine, with a five-year useful life and no salvage value. The machine was depreciated by an accelerated method for book and tax purposes. The machine's carrying amount was $240,000 on December 31, 20x1. On January 1, 20x2, Warren changed to the straight-line method for financial statement purposes. Warren can justify the change. Warren's income tax rate is 30%. In its 20x2 income statement, what amount would be deducted for depreciation?

    **a.** $120,000
    **b.** $ 84,000
    **c.** $ 36,000
    **d.** $0

**104.** On January 1, 20x0, Pell Corp. purchased a machine having an estimated useful life of 10 years and no salvage value. The machine was depreciated by the double-declining balance method for both financial statement and income tax reporting. On January 1, 20x5, Pell changed to the straight-line method for financial statement reporting but not for income tax reporting. Accumulated depreciation at December 31, 20x4, was $560,000. If the straight-line method had been used, the accumulated depreciation at December 31, 20x4, would have been $420,000. Pell's enacted income tax rate for 20x5 and thereafter is 30%. The amount shown in the 20x5 retained earnings statement for the retrospective effect of changing to the straight-line method should be

    **a.** $98,000 debit.
    **b.** $0.
    **c.** $140,000 credit.
    **d.** $140,000 debit.

**105.** Coffey Corp.'s trial balance of income statement accounts for the year ended December 31 was as follows:

| | | |
|---|---:|---:|
| Net sales | | $1,600,000 |
| Cost of goods sold | $ 960,000 | |
| Selling expenses | 235,000 | |
| Administrative expenses | 150,000 | |
| Interest expense | 25,000 | |
| Adjustment due to accounting change in depreciation method | 40,000 | |
| Gain on debt extinguishment | | 10,000 |
| | $1,410,000 | $1,610,000 |

Coffey's income tax rate is 30%. In Coffey's multiple-step income statement for the year, income from operations before income tax is

    **a.** $190,000
    **b.** $200,000
    **c.** $230,000
    **d.** $240,000

**106.** The retrospective application would usually be reported on the face of the financial statements for a

    **a.** Correction of error.
    **b.** Change in depreciation method.
    **c.** Change in accounting estimate.
    **d.** Change in accounting principle.

**107.** The concept of consistency is concerned with the accounting for which of the following income statement items?

    **a.** Discontinued operations.
    **b.** Loss on disposal of a segment of a business.
    **c.** Extraordinary items.
    **d.** Retrospective application of change in accounting principle.

**108.** On January 1 Jay Company changed to the weighted-average cost method from the first-in, first-out (FIFO) cost method for inventory cost flow purposes. Jay can justify the change, which was made for both financial statement and income tax reporting purposes. The change will result in a $120,000 decrease in the beginning inventory at January 1. Ignoring income taxes, the retrospective effect of changing to the weighted-average method from the FIFO method must be reported by Jay for the year's

    **a.** Income statement as a $120,000 debit.
    **b.** Retained earnings statement as a $120,000 debit adjustment to the beginning balance.
    **c.** Income statement as a $120,000 credit.
    **d.** Retained earnings statement as a $120,000 credit adjustment to the beginning balance.

**109.** Goddard has used the FIFO method of inventory valuation since it began operations in 20x0. Goddard decided to change to the weighted-average method for determining inventory costs at the beginning of 20x3. The following schedule shows year-end inventory balances under the FIFO and weighted-average methods:

| Year | FIFO | Weighted-average |
|------|------|------------------|
| 20x0 | $45,000 | $54,000 |
| 20x1 | $78,000 | $71,000 |
| 20x2 | $83,000 | $78,000 |

What amount, before income taxes, should be reported as the adjustment to retained earnings because of the change in accounting principle?

a. $5,000 decrease.
b. $3,000 decrease.
c. $2,000 increase.
d. $0

**110.** Brighton Co. changed from the individual item approach to the aggregate approach in applying the lower of FIFO cost or market to inventories. The retrospective adjustment of this change should be reported in Brighton's financial statements as a

a. Prior period adjustment, with separate disclosure.
b. Component of income from continuing operations, with separate disclosure.
c. Adjustment to beginning retained earnings, with separate disclosure.
d. Component of income after continuing operations, without separate disclosure.

**111.** On August 31 of the current year, Harvey Co. decided to change from the FIFO periodic inventory system to the weighted average periodic inventory system. Harvey is on a calendar year basis. The retrospective effect of the change is determined

a. As of January 1 of the current year.
b. As of August 31 of the current year.
c. During the eight months ending August 31, by a weighted average of the purchases.

d. During the current year by a weighted average of the purchases.

**112.** An example of a change in accounting principle that should be reported by restating the financial statements of prior periods (retrospective adjustment) is the change from the

a. Straight-line method of depreciating plant equipment to the sum-of-the-years-digits method.
b. Sum-of-the-years-digits method of depreciating plant equipment to the straight-line method.
c. LIFO method of inventory pricing to the FIFO method.
d. All of the above.

**113.** On January 1, 20x0, Belmont Company changed its inventory cost flow method to the FIFO cost method from the LIFO cost method. Belmont can justify the change, which was made for both financial statement and income tax reporting purposes. Belmont's inventories aggregated $4,000,000 on the LIFO basis at December 31, 20x9. Supplementary records maintained by Belmont showed that the inventories would have totaled $4,800,000 at December 31, 20x9, on the FIFO basis. Ignoring income taxes, the adjustment for the effect of changing to the FIFO method from the LIFO method should be reported by Belmont in the 20x0

a. Income statement as an $800,000 debit.
b. Retained earnings statement as an $800,000 debit adjustment to the beginning balance.
c. Income statement as an $800,000 credit.
d. Retained earnings statement as an $800,000 credit adjustment to the beginning balance.

**114.** Milton Co. began operations on January 1, 20x0. On January 1, 20x2, Milton changed its inventory method from LIFO to FIFO for both financial and income tax reporting. If FIFO had been used in prior years, Milton's inventories would have been higher by $60,000 and $40,000 at December 31, 20x0 and 20x1, respectively. Milton has a 30% income tax rate. What amount should Milton report as the retrospective adjustment of this accounting change in its financial statements for the year ended December 31, 20x2?

   **a.** $0
   **b.** $14,000
   **c.** $28,000
   **d.** $42,000

**115.** Are the below inventory pricing changes reported on the financial statements as retrospective adjustments?

|  | LIFO to weighted average | FIFO to weighted average |
|---|---|---|
| **a.** | Yes | Yes |
| **b.** | Yes | No |
| **c.** | No | No |
| **d.** | No | Yes |

**116.** On December 31, 20x0, Rapp Co. changed inventory cost methods to FIFO from LIFO for financial statement and income tax purposes. The change will result in a $175,000 increase in the beginning inventory at January 1, 20x0. Assuming a 30% income tax rate, the retrospective effect of this accounting change in reported income for the year ended December 31, 20x0, is

   **a.** $175,000
   **b.** $122,500
   **c.** $ 52,500
   **d.** $0

**117.** The Hastings Company began operations on January 1, 20x6, and uses the FIFO method in costing its raw material inventory. Management is contemplating a change to the LIFO method and is interested in determining what effect such a change will have on net income. Accordingly, the following information has been developed:

| Final Inventory | 20x6 | 20x7 |
|---|---|---|
| FIFO | $240,000 | $270,000 |
| LIFO | 200,000 | 210,000 |

| Net Income (computed under the FIFO method) | 120,000 | 170,000 |
|---|---|---|

Based upon the above information, a change to the LIFO method in 20x7 would result in net income for 20x7 of

   **a.** $110,000.
   **b.** $150,000.
   **c.** $170,000.
   **d.** $230,000.

**118.** During the current year, Krey Co. increased the estimated quantity of copper recoverable from its mine. Krey uses the units of production method. As a result of the change, which of the following should be reported in Krey's financial statements for the year?

|  | Retrospective effect of a change in accounting principle | Pro forma effects of retroactive application of new depletion base |
|---|---|---|
| **a.** | Yes | Yes |
| **b.** | Yes | No |
| **c.** | No | No |
| **d.** | No | Yes |

**119.** The effect of a change in accounting principle that is inseparable from the effect of a change in accounting estimate (for example, change in depreciation method) should be reported

   **a.** By restating the financial statement of all prior periods presented.
   **b.** As a correction of an error.
   **c.** As a component of income from continuing operations, in the period of change and future periods if the change affects both.
   **d.** As a separate disclosure after income from continuing operations, in the period of change and future periods if the change affects both.

**120.** A change in the periods benefited by a deferred cost because additional information has been obtained is

    **a.** A correction of an error.

    **b.** An accounting change that should be reported by restating the financial statements of all prior periods presented.

    **c.** An accounting change that should be reported in the period of change and future periods if the change affects both.

    **d.** Not an accounting change.

**121.** A company has included in its consolidated financial statements this year a subsidiary acquired several years ago that was appropriately excluded from consolidation last year. This results in

    **a.** An accounting change that should be reported prospectively.

    **b.** An accounting change that should be reported by restating the financial statements of all prior periods presented.

    **c.** A correction of an error.

    **d.** Neither an accounting change nor a correction of an error.

**122.** An example of an item which should be reported as a prior period adjustment is the

    **a.** Collection of previously written-off accounts receivable.

    **b.** Payment of taxes resulting from examination of prior year income tax returns.

    **c.** Correction of error in financial statements of a prior year.

    **d.** Receipt of insurance proceeds for damage to building sustained in a prior year.

**123.** While preparing its 20x3 financial statements, Dek Corp. discovered computational errors in its 20x2 and 20x1 depreciation expense. These errors resulted in overstatement of each year's income by $25,000, net of income taxes. The following amounts were reported in the previously issued financial statements:

|  | 20x2 | 20x1 |
|---|---|---|
| Retained earnings, 1/1 | $700,000 | $500,000 |
| Net income | 150,000 | 200,000 |
| Retained earnings, 12/31 | $850,000 | $700,000 |

Dek's 20x3 net income is correctly reported at $180,000. Which of the following amounts should be reported as prior period adjustments and net income in Dek's 20x3 and 20x2 comparative financial statements?

| | Year | Prior period adjustment | Net income |
|---|---|---|---|
| **a.** | 20x2 | – | $150,000 |
| | 20x3 | ($50,000) | 180,000 |
| **b.** | 20x2 | ($50,000) | $150,000 |
| | 20x3 | – | 180,000 |
| **c.** | 20x2 | ($25,000) | $125,000 |
| | 20x3 | – | 180,000 |
| **d.** | 20x2 | – | $125,000 |
| | 20x3 | – | 180,000 |

**124.** Thorpe Co.'s income statement for the year ended December 31 reported net income of $74,100. The auditor raised questions about the following amounts that had been included in net income:

| | |
|---|---|
| Unrealized loss on decline in market value of noncurrent investments in stock | $( 5,400) |
| Gain on early retirement of bonds payable (net of $11,000 tax effect) | 22,000 |
| Adjustment to profits of prior years for errors in depreciation (net of $3,750 tax effect) | ( 7,500) |
| Loss from fire (net of $7,000 tax effect) | (14,000) |

The loss from the fire was an infrequent but not unusual occurrence in Thorpe's line of business. Thorpe's December 31 income statement should report net income of

    **a.** $65,000

    **b.** $66,100

    **c.** $81,600

    **d.** $87,000

**125.** Which of the following should be reported as a prior period adjustment?

| | Change in estimated lives of depreciable assets | Change from unaccepted principle to accepted principle |
|---|---|---|
| a. | Yes | Yes |
| b. | No | Yes |
| c. | Yes | No |
| d. | No | No |

**126.** On January 2 of the current year, Air, Inc. agreed to pay its former president $300,000 under a deferred compensation arrangement. Air should have recorded this expense during the previous year but did not do so. Air's reported income tax expense would have been $70,000 lower in the previous year had it properly accrued this deferred compensation. In its December 31 financial statements for the current year, Air should adjust the beginning balance of retained earnings by a

a. $230,000 credit.
b. $230,000 debit.
c. $300,000 credit.
d. $370,000 debit.

**127.** During 20x2, Dale Corp. made the following accounting changes:

| Method used in 20x1 | Method used in 20x2 | After-tax effect |
|---|---|---|
| Sum-of-the-years' digits depreciation | Straight-line depreciation | $30,000 |
| Weighted-average for inventory valuation | First-in, first-out for inventory valuation | 98,000 |

What amount should be classified in 20x2 as prior period adjustments?

a. $0
b. $ 30,000
c. $ 98,000
d. $128,000

**128.** Earnings per share data should be reported on the face of the income statement for

| | Cumulative effect of a change in accounting principle | Income before extraordinary items |
|---|---|---|
| a. | Yes | No |
| b. | Yes | Yes |
| c. | No | Yes |
| d. | No | No |

**129.** For purposes of computing the weighted-average number of shares outstanding during the year, a midyear event that must be treated as occurring at the beginning of the year is the

a. Declaration and payment of stock dividend.
b. Purchase of treasury stock.
c. Sale of additional common stock.
d. Issuance of stock warrants.

**130.** The following information pertains to Jet Corp.'s outstanding stock for 20x2:

Common stock, $5 par value
| | |
|---|---|
| Shares outstanding, 1/1 | 20,000 |
| 2-for-1 stock split, 4/1 | 20,000 |
| Shares issued, 7/1 | 10,000 |

Preferred stock, $10 par value, 5% cumulative
| | |
|---|---|
| Shares outstanding, 1/1 | 4,000 |

What are the number of shares Jet should use to calculate 20x2 earnings per share?

a. 40,000
b. 45,000
c. 50,000
d. 54,000

**131.** On January 31, 20x2, Pack, Inc. split its common stock 2 for 1, and Young, Inc. issued a 5% stock dividend. Both companies issued their December 31, 20x1, financial statements on March 1, 20x2. Should Pack's 20x1 earnings per share (EPS) take into consideration the stock split, and should Young's 20x1 EPS take into consideration the stock dividend?

| | Pack's 20x1 EPS | Young's 20x1 EPS |
|---|---|---|
| a. | Yes | No |
| b. | No | No |
| c. | Yes | Yes |
| d. | No | Yes |

**132.** Oak Co. offers a three-year warranty on its products. Oak previously estimated warranty costs to be 2% of sales. Due to a technological advance in production at the beginning of 20x4, Oak now believes 1% of sales to be a better estimate of warranty costs. Warranty costs of $80,000 and $96,000 were reported in 20x2 and 20x3, respectively. Sales for 20x4 were $5,000,000. What amount should be disclosed in Oak's 20x4 financial statements as warranty expense?

    **a.** $ 50,000
    **b.** $ 88,000
    **c.** $100,000
    **d.** $138,000

**133.** At December 31 the Suppa Company had 500,000 shares of common stock issued and outstanding, 400,000 of which had been issued and outstanding throughout the year and 100,000 of which were issued on October 1. Net income for the year ended December 31 was $2,144,000. What should be Suppa's basic earnings per common share, rounded to the nearest penny?

    **a.** $4.29
    **b.** $4.76
    **c.** $5.04
    **d.** $5.36

**134.** At December 31, 20x9 Sonic Company had 20,000 shares of common stock issued and outstanding and 5,000 shares of nonconvertible preferred stock issued and outstanding. Sonic's net income for the year ended December 31, 20x0, was $120,000. During 20x0 Sonic declared and paid $50,000 cash dividends on common stock and $8,000 cash dividends on the nonconvertible preferred stock. There were no common stock or preferred stock transactions during the year. The basic earnings per common share for the year ended December 31, 20x0, should be

    **a.** $3.50.
    **b.** $4.80.
    **c.** $5.60.
    **d.** $6.00.

**135.** In determining basic earnings per share, dividends on nonconvertible cumulative preferred stock should be

    **a.** Deducted from net income whether declared or not.
    **b.** Deducted from net income only if declared.
    **c.** Added back to net income whether declared or not.
    **d.** Disregarded.

**136.** Appling Company had 300,000 shares of common stock issued and outstanding at December 31, 20x1. No common stock was issued during 20x2. On January 1, 20x2, Appling issued 200,000 shares of nonconvertible preferred stock. During 20x2 Appling declared and paid $150,000 cash dividends on the common stock and $120,000 on the preferred stock. Net income for the year ended December 31, 20x2, was $660,000. What should be Appling's 20x2 basic earnings per common share?

    **a.** $1.30
    **b.** $1.70
    **c.** $1.80
    **d.** $2.20

**137.** In applying the treasury stock method of computing the dilutive effect of outstanding options or warrants, for quarterly diluted earnings per share, when is it appropriate to use the ending market price of common stock as the assumed repurchase price?

    **a.** Always.
    **b.** When the ending market price is the same as average market price.
    **c.** When the ending market price is higher than the average market price and the exercise price.
    **d.** When the ending market price is lower than the average market price and higher than the exercise price.

**138.** Weaver Company had 100,000 shares of common stock issued and outstanding at December 31, 20x8. On July 1, 20x9, Weaver issued a 10% stock dividend. Unexercised stock options to purchase 20,000 shares of common stock (adjusted for the 20x9 stock dividend) at $20 per share were outstanding at the beginning and end of 20x9. The average market price of Weaver's common stock (which was not affected by the stock dividend) was $25 per share during 20x9. Net income for the year ended December 31, 20x9, was $550,000. What should be Weaver's 20x9 diluted earnings per common share, rounded to the nearest penny?
    **a.** $4.82
    **b.** $5.00
    **c.** $5.05
    **d.** $5.24

**139.** Blaine Corp. reported a net income of $67,000 for the year ending December 31, 20x8. It had the following securities outstanding for the entire year:

- 20,000 shares of $15 par value common stock.
- 1,000, 7%, $100 par value preferred shares. Each share is convertible into 3 shares of common stock.
- 200, $1,000 face value, 4 1/2% convertible bonds. Each bond is convertible into 20 shares of common stock.
- 500, $1,000 face value, 6% convertible bonds. Each bond is convertible into 30 shares of common stock.

Blaine's tax rate for the year was 35%

Which of the following statements is correct with respect to the computation of Blaine's earnings per share?
    **a.** All the convertible securities would be used in the computation of diluted earnings per share since they are all dilutive.
    **b.** The preferred shares and 4 1/2% bonds would both be used in the computation of diluted earnings per share, but the 6% bonds would not since they are antidilutive.
    **c.** Both the bond issues would be used in the computation of diluted earnings per share, but the preferred shares would not since they are antidilutive.
    **d.** The preferred shares and the 6% bonds would be used in the computation of diluted earnings per share, but the 4 1/2% bonds would not since they are antidilutive.

**140.** Antidilutive convertible securities would generally be used in the calculation of

| | Basic earnings per share | Diluted earnings per share |
|---|---|---|
| **a.** | Yes | Yes |
| **b.** | No | Yes |
| **c.** | No | No |
| **d.** | Yes | No |

**141.** Which of the following is not an objective of ASC Topic 260, "Earnings Per Share?"
    **a.** Enhancement of comparability among companies internationally.
    **b.** Elimination of certain complexities in the computation of earnings per share.
    **c.** The introduction of a "fair value" approach to the computation of earnings per share.
    **d.** Simplification of the reporting practices relating to earnings per share.

**142.** In determining earnings per share, interest expense, net of applicable income taxes on convertible debt that is dilutive should be
    **a.** Added back to net income for diluted earnings per share, and ignored for basic earnings per share.
    **b.** Added back to net income for both basic earnings per share and diluted earnings per share.
    **c.** Deducted from net income for diluted earnings per share, and ignored for basic earnings per share.
    **d.** Deducted from net income for both basic earnings per share and diluted earnings per share.

**143.** Fountain, Incorporated, has 5,000,000 shares of common stock outstanding on December 31, 20x6. An additional 1,000,000 shares of common stock were issued on April 1, 20x7, and 500,000 more on July 1, 20x7. On October 1, 20x7, Fountain issued 10,000, $1,000 face value, 7% convertible bonds. Each bond is convertible into 40 shares of common stock. No bonds were converted into common stock in 20x7. What is the number of shares to be used in computing basic earnings per share and diluted earnings per share, respectively?
a. 5,750,000 and 5,950,000
b. 5,750,000 and 6,150,000
c. 6,000,000 and 6,100,000
d. 6,000,000 and 6,900,000

**144.** When computing diluted earnings per share, convertible securities are
a. Ignored.
b. Recognized whether they are dilutive or antidilutive.
c. Recognized only if they are dilutive.
d. Recognized only if they are antidilutive.

**145.** Information relating to the capital structure of Vauxhall Corporation is as follows:

|  | 12/31/x8 | 12/31/x9 |
|---|---|---|
| Outstanding shares of: | | |
| Common stock | 200,000 | 200,000 |
| Preferred 6% stock, | | |
| $100 par, convertible | | |
| into 3 shares of | | |
| common stock for | | |
| each share of preferred | 10,000 | 10,000 |

The preferred stock was issued at par on July 1, 20x8, when the bank prime interest rate was 9.5%. During 20x9 Vauxhall paid dividends of $6 per share on its preferred stock. The net income for the year ended December 31, 20x9, is $860,000. The basic earnings per common share, rounded to the nearest penny, for the year ended December 31, 20x9, should be
a. $3.74.
b. $4.00.
c. $4.10.
d. $4.30.

**Questions 146 and 147 are based on the following data:**

At December 31, 20x1 and 20x0, Gravin Corporation had 90,000 shares of common stock and 20,000 shares of convertible preferred stock outstanding, in addition to 9% convertible bonds payable in the face amount of $2,000,000. During 20x1, Gravin paid dividends of $2.50 per share on the preferred stock. The preferred stock is convertible into 20,000 shares of common stock. The 9% convertible bonds are convertible into 30,000 shares of common stock. Net income for 20x1 was $970,000. Assume an income tax rate of 40%.

**146.** How much is the basic earnings per share for the year ended December 31, 20x1?
a. $ 7.70
b. $ 8.36
c. $ 8.82
d. $10.22

**147.** How much is the diluted earnings per share for the year ended December 31, 20x1?
a. $ 7.70
b. $ 8.21
c. $ 9.35
d. $10.22

**148.** On June 30, 20x0, Lomond, Inc. issued twenty, $10,000, 7% bonds at par. Each bond was convertible into 200 shares of common stock. On January 1, 20x1, 10,000 shares of common stock were outstanding. The bondholders converted all the bonds on July 1, 20x1. The following amounts were reported in Lomond's income statement for the year ended December 31, 20x1:

| | |
|---|---|
| Revenues | $977,000 |
| Operating expenses | 920,000 |
| Interest on bonds | 7,000 |
| Income before income tax | 50,000 |
| Income tax at 30% | 15,000 |
| Net income | $ 35,000 |

What amount should Lomond report as its 20x1 diluted earnings per share?
a. $2.50
b. $2.85
c. $2.92
d. $3.50

**149.** Peters Corp.'s capital structure was as follows at December 31, of both 20x1 and 20x2:

Outstanding shares of stock:

| | |
|---|---|
| Common | 110,000 |
| Convertible preferred | 10,000 |
| 8% convertible bonds | $1,000,000 |

During 20x2, Peters paid dividends of $3.00 per share on its preferred stock. The preferred shares are convertible into 20,000 shares of common stock. The 8% bonds are convertible into 30,000 shares of common stock. Net income for 20x2 was $850,000. Assume that the income tax rate is 30%. The basic earnings per share for 20x2 is

  a. $6.31
  b. $6.54
  c. $7.08
  d. $7.45

**150.** Jones Corp.'s capital structure was as follows at December 31 for both 20x1 and 20x2:

Outstanding shares of stock:

| | |
|---|---|
| Common | 110,000 |
| Convertible preferred | 10,000 |
| | |
| 8% convertible bonds | $1,000,000 |

During 20x2, Jones paid dividends of $3.00 per share on its preferred stock. The preferred shares are convertible into 20,000 shares of common stock. The 8% bonds are convertible into 30,000 shares of common stock. Net income for 20x2 is $850,000. Assume that the income tax rate is 30%.

The diluted earnings per share for 20x2 is

  a. $5.48
  b. $5.66
  c. $5.81
  d. $6.26

**151.** During 20x8, Moore Corp. had the following securities issued and outstanding for the entire year:

- 100,000 shares of common stock, $1 par
- 1,000 shares of 4% preferred stock, $100 par, convertible share for share into common stock.
- 30,000 options exercisable at $15 per share.

Moore's net income for the year was $900,000, and its income tax rate was 30%. The average market price per common share for the year was $20. Year-end market price was $25. Both the convertible preferred shares and the options are dilutive. In the computation of diluted earnings per share, the number of shares to be used in the denominator is

  a. 107,500
  b. 108,500
  c. 112,000
  d. 113,000

**152.** Growing, Inc., had net income for 20x1 of $10,600,000 and basic earnings per share on common stock of $5.00. Included in the net income was $1,000,000 of bond interest expense related to its long-term debt. The income tax rate for 20x7 was 50%. Dividends on preferred stock were $600,000. The dividend payout ratio on common stock was 40%. What were the dividends on common stock in 20x1?

  a. $3,600,000
  b. $3,800,000
  c. $4,000,000
  d. $4,240,000

**153.** Which of the following is used in calculating the income recognized in the fourth and final year of a contract accounted for by the percentage-of-completion method?

| | Actual total costs | Income previously recognized |
|---|---|---|
| a. | Yes | Yes |
| b. | Yes | No |
| c. | No | Yes |
| d. | No | No |

**154.** According to the installment method of accounting, gross profit on an installment sale is recognized in income
  **a.** On the date of sale.
  **b.** On the date the final cash collection is received.
  **c.** In proportion to the cash collection.
  **d.** After cash collections equal to the cost of sales have been received.

**155.** It is proper to recognize revenue prior to the sale of merchandise when

I. The revenue will be reported as an installment sale.
II. The revenue will be reported under the cost recovery method.

  **a.** I only.
  **b.** II only.
  **c.** Both I and II.
  **d.** Neither I nor II.

**156.** Wren Co. sells equipment on installment contracts. Which of the following statements best justifies Wren's use of the cost recovery method of revenue recognition to account for these installments sales?
  **a.** The sales contract provides that title to the equipment only passes to the purchaser when all payments have been made.
  **b.** No cash payments are due until one year from the date of sale.
  **c.** Sales are subject to a high rate of return.
  **d.** There is no reasonable basis for estimating collectability.

**157.** As an inducement to enter a lease, Graf Co., a lessor, granted Zep, Inc., a lessee, twelve months of free rent under a five-year operating lease. The lease was effective on January 1, 20x3, and provides for monthly rental payments to begin January 1, 20x4. Zep made the first rental payment on December 30, 20x3. In its 20x3 income statement, Graf should report rental revenue in an amount equal to

  **a.** Zero.
  **b.** Cash received during 20x3.
  **c.** One-fourth of the total cash to be received over the life of the lease.
  **d.** One-fifth of the total cash to be received over the life of the lease.

**158.** Bill Co. owns a 20% royalty interest in an oil well. Rill receives royalty payments on January 31 for the oil sold between the previous June 1 and November 30, and on July 31 for oil sold between the previous December 1 and May 31. Production reports show the following oil sales:

June 1, 20x3 - November 30, 20x3       $300,000
December 1, 20x3 - December 31, 20x3   50,000
December 1, 20x3 - May 31, 20x4        400,000
June 1, 20x4 - November 30, 20x4       325,000
December 1, 20x4 - December 31, 20x4   70,000

What amount should Rill report as royalty revenue for 20x4?
  **a.** $140,000
  **b.** $144,000
  **c.** $149,000
  **d.** $159,000

**159.** Clark Co.'s advertising expense account had a balance of $146,000 on December 31, 20x3, before any necessary year-end adjustment relating to the following:

- Included in the $146,000 is the $15,000 cost of printing catalogs for a sales promotional campaign in January 20x4.
- Radio advertisements broadcast during December 20x3 were billed to Clark on January 2, 20x4. Clark paid the $9,000 invoice on January 11, 20x4.

What amount should Clark report as advertising expense in its income statement for the year ended December 31, 20x3?
  **a.** $122,000
  **b.** $131,000
  **c.** $140,000
  **d.** $155,000

**160.** Which of the following should be included in general and administrative expenses?

|  | Interest | Advertising |
|---|---|---|
| **a.** | Yes | Yes |
| **b.** | Yes | No |
| **c.** | No | Yes |
| **d.** | No | No |

**161.** Able Co. provides an incentive compensation plan under which its president receives a bonus equal to 10% of the corporation's income before income tax but after deduction of the bonus. If the tax rate is 40% and net income after bonus and income tax was $360,000, what was the amount of the bonus?
- **a.** $36,000
- **b.** $60,000
- **c.** $66,000
- **d.** $90,000

**162.** On April 30, 20x4, Deer Corp. approved a plan to dispose of a segment of its business. For the period January 1 through April 30, 20x4, the segment had revenues of $500,000 and expenses of $800,000. The assets of the segment were sold on October 15, 20x4, at a loss for which no tax benefit is available. In its income statement for the year ended December 31, 20x4, how should Deer report the segment's operations from January 1 to April 30, 20x4?
- **a.** $500,000 and $800,000 should be included with revenues and expenses, respectively, as part of continuing operations.
- **b.** $300,000 should be reported as part of the loss on disposal of a segment.
- **c.** $300,000 should be reported as an extraordinary loss.
- **d.** $300,000 should be reported as a loss from operations of a discontinued segment.

**163.** In open market transactions, Gold Corp. simultaneously sold its long-term investment in Iron Corp. bonds and purchased its own outstanding bonds. The broker remitted the net cash from the two transactions. Gold's gain on the purchase of its own bonds exceeded its loss on the sale of the Iron bonds. Gold should report the
- **a.** Net effect of the two transactions as an extraordinary gain.
- **b.** Net effect of the two transactions in income before extraordinary items.
- **c.** Effect of its own bond transaction gain in income before extraordinary items, and report the Iron bond transaction as an extraordinary item.
- **d.** Effect of its own bond transaction as an extraordinary gain, and report the Iron bond transaction loss in income before extraordinary items.

**164.** Foy Corp. failed to accrue warranty costs of $50,000 in its December 31, 20x2, financial statements. In addition, a change from straight-line to accelerated depreciation made at the beginning of 20x3 resulted in a cumulative effect of $30,000 on Foy's retained earnings. Both the $50,000 and the $30,000 are net of related income taxes. What amount should Foy report as prior period adjustments in 20x3?
- **a.** $0
- **b.** $30,000
- **c.** $50,000
- **d.** $80,000

# CHAPTER 7

## INCOME STATEMENT

### Simulation Questions

**Number 1   (Estimated time - 10 minutes)**

This question consists of 8 items. Select the **best** answer for each item. **Answer all items.** Your grade will be based on the total number of correct answers.

**Items 1 through 8 are based on the following:**

Pucket Corp. is in the process of preparing its financial statements for the year ended December 31. Items 1 through 8 represent various transactions or situations that occurred during the year.

**Required:**

For items 1 through 8, select from the list of financial statement categories below the category in which the item should be presented. A financial statement category may be selected once, more than once, or not at all.

Financial Statement Categories:

A. Income from continuing operations, with **no** separate disclosure.
B. Income from continuing operations, with separate disclosure (either on the face of statement or in the notes).
C. Extraordinary items.
D. Separate component of stockholders' equity.
E. None of the above categories include this item.

**Example:**

The following is an example of the manner in which the answer sheet should be marked:

Item

99. Recording of annual depreciation expense.

| Item | Financial Statement Categories |
|------|-------------------------------|
| 99 | A    B    C    D    E |

**Items to be answered:**

1. An increase in the unrealized excess of cost over market value of short-term marketable equity securities.

2. An increase in the unrealized cost over market value of long-term marketable equity securities.

3. Income from operations of a discontinued segment in the segment's disposal year, but before the measurement date.

4. A gain on remeasuring a foreign subsidiary's financial statement from the local currency into the functional currency.

5. A loss on translating a foreign subsidiary's financial statements from the functional local currency into the reporting currency.

6. A loss caused by a major earthquake in an area previously considered to be subject to only minor tremors.

7. The probable receipt of $100,000 from a pending lawsuit.

8. The purchase of research and development services. There were **no** other research and development activities.

## Number 2 (Estimated time - 15 to 25 minutes)

Question 2 consists of 10 items. Select the **best** answer for each item. **Answer all items.** Your grade will be based on the total number of correct answers.

On January 2, 20x3, Quo, Inc. hired Reed to be its controller. During the year, Reed, working closely with Quo's president and outside accountants, made changes in accounting policies, corrected several errors dating from 20x2 and before, and instituted new accounting policies.

Quo's 20x3 financial statements will be presented in comparative form with its 20x2 financial statements.

### Required:

**Items 1 through 10** represent Quo's transactions. List A represents possible classifications of these transactions as: a change in accounting principle, a change in accounting estimate, a correction of an error in previously presented financial statements, or neither an accounting change nor an accounting error.

List B represents the general accounting treatment required for these transactions. These treatments are:

- Cumulative effect approach - Include the cumulative effect of the adjustment resulting from the accounting change or error correction in the 20x3 financial statements, and do **not** restate the 20x2 financial statements.
- Retroactive restatement approach - Restate the 20x2 financial statements and adjust 20x2 beginning retained earnings if the error or change affects a period prior to 20x2.
- Prospective approach - Report 20x3 and future financial statements on the new basis, but do **not** restate 20x2 financial statements.

For each item, select one from List A and one from List B.

List A (Select one)
A. Change in accounting principle.
B. Change in accounting estimate.
C. Correction of an error in previously presented financial statements.
D. Neither an accounting change nor an accounting error.

List B (Select one)
X. Cumulative effect approach.
Y. Retroactive restatement approach.
Z. Prospective approach.

**Items to be answered:**

1. Quo manufactures heavy equipment to customer specifications on a contract basis. On the basis that it is preferable, accounting for these long-term contracts was switched from the completed-contract method to the percentage-of-completion method.

2. As a result of a production breakthrough, Quo determined that manufacturing equipment previously depreciated over 15 years should be depreciated over 20 years.

3. The equipment that Quo manufactures is sold with a five-year warranty. Because of a production breakthrough, Quo reduced its computation of warranty costs from 3% of sales to 1% of sales.

4. Quo changed from LIFO to FIFO to account for its finished goods inventory.

5. Quo changed from FIFO to average cost to account for its raw materials and work in process inventories.

6. Quo sells extended service contracts on its products. Because related services are performed over several years, in 20x3,Quo changed from the cash method to the accrual method of recognizing income from these service contracts.

7. During 20x3, Quo determined that an insurance premium paid and entirely expensed in 20x2 was for the period January 1, 20x2, through January 1, 20x4.

8. Quo changed its method of depreciating office equipment from an accelerated method to the straight-line method to more closely reflects costs in later years.

9. Quo instituted a pension plan for all employees in 20x3 and adopted ASC Topic 715, Employers' Accounting for Pensions. Quo had not previously had a pension plan.

10. During 20x3, Quo increased its investment in Worth, Inc. from a 10% interest, purchased in 20x2, to 30%, and acquired a seat on Worth's board of directors. As a result of its increased investment, Quo changed its method of accounting for investment in subsidiary from the cost method to the equity method.

# CHAPTER 7

## INCOME STATEMENT

### Multiple Choice Answers

1. /d/ No losses should be included in total revenues on a single-step income statement. Information presented after Income from Continuing Operations has the same content and follows the same format in both multi- and single-step forms.

| | |
|---|---|
| Sales | $187,000 |
| Gain on sale of equipment | 4,700 |
| Interest revenue | 10,200 |
| Total revenues | $201,900 |

2. /c/ A loss from early extinguishment of debt is a specifically identified "extraordinary" item by the FASB. It should be presented after discontinued operations and before cumulative effect of accounting changes, if any.

3. /d/ According to SFAC No. 6, revenues arise from an increase in assets or a decrease in liabilities generated by activities that are related to ongoing, major or central operations. Option A is incorrect because assets are decreasing. Options B and C refer to incidental transactions.

4. /b/ Revenue from the sale of goods should be recognized at the point of sale on October 1. 50,000 gallons at $3 per gallon = $150,000

5. /a/ Gross sales of $1,000,000 less allowance for sales returns of $100,000 ($1M x 10%) = $900,000

6. /b/ Revenue is recognized when earned and realized.

7. /b/ Income previously recognized will be deducted from total income earned to date to arrive at income recognized in Year 3. Progress billings are not considered in the computation.

8. /c/

| | |
|---|---|
| Revenue recognized through 12/31/x1 (0.6 x $6,000,000) | $3,600,000 |
| Revenue recognized in 20x0 (0.2 x $6,000,000) | 1,200,000 |
| Revenue recognized in 20x1 | $2,400,000 |
| Income recognized in 20x1 ($720,000 - 300,000) | 420,000 |
| Actual contract costs, 20x1 | $1,980,000 |

9. /d/ Gross profit 20x2:

| | |
|---|---|
| Estimated gross profit 12/31/x2 [$3M - ($1,800,000 + $600,000)] | $600,000 |
| Percent completed, 12/31/x2 [$1,800,000 -:- ($1,800,000 + $600,000)] | 75% |
| Gross profit earned to date | $450,000 |
| Less gr. profit recognized 20x1 | -300,000 |
| Gross profit, 20x2 | $150,000 |

10. /a/ Remember that Construction in Progress is debited for both expenses and gross profit in the percentage-of-completion method.

| | |
|---|---|
| CIP Balance 20x2 | $364,000 |
| Less total expenses, x1 & x2 | 297,000 |
| Gross profit included in balance | $ 67,000 |
| Gross profit 20x1 ($122,000 - 105,000) | - 17,000 |
| Gross profit 20x2 | $ 50,000 |

11. /d/ $5,400,000 costs incurred -:- ($5,400,000 + $10,800,000 costs to complete) = 33 1/3% completed Year 1.

$18,000,000 revenue - $16,200,000 total estimated costs = $1.8M estimated gross profit x 33 1/3% = $600,000 gross profit, Year 1.

12. /d/ Progress billings are not considered in the determination of income in any year.

13. /b/ Revenue is recognized when the contract is completed. Recognition is not connected to the collection of progress billings nor to the relationship of billings to costs.

14. /d/ The entire amount of gross profit is recognized upon completion of the contract. $600,000 contract price - ($225,000 + $255,000 actual costs incurred) = $120,000

15. /a/ Under either contract revenue method, a loss is recognized in full in the period in which it occurs.

16. /b/ Project #1:

| | |
|---|---|
| Contract revenue | $420,000 |
| Less estimated total costs | |
| ($240,000 + $120,000) | (360,000) |
| Estimated gross profit | $ 60,000 |
| Percent completed | |
| ($240,000 -:- $360,000) | x 2/3 |
| Gross profit recognized | $ 40,000 |

Project #2:

| | |
|---|---|
| Contract revenue | $300,000 |
| Less estimated total costs | |
| ($280,000 + $40,000) | (320,000) |
| Estimated loss | $(20,000) |

$40,000 gross profit (Project #1) - $20,000 loss (Project #2) = $20,000 net gross profit.

17. /d/ When cost estimates are not reliable, the completed contract method is preferable, based on conservatism.

18. /d/ Under either method, conservatism provides that all probable losses be immediately recognized.

19. /d/ The account progress billings, a contra-asset account, is credited in both instances. Revenue recognition is not dependent on progress billings in either method.

20. /c/ AR Balance, 12/31/x2:

| | |
|---|---|
| Total sales, x1 and x2 | $3,000,000 |
| Less cash receipts from x1 sales | |
| [($150,000 + $90,000) -:- 30%] | - 800,000 |
| Less cash receipts from x2 sales | |
| ($200,000 -:- 40%) | - 500,000 |
| Acc. receivable balance, 12/31/x2 | $1,700,000 |

21. /a/ Deferred gross profit = (20x1 sales less related cash collections) x gross profit rate. ($14,000,000 - $1,400,000) x 40% – $5,040,000

22. /d/ Gross profit realized = cash collections times gross profit rate. $2,020,000 x 40% = $808,000

23. /d/ $140,000 total gross profit -:- 40% = $350,000 total installment sales receivable. $350,000 - $200,000 balance December 31 = $150,000 cash collections. $150,000 x 40% = $60,000 realized gross profit. (Note also that Option D is the only one in which the relationship between cash collections and gross profit percent is 40%.)

24. /d/ Installment receivables balance of December 31 x appropriate gross profit rate = deferred revenue. $60,000 sales - $35,000 collections - $5,000 write-offs = $20,000 x 30% = $6,000

25. /b/ $500,000 gross profit -:- $1.5M = 33 1/3% gross profit rate. Collections: cash $300,000 + $300,000 principal on note. $600,000 x 33 1/3% = $200,000 realized gross profit. The interest income on the note is reported separately. It is not a component of the realized gross profit on the installment sale.

26. /c/ The installment method of revenue recognition is acceptable for accounting only when the selling price is not reasonably assured or there is difficulty in estimating the degree of collectability.

27. /c/ Although the account Deferred Gross Profit is most often treated as a liability account for reporting purposes, it is conceptually a contra-asset account offsetting the installment receivables. It is included in current or noncurrent assets according to the estimated months to collection.

**28.** /a/ Total revenue = gross profit realized + interest income. (Contrast wording of this problem with #25 above.)

Gross profit rate: $600,000 -:- $1.8M = 33 1/3%. Collections 20x2, $300,000 payment on note principal x 33 1/3% = $100,000 gross profit realized. $100,000 + $150,000 interest revenue = <u>$250,000</u> total revenue.

**29.** /c/ Under the cost recovery method, no gross profit is recognized until cash equal to the cost of sales ($17,000) has been received. By 3/31/x2, total collections have amounted to $22,000 of which $5,000 represents gross profit to be recognized in the year ended 3/31/x2.

**30.** /d/ No income should be recorded under the cost recovery method until cash collections equal to the carrying amount of the real estate sold have been received.

**31.** /c/ Amar Farms will record its revenues at completion of production because it is assured of selling all it produces at a locked-in price no lower than $.70/pound. 300,000 lb produced in 20x1 x $.70/lb = <u>$210,000</u>.

**32.** /c/ Since Dell Inc. is the city's only supplier, and the contract locks in guaranteed sales between 4,000 and 5,500 desks at a fixed price of $110 per desk, total contract revenue is recognized by Dell on completion of production and is based on 5,000 desks produced at $110/desk = <u>$550,000</u>.

**33.** /d/ Rice has earned the down payment; however, the revenue relating to the installment note depends upon the performance of substantial future services. The present value of these installments, therefore, should be reported as unearned franchise fees.

**34.** /c/ The production 6/1/ through 11/30 yields no 20x1 royalty revenue. Production 12/1/x0 through 5/31/x1: $500,000 x 20% = $100,000 total royalties - $15,000 accrued on 12/31/x0 for December x0 = $85,000 20x1 royalty revenue. Production 6/1/x1 through 12/31/x1: $425,000 + $70,000 = $495,000 x 20% = $99,000. $85,000 + $99,000 = <u>$184,000</u>

**35.** /d/ Royalty revenue earned = sales for year x 10% = $350,000 x 10% = <u>$35,000</u>

**36.** /b/ Only the cash dividends received from Joyce during 20x2, <u>$2,000</u>. Dividends from James are accounted for using the equity method.

**37.** /c/

| | |
|---|---|
| $60,000 | Rent received |
| 10,000 | Amortization of nonrefundable rent deposit ($100,000 x 10%) |
| <u>$70,000</u> | |

**38.** /d/

| | |
|---|---|
| $13,000 | Payment received 10/31/x2 |
| 14,000 | 20% of $70,000 (estimated sales of the last half of 20x2) |
| <u>$27,000</u> | |

**39.** /d/

| | |
|---|---|
| $20,000 | Cash received |
| 700 | Increase in A/R |
| 2,000 | Decrease in unearned rentals |
| <u>$22,700</u> | |

**40.** /a/ Cost of goods sold:

| | |
|---|---|
| Inventory 12/31/x0 | $290,000 |
| Purchases ($490,000 paid to suppliers + $25,000 increase in AP) | 515,000 |
| Less inventory 12/31/x1 | -260,000 |
| Cost of goods sold | <u>$545,000</u> |

**41.** /a/ Selling expenses:

| | |
|---|---:|
| Advertising | $150,000 |
| Freight-out | 80,000 |
| One-half of rent | 110,000 |
| Sales salaries & commissions | 140,000 |
| Total selling expenses | $480,000 |

**42.** /b/ The commission is a direct result of the sale.

**43.** /b/ B is the best answer because A, C, and D are not allocations.

**44.** /a/ Losses are accrued when they become evident under the theory of conservatism.

**45.** /b/ Net sales for the year of $15M x commission rate of 3% = $450,000 commissions expense.

**46.** /c/ Since excess advance wages over commissions earned are not charged back, each salesperson earns the higher of monthly fixed salary or monthly commissions. The amount to accrue is the difference between total expense for the month and fixed salaries already paid and recorded.

Salespersons' monthly earnings:

| | |
|---|---:|
| A (salary is higher figure) | $10,000 |
| B ($400K x 6%) | 24,000 |
| C ($600K x 6%) | 36,000 |
| Total earnings | $70,000 |
| Less salaries recorded | -42,000 |
| Amount to accrue | $28,000 |

**47.** /b/ 

| | |
|---|---:|
| Prepaid insurance 12/31/x2 (Balance of 7/1 premium) | $1,600 |
| Prepaid rent - all to be earned 20x3 | 2,000 |
| Total prepaid expenses | $3,600 |

**48.** /d/ Since Dyur purchased the factory subject to an allowance for accrued taxes, the company is responsible for payment of a full six-months' taxes on November 1 to cover the period 7/1/ through 12/31/x0. Therefore, the payment covers four monthly accruals (7/1/ to 11/1) and two months of prepaid taxes (11/1 through 12/31).

**49.** /a/ Accruals should be recorded on 12/31 for both the salaries for two days in December and the annual bonuses. $224,000 + $3,500 + $62,500 = $290,000

**50.** /b/ $82,000 + $13,000 unrecorded legal fees = $95,000. (The $55,000 consultants' fees are already included in the $82,000 figure.)

**51.** /d/ Periodic payments to a franchisor based on franchisee revenues would be expensed as incurred (matching principle).

**52.** /c/ Both 20x1 and 20x3 were included in the service period contemplated when the stock options were granted.

**53.** /c/ FMV of stock options on date of grant, $5 x 40,000 shares = $200,000 total deferred compensation. $200,000 -:- 2 years = $100,000 expense for year ended 12/31/x1.

**54.** /c/ Do not be distracted by the irrelevant data given; focus on the key points: share market value, exercise price, and benefit period. $47 - $38 = $9/share x 10,000 shares = $90,000 total deferred compensations. $90,000 -:- 3 years = $30,000

**55.** /d/ The account Stock Options Outstanding is reduced when the shares are no longer outstanding; i.e. either on the exercise date or upon expiration.

**56.** /b/ As no benefit period is given and the rights are exercisable at the beginning of the next year, assume that all related cost pertains to the current year. $20 (market value) - $15 (exercise price) = $5/share x 1,000 shares = $5,000.

**57.** /b/ Deferred compensation costs should be allocated to expense over the period of employee service contemplated when the stock options were granted to the employees.

**58.** /c/ The only impact of the change from FIFO to weighted-average is for the beginning inventory figure. Since the change was made in Dec of 20x4, the weighted average inventory figure at December 31 will have been used to compute net income. The result would be an understatement of cost of goods sold by $6,000. The after-tax effect on net income for the period would be an overstatement by $4,200.

**59.** /d/ This is a change in accounting principle that requires the cumulative effect to be reported, net of taxes, as a component of the current year's income.

**60.** /c/ Whether the grant date and measurement date are different or identical, the compensation cost should be recognized over the period that the services are rendered for a compensatory stock option plan.

**61.** /c/ Appreciation to date x percentage of service period completed = total liability to date. $28 (market price 12/31/x1) - $20 = $8 appreciation per share. 30,000 rights x $8 = $240,000 total appreciation. $240,000 x (2/3years) = $160,000

**62.** /c/ Since the rights were granted for past services, no adjustment to the increase in value is needed for the percentage of service period completed. $15 increase per share x 20,000 rights = $300,000.

**63.** /a/ Compensation expense relating to an ESOP is measured at the fair value of assets contributed to the plan during the year. $45,000 cash + (3,000 shares x $18/share) = $99,000. The acquisition of 6,000 shares used funds already in the ESOP and distributions from the fund are not related to the measurement of expense.

**64.** /a/ According to ASC Topic 710, accrual must be made if compensation payment relates to services already rendered, is probable, and pertains to rights that vest or accumulate.

**65.** /b/ Accrue amounts relating only to Ryan since those rights vest or accumulate but Todd's do not. $800 x 2 weeks = $1,600.

**66.** /c/ First, adjust the balance remaining for vacations earned in prior years but not taken during the current year. $35,000 - $20,000 x 10% = $1,500. $30,000 current-year vacations earned + $1,500 adjustment = $31,500.

**67.** /d/ Since the rights either vest or accumulate and are estimable, accrued expense totaling $150,000 should be recorded.

**68.** /b/ Let C = contribution amount.
$$C = .10(\$75,000 - C)$$
$$C = \$7,500 - .1C$$
$$1.1C = \$7,500$$
$$C = \$6,818$$

**69.** /d/ Let B = Bonus
$$B = 0.1(\$430,000 - \$100,000 - B)$$
$$B = \$43,000 - \$10,000 - 0.1B)$$
$$1.1B = \$33,000$$
$$B = \$30,000$$

**70.** /c/ $800,000 x 10% = $80,000

**71.** /a/ The adjusted amount earned by the artist during 20x0 is Bain's royalty expense for the year. Amounts prepaid will be expensed in future periods when related sales are made (matching principle).

**72.** /c/ $250,000
300,000
150,000
$700,000

The $500,000 of cost reimbursed should not be reported in the Trencher, Inc. income statement.

**73.** /d/ All costs presented qualify for inclusion in the income statement as R & D expenses.

**74.** /c/ The legal costs are capitalized as part of the patent costs. R & D expenses include the cost of equipment to be used solely on the development of the product. $60,000 + $200,000 + $80,000 = $340,000

**75.** /d/ Options A, B, and C are not R & D items because they pertain to commercial production of existing products.

**76.** /d/ Research and development expense includes essentially all expenditures up to the point that the product or process is brought into commercial production.

**77.** /b/ Gains or losses from disposal of a segment of a business are shown net of tax as a separate item after continuing operations but before extraordinary items (discontinued operations).

**78.** /a/ Losses during the phase-out period are shown as part of the loss on disposal of the segment.

**79.** /d/ The severance pay and employee relocation costs are properly included as part of the loss on disposal of the segment. Also, the results of operating the segment up through the date of disposal should be included under the heading "Discontinued Operations." Therefore, the total loss should be 475,000 + 75,000 = $550,000. The assumption is that all losses have been realized during the year.

**80.** /a/ All losses from operating the discontinued segment during the year should be included in the loss from discontinued segment. Therefore, the loss from the discontinued segment is $1,200,000 x .60 = $720,000.

**81.** /c/ Losses from operating a discontinued segment prior to the measurement date are included in the loss from discontinued operations, as are losses incurred during the phase-out period.

**82.** /a/ Losses from operating a discontinued segment after the measurement date (September 30 in this case) are included in the loss on disposal.

**83.** /a/ Loss on discontinued operations of Alpha division for 20x1 is the loss up to measurement date (12/31) net of taxes; $1,400,000 - ($1,400,000 x 30%) = $980,000

**84.** /c/ Loss on disposal:

| | |
|---|---|
| 20x2 operating loss | $500,000 |
| Loss on sale of facilities | 300,000 |
| Total loss on disposal | $800,000 |
| Less tax at 30% | -240,000 |
| Loss net of tax | $560,000 |

**85.** /d/ 20x1: Revised income statement should show loss from operations of discontinued segment, $250,000 net of tax at 30% = ($175,000).

20x2: Gain on disposal of $450,000 less loss on operations for 20x2 of $320,000 = overall gain on disposal of $130,000, net of tax at 30% = $91,000.

**86.** /c/ Use the actual figures for both years when these figures were known.

20x0: Loss of $300,000
20x1: Gain $650,000 less $300,000 loss = $350,000 gain.

**87.** /c/

| Operations to measurement | |
|---|---|
| date during year | $(130,000) |
| Disposal costs incurred | (75,000) |
| Loss on operations after | |
| measurement date | (50,000) |
| Write down of segment to FV | (350,000) |
| Loss on disposal of a | |
| segment before taxes | $(605,000) |

The additional losses incurred in 20x2 will be recognized as losses on the 20x2 financial statements.

**88.** /b/ An item must be either unusual and infrequently occurring to be classified as unusual.

**89.** /b/ Since hailstorms are not unusual in nature and frequently occur in Toncan's operating environment, hail damage loss does not qualify for "extraordinary" treatment. The actual loss amount should be reported as a component of income from continuing operations.

**90.** /a/ Loss from hurricane damage: $800,000 (equipment) + $300,000 (building) = $1,100,000 less $1,000,000 insurance recovery = $100,000 extraordinary loss before taxes. Note that the foreign currency exchange loss and loss from discontinued operations are specifically cited by the FASB as never being "extraordinary."

**91.** /a/ Neither item qualifies for extraordinary treatment. Foreign currency transactions are specifically cited by the FASB as not extraordinary, and a court-ordered increase in a contract's price is neither unusual in nature nor infrequent in occurrence.

**92.** /a/ Book value of the bonds is the face amount plus the unamortized premium for 1/2 of the bonds, $300,000 + 4,500 = $304,500. Cost to repurchase the bonds in the open market is $291,000. Therefore, the

gain is $13,500 and it is classified normally as "Other Income" if considered unusual or infrequent. If it is considered unusual and infrequent it would be considered extraordinary.

**93.** /d/ Gains or losses from early extinguishment of debt should normally be shown as other income unless they are considered both unusual and infrequent. This applies when funds to extinguish the debt are the proceeds from new debt or when new bonds are directly exchanged for old bonds.

**94.** /b/

| Gain on the sale of equipment | $275,000 |
|---|---|
| Loss on the write-down | |
| of inventories. | (70,000) |
| Total infrequent net gains | $205,000 |

The gain from selling the only investment Pierre has ever owned would be considered an extraordinary gain.

**95.** /c/ Losses resulting from a strike are specifically cited as not extraordinary by the FASB. However, since this was Teller's first loss from an antitrust action, it would meet both the unusual in nature and infrequent in occurrence criteria or treatment as an extraordinary item.

**96.** /b/ All three listed events are considered infrequent losses that are not considered extraordinary. $20,000 + $50,000 + $70,000 = $140,000.

**97.** /a/ Neither losses on disposal of a segment of a business nor losses on translation of foreign currency are considered extraordinary items.

**98.** /a/ Transactions which are unusual in nature or occur infrequently, but not both, can be shown as separate components of income but must not be shown net of tax.

**99.** /b/ $260,000 gain on disposal of a segment plus the $190,000 gain on reacquisition and retirement of bonds less $90,000 loss on abandonment of equipment = $360,000 net gain. All items are considered to be infrequent gains and losses (not extraordinary).

**100.** /a/ Although none of the items is extraordinary, all qualify as infrequent (or should be infrequent!).

**101.** /d/ D is the only option which is not a change in accounting principle. This is a correction of an error. Options A, B, and C are all changes in accounting principle that require a retrospective approach.

**102.** /a/ The change in depreciation methods is not considered a retrospective adjustment to income for prior years. It is considered a change in accounting estimate and accounted for prospectively. Therefore, no adjustment to prior years is required and the current year's depreciation is recalculated using the new depreciation method.

**103.** /a/

| | |
|---|---|
| Current book value | $240,000 |
| Years of life remaining | 2 years |
| Straight-line depreciation | $120,000 |

There is no retroactive adjustment required for the change in depreciation methods, so the current book value is depreciated over the remaining two years of life.

**104.** /b/ There is no retrospective treatment of changes in depreciation methods as it is considered a change in estimate. The only change would be a recalculation of the annual depreciation using the new depreciation method.

**105.** /d/ There is no adjustment required due to the change in depreciation method, only the current calculated depreciation expense is shown on the income statement (no retrospective change is made, only prospective). The gain on debt extinguishment is reported separately as an ordinary gain (not extraordinary) and thus a component of income from operations. All other items are used in determination of income from operations before income taxes. Therefore, the only adjustment to income required is to remove the adjustment for depreciation from expense (increase net income by $40,000). If the gain on debt extinguishment is considered extraordinary then it would not be part of income from continuing operations and the answer would be C.

**106.** /d/ Retrospective effects of retroactive application are reported on the face of the financial statements for a change in accounting principle. All other items affect the current and future periods.

**107.** /d/ The retrospective application of a change in accounting principle is shown as an adjustment to income in prior years, but this is not consistent with the principle used in prior years. The retrospective application restates prior years to make all financial statements presented consistent.

**108.** /b/ The retrospective effect of the change would be to decrease the value of inventory and increase the amount charged to Cost of Goods Sold in prior years as a $120,000 debit. Therefore, a $120,000 debit adjustment (decrease) to beginning retained earnings is required.

**109.** /a/ Do not simply compare totals over the three years in this question (Option B). Differences in net income arising from under- or over-stating inventory amounts are self-correcting over a two-year period. This is because the ending inventory amount of the first period becomes the beginning inventory amount for the second period, thus canceling the effect of the difference in amounts. Compare only the 20x2 figures. FIFO inventory exceeded weighted-average by $5,000, causing cost of goods sold to be lower by $5,000 than it would have been had the weighted-average figure been used. A decrease of $5,000, therefore, needs to be reported as the retrospective adjustment to retained earnings.

**110.** /c/ This is a change in the method of inventory pricing and is reported as a retrospective adjustment to beginning retained earnings with separate disclosure required.

**111.** /a/ The retrospective effect of a change in accounting principle is determined as of the beginning of the year in which the change is made.

**112.** /c/ C, a change from the LIFO method of inventory pricing to FIFO, requires a retrospective restatement of prior years statements. The change must be disclosed, including justification for the change.

**113.** /d/ A change from the LIFO method to another method of inventory pricing requires retrospective adjustment treatment. The effect of the change would be to increase the value of inventory and decrease the amount charged to Cost of Goods Sold in prior years by $800,000. This is shown in the 20x0 retained earnings statement as an $800,000 credit (increase).

**114.** /a/ A change from the LIFO method to another method of inventory pricing requires retrospective adjustment treatment. The effect of the change would be to increase the value of inventory and decrease the amount charged to Cost of Goods Sold in prior years. Therefore, there is no retrospective effect on the income statement.

**115.** /a/ A change from LIFO requires retrospective adjustment. Likewise, a change from FIFO to weighted average is a also a retrospective adjustment change.

**116.** /b/ A change from LIFO is a retrospective change that should be reflected in the earliest period reported. (Note: if it is impracticable to determine the cumulative effect, it should be applied prospectively.) $175,000 less 30% taxes is a $122,500 change in income.

**117.** /a/ For a change to the LIFO method of inventory valuation, only disclosure of the effect on the current year's income and the justification for the change is required. Thus, the change to the LIFO method of inventory valuation would decrease Ending Inventory by $60,000, thereby increasing Cost of Goods Sold by $60,000 and decreasing Net Income to $110,000.

**118.** /c/ This is not a change in accounting principle; rather, it is a change in estimate. It is not, therefore, reported as a retrospective effect change. As a change in estimate, it is accounted for in the period of the change and in any future periods affected.

**119.** /c/ The effect of a change in accounting principle that is inseparable from a change in estimate is accounted for as a change in estimate. This requires reporting the effect as a component of income from continuing operations in the period of the change and in any future periods affected.

**120.** /c/ A change in benefit periods is a change in estimate. It is accounted for prospectively; i.e. in the period of change and any future periods benefited.

**121.** /b/ This is a change in reporting entity which requires restatement of financial statements for all prior periods presented.

**122.** /c/ A correction of an error is accounted for as a prior period adjustment.

**123.** /c/ 20x2's retained earnings' statement should show a prior-period adjustment of $(25,000) relating to the overstatement of 20x1's income (correction of an error). 20x2 income should be $125,000 ($150,000 originally reported less the $25,000 overstated in 20x2). 20x3's income is correctly stated at $180,000.

**124.** /d/ Unrealized losses on noncurrent MES are reported in the stockholders' equity section of the balance sheet. Prior-period adjustments for errors are not components of net income; they are direct adjustments to beginning retained earnings. The gain on retirement of bonds is a component of net income. The loss from the fire would be included in net income. It would not be shown net of tax as it is not "extraordinary." However, the tax effect would reduce net income by $7,000 so no amount is added back for the tax.

| | |
|---|---|
| Net income as reported | $74,100 |
| Add back: | |
| Unrealized loss on | |
| noncurrent MES | 5,400 |
| Adjustment for errors | 7,500 |
| Corrected net income | $87,000 |

**125.** /b/ A change from an unaccepted to an accepted accounting principle is treated as the correction of an error and would be reported as a prior period adjustment. A change in the lives of depreciable assets is a change in estimate.

**126.** /b/ Air Inc.'s prior year income was overstated by the $300,000 deferred compensation expense net of $70,000 tax benefit. A debit of $230,000 is needed to adjust beginning retained earnings.

**127.** /a/ Neither change is the correction of an error; the change in depreciation methods is accounted for as a change in estimate and the change in inventory methods is a change in accounting principle requiring retrospective effect treatment.

**128.** /b/ ASC Topic 260 requires that earnings per share data be presented for both income before extraordinary items and the cumulative effect of change in accounting principle if both extraordinary item/s and accounting changes exist.

**129.** /a/ Declaration of a stock dividend constitutes a redefinition of a share of the firm and thus requires retroactive adjustment to year-end equivalents, i.e., it is treated as occurring at the beginning of the year.

**130.** /b/ The 2-for-1 stock split is treated as having occurred at the beginning of the year.

| | | |
|---|---|---|
| 1/1 - 4/1 | 20,000 x 2 x 3/12 | 10,000 |
| 4/1 - 7/1 | 40,000 x 3/12 | 10,000 |
| 7/1 - 12/31 | 50,000 x 6/12 | 25,000 |
| Weighted average shares | | 45,000 |

**131.** /c/ Both the declaration of a stock dividend and a stock split require consideration in the 20x1 statements. They occurred between balance sheet date and presentation date of the statements and have a material effect on the presentation of EPS information.

**132.** /a/ This is a change in estimate and is accounted for prospectively; i.e. in the period of change and thereafter. Financial statements for prior periods are not restated and no cumulative effect or pro forma amounts are reported. The warranty expense for 20x4 is, therefore, 1% of the sales for that period ($5,000,00 x 1% = $50,000).

**133.** /c/

| | | | |
|---|---|---|---|
| Jan-Sept | 400,000 | 9/12 | 300,000 |
| Oct-Dec | 500,000 | 3/12 | 125,000 |
| | | | 425,000 |

Basic EPS = 2,144,000/425,000 = $5.04

**134.** /c/ Numerator = $120,000 - 8,000 (preferred dividends) = $112,000. Denominator = 20,000 shares. Basic EPS = $5.60.

**135.** /a/ Dividends on cumulative preferred stock are deducted from net income in calculating earnings available to common whether the dividends are declared or not because even if the dividends are not declared, they accumulate or carry over to subsequent years.

**136.** /c/ Numerator = $660,000 - 120,000 (preferred dividends) = $540,000. Denominator = 300,000 shares. Basic EPS = $1.80.

**137.** /b/ One of the more significant changes in the computation of EPS under ASC Topic 260 is in the application of the treasury stock method for the dilutive effect of outstanding options, rights, and warrants. Under the new standard, it is always assumed that the proceeds of the exercise of the options will be used to purchase treasury shares at the average market price for the year. The period-end market price now has no impact on the calculation. (You are also reminded that conversion of the options is not assumed unless the average market price is higher than the exercise price.)

**138.** /a/ The denominator effect of conversion of the options is an increase of 4,000 shares. 20,000 shares issued at $20/share yields $400,000 -:- $25/share average market price per share = 16,000 treasury shares. 20,000 - 16,000 = 4,000 incremental denominator.

| | Numerator | Denominator | EPS |
|---|---|---|---|
| Basic EPS | $550,000 | 110,000 | $5.00 |
| Incremental from options | -0- | 4,000 | |
| Diluted EPS | $550,000 | 114,000 | $4.82 |

**139.** /c/ The solution requires computation of the incremental ratios for each of the convertible securities and their use in the determination of diluted EPS.

| | Num. | Denom. | Ratio |
|---|---|---|---|
| Preferred | $7,000 | 3,000 | 2.33 |
| 4 1/2% bonds | $5,850[1] | 4,000 | 1.46 |
| 6% bonds | $19,500[2] | 15,000 | 1.30 |

[1] Interest saved of $9,000 ($200,000 x 4.5%) net of taxes at 35% = $5,850.

[2] Interest saved of $30,000 ($500,000 x 6%) net of taxes at 35% = $19,500

Starting from basic EPS, add the denominators and numerators from each convertible security as indicated by ascending order of the ratios. Stop if an antidilutive effect occurs.

Basic EPS is $67,000 - $7,000 (preferred dividends) -:- 20,000 common shares = $3.00

Add 6% bonds effect (lowest ratio):
($60,000 + $19,500) / (20,000 + 15,000) = $2.27

Add 4 1/2% bonds effect (next highest ratio):
($60,000 + $19,500 + $5,850) / (20,000 + 15,000 + 4,000) = $2.19

Add preferred stock effect:
($60,000 + $19,500 + $5,850 + $7,000)/(20,000 + 15,000 + 4,000 + 3,000) = $2.20

Since the effect of adding the preferred stock numerator and denominator is to increase diluted EPS from $2.19 to $2.20, they are antidilutive and are excluded from the computation. Diluted EPS is $2.19.

**140.** /c/ Antidilutive convertible securities are not used in the calculation of either basic or diluted EPS.

**141.** /c/ Options A, B, and D are stated objectives of ASC Topic 260. Option C, however, is not applicable to EPS computations and is a nonsense answer.

**142.** /a/ Basic earnings per share does not consider the effect on EPS of the conversion of convertible securities. This is a factor, however, in the determination of diluted EPS.

**143.** /c/

| | | | |
|---|---|---|---|
| Jan-Mar | 5,000,000 | 3/12 | 1,250,000 |
| Apr-June | 6,000,000 | 3/12 | 1,500,000 |
| Jul-Dec | 6,500,000 | 6/12 | 3,250,000 |
| | | | 6,000,000 |

The number of shares added for computing diluted EPS are 10,000 bonds x 40 shares per bond = 400,000 x 3/12 = 100,000. Therefore, the number of shares to be used in calculating diluted EPS would be 6,100,000. Note that there is not enough information to tell whether the bonds are dilutive or antidilutive, so you don't know whether the correct number of shares to use in calculating diluted EPS would be 6,000,000 or 6,100,000. However, there is no answer corresponding to the first possibility, so the best answer is 6,100,000.

**144.** /c/ When calculating diluted EPS, only dilutive securities are considered.

**145.** /b/ $860,000 - $60,000 (preferred dividend) -:- 200,000 shares = Basic EPS of $4.00.

**146.** /d/ $970,000 - $50,000 (preferred dividend) -:- 90,000 common shares = basic EPS of $10.22.

**147.** /a/ Incremental ratio for conversion of preferred shares is $50,000 dividends saved -:- 20,000 additional shares = 2.5.

Incremental ratio for conversion of 9% bonds is $108,000 ($180,000 interest net of taxes at 40%) -:- 30,000 additional shares = 3.6.

Basic EPS = $10.22 (from #146)

Consider effect of preferred shares:
($920,000 + $50,000)/(90,000 + 20,000) = $8.82

Consider effect of 9% bonds:
($920,000 + $50,000 + $108,000) / (90,000 + 20,000 + 30,000) = $7.70.

Since the effect of both convertible securities is dilutive, diluted EPS is $7.70

**148.** /b/ Weighted average shares:

| | |
|---|---|
| 10,000 shares outstanding x 6/12 | 5,000 |
| 14,000 shares outstanding x 6/12 | 7,000 |
| Denominator for basic EPS | 12,000 |
| 4,000 shares x 50% if bonds converted for first six months of year | 2,000 |
| Denominator for diluted EPS | 14,000 |

Numerator for Basic EPS is $35,000. Incremental numerator for diluted is $4,900 ($7,000 bond interest expense saved net of increased taxes at 30%)

Basic EPS: $35,000 -:- 12,000 shares = $2.92

Diluted EPS: ($35,000 + $4,900) -:- 14,000 shares = $2.85

**149.** /d/ Numerator of $850,000 - $30,000 (preferred dividends) -:- 110,000 shares = Basic EPS of $<u>7.45</u>.

**150.** /b/ Determine incremental ratios, then proceed from basic EPS to diluted EPS.

Preferred shares: Numerator $30,000; denominator 20,000 shares. Ratio is 1.5

8% bonds: Numerator is $56,000 ($80,000 interest expense saved, net of $24,000 tax); denominator is 30,000 shares. Ratio is 1.87.

Basic EPS is $850,000 - $30,000 (preferred dividends) -:- 110,000 shares = $7.45.

<u>Consider effect of preferred shares:</u> ($820,000 + $30,000)/(110,000 + 20,000) = $6.54.

<u>Consider effect of 8% bonds:</u> ($820,000 + $30,000 + $56,000)/(110,000 + 20,000 + 30,000) = $5.66.

Since both convertible securities are dilutive, diluted EPS is $<u>5.66</u>.

**151.** /b/ The denominator is the sum of the 100,000 shares outstanding and the incremental shares relating to the "if converted" preferred stock (1,000) and the options (7,500 -- see below).

From options: 30,000 exercisable at $15 each yields proceeds of $450,000. Purchase of treasury shares at average market price of $20 per share provides buy-back of 22,500 shares. Incremental shares outstanding would be 30,000 - 22,500 = 7,500.

Using the stock options, EPS = $900,000 + 0 / 107,500 shares = $8.37 per share.

The preferred stock will add $4,000 to the numerator ($100,000 x 4%) and 1,000 shares to the denominator. Therefore, the new EPS = (900,000 + 4,000) / (107,500 + 1,000) = $904,000 / 108,500 = $8.33 per share. Thus, the preferred stock is also dilutive (EPS went down).

**152.** /c/ Earnings available to common shareholders are $10,600,000 - 600,000 (preferred dividends) = $10,000,000. Since the dividend payout ratio was 40%, the dividends to common shareholders must have been $4,000,000.

**153.** /a/ Actual total costs are used in the calculation of the percent completion during the final year. Income previously recognized is subtracted from total income to date to arrive at income to be recognized for the final period.

**154.** /c/ Under the installment method of revenue recognition, each payment received is treated as partly a return of costs and partly profit. The profit recognized is determined by applying the appropriate gross profit rate(s) to the cash collections received.

**155.** /d/ It is proper to recognize revenue prior to sale only when it is guaranteed that merchandise will be sold at a locked-in minimum price. The rationale is that the earnings process is virtually complete at the time of acquisition of the merchandise or upon completion of production. Neither circumstance listed is applicable to revenue recognition prior to sale.

**156.** /d/ Under the cost recovery method of revenue recognition, equal amounts of revenue and cost are recognized as collections are made until all the costs have been recovered. Recognition of profit is thus postponed until costs have been recovered. It is a conservative approach to revenue recognition that is appropriate when there is no reasonable basis upon which to base an estimate of collectability.

**157.** /d/ Lease revenues are to be recognized ratably over the period benefited. Even though only four annual payments will be received, the lease is for five years. Therefore, one-fifth of the total cash to be received over the lease is recognized in the 20x3 income statement.

**158.** /c/ Royalty interest to be recognized is 20% of oil sales for 20x4.

| Oil sales, 20x4: | |
| --- | --- |
| Dec 1, x3 - May 31, x4 | $400,000 |
| Less Dec x3 sales | (50,000) |
| Sales 1/1/x3 - 5/31/x4 | $350,000 |
| Plus: | |
| June 1 - Nov 30, x4 | 325,000 |
| December 20x4 | 70,000 |
| Total oil sales, x4 | $745,000 |
| x 20% | |
| Royalty income 20x4 | $149,000 |

**159.** /c/ The $15,000 printing cost for catalogs for the January sales promotion should not be deducted until the related revenues are earned (January of next year -- matching principle). The $9,000 cost for radio advertisements has to be recognized in the period in which the advertisements were run -- December, 20x4. Advertising expense for the year ended December 31, 20x3, should therefore be $140,000 ($146,000 - $15,000 + $9,000).

**160.** /d/ Interest expense is classified as an "other" expense. Advertising expense is a selling expense.

**161.** /b/ Since the bonus is based on income after bonus but before taxes, the first step is to compute that base. Income after taxes (40% tax rate) and bonus is $360,000. Therefore, income after bonus but before taxes is $360,000/60% = $600,000. The bonus is $600,000 x 10% = $60,000.

**162.** /d/ Income or loss from operating a discontinued segment up through the measurement date (April 30) is shown net of tax as income or loss from operations of discontinued operations. The loss during the period January 1 through April 30 was $300,000.

**163.** /d/ The two bond transactions are separate events and must be recorded separately - no netting is allowed, even though the proceeds of one transaction were used to effect the repurchase of the company's own bonds. Gold's loss on the sale of its investment in Iron Corp.'s bonds is reported as a component of income from continuing operations -- other gains and losses. The early extinguishment of its own bonds is reported as an extraordinary item, net of taxes.

**164.** /c/ The correction of the failure to accrue warranty costs of $50,000 in the previous year is the only prior period adjustment to be made. The change in depreciation method is a change in accounting principle. The cumulative effect of such a change is reported, net of taxes, as a component of income reported after extraordinary items.

# CHAPTER 7

# INCOME STATEMENT

## Simulation Answers

### Number 1 Answer

1. /B/ Increases in unrealized excess of cost over market value on short-term MES are recognized in the income statement as a component of income from continuing operations.

2. /D/ Increases in unrealized losses relating to long-term MES are not reported on the income statement. They are included in a special contra account as a component of stockholders' equity.

3. /E/ Income from operations of a discontinued segment is one of the two major components of the results of discontinued operations. It is reported after income from continuing operations, but before extraordinary items and cumulative effect of a change in accounting principles, if any.

4. /B/ Translation losses using the remeasurement method are included in the income statement as a component of income from continuing operations. (See Chapter 5, "Special Topics," - Foreign Exchange.)

5. /D/ In this instance, the functional currency is the local currency; therefore, the current rate method would be used to translate the financial statements. The loss would be reported as an adjustment in the stockholders' equity section of the balance sheet. (See Chapter 5, "Special Topics," - Foreign Exchange.)

6. /C/ Losses arising from events that are both unusual in nature and infrequent in occurrence are considered to be extraordinary items.

7. /E/ A probable receipt from a pending lawsuit is a gain contingency. Such gains are not recognized until they are realized.

8. /B/ All research and development costs are expensed in the period incurred, whether self-performed or provided as a service by another company. The absence of other research and development activities is irrelevant.

### Number 2 Answer

1. /A/Y/ A change in the method of accounting for long-term construction contracts is one of the five specific changes in principle that require retroactive restatement. Such changes are likely to have significantly large cumulative amounts relative to the income of the period. Any part of the cumulative effect attributable to years earlier than 20x2 would be shown as an adjustment to the beginning balance of retained earnings for that year. See text discussion under Section VI.A.2.b.

2. /B/Z/ This is a change in the estimated service life of an asset and is, accordingly, treated as a change in estimate. No retroactive adjustments are made. The new service life is used in the current period and into the future (prospectively).

3. /B/Z/ This also is a change in estimate and treated prospectively.

**4.** /A/Y/ A change in accounting for inventories from LIFO to any other method is another one of the five specific situations where a change in accounting principle requires retroactive restatement. See answer to Item 1 for further explanation.

**5.** /A/X/ This is a change in accounting principle, but it does not require restatement. The cumulative effect of the change (net of tax) will be included as an element of net income and will be reported on the income statement after extraordinary items.

**6.** /C/Y/ This is not a change in principle, rather it is the correction of an error. Quo should have been using the accrual method to record service contract revenues since the revenues pertain to contracts that are performed over several years. Use of the cash basis method was incorrect. Corrections of errors are accounted for as prior period adjustments. Comparative statements for prior periods presented are restated. Any cumulative effect attributable to years prior to 20x2 would be adjusted to the beginning balance of retained earnings for that year.

**7.** /C/Y/ This also is correction of an error and requires retroactive restatement. However, since the error was made in 20x2, there will be no amount attributable to years prior to 20x2 that would require an adjustment to beginning retained earnings for that year.

**8.** /A/X/ This is a change in accounting principle that is treated using the cumulative effect approach. Notice that this affects existing depreciable assets. If this were adoption of a different depreciation method for newly acquired assets only, the cumulative effect approach would not be used.

**9.** /D/Z/ Since Quo did not have a pre-existing pension plan, this is not a change in accounting principle. The implementation of accounting procedures following ASC Topic 715 are coincident with the institution of the plan itself and will be accounted for prospectively.

**10.** /D/Y/ When ownership of an investee reaches the point at which significant influence can be exerted (30% interest and a seat on the board of directors in this case), the equity method of accounting for the investment is implemented. Although it is not a change in principle or correction of an error, there is a retroactive restatement of the investment account. The adjustment is equal to the difference between the actual balance and what the balance would have been had the equity method always been used. 20x2 income will be adjusted for the difference between investment income as recorded under the previous method and investment income as it would have been recorded under the equity method.

# CHAPTER 8

## STATEMENT OF CASH FLOWS AND RATIO ANALYSIS

### Question Map

IX.    CONVERSION FROM CASH TO ACCRUAL BASIS -- 31, 32, 33, 57

X.    RATIO ANALYSIS
    A.  Introduction
    B.  Liquidity Ratios—34, 35, 36, 37, 39
    C.  Activity Ratios -- 38, 40, 41,42, 43, 52, 54, 55, 56
    D.  Leverage Ratios – 52, 53
    E.  Coverage Ratios -- 51
    F.  Profitability Ratios– 34, 44, 46, 47, 48, 50, 52
    G.  The DuPont System
    H.  Comprehensive Example

## Multiple Choice Questions

**1.** The primary purpose of a statement of cash flows is to provide relevant information about

a. Differences between net income and associated cash receipts and disbursements.

b. An enterprise's ability to generate future positive net cash flows.

c. The cash receipts and cash disbursements of an enterprise during a period.

d. An enterprise's ability to meet cash operating needs.

**2.** Cook Co. had the following balances at December 21, 20x2:

Cash in checking account        $350,000
Cash in money-market account    250,000
U.S. Treasury bill, purchased
  12/1/x2,maturing 2/28/x3      800,000
U.S. Treasury bond, purchased 3/1/x2,
  maturing 2/28/x3              500,000

Cook's policy is to treat as cash equivalent all highly-liquid investments with a maturity of three months or less when purchased. What amount should Cook report as cash and cash equivalents in it December 31, 20x2, balance sheet?

a. $ 600,000
b. $1,150,000
c. $1,400,000
d. $1,900,000

**3.** Deed Co. owns 2% of Beck Cosmetic Retailers. A property dividend by Beck consisted of merchandise with a fair value lower than the listed retail price. Deed in turn gave the merchandise to its employees as a holiday bonus. How should Deed report the receipt and distribution of the merchandise in its statement of cash flows?

a. As both an inflow and outflow for operating activities.

b. As both an inflow and outflow for investing activities.

c. At fair value for dividend revenue and listed retail price for employee compensation expense.

d. As a noncash activity.

**4.** Which of the following must be included as part of the statement of cash flows?

a. Acquisition of fixed assets in exchange for capital stock.

b. Payment of cash dividends.

c. Retirement of a bond issue through the issuance of another bond issue.

d. Conversion of convertible debt to capital stock.

**5.** Which of the following cash flows per share should be reported in a statement of cash flows?

a. Primary cash flows per share only.

b. Fully diluted cash flows per share only.

c. Both primary and fully diluted cash flows per share.

d. Cash flows per share should **not** be reported.

**6.** The following information was taken from the financial statement of Planet Corp. for the year:

Accounts receivable, 1/1        $ 21,600
Accounts receivable, 12/31      30,400
Sales on account and cash sales 438,000
Uncollectible accounts          1,000

No accounts receivable were written off or recovered during the year.

If the direct method is used in the statement of cash flows for the year, Planet should report cash collected from customers as

a. $447,800
b. $446,800
c. $429,200
d. $428,200

**7.** In a statement of cash flows, which of the following would increase reported cash flows from operating activities using the direct method? (Ignore income tax considerations.)
- **a.** Dividends received from investments.
- **b.** Gain on sale of equipment.
- **c.** Gain on early retirement.
- **d.** Change from straight-line to accelerated depreciation.

**8.** The cash outflow associated with the payment of taxes on an unusual gain on the extinguishment of debt is classified on the statement of cash flows as an:

| | Operating Activity | Financing Activity |
|---|---|---|
| **a.** | Yes | No |
| **b.** | No | Yes |
| **c.** | Yes | Yes |
| **d.** | No | No |

**Items 9 through 13 are based on the following:**

Flax Corp. uses the direct method to prepare its statement of cash flows. Flax's trial balances at December 31, 20x1 and 20x0, are as follows:

| | December 31 | |
|---|---|---|
| | 20x1 | 20x0 |
| Debits: | | |
| Cash | $ 35,000 | $ 32,000 |
| Accounts receivable | 33,000 | 30,000 |
| Inventory | 31,000 | 47,000 |
| Property, plant and equipment | 100,000 | 95,000 |
| Unamortized bond discount | 4,500 | 5,000 |
| Cost of goods sold | 250,000 | 380,000 |
| Selling expenses | 141,500 | 172,000 |
| General and admin. expenses | 137,000 | 151,300 |
| Interest expense | 4,300 | 2,600 |
| Income tax expense | 20,400 | 61,200 |
| | $756,700 | $976,100 |

| | 20x1 | 20x0 |
|---|---|---|
| Credits: | | |
| Allowance for uncollectible accounts | $ 1,300 | $ 1,100 |
| Accumulated depreciation | 16,500 | 15,000 |
| Trade accounts payable | 25,000 | 17,500 |
| Income taxes payable | 21,000 | 27,100 |
| Deferred income taxes | 5,300 | 4,600 |
| 8% callable bonds payable | 45,000 | 20,000 |
| Common stock | 50,000 | 40,000 |
| Additional paid-in Capital | 9,100 | 7,500 |
| Retained earnings | 44,700 | 64,600 |
| Sales | 538,800 | 778,700 |
| | $756,700 | $976,100 |

- Flax purchased $5,000 in equipment during 20x1.
- Flax allocated one-third of its depreciation expense to selling expenses and the remainder to general and administrative expenses.

What amounts should Flax report in its statement of cash flows for the year ended December 31, 20x1, for the following:

**9.** Cash collected from customers?
- **a.** $541,800
- **b.** $541,600
- **c.** $536,000
- **d.** $535,800

**10.** Cash paid for goods to be sold?
- **a.** $258,500
- **b.** $257,500
- **c.** $242,500
- **d.** $226,500

**11.** Cash paid for interest?
- **a.** $4,800
- **b.** $4,300
- **c.** $3,800
- **d.** $1,700

**12.** Cash paid for income taxes?
- **a.** $25,800
- **b.** $20,400
- **c.** $19,700
- **d.** $15,000

13. Cash paid for selling expenses?
   a. $142,000
   b. $141,500
   c. $141,000
   d. $140,000

14. Kresley Co. has provided the following current-year account balances for the preparation of the annual statement of cash flows:

|  | Jan. 1 | Dec. 31 |
|---|---|---|
| Accounts receivable | $11,500 | $14,500 |
| Allowance for uncollectible accounts | 400 | 500 |
| Prepaid rent expense | 6,200 | 4,100 |
| Accounts payable | 9,700 | 11,200 |

Kresley's net income for the year is $75,000. Net cash provided by operating activities in the statement of cash flows should be
   a. $72,700
   b. $74,300
   c. $75,500
   d. $75,700

15. Token Company sold some of its fixed assets during 20x8. The original cost of the fixed assets was $750,000 and the allowance for accumulated depreciation at the date of sale was $600,000. The proceeds from the sale of the fixed assets were $210,000. The information concerning the sale of the fixed assets should be shown on Token's statement of cash flows for the year ended December 31, 20x8, using the indirect method of:
   a. A subtraction from net income of $60,000 and an investing inflow of $150,000.
   b. An addition to net income of $60,000 and an investing inflow of $150,000.
   c. A subtraction from net income of $60,000 and an investing inflow of $210,000.
   d. An investing inflow of $150,000.

16. Kirt, Incorporated, had net income for 20x8 of $3,000,000. Additional information is as follows:

| | |
|---|---|
| Amortization of goodwill | $ 80,000 |
| Depreciation on fixed assets | 3,200,000 |
| Long-term debt: | |
| Bond discount amortization | 130,000 |
| Interest expense | 2,600,000 |
| Provision for doubtful accounts: | |
| Current receivables | 700,000 |
| Long-term receivables | 210,000 |

In the 20x8 statement of cash flows the net cash flow from operating activities would be
   a. $6,200,000
   b. $6,410,000
   c. $6,620,000
   d. $7,320,000

17. Metro, Inc. reported net income of $150,000 for 20x0. Changes occurred in several balance sheet accounts during the year as follows:

| | |
|---|---|
| Investment in Videogold, Inc. stock, carried on the equity basis | $5,500 increase |
| Accumulated depreciation, caused by major repair to equipment | 2,100 decrease |
| Premium on bonds payable | 1,400 decrease |
| Deferred income tax liability (long-term) | 1,800 increase |

In Metro's 20x0 cash flow statement, the reported net cash provided by operating activities should be
   a. $150,400
   b. $148,300
   c. $144,900
   d. $142,800

18. In a statement of cash flows, if used equipment is sold at a loss, the amount shown as a cash inflow from investing activities equals the carrying amount of the equipment
   a. Less the loss and plus the amount of tax attributable to the loss.
   b. Less both the loss and the amount of tax attributable to the loss.
   c. Less the loss.
   d. With no addition or subtraction.

**19.** In 20x0, a tornado completely destroyed a building belonging to Holland Corp. The building cost $100,000 and had accumulated depreciation of $48,000 at the time of the loss. Holland received a cash settlement from the insurance company and reported an extraordinary loss of $21,000. In Holland's 20x0 cash flow statement, the net change reported in the cash flows from investing activities section should be

    **a.** $10,000 increase.
    **b.** $21,000 decrease.
    **c.** $31,000 increase.
    **d.** $52,000 decrease.

**20.** Alp, Inc. had the following activities during the year:

- Acquired 2,000 shares of stock in Maybel, Inc. for $26,000.
- Sold an investment in Rate Motors, Inc. for $35,000 when carrying value was $33,000.
- Acquired a $50,000, 4-year certificate of deposit from a bank. (During the year, interest of $3,750 was paid to Alp.)
- Collected dividends of $1,200 on stock investments.

In Alp's statement of cash flows for the year, net cash used in investing activities should be

    **a.** $37,250
    **b.** $38,050
    **c.** $39,800
    **d.** $41,000

**Items 21 and 22 are based on the following information:**

Clark Company is preparing a statement of cash flows for the year ended December 31, 20x8. It has the following account balances:

| | 12/31/x7 | 12/31/x8 |
|---|---|---|
| Machinery | $1,000,000 | $1,280,000 |
| Accumulated depreciation -- machinery | 408,000 | 480,000 |
| Loss on sale of machinery | | 16,000 |

During 20x8, Clark sold for $104,000 a machine that cost $160,000 and purchased several items of machinery.

**21.** Depreciation on machinery for 20x8 was
    **a.** $ 72,000
    **b.** $ 96,000
    **c.** $112,000
    **d.** $128,000

**22.** Machinery purchases for 20x8 amounted to
    **a.** $136,000
    **b.** $280,000
    **c.** $384,000
    **d.** $440,000

**23.** The following information for the year has been provided by the Edward Company:

| | |
|---|---|
| Proceeds from short-term borrowings | $ 600,000 |
| Proceeds from long-term borrowings | 2,000,000 |
| Purchases of fixed assets | 1,600,000 |
| Purchases of inventories | 4,000,000 |
| Proceeds from sale of Edward's common stock | 1,000,000 |

In a statement of cash flows, the net cash out flow from investing activities would be
    **a.** $5,600,000
    **b.** $4,600,000
    **c.** $ 600,000
    **d.** $1,600,000

**24.** In a statement of cash flows, which of the following items is reported as a cash outflow from financing activities?

I. Payments to retire mortgage notes.
II. Interest payments on mortgage notes.
III. Dividend payments.

    **a.** I, II, and III.
    **b.** II and III.
    **c.** I only.
    **d.** I and III.

**25.** The proceeds from the reissuance of treasury stock at an amount in excess of its costs is classified on the statement of cash flows as an:

|    | Financing Activity | Investing Activity |
|----|--------------------|--------------------|
| a. | Yes                | No                 |
| b. | No                 | Yes                |
| c. | Yes                | Yes                |
| d. | No                 | No                 |

**26.** Selected information from Basket Company's accounting records for the year is as follows:

| Proceeds from issuance of common stock | $8,000,000 |
|---|---|
| Proceeds from issuance of preferred stock | 2,000,000 |
| Dividends paid on common stock | 1,000,000 |
| Dividends paid on preferred stock | 400,000 |
| Purchases of treasury stock | 300,000 |
| Sales of stock to officers and employees not included above | 200,000 |

In a statement of cash flows, the net cash flow from financing activities would be
- a. $ 8,500,000
- b. $10,000,000
- c. $ 9,500,000
- d. $ 8,300,000

**27.** During the year, Teb, Inc. had the following activities related to its financial operations:

| Payment for the early retirement of long-term bonds payable | $750,000 |
|---|---|
| Distribution in current year of cash dividend declared in previous year to preferred stockholders | 62,000 |
| Carrying value of convertible preferred stock in Teb, converted into common shares | 120,000 |
| Proceeds from sale of treasury stock (carrying value at cost, $86,000) | 95,000 |

In Teb's statement of cash flows for the year, net cash used in financing activities should be

- a. $717,000
- b. $716,000
- c. $597,000
- d. $535,000

**Items 28 through 30 are based on the following:**

The differences in Beal Inc.'s balance sheet accounts at December 31, 20x0 and 20x9, are presented below:

|  | Increase (Decrease) |
|---|---|
| **Assets** | |
| Cash and cash equivalents | $ 120,000 |
| Short-term investments | 300,000 |
| Accounts receivable, net | – |
| Inventory | 80,000 |
| Long-term investments | (100,000) |
| Plant assets | 700,000 |
| Accumulated depreciation | – |
| | $1,100,000 |
| | |
| **Liabilities and Stockholders' Equity** | |
| Accounts payable and accrued liabilities | $ (5,000) |
| Dividends payable | 160,000 |
| Short-term bank debt | 325,000 |
| Long-term debt | 110,000 |
| Common stock, $10 par | 100,000 |
| Additional paid-in capital | 120,000 |
| Retained earnings | 290,000 |
| | $1,100,000 |

The following additional information relates to 20x0:

- Net income was $790,000.
- Cash dividends of $500,000 were declared.
- Building costing $600,000 and having a carrying amount of $350,000 was sold for $350,000.
- Equipment costing $110,000 was acquired through issuance of long-term debt.
- A long-term investment was sold for $135,000. There were no other transactions affecting long-term investments.

- 10,000 shares of common stock were issued for $22 a share.

In Beal's 20x0 statement of cash flows,

**28.** Net cash provided by operating activities was

a. $1,160,000
b. $1,040,000
c. $920,000
d. $705,000

**29.** Net cash used in investing activities was

a. $1,005,000
b. $1,190,000
c. $1,275,000
d. $1,600,000

**30.** Net cash provided by financing activities was

a. $20,000
b. $45,000
c. $150,000
d. $205,000

**31.** Class Corp. maintains its accounting records on the cash basis but restates its financial statements to the accrual method of accounting. Class had $60,000 in cash-basis pretax income for 20x2. The following information pertains to Class's operations for the years ended December 31, 20x2 and 20x1:

| | 20x2 | 20x1 |
|---|---|---|
| Accounts receivable | $40,000 | $20,000 |
| Accounts payable | 15,000 | 30,000 |

Under the accrual method, what amount of income before taxes should Class report in its December 31, 20x2, income statement?

a. $25,000
b. $55,000
c. $65,000
d. $95,000

**32.** White Co. wants to convert its 20x1 financial statements from the accrual basis of accounting to the cash basis. Both supplies inventory and office salaries payable increased between January 1 and December 31 of 20x1. To obtain 20x1 cash basis net income how should these increases be added to or subtracted from accrual basis net income?

| | Supplies inventory | Office salaries payable |
|---|---|---|
| a. | Deducted | Deducted |
| b. | Deducted | Added |
| c. | Added | Deducted |
| d. | Added | Added |

**33.** Zeta Co. reported sales revenue of $4,600,000 in its income statement for the year ended December 31, 20x1. Additional information is as follows:

Accounts receivable:

| | |
|---|---|
| 12/31/x0 | $1,000,000 |
| 12/31/x1 | $1,300,000 |

Allowance for uncollectible accounts:

| | |
|---|---|
| 12/31/x0 | (60,000) |
| 12/31/x1 | (110,000) |

Zeta wrote off uncollectible accounts totaling $20,000 during the year. Under the cash basis of accounting, Zeta would have reported 20x1 sales of

a. $4,900,000
b. $4,350,000
c. $4,300,000
d. $4,280,000

**34.** Are the following ratios useful in assessing the liquidity position of a company?

| | Defensive-interval ratio | Return on stockholders' equity |
|---|---|---|
| a. | Yes | Yes |
| b. | Yes | No |
| c. | No | Yes |
| d. | No | No |

**35.** Inventories would be included in the calculation of which of the following?

| | Acid test (quick) ratio | Working capital (current) ratio |
|---|---|---|
| a. | Yes | Yes |
| b. | Yes | No |
| c. | No | Yes |
| d. | No | No |

**36.** At December 30, 20x0, Solomon Co. had a current ratio greater than 1:1 and a quick ratio less than 1:1. On December 31, 20x0, all cash was used to reduce accounts payable. How did these cash payments affect the ratios?

|    | Current ratio | Quick Ratio |
|----|---------------|-------------|
| a. | Decreased     | Decreased   |
| b. | Decreased     | Increased   |
| c. | Increased     | Decreased   |
| d. | Increased     | Increased   |

**Questions 37 through 39 are based on the following information:**

Alpha Corporation
SELECTED FINANCIAL DATA

|                              | As of December 31 | |
|                              | 20x0      | 20x9      |
|------------------------------|-----------|-----------|
| Cash                         | $ 10,000  | $ 80,000  |
| Accounts receivable (net)    | 50,000    | 150,000   |
| Merchandise inventory        | 90,000    | 150,000   |
| Short-term marketable        |           |           |
| Securities                   | 30,000    | 10,000    |
| Land and buildings (net)     | 340,000   | 360,000   |
| Mortgage payable             |           |           |
| (no current portion)         | 270,000   | 280,000   |
| Accounts payable (trade)     | 70,000    | 110,000   |
| Short-term notes payable     | 20,000    | 40,000    |

|                    | Year ended December 31 | |
|                    | 20x0        | 20x9        |
|--------------------|-------------|-------------|
| Cash sales         | $1,800,000  | $1,600,000  |
| Credit sales       | 500,000     | 800,000     |
| Cost of goods sold | 1,000,000   | 1,400,000   |

**37.** Alpha's quick (acid test) ratio as of December 31, 20x0, is
  a. 0.5 to 1.
  b. 0.7 to 1.
  c. 1.0 to 1.
  d. 2.0 to 1.

**38.** Alpha's merchandise inventory turnover for 20x0 is
  a. 8.3 times.
  b. 10.0 times.
  c. 11.1 times.
  d. 13.3 times.

**39.** Alpha's current ratio at December 31, 20x0, is
  a. 0.5 to 1.
  b. 0.7 to 1.
  c. 1.0 to 1.
  d. 2.0 to 1.

**40.** Selected information from the accounting records of Dalton Manufacturing Company is as follows:

| | |
|---|---|
| Net sales for 20x2 | $1,800,000 |
| Cost of goods sold for 20x2 | 1,200,000 |
| Inventories at December 31, 20x1 | 336,000 |
| Inventories at December 31, 20x2 | 288,000 |

Assuming there are 300 working days per year, what is the number of days' sales in average inventories for 20x2?
  a. 78
  b. 72
  c. 52
  d. 48

**41.** The following computations were made from Clay Co.'s 20x1 books:

| | |
|---|---|
| Number of days' sales in inventory | 61 |
| Number of days' sales in trade accounts receivable | 33 |

What was the number of days in Clay's 20x1 operating cycle?
  a. 33
  b. 47
  c. 61
  d. 94

**42.** On December 31, 20x1, Northpark Co. collected a receivable due from a major customer. Which of the following ratios would be increased by this transaction?
  a. Inventory turnover ratio.
  b. Receivable turnover ratio.
  c. Current ratio.
  d. Quick ratio.

**Questions 43 and 44 are based on the following data:**

Bretton Corporation's books disclosed the following information as of and for the year ended December 31:

| | |
|---|---|
| Net credit sales | $2,000,000 |
| Net cash sales | 500,000 |
| Merchandise purchases | 1,000,000 |
| Inventory at beginning | 600,000 |
| Inventory at end | 200,000 |
| Accounts receivable at beginning | 300,000 |
| Accounts receivable at end | 700,000 |
| Net income | 100,000 |

**43.** Bretton's accounts receivable turnover is
  a. 2.9 times.
  b. 3.6 times.
  c. 4.0 times.
  d. 5.0 times.

**44.** Bretton's percent of net income on sales is
  a. 4%.
  b. 9%.
  c. 44%.
  d. 56%.

**Questions 45 and 46 are based on the following information:**

Tudor Corporation's condensed financial statements provide the following information:

**BALANCE SHEET**
December 31, 20x1 and 20x0

| | 20x1 | 20x0 |
|---|---|---|
| Cash | $ 60,000 | $ 50,000 |
| Accounts receivable (net) | 220,000 | 200,000 |
| Inventories | 260,000 | 230,000 |
| Property, plant and equipment | 730,000 | 650,000 |
| Accumulated depreciation | (330,000) | (260,000) |
| Total assets | $940,000 | $870,000 |
| | | |
| Current liabilities | $270,000 | $330,000 |
| Stockholders' equity | 670,000 | 540,000 |
| Total liabilities and stockholders' equity | $940,000 | $870,000 |

**STATEMENT OF INCOME**
For the Year Ended December 31, 20x1

| | |
|---|---|
| Net sales | $1,200,000 |
| Cost of goods sold | 780,000 |
| Gross profit | 420,000 |
| Operating expenses | 240,000 |
| Net income | $ 180,000 |

**45.** Assuming that all sales are credit sales, what is Tudor's accounts receivable turnover ratio for 20x1?
  a. 3.18
  b. 5.45
  c. 5.71
  d. 6.00

**46.** What is Tudor's rate of return on average assets for 20x1?
  a. 14.17%
  b. 19.15%
  c. 19.89%
  d. 29.75%

**47.** A company's return on investment (ROI) would generally increase when
  a. Assets increase.
  b. Selling prices decrease.
  c. Costs decrease.
  d. Costs increase.

**48.** Selected information for Irvington Company is as follows:

| | December 31, | |
|---|---|---|
| | 20x8 | 20x9 |
| Preferred stock, 8%, par $100, nonconvertible, noncumulative | $125,000 | $125,000 |
| Common stock | 300,000 | 400,000 |
| Retained earnings | 75,000 | 185,000 |
| Dividends paid on preferred stock for year ended | 10,000 | 10,000 |
| Net income for year ended | 60,000 | 120,000 |

Irvington's return on common stockholders' equity, rounded to the nearest percentage point, for 20x9 is

a. 17%.
b. 19%.
c. 23%.
d. 25%.

**49.** In its 20x6 income statement, Kilm Co. reported cost of goods sold of $450,000. Changes occurred in several balance sheet accounts as follows:

| | |
|---|---|
| Inventory | $160,000 decrease |
| Accounts payable – suppliers | 40,000 decrease |

What amount should Kilm report as cash paid to suppliers in its 20x6 cash flow statement, prepared under the direct method?
   a. $250,000
   b $330,000
   c. $570,000
   d. $650,000

**50.** Information concerning the Gas Company's common stock is as follows:

| | Per Share |
|---|---|
| Book value at December 31 | $12.00 |
| Quoted market value on New York Stock Exchange on December 31 | 9.00 |
| Earnings for the year | 3.00 |
| Par value | 2.00 |
| Dividend for the year | 1.00 |

What was the price-earnings ratio on common stock for the year?
   a. 2 to 1
   b. 2.67 to 1
   c. 3 to 1
   d. 4 to 1

**51.** The following data pertains to Ruhl Corp.'s operations for the year ended December 31:

| | |
|---|---|
| Operating income | $800,000 |
| Interest expense | 100,000 |
| Income before income taxes | 700,000 |
| Income tax expense | 210,000 |
| Net income | $490,000 |

The times interest earned ratio is
   a. 8.0 to 1
   b. 7.0 to 1
   c. 5.6 to 1
   d. 4.9 to 1

**52.** The following information pertains to Ali Corp. as of and for the year ended December 31, 20x1:

| | |
|---|---|
| Liabilities | $ 60,000 |
| Stockholders' equity | $500,000 |
| Shares of common stock issued and outstanding | 10,000 |
| Net income | $ 30,000 |

During 20x1, Ali's officers exercised stock options for 1,000 shares of stock at an option price of $8 per share. What was the effect of exercising the stock options?
   a. Debt to equity ratio decreased to 12%.
   b. Earnings per share increased by $0.33.
   c. Asset turnover increased to 5.4%.
   d. No ratios were affected.

**53.** Successful use of leverage is evidenced by a
   a. Rate of return on investment greater than the rate of return on stockholders' equity.
   b. Rate of return on investment greater than the cost of debt.
   c. Rate of return on sales greater than the rate of return on stockholders' equity.
   d. Rate of return on sales greater than the cost of debt.

**Items 54 through 56 are based on the following:**

Selected data pertaining to Lore Co. for the calendar year 20x4 are as follows:

| | |
|---|---|
| Net cash sales | $ 3,000 |
| Cost of goods sold | 18,000 |
| Inventory at beginning of year | 6,000 |
| Purchases | 24,000 |
| Accounts receivable at beginning of year | 20,000 |
| Accounts receivable at end of year | 22,000 |

**54.** The accounts receivable turnover for 20x4 was 5.0 times. What were Lore's 20x4 net credit sales?
 **a.** $105,000
 **b.** $107,000
 **c.** $110,000
 **d.** $210,000

**55.** What was the inventory turnover for 20x4?
 **a.** 1.2 times.
 **b.** 1.5 times.
 **c.** 2.0 times.
 **d.** 3.0 times.

**56.** Lore would use which of the following to determine the average days sales in inventory?

| | Numerator | Denominator |
|---|---|---|
| **a.** | 365 | Average inventory |
| **b.** | 365 | Inventory turnover |
| **c.** | Average inventory | Sales divided by 365 |
| **d.** | Sales divided by 365 | Inventory turnover |

**57.** Ward, a consultant, keeps her accounting records on a cash basis. During 20x4, Ward collected $200,000 in fees from clients. At December 31, 20x3, Ward had accounts receivable of $40,000. At December 31, 20x4, Ward had accounts receivable of $60,000, and unearned fees of $5,000. On an accrual basis, what was Ward's service revenue for 20x4?
 **a.** $175,000
 **b.** $180,000
 **c.** $215,000
 **d.** $225,000

**Items 58 and 59 are based on the following**:

In preparing its cash flow statement for the year ended December 31, 20x4, Reve Co. collected the following data:

| | |
|---|---|
| Gain on sale of equipment | $ (6,000) |
| Proceeds from sale of equipment | 10,000 |
| Purchase of A.S., Inc. bonds (par value $200,000) | (180,000) |
| Amortization of bond discount | 2,000 |
| Dividends declared | (45,000) |
| Dividends paid | (38,000) |
| Proceeds from sale of treasury stock (carrying amount $65,000) | 75,000 |

In its December 31, 20x4, statement of cash flows,

**58.** What amount should Reve report as net cash used in investing activities?
 **a.** $170,000
 **b.** $176,000
 **c.** $188,000
 **d.** $194,000

**59.** What amount should Reve report as net cash provided by financing activities?
 **a.** $20,000
 **b.** $27,000
 **c.** $30,000
 **d.** $37,000

**60.** Which of the following information should be disclosed as supplemental information in the statement of cash flows?

| | Cash flow per share | Conversion of debt to equity |
|---|---|---|
| **a.** | Yes | Yes |
| **b.** | Yes | No |
| **c.** | No | Yes |
| **d.** | No | No |

**61.** Which of the following is **not** disclosed on the statement of cash flows when prepared under the direct method, either on the face of the statement or in a separate schedule?
 **a.** The major classes of gross cash receipts and gross cash payments.
 **b.** The amount of income taxes paid.
 **c.** A reconciliation of net income to net cash flow from operations.
 **d.** A reconciliation of ending retained earnings to net cash flow from operations.

# CHAPTER 8

## STATEMENT OF CASH FLOWS AND RATIO ANALYSIS

### Simulation Questions

**Simulation Task Question 1**                    **(Estimated time  20 - 25 minutes)**

This question consists of 5 items.  These items require numerical answers and selection of the proper cash flow category.  **Answer all items.**  Your grade will be based on the total number of correct answers.

Following are selected balance sheet accounts of Zach Corp. at December 31, 20x1 and 20x0, and the increases or decreases in each account from 20x0 to 20x1.  Also presented is selected income statement information for the year ended December 31, 20x1, and additional information.

| Selected balance sheet accounts | 20x1 | 20x0 | Increase (Decrease) |
|---|---|---|---|
| Assets: | | | |
| Accounts receivable | $ 34,000 | $ 24,000 | $ 10,000 |
| Property, plant, and equipment | 277,000 | 247,000 | 30,000 |
| Accumulated depreciation | (178,000) | (167,000) | (11,000) |
| | | | |
| Liabilities and stockholders' equity: | | | |
| Bonds payable | 49,000 | 46,000 | 3,000 |
| Dividends payable | 8,000 | 5,000 | 3,000 |
| Common stock, $1 par | 22,000 | 19,000 | 3,000 |
| Additional paid-in capital | 9,000 | 3,000 | 6,000 |
| Retained earnings | 104,000 | 91,000 | 13,000 |

Selected income statement information for the year ended December 31, 20x1

| | |
|---|---|
| Sales revenue | $155,000 |
| Depreciation | 33,000 |
| Gain on sale of equipment | 13,000 |
| Net income | 28,000 |

Additional information

- Accounts receivable relate to sales of merchandise.
- During 20x1, equipment costing $40,000 was sold for cash.
- During 20x1, $20,000 of bonds payable were issued in exchange for property, plant, and equipment.  There was no amortization of bond discount or premium.

## Required:

Items 1 through 5 represent activities that will be reported in Zach's statement of cash flows for the year ended December 31, 20x1. The following two responses are required for each item:

- Determine the amount that should be reported in Zach's 20x1 statement of cash flows.

- Using the list below, determine the category in which the amount should be reported in the statement of cash flows.

     O.  Operating activity
     I.  Investing activity
     F.  Financing activity

## Items to be Answered:

1. Cash collections from customers (direct method).
2. Payments for purchase of property, plant, and equipment.
3. Proceeds from sale of equipment.
4. Cash dividends paid.
5. Redemption of bonds payable.

This question consists of 6 items. Select the **best** answer for each item. Your grade will be based on the total number of correct answers.

The following condensed trial balance of Probe Co., a publicly-held company, has been adjusted except for income tax expense.

Probe Co.
**CONDENSED TRIAL BALANCE**

|  | 12/1/x3 | 1/1/x3 | (Change) |
|---|---|---|---|
| Cash | $ 473,000 | $ 817,000 | $(344,000) |
| Accounts receivable, net | 670,000 | 610,000 | 60,000 |
| Property, plant, and equipment | 1,070,000 | 995,000 | 75,000 |
| Accumulated depreciation | (345,000) | (280,000) | (65,000) |
| Dividends payable | (25,000) | (10,000) | (15,000) |
| Income taxes payable | 35,000 | (150,000) | 185,000 |
| Deferred income tax liability | (42,000) | (42,000) | --- |
| Bonds payable | (500,000) | (1,000,000) | 500,000 |
| Unamortized premium on bonds | (71,000) | (150,000) | 79,000 |
| Common stock | (350,000) | (150,000) | (200,000) |
| Additional paid-in capital | (430,000) | (375,000) | (55,000) |
| Retained earnings | (185,000) | (265,000) | 80,000 |
|  |  |  |  |
| Sales | (2,420,000) |  |  |
| Cost of sales | 1,863,000 |  |  |
| Selling and administrative expenses | 220,000 |  |  |
| Interest income | (14,000) |  |  |
| Interest expense | 46,000 |  |  |
| Depreciation | 88,000 |  |  |
| Loss on sale of equipment | 7,000 |  |  |
| Gain on extinguishment of bonds | (90,000) |  |  |
|  | $ 0 | $ 0 | $300,000 |

Additional Information:

- During 20x3, equipment with an original cost of $50,000 was sold for cash, and equipment costing $125,000 was purchased.

- On January 1, 20x3, bonds with a par value of $500,000 and related premium of $75,000 were redeemed. The $1,000 face value, 10-year, 10% par bonds had been issued on January 1 nine years earlier, to yield 8%. Interest is payable annually every December 31.

- Probe's tax payments during 20x3 were debited to Income Taxes Payable. Probe elected early adoption of ASC Topic 740, <u>Accounting for Income Taxes</u>, for the year ended December 31, 20x2, and recorded a deferred income tax liability of $42,000 based on temporary differences of $120,000 and an enacted tax rate of 35%. Probe's 20x3 financial statement income before income taxes was greater than it 20x3 taxable income, due entirely to temporary differences, by $60,000. Probe's cumulative net taxable temporary differences at December 31, 20x3, were $180,000. Probe's enacted tax rate for the current and future years is 30%.

- 60,000 shares of common stock, $2.50 par, were outstanding on December 31, 20x2. Probe issued an additional 80,000 shares on April 1, 20x3.

- There were no changes to retained earnings other than dividends declared.

**Required:**

For each transaction in **items 1 through 6**, the following **two** responses are required:

- Determine the amount to be reported in Probe's 20x3 statement of cash flows prepared using the indirect method.

- Select from the list below where the specific item should be separately reported on the statement of cash flows prepared using the indirect method.

  O. Operating.
  I. Investing.
  F. Financing.
  S. Supplementary information.
  N. Not reported on Probe's statement of cash flows.

1. Cash paid for income taxes.
2. Cash paid for interest.
3. Redemption of bonds payable.
4. Issuance of common stock.
5. Cash dividends paid.
6. Proceeds from sale of equipment.

# CHAPTER 8

## STATEMENT OF CASH FLOWS AND RATIO ANALYSIS

### Multiple Choice Answers

**1** /c/ The primary purpose of the cash flows statement is to provide information about the entity's cash receipts and disbursements during a period. Choices a, b and d are all items that a user of the statement may assess from the information provided on the statement. None of them is, of itself, the primary purpose of the statement.

**2.** /c/ The U.S. Treasury bond is not considered a cash equivalent because it does not have an original maturity date of three months or less.

**3.** /d/ Property dividends are not cash flows. They are included in the cash flow statement through presentation in a supporting schedule of non-cash financing and investing activities.

**4.** /b/ Cash dividends represent a financing outflow. All other items are non-cash activities that would be reported in a separate disclosure outside the body of the formal statement.

**5.** /d/ Cash flows per share are not reported.

**6.** /c/ Since no accounts were written off or recovered, assume that AR activity involved only credit sales and cash collections.

| | |
|---|---|
| Sales | $438,000 |
| Less increase in AR | - 8,800 |
| Cash collections | $429,200 |

**7.** /a/ Dividends received from investments are cash flows from operating activities. Options B and C are not operating activities. Option D would not be included in the statement using the direct method.

**8.** /a/ All income taxes paid are recorded as an operating activity regardless of the cause of the tax payment.

**9.** /d/ Cash collected from customers in 20x1:

| | |
|---|---|
| Sales | $538,800 |
| Deduct increase in | |
| Accounts Receivable | -3,000 |
| | $535,800 |

**10.** /d/ Cash paid for goods to be sold:

| | |
|---|---|
| Cost of Goods Sold | $250,000 |
| Deduct: | |
| Inventory decrease | |
| ($47,000 - 31,000) | -16,000 |
| Increase in Trade | |
| Accounts Payable | |
| ($25,000 - 17,500) | - 7,500 |
| | $226,500 |

**11.** /c/ Cash paid for interest:

| | |
|---|---|
| Interest expense | $4,300 |
| Less decrease in | |
| Unamortized Bond | |
| Discount | |
| ($5,000 - 4,500) | -500 |
| | $3,800 |

**12.** /a/ Cash paid for income taxes:

| | |
|---|---|
| Income tax expense | $20,400 |
| Add decrease in | |
| Income Tax Payable | 6,100 |
| Less increase in | |
| Deferred Income Tax | -700 |
| | $25,800 |

**13.** /c/ Cash paid for selling expenses:

| | |
|---|---|
| Selling expense | $141,500 |
| Deduct depreciation | |
| expense (1/3 of | |
| $1,500, the increase | |
| in Accumulated Depreciation) | -500 |
| | $141,000 |

**14.** /d/ Net Cash Provided by Operations:

| | |
|---|---|
| Net income | $75,000 |
| Less increase in net AR | |
| ($11,100 - $14,000) | - 2,900 |
| Plus: | |
| Decrease in prepaid rent | 2,100 |
| Increase in AP | 1,500 |
| Net cash flows | $75,700 |

**15.** /c/ The total cash received of $210,000 must be reported as an investing inflow. The gain on sale of $60,000 must be subtracted from net income to arrive at the net cash flow from operating activities.

**16.** /d/ $3,000,000
+   80,000
+3,200,000
+   130,000
+   700,000
+   210,000
$7,320,000

**17.** /c/ Net Cash Provided by Operations:

| | |
|---|---|
| Net income | $150,000 |
| Equity in investee income | - 5,500 |
| Bond premium amortized | - 1,400 |
| Increase in deferred taxes | + 1,800 |
| Net cash flows | $144,900 |

The decrease in accumulated depreciation was caused by an extraordinary repair to an asset (see Chapter 2). At the same time, the cost of the asset account was increased; thus, this was an investing activity, not an operations activity.

**18.** /c/ The proceeds of the sale (carrying amount less the loss) are reported as an investing activity in the statement of cash flows.

**19.** /c/
| | |
|---|---|
| Carrying amount | |
| ($100,000 - $48,000) | $52,000 |
| Loss reported | 21,000 |
| Cash settlement - insurance | $31,000 |

**20.** /d/ Net Cash Used in Investing Activities:

| | |
|---|---|
| Sale of Rate Motors, Inc. | |
| investment | $ 35,000 |
| Maybel stock purchase | -26,000 |
| Purchase of certificate of | |
| deposit | -50,000 |
| | $(41,000) |

**21.** /c/ Proceeds $104,000    Cost $160,000
+ Loss    + 16,000    - B.V.-120,000
= B.V. of                = Acc.
  Asset    $120,000    Depr.$ 40,000

$480,000 - 408,000 + 40,000 = $112,000

**22.** /d/ $1,280,000 - 1,000,000 + 160,000 = $440,000

**23.** /d/ The only investing activity presented is the purchase of fixed assets for $1,600,000. All other items are financing or operating activities.

**24.** /d/ Interest payments are operating cash outflows.

**25.** /a/ The full amount of the proceeds from the sale of treasury stock is treated as a financing activity because the firm is generating cash from the sale of its own stock.

**26.** /a/ $8,000,000
+2,000,000
-1,000,000
-   400,000
-   300,000
+   200,000
$8,500,000

**27.** /a/ Net Cash Used in Financing Activities:

| | |
|---|---|
| Sale of treasury stock | $ 95,000 |
| Retirement of bonds | -750,000 |
| Cash dividend | - 62,000 |
| | $717,000 |

**28.** /c/ Net cash provided by operating activities:

| | |
|---|---:|
| Net Income | $790,000 |
| Deduct: | |
| Increase in Inventory | - 80,000 |
| Decrease in Accounts Payable and Accrued Liabilities | - 5,000 |
| Gain on sale of long-term investment ($135,000 - 100,000) | - 35,000 |
| Add Depreciation expense | +250,000 |
| | $920,000 |

**29.** /a/ Net cash used in investing activities:

| | |
|---|---:|
| Cash used: | |
| Increase in short-term investment | $(300,000) |
| Increase in plant assets* | (1,190,000) |
| Cash provided: | |
| Proceeds from sale: | |
| Long-term investments | 135,000 |
| Building | 350,000 |
| | $(1,005,000) |

| | |
|---|---:|
| *Increase in balance of Plant Assets a/c | $ 700,000 |
| Add cost of building sold | 600,000 |
| Less Plant Assets acquired from issuance of long-term debt | -110,000 |
| Cash used for purchase of plant assets | $1,190,000 |

**30.** /d/ Net cash provided by financing activities:

| | |
|---|---:|
| Cash dividends paid: | |
| Dividends declared | $(500,000) |
| Increase in Dividends Payable | 160,000 |
| | (340,000) |
| Cash provided by: | |
| Sale of Common Stock (10,000 x $22) | 220,000 |
| Increase in short-term bank debt | 325,000 |
| | $205,000 |

**31.** /d/

| | |
|---|---:|
| Cash basis income | $60,000 |
| Add: | |
| Increase in AR | 20,000 |
| Decrease in AP | 15,000 |
| Accrual income | $95,000 |

**32.** /b/ It is assumed that the supplies inventory increase was from a cash purchase, which would reduce cash basis income. An increase in salaries payable, by definition, implies no cash outflow occurred. The accrual income would deduct the related expense; cash basis would not.

**33.** /d/

| | |
|---|---:|
| Accrual sales | $4,600,000 |
| Less: | |
| Increase in AR | - 300,000 |
| Accounts written off | - 20,000 |
| Cash sales | $4,280,000 |

**34.** /b/ "Liquidity" means "nearness to cash;" the term is often used synonymously with "solvency," which means the ability to repay debt. The defensive interval ratio is an indicator of ability to pay debts with quick assets, whereas the return on stockholders' equity is an indicator of return, not of the ability to pay debts.

**35.** /c/ Quick ratio: (Cash + Accounts Receivable + Marketable Securities)/Current Liabilities

Current Ratio: Current Assets/Current Liabilities

**36.** /c/ Most ratios can be greater than, equal to, or less than one. Here, the numerator and denominator are changing equally, which causes the current ratio to increase and the quick ratio to decrease.

**37.** /c/ $\dfrac{\$10,000 + \$50,000 + \$30,000}{\$70,000 + \$20,000}$

$= \$90,000/\$90,000$  $= 1{:}1$

**38.** /a/ $\dfrac{\$1,000,000}{(\$90,000 + \$150,000)/2}$  $= 8.3$

**39.** /d/

$\dfrac{\$10,000 + \$50,000 + \$90,000 + \$30,000}{\$70,000 + \$20,000}$

$= \$180,000/\$90,000$  $= 2{:}1$

**40.** /a/ Average daily cost of goods sold
= Cost of Goods Sold/300
= \$1,200,000/300
= \$4,000.

Days sales in avg. inventory
= Avg. Inventory/Avg. Daily COGS
= \$312,000/\$4,000
= 78 days.

**41.** /d/ Number of days' sales in
    inventory                 61
Number of days' sales in
    trade accounts receivable   <u>33</u>
Number of days in the
    operating cycle           94

**42.** /b/ Collecting a receivable has no effect on either the current ratio or the quick ratio (Answers C and D). Answer A is incorrect because Inventory is not involved in this situation. Answer b decreases the ratio's denominator and therefore increases the ratio.

**43.** /c/ $\dfrac{\$2,000,000}{(\$300,000 + \$700,000)/2}$  $=$  $4$

**44.** /a/ $\dfrac{\$100,000}{\$2,000,000 + \$500,000}$  $=$  $4\%$

**45.** /c/ Accounts receivable turnover = Credit Sales/(Avg. A/R)

= \$1,200,000/[(\$220,000 + \$200,000)/2]
= 5.71.

**46.** /c/ Rate of Return on average assets = Net Income/Avg. Assets

= \$180,000/[(\$940,000 + \$870,000)/2] = 19.89%.

**47.** /c/ ROI = Net Income After Tax/Average Total Assets. A reduction in costs would increase this ratio.

**48.** /c/ $\dfrac{120,000 - 10,000}{(375,000 + 585,000) / 2}$

= approx. 23%.

**49.** /b/ Cost of goods sold must be reduced for amounts relating to inventory decrease (selling inventory that was on hand from the previous period) and increased for the pay-down of the accounts payable balance. \$450,000 - \$160,000 + \$ 40,000 = \$330,000.

**50.** /c/ \$9.00/\$3.00 = 3:1

**51.** /a/ Income available for interest (\$800,000) -:- interest expense (\$100,000) = 8:1

**52.** /a/ Exercising stock options leads to an increase in the number of shares outstanding, increasing the denominator of the debt to equity ratio and causing the ratio to decrease. Also note that exercising took place before the year-end figures and the year-end debt to equity ratio is 12% (\$60,000 / \$500,000) Options B and C are incorrect, because both would decrease.

**53.** /b/ Successful use of debt is evidenced by the return on assets being greater than the average cost of debt, which leads to the return on equity being greater than the return on assets. Unfavorable leverage would have the reverse effect.

**54.** /a/ AR turnover = net credit sales/average accounts receivable. Therefore, AR turnover X average accounts receivable = net credit sales. $21,000 (average AR) x 5 = $105,000

**55.** /c/ COGS -:- average inventory. $18,000 -:- $9,000* = 2.0 times

| *Beginning inventory | $ 6,000 |
|---|---|
| Purchases | 24,000 |
| Goods available for sale | $30,000 |
| Less cost of goods sold | 18,000 |
| Ending inventory | $12,000 |

Average inventory = ($6,000 + $12,000) / 2 = $9,000

**56.** /b/ 365 -:- inventory turnover is the formula needed.

**57.** /c/ The revenue to be recorded on an accrual basis is the amount of credit sales earned and realized/realizable for the period. This is $200,000 cash received, decreased by the $40,000 relating to prior period's receivables and the $5,000 of unearned fees, increased by the $60,000 ending balance of accounts receivable. $200,000 - $40,00 - $5,000 + $60,000 = $215,000.

**58.** /a/
| Proceeds from sale of equipment | $ 10,000 |
|---|---|
| Less purchase of bonds | (180,000) |
| Net cash used in investing activities | ($170,000) |

Note that the gain on sale of equipment is not relevant in this computation of cash flows from investing activities since the entire proceeds from sale were given.

**59.** /d/
| Sale of treasury stock | $75,000 |
|---|---|
| Less dividends paid | (38,000) |
| Net cash provided by financing activities | $37,000 |

Reminder: Dividends declared are not relevant. Amortization of discount is only useful when determining cash flows from operations.

**60.** /c/ Cash flow per share is never disclosed. Conversion of debt to equity would be disclosed as part of a supplementary schedule of significant non-cash financing and investing activities.

**61.** /d/ The major classes of gross cash receipts and gross cash payments, as well as the amount of income taxes paid (Options A and B) are disclosed within the body of the statement itself. A reconciliation of net income to net cash flow from operations (Option C) is disclosed in a separate schedule. A reconciliation of ending retained earnings to net cash flow from operations is the only option listed that is not a requirement.

# CHAPTER 8

## STATEMENT OF CASH FLOWS AND RATIO ANALYSIS

### Simulation Answers

## Number 1 Answer

1. Cash collections from customers:

| | |
|---|---|
| Sales Revenue | $155,000 |
| Less: Increase in Accounts Receivable | -10,000 |
| Collected from customers | $145,000 |

/O/    Cash Flow Category: Operating Activity

2. Payments for purchase of Property, Plant and Equipment:

| | |
|---|---|
| PPE balance 12/31/x0 | $247,000 |
| Less cost of equipment sold | -40,000 |
| | 207,000 |
| PPE balance 12/31/x1 | 277,000 |
| Cost of PPE purchased during 20x1 | 70,000 |
| Less: Cost of PPE acquired by exchange for bonds payable | -20,000 |
| Cost of PPE purchased for cash in 20x1 | $ 50,000 |

/I/    Cash Flow Category: Investing Activity

3. Proceeds from sale of equipment:

| | |
|---|---|
| Accumulated Depreciation - balance 12/31/x0 | $167,000 |
| Depreciation Expense for 20x1 | 33,000 |
| | 200,000 |
| Less: Accumulated Depreciation, balance 12/31/x1 | -178,000 |
| Depreciation attributable to equipment sold | $ 22,000 |

| | |
|---|---|
| Cost of equipment sold | $ 40,000 |
| Less depreciation (above) | -22,000 |
| Book value of equipment sold | 18,000 |
| Gain on sale of equipment | 13,000 |
| Cash proceeds | $ 31,000 |

/I/    Cash Flow Category: Investing Activity

4. Cash Dividends Paid:

| | |
|---|---|
| Retained Earnings - balance 12/31/x0 | $ 91,000 |
| Net Income, 20x1 | 28,000 |
| | 119,000 |
| Retained Earnings - balance 12/31/x1 | -104,000 |
| Dividends declared | 15,000 |
| Less: Increase in Dividends Payable | -3,000 |
| Cash dividends paid in 20x1 | $ 12,000 |

/F/    Cash Flow Category: Financing Activity

5. Redemption of Bonds Payable:

| | |
|---|---|
| Bonds Payable - balance 12/31/x0 | $ 46,000 |
| Bonds issued in exchange for equipment | 20,000 |
| | 66,000 |
| Less: Bonds Payable - balance 12/31/x1 | - 49,000 |
| Bonds redeemed during 20x1 | $ 17,000 |

/F/    Cash Flow Category: Financing Activity

## Number 2 Answer

1. Cash paid for income taxes is equal to the decrease in the Income Taxes Payable account for the period - $185,000.

   /O/    Cash Flow Category:
          Operating Activity

2. Interest paid is equal to interest expense recorded ($46,000) plus bond premium amortized for the period ($4,000), for a total of $50,000.

| | |
|---|---|
| Unamortized bond premium 1/1 | $150,000 |
| Less premium reduction due to bond redemption | 75,000 |
| Balance after redemption | $ 75,000 |
| Less unamortized premium 12/31 | 71,000 |
| Premium amortized for period | $ 4,000 |

   Alternative computation:

| | |
|---|---|
| Interest recorded, $575,000 x 8% | $46,000 |
| Interest paid, $500,000 x 10% | 50,000 |
| Amortization amount | $ 4,000 |

   /O/    Cash Flow Category:
          Operating Activity

3. The bonds were redeemed at a gain of $90,000. Carrying value 1/1/x3, $575,000, less $90,000 gain = $485,000 cash paid.

   /F/    Cash flow Category:
          Financing Activity

4. Since there were no other stock transactions during the year, the cash received from the issuance of stock is the sum of the increases in the common stock and APIC accounts. $200,000 + $55,000 = $255,000.

   /F/    Cash Flow Category:
          Financing Activity

5.
| | |
|---|---|
| Dividends payable 12/31/x2 | $10,000 |
| Dividends declared | 80,000 |
| Less dividends payable 12/31/x3 | (25,000) |
| Cash dividends paid | $65,000 |

   /F/    Cash Flow Category:
          Financing Activity

6. Proceeds of sale of equipment are book value of asset less loss of $7,000.

| | |
|---|---|
| Acc. depreciation 12/31/x2 | $280,000 |
| Add depreciation expense | 88,000 |
| Subtotal | $368,000 |
| Less acc. depreciation 12/31/x3 | 345,000 |
| Depreciation relating to asset sold | $ 23,000 |

| | |
|---|---|
| Original cost of asset | $50,000 |
| Less acc. depreciation | 23,000 |
| Book value at time of sale | $27,000 |
| Less loss on sale | 7,000 |
| Cash proceeds from sale | $20,000 |

   /I/    Cash Flow Category:
          Investing Activity

# CHAPTER 9

# CONSOLIDATIONS

## Question Map

D. Push-down Accounting
E. Post-Acquisition Consolidated Financial Statements (Basic Concepts) – 19, 20, 30-33, 47, 48, 49
    1. Reverse Equity Entries
    2. Eliminate Investment Account – 51
    3. Allocate Differential
    4. Amortization of Differential Elements
    5. Eliminate Intercompany Items

IV.  POST-ACQUISITION FINANCIAL STATEMENTS: INTERCOMPANY TRANSACTIONS
A. Overview
    1. Avoidance of Double Counting
    2. Upstream/Downstream Transactions
B. Intercompany Inventory Transactions
    1. Eliminate Sales and Intercompany Profits
    2. Inventory Complications
C. Fixed Asset Transactions
D. Intercompany Bonds
    1. Constructively Retired
    2. Gains (Losses) From Constructive Retirement

V.   DISCLOSURES REQUIRED – 4

VI.  SPECIAL TOPICS
A. Interim Purchases
B. Piecemeal Acquisitions
C. Theories of Consolidation
    1. Parent Company Theory
    2. Modified Parent Company Theory
    3. Entity Theory
D. Combined Financial Statements
E. Variable Interest Entities

# CHAPTER 9

## CONSOLIDATIONS

### Multiple Choice Questions

**1.** On July 1 Diamond, Inc., paid $1,000,000 for 100,000 shares (40%) of the outstanding common stock of Ashley Corporation. At that date the net assets of Ashley totaled $2,500,000 and the fair values of all of Ashley's identifiable assets and liabilities were equal to their book values. Ashley reported net income of $500,000 for the year ended December 31 of which $300,000 was for the six months ended December 31. Ashley paid cash dividends of $250,000 on September 30. In its income statement for the year ended December 31, what amount of income should Diamond report from its investment in Ashley?

   **a.** $ 80,000
   **b.** $100,000
   **c.** $120,000
   **d.** $200,000

**2.** Ownership of 51 percent of the outstanding voting stock of a company would usually result in
   **a.** The use of the cost method.
   **b.** The use of the lower of cost or market method.
   **c.** A pooling of interests.
   **d.** A consolidation.

**3.** Consolidated financial statements are typically prepared when one company has
   **a.** Accounted for its investment in another company by the equity method.
   **b.** Accounted for its investment in another company by the cost method.
   **c.** Significant influence over the operating and financial policies of another company.
   **d.** The controlling financial interest in another company.

**4.** Which of the following should be disclosed in the Summary of Significant Accounting Policies?

   **a.** Composition of inventory (raw materials, work-in-process, and finished goods).
   **b.** Basis of consolidation.
   **c.** Depreciation expense amount.
   **d.** Adequacy of pension plan assets in relationship to vested benefits.

**5.** Which of the following is the appropriate basis for valuing fixed assets acquired in a business combination accounted for as a purchase carried out by exchanging cash for common stock?
   **a.** Historic cost.
   **b.** Book value.
   **c.** Cost plus any excess of purchase price over book value of asset acquired.
   **d.** Fair value.

**6.** Company X acquired for cash all of the outstanding common stock of Company Y. How should Company X determine in general the amounts to be reported for the inventories and long-term debt acquired from Company Y?

| | Inventories | Long-term Debt |
|---|---|---|
| **a.** | Fair value | Fair value |
| **b.** | Fair value | Recorded value |
| **c.** | Recorded value | Fair value |
| **d.** | Recorded value | Recorded value |

**7.** The Action Corporation issued non-voting preferred stock with a fair market value of $4,000,000 in exchange for all of the outstanding common stock of Master Corporation. On the date of the exchange, Master had tangible net assets with a book value of $2,000,000 and a fair value of $2,500,000. In addition, Action issued preferred stock valued at $400,000 to an individual as a finder's fee in arranging the transaction. As a result of this transaction, Action should record an increase in net assets of

   **a.** $2,000,000.
   **b.** $2,500,000.
   **c.** $2,900,000.
   **d.** $4,400,000.

**8.** On March 1 Agront Corporation issued 10,000 shares of its $1 par value common stock for all of the outstanding stock of Barcelo Corporation, when the fair market value of Agront's stock was $50 per share. In addition, Agront made the following payments in connection with this business combination:

Finder's and consultants' fees     $20,000
SEC registration costs                7,000

Agront's acquisition cost would be capitalized at
- **a.** $0.
- **b.** $500,000.
- **c.** $520,000.
- **d.** $527,000.

**9.** On November 30 File, Incorporated, purchased for cash of $25 per share all 300,000 of the outstanding common stock of Mooney Company. Mooney's balance sheet at November 30 showed a book value of $6,000,000. Additionally, the fair value of Mooney's property, plant, and equipment on November 30 was $800,000 in excess of its book value. What amount, if any, will be shown in the balance sheet caption "Goodwill" in the November 30 consolidated balance sheet of File, Incorporated, and its wholly-owned subsidiary, Mooney Company?
- **a.** $0
- **b.** $  700,000
- **c.** $  800,000
- **d.** $1,500,000

**10.** On April 1 Union Company paid $1,600,000 for all the issued and outstanding common stock of Cable Corporation in a transaction properly accounted for as a purchase. The recorded assets and liabilities of Cable on April 1 were as follows:

Cash                              $160,000
Inventory                          480,000
Property, plant and
  equipment (net)                  960,000
Liabilities                       (360,000)

On April 1 it was determined that Cable's inventory had a fair value of $460,000, and the property, plant and equipment (net) had a fair value of $1,040,000. What is the amount of goodwill resulting from the business combination?
- **a.** $0
- **b.** $20,000
- **c.** $300,000
- **d.** $360,000

**11.** On July 31 Light Company purchased for cash of $8,000,000, all of the outstanding common stock of Shirk Company when Shirk's balance sheet showed net assets of $6,400,000. Shirk's assets and liabilities had fair values different from the book values as follows:

|  | Book Value | Fair Value |
|---|---|---|
| Property, plant, | | |
| and equipment, net | $10,000,000 | $11,500,000 |
| Other assets | 1,000,000 | 700,000 |
| Long-term debt | 6,000,000 | 5,600,000 |

As a result of the transaction above, what amount, if any, will be shown as goodwill in the July 31 consolidated balance sheet of Light Company and its wholly-owned subsidiary, Shirk Company?
- **a.** $0
- **b.** $100,000
- **c.** $1,200,000
- **d.** $1,600,000

**12.** On April 1 the Jack Company paid $800,000 for all the issued and outstanding common stock of Ann Corporation in a transaction properly accounted for as a purchase. The recorded assets and liabilities of Ann Corporation on April 1 follows:

Cash                                    $ 80,000
Inventory                                240,000
Property and equipment (net of
  Accumulated depreciation
  of $320,000)                           480,000
Liabilities                             (180,000)

On April 1 it was determined that the inventory of Ann had a fair value of $190,000, and the property and equipment (net) had a fair value of $560,000.

What is the amount of goodwill resulting from the business combination?

   a. $0
   b. $ 50,000
   c. $150,000
   d. $180,000

**Questions 13 and 14 are based on the following:**

The Nugget Company's balance sheet on December 31 is as follows:

| Assets | |
|---|---|
| Cash | $ 100,000 |
| Accounts receivable | 200,000 |
| Inventories | 500,000 |
| Property, plant and | |
|   equipment | 900,000 |
| | $1,700,000 |

| Liabilities and Stockholders' Equity | |
|---|---|
| Current liabilities | $ 300,000 |
| Long-term debt | 500,000 |
| Common stock (par $1/share) | 100,000 |
| Additional paid-in capital | 200,000 |
| Retained earnings | 600,000 |
| | $1,700,000 |

On December 31 the Bronc Company purchased all of the outstanding common stock of Nugget for $1,500,000 cash. On that date, the fair (market) value of Nugget's inventories was $450,000 and the fair value of Nugget's property, plant and equipment was $1,000,000. The fair values of all other assets and liabilities of Nugget were equal to their book values.

**13.** As a result of the acquisition of Nugget by Bronc, the consolidated balance sheet of Bronc and Nugget should reflect goodwill in the amount of

   a. $500,000.
   b. $550,000.
   c. $600,000.
   d. $650,000.

**14.** Assuming that the balance sheet of Bronc (unconsolidated) at December 31 reflected retained earnings of $2,000,000, what amount of retained earnings should be shown in the December 31 consolidated balance sheet of Bronc and its new subsidiary, Nugget?

   a. $2,000,000
   b. $2,600,000
   c. $2,800,000
   d. $3,150,000

**15.** In a business combination what is the appropriate method of accounting for an excess of fair value assigned to net assets over the cost paid for them?

   a. Record as negative goodwill.
   b. Record as additional paid-in capital from combination on the books of the combined company.
   c. Proportionately reduce values assigned to nonmonetary assets and record any remaining excess as a deferred credit.
   d. Allocate the amount to income on the transaction closing date.

**16.** On June 30 Needle Corporation purchased for cash at $10 per share all 100,000 shares of the outstanding common stock of Thread Company. The total appraised value of identifiable assets less liabilities of Thread Company was $1,400,000 at June 30 including the appraised value of Thread's property, plant and equipment (its only noncurrent asset) of $250,000. The consolidated balance sheet of Needle Corporation and its wholly owned subsidiary at June 30 should reflect

   a. A deferred credit (negative goodwill) of $150,000.
   b. Goodwill of $150,000.
   c. A deferred credit (negative goodwill) of $400,000.
   d. Goodwill of $40,000.

**17.** Beni Corp. purchased 100% of Carr Corp.'s outstanding capital stock for $430,000 cash. Immediately before the purchase, the balance sheet of both corporations reported the following:

| | Beni | Carr |
|---|---|---|
| Assets | $2,000,000 | $750,000 |
| | | |
| Liabilities | $ 750,000 | $400,000 |
| Common stock | 1,000,000 | 310,000 |
| Retained Earnings | 250,000 | 40,000 |
| Liabilities and stockholders' equity | $2,000,000 | $750,000 |

At the date of purchase, the fair value of Carr's assets was $50,000 more than the aggregate carrying amounts. In the consolidated balance sheet prepared immediately after the purchase, the consolidated stockholders' equity should amount to
- **a.** $1,680,000
- **b.** $1,650,000
- **c.** $1,600,000
- **d.** $1,250,000

**18.** On October 1, Company X acquired for cash all of the outstanding common stock of Company Y. Both companies have a December 31 year end and have been in business for many years. Consolidated net income for the year ended December 31 should include net income of
- **a.** Company X for 3 months and Company Y for 3 months.
- **b.** Company X for 12 months and Company Y for 3 months.
- **c.** Company X for 12 months and Company Y for 12 months.
- **d.** Company X for 12 months; but no income from Company Y until Company Y distributes a dividend.

**Items 19 and 20 are based on the following:**

On January 1, 20x1, Dallas, Inc. purchased 80% of Style, Inc.'s outstanding common stock for $120,000. On that date, the carrying amounts of Style's assets and liabilities approximated their fair values. During the year, Style paid $5,000 cash dividends to its stockholders. Summarized balance sheet information for the two companies follows:

| | Dallas 12/31/x1 | Style 12/31/x1 | Style 1/1/x1 |
|---|---|---|---|
| Investment in Style (equity method) | $132,000 | | |
| Other assets | 138,000 | $115,000 | $100,000 |
| | $270,000 | $115,000 | $100,000 |
| | | | |
| Common stock | $50,000 | $20,000 | $20,000 |
| Additional paid-in capital | 80,250 | 44,000 | 44,000 |
| Ret. Earnings | 139,750 | 51,000 | 36,000 |
| | $270,000 | $115,000 | $100,000 |

**19.** What amount should Dallas report as earnings from subsidiary in its 20x1 income statement?
- **a.** $12,000
- **b.** $15,000
- **c.** $16,000
- **d.** $20,000

**20.** What amount of stockholders' equity should be reported in Dallas' December 31, 20x1, consolidated balance sheet?
- **a.** $270,000
- **b.** $286,000
- **c.** $362,000
- **d.** $385,000

**21.** Grant, Inc., has current receivables from affiliated companies at December 31 as follows:

- A $50,000 cash advance to Adams Corporation. Grant owns 30% of the voting stock of Adams and accounts for the investment by the equity method.
- A receivable of $160,000 from Bullard Corporation for administrative and selling services. Bullard is 100% owned by Grant and is included in Grant's consolidated statements.
- A receivable of $100,000 from Carpenter Corporation for merchandise sales on open account. Carpenter is a 90% owned, unconsolidated subsidiary of Grant.

In the current assets section of its December 31 consolidated balance sheet, Grant should report accounts receivable from investees in the total amount of
- **a.** $ 90,000.
- **b.** $140,000.
- **c.** $150,000.
- **d.** $310,000.

**22.** Bibi Corporation owns 80% of the outstanding capital stock of Daniels Corporation. On July 1 Bibi advanced $50,000 in cash to Daniels. On the consolidated balance sheet at December 31 how much of the advance should be eliminated?
- **a.** $0.
- **b.** $10,000.
- **c.** $40,000.
- **d.** $50,000.

**Items 23 through 26 are based on the following:**

Selected information from the separate and consolidated balance sheets and income statements of Pard, Inc. and its subsidiary, Spin Co., as of December 31, 20x1, and for the year then ended is as follows:

| | Pard | Spin | Consolidated |
|---|---|---|---|
| **Balance Sheet** | | | |
| Acc. receivable | $ 26,000 | $ 19,000 | $ 39,000 |
| Inventory | 30,000 | 25,000 | 52,000 |
| Investment in Spin | 67,000 | | |
| Goodwill | | | 30,000 |
| Minority Interest | | | 10,000 |
| Stockholder's Equity | 154,000 | 50,000 | 154,000 |
| | | | |
| **Income Statement** | | | |
| Revenues | $200,000 | $140,000 | $308,000 |
| COGS | 150,000 | 110,000 | 231,000 |
| Gr. Profit | $ 50,000 | $ 30,000 | $ 77,000 |
| Equity in earnings of Spin | 11,000 | | |
| Net income | 36,000 | 20,000 | 40,000 |

Additional information:
- During 20x1, Pard sold goods to Spin at the same markup on cost that Pard uses for all sales. At December 31, 20x1, Spin had not paid for all of these goods and still held 37.5% of them in inventory.
- Pard acquired its interest in Spin on January 2, 20x8 (3 years earlier).

**23.** What was the amount of intercompany sales from Pard to Spin during 20x1?
- **a.** $ 3,000
- **b.** $ 6,000
- **c.** $29,000
- **d.** $32,000

**24.** At December 31, 20x1, what was the amount of Spin's payable to Pard for intercompany sales?
- **a.** $ 3,000
- **b.** $ 6,000
- **c.** $29,000
- **d.** $32,000

**25.** In Pard's consolidated balance sheet, what was the carrying amount of the inventory that Spin purchased from Par?

    **a.** $ 3,000
    **b.** $ 6,000
    **c.** $ 9,000
    **d.** $12,000

**26.** What is the percent of minority interest ownership in Spin?

    **a.** 10%
    **b.** 20%
    **c.** 25%
    **d.** 45%

**27.** During 20x0, Pard Corp. sold goods to its 90%-owned subsidiary, Seed Corp. At December 31, 20x0, one-half of these goods were included in Seed's ending inventory. Reported 20x0 selling expenses were $1,100,000 and $400,000 for Pard and Seed respectively. Pard's selling expenses included $50,000 in freight-out costs for goods sold to Seed. What amount of selling expenses should be reported in Pard's 20x0 consolidated income statement?

    **a.** $1,500,000
    **b.** $1,480,000
    **c.** $1,475,000
    **d.** $1,450,000

**28.** On January 1 Harry Corporation sold equipment costing $2,000,000 with accumulated depreciation of $500,000 to Anna Corporation, its wholly-owned subsidiary, for $1,800,000. Harry was depreciating the equipment on the straight-line method over twenty years with no salvage value, which Anna continued. In consolidation at December 31 the cost and accumulated depreciation, respectively, should be

    **a.** $1,500,000 and $100,000
    **b.** $1,800,000 and $100,000
    **c.** $2,000,000 and $100,000
    **d.** $2,000,000 and $600,000

**29.** Wagner, a holder of a $1,000,000 Palmer, Inc. bond, collected the interest due on March 31, 20x2, and then sold the bond to Seal, Inc. for $975,000. On that date, Palmer, a 75% owner of Seal, had a $1,075,000 carrying amount for this bond. What was the effect of Seal's purchase of Palmer's bond on the retained earnings and minority interest amounts reported in Palmer's March 31, 20x2, consolidated balance sheet?

| | Retained earnings | Minority interest |
|---|---|---|
| **a.** | $100,000 increase | $0 |
| **b.** | $ 75,000 increase | $ 25,000 increase |
| **c.** | $0 | $ 25,000 increase |
| **d.** | $0 | $100,000 increase |

**Items 30 through 33 are based on the following:**

The separate condensed balance sheets and income statements of Purl Corp. and its wholly-owned subsidiary, Scott Corp., are as follows:

**BALANCE SHEET**
December 31, 20x0

| | Purl | Scott |
|---|---|---|
| Assets | | |
| Current assets | | |
| Cash | $ 80,000 | $ 60,000 |
| Acc. receivable (net) | 140,000 | 25,000 |
| Inventories | 90,000 | 50,000 |
| Total current assets | 310,000 | 135,000 |
| Property, plant and | | |
| equipment (net) | 625,000 | 280,000 |
| Investment in Scott | | |
| (equity method) | 390,000 | |
| Total assets | $1,325,000 | $415,000 |

Liabilities and Stockholders' Equity

| | Purl | Scott |
|---|---|---|
| Current liabilities: | | |
| Accounts payable | $ 160,000 | $ 95,000 |
| Accrued liabilities | 110,000 | 30,000 |
| Stockholders' equity: | | |
| Common stock ($10 par) | 300,000 | 50,000 |
| APIC | | 10,000 |
| Retained earnings | 755,000 | 230,000 |
| Total liabilities and | | |
| stockholders' equity | $1,325,000 | $415,000 |

## INCOME STATEMENTS
## For the Year Ended December 31, 20x0

| | Purl | Scott |
|---|---|---|
| Sales | $2,000,000 | $750,000 |
| Cost of goods sold | 1,540,000 | 500,000 |
| Gross margin | 460,000 | 250,000 |
| Operating expenses | 260,000 | 150,000 |
| Operating income | 200,000 | 100,000 |
| Equity in earnings of Scott | 60,000 | _____ |
| Income before income taxes | 260,000 | 100,000 |
| Provision for income taxes | 60,000 | 30,000 |
| Net income | $ 200,000 | $ 70,000 |

### Additional information:

- On January 1, 20x0, Purl purchased for $360,000 all of Scott's $10 par, voting common stock. On January 1, 20x0, the fair value of Scott's assets and liabilities equaled their carrying amount of $410,000 and $160,000, respectively, except that the fair values of certain items identifiable in Scott's inventory were $10,000 more than their carrying amounts. These items were still on hand at December 31, 20x0. Purl's policy is to amortize intangible assets over a 10-year period, unless a definite life is ascertainable.

- During 20x0, Purl and Scott paid cash dividends of $100,000 and $30,000, respectively. For tax purposes, Purl receives the 100% exclusion for dividends received from Scott.

- There were no intercompany transactions, except for Purl's receipt of dividends from Scott and Purl's recording of its share of Scott's earnings.

- Both Purl and Scott paid income taxes at the rate of 30%.

In the December 31, 20x0, consolidated financial statements of Purl and its subsidiary:

**30.** Total current assets should be
- **a.** $455,000
- **b.** $445,000
- **c.** $310,000
- **d.** $135,000

**31.** Total assets should be
- **a.** $1,740,000
- **b.** $1,450,000
- **c.** $1,350,000
- **d.** $1,460,000

**32.** Total retained earnings should be
- **a.** $985,000
- **b.** $825,000
- **c.** $795,000
- **d.** $755,000

**33.** Net income should be
- **a.** $270,000
- **b.** $200,000
- **c.** $190,000
- **d.** $170,000

**34.** On January 1, Rolan Corporation issued 10,000 shares of common stock in exchange for all of Sandin Corporation's outstanding stock. Condensed balance sheets of Rolan and Sandin immediately prior to the combination are as follows:

| | Rolan | Sandin |
|---|---|---|
| Total assets | $1,000,000 | $500,000 |
| Liabilities | 300,000 | 150,000 |
| Common stock ($10 par) | 200,000 | 100,000 |
| Retained earnings | 500,000 | 250,000 |
| Total equities | $1,000,000 | $500,000 |

Rolan's common stock had a market price of $60 per share on January 1. The market price of Sandin's stock was not readily ascertainable.

The combination of Rolan and Sandin is properly accounted for as a purchase. Rolan's investment in Sandin's stock will be stated in Rolan's balance sheet immediately after the combination in the amount of
- **a.** $100,000.
- **b.** $350,000.
- **c.** $500,000.
- **d.** $600,000.

**35.** On June 30, 20x2, Pane Corp. exchanged 150,000 shares of its $20 par value common stock for all of Sky Corp.'s common stock. At that date, the fair value of Pane's common stock issued was equal to the book value of Sky's net assets. Both corporations continued to operate as separate businesses, maintaining accounting records with years ending December 31. Information from separate company operations follows:

|  | Pane | Sky |
|---|---|---|
| Retained earnings - 12/31/x1 | $3,200,000 | $925,000 |
| Net income - six months ended 6/30/x2 | 800,000 | 275,000 |
| Dividends paid | 750,000 | -- |

If the business is accounted for as a purchase, what amount of retained earnings would Pane report in its June 30 consolidated balance sheet?

    **a.** $5,200,000
    **b.** $4,450,000
    **c.** $3,525,000
    **d.** $3,250,000

**36.** On December 31, Saxe Corporation was merged into Poe Corporation. In the business combination, Poe issued 200,000 shares of its $10 par common stock, with a market price of $18 a share, for all of Saxe's common stock. The stockholders' equity section of each company's balance sheet immediately before the combination was:

|  | Poe | Saxe |
|---|---|---|
| Common stock | $3,000,000 | $1,500,000 |
| Additional PIC | 1,300,000 | 150,000 |
| Retained earnings | 2,500,000 | 850,000 |
|  | $6,800,000 | $2,500,000 |

Assume that the merger qualifies for treatment as a purchase. In the December 31 consolidated balance sheet, additional paid-in capital should be reported at

    **a.** $ 950,000
    **b.** $1,300,000
    **c.** $1,450,000
    **d.** $2,900,000

**37.** Mr. Cord owns four corporations. Combined financial statements are being prepared for these corporations, which have intercompany loans of $200,000 and intercompany profits of $500,000. What amount of these intercompany loans and profits should be included in the combined financial statements?

|  | Loans | Profits |
|---|---|---|
| **a.** | $200,000 | $0 |
| **b.** | $200,000 | $500,000 |
| **c.** | $0 | $0 |
| **d.** | $0 | $500,000 |

**38.** Combined statements may be used to present the results of operations of

|  | Unconsolidated subsidiaries | Companies under common management |
|---|---|---|
| **a.** | Yes | Yes |
| **b.** | Yes | No |
| **c.** | No | Yes |
| **d.** | No | No |

**39.** The following information pertains to shipments of merchandise from Home Office to Branch during the year:

| | |
|---|---|
| Home Office's cost of merchandise | $160,000 |
| Intracompany billing | 200,000 |
| Sales by Branch | 250,000 |
| Unsold merchandise at Branch on December 31 | 20,000 |

In the combined income statement of Home Office and Branch for the year ended December 31, what amount of the above transactions should be included in sales?

    **a.** $250,000
    **b.** $230,000
    **c.** $200,000
    **d.** $180,000

**40.** For which of the following reporting units is the preparation of combined financial statements most appropriate?

    **a.** A corporation and a majority-owned subsidiary with non-homogeneous operations.

    **b.** A corporation and a foreign subsidiary with nonintegrated homogeneous operations.

    **c.** Several corporations with related operations with some common individual owners.

    **d.** Several corporations with related operations owned by one individual.

**41.** Which of the following items should be treated in the same manner in both combined financial statements and consolidated statements?

| | Different fiscal periods | Foreign operations |
|---|---|---|
| **a.** | No | No |
| **b.** | No | Yes |
| **c.** | Yes | Yes |
| **d.** | Yes | No |

**42.** Consolidated financial statements are typically prepared when one company has a controlling financial interest in another unless:

    **a.** The subsidiary is a finance company.

    **b.** The fiscal year-ends of the two companies are more than three months apart.

    **c.** Such control is likely to be temporary.

    **d.** The two companies are in unrelated industries, such as manufacturing and real estate.

**Items 43 and 44 are based on the following:**

On January 1, 20x3, Owen Corp. purchased all of Sharp Corp.'s common stock for $1,200,000. On that date, the fair values of Sharp's assets and liabilities equaled their carrying amounts of $1,320,000 and $320,000 respectively. Owen's policy is to amortize intangibles over 10 years. During 20x3, Sharp paid cash dividends of $20,000.

Selected information from the separate balance sheets and income statements of Owen and Sharp as of December 31, 20x3, and for the year then ended follows:

| | Owen | Sharp |
|---|---|---|
| Balance sheet accounts: | | |
| Investment in subsidiary | $1,300,000 | – |
| Retained earnings | 1,240,000 | 560,000 |
| Total stockholders' equity | 2,620,000 | 1,120,000 |
| | | |
| Income statement accounts: | | |
| Operating income | 420,000 | 200,000 |
| Equity in earnings of Sharp | 120,000 | – |
| Net income | 400,000 | 140,000 |

**43.** In Owen's 20x3 consolidated income statement, what amount should be reported for amortization of goodwill?

    **a.** $0

    **b.** $12,000

    **c.** $18,000

    **d.** $20,000

**44.** In Owen's December 31, 20x4, consolidated balance sheet, what amount should be reported as total retained earnings?

    **a.** $1,240,000

    **b.** $1,360,000

    **c.** $1,380,000

    **d.** $1,800,000

**45.** On January 2, 20x3, Paye Co. purchased Shef Co. at a cost that resulted in recognition of goodwill of $200,000, having an expected benefit period of 10 years. During the first quarter of 20x3, Paye spent an additional $80,000 on expenditures designed to maintain goodwill. Due to these expenditures, at December 31, 20x3, Paye estimated that the benefit period of goodwill was 40 years. In its December 31, 20x3, balance sheet, what amount should Paye report as goodwill?

    **a.** $180,000

    **b.** $195,000

    **c.** $200,000

    **d.** $280,000

**Items 46 through 48 are based on the following:**

On January 2, 20x4, Pare Co. purchased 75% of Kidd Co.'s outstanding common stock. Selected balance sheet data at December 31, 20x4, is as follows:

|  | Pare | Kidd |
|---|---|---|
| Total assets | $420,000 | $180,000 |
| Liabilities | $120,000 | $ 60,000 |
| Common stock | 100,000 | 50,000 |
| Retained earnings | 200,000 | 70,000 |
|  | $420,000 | $180,000 |

During 20x4, Pare and Kidd paid cash dividends at $25,000 and $5,000 respectively, to their shareholders. There were no other intercompany transactions.

**46.** In its December 31, 20x4, consolidated statement of retained earnings, what amount should Pare report as dividends paid?
   - a. $5,000
   - b. $25,000
   - c. $26,250
   - d. $30,000

**47.** In Pare's December 31, 20x4, consolidated balance sheet, what amount should be reported as minority interest in net assets?
   - a. $0
   - b. $ 30,000
   - c. $ 45,000
   - d. $105,000

**48.** In its December 31, 20x4, consolidated balance sheet, what amount should Pare report as common stock?
   - a. $ 50,000
   - b. $100,000
   - c. $137,500
   - d. $150,000

**49.** Sun, Inc. is a wholly-owned subsidiary of Patton, Inc. On June 1, 20x3, Patton declared and paid a $1 per share cash dividend to stockholders of record on May 15, 20x3. On May 1, 20x3, Sun bought 10,000 shares of Patton's common stock for $700,000 on the open market, when the book value per share was $30. What amount of gain should Patton report from this transaction on its consolidated income statement for the year ended December 31, 20x3?
   - a. $0
   - b. $390,000
   - c. $400,000
   - d. $410,000

**50.** The primary reason that ASC Topic 805, Business Combinations, was adopted is
   - a. The pooling method is superior to the purchase method.
   - b. It more accurately reflects the effects of the business combination.
   - c. The purchase method is superior to the pooling method.
   - d. The method improves the comparability of financial statements.

# CHAPTER 9

## CONSOLIDATIONS

## Simulation Task Questions

**Number 1**                                **(Estimated time - 45 to 55 minutes)**

**Task Question Number 1** consists of 16 items. Select the **best** answer for each item.

Presented below are selected amounts from the separate unconsolidated financial statements of Poe Corp. and its 90%-owned subsidiary, Shaw Co., at December 31, 20x2. Additional information follows:

| | Poe | Shaw |
|---|---|---|
| **Selected income statement amounts** | | |
| Sales | $710,000 | $530,000 |
| Cost of goods sold | 490,000 | 370,000 |
| Gain on sale of equipment | --- | 21,000 |
| Earnings from investment in subsidiary | 61,000 | --- |
| Interest expense | --- | 16,000 |
| Depreciation | 25,000 | 20,000 |
| | | |
| **Selected balance sheet amounts** | | |
| Cash | $ 50,000 | $ 15,000 |
| Inventories | 229,000 | 150,000 |
| Equipment | 440,000 | 360,000 |
| Accumulated depreciation | (200,000) | (120,000) |
| Investment in Shaw | 189,000 | --- |
| Investment in bonds | 100,000 | --- |
| Discount on bonds | (9,000) | --- |
| Bonds payable | --- | (200,000) |
| Common stock | (100,000) | (10,000) |
| Additional paid-in capital | (250,000) | (40,000) |
| Retained earnings | (402,000) | (140,000) |
| | | |
| **Selected statement of retained earnings amounts** | | |
| Beginning balance, December 31, 20x1 | $272,000 | $100,000 |
| Net income | 210,000 | 70,000 |
| Dividends paid | 80,000 | 30,000 |

Additional information:
- On January 2, 20x2, Poe, Inc. purchased 90% of Shaw, Co.'s outstanding common stock for cash of $155,000. On that date, Shaw's stockholders' equity equaled $150,000 and the fair values of Shaw's assets and liabilities equaled their carrying amounts. Poe has accounted for the acquisition as a purchase. Poe's policy is to amortize intangibles over 10 years.

- On September 4, 20x2, Shaw paid cash dividends of $30,000.

- On December 31, 20x2, Poe recorded its equity in Shaw's earnings.

**Required:**

**a.** **Items 1 through 3** below represent transactions between Poe and Shaw during 20x2. Determine the dollar amount effect of the consolidating adjustment on 20x2 consolidated income before considering minority interest. Ignore income tax considerations.

1. On January 3, 20x2, Shaw sold equipment with an original cost of $30,000 and a carrying value of $15,000 to Poe for $36,000. The equipment had a remaining life of three years and was depreciated using the straight-line method by both companies.

2. During 20x2, Shaw sold merchandise to Poe for $60,000, which included a profit of $20,000. At December 31, 20x2, half of this merchandise remained in Poe's inventory.

3. On December 31, 20x2, Poe paid $91,000 to purchase 50% of the outstanding bonds issued by Shaw. The bonds mature on December 31, 20x8, and were originally issued at par. The bonds pay interest annually on December 31 of each year, and the interest was paid to the prior investor immediately before Poe's purchase of the bonds.

**b.** **Item 4.** Determine the amount recorded by Poe as amortization of goodwill for 20x2.

**c.** **Items 5 through 16** below refer to accounts that may or may not be included in Poe and Shaw's consolidated financial statements. The list on the right refers to the various possibilities of those amounts to be reported in Poe's consolidated statements for the year ended December 31, 20x2. Consider all transactions stated in items 1 through 4 in determining your answer. Ignore income tax considerations.

**Items to be Answered:**
5. Cash
6. Equipment
7. Investment in subsidiary
8. Bonds payable
9. Minority interest
10. Common stock
11. Beginning retained earnings
12. Dividends paid
13. Gain on retirement of bonds
14. Cost of goods sold
15. Interest expense
16. Depreciation expense

**Responses to be selected:**
A. Sum of amounts on Poe and Shaw's separate unconsolidated financial statements.
B. Less than the sum of amounts on Poe and Shaw's separate unconsolidated financial statements but not the same as the amount on either.
C. Same as amount for Poe only.
D. Same as amount for Shaw only.
E. Eliminated entirely in consolidation.
F. Shown in consolidated financial statements but not in separate unconsolidated financial statements.
G. Neither in consolidated nor in separate unconsolidated financial statements.

**Number 2.**

**Question Number 2** consists of 10 items. Select the best answer for each item.

On January 2, 20x5, Purl Co. purchased 90% of Strand Co.'s outstanding common stock at a purchase price that was in excess of Strand's stockholders' equity. On that date, the fair values of Strand's assets and liabilities equaled their carrying amounts. Purl has accounted for the acquisition as a purchase. Transactions during 20x5 were as follows:

- On February 15, 20x5, Strand sold equipment to Purl at a price higher than the equipment's carrying amount. The equipment had a remaining life of three years and was depreciated using the straight-line method by both companies.
- During 20x5, Purl sold merchandise to Strand under the same terms it offered to third parties. At December 31, 20x5, one-third of this merchandise remained in Strand's inventory.
- On November 15, 20x5, both Purl and Strand paid cash dividends to their respective shareholders.
- On December 31, 20x5, Purl recorded its equity in Strand earnings.

**Required: Items 6 through 15** relate to accounts that may or may not be included in Purl and Strand's consolidated financial statements. The alphabetized list refers to the possible ways those accounts may be reported in Purl's consolidated financial statements for the year ended December 31, 20x5. For each item, select a corresponding letter. An answer may be selected once, more than once, or not at all.

A. Sum of the amounts on Purl and Strand's separate unconsolidated financial statements.
B. Less than the sum of the amounts on Purl and Strand's separate unconsolidated financial statements, but not the same as the amount on either separate unconsolidated financial statement.
C. Same as the amount for Purl only.
D. Same as the amount for Strand only.
E. Eliminated entirely in consolidation.
F. Shown in the consolidated financial statements but not in the separate unconsolidated financial statements.

**Items:**
6. Cash.
7. Equipment.
8. Investment in subsidiary.
9. Minority interest.
10. Common stock.
11. Beginning retained earnings.
12. Dividends paid.
13. Cost of goods sold.
14. Interest expense.
15. Depreciation expense.

# CHAPTER 9

# CONSOLIDATIONS

## Multiple Choice Answers

1. /c/ 40% interest presumes the equity method, therefore 40% of NI since acquisition of investment (0.40 x $300,000 = $120,000)

2. /d/ When an investor has over a 50% interest in an investee, consolidated financial statements should be prepared. A and B are incorrect because an investment of over 20% should be accounted for by the equity method, while investments of less than 20% would use the cost method. C is incorrect because the pooling of interests method of recording a business combination is no longer acceptable.

3. /d/ Consolidated financial statements should be prepared when over 50% ownership occurs because the investor has control over the resources of the investee. C is incorrect because significant influence is assumed when a 20% ownership applies, yet control (over 50%) is needed before consolidated financial statements should be prepared. A is incorrect because the equity method is applied to all investments of over 20%, whereas 50% is needed for control. B is incorrect because the cost method applies to investments of under 20% and so no control would exist.

4. /b/ The basis of consolidation is a required disclosure while the other items are not required under ASC Topic 235.

5. /d/ Assets and liabilities are recorded at their fair value at the date of acquisition under the purchase method.

6. /a/ Since the acquisition was cash for stock, the purchase method states that all assets and liabilities are to be recorded at their fair values at the date of acquisition.

7. /d/ Cost of Acquisition:

| | |
|---|---|
| Preferred Stock | $4,000,000 |
| Finder's Fee | 400,000 |
| | $4,400,000 |

Action would record an increase in net assets for the entire cost of acquisition of $4,400,000. Tangible assets would be written up to $2,500,000 and goodwill of $1,900,000 would be recorded.

Writing all of the net assets up (down) to their fair values resulted in no remaining excess in this case, and thus zero goodwill is recorded.

8. /c/ The capitalized cost would be the fair value of the stock issued plus the finder's and the consultant's fees. The SEC registration costs are costs associated with issuing stock and thus are recorded as a reduction to additional paid-in capital.

9. /b/ The excess of the cost over the net book value should be allocated first to write net tangible assets up to their fair values and any remaining excess to goodwill.

| | |
|---|---|
| Cost ($25 x 300,000 shares) | $7,500,000 |
| Net book value | (6,000,000) |
| Excess of cost over book value | $1,500,000 |
| Write up PP&E to fair value | (800,000) |
| Remaining excess to goodwill | $ 700,000 |

10. /c/

| | |
|---|---|
| Cost of investment | $1,600,000 |
| Book value of net assets | (1,240,000) |
| Excess cost over book value | $ 360,000 |
| Inventory write-down | 20,000 |
| PP&E writeup | (80,000) |
| Remaining excess to goodwill | $ 300,000 |

**11.** /a/ The excess of the cost over the book value of the net assets is allocated to the net assets to bring them up to their fair values. The excess of cost over book value is $1,600,000 (8,000,000 - 6,400,000) in this case, and is all accounted for by FMV greater than BV of assets. No amount remains to allocate to goodwill

This excess is allocated to the net assets as follows:

|  | Book Value | Fair Value | Allocation |
|---|---|---|---|
| Property, Plant, & Equipment | $10,000,000 | $11,500,000 | $1,500,000 |
| Other Assets | 1,000,000 | 700,000 | (300,000) |
| Long-term Debt | 6,000,000 | 5,600,000 | 400,000 |
|  |  |  | $1,600,000 |

**12.** /c/

| Cost of investment | $800,000 |
|---|---|
| Book value of net assets | (620,000) |
| Excess cost over book value | $180,000 |
| Inventory write-down | 50,000 |
| Property and equipment writeup | (80,000) |
| Remaining excess to goodwill | $150,000 |

**13.** /b/

| Cost of investment | $1,500,000 |
|---|---|
| Book value of net assets | (900,000) |
| Excess cost over book value | $ 600,000 |
| Inventory writedown | 50,000 |
| PP&E writeup | (100,000) |
| Remaining excess to goodwill | $ 550,000 |

**14.** /a/ The entire stockholders' equity section of Nuggett Company is eliminated against the investment account when consolidated financial statements are prepared.

**15.** /d/ ASC Topic 805 and ASC Topic 810 states that any fair value in excess of cost should be allocated to income on the transaction closing date.

**16.** /a/ A deferred credit (negative goodwill) of $150,000

| Fair value of net assets | $1,400,000 |
|---|---|
| Purchase price (100,000 shares at $10/share) | (1,000,000) |
| Excess of fair value over cost | $ 400,000 |
| Noncurrent assets | (250,000) |
| Negative goodwill | $ 150,000 |

Any excess of fair value over cost must be allocated to noncurrent assets (excluding long-term investments) based on their relative adjusted values, but not to below zero. Any remaining excess should be recorded as a deferred credit and amortized over 40 years or the period to be benefited, if less.

**17.** /d/ In preparing the consolidated balance sheet, the subsidiary stockholders' equity is either eliminated (the parent's share) or reclassified (MI share). Here, the parent owns 100%, so there is no MI. Therefore, the consolidated stockholders' equity is the parents' stockholder's equity.

| Common stock | $1,000,000 |
|---|---|
| Retained earnings | 250,000 |
|  | $1,250,000 |

**18.** /b/ This combination would be recorded as a purchase because cash was given in exchange for stock. Under the purchase method, the consolidated net income includes the investee's net income from the date of combination through year-end.

**19.** /c/ The question asks for the parent's (Dallas') share of the subsidiary's (Style's) net income, before amortization of goodwill, for the year. The net income is determined through the change in retained earnings:

| | |
|---|---|
| Retained earnings, 12/31 | $51,000 |
| Retained earnings, 1/1 | 36,000 |
| | $15,000 |
| Dividends paid by Style | + 5,000 |
| Change in RE due to net income | $20,000 |
| Dallas' share (80%) | $16,000 |

**20.** /a/ The consolidated stockholders' equity accounts are always the parent's balances when the equity method has been applied by parent. Further, following the purchase method of consolidation, the subsidiary's stockholders' equity accounts are eliminated along with the Investment in Subsidiary account, or reclassified as minority interest. In this case, 80% of Style's stockholders' equity accounts would be eliminated and 20% reclassified as minority interest.

**21.** /c/ Any intercompany receivables from a <u>consolidated</u> affiliate will be eliminated when preparing consolidated financial statements. Adams Corporation is a 30% investee and thus isn't consolidated, so this receivable will remain on the consolidated balance sheet. Bullard Corporation is a consolidated affiliate and so its receivable will be eliminated. Even though Carpenter Corporation is 90% owned, it isn't a consolidated affiliate and thus the receivable would remain on the consolidated balance sheet.

**22.** /d/ All intercompany receivables and payables should be eliminated when consolidated financial statements are presented.

**23.** /d/ Intercompany sales would be included in the gross sales of the seller, parent or subsidiary. They are not included in consolidated sales, however, since they did not result from an arm's-length transaction.

| | |
|---|---|
| Parent gross revenues | $200,000 |
| Subsidiary gross revenues | 140,000 |
| | $340,000 |
| Less consolidated gross revenues | (308,000) |
| Intercompany sales | $ 32,000 |

**24.** /b/ Any intercompany payable by Spin to Pard would be matched by an intercompany receivable on Pard's books. Further, any such intercompany account would be eliminated.

| | |
|---|---|
| Parent's gross AR | $26,000 |
| Subsidiary's gross AR | 19,000 |
| | $45,000 |
| Less consolidated gross receivables | (39,000) |
| Interco. AR/AP | $ 6,000 |

**25.** /c/ Intercompany profit must be eliminated from the carrying amount of the inventory.

| | |
|---|---|
| Parent's inventory | $30,000 |
| Subsidiary's inventory | 25,000 |
| | $55,000 |
| Consolidated inventory | (52,000) |
| Intercompany profit | $ 3,000 |

Since the requirement calls for the carrying amount of the inventory that Spin purchased from Pard, use the $3,000 gross profit figure as follows:

Pard's markup = gross profit/COGS
Pard's markup = 1/3 ($50,000 -:- $150,000)

When gross profit is $3,000, related cost must be $3,000 -:- 1/3 = $9,000.

**26.** /b/ In the consolidated balance sheet, we are given minority interest ownership in the subsidiary as $10,000 and total stockholders' equity of $50,000. Ownership percent is $10,000 -:- $50,000 = 20%.

**27.** /d/ When there are intercompany transactions, be alert for double counting and eliminate any found that does not net itself. This question asks for consolidated selling expenses where some selling expenses were charged by parent to subsidiary.

| | |
|---|---:|
| Pard's selling expenses | $1,100,000 |
| Less freight-out charged to Seed | - 50,000 |
| Third-party selling expenses | $1,050,000 |
| Plus Seed's selling expenses | 400,000 |
| Consolidated selling exp. | $1,450,000 |

**28.** /d/ When consolidated financial statements are prepared the intercompany sale is treated as though it never occurred. The consolidated entity would show the assets as though it was never sold. The cost would remain at $2,000,000 and accumulated depreciation would increase $100,000 for the current year's depreciation expense ($2,000,000/20 years = $100,000/year).

**29.** /a/ The parent has issued a bond payable, i.e. Palmer is the debtor. When the subsidiary, Seal, acquired that bond (or any portion of it), there are no longer third parties holding debt. Therefore, the debt is treated as extinguished. When debt is extinguished, a gain or loss is calculated by comparing the carrying value of the debt with the reacquisition price paid. In this case:

| | |
|---|---:|
| Carrying value: | |
| Face value of bond | $1,000,000 |
| Plus premium remaining | 75,000 |
| Carrying value | $1,075,000 |
| Reacquisition price: | |
| Investment in Bond Payable | $1,000,000 |
| Less discount remaining | - 25,000 |
| Reacquisition price | $ 975,000 |

$1,075,000 - $975,000 = $100,000 gain on intercompany bond acquisition. There is no effect on minority interest because the parent was the issuer of the bond. Had the facts been reversed and Seal, the subsidiary, been the issuer of the bond, then the MI would have been allocated 25% of the gain, ($25,000).

**30.** /a/ The business combination was accounted for as an acquisition. The question asks for total (i.e. consolidated) current assets one year later. Using the acquisition method, the parent's book value is added to the subsidiary's book value, reflecting the parent's ownership percentage (here 100%) of adjustments to fair market value as of the date of combination.

| | |
|---|---:|
| Parent's current assets | $310,000 |
| Subsidiary's current assets | 135,000 |
| Adjust inventory to fair value | 10,000 |
| Total current assets | $455,000 |

The inventory adjustment is required because the original items were still on hand at year end.

**31.** /d/ Calculation of consolidated total assets must reflect the consolidation eliminations, so the investment in subsidiary account is not included.

| | |
|---|---:|
| Parent's total assets | $1,325,000 |
| Less Investment in Scott | - 390,000 |
| | $ 935,000 |
| Subsidiary's assets | 415,000 |
| Plus inventory adjustment | 10,000 |
| Plus goodwill* | 100,000 |
| Consolidated assets | $1,460,000 |

| | |
|---|---:|
| *Computation for goodwill: | |
| Price paid on acquisition | $360,000 |
| Less book value of Sub.'s net assets. ($410,000 - 160,000) | 250,000 |
| Differential | $110,000 |
| Adjust book value of inventory to market value | -10,000 |
| Goodwill | $100,000 |

**32.** /d/ The consolidated retained earnings is the parent's balance when the equity method is used to account for the investment in subsidiary account.

**33.** /b/ Consolidated net income is the parent's net income when the equity method is used to account for the investment in subsidiary account.

**34.** /d/ Under the purchase method the investment is recorded at the fair value of the stock issued.

**35.** /d/ Watch the dates in this question! Retained earnings given is for the beginning of the year; i.e. prior to the business combination. If the business combination is recorded as an acquisition, the consolidated retained earnings as of the date of acquisition will be the parent's balance only. Notice that in purchase transactions, the parent records its share of subsidiary net income and dividends only from the date of acquisition forward.

| | |
|---|---:|
| Pane's retained earnings, 1/1 | $3,200,000 |
| Pane's income | 800,000 |
| Pane's dividends | - 750,000 |
| Consolidated RE, 6/30 | $3,250,000 |

**36.** /d/ The requirement is to calculate consolidated paid-in capital in a purchase accounting business combination. The fair market value of Saxe was calculated as follows: 200,000 shares issued times $18/share = $3,600,000. Since the par value of the stock issued was (200,000 shares x $10 par value) $2,000,000, the balance of $1,600,000 must increase paid-in capital.

| | |
|---|---:|
| Poe paid-in capital beginning balance | $1,300,000 |
| Amount recorded in purchase of Saxe | 1,600,000 |
| Consolidated PIC | $2,900,000 |

**37.** /c/ The process of preparing combined financial statements is analogous to the consolidation process to the extent that intercompany transactions are eliminated in both cases. Here, no portion of intercompany loans or profits is included in combined financial statements.

**38.** /a/ Combined financial statements may be used to present the operations of both unconsolidated subsidiaries and for companies under common management.

**39.** /a/ Often, companies will have geographically separate operations owned under one corporation but operated with varying degrees of independence. The home office/branch office structure is an example of such operations. A combined set of financial statements provides useful information about the company as a whole. Intracompany transactions, however, must not be included in the combined balances. The facts here indicate sales by Home Office to Branch of $200,000, which would not be added to the sales to outside third parties by Branch. On the facts, only the $250,000 sales by Branch are to be shown as sales.

**40.** /d/ Combined financial statements are likely to be prepared for separate corporations under common ownership. Notice they are "brother-sisters," not parent-subsidiary. A and B are not correct answers because consolidation is required for a corporation and non-homogeneous subsidiaries, whether they are domestic or foreign. As to C, neither combined nor consolidated financial statements may be prepared.

**41.** /c/ Foreign corporations are included in combined financial statements as well as in consolidated financial statements. Operations with fiscal periods that differ by more than three months must conform them under both methods.

**42.** /c/ If control is likely to be temporary or future control is in doubt due to some unpredictable circumstances, consolidated reports are not prepared.

**43.** /a/

| | |
|---|---|
| Price paid for purchase of common stock | $1,200,000 |
| Book value/fair value of equity when purchased ($1,320,000 assets less $320,000 liabilities | (1,000,000) |
| Goodwill | $ 200,000 |

Goodwill is not amortized, but rather uses an impairment test to determine any loss in value. Since no information is given as to any impairment, there is no cost allocated to expense.

**44.** /a/ Although not expressly stated, the fact pattern indicates that this transaction was accounted for using the purchase method (presence of goodwill, etc.). In that case, the retained earnings figure carried through to the consolidated balance sheet is the $1,240,000 of the parent company, Owen Corp.

**45.** /c/ The cost of goodwill is measured as that which arose in the purchase transaction. The additional $80,000 spent internally to enhance it is not recorded. Goodwill is not amortized and thus, without additional information, would remain at the reported cost, $200,000.

**46.** /b/ Dividends paid by the consolidated entity are those paid by Pare -- $25,000. The amount paid by Kidd include intercompany dividends of $3,750 to Pare (eliminated), and $1,250 to the minority interest. Dividends paid to the minority owners are not dividends of the consolidated entity.

**47.** /b/ Minority interest to be reported is 25% of the net assets of Kidd -- $120,000 x 25% = $30,000. (Net assets are total assets of $180,000 less liabilities of $60,000.)

**48.** /b/ Common stock reported on the consolidated balance sheet is the stock of Pare (the parent company) -- $100,000.

**49.** /a/ The intercompany purchase and sale of the shares results in a simultaneous gain and loss as far as the consolidated entity is concerned. These items would be eliminated in the preparation of the consolidated financial statements.

**50.** /d/ ASC Topic 805 requires all business combinations to be accounted for by one method (the acquisition method). This improves the comparability of financial statements. A and C are incorrect because neither the pooling nor the purchase method was superior in comparison to the other method. Answer B is incorrect because the pooling and purchase methods accurately reflect the effects of the combination.

# CHAPTER 9

## CONSOLIDATIONS

### Simulation Answers

**Number 1 Answer** (Note: The exam called for the answers to be marked on a sense sheet.)

a. 1. $\underline{14,000}$ decrease. Gain on intercompany sale of equipment of $21,000 less $7,000 excess depreciation taken by Poe Co. based on the $36,000 cost. $36,000 -:- 3 years = $12,000. Undepreciated historical cost of $15,000 -:- 3 years = $5,000. $12,000 - $5000 = $7,000.

2. $\underline{10,000}$ decrease. Half of the $60,000 intercompany sales amount has not been realized in sales to outside parties. Therefore, the related unconfirmed profit ($20,000 X 50%) would not be included in consolidated income.

3. $\underline{9,000}$ increase. Since the bonds have been constructively retired at a price $9,000 lower than their $100,000 carrying value, a gain must be reported in the consolidated statements. The gain amount would be adjusted against Poe's Discount on Bonds Payable account.

b. 4. $\underline{0}$. Total goodwill, $155,000 price paid less ($150,000 X 90% interest acquired) = $20,000. However, goodwill is not amortized and there is no information given as to any impairment of value.

c. 5. /A/ Cash amounts are not adjusted in consolidated statements. The balances are combined.

6. /B/ The consolidated total for equipment must be $6,000 lower than the sum of the separate entities' account balances. This is to eliminate the excess price paid by Poe over the historical cost of equipment sold to it by Shaw. ($36,000 - $30,000)

7. /E/ The investment account is completely eliminated in the consolidated reporting process.

8. /B/ Bonds payable are reduced by the face value of those bonds constructively retired.

9. /F/ Since minority interest represents the ownership interest relating to owners external to the consolidated entity, it follows that it only appears in consolidated reporting. When the companies issue their own, separate statements, there are no minority owners to be represented.

10. /C/ The acquisition method requires that the equity accounts of only the parent company be reported on the consolidated statements. Combining the accounts would "double count" the subsidiary's equity.

11. /C/ See answer to 10 above.

12. /C/ Only the dividends paid by Poe are reported. Those paid by Shaw to Poe are eliminated ($30,000 X 90%), and those paid to minority stockholders are a part of minority interest.

**13.** /F/ The gain on retirement of bonds occurred because the consolidated entity "invested in its own debt." Thus, from the consolidated entity's point of view, a gain has occurred because "it paid itself" $9,000 less than the carrying value of the bonds. However, when looking at the companies separately, the debt is still outstanding and no retirement has occurred. Thus, the gain exists only within the consolidated framework.

**14.** /B/ The cost of goods sold needs to be reduced to allow for the cost relating to the unconfirmed gross profit in the inventories.

**15.** /D/ Interest expense was incurred only by Shaw and it was paid to outside entities, therefore it is not eliminated in the consolidation process.

**16.** /B/ Consolidated depreciation expense is too high by $7,000. See answer to a.1 above.

**Number 2 Answer**

1. /A/    Cash amounts are not adjusted in consolidated statements. The balances are combined.

2. /B/    The separate statements will reflect the inter-company purchase/sale of the item of equipment at a price in excess of its book value. However, since the equipment was not sold to an external entity, the consolidated balance sheet must report the equipment at its book value based on its original historical cost. Furthermore, the inter-company gain relating to this non-external sale must also be eliminated so as not to be included in the consolidated income statement.

3. /E/    The investment in subsidiary account is completely eliminated in the consolidated reporting process.

4. /F/    Minority interest represents ownership interest external only to the consolidated entity. When the companies publish their own, separate statements, there are no minority owners to be represented.

5. /C/    The purchase method requires that the equity accounts of only the parent company be reported on the consolidated statements. The parent company's investment account is eliminated against the equity accounts of the subsidiary corporation.

6. /C/    Beginning retained earnings of the subsidiary company are eliminated in the worksheet entry against the investment in subsidiary account. This leaves the beginning retained earnings of only the parent company to be reported on the consolidated statements.

7. /C/    Only the dividends paid by the parent company, Purl, are reported. Those paid by Strand to Purl are eliminated, and those paid by Strand to minority stockholders are included in the minority interest figure reported.

8. /B/    Cost of goods sold is adjusted to remove amounts pertaining to intercompany sales and any unconfirmed gross profit in cost of goods sold. The worksheet entry to eliminate the intercompany sales and related costs would result in the cost of goods sold of the combined entity being less than that of the sum of the separate entities.

9. /A/    Interest expense is not specifically identified in any transactions in the fact pattern, and there appear to be no intercompany loans/receivables that would give rise to intercompany interest transactions. It is assumed, therefore, that any interest paid by both companies would be to external entities, and would therefore be summed on the consolidated statements.

10. /B/    Depreciation expense on Purl's statement would be based on the price it paid for the equipment purchased from Strand. However, as far as the consolidated entity is concerned, there has been no external sale, and the depreciation expense should be based on the original historical cost of the equipment when Strand acquired it. Therefore, an adjustment to reduce depreciation expense is necessary to produce the amount to be reported in the consolidated statements.

# CHAPTER 10

# INCOME TAX ACCOUNTING AND OTHER TOPICS

## Question Map

II.  CURRENT LIABILITY FOR TAXES OWED
   A.  Current Liability - No Temporary or Permanent Differences
   B.  Current Liability - Permanent Differences -- 9, 18, 19
   C.  Effective Tax Rate   Permanent Differences – 11

III. CURRENT ASSET FOR REFUNDABLE TAXES – 12, 51

IV.  DEFERRED TAX ASSETS AND LIABILITIES (DTA/DTL)
   A.  Types of Temporary Differences
   B.  Theoretical Approaches to Interperiod Tax Allocation
   C.  Determine DTL/DTA
       1.  Compute Temporary Differences
       2.  Compute Current Income Tax Expense – 4, 7, 17, 50
       3.  Compute Balance in DTA/DTL – 1, 2, 3, 8, 16
       4.  Consider Valuation Allowance
       5.  Compute Deferred Income Tax Expense and Prepare JE – 5, 10
   D.  Effect on DTA/DTL in the Future

V.   ADDITIONAL DEFERRED TAX ISSUES
   A.  Valuation Allowance for Deferred Tax Asset – 13, 54
   B.  Tax Laws and Rates – 48
   C.  Classifying DTA/DTL as Current/Noncurrent – 14, 15, 49
   D.  Netting DTA and DTL for Reporting Purposes -- 6
   E.  Intraperiod Versus Interperiod Tax Allocation

X.   SUMMARY OF SIGNIFICANT ACCOUNTING POLICIES -- 20

XI.  RELATED PARTY DISCLOSURES – 21, 56

XII. INTERIM FINANCIAL STATEMENTS
   A.  Modified GAAP – 52, 55
   B.  Statement Content – 22, 23, 29
   C.  Principles/Methods Underlying Statement Preparation
       1.  Product Costs -- 24, 25, 26
       2.  Period Costs -- 27, 28, 29, 30

# CHAPTER 10

## INCOME TAX ACCOUNTING AND OTHER TOPICS

### Multiple Choice Questions

**1.** West Corp. leased a building and received the $36,000 annual rental payment on June 15, 20x2. The beginning of the lease was July 1, 20x2. Rental income is taxable when received. West's tax rates are 30% for 20x2 and 40% thereafter. West had no other permanent or temporary differences. West determined that no valuation allowance was needed. What amount of deferred tax asset should West report on its December 31, 20x2, balance sheet?

    **a.** $5,400
    **b.** $7,200
    **c.** $10,800
    **d.** $14,400

**2.** Taft Corp. uses the equity method to account for its 25% investment in Flame, Inc. During 20x2, Taft received dividends of $30,000 from Flame and recorded $180,000 as its equity in the earnings of Flame. Additional information follows:

- All the undistributed earnings of Flame will be distributed as dividends in future periods.

- The dividends received from Flame are eligible for the 80% dividends received deduction.

- There are no other temporary differences.

- Enacted income tax rates are 30% for 20x2 and thereafter.

In its December 31, 20x2 balance sheet, what amount should Taft report for deferred income tax liability?

    **a.** $9,000
    **b.** $10,800
    **c.** $45,000
    **d.** $54,000

**3.** Stone Co. began operations in 20x2 and reported $225,000 in income before income taxes for the year. Stone's 20x2 tax depreciation exceeded its book depreciation by $25,000. Stone also had nondeductible book expenses of $10,000 related to permanent differences. Stone's tax rate for 20x2 was 40%, and the enacted rate for years after 20x2 is 35%. In its December 31, 20x2, balance sheet, what amount of deferred income tax liability should stone report?

    **a.** $8,750
    **b.** $10,000
    **c.** $12,250
    **d.** $14,000

**4.** Venus Corp.'s worksheet for calculating current and deferred income taxes for 20x2 follows:

| | 20x2 | 20x3 | 20x4 |
|---|---|---|---|
| Pretax F/S income | $1,400 | | |
| Temporary differences: | | | |
|   Depreciation | (800) | (1,200) | $2,000 |
|   Warranty costs | 400 | (100) | (300) |
| Taxable income | $1,000 | (1,300) | 1,700 |
| | | | |
| Loss carryback | (1,000) | 1,000 | |
| Loss carryforward | | 300 | (300) |
| | $ 0 | $ 0 | $1,400 |
| | | | |
| Enacted rate | 30% | 30% | 25% |
| | | | |
| Deferred tax liability (asset): | | | |
|   Current | $ (300) | | |
|   Noncurrent | | | $ 350 |

Venus had no prior deferred tax balances. In its 20x2 income statement, what amount should Venus report as current income tax expense?

    **a.** $420
    **b.** $350
    **c.** $300
    **d.** $0

**5.** Quinn Co. reported a net deferred tax asset of $9,000 in its December 31, 20x3, balance sheet. For 20x4, Quinn reported pretax financial statement income of $300,000. Temporary differences of $100,000 resulted in taxable income of $200,000 for 20x4. At December 31, 20x4, Quinn had cumulative taxable differences of $70,000. Quinn's income tax rate is 30%. In its December 31, 20x4, income statement, what should Quinn report as deferred income tax expense?

- **a.** $12,000
- **b.** $21,000
- **c.** $30,000
- **d.** $60,000

**6.** Bravo Company operates in a single tax jurisdiction and considers itself to be a single tax paying component. It has identified the following deferred tax differences:

|  | Taxable | Deductible |
|---|---|---|
| Current | $100,000 | $30,000 |
| Noncurrent | $300,000 | $50,000 |

What amounts should be reported on Bravo's classified balance sheet?

- **a.** All four amounts should appear separately according to their category and classification as shown above.
- **b.** Single amounts of $400,000 and $80,000 should be presented respectively as a deferred tax liability and asset.
- **c.** $70,000 should be classified as a current liability and $250,000 should be classified as a long-term liability.
- **d.** $320,000 should be presented as a net long-term liability.

**Questions 7 and 8 are based on the following information:**

Zeff Co. prepared the following reconciliation of its pretax financial statement income to taxable income for the year ended December 31, 20x4, its first year of operations.

| | |
|---|---|
| Pretax financial statement income | $160,000 |
| Nontaxable interest received on municipal securities | (5,000) |
| Long-term loss accrual in excess of deductible amount | 10,000 |
| Depreciation in excess of financial statement amount | (25,000) |
| Taxable income | $140,000 |

Zeff's tax rate for 20x4 is 40%

**7.** In its 20x4 income statement, what amount should Zeff report as current income tax expense?

- **a.** $52,000
- **b.** $56,000
- **c.** $62,000
- **d.** $64,000

**8.** In its December 31, 20x4, balance sheet, what should Zeff report as deferred income tax liability?

- **a.** $2,000
- **b.** $4,000
- **c.** $6,000
- **d.** $8,000

**Items 9 through 11 are based on the following:**

Aardvark Inc. had pretax financial income (PTFI) of $420,000, which included the amounts below.

| | |
|---|---|
| Municipal bond interest | $ 20,000 |
| Proceeds of life insurance policy | 100,000 |
| Dividend income from investments (subject to 80% exclusion from taxable income) | 50,000 |
| Fines and penalties | 10,000 |
| Statutory tax rate | 40% |

**9.** What is Aardvark's taxable income?

- **a.** $260,000
- **b.** $270,000
- **c.** $360,000
- **d.** $380,000

**10.** By what amount does current income tax expense differ from total income tax expense?
 a. $0
 b. $ 6,000
 c. $18,000
 d. $30,000

**11.** What is Aardvark's effective tax rate?
 a. $108,000 ÷ $420,000
 b. $108,000 ÷ $270,000
 c. $270,000 ÷ $420,000
 d. $270,000 ÷ $108,000

**12.** Echone Company realized a $12,000 operating loss in 20x4. In the previous three years, it had taxable income of $9,000 (20x3), $4,000 (20x2), and $8,000 (20x1). The tax rate in 20x4 was 40%. In the four prior years it was 30%. If Echone Company elects to carry back the loss, what amount of tax refund can it expect to receive?
 a. $6,300
 b. $4,800
 c. $3,900
 d. $3,600

**13.** At the end of its first year of operations (20x4), year-end financial statements of Wells Inc. showed a deferred tax asset of $20,000 and a related valuation allowance of $4,000. At the end of 20x5, the deferred tax asset had grown to $25,000. For 20x6 and beyond, Wells anticipated the following:

- No taxable temporary differences or reversals of prior taxable temporary differences.

- $200,000 of future taxable income, judged to be less than 50% sure of arising.

- No tax-planning strategies to create taxable income would be available.

Assuming a carryforward option is available, what actions should be taken relative to the valuation account?

| | Action | Amount |
|---|---|---|
| a. | Debit | $25,000 |
| b. | Credit | $21,000 |
| c. | Credit | $25,000 |
| d. | None | ---- |

**14.** In its first four years of operations ending December 31, 20x2, Alder, Inc.'s depreciation for income tax purposes exceeded its depreciation for financial statement purposes. This temporary difference was expected to reverse in 20x3, 20x4, and 20x5. Alder had no other temporary differences. Alder's 20x2 balance sheet should include
 a. A noncurrent contra asset for the effects of the differences between asset bases for financial statement and income tax purposes.
 b. Both current and noncurrent deferred tax assets.
 c. A current deferred tax liability only.
 d. A noncurrent deferred tax liability only.

**15.** At the end of 20x3, the tax effects of temporary differences for the Thorn Co. were as follows:

| | Deferred tax assets (liabilities) | Related asset classification |
|---|---|---|
| Accelerated tax depreciation | ($75,000) | Noncurrent asset |
| Additional costs in inventory for tax purposes | 25,000<br>($50,000) | Current asset |

A valuation allowance was not considered necessary. Thorn anticipates that $10,000 of the deferred tax liability will reverse in 20x4. In Thorn's December 31, 20x3, balance sheet, what amount should Thorn report as noncurrent deferred tax liability?
 a. $40,000
 b. $50,000
 c. $65,000
 d. $75,000

**Items 16 and 17 are based on the following:**

Kent, Inc.'s reconciliation between financial statement and taxable income for 20x3 follows:

| | |
|---|---|
| Pretax financial statement income | $150,000 |
| Permanent difference | ( 12,000) |
| | 138,000 |
| Temporary difference – depreciation | ( 9,000) |
| Taxable income | $129,000 |

| Additional information: | At | |
|---|---|---|
| | 12/31/x2 | 12/31/x3 |
| Cumulative temporary differences (future taxable amounts) | $11,000 | $20,000 |

The enacted tax rate was 34% for 20x2, and 40% for 20x3 and years thereafter.

**16.** In its December, 20x3, balance sheet, what amount should Kent report as deferred tax liability?
 a. $3,600
 b. $6,800
 c. $7,340
 d. $8,000

**17.** In its 20x3 income statement, what amount should Kent report as current income tax expense?
 a. $51,600
 b. $55,200
 c. $55,860
 d. $60,000

**18.** In its 20x3 income statement, Cere Co. reported income before income taxes of $300,000. Cere estimated that, because of permanent differences, taxable income for 20x3 would be $280,000. During 20x3 Cere made estimated tax payments of $50,000, which were debited to income tax expense. Cere is subject to a 30% tax rate. What amount should Cere report as income tax expense on the income statement?
 a. $34,000
 b. $50,000
 c. $84,000
 d. $90,000

**19.** For the year ended December 31, 20x3, Grim Co.'s pretax financial statement income was $200,000 and its taxable income was $150,000. The difference is due to the following:

| | |
|---|---|
| Interest on municipal bonds | $ 70,000 |
| Premium expense on key officer life insurance | (20,000) |
| Total | $ 50,000 |

Grim's enacted income tax rate is 30%. In its 20x3 income statement, what amount should Grim report as current income tax expense?
 a. $45,000
 b. $51,000
 c. $60,000
 d. $66,000

**20.** The summary of significant accounting policies should disclose the
 a. Pro forma effect of retroactive application of an accounting change.
 b. Basis of profit recognition on long-term construction contracts.
 c. Adequacy of pension plan assets in relation to vested benefits.
 d. Future minimum lease payments in the aggregate and for each of the five succeeding fiscal years.

**21.** Dean Co. acquired 100% of Morey Corp. prior to 20x9. During 20x9, the individual companies included in their financial statements the following:

| | Dean | Morey |
|---|---|---|
| Officers' salaries | $ 75,000 | $ 50,000 |
| Officers' expenses | 20,000 | 10,000 |
| Loans to officers | 125,000 | 50,000 |
| Intercompany sales | 150,000 | -- |

What amount should be reported as related party disclosures in the notes to Dean's 20x9 consolidated financial statements?
 a. $150,000
 b. $155,000
 c. $175,000
 d. $330,000

**22.** For interim financial reporting, a company's income tax provision for the second quarter of 20x1 should be determined using the
  a. Statutory tax rate for 20x1.
  b. Effective tax rate expected to be applicable for the second quarter of 20x1.
  c. Effective tax rate expected to be applicable for the full year of 20x1 as estimated at the end of the first quarter of 20x1.
  d. Effective tax rate expected to be applicable for the full year of 20x1 as estimated at the end of the second quarter of 20x1.

**23.** For interim financial reporting, an unusual gain occurring in the second quarter should be
  a. Recognized ratably over the last three quarters.
  b. Recognized ratably over all four quarters with the first quarter being restated.
  c. Recognized in the second quarter.
  d. Disclosed by footnote only in the second quarter.

**24.** For external reporting purposes, it is appropriate to use estimated gross profit rates to determine the cost of goods sold for

| | Interim financial reporting | Year-end financial reporting |
|---|---|---|
| a. | Yes | Yes |
| b. | Yes | No |
| c. | No | Yes |
| d. | No | No |

**25.** An inventory loss from a market price decline occurred in the first quarter, and the decline was not expected to reverse during the fiscal year. However, in the third quarter the inventory's market price recovery exceeded the market decline that occurred in the first quarter. For interim financial reporting, the dollar amount of net inventory should
  a. Decrease in the first quarter by the amount of the market price decline and increase in the third quarter by the amount of the decrease in the first quarter.
  b. Decrease in the first quarter by the amount of the market price decline and increase in the third quarter by the amount of the market price recovery.
  c. Decrease in the first quarter by the amount of the market price decline and not be affected in the third quarter.
  d. Not be affected in either the first quarter or the third quarter.

**26.** A planned volume variance in the first quarter, which is expected to be absorbed by the end of the fiscal period, ordinarily should be deferred at the end of the first quarter if it is

| | Favorable | Unfavorable |
|---|---|---|
| a. | Yes | No |
| b. | No | Yes |
| c. | No | No |
| d. | Yes | Yes |

**27.** In January Horner Company paid $80,000 in property taxes on its plant for the calendar year. Also in January Horner estimated that its year-end bonus to executives for the year would be $320,000. What is the amount of the expenses related to these two items that should be reflected in Horner's quarterly income statement for the three months ended June 30 (second quarter)?
  a. $0
  b. $20,000
  c. $80,000
  d. $100,000

**28.** On March 15, 20x2, Krol Co. paid property taxes of $90,000 on its office building for the calendar year 20x2. On April 1, 20x2, Krol paid $150,000 for unanticipated repairs to its office equipment. The repairs will benefit operations for the remainder of 20x2. What is the total amount of these expenses that Krol should include in its quarterly income statement for the three months ended June 30, 20x2?
  a. $172,500
  b. $ 97,500
  c. $ 72,500
  d. $ 37,500

**29.** Farr Corp. had the following transactions during the quarter ended March 31, 20x0:

Loss on early extinguishment
  of debt                                 $ 70,000
Payment of fire insurance premium
  for calendar year 20x0              100,000

What amount should be included in Farr's income statement for the quarter ended March 31, 20x0?

| | Loss | Insurance expense |
|---|---|---|
| a. | $70,000 | $100,000 |
| b. | $70,000 | $ 25,000 |
| c. | $17,500 | $ 25,000 |
| d. | $0 | $100,000 |

**30.** In May Roy Company spent $200,000 on an advertising campaign for subscriptions to the school magazine it sells. The subscriptions do not start until September and the magazine is only sold on a yearly subscription basis. What amount of expense should be included in Roy's quarterly income statement for the three months ended June 30 as a result of this expenditure?
- a. $0
- b. $50,000
- c. $66,667
- d. $200,00

**31.** Financial reporting by a development stage enterprise differs from financial reporting for an established operating enterprise in regard to footnote disclosures
- a. Only.
- b. And expense recognition principles only.
- c. And revenue recognition principles only.
- d. And revenue and expense recognition principles.

**32.** Deficits accumulated during the development stage of a company should be
- a. Reported as organization costs.
- b. Reported as a part of stockholders' equity.
- c. Capitalized and written off in the first year of principal operations.
- d. Capitalized and amortized over a five year period beginning when principal operations commence.

**33.** Lex Corp. was a development stage enterprise from October 10, 20x7 (inception) to December 31, 20x8. The year ended December 31, 20x9 is the first year in which Lex is an established operating enterprise. The following are among the costs incurred by Lex:

| | For the period 10/10/x7 to 12/31/x8 | For the year ended 12/31/x9 |
|---|---|---|
| Leasehold improvements, equipment and furniture | $1,000,000 | $ 300,000 |
| Security deposits | 60,000 | 30,000 |
| Research and Development | 750,000 | 900,000 |
| Laboratory operations | 175,000 | 550,000 |
| General and Administrative | 225,000 | 685,000 |
| Depreciation | 25,000 | 115,000 |
| | $2,235,000 | $2,580,000 |

From its inception through the period ended December 31, 20x9, what is the total amount of costs incurred by Lex that should be charged to operations?
- a. $3,425,000
- b. $2,250,000
- c. $1,775,000
- d. $1,350,000

**34.** A statement of cash flows for a development stage enterprise
- a. Is the same as that of an established operating enterprise and, in addition, shows cumulative amounts from the enterprise's inception.
- b. Shows only cumulative amounts from the enterprise's inception.
- c. Is the same as that of an established operating enterprise, but does **not** show cumulative amounts from the enterprise's inception.
- d. Is **not** presented.

**35.** Personal financial statements should report assets and liabilities at
  a. Historical cost.
  b. Historical cost and, as additional information, at estimated current values at the date of the financial statements.
  c. Estimated current values at the date of the financial statements.
  d. Estimated current values at the date of the financial statements and, as additional information, at historical cost.

**36.** The following information pertains to marketable equity securities owned by Kent:

| Stock | Fair value at December 31, 20x9 | Fair value at December 31, 20x8 | Cost in 20x7 |
|---|---|---|---|
| City Mfg. Inc. | $95,500 | $93,000 | $89,900 |
| Tri Corp. | 3,400 | 5,600 | 3,600 |
| Zee, Inc. | – | 10,300 | 15,000 |

The Zee stock was sold in January 20x9 for $10,200. In Kent's personal statement of financial condition at December 31, 20x9, what amount should be reported for marketable equity securities?
  a. $93,300
  b. $93,500
  c. $94,100
  d. $98,900

**37.** The following information pertains to an insurance policy that Barton owns on his life:

| | |
|---|---|
| Face amount | $100,000 |
| Accumulated premiums paid up to December 31, 20x1 | 8,000 |
| Cash value at December 31, 20x1 | 12,000 |
| Policy loan | 3,000 |

In Barton's personal statement of financial condition at December 31, 20x1, what amount should be reported for the investment in life insurance?
  a. $97,000
  b. $12,000
  c. $9,000
  d. $8,000

**38.** Moran is preparing a personal statement of financial condition as of April 30, 20x1. Included in Moran's assets are the following:

- 50% of the voting stock of Crow Corp. A stockholders' agreement restricts the sale of the stock and, under certain circumstances, requires Crow to repurchase the stock based on carrying amounts of net assets plus an agreed amount for goodwill. At April 30, 20x1, the buyout value of this stock is $337,500. Moran's tax basis for the stock is $215,000.
- Jewelry with a fair value aggregating $35,000 based on an independent appraisal on April 30, 20x1, for insurance purposes. This jewelry was acquired by purchase and gift over a 10-year period and has a total tax basis of $20,000.

At what total amount should the Crow stock and jewelry be reported in Moran's April 30, 20x1, personal statement of financial condition?
  a. $372,500
  b. $357,500
  c. $250,000
  d. $235,000

**39.** Clint owns 50% of Vohl Corp.'s common stock. Clint paid $20,000 for this stock in 20x6. At December 31, 20x1, Clint's 50% stock ownership in Vohl had a fair value of $180,000. Vohl's cumulative net income and cash dividends declared for the five years ended December 31, 20x1, were $300,000 and $40,000, respectively. In Clint's personal statement of financial condition at December 31, 20x1, what amount should be shown as the investment in Vohl?
  a. $20,000
  b. $150,000
  c. $170,000
  d. $180,000

**40.** Ely had the following personal investments at December 31, 20x0:

- Realty held as a limited business activity not conducted in a separate business entity. Mortgage payments were made with funds from sources unrelated to the realty. The cost of this realty was $500,000, and the related mortgage payable was $100,000 at December 31, 20x0.
- Sole proprietorship marketable as a going concern. Its cost was $900,000, and it had related accounts payable of $80,000 at December 31, 20x0.

The costs of both investments equal estimated current values. The balances of liabilities equal their estimated current amounts.

How should the foregoing information be reported in Ely's statement of financial condition at December 31, 20x0?

| | Assets | Liabilities |
|---|---|---|
| **a.** Investment in | | |
| real estate | $400,000 | |
| Investment in sole | | |
| Proprietorship | 820,000 | |
| | | |
| **b.** Investment in | | |
| real estate | $ 500,000 | |
| Investment in sole | | |
| Proprietorship | 820,000 | |
| Mortgage payable | | $100,000 |
| | | |
| **c.** Investment in | | |
| real estate | $500,000 | |
| Investment in sole | | |
| Proprietorship | 900,000 | |
| Mortgage payable | | $100,000 |
| Accounts payable | | 80,000 |
| | | |
| **d.** Investments | $1,400,000 | |
| Accounts and | | |
| mortgage payable | | $180,000 |

**41.** Smith owns several works of art. At what amount should these art works be reported in Smith's personal financial statements?

a. Original cost.
b. Insured amount.
c. Smith's estimate.
d. Appraised value.

**42.** Jen has been employed by Komp, Inc. since February 1, 20x9. Jen is covered by Komp's Section 401(k) deferred compensation plan. Jen's contributions have been 10% of salaries. Komp has made matching contributions of 5%. Jen's salaries were $21,000 in 20x9, $23,000 in 20x0, and $26,000 in 20x1. Employer contributions vest after an employee completes three years of continuous employment. The balance in Jen's 401(k) account was $11,900 at December 31, 20x1, which included earnings of $1,200 on Jen's contributions. What amount should be reported for Jen's vested interest in the 401(k) plan in Jen's December 31, 20x1, personal statement of financial condition?
a. $11,900
b. $8,200
c. $7,000
d. $1,200

**43.** At December 31, 20x0, Ryan had the following noncancelable personal commitments:

- Pledge to be paid to County Welfare Home 30 days after volunteers paint the walls and ceiling of the Home's recreation room ........................ $ 5,000
- Pledge to be paid to City Hospital on the recovery of Ryan's comatose sister ........ 25,000

What amount should be included in liabilities in Ryan's personal statement of financial condition at December 31, 20x0?
a. $0
b. $5,000
c. $25,000
d. $30,000

**44.** Shea, a calendar-year taxpayer, is preparing a personal statement of financial condition as of April 30, 20x2. Shea's 20x1 income tax liability was paid in full on April 15, 20x2. Shea's tax on income earned from January through April 20x2 is estimated at $30,000. In addition, $25,000 is estimated for income tax on the differences between the estimated current values of Shea's assets and the current amounts of liabilities and their tax bases at April 30, 20x2. No withholdings or payments have been made towards the 20x2 income tax liability. In Shea's statement of financial condition at April 30, 20x2, what is the total of the amount or amounts that should be reported for income taxes?
   a. $0
   b. $25,000
   c. $30,000
   d. $55,000

**45.** In personal financial statements, how should estimated income taxes on the excess of the estimated current values of assets over their tax bases by reported in the statement of financial condition?
   a. As liabilities.
   b. As deductions from the related assets.
   c. Between liabilities and net worth.
   d. In a footnote disclosure only.

**46.** The estimated current values of Lane's personal assets at December 31, 20x0, totaled $1,000,000, with tax bases aggregating $600,000. Included in these assets was a vested interest in a deferred profit-sharing plan with a current value of $80,000 and a tax basis of $70,000. The estimated current amounts of Lane's personal liabilities equaled their tax bases at December 31, 20x0. Lane's 20x0 effective income tax rate was 30%. In Lane's personal statement of financial condition at December 31, 20x0, what amount should be provided for estimated income taxes relating to the excess of current values over tax bases?
   a. $120,000
   b. $117,000
   c. $3,000
   d. $0

**47.** The following information pertains to Smith's personal assets and liabilities at December 31, 20x0:

|  | Historical cost | Estimated current values | Estimated current amounts |
|---|---|---|---|
| Assets | $500,000 | $900,000 | |
| Liabilities | 100,000 | | $80,000 |

Smith's 20x0 income tax rate was 30%. In Smith's personal statement of financial condition at December 31, 20x0, what amount should be reported as Smith's net worth?
   a. $294,000
   b. $420,000
   c. $694,000
   d. $820,000

**48.** As a result of differences between depreciation for financial reporting purposes and tax purposes, the financial reporting basis of Noor Co.'s sole depreciable asset, acquired in 20x4, exceeded its tax basis by $250,000 at December 31, 20x4. This difference will reverse in future years. The enacted tax rate is 30% for 20x4, and 40% for future years. Noor has no other temporary differences. In its December 31, 20x4, balance sheet, how should Noor report the deferred tax effect of this difference?
   a. As an asset of $75,000.
   b. As an asset of $100,000.
   c. As a liability of $75,000.
   d. As a liability of $100,000.

**49.** At December 31, 20x4, Bren Co. had the following deferred income tax items:

- A deferred income tax liability of $15,000 related to a noncurrent asset.
- A deferred income tax asset of $3,000 related to a noncurrent liability.
- A deferred income tax asset of $8,000 related to a current liability.

Which of the following should Bren report in the noncurrent section of its December 31, 20x4, balance sheet?
   a. A noncurrent asset of $3,000 and a noncurrent liability of $15,000.
   b. A noncurrent liability of $12,000.
   c. A noncurrent asset of $11,000 and a noncurrent liability of $15,000.
   d. A noncurrent liability of $4,000.

**50.** For the year ended December 31, 20x4, Tyre Co. reported pretax financial statement income of $750,000. Its taxable income was $650,000. The difference is due to accelerated depreciation for income tax purposes. Tyre's income tax rate is 30%, and Tyre made estimated tax payments during 20x4 of $90,000. What amount should Tyre report as current income tax expense for 20x4?

    **a.** $105,000
    **b.** $135,000
    **c.** $195,000
    **d.** $225,000

**51.** Mobe Co. reported the following operating income (loss) for its first three years of operations:

| | |
|---|---|
| 20x2 | $ 300,000 |
| 20x3 | (700,000) |
| 20x4 | 1,200,000 |

For each year, there were no deferred income taxes, and Mobe's income tax rate was 30%. In its 20x3 income tax return, Mobe elected to carry back the maximum amount of loss possible. In its 20x4 income statement, what amount should Mobe report as total income tax expense?

    **a.** $120,000
    **b.** $150,000
    **c.** $240,000
    **d.** $360,000

**52.** Interim financial reporting should be viewed primarily in which of the following ways?

    **a.** As useful only if activity is spread evenly throughout the year.
    **b.** As if the interim period were an annual accounting period.
    **c.** As reporting for an integral part of an annual period.
    **d.** As reporting under a comprehensive basis of accounting other than GAAP.

**53.** Personal financial statements usually consist of

    **a.** A statement of net worth and a statement of changes in net worth.
    **b.** A statement of net worth, an income statement, and a statement of changes in net worth.
    **c.** A statement of financial condition and a statement of changes in net worth.
    **d.** A statement of financial condition, a statement of changes in net worth, and a statement of cash flows.

**54.** On its December 31, 20x4, balance sheet, Shin Co. had income taxes payable of $13,000 and a current deferred tax asset of $20,000 before determining the need for a valuation account. Shin had reported a current deferred tax asset of $15,000 at December 31, 20x3. No estimated tax payments were made during 20x4. At December 31, 20x4, Shin determined that it was more likely than not that 10% of the deferred tax asset would not be realized. In its 20x4 income statement, what amount should Shin report as total income tax expense?

    **a.** $ 8,000
    **b.** $ 8,500
    **c.** $10,000
    **d.** $13,000.

**55.** Conceptually, interim financial statements can be described as emphasizing

    **a.** Timeliness over reliability.
    **b.** Reliability over relevance.
    **c.** Relevance over comparability.
    **d.** Comparability over neutrality.

**56.** Which type of material related-party transactions requires disclosure?

    **a.** Only those not reported in the body of the financial statements.
    **b.** Only those that receive accounting recognition.
    **c.** Only those that contain possible illegal acts.
    **d.** All those other than compensation arrangements, expense allowances, and other similar items in the ordinary course of business.

# CHAPTER 10

## INCOME TAX ACCOUNTING
## AND OTHER TOPICS

### Simulation Task Questions

**Number 1**

**Task Question Number 1** consists of 2 parts. Each part consists of 4 items. **Answer all items.**

**a. Required:** **Items 1 through 4** describe circumstances resulting in differences between financial statement income and taxable income. For each numbered item, determine whether the difference is:

A. A temporary difference resulting in a deferred tax asset.
B. A temporary difference resulting in a deferred tax liability.
C. A permanent difference.

An answer may be selected once, more than once, or not at all.

1. For plant assets, the depreciation expense deducted for tax purposes is in excess of the depreciation expense used for financial reporting purposes.

2. A landlord collects some rents in advance. Rents received are taxable in the period in which they are received.

3. Interest is received on an investment in tax-exempt municipal obligations.

4. Costs of guarantees and warranties are estimated and accrued for financial reporting purposes.

**b.** The following partially completed worksheet contains Lane Co.'s reconciliation between financial statement income and taxable income for the three years ended April 30, 20x7, and additional information.

### Lane Co.
### INCOME TAX WORKSHEET
For the Three Years Ended April 30, 20x7

|  | 4/30/x5 | 4/30/x6 | 4/30/x7 |
|---|---|---|---|
| Pretax financial income | $900,000 | $1,000,000 | $1,200,000 |
| Permanent differences | 100,000 | 100,000 | 100,000 |
| Temporary differences | 200,000 | 100,000 | 150,000 |
| Taxable income | $600,000 | $ 800,000 | $ 950,000 |
|  |  |  |  |
| Cumulative temporary differences |  |  |  |
| (future taxable amounts) | $200,000 | $ **(6)** | $ 450,000 |
| Tax rate | 20% | 25% | 30% |
| Deferred tax liability | $ 40,000 | $ 75,000 | $ **(8)** |
| Deferred tax expense | $ --- | $ **(7)** | $ --- |
| Current tax expense | $ **(5)** | $ --- | $ --- |

The tax rate changes were enacted at the beginning of each tax year and were not known to Lane at the end of the prior year.

**Required: Items 5 through 8** represent amounts omitted from the worksheet. For each item, determine the amount omitted from the worksheet. Select the amount from the following list. An answer may be used once, more than once, or not at all.

A. $ 25,000
B. $ 35,000
C. $ 45,000
D. $ 75,000
E. $100,000
F. $112,500
G. $120,000

H. $135,000
I. $140,000
J. $160,000
K. $180,000
L. $200,000
M. $300,000
N. $400,000

5. Current tax expense for the year ended April 30, 20x5.

6. Cumulative temporary differences at April 30, 20x6.

7. Deferred tax expense for the year ended April 30, 20x6.

8. Deferred tax liability at April 30, 20x7

# CHAPTER 10

## INCOME TAX ACCOUNTING AND OTHER TOPICS

### Multiple Choice Answers

1. /b/ Of the $36,000 cash rental payment received, $18,000 is recognized in the financial statements; however, IRS considers all of it as taxable income. They want their money NOW. This produces a temporary difference which will reverse next year. To recognize the DTA, multiply the deferred income amount of $18,000 by the enacted tax rate of 40%, which equals $7,200.

2. /a/
| Total equity in earnings | $180,000 |
|---|---|
| Less dividends received | (30,000) |
| Undistributed equity | $150,000 |
| Tax exclusion at 80% | -120,000 |
| Future taxable income | $ 30,000 |
| Enacted tax rate | x 30% |
| Deferred Tax Liability | $ 9,000 |

3. /a/ Stone Co.'s tax depreciation is $25,000 greater than book depreciation this year, therefore sometime in the future this difference will reverse producing a lower tax deduction. Smaller tax deductions means higher taxable income and higher taxes payable. $25,000 x .35 enacted tax rate = $8,750 DTL

4. /c/ Beware of the wording here. The current tax expense is the amount of taxes that are to be paid; i.e. taxes payable per the income tax return. Taxable income ($1,000) x enacted tax rate (30%) = $300.

5. /c/ Deferred income tax expense for 20x4 is the sum of the deferred taxes to be paid in the future ($70,000 taxable at 30% = $21,000) and the reduction in the deferred tax asset from the 20x3 balance of $9,000 down to zero at the end of 20x4. Note that the DTA was current. Therefore, as of 20x3 it was expected to be used against taxable amounts of 20x4.

6. /c/ Deferred tax assets and liabilities must be separated into current and noncurrent portions for financial reporting purposes, based on the classification of the related asset or liability, or, if indeterminable, the expected reversal date. Assets and liabilities (current and noncurrent) must then be offset against each other and presented as a single amount.

7. /b/ Current income tax expense is the taxes to be paid for the current period according to the income tax return. It is computed as taxable income of $140,000 times the tax rate of 40%, $56,000.

8. /c/ Deferred income tax liability is the taxes to be paid in the future as a result of temporary differences between PTFI and TI. The temporary differences are excess depreciation taken in the current period, but taxable in the future; and excess long-term loss not deductible currently, but which will be deductible in the future. The net of these two amounts produces a future taxable amount of $15,000. At the 40% tax rate, the DTL is $6,000. The interest on municipal securities is a permanent difference. It will never be taxable.

**9.** /b/

| | |
|---|---:|
| Pretax financial income | $420,000 |
| Add back nondeductible expenses: | |
| Fines and penalties | 10,000 |
| Deduct exempt revenue: | |
| Municipal bond interest | (20,000) |
| Life insurance proceeds | (100,000) |
| 80% dividend deduction | (40,000) |
| Taxable income | $270,000 |

**10.** /a/ All differences in the question are attributable to permanent differences. Permanent differences do not cause differences between current income tax expense and total income tax expense, i.e., permanent differences do not affect deferred income tax expense.

**11.** /a/ Before adjustments to taxable income, Aardvark would have a tax liability computed at 40%. Due to the reduction in taxable income to $270,000, it paid only $108,000 on $420,000 of pretax financial income, for a 25.71% effective tax rate.

**12.** /d/ Operating losses may be applied either to two prior years and then 20 years in the future, or to 20 years in the future. Losses carried forward or backward are valued using the tax rate in existence in the period in which they are to be applied. ($12,000 x 30% = $3,600)

**13.** /b/ All available evidence, both positive and negative, should be considered to determine whether, based on the weight of that evidence, a valuation allowance is needed. That evidence includes examination of four sources, three of which are stated in the question, and loss carry-back possibilities (not applicable since this is the first year of operations). The deferred tax asset is not able to be realized in its entirety, requiring a balance in the valuation allowance account equal to the balance in the deferred asset account, $25,000. A credit of $21,000 to the account, when added to the prior balance of $4,000, will bring the balance to $25,000.

**14.** /d/ If deduction for income tax purposes is greater than deduction for financial statement purposes in earlier years, taxable income for tax purposes in later years will be higher, thereby generating a deferred liability. The deferred tax liability is classified as long-term.

**15.** /d/ Deferred tax liabilities are classified as noncurrent, even though $10,000 will reverse in the next period.

**16.** /d/ Future taxable amount as of 12/31/x2 of $20,000 x enacted tax rate for 20x3 of 40% = $8,000.

**17.** /a/ The current income tax expense is equal to taxes payable per the income tax return, or $51,600 ($129,000 x 40%).

**18.** /c/ Permanent differences do not cause any difference between total income tax expense and current income tax expense. Therefore, total income tax expense is $84,000 (taxable income of $280,000 x 30%).

**19.** /a/

| | |
|---|---:|
| PTFI | $200,000 |
| Less municipal interest | ( 70,000) |
| Plus insurance premium | 20,000 |
| Taxable income | $150,000 |
| x Tax rate of 20% | |
| = Current income tax expense | $45,000 |

**20.** /b/ In the summary of significant accounting policies section, only subjects dealing with methods are discussed. Answers a, c, and d would probably be included in the footnotes to the financial statements, but not under the caption of the summary of significant accounting policies.

**21.** /c/ Certain types of intercompany related party transactions don't require special disclosure, including compensation agreements, expense allowances and other similar events in the normal course of business, as well as transactions eliminated when consolidating or combining statements. Officers' salaries, officers' expenses, and intercompany sales are accordingly all eliminated as amounts to be reported as related party transactions, leaving only loans to officers:

| Loans to officers: | |
|---|---:|
| Dean | $125,000 |
| Morey | 50,000 |
| | $175,000 |

**22.** /d/ For the second quarter 20x1 interim financial statements, the best estimate available at that time of the full year's effective tax rate would be used.

**23.** /c/ In general, circumstances should be recognized in the period in which they occur. No exception is made for unusual gain/loss.

**24.** /b/ For interim financial reporting the gross profit method is acceptable; however, this fact must be disclosed. The gross profit method is not acceptable for year-end financial reporting.

**25.** /a/ Events should be recorded in the interim period in which they occur. An inventory loss not expected to be recovered later in the reporting year would therefore be recorded in the first quarter, when it occurred. Recovery of that loss in the third quarter would be reported at that time only to the extent of the loss reported in the first quarter (conservatism).

**26.** /d/ Generally, planned volume variances (favorable or unfavorable) which are expected to be absorbed by year-end are ignored in interim statements. However, unplanned variances should be reported in the interim period in which they occur.

**27.** /d/

| | |
|---|---:|
| Property taxes ($80,000 x 1/4) | $ 20,000 |
| Bonus ($320,000 x 1/4) | 80,000 |
| | $100,000 |

**28.** /c/ Expenses to be included in the quarterly income statement are:

| | | |
|---|---|---:|
| Property tax: | (1/4 of $90,000) | $22,500 |
| Repairs:* | (1/3 of $150,000) | 50,000 |
| | | $72,500 |

    \* The $150,000 repairs are allocated to each of the three remaining quarters in 20x2.

**29.** /b/ The full amount of the $70,000 loss should be recognized in the period when it occurred. Insurance expense would be allocated over the entire year, or $25,000 per quarter.

**30.** /a/ The $200,000 spent on advertising should be matched against the revenue derived from the sales of subscriptions, thus, no expense should be reported for the quarter ended June 30.

**31.** /a/ All accounting and reporting procedures applicable to established companies must be followed by development stage enterprises, with only a few exceptions.

**32.** /b/ Cumulative net losses from the development stage should be reported in the Stockholders' Equity section, captioned "Deficit accumulated during the developmental stage."

**33.** /a/ The question asks for the amount of costs to be charged to operations. The first two items given, leasehold improvements, equipment and furniture and security deposits are balance sheet items; only the remainder are income statement items. Total amount of costs would be calculated as follows:

|  | 10/10/x7 to 12/31/x8 | FYE 12/31/x9 |
|---|---|---|
| R & D | $ 750,000 | $ 900,000 |
| Lab Op. | 175,000 | 550,000 |
| G & A | 225,000 | 685,000 |
| Depr. | 25,000 | 115,000 |
|  | $1,175,000 | $2,250,000 |

|  |  |
|---|---|
|  | $1,175,000 |
|  | 2,250,000 |
|  | $3,425,000 |

**34.** /a/ In addition to reporting normal cash flows, the cumulative amounts of operating, investing, and financing cash flows since commencement of the DSE should be shown.

**35.** /c/ The most current representative values of assets, liabilities and taxes due as of the date of the statements should be provided.

**36.** /d/ In preparing personal financial statements, marketable securities are valued using the most current information, including quoted prices where available:

| City Mfg. Co. | $95,500 |
|---|---|
| Tri Corp. | 3,400 |
| Zee, Inc. (sold) | 0 |
|  | $98,900 |

**37.** /c/

| Cash value | $12,000 |
|---|---|
| Less loan outstanding | - 3,000 |
| Balance | $ 9,000 |

**38.** /a/

| Crow Corp. stock (buyout value) | $337,500 |
|---|---|
| Jewelry (appraisal value) | 35,000 |
|  | $372,500 |

**39.** /d/ The fair market value of the stock, $180,000, should be shown on the personal financial statement.

**40.** /b/ Assets and liabilities connected with a business should be valued using any acceptable means and then netted and reported as a single figure. If the assets and liabilities are not operated as a business, they should not be combined with business-like items. Therefore, the $500,000 asset and $100,000 liability should be reported separately. For the sole proprietorship operated as a business (determined from the "going concern" comment), the $900,000 asset and $80,000 liability should be combined to produce a net valuation of $820,000.

**41.** /d/ For a personal financial statement, to report the most current value of the art works, appraised value should be used.

**42.** /b/ Nonforfeitable rights to future cash flows that are fixed and determinable and not contingent on occurrence of any future event (such as life expectancy or future performance), are an asset. If noncancelable commitments exist, they are considered a liability. But if the cash flows are contingent on some future event, they should not be recognized as an asset or a liability. Here, at the end of 20x1, Jen is not yet vested and cannot claim any contribution made by her employer. She can only claim her contribution of $7,000 plus $1,200 earnings on her contribution.

**43.** /a/ The commitments are both contingent upon the occurrence of future events and are therefore not included in a personal financial statement.

**44.** /d/ Estimated tax for

| | |
|---|---|
| Jan - April 20x2 | $30,000 |
| Less withholding | -0- |
| Taxes owed | $30,000 |
| Plus estimated taxes on difference between assets and liabilities | 25,000 |
| Total tax owed | $55,000 |

**45.** /c/ The basic accounting equation is modified for personal financial statements:

$$Assets = Liabilities + Est. Tax + Net Worth$$

**46.** /a/ Assume for purposes of this calculation that all assets are sold and liabilities liquidated at their current values with the difference between current values and tax bases taxed at current rates.

Current value
| | |
|---|---|
| Assets | $1,000,000 |
| Tax bases | |
| Assets | - 600,000 |
| Excess of current value over tax bases* | $ 400,000 |
| Effective tax rate | x .30 |
| Estimated income tax | $ 120,000 |

The estimated income tax is shown on the statement between liabilities and equity.

* Note that the current value of the liabilities equals their tax bases, so liabilities are not included in this computation.

**47.** /c/ Assets:
| | |
|---|---|
| Estimated current values | $900,000 |
| Cost | -500,000 |
| Excess of current values over cost | 400,000 |

Liabilities:
| | | |
|---|---|---|
| Cost | $100,000 | |
| Estimated current values | 80,000 | |
| Excess of cost over current values | | -( 20,000) |
| | | 420,000 |
| Tax rate | | x .30 |
| Estimated tax | | $126,000 |

| | |
|---|---|
| Assets (Current value) | $900,000 |
| Liabilities (Current value) | - 80,000 |
| Estimated tax (see above) | -126,000 |
| Net Worth | $694,000 |

**48.** /d/ Future reversal of differences of $250,000 at enacted tax rate of 40% = $100,000. This is a liability because it represents future taxable amounts.

**49.** /b/ DTA and DTL may be netted by category (current and noncurrent) and reported as a single amount. In the noncurrent category, DTL of $15,000 less DTA of $3,000 is $12,000.

**50.** /c/ The currently taxable income of $650,000 x 30% = $195,000.

**51.** /c/ Of the $700,000 loss in 20x3, a maximum of $300,000 can be carried back to offset the income of 20x2. This leaves $400,000 unused to carry forward. In 20x4, $1,200,000 - $400,000 = $800,000 taxable income. $800,000 x 30% = $240,000

**52.** /c/ Each interim period is to be viewed as an integral part of the annual fiscal period rather than a self-contained period.

**53.** /c/ Personal financial statements consist of a statement of financial condition and a statement of changes in net worth. Neither an income statement nor a statement of cash flows is presented.

**54.** /c/

| | |
|---|---|
| Income taxes payable | $13,000 |
| Plus valuation allowance needed ($20,000 x 10%) | 2,000 |
| Total credit entries | $15,000 |
| Less: | |
| Increase in DTA from 12/x3 to 12/x | (5,000) |
| Total income tax exp. | $10,000 |

**55.** /a/ Interim statements do not constitute full and fair presentation in accordance with GAAP. They provide timely, abbreviated information that is needed by users on an interim basis. As such, they emphasize timeliness over reliability.

**56.** /d/ The only correct answer. Special disclosures are not required relating to material related-party transactions if those transactions relate to compensation agreements, expense allowances, and other similar events in the normal course of business.

# CHAPTER 10

## INCOME TAX ACCOUNTING
## AND OTHER TOPICS

### Simulation Task Answers

**Task Number 1 Answer**

**Part a**

**1.** /B/    A deferred tax liability arises from temporary differences that cause future taxable income to be higher than current taxable income. Accelerated depreciation methods used for tax purposes cause higher deductions for tax purposes in the early years in the life of an asset. However, at some point in the future, the depreciation for tax purposes will be less than that taken for financial reporting purposes. From that point on (reversal point) taxable income will be higher than pretax financial income so far as depreciation expense is concerned.

**2.** /A/    A deferred tax asset arises from temporary differences that cause future taxable income to be lower than current taxable income. Rents collected in advance are recognized for tax purposes in the year received and thus taxed in that year; however, they are not recognized for financial reporting purposes until earned. In the years in which they are earned, they will be included in financial reporting revenues, but will not be included in taxable revenues. Thus, future taxable income will be lower than future pretax financial income so far as these advance rent receipts are concerned.

**3.** /C/    A permanent difference is an item which is consistently treated differently for tax and financial reporting purposes. In other words, it is either an element of pretax financial income but never taxable income, or is an element of taxable income but never pretax financial income. Interest on state and municipal bonds is always an element of pretax financial income but is never included in income for tax purposes.

**4.** /A/    Warranty and guarantee expense, deducted as accrued for financial reporting purposes, may not be deducted for tax purposes until actually paid. Therefore, this accrued expense is a future deductible amount. It will be available to deduct in (and therefore benefit) future tax periods -- but not the current one.

**Part b.**

5. /G/    Current tax expense is current taxable income times the current tax rate.  $600,000 x 20% = $120,000.

6. /M/    First, it is important to understand that the temporary differences listed in each of the years are those originating in each of the years.  No information has been given as to when those differences reverse.  Therefore, it is to be assumed that they will all begin to reverse at some point beyond April 30, 20x7.  As of April 30, 20x6, the cumulative temporary differences is the sum of the $200,000 originating in 20x5 and the $100,000 originating in 20x6; namely, $300,000.

7. /B/    Deferred tax expense is the increase in deferred tax liability during the year. DTL at 4/30/x5 was $40,000.  It increased to $75,000 at 4/30/x6.  Therefore, the deferred tax expense is $35,000.

8. /H/    Deferred tax liability at 4/30/x7 is the cumulative future taxable amount of $450,000 (given) times the enacted tax rate known to Lane.  The 30% tax rate was known to Lane at 4/30/x7.  DTL is $450,000 x 30% = $135,000.

# FINANCIAL ACCOUNTING

## CHAPTER 11

## GOVERNMENTAL ACCOUNTING AND REPORTING

### Question Map

III. SPECIAL ISSUES IN GOVERNMENTAL ACCOUNTING
   A. Budgets – 21, 22, 23, 26, 27, 31, 75, 76, 77, 89, 94, 95, 102
   B. Encumbrances – 11, 12, 78, 87, 89, 96
   C. Modified Accrual Basis of Accounting – 25, 36, 40
      1. Revenues – 37
         a. Measurable and Available – 16, 18, 97, 98
         b. Deferred Revenue – 66
         c. Property Tax Revenues – 14, 15, 17, 33, 66, 83
         d. Grants – 28, 84
         e. Licenses, Fees, and Permits
         f. Taxpayer Assessed Revenues – 18
      2. Expenditures – 70
         a. Recognition – 29, 80, 96
            (1) Purchase of General Fixed Assets – 6, 10, 47, 48, 54, 55, 67, 71, 92
            (2) Interest on General Long-Term Debt – 40, 57, 85
            (3) Principal Payment on General Long-Term Debt – 57, 85
         b. Classification – 74
      3. Other Financing Sources/Uses – 37, 84, 92, 109
      4. Funds Using Modified Accrual Basis – 13, 19, 20, 31, 69
   D. Fixed Assets – 81, 86
      1. Purchase of Fixed Assets – 6, 10, 47, 48, 54, 55, 67, 71, 92
      2. Capital Leases – 53, 54, 55, 56, 57, 58, 59, 60, 71, 105
      3. Depreciation – 65, 67, 114
      4. Sale of Fixed Assets – 67, 99, 100
   E. Inventory Accounting
      1. Purchases Method
      2. Consumption Method
   F. Long-Term Debt – 52, 72, 80, 91
      1. Proceeds of Long-Term Debt – 33, 37, 50
      2. Principal Payments – 85
      3. Interest Payments – 40, 85
      4. Bond Issuance Costs – 49
      5. Bond Premium – 33, 79
      6. Bond Anticipation or Tax Anticipation Notes – 36, 91

IV. INTERFUND TRANSFERS AND ACTIVITIES
   A. Reciprocal Interfund Activities
      1. Interfund Services Provided and Used – 68, 101
      2. Interfund Loans
   B. Nonreciprocal Interfund Activities
      1. Interfund Transfers – 37, 70, 92, 109
      2. Interfund Reimbursements

# CHAPTER 11

## GOVERNMENTAL ACCOUNTING AND REPORTING

### Multiple Choice Questions

1. The primary authoritative body for determining the measurement focus and basis of accounting standards for governmental fund operating statements is the
   a. Governmental Accounting Standards Board (GASB).
   b. National Council on Governmental Accounting (NCGA).
   c. Government Accounting and Auditing Committee of the AICPA (GAAC).
   d. Financial Accounting Standards Board (FASB).

2. Central County received proceeds from various towns and cities for capital projects financed by each local government, and a portion of the tax was restricted to repay the long-term debt of Central's capital projects. Central should account for the restricted portion of the special tax in which of the following funds?
   a. Internal service fund.
   b. Enterprise fund.
   c. Capital projects fund.
   d. Debt service fund.

3. The town of Hill operates municipal electric and water utilities. In which of the following funds should the operations of the utilities be accounted for?
   a. Enterprise fund.
   b. Internal service fund.
   c. Agency fund.
   d. Special revenue fund.

4. Bay Creek's municipal motor pool maintains all city-owned vehicles and charges the various departments for the cost of rendering those services. In which of the following funds should Bay account for the cost of such maintenance?

   a. General fund.
   b. Internal service fund.
   c. Special revenue fund.
   d. Special assessment fund.

5. Stone Corp. donated investments to Pine City and stipulated that the principal must remain intact, while income from the investments be used to acquire art for the city's museum. Assuming that Pine City has already adopted GASB Statement 34, which of the following funds should be used to account for the investments?
   a. Permanent fund.
   b. Special revenue fund.
   c. Expendable trust fund.
   d. Nonexpendable trust fund.

6. When equipment was purchased with general fund resources, an appropriate entry was made in the general fixed asset account group. In the fund financial statements, which of the following accounts would have been increased in the general fund?
   a. Due from general fixed asset account group.
   b. Expenditures.
   c. Appropriations.
   d. No entry should be made in the general fund.

7. The following revenues were among those reported by Ariba Township for the fiscal year:

| | |
|---|---|
| Net rental revenue (after depreciation) from parking garage owned by Ariba | $40,000 |
| Interest earned on investments held for employees' retirement benefits | 100,000 |
| Property taxes | 6,000,000 |

What amount of the foregoing revenues should be accounted for in Ariba's governmental-type funds?
   a. $6,140,000
   b. $6,100,000
   c. $6,040,000
   d. $6,000,000

**8.** One characteristic of state and local governments is that fixed assets used for general government activities

    **a.** Often are not expected to contribute to the generation of revenues.

    **b.** Do not depreciate as a result of such use.

    **c.** Are acquired only when direct contribution to revenues is expected.

    **d.** Should not be maintained at the same level as those of businesses so that current financial resources can be used for other government services.

**9.** Which of the following fund types or account group should account for fixed assets in a manner similar to a "for-profit" organization in the fund financial statements?

    **a.** Special revenue fund.

    **b.** Capital projects fund.

    **c.** General fixed assets account group.

    **d.** Enterprise fund.

**10.** In the fund financial statements, fixed assets used by a governmental unit should be accounted for in the

| | Capital Projects Fund | General Fund |
|---|---|---|
| **a.** | Yes | Yes |
| **b.** | Yes | No |
| **c.** | No | No |
| **d.** | No | Yes |

**11.** Which of the following amounts are included in a general fund's encumbrance account?

  I. Outstanding vouchers payable amounts.

  II. Outstanding purchase order amounts.

  III. Excess of the amount of a purchase order over the actual expenditure for that order.

    **a.** I only.

    **b.** I and III.

    **c.** II only.

    **d.** II and III.

**12.** Alto Township's commitment for appropriations that had not been expended during the fiscal year ended December 31 totaled $10,000. These appropriations do not lapse at year-end. On its December 31 balance sheet, the $10,000 should be reported as

    **a.** Vouchers payable - prior year.

    **b.** Deferred expenditures.

    **c.** Fund balance reserved for encumbrances.

    **d.** Budgetary fund balance - reserved for encumbrances.

**13.** The modified accrual basis of accounting should be used in the fund financial statements for which of the following funds?

    **a.** Capital projects fund.

    **b.** Enterprise fund.

    **c.** Pension trust fund.

    **d.** Proprietary fund.

**14.** In its fund financial statements, a public-school district would recognize revenue from property taxes levied for its debt service fund when

    **a.** Bonds to be retired by the levy are due and payable.

    **b.** Assessed valuations of property subject to the levy are known.

    **c.** Funds from the levy are measurable and available to the district.

    **d.** Proceeds from collection of the levy are deposited in the district's bank account.

**15.** Pine City's year-end is June 30. Pine levies property taxes in January of each year for the calendar year. One-half of the levy is due in May and one-half is due in October. Property tax revenue is budgeted for the period in which payment is due. The following information pertains to Pine's property taxes for the period from July 1, 20x0, to June 30, 20x1:

|  | Calendar year | |
|  | 20x0 | 20x1 |
| Levy | $2,000,000 | $2,400,000 |
| Collected in: | | |
| May | 950,000 | 1,100,000 |
| July | 50,000 | 60,000 |
| October | 920,000 | |
| December | 80,000 | |

The $40,000 balance due for the May 20x1 installments was expected to be collected in August 20x1. What amount should Pine recognize for property tax revenue in its fund financial statements for the year ended June 30, 20x1?

    a. $2,160,000
    b. $2,200,000
    c. $2,360,000
    d. $2,400,000

**16.** Under the modified accrual basis of accounting for a governmental unit, revenues that are measurable should be recognized in the accounting period in which they are

    a. Earned.
    b. Available.
    c. Budgeted.
    d. Collected.

**17.** Property taxes levied in fiscal year 20x1 to finance the general fund budget of fiscal year 20x2 should be reported as general fund revenues in the fund financial statements during fiscal year 20x2

    a. Regardless of the fiscal year in which collected.
    b. For the amount collected in fiscal year 20x2 only.
    c. For the amount collected before the end of fiscal year 20x2 only.
    d. For the amount collected before the end of fiscal year 20x2 or shortly thereafter.

**18.** The following pertains to governmental funds of Cobb City:

- 20x0 governmental fund revenues that became measurable and available in time to be used for payment of 20x0 liabilities    $16,000,000
- Revenues in prior years and included in the $16,000,000 indicated above    2,000,000
- Sales taxes collected by merchants in 20x0 but not required to be remitted to Cobb until Jan. 20x1    3,000,000

For the year ended December 31, 20x0, Cobb should recognize revenues in the fund financial statements of

    a. $14,000,000
    b. $16,000,000
    c. $17,000,000
    d. $19,000,000

**19.** The modified accrual basis of accounting is appropriate in the fund financial statements for which of the following fund categories of a county government?

| | Governmental | Proprietary |
|---|---|---|
| a. | No | No |
| b. | No | Yes |
| c. | Yes | Yes |
| d. | Yes | No |

**20.** A local governmental unit could have funds using which of the following accounting bases in the fund financial statements?

| | Accrual basis | Modified accrual basis |
|---|---|---|
| a. | No | Yes |
| b. | No | No |
| c. | Yes | No |
| d. | Yes | Yes |

**21.** The estimated revenues control account balance of a governmental fund type is eliminated when

    a. The budget is recorded.
    b. The budgetary accounts are closed.
    c. Appropriations are closed.
    d. Property taxes are recorded.

**22.** The appropriations control account of a governmental unit is debited when
   a. Supplies are purchased.
   b. Expenditures are recorded.
   c. The budgetary accounts are closed.
   d. The budget is recorded.

**23.** The budgetary fund balance reserved for encumbrances account of a governmental-type fund is increased when
   a. The budget is recorded.
   b. Appropriations are recorded.
   c. Supplies previously ordered are received.
   d. A purchase order is approved.

**24.** Which of the following accounts should Moon City close at the end of its fiscal year?
   a. Vouchers payable.
   b. Expenditures.
   c. Fund balance.
   d. Fund balance - reserved for encumbrances.

**25.** The following information pertains to Pine City's general fund for the year:

| | |
|---|---|
| Appropriations | $6,500,000 |
| Expenditures | 5,000,000 |
| Other financing sources | 1,500,000 |
| Other financing uses | 2,000,000 |
| Revenues | 8,000,000 |

After Pine's general fund accounts were closed at the end of the year, the fund balance increased by
   a. $3,000,000
   b. $2,500,000
   c. $1,500,000
   d. $1,000,000

**26.** Oro County's expenditures control account at year end had a balance of $9,000,000. When Oro's books were closed, this $9,000,000 expenditures control balance should have
   a. Been debited.
   b. Been credited.
   c. Remained open.
   d. Appeared as a contra account.

**27.** When Rolan County adopted its budget for the year, $20,000,000 was recorded for estimated revenues control. Actual revenues for the year amounted to $17,000,000. In closing the budgetary accounts,
   a. Revenues control should be debited for $3,000,000.
   b. Estimated revenues control should be debited for $3,000,000.
   c. Revenues control should be credited for $20,000,000.
   d. Estimated revenues control should be credited for $20,000,000.

**28.** Todd City received a state grant to buy a bus, and an additional grant for bus operation during the year. Only 90% of the capital grant was used for the bus purchase during the year, but 100% of the operating grant was disbursed. In reporting the state grants for the bus purchase and operation, what should Todd include as grant revenues for the year?

| | 90% of the capital grant | 100% of the capital grant | 100% of the operating grant |
|---|---|---|---|
| a. | Yes | No | No |
| b. | No | Yes | No |
| c. | No | Yes | Yes |
| d. | Yes | No | Yes |

**29.** Lake City incurred $300,000 of salaries and wages expense in its general fund for the month. For this $300,000 expense, Lake should debit
   a. Fund balance - unreserved, undesignated.
   b. Encumbrances control.
   c. Appropriations control.
   d. Expenditures control.

**30.** Lake County received the following proceeds that are legally restricted to expenditure for specified purposes:

Levies on affected property
  owners to install sidewalks     $500,000
Gasoline taxes to finance
  road repairs                     900,000

What amount should be accounted for in Lake County's special revenue funds?

  a. $1,400,000
  b. $900,000
  c. $500,000
  d. $0

**31**. Should a special revenue fund with a legally adopted budget recognize revenues and expenditures on an accrual basis for the fund financial statements and integrate budgetary accounts into its accounting system?

| | Accrual basis for fund financial statements | Integrate budgetary accounts |
|---|---|---|
| a. | Yes | Yes |
| b. | Yes | No |
| c. | No | Yes |
| d. | No | No |

**32.** Kew City received a $15,000,000 federal grant to finance the construction of a center for rehabilitation of drug addicts. The proceeds of this grant should be accounted for in the

  a. Special revenue fund.
  b. General fund.
  c. Capital projects fund.
  d. Trust funds.

**33.** The following information pertains to property taxes received or receivable by the City of Newberry governmental funds for the year ended December 31, 20x5:

20x4 property tax levy:
  20x4 taxes collected during
    January and February
    20x5                          $ 250,000
  20x4 taxes collected
    during March through
    December 20x5                   180,000

20x5 property tax levy:
  Levied and collected
    during 20x5                   4,000,000
  20x5 taxes collected
    during January and
    February 20x6                   300,000
  20x5 taxes expected to be
    collected after February
    20x6                            200,000

In the city's Statement of Revenues, Expenditures, and Changes in Fund Balances, the total net increase in fund balances for governmental funds was $30,000 during 20x5. If property taxes are the only reconciling item, what was the city's change in net assets of governmental activities on its government-wide Statement of Activities during 20x5?

  a. Increase of $10,000.
  b. Increase of $50,000.
  c. Increase of $100,000.
  d. Decrease of $40,000.

**Items 34 and 35 are based on the following:**

On March 2, 20x1, Finch City issued 10-year general obligation bonds at face amount, with interest payable March 1 and September 1. The proceeds were to be used to finance the construction of a civic center over the period April 1, 20x1 to March 31, 20x2. The city's accounting system includes account groups for general fixed assets and general long-term debt.

**34.** Proceeds from the general obligation bonds should be recorded in the

  a. General fund.
  b. Capital projects fund.
  c. General long-term debt account group.
  d. Debt service fund.

**35.** The liability for the general obligation bonds should be recorded in the

  a. General fund.
  b. Capital projects fund.
  c. General long-term debt account group.
  d. Debt service fund.

**36.** Grove Township issued $50,000 of bond anticipation notes at face amount and placed the proceeds into its capital projects fund. All legal steps were taken to refinance the notes, but Grove was unable to consummate refinancing. In the capital projects fund, what account should be credited to record the $50,000 proceeds?

    **a.** Other financing sources control.
    **b.** Revenues control.
    **c.** Deferred revenues.
    **d.** Bond anticipation notes payable.

**37.** On December 31, Park Township paid a contractor $4,000,000 for the total cost of a new police building built during the year. Financing was by means of a $3,000,000 general obligation bond issue sold at face amount on December 31, with the remaining $1,000,000 transferred from the general fund. What amount should Park record as revenues in the fund financial statements of its capital projects fund in connection with the bond issue proceeds and the transfer?

    **a.** $0
    **b.** $1,000,000
    **c.** $3,000,000
    **d.** $4,000,000

**38.** During the current year, Beach issued $400,000 of bonds, the proceeds of which were restricted to the financing of a capital project. The bonds will be paid wholly from special assessment against benefited property owners. However, Beech is obligated to provide a secondary source of funds for repayment of the bonds in the event of default by the assessed property owners. In Beech's government-wide financial statements, this $400,000 special assessment debt should

    **a.** Not be reported.
    **b.** Be reported as a liability under business type activities.
    **c.** Be reported as a liability under governmental activities.
    **d.** Be reported as a liability under component units.

**39.** Dale City is accumulating financial resources that are legally restricted to payments of general long-term debt principal and interest maturing in future years. At December 31, $5,000,000 has been accumulated for principal payments and $300,000 has been accumulated for interest payments. These restricted funds should be accounted for in the

| | Debt service fund | General fund |
|---|---|---|
| **a.** | $0 | $5,300,000 |
| **b.** | $300,000 | $5,000,000 |
| **c.** | $5,000,000 | $300,000 |
| **d.** | $5,300,000 | $0 |

**40.** On March 2, 20x1, Finch City issued 10-year general obligation bonds at face amount, with interest payable March 1 and September 1. The proceeds were to be used to finance the construction of a civic center over the period April 1, 20x1, to March 31, 20x2. During the fiscal year ended June 30, 20x1, no resources had been provided to the debt service fund for the payment of principal and interest. On June 30, 20x1, Finch's fund financial statements should include interest payable on the general obligation bonds for

    **a.** 0 months.
    **b.** 3 months.
    **c.** 4 months.
    **d.** 6 months.

**41.** During the year, Spruce City reported the following receipts from self-sustaining activities paid for by users of the services rendered:

Operation of water supply plant $5,000,000
Operation of bus system            900,000

What amount should be accounted for in Spruce's enterprise funds?

    **a.** $0
    **b.** $900,000
    **c.** $5,000,000
    **d.** $5,900,000

**42.** Sunnydate City's accounting system includes a general fixed asset account group. In the fund financial statements, fixed assets of the city's enterprise fund should be accounted for in the

  a. Enterprise fund but **no** depreciation on the fixed assets should be recorded.
  b. Enterprise fund and depreciation on the fixed assets should be recorded.
  c. General fixed asset account group but **no** depreciation on the fixed assets should be recorded.
  d. General fixed asset account group and depreciation on the fixed assets should be recorded.

**43.** The following information for the year ended June 30 pertains to a proprietary fund established by Burwood Village in connection with Burwood's public parking facilities:

| | |
|---|---|
| Receipts from users of parking facilities | $400,000 |
| Expenditures: | |
| Parking meters | 210,000 |
| Cash expenses including salaries | 90,000 |
| Depreciation of parking meters | 70,000 |

For the year ended June 30, this proprietary fund should report income in its fund financial statements of

  a. $0
  b. $30,000
  c. $100,000
  d. $240,000

**44.** Glen County is the administrator of a multiple-jurisdiction deferred compensation plan covering both its own employees and those of other governments participating in the plan. This plan is an eligible deferred compensation plan under the U.S. Internal Revenue Code and Income Tax Regulations. Glen has legal access to the plan's $40,000,000 in assets, comprising $2,000,000 pertaining to Glen and $38,000,000 pertaining to the other participating governments. In Glen's fund financial statements, what amount should be reported in a fiduciary fund for plan assets and as a corresponding liability?

  a. $0
  b. $2,000,000
  c. $38,000,000
  d. $40,000,000

**45.** A state government collected income taxes of $8,000,000 for the benefit of one of its cities that imposes an income tax on its residents. The state remitted these collections periodically to the city. The state should account for the $8,000,000 in the

  a. General fund.
  b. Agency funds.
  c. Internal service funds.
  d. Special assessment funds.

**46.** The following fund types used by Cliff City had total assets at December 31 as follows:

| | |
|---|---|
| Special revenue funds | $100,000 |
| Permanent funds | 175,000 |
| Agency funds | 150,000 |
| Trust funds | 200,000 |

Total fiduciary fund assets amounted to

  a. $200,000
  b. $300,000
  c. $350,000
  d. $450,000

**47.** Which of the following expenditures by a city's general fund should be classified as fixed assets on the statement of net assets in the government-wide financial statements?

| | Structural alterations to fire house | Mayor's office furniture |
|---|---|---|
| a. | No | No |
| b. | No | Yes |
| c. | Yes | No |
| d. | Yes | Yes |

**48.** Which of the following expenditures by a city's general fund should be classified as fixed assets on the balance sheet in the fund financial statements?

| | Structural alterations to fire house | Mayor's office furniture |
|---|---|---|
| **a.** | No | No |
| **b.** | No | Yes |
| **c.** | Yes | No |
| **d.** | Yes | Yes |

**49.** On April 1, Oak County incurred the following expenditures in issuing general long-term bonds:

| | |
|---|---|
| Issue costs | $400,000 |
| Debt insurance | 90,000 |

In Oak's fund financial statements, what amount should be deferred and amortized over the life of the bonds?
- **a.** $0
- **b.** $90,000
- **c.** $400,000
- **d.** $490,000

**50.** Silver City uses a general long-term debt account group. On June 28, Silver City's debt service fund received funds for the future repayment of bond principal. As a consequence, the long-term debt account group reported
- **a.** An increase in the amount available in debt service funds and an increase in the fund balance.
- **b.** An increase in the amount available in debt service funds and an increase in the amount to be provided for bonds.
- **c.** An increase in the amount available in debt service funds and a decrease in the amount to be provided for bonds.
- **d.** No changes in any amount until the bond principal is actually paid.

**51.** Maple Township issued the following bonds during the year ended June 30:

| | |
|---|---|
| Bonds issued for the garbage collection enterprise fund that will service the debt | $500,000 |
| Revenue bonds to be repaid from admission fees collected by the Township zoo enterprise fund | 350,000 |

What amount of these bonds should be reported as a liability under governmental activities in Maple's government-wide statement of net assets?
- **a.** $0
- **b.** $350,000
- **c.** $500,000
- **d.** $850,000

**52.** Todd City has incurred the following long-term obligations:

- General obligation bonds issued for the water and sewer fund which will service the debt.
- Revenue bonds to be repaid from admission fees collected from users of the municipal recreation center.

These bonds are expected to be paid from enterprise funds, and secured by Todd's full faith, credit, and taxing power as further assurance that the obligations will be paid. Which of these long-term obligations should be accounted for as general long-term debt?

| | General obligation bonds | Revenue bonds |
|---|---|---|
| **a.** | Yes | Yes |
| **b.** | Yes | No |
| **c.** | No | Yes |
| **d.** | No | No |

**53.** Bell City entered into a capital lease agreement at year-end December 31, 20x1 to acquire a general fixed asset. Under this agreement, Bell is to make three annual payments of $75,000 each on principal, plus interest of $22,000, $15,000, and $8,000 at the end of each of the next three years. In its 20x1 fund financial statements, what amount should be recognized as an expenditure in Bell's general fund?

    **a.** $270,000
    **b.** $225,000
    **c.** $75,000
    **d.** $0

**Items 54 through 59 are based on the following:**

Rock County has acquired equipment through a noncancelable lease-purchase agreement dated December 31, 20x0. This agreement requires no down payment and the following minimum lease payments:

| Year | Principal | Interest | Total |
|------|-----------|----------|-------|
| 20x1 | $50,000 | $15,000 | $65,000 |
| 20x2 | 50,000 | 10,000 | 60,000 |
| 20x3 | 50,000 | 5,000 | 55,000 |

**54.** Assume the equipment is used for general county administration. For the fund financial statements, what account in the general fund should be debited for $150,000 at inception of the lease?

    **a.** Other financing uses control.
    **b.** Equipment.
    **c.** Expenditures control.
    **d.** Memorandum entry only.

**55.** Assume the equipment is used for general county administration. For the government-wide financial statements, what account in the general fund should be debited for $150,000 at inception of the lease?

    **a.** Other financing uses control.
    **b.** Equipment.
    **c.** Expenditures control.
    **d.** Memorandum entry only.

**56.** Assume the lease payments will be financed with general government resources and the county uses a general long-term debt account group. What journal entry is required for $150,000 in the account group at inception of the lease?

| | Debit | Credit |
|----|-------|--------|
| **a.** | Expenditures control | Other financing sources control |
| **b.** | Other financing uses control | Expenditures control |
| **c.** | Amount to be provided for lease payments | Capital lease obligation payable |
| **d.** | Capital lease obligation payable | Amount to be provided for lease payments |

**57.** Assume the lease payments are required to be made from a debt service fund. For the fund financial statements, what account or accounts should be debited in the debt service fund for the 20x1 lease payment of $65,000?

    **a.** Expenditures control    $65,000
    **b.** Other financing sources
        control    $50,000
        Expenditures control    15,000
    **c.** Amount to be provided
        for lease payments    $50,000
        Expenditures control    15,000
    **d.** Expenditures control    $50,000
        Amount to be provided
        for lease payments    15,000

**58.** Assume the equipment is used in enterprise fund operations and the lease payments are to be financed with enterprise fund revenues. For the fund financial statements, what account should be debited for $150,000 in the enterprise fund at inception of the lease?

    **a.** Expenses control.
    **b.** Expenditures control
    **c.** Other financing sources control.
    **d.** Equipment.

**59.** Assume the equipment is used in internal service fund operations and the lease payments are financed with internal service fund revenues. For the fund financial statements, what account or accounts should be debited in the internal service fund for the December 31, 20x1, lease payment of $65,000?

a. Expenditures control     $65,000

b. Expenses control     $65,000

c. Capital lease obligation
    payable     $50,000
    Expenses control     15,000

d. Expenditures control     $50,000
    Expenses control     15,000

**60.** The following information pertains to a computer that Pine Township leased from Karl Supply Co. on July 1 for general township use:

| | |
|---|---|
| Karl's cost | $5,000 |
| Fair value at lease inception | $5,000 |
| Estimated economic life | 5 years |
| Fixed noncancelable term | 30 months |
| Rental at beginning of each month | $135 |
| Guaranteed residual value | $2,000 |

Present value of minimum lease payments using:

| | |
|---|---|
| Pine's incremental borrowing rate of 10.5% | $5,120 |
| Karl's implicit interest rate of 12.04% | $5,000 |

What amount should Pine recognize as the cost of an asset in its government-wide statement of net assets for this leased computer?

a. $0
b. $3,000
c. $5,000
d. $5,120

**61.** The primary emphasis in accounting and reporting in the fund financial statements for governmental funds is on
a. Flow of financial resources.
b. Income determination.
c. Capital maintenance.
d. Transfers relating to proprietary activities.

**62.** Governmental financial reporting should provide information to assist users in which situation(s)?

I. Making social and political decisions.
II. Assessing whether current-year citizens received services but shifted part of the payment burden to future-year citizens.

a. I only.
b. II only.
c. Both I and II.
d. Neither I nor II.

**63.** The orientation of accounting and reporting for all proprietary funds of governmental units is
a. Income determination.
b. Project.
c. Flow of funds.
d. Program.

**64.** Taxes collected and held by Franklin County for a separate school district would be accounted for in which fund?
a. Special revenue.
b. Internal service.
c. Trust.
d. Agency.

**65.** For state and local governments, depreciation expense on assets acquired with capital grants externally restricted for capital acquisitions should be reported in the fund financial statements for which type of fund?

| | Governmental fund | Proprietary fund |
|---|---|---|
| a. | Yes | No |
| b. | Yes | Yes |
| c. | No | No |
| d. | No | Yes |

**66.** In which situation(s) should property taxes due to a governmental unit be recorded as deferred revenue?

I. Property taxes receivable are recognized in advance of the year for which they are levied.

II. Property taxes receivable are collected in advance of the year in which they are levied.

a. I only.
b. Both I and II.
c. II only.
d. Neither I nor II.

**67.** The Western City Fire District accounting system includes the following information for governmental funds related to the year ended December 31, 20x5:

| | |
|---|---|
| Expenditures for purchase of general fixed assets | $500,000 |
| Depreciation of general fixed assets | 225,000 |
| Sale of general fixed assets: | |
| Proceeds | 50,000 |
| Cost | 300,000 |
| Accumulated depreciation | 280,000 |

In the fire district's Statement of Revenues, Expenditures, and Changes in Fund Balances, the total net decrease in fund balances for governmental funds was $10,000 during 20x5. If accounting for general fixed assets is the only type of reconciling item, what was the fire district's change in net assets of governmental activities on its government-wide Statement of Activities during 20x5?
a. Increase of $245,000.
b. Increase of $265,000.
c. Increase of $520,000.
d. Decrease of $540,000.

**68.** A city's electric utility, which is operated as an enterprise fund, rendered billings for electricity supplied to the general fund. Which of the following accounts should be debited in the general fund?
a. Appropriations.
b. Expenditures.
c. Due to electric utility enterprise fund.
d. Other financing uses – Interfund transfers.

**69.** The modified accrual basis of accounting is appropriate in the government-wide statements for which of the following fund categories of a county government?

| | Governmental | Proprietary |
|---|---|---|
| a. | No | No |
| b. | No | Yes |
| c. | Yes | Yes |
| d. | Yes | No |

**70.** For the fund financial statements, which of the following transactions is an expenditure of a governmental unit's general fund?
a. Contribution of enterprise fund capital by the general fund.
b. Transfer from the general fund to a capital projects fund.
c. Operating subsidy transfer from the general fund to an enterprise fund.
d. Routine employer contributions from the general fund to a pension trust fund.

**71.** When a governmental unit acquires a general fixed asset through a capital lease, the acquisition should be reflected in the fund financial statements as
a. An expenditure but **not** as an other financing source.
b. An other financing source but **not** as an expenditure.
c. Both an expenditure and an other financing source.
d. Neither an expenditure nor an other financing source.

**72.** The portion of a special assessment debt to be repaid from general resources of the government and maturing in 5 years should be reported as a liability in the fund financial statements of a/an
a. General fund.
b. Agency fund.
c. Capital projects fund.
d. None of the above.

**73.** The debt service fund of a governmental unit is used to account for the accumulation of resources for and payment of principal and interest in connection with a

| | Trust Fund | Proprietary Fund |
|---|---|---|
| a. | No | No |
| b. | No | Yes |
| c. | Yes | Yes |
| d. | Yes | No |

**74.** The expenditure element "salaries and wages" is an example of which type of classification?
- a. Object.
- b. Program.
- c. Function.
- d. Activity.

**Items 75 and 76 are based on the following:**

Ridge Township's governing body adopted its general fund budget for the year ended July 31, 20x4, comprised of estimated revenues of $100,000 and appropriations of $80,000. Ridge formally integrates its budget into the accounting records.

**75.** To record the appropriations of $80,000, Ridge should
- a. Credit appropriations control.
- b. Debit appropriations control.
- c. Credit estimated expenditures control.
- d. Debit estimated expenditures control.

**76.** To record the $20,000 budgeted excess of estimated revenues over appropriations, Ridge should
- a. Credit estimated excess revenues control.
- b. Debit estimated excess revenues control.
- c. Credit budgetary fund balance.
- d. Debit budgetary fund balance.

**77.** For the budgetary year ending December 31, 20x3, Maple City's general fund expects the following inflows of resources:

| | |
|---|---|
| Property taxes, licenses & fines | $9,000,000 |
| Proceeds of debt issue | 5,000,000 |
| Interfund transfers for debt service | 1,000,000 |

In the budgetary entry, what amount should Maple record for estimated revenues?
- a. $9,000,000
- b. $10,000,000
- c. $14,000,000
- d. $15,000,000

**78.** During its fiscal year ended June 30, 20x3, Cliff City issued purchase orders totaling $5,000,000, which were properly charged to encumbrances at that time. Cliff received goods and related invoices at the encumbered amounts totaling $4,500,000 before year end. The remaining goods of $500,000 were not received until after year end. Cliff paid $4,200,000 of the invoices received during the year. What amount of Cliff's encumbrances were outstanding at June 30, 20x3?
- a. $0
- b. $300,000
- c. $500,000
- d. $800,000

**79.** Wood City, which is legally obligated to maintain a debt service fund, issued the following general obligation bonds on July 1, 20x2:

| | |
|---|---|
| Term of bonds | 10 years |
| Face amount | $1,000,000 |
| Issue price | 101 |
| Stated interest rate | 6% |

Interest is payable on January 1 and July 1. In the fund financial statements, what amount of bond premium should be amortized in Wood's debt service fund for the year ended December 31, 20x2?
- a. $1,000
- b. $500
- c. $250
- d. $0

**80.** The following information pertains to Spruce City's liability for general fund claims and judgments:

| | |
|---|---|
| Current liability at 1/1/x2 | $100,000 |
| Claims paid during 20x2 | 800,000 |
| Current liability at 12/31/x2 | 140,000 |
| Noncurrent liability at 12/31/x2 | 200,000 |

In its fund financial statements, what amount should Spruce report for 20x2 claims and judgments expenditures?
- **a.** $1,040,000
- **b.** $940,000
- **c.** $840,000
- **d.** $800,000

**81.** Fixed assets of a governmental unit should be reported on the balance sheet in the fund financial statements of a/an
- **a.** General fund.
- **b.** Capital projects fund.
- **c.** Special revenue fund.
- **d.** Enterprise fund.

**82.** Cal City maintains several major fund types. The following were among Cal's cash receipts during 20x3:

| | |
|---|---|
| Unrestricted state grant | $1,000,000 |
| Interest on bank accounts held for employees' pension plan | 200,000 |

What amount of these cash receipts should be accounted for in Cal's general fund?
- **a.** $1,200,000
- **b.** $1,000,000
- **c.** $200,000
- **d.** $0

**83.** The following information pertains to property taxes levied by Oak City for the calendar year 20x2:

| | |
|---|---|
| Collections during 20x2 | $500,000 |
| Expected collections during the first 60 days of 20x3 | 100,000 |
| Expected collections during the balance of 20x3 | 60,000 |
| Expected collections during January 20x4 | 30,000 |
| Estimated to be uncollectible | 10,000 |
| Total levy | $700,000 |

In its fund financial statements, what amount should Oak report for the 20x2 net property tax revenues?

- **a.** $700,000
- **b.** $690,000
- **c.** $600,000
- **d.** $500,000

**84.** Financing for the renovation of Fir City's municipal park, begun and completed during 20x2, came from the following sources:

| | |
|---|---|
| Grant from state government | $400,000 |
| Proceeds from general obligation bond issue | 500,000 |
| Transfer from Fir's general fund | 100,000 |

In the 20x2 fund financial statements for its capital projects fund, Fir should report these amounts as

| | Revenues | Other Financing Sources |
|---|---|---|
| **a.** | $1,000,000 | $0 |
| **b.** | $900,000 | $1,000,000 |
| **c.** | $400,000 | $600,000 |
| **d.** | $0 | $1,000,000 |

**85.** A major exception to the general rule of expenditure accrual for the fund financial statements of governmental units relates to unmatured

| | Principal of general long-term debt | Interest on general long-term debt |
|---|---|---|
| **a.** | Yes | Yes |
| **b.** | Yes | No |
| **c.** | No | Yes |
| **d.** | No | No |

**86.** Dodd Village received a gift of a new fire engine from a local civic group. The fair value of this fire engine was $400,000. Assuming the Village uses a general fixed asset account group, the entry to be made in the account group for this gift is

|  | | Debit | Credit |
|---|---|---|---|
| a. | Memorandum entry only | -- | -- |
| b. | General fund assets | 400,000 | |
| | Private gifts | | 400,000 |
| c. | Investment in general fixed assets | 400,000 | |
| | Gift revenue | | 400,000 |
| d. | Machinery & equip. | 400,000 | |
| | Investment in general fixed assets from private gifts | | 400,000 |

**87.** In 20x4, New City issued purchase orders and contracts of $850,000 that were chargeable against 20x4 budgeted appropriations of $1,000,000. The journal entry to record the issuance of the purchase orders and contracts should include a

a. Credit to vouchers payable of $1,000,000.
b. Credit to reserve for encumbrances of $850,000.
c. Debit to expenditures of $1,000,000.
d. Debit to expenditures of $850,000.

**88.** Hill City's water utility fund held the following investments in U.S. Treasury securities at June 30, 20x4:

| Investment | Date purchased | Maturity date | Carrying amount |
|---|---|---|---|
| 3-month T-bill | 5/31/x4 | 8/31/x4 | $ 30,000 |
| 3-yr T-note | 6/15/x4 | 8/31/x4 | 50,000 |
| 5-yr T-note | 10/1/x0 | 9/30/x5 | 100,000 |

In the fund's balance sheet, what amount of these investments should be reported as cash and cash equivalents at June 30, 20x4?

a. $0
b. $30,000
c. $80,000
d. $180,000

**89.** The following information pertains to Park Township's general fund at December 31, 20x2:

| Total assets, including $200,000 of cash | $1,000,000 |
|---|---|
| Total liabilities | 600,000 |
| Reserved for encumbrances | 100,000 |

Appropriations do not lapse at year-end. At December 31, 20x2, what amount should Park report as unreserved fund balance in the fund financial statements of its general fund?

a. $200,000
b. $300,000
c. $400,000
d. $500,000

**90.** Deferred compensation plans, for other than proprietary fund employees, adopted under IRC Sec. 457, should be reported in a(an)

a. Governmental fund.
b. Agency fund.
c. Trust fund.
d. Account group.

**91.** The following obligations were among those reported by Fern Village at December 31, 20x2:

| Vendor financing with a term of 10 months when incurred, in connection with a capital asset acquisition that is not part of a long-term financing plan | $ 150,000 |
|---|---|
| Long-term bonds for financing of capital asset acquisition | 3,000,000 |
| Bond anticipation notes due in six months, issued as part of a long-term financing plan for capital purposes | 400,000 |

What aggregate amount should Fern report as long-term debt under governmental activities in its government-wide financial statements at December 31, 20x2?

a. $3,000,000
b. $3,150,000
c. $3,400,000
d. $3,550,000

**92.** On December 31, 20x0, Elm Village paid a contractor $4,500,000 for the total cost of a new Village Hall built in 20x0 on Village-owned land. Financing for the capital project was provided by a $3,000,000 general obligation bond issue sold at face amount during 20x0, with the remaining $1,500,000 transferred from the general fund. What account and amount should be reported in Elm's 20x0 fund financial statements for the general fund?

    **a.** Other financing sources, $4,500,000.
    **b.** Expenditures, $4,500,000.
    **c.** Other financing sources, $3,000,000.
    **d.** Other financing uses, $1,500,000.

**93.** Fixed assets donated to a governmental unit should be recorded

    **a.** At estimated fair value when received.
    **b.** At the lower of donor's carrying amount or estimated fair value when received.
    **c.** At the donor's carrying amount.
    **d.** As a memorandum entry only.

**94.** The budget of a governmental unit, for which the appropriations exceed the estimated revenues, was adopted and recorded in the general ledger at the beginning of the year. During the year, expenditures and encumbrances were less than appropriations; whereas revenues equaled estimated revenues. The budgetary fund balance account is

    **a.** Credited at the beginning of the year and debited at the end of the year.
    **b.** Credited at the beginning of the year and **not** changed at the end of the year.
    **c.** Debited at the beginning of the year and credited at the end of the year.
    **d.** Debited at the beginning of the year and **not** changed at the end of the year.

**95.** A budgetary fund balance reserved for encumbrances in excess of a balance of encumbrances indicates

    **a.** An excess of vouchers payable over encumbrances.
    **b.** An excess of purchase orders over invoices received.
    **c.** An excess of appropriations over encumbrances.
    **d.** A recording error.

**96.** Gold County received goods that had been approved for purchase but for which payment had not yet been made. Should the accounts listed below be increased?

| | Encumbrances | Expenditures |
|---|---|---|
| **a.** | No | No |
| **b.** | No | Yes |
| **c.** | Yes | No |
| **d.** | Yes | Yes |

**97.** For the government-wide financial statements, which of the following funds of a governmental unit recognizes revenues in the accounting period in which they become measurable and available?

| | General fund | Enterprise fund |
|---|---|---|
| **a.** | Yes | No |
| **b.** | No | Yes |
| **c.** | Yes | Yes |
| **d.** | No | No |

**98.** For the fund financial statements, which of the following funds of a governmental unit recognizes revenues in the accounting period in which they become measurable and available?

| | General fund | Enterprise fund |
|---|---|---|
| **a.** | Yes | No |
| **b.** | No | Yes |
| **c.** | Yes | Yes |
| **d.** | No | No |

**99.** Old equipment owned by the general fund of Western County is sold for $1,000. The original cost of the equipment was $5,000, and the accumulated depreciation at the time of sale was $3,800. In the Statement of Revenues, Expenditures, and Changes in Fund Balances, the sale is recognized as

a. A loss of $200.
b. A loss of $4,000.
c. An other financing source of $1,000.
d. This transaction is not recognized in the Statement of Revenues, Expenditures, and Changes in Fund Balances.

**100.** Old equipment owned by the general fund of Western County is sold for $1,000. The original cost of the equipment was $5,000, and the accumulated depreciation at the time of sale was $3,800. In the government-wide Statement of Activities, the sale is recognized as
a. A loss of $200.
b. A loss of $4,000.
c. An other financing source of $1,000.
d. This transaction is not recognized in the Statement Activities.

**101.** The billings for transportation services provided to other governmental units are recorded by the internal service fund as
a. Transportation appropriations.
b. Operating revenues.
c. Interfund exchanges.
d. Intergovernmental transfers.

**102.** The estimated revenues control account of a governmental unit is debited when
a. Actual revenues are recorded.
b. Actual revenues are collected.
c. The budget is recorded.
d. The budget is closed at the end of the year.

**103.** What is the basic criterion used to determine the reporting entity for a governmental unit?
a. Special financing arrangement.
b. Geographic boundaries.
c. Scope of public services.
d. Financial accountability.

**104.** Tuston Township owed the following principal amounts for bonds as of June 30, 20x5:

Bonds issued for the garbage
collection enterprise fund
that will service the debt        $700,000

Revenue bonds to be repaid
from admission fees
collected by the Township
zoo enterprise fund               500,000

What amount of these bonds should be reported under governmental activities on Tuston's government-wide statement of net assets on June 30, 20x5?
a. $1,200,000
b. $700,000
c. $500,000
d. $0

**105.** Frome City signed a 20-year office property lease for its general staff. Frome could terminate the lease at any time after giving one year's notice, but termination is considered a remote possibility. The lease meets the criteria for a capital lease. In the city's government-wide statement of net assets, what is the effect of the lease on assets and liabilities?

|  | Asset amount | Liability amount |
|---|---|---|
| a. | Increase | Increase |
| b. | Increase | No effect |
| c. | No effect | Increase |
| d. | No effect | No effect |

**106.** Eureka City should issue a statement of cash flows for which of the following funds?

|  | Eureka City Hall capital projects fund | Eureka Water enterprise fund |
|---|---|---|
| a. | No | Yes |
| b. | No | No |
| c. | Yes | No |
| d. | Yes | Yes |

**107.** The following transactions were among those reported by Cliff County's water and sewer enterprise fund for the year:

| | |
|---|---|
| Proceeds from sale of revenue bonds | $5,000,000 |
| Cash received from customer households | 3,000,000 |
| Capital contributed by subdividers | 1,000,000 |

In the water and sewer enterprise fund's statement of cash flows for the year, what amount should be reported as cash flows from capital and related financing activities?
a. $9,000,000
b. $8,000,000
c. $6,000,000
d. $5,000,000

**108.** The annual financial statements of a city should contain a Statement of Revenues, Expenditures, and Changes in Fund Balances for

| | Fiduciary funds | Proprietary funds |
|---|---|---|
| a. | Yes | Yes |
| b. | Yes | No |
| c. | No | Yes |
| d. | No | No |

**109.** Interfund transfers received by a governmental-type fund should be reported in the Statement of Revenues, Expenditures, and Changes in Fund Balances as a (an)
a. Addition to contributed capital.
b. Addition to retained earnings.
c. Other financing source.
d. Reimbursement.

**110.** The operating statements of governmental units should embody the
a. All-inclusive approach.
b. Current performance approach.
c. Prospective approach.
d. Retroactive approach.

**111.** If a city legally adopts its annual general fund budget on the modified accrual basis of accounting, its estimated revenues should be

a. Reported on the modified accrual basis of accounting in the general fund statement of revenues, expenditures, and changes in fund balance - budget and actual.
b. Converted to the cash basis of accounting and reported in the general fund statement of revenues, expenditures, and other changes in fund balance - budget and actual.
c. Reported as current assets in the general fund balance sheet.
d. Reported as noncurrent assets in the general fund balance sheet.

**112.** Which event(s) should be included in a statement of cash flows for a governmental entity?

I. Cash inflow from issuing bonds to finance city hall construction.
II. Cash outflow from a city utility representing payments in lieu of taxes.

a. I only.
b. II only.
c. Both I and II.
d. Neither I nor II.

**113.** Vale City legally adopts a cash-basis budget. What basis should be used in Vale's statement of revenues, expenditures, and changes in fund balances -- budget and actual?
a. Cash.
b. Modified accrual.
c. Accrual.
d. Modified cash.

**114.** The City of Benton is required to recognize depreciation for the fixed assets of governmental funds in:

| | Fund Financial Statements | Government-Wide Financial Statements |
|---|---|---|
| a. | Yes | Yes |
| b. | No | No |
| c. | Yes | No |
| d. | No | Yes |

# CHAPTER 11

## GOVERNMENTAL ACCOUNTING AND REPORTING

### Simulation Task Questions

**Task Question 1**                                   **(Estimated time: 7 - 12 minutes)**

Question No. 1 consists of 4 items.  Select the **best** answer for each item.  **Answer all items.** Your grade will be based on the total number of correct answers.

### Items 1 through 4 are based on the following:

During 20x1, Krona City issued bonds for financing the construction of a civic center, and bonds for financing improvements in the environmental controls for its water and sewer enterprise. The latter bonds require a sinking fund for their retirement.  The City uses a general fixed asset account group and a general long-term debt account group.

**Required:**

Financial Statement Items

Items 1 through 4 represent items Krona should report in its 20x1 fund financial statements. For each item, determine whether it would be included in each of the fund types and account groups listed below.  Answer **Y** if the item would be included and **N** if the item would not be included.

Krona's Fund Types and Account Groups:
A.  General fund
B.  Enterprise funds
C.  Capital projects funds
D.  Debt service funds
E.  General fixed assets account group
F.  General long-term debt account group

**Items to be Answered:**

1.  Bonds payable.
2.  Accumulated depreciation.
3.  Amounts identified for the repayment of the two bond issues.
4.  Reserve for encumbrances.

**Task Question 2**                                   **(Estimated time - 45 to 55 minutes)**

Question No. 2 consists of 20 items relating to a municipal government.  Select the **best** answer for each item. **Answer all items.**  Your grade will be based on the total number of correct answers.

Items 1 through 10, in the left-hand column, represent various transactions pertaining to a municipality that uses encumbrance accounting and account groups for general fixed assets and general long-term debt.  To the right of these items is a listing of the possible ways to record the transactions.  Items 11 through 20, also listed in the left-hand column, represents the funds, accounts, and account groups used by the municipality. To the right of these items is a list of possible accounting and reporting methods.

**Required:**

**a.** For each of the municipality's transactions (Items 1 through 10), select the appropriate recording of the transaction for the fund financial statements. A method of recording the transactions may be selected once, more than once, or not at all.

**b.** For each of the municipality's funds, accounts, and account groups (Items 11 through 20), select the appropriate method of accounting and reporting for the fund financial statements. An accounting and reporting method may be selected once, more than once, or not at all.

<u>Item</u>

**Items to be Answered:**

**a.**　　　　　　<u>Transactions</u>

1. General obligation bonds were issued at par.

2. Approved purchase orders were issued for supplies.

3. The above-mentioned supplies were received and the related invoices were approved.

4. General fund salaries and wages were incurred.

5. The internal service fund had interfund billings.

6. Revenues were earned from a previously awarded grant.

7. Property taxes were collected in advance.

8. Appropriations were recorded on adoption of the budget.

9. Short-term financing was received from a bank, secured by the city's taxing power.

10. There was an excess of estimated inflows over estimated outflows.

<u>Recording of Transactions</u>

A. Credit appropriations control.

B. Credit budgetary fund balance - unreserved.

C. Credit expenditures control.

D. Credit deferred revenues.

E. Credit interfund revenues.

F. Credit tax anticipation notes payable.

G. Credit other financing sources.

H. Credit other financing uses.

I. Debit appropriations control.

J. Debit deferred revenues.

K. Debit encumbrances control.

L. Debit expenditures control.

**b.** Funds, Accounts, and Account Groups

11. Enterprise fund fixed assets.

12. Capital projects fund.

13. General fixed assets.

14. Infrastructure fixed assets.

15. Enterprise fund cash.

16. General fund.

17. Agency fund cash.

18. General long-term debt.

19. Special revenue fund.

20. Debt services fund.

Accounting and Reporting by Funds and Account Groups

A. Accounted for in a fiduciary fund.

B. Accounted for in a proprietary fund.

C. Accounted for in a permanent fund.

D. Accounted for in a self-balancing account group.

E. Accounted for in a special assessment fund.

F. Accounts for major construction activities.

G. Accounts for property tax revenues.

H. Accounts for payment of interest and principal on tax supported debt.

I. Accounts for revenues from earmarked sources to finance designated activities.

J. Reporting may require retroactive recognition.

---

**Task Question 3** **(Estimated time – 25 to 40 minutes)**

**Question Number 3** consists of 23 items. Select the **best** answer for each item.

The following information relates to Bel City, whose first fiscal year ended December 31, 20x4. Assume Bel has only the long-term debt specified in the information and only the funds necessitated by the information. The city uses account groups to keep track of general fixed assets and general long-term debt.

1. General fund:

The following selected information is taken from Bel's 20x4 general fund financial records:

| | Budget | |
|---|---|---|
| Actual | | |
| Property taxes | $5,000,000 | $4,700,000 |
| Other revenues | 1,000,000 | 1,050,000 |
| Total revenues | $6,000,000 | $5,750,000 |
| Total expenditures | $5,600,000 | $5,700,000 |

| | |
|---|---|
| Property taxes receivable | $420,000 |
| Less: Allowance for estimated uncollectible taxes | 50,000 |
| | $370,000 |

- There were no amendments to the budget as originally adopted.

- There were no encumbrances outstanding at December 31, 20x4.

## 2. Capital project fund:

- Finances for Bel's new civic center were provided by a combination of general fund transfers, a state grant, and an issue of general obligation bonds. Any bond premium on issuance is to be used for the repayment of the bonds at their $1,200,000 par value. At December 31, 20x4, the capital project fund for the civic center had the following closing entries:

| | | |
|---|---|---|
| Revenues | $ 800,000 | |
| Other financing sources | | |
| - bond proceeds | 1,230,000 | |
| Other financing sources | | |
| - interfund transfers | 500,000 | |
| Expenditures | | $1,080,000 |
| Other financing uses | | |
| - interfund transfers | | 30,000 |
| Unreserved fund balance | | 1,420,000 |

- Also, at December 31, 20x4, capital project fund entries reflected Bel's intention to honor the $1,300,000 purchase orders and commitments outstanding for the center.

- During 20x4, total capital project fund encumbrances exceeded the corresponding expenditures by $42,000. All expenditures were previously encumbered.

- During 20x5, the capital project fund received no revenues and no other financing sources. The civic center building was completed in early 20x5 and the capital project fund was closed by a transfer of $27,000 to the general fund.

## 3. Water utility enterprise fund:

- Bel issued $4,000,000 revenue bonds at par. These bonds, together with a $700,000 transfer from the general fund, were used to acquire a water utility. Water utility revenues are to be the sole source of funds to retire these bonds beginning in the year 20x9.

## Required:

For items **1 through 15**, indicate if the answer to each item is yes (Y) or no (N).

**Items 1 through 7** relate to the fund financial statements of Bel's general fund.

1. Did recording budgetary accounts at the beginning of 20x4 increase the fund balance by $50,000?

2. Should the budgetary accounts for 20x4 include an entry for the expected transfer of funds from the general fund to the capital projects fund?

3. Should the $700,000 payment from the general fund, which was used to help to establish the water utility fund, be reported as an "other financing use – interfund transfer"?

4. Did the general fund receive the $30,000 bond premium from the capital projects fund?

5. Should the payment from the general fund for water received for normal civic center operations be reported as an "other financing use – interfund transfer"?

6. Would closing budgetary accounts cause the fund balance to increase by $400,000?

7. Would the interaction between budgetary and actual amounts cause the fund balance to decrease by $350,000?

**Items 8 through 15** relate to Bel's account groups and accounting for the fund financial statements of funds other than the general fund.

8. In the general fixed assets account group, should a credit amount be recorded for 20x4 in "Investment in general fixed assets - capital projects fund"?

9. In the general fixed assets account group, could Bel elect to record depreciation in 20x5 on the civic center?

10. In the general fixed assets account group, could Bel elect to record depreciation on water utility equipment?

11. Should the capital project fund be included in Bel's combined statement of revenues, expenditures, and changes in fund balances?

12. Should the water utility enterprise fund be included in Bel's combined balance sheet?

In which fund should Bel report capital and related financing activities in its 20x4 statement of cash flows?

13. Debt service fund.

14. Capital project fund.

15. Water utility enterprise fund.

For **Items 16 through 23**, determine the proper amount.

**Items 16 and 17** relate to the fund financial statements of Bel's general fund.

16. What was the amount recorded in the opening entry for appropriations?

17. What was the total amount debited to property taxes receivable?

**Items 18 through 23** relate to Bel's account groups and accounting for the fund financial statements of funds other than the general fund.

18. In the general long-term debt account group, what amount should be reported for bonds payable at December 31, 20x4?

19. In the general fixed assets account group, what amount should be recorded for "Investment in general fixed assets - capital project fund" at December 31, 20x4?

20. What was the completed cost of the civic center?

21. How much was the state capital grant for the civic center?

22. In the capital project fund, what was the amount of the total encumbrances recorded during 20x4?

23. In the capital project fund, what was the unreserved fund balance reported at December 31, 20x4?

**Task Question 4**            **(Estimated time –**
                                      **20 minutes)**

**Question Number 4** consists of 10 items. Select the **best** answer for each item

The following information relates to Dane City during its fiscal year ended December 31, 20x4:

- The city uses account groups to keep track of general fixed assets and general long-term debt.

- On October 31, 20x4, to finance the construction of a city hall annex, Dane issued 8% 10-year general obligation bonds at their face value of $600,000. Construction expenditures during the period equaled $364,000.

- Dane reported $109,000 from hotel room taxes, restricted for tourist promotion, in a special revenue fund. The fund paid $81,000 for general promotions and $22,000 for a motor vehicle.

- 20x4 general fund revenues of $104,500 were transferred to a debt service fund and used to repay $100,000 of 9% 15-year term bonds, and to pay $4,500 of interest. The bonds were used to acquire a citizens' center.

- At December 31, 20x4, as a consequence of past services, city firefighters had accumulated entitlements to compensated absences valued at $86,000. General fund resources available at December 31, 20x4, are expected to be used to settle $17,000 of this amount, and $69,000 is expected to be paid out of future general fund resources.

- At December 31, 20x4, Dane was responsible for $83,000 of outstanding general fund encumbrances, including the $8,000 for supplies indicated below.

- Dane uses the purchases method to account for supplies. The following information relates to supplies:

| | |
|---|---|
| Inventory - 1/1/x4 | $39,000 |
| Inventory - 12/31/x4 | 42,000 |
| Encumbrances outstanding - | |
| 1/1/x4 | 6,000 |
| 12/31/x4 | 8,000 |
| Purchase orders during 20x4 | 190,000 |
| Amounts credited to vouchers payable during 20x4 | 181,000 |

**Required:**

**For Items 1 through 10,** determine the amounts to be recognized in the fund financial statements based solely on the above information.

1. What is the amount of 20x4 general fund other financing uses - interfund transfers?

2. How much should be reported as 20x4 general fund liabilities from entitlements for compensated absences?

3. What is the 20x4 reserved amount of the general fund balance?

4. What is the 20x4 capital projects fund balance?

5. What is the 20x4 fund balance on the special revenue fund for tourist promotion?

6. What is the amount of 20x4 debt service fund expenditures?

7. What amount should be included in the general fixed assets account group for the cost of assets acquired in 20x4?

8. What amount stemming from 20x4 transactions and events decreased the liabilities reported in the general long-term debt account group?

9. Using the purchases method, what is the amount of 20x4 supplies expenditures?

10. What was the total amount of 20x4 supplies encumbrances?

**Task Question 5**    (Estimated time – 15 minutes)

Dease City is a governmental organization that has governmental-type funds and account groups. The following is selected information taken from the city's financial records. The financial records are prepared on the basis of accounting used in the fund financial statements.

General Fund

| | |
|---|---|
| Fund balance 1/1/x6 | $ 700,000 |
| 20x6 estimated revenues | 10,000,000 |
| 20x6 actual revenues | 10,500,000 |
| 20x6 appropriations | 9,000,000 |
| Encumbrances at end of 20x6 | 500,000 |
| Vouchers payable 12/31/x6 | 300,000 |
| 20x6 interfund transfers in | 100,000 |
| 20x6 property tax levy | 9,500,000 |
| 20x6 property taxes estimated to be uncollectible when property tax levy for 20x6 recorded. | 100,000 |
| 20x6 property taxes delinquent at end of 20x6 | 150,000 |

Capital projects fund

| | |
|---|---|
| 20x6 interfund transfers in | 100,000 |
| Construction of new library wing started and completed in 20x6: | |
| Proceeds from bonds issued at 100 in 20x6 | 2,000,000 |
| Expenditures for 20x6 | 2,100,000 |

**Required:**

**Items 1 through 5** represent transactions by governmental-type funds and account groups based on the above information. For each item, determine the amounts based solely on the above information.

1. What was the net amount credited to the budgetary fund balance when the budget was recorded?

2. What was the amount of property taxes collected on the property tax levy for 20x6?

3. What amount for the new library wing was included in the capital projects fund balance at the end of 20x6?

4. What amount for the new library wing was charged to the general fixed assets account group at the end of 20x6?

5. What amount for the new library wing bonds was included in the general long-term debt account group at the end of 20x6?

# CHAPTER 11

## GOVERNMENTAL ACCOUNTING AND REPORTING

### Multiple Choice Answers

1.  /a/ The GASB is the body charged with promulgating GAAP for governmental organizations. The NCGA was the association of governmental accountants that was authoritative prior to the formation of the GASB. GASB has provided that many of the standards set by NCGA remain in effect until GASB provides otherwise. The FASB is the authoritative body for non-governmental, non-profit organizations, as well as for profit making companies.

2.  /d/ The portion of the tax restricted, presumably by law, for use to repay or service long-term debt would be transferred to the Debt Service Fund (DSF). The DSF then receives and accounts for the resources and expends them to pay interest and principal when mature (due and owing). The purpose here is to assure that the restrictions on use of resources are complied with.

3.  /a/ Generally, assume that, in the case of utilities, customer fees are expected to pay the predominance of the costs incurred for services rendered to them. In such cases, the enterprise fund (a type of proprietary fund) is appropriately used, because determining full costs to charge customers is essential. An internal service fund is a proprietary fund as well, but it is used to account for services performed for other governmental units rather than for outside customers. A special revenue fund could be appropriate if user fees paid less than a predominance of the costs of services rendered, but this is generally not the case for utilities.

4.  /b/ When a governmental agency such as a municipal motor pool, renders services for other governmental funds (various departments), the internal service fund type is used. The various departments are billed for the full cost of services rendered, including allocated fixed costs. Full accrual accounting is used in this proprietary fund type. Although special assessments are still levied against taxpayers who directly receive benefits, the special assessment fund is no longer used to account for such transactions. Rather, the transaction is analyzed by its parts and other governmental funds are used s is appropriate. The concept is not applicable to this problem, but use of this terminology demonstrates the need to be aware of the transaction type.

5.  /a/ When a third-party grantor transfers assets (in this case, investments) with instructions to use only the interest (therefore maintaining the principal intact) for purposes that benefit the government, the principal is accounted for in a Permanent fund.

6.  /b/ The modified accrual method of accounting is used for the general fund in the fund financial statements. When resources are expended in the general fund, the debit (increase) is ultimately to "expenditures" since an appropriate current use was made of the funds. The credit would presumably be to "Vouchers Payable." The expenditures account normally has a debit balance. Appropriations is the wrong answer since that account normally carries a credit balance and because the appropriation is

legislative permission to use resources. An entry would have to be made in the general fund because its resources are ultimately going to decrease as a result of this transaction.

7. /d/ Governmental funds are accounted for on the modified accrual basis of accounting, so depreciation is not used. Mention of depreciation in the parking garage case tells us that this is an enterprise fund. Governmental employee retirement benefits are accounted for in a fiduciary fund type, a pension trust fund. Property taxes are liens against the land and are measurable and available when levied by the government. They may, therefore, be recognized currently in governmental funds.

8 /a/ A is the best answer in that the assets of governmental funds are not expected to generate revenues. Depreciation does not use current resources, so is not treated as an expenditure in governmental fund types. Accumulated Depreciation may be allocated wholly within the General Fixed Asset Group. Answer C is mutually exclusive of A and is just plain incorrect. Answer D is incorrect because fixed assets exist so that governmental funds may provide services by using them. Failure to keep them maintained will result in services not being performed.

9. /d/ Enterprise funds are a type of proprietary fund and account for fixed assets within their own balance sheet. Further, fixed assets are depreciated and depreciation expense is allocated against revenues. Unlike "for-profit" organizations, special revenue funds and capital projects funds do not account for their fixed assets as part of fund records. Fixed assets of

governmental funds are accounted for in the general fixed asset account group. Depreciation is not accounted for in governmental funds.

10. /c/ The modified accrual method of accounting is used for governmental funds – including capital projects and the general fund – in the fund financial statements. Under the modified accrual method, no fixed assets are carried on the balance sheet. Instead, purchases of fixed assets are recorded as expenditures.

11. /c/ Outstanding vouchers payable are carried in the account of that name, analogously to accounts payable. The excess of the amount of a purchase order (the expected cost of the item) over the actual expenditure for that item would, in effect, increase the amount available for future expenditure. Example: goods expected to cost $100 were ordered and actually cost $80. Encumbrances, which are closed when goods are received, would exceed expenditures. So the excess amount of $20 would be available to encumber.

12. /c/ The trick to this question is to interpret what a "commitment appropriation" is. Since the problem speaks of amounts not yet expended, and about appropriations that do not lapse, it becomes clear that commitment appropriations means encumbrances for goods not yet received. In other words, an encumbrance represents a burden or commitment of appropriated amounts from the time the order is approved for purchase to the time the items are received. At the period end, open encumbrances are credited (closed), but the Fund Balance Reserved for Encumbrances remains open. D is

not the correct answer because budgetary fund balance is a title used for the account to balance the entry to record the budget at the start of the period. Encumbrances are not budgeted. Permission to expend resources is given by the "appropriation" account. If appropriations lapse at the end of a period, authority to place orders for goods or services ends. Therefore, the entire encumbrancing entry is reversed. None of the answers available provides for this event, so there is no ambiguity.

13. /a/ The governmental funds (here the capital projects fund) use the modified accrual basis of accounting in the fund financial statements. This means that revenues are recognized when they are both measurable and available as cash within the budget period, or shortly thereafter. Proprietary funds (enterprise and internal service funds) use full accrual accounting for all types of financial statements. The fiduciary fund type, pension trust fund, also uses full accrual accounting.

14. /c/ The debt service fund is a governmental fund, which must use the modified accrual basis of accounting in the fund financial statements. Under the modified accrual method of accounting, revenues are recognized when both measurable and available.

15. /b/ The problem does not state the type of fund, but city property taxes are usually recognized in a governmental-type fund. In the fund financial statements of governmental funds, revenues are recognized under the modified accrual method – i.e., when they are measurable and available. Taxes in this jurisdiction are due May 1 and

October 1, with a fiscal year end of June 30. Revenues may thus be recognized if they are due prior to June 30 and will be collected within 60 days of that date (i.e. on or before August 30). For the period July 1, 20x0 to June 30, 20x1, collections include the following:

| October 20x0 | $ 920,000 |
| December 20x0 | 80,000 |
| May 20x1 | 1,100,000 |
| July 20x1 | 60,000 |
| August 20x1 | 40,000 |
| Total | $2,200,000 |

Note that the May and July payments of 20x0 pertain to the fiscal year ending June 30, 20x0.

16. /b/ Under the modified accrual basis of accounting, revenues are recognized when they are both measurable in dollars and available for cash collection within the period or shortly thereafter.

17. /d/ The general fund (a governmental-type fund) must use the modified accrual method of accounting in the fund financial statements. Thus, revenues are recognized when measurable and available. Available means due and collected in cash within the fiscal year or shortly (generally within 60 days) after its ending.

18. /b/ Governmental funds must use the modified accrual method of accounting in the fund financial statements. The problem states that the $2,000,000 is included in the $16,000,000 that is both measurable and available in that year. Therefore, that total amount is correctly recognized in 20x0. The $3,000,000 of sales taxes is available because it will be received within 60 days of the end of the year.

19. /d/ Governmental funds follow the modified accrual basis of accounting in the fund financial statements. Proprietary funds use full accrual basis accounting for all financial statements.

20. /d/ Since a local government may have all of governmental, proprietary, and fiduciary fund types, depending on the number and sophistication of the transactions it experiences, both modified accrual basis (for governmental funds in the fund financial statements) and accrual basis (for proprietary and fiduciary funds in the fund financial statements) could be used.

21. /b/ The estimated revenue control account is the sum of all expected cash revenue inflows for the period. It is debited when the budget is recorded and credited (eliminated) when the budgetary entries are closed at the end of the period. Appropriations and property taxes have nothing to do with this question.

22. /c/ Legislatively granted permission to expend resources is recognized in the budgetary entry as a credit to the account "appropriations." When the budgetary accounts are closed, the appropriations account is debited. Supplies and expenditures have nothing to do with this question.

23. /d/ Encumbrances are recognized when the purchase order for goods or services is approved by the appropriate authorities. The budgetary entry precedes, but does not directly involve, entries made for encumbering the appropriated amounts, so A and B are irrelevant to this problem. When supplies previously ordered are received, the fund balance reserved for encumbrances is reduced (debited), not increased.

24. /b/ Only the expenditures account is nominal. The vouchers payable balance, the (unreserved) fund balance, and the fund balance reserved for encumbrances are all balance sheet accounts and are not closed at the end of an accounting period.

25. /b/ Since estimated revenues are not given, nor are encumbrances, the appropriation closing will have no effect on fund balance here.

Inflows which increase
fund balance:
Revenues                         $8,000,000
Other financing sources   1,500,000
                                        $9,500,000

Outflows which decrease
fund balance:
Expenditures                   $5,000,000
Other financing uses        2,000,000
                                       $7,000,000

Net increase to fund balance is $9,500,000 total inflows less $7,000,000 total outflows = $2,500,000.

26. /b/ The expenditures account is debited when resources are used to accomplish fund purposes. Therefore, to close the expenditures account, credit it. Further, it is a nominal account, requiring closure at the end of the period. It is analogous to the expense account in for-profit accounting, with the important proviso that cost expiration is irrelevant to governmental accounting. Resource outflows are what are measured.

27. /d/ When recording the budget, estimated revenues control is debited, here for $20,000,000. When actual revenues are recognized, the revenue account is credited. The closing entry would be:

| | | |
|---|---|---|
| Revenue | 17,000,000 | |
| Fund balance | 3,000,000 | |
| Estimated revenues control | | 20,000,000 |

28. /d/ When restricted grants are received, the accounting must enable assurance of compliance with the restriction. Therefore, amounts are recorded as "deferred revenues." When the actual expenditure occurs, and thus compliance is known, the deferred revenue is debited and an actual revenue recognized. Here the capital grant has been 90% expended, so 90% of the grant is recognized as revenue in the period expended. The remaining 10% is still deferred.

Since the operating grant has been totally expended, all of it is recognized as revenue.

29. /d/ Wages of civil service employees are usually budgeted as part of the appropriated amount. Therefore, encumbrancing would not provide any useful information. Debit "expenditure" directly for $300,000.

30. /b/ Gasoline taxes restricted for use to finance road repairs is the classic example of transactions to be recorded in a special revenue fund. There is an inflow from a specific and limited source. The outflow is restricted as to specific purposes. The use of the specific purpose fund makes compliance tracking much easier.

The levies against property owners who are going to pay for improvements that directly benefit their property are an example of a special assessment. Special assessments are not accounted for in one separate fund, but analyzed by their component parts. Here the levies are going to be used to build sidewalks, which is a capital project. Therefore, the property taxes receivable resulting from the levy would be recognized as revenue in a capital projects fund, not in a special revenue fund.

31. /c/ Special revenue funds are a type of governmental fund, so they must use the same modified accrual basis of accounting in the fund financial statements. Budgets are incorporated into the accounts assuming there is a legally adopted budget.

32. /c/ Amounts which are to be used to construct or acquire fixed assets (here a rehabilitation center for drug addicts) are accounted for in a capital projects fund.

33. /b/ In the Statement of Revenues, Expenditures, and Changes in Fund Balances, property tax revenues for governmental funds are accounted for using the modified accrual basis of accounting. In the Statement of Activities, property tax revenues are accounted for using full accrual accounting.

Modified accrual property tax revenues:

| | |
|---|---|
| 20x4 taxes collected Mar-Dec 20x5 | $ 180,000 |
| 20x5 levied & collected | 4,000,000 |
| 20x5 taxes collected Jan-Feb 20x6 | 300,000 |
| Total | $4,480,000 |

Accrual property tax revenues:

| | |
|---|---|
| 20x5 levied & collected | $4,000,000 |
| 20x5 taxes collected Jan-Feb 20x6 | 300,000 |
| 20x5 taxes expected to be Collected after Feb x6 | 200,000 |
| Total | $4,500,000 |

Reconciliation:

| | |
|---|---|
| Change in fund balances – governmental funds | $ 30,000 |
| 20x4 taxes collected Mar-Dec 20x5 | (180,000) |
| 20x5 taxes expected to be Collected after Feb 20x6 | 200,000 |
| Change in net assets – governmental activities | $ 50,000 |

**34.** /b/ Funds to be used to finance construction of a civic center are recorded in the capital projects fund.

**35.** /c/ The principal amount of the bond, which is a general obligation of the city, will be recorded in the General Long-term Debt Account Group.

**36.** /d/ Bond Anticipation Notes (BANs) are short-term debt instruments issued pending securing other financing. This type of interim financing would be considered a current liability of the capital projects fund. BANs would not be recorded as a general long-term debt group item unless the underlying bond were definitely issuable and the BAN were legally to be paid from the bond issue proceeds. Since we are not told either, when both are required, the BAN is recorded in the capital projects fund.

**37.** /a/ Both bond issue proceeds and Interfund transfers of cash from the general fund are other financing sources, not revenues, in the capital projects fund. Therefore, the amount of revenue recognized is zero.

**38.** /c/ Special Assessment Debt will be paid by taxes levied against the benefited property owners. When the governmental unit guarantees payments, that is, when the full faith and credit of the government is pledged, the principal amount of the debt is accounted for in a special revenue fund. Special revenue funds are combined with other governmental funds in the "governmental activities" column of the government-wide financial statements. Note: The debt would not appear as a liability for this fund in the governmental fund financial statements.

**39** /d/ Principal and interest on the debt of governmental funds is paid by the Debt Service Fund (DSF). Therefore, any amounts accumulated to pay principal and interest are recorded in the DSF.

**40.** /a/ The problem describes general long-term debt activities, which would be accounted for in governmental funds that use the modified actual basis of accounting in the fund financial statements. The government fiscal year runs from July 1 to June 30. The interest payments on the bond are due March 1 and October 1. The bond was issued March 2. Therefore, no interest is due and owing between March 2 and June 30, the fiscal year-end. Under the modified accrual basis, we are measuring use of resources. No cash is required until October 1, so no interest is accrued on June 30 in the fund financial statements. (Note, however, that interest would be accrued in the usual manner for the government-wide financial statements.)

**41.** /d/ If an activity is self-sustaining due to payments by users, the definition of enterprise fund is met. So both the water supply plant and bus system resources would be accounted for in enterprise funds. The answer is the sum of $5,000,000 and $900,000 = $5,900,000.

**42.** /b/ The problem states that the city uses a general fixed asset account group, but this information is irrelevant because account groups are not used for proprietary (including enterprise) funds. Enterprise funds account for fixed assets and long-term debt associated with the fund within their own balance sheet accounts. Full accrual methods are followed. Therefore, depreciation expense is allocated and recorded for the fund financial statements as well as the government-wide financial statements.

**43.** /d/ Proprietary funds always use full accrual accounting, so net income is calculated in the usual fashion. Note that amounts spent on fixed assets (such as parking meters) are capitalized, not expensed.

| | |
|---|---:|
| Revenues from user fees | $400,000 |
| Cash expenses | (90,000) |
| Depreciation expense | (70,000) |
| Net income | $240,000 |

**44.** /d/ Fiduciary funds are used when a governmental unit administers funds held in trust or as an agent for others. In this case, the account receives and administers funds from a deferred compensation program, which benefits its employees and also the employees of other jurisdictions. This plan would be accounted for as a trust fund because the funds are held long term.

**45.** /b/ The state government is collecting taxes that are to be paid over to one of the cities within the state. It therefore would use an agency fund to account for the $8,000,000. An agency fund is used when a governmental unit administers funds for others on a short-term basis.

**46.** /c/ The fiduciary funds include both the trust funds and the agency funds. The trust funds include the expendable, nonexpendable, and pension trusts.

**47.** /d/ In the government-wide financial statements, general fund fixed assets are reported as assets on the statement of net assets. The fixed assets are reported net of accumulated depreciation and also net of any impairment write-downs.

**48.** /a/ This is the same question as the preceding one, but it refers to the fund financial statements instead of the government-wide financial statements. The modified accrual basis of accounting is used for the general fund in the fund financial statements, so no fixed assets are recognized on the balance sheet. Instead, the cost would be recognized as an expenditure.

**49.** /a/ General long-term debt is accounted for using the modified accrual method of accounting in the fund financial statements. Under modified accrual accounting, debt issuance costs represent a current reduction of available resources and are therefore expenditures when incurred. If the bond underwriter pays them, they could be reductions in bond proceeds. (Note, however, that these costs would be deferred and amortized for the government-wide financial statements.)

**50.** /c/ Payment of principal, when due, is done by the debt service fund. Amounts accumulated in the debt service fund for payment of principal are reflected in the General Long-term Debt Account Groups as reductions of "Amounts to be Provided" and increases in "Amounts Available in Debt Service Funds" (given that the statement in the fact pattern that the city uses a GLTDAG). The sum of the debits "Amounts Available" and "Amounts to be Provided" will equal the credit balance in the GLTDAG.

**51.** /a/ The proprietary and fiduciary funds reflect debt issued by and to be repaid from those funds directly in those funds. Both of the debt issuances in this problem relate to an enterprise fund and would be reported as liabilities under business type activities in the government-wide financial statements.

**52.** /d/ Long-term debt issued by and expected to be repaid by proprietary funds is carried in those funds. This is true even though the principal amount is guaranteed by the full faith and credit of the city, provided that the risk of loss is remote. In the typical case, the proprietary fund adjusts its rates to provide for the debt repayment. The city would disclose its contingent liability in a footnote.

**53.** /b/ In the general fund, a capital lease represents an expenditure in the fund financial statements (which use the modified accrual method of accounting) because a resource has been acquired in exchange for a commitment to make future payments to the lessor. Further, the lessor has financed the acquisition for the general fund, so the credit is to "Other Financing Sources." The amount to be recorded is the net discounted present value of the minimum lease payments. The effect of discounting is that only the principal amount owing is reflected. In this case, the principal payments are stated to be three payments of $75,000 each, totaling $225,000. No interest is recorded as an expenditure until an actual payment is made.

**54.** /c/ In the fund financial statements, fixed assets acquired by a governmental-type fund are accounted for as expenditures. At the inception of a capital lease, the governmental fund debits "expenditures" for the present value of the future minimum lease payments (in this problem, the total expected future principal payments).

**55.** /b/ This question is the same as the preceding one, except it refers to the government-wide financial statements rather than the fund financial statements. The fixed assets of governmental funds are accounted for using usual accrual accounting in the government-wide financial statements. Thus, the present value of the future minimum lease payments would be recorded as equipment.

**56.** /c/ The entry to record new debt in the General Long-Term Debt Account Group includes a credit to the liability account. Answer c is the only possible answer, because it is the only one in which the lease liability is credited. The complete entry to record the leasehold obligation in the General Long-Term Debt Account Group would be:

Amount to be provided for
  lease payments        debit
    Capital lease obligation
      payable                  credit

**57.** /a/ Payments of long-term debt, including payments on capital lease obligations, are made in the debt service fund, which is a governmental-type fund. In the fund financial statements, governmental-type funds use the modified accrual method of accounting. Therefore, both principal and interest are recorded as expenditures when due. The entry would be:

Expenditure - principal   50,000
Expenditure - interest    15,000
    Cash                           65,000

**58.** /d/ Proprietary funds account for assets used by those funds, together with any debit incurred to acquire assets, using regular accrual accounting for all financial statements. Therefore, capital leasing activities are accounted for just as in for-profit firms: Equipment is debited, and Capital Lease Obligation Payable is credited at the inception of the lease.

**59.** /c/ Internal service funds account for assets used by those funds, together with any debit incurred to acquire assets, using regular accrual accounting for all financial statements. Therefore, capital leasing activities are accounted for just as in for-profit firms. Each lease payment would be broken down between the principal portion, which reduces the lease liability, and the interest portion, which is an expense.

**60.** /c/ The amount recognized as the cost of the asset in the government-wide statement of net assets is the net discounted present value of minimum lease payments, but not to exceed the fair market value of the leased asset. Here, the present value amount is $5,120, which exceeds the fair market value at lease inception of $5,000, so record the fair market value.

**61.** /a/ In governmental funds, the primary focus is on accounting for and reporting the flows of current financial resources. Income determination and capital maintenance are objectives of accounting and reporting for proprietary, nonexpendable trust, and pension trust funds. Transfers relating to proprietary activities are simply events that are recorded in appropriate funds. They are not an emphasis in accounting and reporting procedures.

**62.** /c/ Information reported in governmental financial statements is useful for citizens to make social and political decisions about which legislatures to elect based on their position and performance relating to fiscal issues. The financial statements also provide useful information about interperiod equity; i.e. has the governmental unit provided sufficient current resources to maintain current services without passing payment burden into the future?

**63.** /a/ The focus of accounting and reporting for proprietary (business-type) funds of governmental units is the determination of income and capital maintenance. Answer (c), flow of funds, is relevant to governmental type funds. Answers (b) project and (d) program refer to classifications of expenditures and are not relevant to the question.

**64.** /d/ Agency funds are used when one governmental unit collects and holds resources for others on a short-term basis. The collecting governmental entity is acting in a custodial capacity.

**65.** /d/ Fixed assets of governmental funds are not capitalized for the fund financial statements. Rather, they are fully expended in the period of acquisition. For this reason, depreciation is not relevant and is not used in such funds. However, in proprietary funds, where determination of periodic income is an objective, assets are capitalized and depreciated.

**66.** /b/ If property taxes receivable are recorded before they are levied, they are not current revenue. Their recognition is deferred. Similarly, any property taxes collected prior to the levy year are unearned and also recorded as deferred revenues.

**67.** /a/ The modified accrual method of accounting is used in the Statement of Revenues, Expenditures, and Changes in Fund Balances for governmental funds, while full accrual accounting is used in the Statement of Activities. Here is the reconciliation:

| | |
|---|---|
| Change in fund balances – governmental funds | $ (10,000) |
| Expenditures for purchased assets | 500,000 |
| Depreciation | (225,000) |
| Proceeds from sale | (50,000) |
| Gain on sale [50 – (300 – 280)] | 30,000 |
| Change in net assets – governmental activities | $245,000 |

**68.** /b/ Although the electric utility is an enterprise fund, it is an internal service fund as far as the general fund is concerned when it provides electricity to the governmental fund. This is a quasi-external transaction.

Although there will be a transfer of resources between two funds of the same government, the transaction is treated "as though" the general fund was utilizing current resources to acquire service from an external supplier. Thus, the general fund will debit expenditures and the electric utility enterprise fund will credit operating revenues. This is not an interfund transfer.

**69.** /a/ Full accrual accounting is used for all funds in the government-wide financial statements.

**70.** /d/ The general fund uses the modified accrual method of accounting in the fund financial statements. Under the modified accrual method, item D is the only activity described that is classified as an expenditure. Each of the other answers would be classified as an Other Financing Use (interfund transfer).

**71.** /c/ General fixed assets are accounted for using the modified accrual method of accounting in the fund financial statements. Thus, the acquiring fund records an expenditure in the amount of the present value of the periodic lease payments. This expenditure is financed through a long-term debt arrangement. Long-term debt arrangements are classified as other financing sources.

**72.** /d/ Where a government is primarily or secondarily obligated to repay special assessment debt from general government resources, that debt must be recognized as debt in the government-wide financial statements. However, it is not recognized as debt in the fund financial statements.

**73.** /a/ The debt service fund is used to service the only the general obligation debt that is recorded in the long-term debt account group. To the extent that trust funds may borrow, they generally service their own debt. The debt to finance a proprietary fund's activities is serviced within its own fund.

**74.** /a/ Object classification identifies the specific items purchased or services acquired. Function or program classification relates to major services provided by the government, e.g. public safety. Activity classification is used to identify a unit of operations, such as the police department.

**75.** /a/ Appropriations control is credited when the budget is recorded. Since there is no such account as "estimated expenditures control," options C and D would both be incorrect. A debit to appropriations control (option B) would be recorded to close out the budget entries at the end of the period.

**76.** /c/ An excess of anticipated revenues and other financing sources over appropriations and other financing uses would require a credit to budgetary fund balance in the amount of $20,000

**77.** /a/ $9,000,000. The only anticipated receipts that are classified as revenues are the property taxes, licenses and fines. Proceeds of debt issue are classified as other financing sources. The anticipated transfer for debt service is an interfund transfer. This would also be classified as other financing activity.

**78.** /c/ $500,000. The amount of encumbrances outstanding at June 30, 20x3, is equal to the total of encumbrances for the period relating to purchase orders issued ($5,000,000) less the amount unencumbered relating to goods received ($4,500,000).

**79.** /d/ General debt obligations are accounted for using the modified accrual method of accounting in the fund financial statements. Thus, interest expense is accrued only when payable. Any premium realized upon issuance of the bonds is included as part of the bond proceeds and is available to service both interest and principal payments to be made from the debt service fund. Since allocation of resources and expenditures among time periods is not a measurement focus, it follows, therefore, that any premium (or discount) relating to a bond issue is not amortized.

**80.** /c/ The general fund uses the modified accrual method of accounting in the fund financial statements. Of the $800,000 paid in 20x2, $700,000 relates to 20x2 (see $100,000 balance of current liability as of 1/1/x2). An additional $140,000 of expenditures must have been recorded prior to 12/31/x2 relating to current liability incurred in 20x2. The total of these two amounts ($840,000) would be reported as claims and judgments and expenditures for 20x2. The noncurrent liability is not an expenditure until it matures.

**81.** /d/ Only the fixed assets of a proprietary fund or a trust fund are reported on the balance sheet in the fund financial statements of a governmental unit.

**82.** /b/ Since the resources are unrestricted as to use, the state grant would be accounted for in Cal's general fund. The interest on bank accounts held for employees' pension plan, however, would be accounted for in a pension trust fund.

**83.** /c/ $600,000. The problem does not state the type of fund, but property taxes are usually related to governmental-type funds, which use the modified accrual method of accounting in the fund financial statements. Net property tax revenues for 20x2 are equal to expected collections during 20x2 ($500,000) + expected collection within 60 days of the end of 20x2 ($100,000). Alternatively, the same answer can be derived by subtracting from the total levy of $700,000 the deferred revenues portion anticipated during the balance of 20x3 ($60,000) and 20x4 ($30,000), as well as the estimated uncollectible amount of $10,000.

**84.** /c/ The grant from the state government is classified as revenues ($400,000). The proceeds from the issuance of bonds and the transfer in from Fir's general fund are both other financing sources in the fund financial statements of governmental funds (including capital projects funds): $500,000 + $100,000 = $600,000.

**85.** /a/ This question is asking about the major items that are different between the modified accrual method of accounting used by governmental funds (including debt service funds) in the fund financial statements, and full accrual accounting. Under the modified accrual method, both principal and interest are accrued as expenditures when they mature. Under regular accrual accounting, principal payments are not recorded as charges against revenues, and interest expense is accrued over time.

**86.** /d/ The entry to be made in the general fixed assets account group requires a debit to an appropriate asset account and a credit to an investment account that indicates the source of the resources. The entry would be measured at the fair value of the asset when it was received. Option A is incorrect because a memorandum entry only is not sufficient. Option B is incorrect, because the account general fixed assets is too vague and the credit private gifts is not correct. Option C is incorrect because the investment account needs to be credited, and this is not a revenue transaction.

**87.** /b/ When the purchase orders and contracts were issued, an entry would have been made to record an encumbrance of $850,000. This entry would have consisted of a debit to encumbrances and a credit to budgetary fund balance reserved for encumbrances.

**88.** /c/ Cash and cash equivalents includes highly liquid investments that have a maturity of three months or less as of the date of purchase. The T-bill purchased 5/31/x4 and the T-note purchased 6/15/x4 both satisfy this requirement. They total $80,000. Although the 5-year note will mature within three months of the balance sheet date, it did not have a 3-month maturity as of its date of purchase.

**89.** /b/ Total fund balance is equal to $1,000,000 less $600,000 of liabilities, or $400,000. Of this $400,000, $100,000 is reserved for encumbrances. Unreserved fund balance is, therefore, $300,000.

**90.** /c/ Deferred compensation plans represent amounts held on behalf of others. A trust fund is the appropriate account to use for such an activity, because the funds are held long term for the benefit of others.

**91.** /c/ For the government-wide financial statements, governmental funds report both short-term and long-term debt. The governmental activity long-term debt relating to capital activities is the sum of the long-term bonds issued for capital acquisition ($3,000,000) and the $400,000 of bond anticipation notes that are to be repaid from proceeds that are to be realized as part of a long-term financing plan. The vendor financing is short-term and is not part of long-term debt.

**92.** /d/ The general fund uses the modified accrual method of accounting in the fund financial statements. The only possible answer is d. The interfund transfer of $1,500,000 from the general fund to the capital projects fund is recorded in the general fund as an other financing use – interfund transfer. Option A is not correct because it assumes that the $3,000,000 proceeds from the bond issue would be recorded first as a receipt in the general fund, followed by a transfer to the capital projects fund. However, the bond proceeds would be recorded directly in the capital projects fund as an other financing source. Option B is not correct because $4,500,000 is not being transferred from the general to the capital projects fund; furthermore, such a transfer (if made) would not be recorded as an expenditure; it would be an other financing use – interfund transfer. Option C is not correct because the transfer from the general to the capital projects fund is in the amount of $1,500,000, not $3,000,000.

**93.** /a/ Fixed assets donated to a governmental unit should be measured at the estimated fair value of the asset on the date of receipt.

**94.** /c/ This question has a powerful distracter to influence the unwary! Focus on the budget entries. If appropriations exceeded anticipated revenues, the budget entry at the beginning of the period would have required a debit to the budgetary fund balance. At the end of the period, this entry would be reversed, requiring a credit to the budgetary fund balance. Option C applies. The actual activity level of expenditures and encumbrances have no effect on the closing budget entry. They affect the closing entries relating to actual activity.

**95.** /d/ When encumbrances are initially recorded and then reversed upon receipt of goods and/or services, the accounts encumbrances and budgetary fund balance reserved for encumbrances are affected equally. If the balance of one of these accounts is not equal to the balance of the other, an error must have been made.

**96.** /b/ Under the encumbrancing procedure, the encumbrance entry is reversed when goods are received, and an expenditure and corresponding liability is set up. Since the issue of a purchase order stimulates a debit to encumbrances, receipt of the goods requires a credit (or decrease) to that account. At the same time, the expenditures control account would be increased, with a corresponding increase to an appropriate liability account (vouchers or accounts payable).

**97.** /d/ This description "measure and available" applies to revenue recognition under the modified accrual method of accounting. However, this method of accounting is not used for any funds in the government-wide financial (all funds use regular accrual accounting).

**98.** /a/ This question is the same as the preceding one, except it refers to the fund financial statements rather than the government-wide financial statements. In the fund financial statements, governmental-type funds (including the general fund) use the modified accrual method of accounting. Proprietary-type funds (including the enterprise fund) use regular accrual accounting.

**99.** /d/ The Statement of Revenues, Expenditures, and Changes in Fund Balances is one of the fund financial statements, which requires the modified accrual method of accounting for governmental-type funds (including the general fund). Under the modified accrual method, no gain or loss on sale of fixed assets is recorded. Instead, the sale proceeds are recorded as an other financing source.

**100.** /a/ This question is the same as the preceding one, except it refers to the government-wide financial statements instead of the fund financial statements. Regular accrual accounting is used for all funds in the government-wide financial statements, so a gain or loss on the sale of a fixed asset is recorded as usual: [$1,000 − ($5,000 − $3,800)] = $(200).

**101.** /b/ An internal service fund is a business-type fund. Therefore, billings for services rendered to other governmental units are recorded as operating revenues. Note that all other answer options are items or transaction names that are outside the terminology of governmental accounting practices (i.e. nonsense items!).

**102.** /c/ The account "estimated revenues control" is a budget account. It is debited when the budget is recorded at the beginning of the year and credited when the budget is closed at the end of the year.

**103.** /d/ The reporting entity must be the entity which is financially accountable for the governmental unit. A governmental financial reporting entity consists of a primary government and its component units. Component units are legally separate organizations for which the primary government is financially accountable.

**104.** /d/ Debt arising from proprietary funds is recorded within those funds and is classified under business type activities on the government-wide statement of net assets. Since all the bonds in the fact pattern pertain to enterprise funds and would be recorded directly in those funds, no amount relating to these bonds should be recognized as governmental activity debt.

**105.** /a/ Since this is a capital lease that will benefit the general government staff, it should be accounted for in a governmental fund. In the government-wide financial statements, the lease asset will be recognized as an asset, and the lease obligation will be recognized as a liability.

**106.** /a/ Statements of Cash Flows are required for proprietary funds but not for governmental funds.

**107.** /c/ In the enterprise fund, sale of bonds provides cash presumably for capital activities, i.e. to fund acquisition or construction of fixed assets. Capital contributed by subdividers is paid in to permit expansion of water and sewer facilities to a greater number of households. Capital improvements are to be paid for from these funds. Therefore, they too are for capital and related financing activities.

Amounts paid in by customers are presumably for services rendered. Customers have paid their water and sewer bills. These are revenues to the enterprise fund, and are therefore cash inflows from operating activities.

**108.** /d/ A statement of revenues, expenditures, and changes in fund balances is used only by governmental-type funds in the fund financial statements. Proprietary funds report a statement of revenues, expenses, and changes in fund net assets. Fiduciary funds report a statement of changes in fiduciary net assets.

**109.** /c/ Interfund transfers are transfers of resources from one fund to another for operational purposes in the receiving fund. They are classified as "other financing sources" upon receipt. The transferring fund would classify them as "other financing uses." Reimbursements are handled as reductions in expenditures in the receiving fund.

**110.** /a/ The operating statements of governmental units should include all changes that affected the fund balance for the period, both operating and non-operating. This is called the "all-inclusive approach."

**111.** /a/ The estimated revenues of the general fund are reported on the statement of revenues, expenditures, and changes in fund balances - budget and actual. They should be reported on the basis of accounting used to prepare the budget, which in this problem is the modified accrual basis of accounting.

**112.** /b/ A statement of cash flows is published only for funds using proprietary fund accounting methods. Cash inflows from issuing bonds to finance city hall construction would be reported in the capital projects fund -- a governmental fund for which no cash statement is presented. A city utility would be operated as an enterprise (i.e. proprietary) fund. Therefore, the cash outflow representing payments in lieu of property taxes would be included in that fund's cash flow statement.

**113.** /a/ GASB 34 requires the statement of revenues, expenditures, and changes in fund balance – budget and actual to be presented using the method of accounting used in preparing the budget, which might or might not comply with GAAP. If the budgetary accounting method is different than GAAP, then the financial statements must also include a schedule that reconciles the budgetary and GAAP amounts.

**114.** /d/ Depreciation is required for governmental funds only in the government-wide financial statements.

.

# CHAPTER 11
## GOVERNMENTAL ACCOUNTING AND REPORTING

### Simulation Task Answers

**Task Number 1 Answer**

| | General Fund | Enterprise Funds | Capital Projects Funds | Debt Service Funds | General Fixed Assets Account Group | General Long-Term Debt Acct. Group |
|---|---|---|---|---|---|---|
| 1. | N | Y | N | N | N | Y |
| 2. | N | Y | N | N | Y | N |
| 3. | N | Y | N | Y | N | Y |
| 4. | Y | N | Y | N | N | N |

1. Bonds payable would be included in the Enterprise Fund (water and sewer bonds) and the General Long-Term Debt Group (civic center construction bonds).

2. Accumulated depreciation would be included in the Enterprise Fund, which uses accrual accounting; accumulated depreciation may be treated as an allocation of the General Fixed Asset Account Group credit balance. Its use is optional.

3. Amounts identified for the repayment of the two bond issues would be included in the Enterprise Fund (water and sewer bonds) and the General Long-Term Debt Account Group (civic center construction bonds).

4. Both the General Fund and the Capital Projects Fund use encumbrances and thus the reserve for encumbrances account.

**Task Number 2 Answer**

1. /G/ Proceeds from the issuance of general obligation bonds are other financing sources, as opposed to revenues.

2. /K/ When a purchase order is issued relating to the use of resources accounted for in governmental funds, an encumbrance is recorded. The entry would debit encumbrances control account and credit "Fund balance reserved for encumbrances."

3. /L/ When items previously ordered are received, the encumbrance entry recorded when the items were ordered is reversed, and an entry to record an expenditure and related liability is made.

4. /L/ Note that this is an example of a regularly recurring expenditure for a governmental commitment that is known. The encumbrancing procedure is not used, and the account Expenditures is debited directly.

5. /E/ Internal service funds record revenues upon providing services to other governmental departments. Since accrual accounting is used in these funds, these revenues are recorded when earned, i.e. when billed.

6. /J/ Restricted grants are not recognized as revenues until the related expenditure for the appropriate purpose has been made.

7. /D/ Taxes collected in advance are recorded as deferred revenues. They will be recognized as revenues in the budgetary period in which they are due.

8. /A/ The entry to record the legislated amounts of spending authority are incorporated into the accounts by crediting appropriations control when the budget entry is made.

9. /F/ By recording the debt in the account "tax anticipation notes payable," the government is disclosing the fact that the obligation is secured by the city's taxing power.

10. /B/ When the budget entry is made, the excess of anticipated inflows of resources over outflows is recorded as a credit to "budgetary fund balance - unreserved."

11. /B/ An enterprise fund is a proprietary fund. Fixed assets of such funds are accounted for within their own balance sheets.

12. /F/ By definition.

13. /D/ The general fixed assets of a governmental entity are accounted for in the General Fixed Asset Account Group. This is an accounting device only. The outflows of resources used to acquire the assets are recorded as expenditures in the appropriate funds from which payments are made.

14. /J/ Infrastructure fixed assets are the basic installations of a community, such as roads, communication systems, etc. Reporting of such items was optional prior to GASB 34. Governments (other than those smaller than $10 million in revenues) that did not previously capitalize infrastructure assets are required to capitalize them retroactively for major infrastructure acquired subsequent to fiscal years beginning after June 15, 1980.

15. /B/ An enterprise fund is a proprietary fund.

16. /G/ The general fund is used to account for all transactions that are not "special" or related to a particular activity (such as capital projects, debt service, etc.) of a governmental entity. One of its most significant revenue sources is taxation of property - both real and personal.

17. /A/ An agency fund is a fiduciary fund. That is, its purpose is to act as a custodian for other funds.

18. /D/ The general long-term debt that is secured by the "full faith and credit" of the governmental entity is known as general obligation debt. It is accounted for in the General Long-term Debt Account group. As with the General Fixed Asset Account Group, this is a self-balancing accounting device.

19. /I/ A special revenue fund is used to account for the proceeds of specific revenue sources that are legally restricted to expenditures for particular, designated purposes.

20. /H/ Payments of principal and interest related to general obligation long-term debt are accounted for in the debt-service fund.

**Number 3 Answer**

1.  /N/  The answer is No to this question for two reasons. (1) Recording the budgetary accounts at the beginning of 20x4 would have increased the <u>budgetary</u> fund balance, not the actual fund balance. (2) The amount by which the budgetary fund balance would increase would be $400,000.

2.  /Y/  Anticipated transfers included in the budget should be included in the opening budgetary entry. It would be identified as an estimated other financing use, interfund transfer.

3.  /Y/  The $700,000 payment to establish the water utility fund is a type of interfund transfer out.

4.  /N/  The information states that any premium on issuance of bonds is to be used for the repayment of the bonds. This means that the debt service fund, not the general fund, received the premium from the capital projects fund.

5.  /N/  Payment by the general fund for water received for normal civic operations is recorded as an expenditure in the general fund. It is not an other financing use.

6.  /N/  As in Item 1 above, the account named used to refer to the fund balance does not include the word <u>budgetary</u>. Therefore, again there are two issues in this question. (1) Closing budgetary accounts does not affect the actual fund balance, and (2) the closing budget entry would include a debit to budgetary fund balance for $400,000, not a credit.

7.  /N/  There is no interaction between the budgetary and actual amounts. The only entries that affect the fund balance are the actual amounts.

8.  /Y/  When expenditures are incurred for the construction of the new civic center in the capital projects fund, a simultaneous entry is made in the general fixed asset account group in the amount of the expenditure. This entry debits the account "Construction in Progress" and credits "Investment in General Fixed Assets - Capital Projects Fund." This credit identifies the fund where resources were used for the acquisition of the asset.

9.  /Y/  A portion of the credit balances in the general fixed asset account group may be described as accumulated depreciation. This practice is optional. Note that the question uses only the word <u>depreciation</u>, it does not include <u>accumulated</u>. For this reason, the question could, arguably, be answered NO. However, the CPA exam uses both the terms accumulated depreciation and depreciation in questions on this topic.

10. /N/  The assets of the water utility fund will be recorded directly in that enterprise fund. They will be capitalized and depreciated in that fund. Only the assets acquired using governmental funds' resources are recorded in the general fixed asset account group.

11. /Y/  Bel's combined statement of revenues, expenditures, and changes in fund balances is presented for governmental funds. Since the capital project fund is a governmental fund, it would be included in the statement.

12. /Y/  Bel's combined balance sheet should be presented for all fund types and account groups.

13. /N/  The debt service fund is a governmental fund. Governmental funds are not included in the statement of cash flows.

14. /N/  The capital project fund is a governmental fund. Governmental funds are not included in the statement of cash flows.

**15.** /Y/ The cash flows statement should include all proprietary fund types and all non-expendable fund types. Since the water utility is an enterprise (i.e. proprietary) fund, its capital and related financing activities will be presented in the statement of cash flows.

**16.** $5,600,000. The amount recorded for appropriations should be equal to the budgeted expenditures.

**17.** $4,750,000. Property taxes receivable are recorded at gross. Thus, the account would have been debited for the sum of the actual tax revenue of $4,700,000 and the $50,000 allowance for uncollectible taxes.

**18.** $1,200,000. The face amount of debt, i.e. the amount that has to be repaid, is recorded in the general long-term debt account group. The premium of $30,000 is not included.

**19.** $1,080,000. The amount recorded in the general fixed asset account group for the construction to date of the civic center must be equal to the expenditures of the period. The expenditures are identified in the closing entry as $1.08 million.

**20.** $2,473,000. The completed cost is equal to the sum of the resources accumulated in the capital projects fund for purposes of building the civic center less the remaining equity transferred to the general fund upon completion of the project. $800,000 grant + $1,200,000 face amount of bonds + $500,000 interfund transfer - $27,000 residual equity.

**21.** $800,000. The state grant would be recorded as revenues in the capital project fund. Since the only revenue source identified is the grant, and the total revenue in the closing entry is $800,000, the grant must have been $800,000.

**22.** $2,422,000. Total encumbrances are equal to expenditures recorded, plus the $42,000 of encumbrances that exceeded expenditures, and the open encumbrance at year-end of $1,300,000.

**23.** $120,000. The unreserved fund balance as shown in the closing entry must be adjusted to reserve $1,300,000 for the outstanding encumbrances at year end that are not going to be cancelled. This will leave only $120,000 as unreserved fund balance.

## Task Number 4 Answer

**1.** $104,500. The only 20x4 general fund interfund transfer out was $104,500 to the debt service fund for repayment of bond debt and the interest due during the period.

**2.** $17,000. This question requires careful reading. The portion of the liability for compensated absences that will be recorded in the general fund for the fund financial statements will be the amount that is due to be paid out of currently available resources; namely, the $17,000 settlements. The balance of $69,000 will be recorded as long-term debt only in the government-wide financial statements.

**3.** $125,000. Two reserves need to be placed on the general fund balance. The first is for $83,000 relating to open encumbrances at 12/31/x4. The second in the amount of $42,000 is for the material amount of inventory balance at the end of the year.

**4.** $236,000. The capital projects fund balance is the difference between the bond proceeds of $600,000 received into the fund and the $364,000 of expenditures recorded during the period.

5.  $6,000. The special revenue fund balance is the difference between resource inflows of $109,000 and expenditures during the period. Recall that asset acquisitions are not capitalized in governmental funds. Therefore, since the special revenue is a governmental fund, both the $81,000 paid for general promotion and the $22,000 paid for the motor vehicle, were expenditures of the fund during the period. $109,000 - ($81,000 + $22,000) = $6,000.

6.  $104,500. Payments of both principal and interest are recorded as expenditures in the debt service fund. $100,000 principal + $4,500 interest = $104,500.

7.  $386,000. Assets acquired by governmental funds are recorded as increases in the general fixed asset account group. Two assets were acquired: construction in progress of $364,000 relating to the capital projects fund and $22,000 relating to the motor vehicle purchased with special revenue funds. Note that it would not be correct to include any amounts relating to the citizens' center. That asset was acquired in a prior period when the bonds were issued. It was not an acquisition during 20x4.

8.  $100,000. Payments relating to general obligation debt principal decrease the liabilities recorded in the general long-term debt account group. The only such payment during 20x4 was the $100,000 repayment of the 9%, 15-year bonds.

9.  $181,000. Expenditures for purchases during the period are equal to the amounts credited to vouchers payable during the year -- $181,000. Remember that amounts actually expended are equal to the actual acquisition cost incurred when the purchases are received and the related liability recorded. Unfilled purchase orders are not expenditures.

10. $190,000. Avoid the temptation to do some fancy computations involving open encumbrances at the beginning and end of the period. Encumbrances open at the beginning of the year do not become current year encumbrances. The actual total amount encumbered during 20x4 was $190,000.

## Task Number 5 Answer

1.  $1,000,000. When the budget was recorded, budgetary fund balance would have been credited for the difference between the debit to Estimated Revenues for $10,000,000 and the credit to Appropriations for $9,000,000.

2.  $9,350,000. Property taxes collected in this instance is the difference between the tax levy of $9,500,000 and the balance classified as delinquent as of the end of the year, $150,000. Note that had any receivables been written off during the period, that also would have been deducted from the gross amount levied.

3.  $0. Total expenditures of $2,100,000 in the capital projects fund was equal to the total resources received into the fund. Therefore, there was no balance remaining in the fund as of December 31, 20x6.

4.  $2,100,000. In the general fixed asset account group, an amount equal to the construction costs expended to date on the new library wing would have been recorded. This amounted to $2,100,000.

5.  $2,000,000. The outstanding balance relating to the face amount of the bonds would be included in the general long-term debt account group at the end of 20x6. They were issued at face value of $2,000,000, and no principal payment was made on them during the year.

# CHAPTER 12

## ACCOUNTING FOR NOT-FOR-PROFIT ORGANIZATIONS

### Question Map

IV.  COLLEGES AND UNIVERSITIES – 12, 13
  A. Tuition Revenue – 10, 11
  B. Grant Revenue

V.   HEALTH CARE ORGANIZATIONS -- See Task Problem Number 1
  A. Basic Financial Statements
  B. Liquidity Information on the Balance Sheet
  C. Net Assets or Equity or Fund Balance – 15, 19
  D. Statement of Cash Flows
  E. Statement of Operations -- 23
  F. Health Care Service Revenues and Receivables – 14, 16, 17
  G. Other Revenues, Gains, or Losses -- 18

# CHAPTER 12

## ACCOUNTING FOR NOT-FOR-PROFIT ORGANIZATIONS

### Multiple Choice Questions

**1.** Securities donated to a voluntary health and welfare organization should be recorded at the
    **a.** Donor's recorded amount.
    **b.** Fair market value at the date of the gift.
    **c.** Fair market value at the date of the gift, or the donor's recorded amount, whichever is lower.
    **d.** Fair market value at the date of the gift, or the donor's recorded amount, whichever is higher.

**2.** The League, a not-for-profit organization, received the following pledges:

| | |
|---|---|
| Unrestricted | $200,000 |
| Restricted for capital additions | 150,000 |

All pledges are legally enforceable; however, the League's experience indicates that 10% of all pledges are not collectible. What amount should the League report as pledges receivable net of any required allowance account?
    **a.** $135,000
    **b.** $180,000
    **c.** $315,000
    **d.** $350,000

**3.** Lea Meditators is a not-for-profit religious organization. A storm broke glass windows in Lea's building. A member of Lea's congregation, a professional glazier, replaced the windows at no charge. In Lea's statement of activities, the breakage and replacement of the windows should
    **a.** Not be reported.
    **b.** Be reported by note disclosure only.
    **c.** Be reported as an increase in both expenses and contributions.
    **d.** Be reported as an increase in both net assets and contributions.

**4.** Financial statements of not-for-profit organizations focus on
    **a.** Basic information for the organization as a whole.
    **b.** Standardization of funds nomenclature.
    **c.** Inherent differences of not-for-profit organizations that impact reporting presentations.
    **d.** Distinctions between current fund and non-current fund presentation.

**5.** In a statement of activities of the People's Environmental Protection Association, a voluntary community organization, depreciation expense should
    **a.** Not be included.
    **b.** Be included as an element of support.
    **c.** Be included as an element of other changes in fund balances.
    **d.** Be included as an element of expense.

**6.** United Together, a labor union, had the following expenses for the year ended December 31:

| | |
|---|---|
| Labor negotiations | $500,000 |
| Fund-raising | 100,000 |
| Membership development | 50,000 |
| Administrative and general | 200,000 |

In United Together's statement of activity for the year ended December 31, what amount should be reported under the classification of program services?
    **a.** $850,000
    **b.** $600,000
    **c.** $550,000
    **d.** $500,000

7. Cancer Educators, a not-for-profit organization, incurred costs of $10,000 when it combined program functions with fund raising functions. Which of the following cost allocations might Cancer report in its statement of activities?

|   | Program Services | Fund Raising | General Services |
|---|---|---|---|
| a. | $0 | $0 | $10,000 |
| b. | $0 | $6,000 | $4,000 |
| c. | $6,000 | $4,000 | $0 |
| d. | $10,000 | $0 | $0 |

8. When a nonprofit organization combines fund-raising efforts with educational materials or program services, the total combined costs incurred are
   a. Reported as program services expenses.
   b. Allocated between fund-raising and program services expenses using an appropriate allocation basis.
   c. Reported as fund-raising costs.
   d. Reported as management and general expenses.

9. The following expenditures were made by Green Services, a society for the protection of the environment:

| | |
|---|---|
| Printing the annual report | $12,000 |
| Unsolicited merchandise sent to encourage contributions | 25,000 |
| Cost of audit performed by CPA firm | 3,000 |

What amount should be classified as fund-raising costs in the society's activity statement?
   a. $37,000
   b. $28,000
   c. $25,000
   d. $0

10. For the summer session of the year Ariba University assessed its students $1,700,000 (net of refunds), covering tuition and fees for educational and general purposes. However, only $1,500,000 was expected to be realized because scholarships totaling $150,000 were granted to students, and tuition remissions of $50,000 were allowed to faculty members' children attending Ariba. What amount should Ariba report as revenues from student tuition and fees?
   a. $1,500,000
   b. $1,550,000
   c. $1,650,000
   d. $1,700,000

11. Tuition waivers for which there is no intention of collection from the student should be classified by a not-for-profit university as

|   | Revenue | Expense |
|---|---|---|
| a. | No | No |
| b. | No | Yes |
| c. | Yes | Yes |
| d. | Yes | No |

12. Community College had the following encumbrances at December 31, 20x1:

| | |
|---|---|
| Outstanding purchase orders | $12,000 |
| Commitments for services not received | 50,000 |

What amount should be reported as liabilities in Community's balance sheet at December 31, 20x1?
   a. $62,000
   b. $50,000
   c. $12,000
   d. $0

13. Is the recognition of depreciation expense required for public colleges' fund financial statements and private not-for-profit colleges?

|   | Public | Private |
|---|---|---|
| a. | No | Yes |
| b. | No | No |
| c. | Yes | Yes |
| d. | Yes | No |

**14.** Valley's community hospital normally includes proceeds from sale of cafeteria meals in
   a. Deductions from dietary service expenses.
   b. Ancillary service revenues.
   c. Patient service revenues.
   d. Other revenues.

**15.** Ross Hospital's accounting records disclosed the following information:

| | |
|---|---|
| Net resources invested in plant assets | $10,000,000 |
| Board-designated funds | 2,000,000 |

What amount should be included as part of unrestricted net assets?
   a. $12,000,000
   b. $10,000,000
   c. $ 2,000,000
   d. $0

**16.** Palma Hospital's patient service revenues for services provided during the year, at established rates, amounted to $8,000,000 on the accrual basis. For internal reporting, Palma uses the discharge method. Under this method, patient service revenues are recognized only when patients are discharged, with no recognition given to revenues accruing for services to patients not yet discharged. Patient service revenues at established rates using the discharge method amounted to $7,000,000 for the year. According to generally accepted accounting principles, Palma should report patient service revenues for the year of
   a. Either $8,000,000 or $7,000,000, at the option of the hospital.
   b. $8,000,000
   c. $7,500,000
   d. $7,000,000

**17.** Under Cura Hospital's established rate structure, patient service revenues of $9,000,000 would have been earned for the year ended December 31. However, only $6,750,000 was collected because of charity allowances of $1,500,000 and discounts of $750,000 to third-party payors. For the year ended December 31, what amount should Cura record as patient service revenues?
   a. $6,750,000
   b. $7,500,000
   c. $8,250,000
   d. $9,000,000

**18.** Which of the following normally would be included in other operating revenues of a hospital?

| | Revenues from educational programs | Unrestricted gifts |
|---|---|---|
| a. | No | No |
| b. | No | Yes |
| c. | Yes | No |
| d. | Yes | Yes |

**19.** In hospital accounting, restricted net assets are
   a. Not available unless the board of directors remove the restrictions.
   b. Restricted as to use only for board-designated purposes.
   c. Not available for current operating use; however, the income generated by the funds is available for current operating use.
   d. Restricted as to use by the donor, grantor, or other source of the resources.

**20.** The Pel Museum is a not-for-profit organization. If Pel received a contribution of historical artifacts, it need not recognize the contribution if the artifacts are to be sold and the proceeds used to
   **a.** Support general museum activities.
   **b.** Acquire other items for collections.
   **c.** Repair existing collections.
   **d.** Purchase buildings to house collections.

**21.** The Jones family lost its home in a fire. On December 25, 20x4, a philanthropist sent money to the Amer Benevolent Society to purchase furniture for the Jones family. During January 20x5, Amer purchased this furniture for the Jones family. Amer is a not-for-profit organization. How should Amer report the receipt of the money in its 20x4 financial statements?
   **a.** As an unrestricted contribution.
   **b.** As a temporarily restricted contribution.
   **c.** As a permanently restricted contribution.
   **d.** As a liability.

**22.** On December 30, 20x4, Leigh Museum, a not-for-profit organization, received a $7,000,000 donation of Day Co. shares with donor stipulated requirements as follows:

- Shares valued at $5,000,000 are to be sold with the proceeds used to erect a public viewing building.
- Shares valued at $2,000,000 are to be retained with the dividends used to support current operations.

As a consequence of the receipt of the Day shares, how much should Leigh report as temporarily restricted net assets on its 20x4 statement of financial position?
   **a.** $0
   **b.** $2,000,000
   **c.** $5,000,000
   **d.** $7,000,000

**23.** In April 20x5, Delta Hospital purchased medicines from Field Pharmaceutical Co. at a cost of $5,000. However, Field notified Delta that the invoice was being canceled and that the medicines were being donated to Delta. Delta should record this donation of medicines as
   **a.** A memorandum entry only.
   **b.** A $5,000 credit to non-operating expenses.
   **c.** A $5,000 credit to operating expenses.
   **d.** Other operating revenue of $5,000.

# CHAPTER 12

## ACCOUNTING FOR
## NOT-FOR-PROFIT ORGANIZATIONS

### Simulation Task Questions

**Task Question 1**   (Est. time – 5 to 10 min.)

**Question Number 1** consists of 6 items. Select the best answer for each item.

Alpha Hospital, a large not-for-profit organization, has adopted an accounting policy that does not imply a time restriction on gifts of long-lived assets.

**Required:**

For **Items 1 through 6,** indicate the manner in which the transaction affects Alpha's financial statements.

**A** Increase in unrestricted revenues, gains, and other support.
**B** Decrease in an expense.
**C** Increase in temporarily restricted net assets.
**D** Increase in permanently restricted net assets.
**E** No required reportable event.

1. Alpha's board designates $1,000,000 to purchase investments whose income will be used for capital improvements.

2. Income from investments in Item 1 above, which was not previously accrued, is received.

3. A benefactor provided funds for building expansion.

4. The funds in Item 3 above are used to purchase a building in the fiscal period following the period the funds were received.

5. An accounting firm prepared Alpha's annual financial statements without charge to Alpha.

6. Alpha received investments subject to the donor's requirement that investment income be used to pay for outpatient services.

## Task Question 2

**Question Number 2** consists of 3 parts concerning non-governmental not-for-profit organizations. Part **A** consists of 4 items, Part **B** consists of 7 items, and Part **C** consists of 8 items. Select the **best** answer for each item.

### Part A. Items 1 through 4 are based on the following:

Community Service is a non-governmental not-for-profit voluntary health and welfare calendar-year organization that began operations on January 1, 20x6. It performs voluntary services and derives its revenue primarily from voluntary contributions from the general public. Community implies a time restriction on all promises to contribute cash in future periods. However, no such policy exists with respect to gifts of long-lived assets.

Selected transactions that occurred during Community's 20x7 calendar year are as follows:

- Unrestricted written promises to contribute cash -- 20x6 and 20x7

| | |
|---|---|
| 20x6 promises (collected in 20x7) | $22,000 |
| 20x7 promises (collected in 20x7) | 95,000 |
| 20x7 promises (uncollected) | 28,000 |

- Written promises to contribute cash restricted to use for community college scholarships -- 20x6 and 20x7

| | |
|---|---|
| 20x6 promises (collected and expended in 20x7) | $10,000 |
| 20x7 promises (collected and expended in 20x7) | 20,000 |
| 20x7 promises (uncollected) | 12,000 |

- Written promise to contribute $25,000 if matching funds are raised for the capital campaign during 20x7

| | |
|---|---|
| Cash received in 20x7 from contributor as good-faith advance | $25,000 |
| Matching funds received in 20x7 | -0- |

- Cash received in 20x6 with donor's only stipulation that a bus be purchased.

| | |
|---|---|
| Expenditure of full amount of donation 7/1/x7 | $37,000 |

**Required: Items 1 through 4** represent 20x7 amounts that Community reported for selected financial statement elements in its December 31, 20x7, statement of financial position and 20x7 statement of activities.

For each item, indicate whether the amount was overstated (O), understated (U), or correctly stated (C).

1. Community reported $28,000 as contributions receivable.

2. Community reported $37,000 as net assets released from restrictions (satisfaction of use restrictions).

3. Community reported $22,000 as net assets released from restrictions (due to the lapse of time restrictions).

4. Community reported $97,000 as contributions -- temporarily restricted.

**Part B.** **Items 5 through 11** are based on the following additional selected transactions that occurred during Community's 20x7 calendar year:

- Debt security endowment received in 20x7; income to be used for community services

| | |
|---|---:|
| Face value | $90,000 |
| Fair value at time of receipt | 88,000 |
| Fair value at 12/31/x7 | 87,000 |
| Interest earned in 20x7 | 9,000 |

- 10 concerned citizens volunteered to serve meals to the homeless (400 hours free; fair market value of services $5 per hour) $2,000

- Short-term investment in equity securities in 20x7

| | |
|---|---:|
| Cost | $10,000 |
| Fair value 12/31/x7 | 12,000 |
| Dividend income | 1,000 |

- Music festival to raise funds for a local hospital

| | |
|---|---:|
| Admission fees | $5,000 |
| Sales of food and drinks | 14,000 |
| Expenses | 4,000 |

- Reading materials donated to Community and distributed to the children in 20x7

| | |
|---|---:|
| Fair market value | $8,000 |

- Federal youth training fee for service grant

| | |
|---|---:|
| Cash received during 20x7 | $30,000 |
| Instructor salaries paid | 26,000 |

- Other cash operating expenses

| | |
|---|---:|
| Business manager salary | $60,000 |
| General bookkeeper salary | 40,000 |
| Director of community activities salary | 50,000 |
| Space rental (75% for community activities; 25% for office activities) | 20,000 |
| Printing and mailing costs for pledge cards | 2,000 |

- Interest payment on short-term bank loan in 20x7 $1,000

- Principal payment on short-term bank loan in 20x7 $20,000

**Required:** **For Items 5 through 11,** determine the amounts for the following financial statement elements in the 20x7 statement of activities. Select your answer from the following list of amounts. An amount may be selected once, more than once, or not at all.

| | | |
|---|---|---|
| A. $0 | F. $ 9,000 | K. $87,000 |
| B. $2,000 | G. $14,000 | L. $88,000 |
| C. $3,000 | H. $16,000 | M. $90,000 |
| D. $5,000 | I. $26,000 | N. $94,000 |
| E. $8,000 | J. $50,000 | O. $99,000 |

5. Contributions -- permanently restricted.

6. Revenues -- fees.

7. Investment income -- debt securities.

8. Program expenses.

9. General fund-raising expenses (excludes special events.)

10. Income on long-term investments -- unrestricted.

11. Contributed voluntary services.

**Part C. Items 12 through 19** are based on the fact pattern and financial information found in **both Part A and Part B.**

**Required: Items 12 through 19** represent Community's transactions reportable in the statement of cash flows. For each item listed, select the classification that best describes that item. A classification may be selected once, more than once, or not at all.

     O  Cash flows from operating activities.
     I  Cash flows from investing activities.
     F  Cash flows from financing activities.

**12.** Unrestricted 20x6 promises collected.

**13.** Cash received from a contributor as a good faith advance on a promise to contribute matching funds.

**14.** Purchase of bus.

**15.** Principal payment on short-term bank loan.

**16.** Purchase of equity securities.

**17.** Dividend income earned on equity securities.

**18.** Interest payment on short-term bank loan.

**19.** Interest earned on endowment.

# CHAPTER 12

## ACCOUNTING FOR
## NOT-FOR-PROFIT ORGANIZATIONS

### Multiple Choice Answers

1. /b/ The rule applied when donated assets are received is to record them at fair market value as of the date of gift.

2. /c/ Pledges receivable are recognized as the amount expected to be realized:

| | |
|---|---|
| Unrestricted Pledges Receivable | $200,000 |
| Estimated uncollectible | (20,000) |
| Restricted Pledges Receivable | $150,000 |
| Estimated uncollectible | (15,000) |
| Total | $315,000 |

3. /c/ Contribution of services is limited to those professional services (see narrative) that would normally have had to be contracted for. When appropriate to record them, both an inflow (contribution) and outflow (expense) are recognized in equal amounts.

4. /a/ The terminology "basic information" is extracted directly from the language of FASB Statements.

5. /d/ NFPs that are voluntary community organizations must follow GAAP as defined by the FASB unless specifically exempted. Accrual accounting procedures, including recognition of depreciation expense, are used.

6. /d/ Program services are those functions which fulfill the purpose for the organization's existence. Supporting services are those expenses which are managerial or administrative in nature. Supporting services also include fund-raising expenses. "Membership development" is a term for that support purpose.

7. /c/ The question explicitly states that costs were combined for program functions with fund raising functions. Because "general services" does not fall within either of these categories, none of the cost could be allocated to that function. Thus, only C and D are possible answers. Between those 2 answers, Answer C is the only one which shows some of the cost allocated to both program functions and fund raising. If a cost is incurred for more than one function, then it must be allocated to those functions.

8. /b/ When fund raising efforts are combined with educational materials or with program services, the combined cost must be allocated among fund raising and any program functional services involved.

9. /c/ Fund raising costs include such items as advertising, mailing lists, printing, wages, and costs of unsolicited merchandise sent to encourage contributions. The costs of printing the annual report and the CPA audit fee are management and general services costs.

10. /d/ Financial statements should show relevant information, including, for a college or university, the extent to which scholarships are granted, or tuition remitted for faculty and staff. Therefore, tuition and fees for educational and general purposes should be shown at gross. In this problem the gross amount (and the answer) is $1,700,000.

    The amount of student aid (scholarships and fee remissions) are then shown as expenses. The problem does not ask, but the expenses would total $200,000, consisting of $150,000 in scholarships and $50,000 in fee remissions.

**11.** /c/ Colleges wish to show the volume of services actually rendered. By recording the tuition as if it were to be received, together with an appropriate expense, the service is recorded, but the net amount is not otherwise affected.

**12.** /d/ The fact pattern indicates that Community College uses encumbrance accounting. (See the governmental chapter for more details.) Since the items described represent goods and services that have not yet been received, they are outstanding encumbrances. Outstanding encumbrances are not outstanding liabilities or expenses for the period. Liabilities are incurred when goods or services are received.

**13.** /a/ Because government-owned colleges are required to record the full cost of capital assets as expenditures when they are acquired on the fund financial statements, depreciation expense is not recognized. Private not-for-profit colleges, however, capitalize assets and recognize depreciation expense as part of normal accrual accounting procedures. (Note that government-owned colleges must also recognize depreciation in the government-wide financial statements.)

**14.** /d/ There are three classifications of revenues recorded by hospitals: patient service revenues, other operating revenues, and nonoperating revenues/gains and expenses/losses. Other operating revenues properly include nonprofessional revenues such as the sale of cafeteria meals identified in this question. Patient service revenues are inflows from the professional services supplied to or on behalf of patients. There is no such classification as "ancillary service revenues." Option (a) is an inappropriate accounting procedure.

**15.** /a/ The balance sheet for the unrestricted net assets of a health care organization reflect both current and noncurrent assets and liabilities, including property, plant, and equipment in active service. Although board-designated funds may appear to be restricted, they are classified as unrestricted.

**16.** /b/ Hospitals recognize revenues on an accrual basis. Patient service revenues are those related to the hospital functions: nursing, bed fees, laboratory, pharmacy, and x-ray fees. To comply with GAAP, hospitals recognize patient service revenues in the gross amount billed, whether or not this amount will be collected or collectible (except for charity services). In this problem, that amount is given to be $8,000,000. The hospital may use other accounting methods internally, but these are not acceptable for external reporting purposes.

**17.** /b/ Patient service revenues are booked (recorded) in the gross amount that would be billed except for amounts expected to be uncollectible because of charity care. Amounts not expected to be collected are carried in allowance accounts. These include courtesy discounts to health care professionals and third-party payer adjustments. When reported on the statement of revenues and expenses, provision accounts are subtracted, and only net patient service revenues are reported. Note that uncollectible accounts (i.e. bad debts) are classified among the functional expenses.

**18.** /c/ There are three classes of revenues for health care organizations. Patient service revenues include earnings resulting from providing health care services to patients. Other operating revenues are earnings from activities in which the hospital regularly engages that are not related to patient care. Nonoperating revenues include earnings from unrestricted gifts and bequests, from investment earnings, and other activities.

**19.** /d/ To be referred to as restricted net assets, the limitation, either as to purpose for which the resources may be used, or the time as to when the resource may be used, must be specified by an outside party. This is usually the donor (the grantor). If the Board of Directors specifies or designates a purpose for which or a time when resources must be used, the resources are classified as "unrestricted."

**20.** /b/ Collection items contributed that are historical treasure do not need to be recognized if they are sold and the proceeds used to acquire other collectable items.

**21.** /b/ Because there is a donor-imposed restriction that the money be used for a particular purpose, the receipt of the money should be recorded as temporarily restricted. When the money is used to purchase the furniture, the money will be transferred from temporarily restricted to unrestricted ("net assets released from restrictions").

The preceding answer assumes that the receipt and transfer of funds is part of Amer's operating activities. If Amer is acting merely as an agent, then the receipt of funds would be treated as a liability (answer D).

**22.** /c/ The group of shares valued at $2,000,000 are permanently restricted as only income relating to them may be used. The $5,000,000 amount is temporarily restricted as of the date of the statement of financial position. If the shares had been sold and the monies spent in 20x4, the contribution could have been recorded as unrestricted net assets since it would have been used in the same year as receipt (depending on the accounting policy adopted by the organization).

**23.** /d/ Donated medicines will eventually be expensed as part of operations. Thus, the donation is classified as operating revenue. An unrestricted donation would be classified as nonoperating.

# CHAPTER 12

## ACCOUNTING FOR
## NOT-FOR-PROFIT ORGANIZATIONS

### Task Answers

### Task Number 1 Answer

1.  /E/ This is not a recordable event. No journal entry is made to change the status of the funds from undesignated to designated within the accounting system. Note also that all board-designated funds are accounted for in the general (i.e. unrestricted) fund. Restrictions are placed on net assets only as a result of externally imposed (i.e. donor imposed) directives. (It is possible to argue that the financial statements would show, as a reporting distinction, a portion of the general funds net assets designated for specific use by the board; however, since all of the answers A through D are clearly incorrect, Option E is the best selection for the reasons presented above.)

2.  /A/ Since the board-designated funds remain in the unrestricted general fund, earnings on those funds are recorded as an increase in unrestricted revenues, even though the funds will be used for a particular purpose. Again, the essential difference is that the restriction is not externally imposed by a donor.

3.  /C/ Here the funds are restricted by the donor to be used for a particular purpose. When the funds are received, the recording entry will show recognition of support in the form of temporarily restricted net assets.

4.  /A/ When temporarily restricted funds are used for the purpose specified by the donor, they are released from restriction. The two entries that would be made to reflect this would record a decrease in temporarily restricted net assets with a corresponding increase in unrestricted net assets.

5.  /A/ When contributed services are provided that require special skills, are provided by those possessing such skills, and which would probably have to be purchased if not donated (clearly the case here), the services are recognized as contribution revenue and expense in equal amounts.

6.  /D/ Here the donor has stipulated that only the income from investments may be spent, not the principal (i.e. the investments) being donated. As a result, the investments themselves must be kept permanently restricted. Income will be recorded as temporarily restricted support as it is earned.

**Task Number 2 Answer.**

1.  /U/ Contributions receivable are any 20x7 promises to give not yet collected. Of the items listed in the Part A fact pattern, the only 20x7 uncollected promises to give were the $28,000 in the unrestricted category and the $12,000 restricted for community college scholarships. These total $40,000. Since Community reported $28,000, the contributions receivable was understated.

2.  /U/ Net assets that are categorized as temporarily restricted as to use are released from restriction on the statement of activities in the period in which they are expended for the purpose the donor intended. During 20x7, the items in the fact pattern to which this applies are as follows:

    -   Contributions restricted for use for community college scholarships:

        | | |
        |---|---|
        | 20x6 promises collected and expended in 20x7 | $10,000 |
        | 20x7 promises collected and expended in 20x7 | 20,000 |

    -   Contribution restricted for purchase of bus:

        | | |
        |---|---|
        | Full amount of 20x6 donation expended in 20x7 | 37,000 |
        | Total net assets released from use restriction in 20x7 | $67,000 |

        Since Community reported $37,000, this was an underreported amount.

3.  /C/ Net assets released from time restrictions would be any contributions that become available for use during 20x7 on which a time restriction had been placed previously been placed. In this fact pattern, time restrictions are implied on any unrestricted cash contributions where collection will occur in a future period. The only contribution that meets that criterion is the $22,000 unrestricted cash contribution made in 20x6 and collected in 20x7. The $22,000 would be released from time restriction upon receipt in 20x7. Community reported this amount correctly.

4.  /O/ Community's 20x7 statement of activities would report all contributions promised during 20x7 according to their being unrestricted, temporarily or permanently restricted. The following items from the fact pattern for Part A would be reported on the statement as 20x7 contributions temporarily restricted either as to time or to use:

    | | |
    |---|---|
    | Unrestricted written promise to contribute cash. Promise made in 20x7. Cash to be collected in future period. Time restriction implied according to Community policy. | $28,000 |

    20x7 written promises to contribute cash to be used for community college scholarships:

    | | |
    |---|---|
    | 1. Contribution collected and expended in 20x7 -- categorized as use restricted when contribution promised | 20,000 |
    | 2. Contribution promised in 20x7, to be received in the future. Categorized as use restricted when contribution promised | 12,000 |
    | Total temporarily restricted 20x7 contributions | $60,000 |

Since the correct reportable amount of contributions temporarily restricted is $60,000, the $97,000 was an overstatement.

Note the following points about items not included in the above determination:

1. The $95,000 of unrestricted 20x7 cash promises had no time restriction placed on them because they were received in the same period in which they were promised.

2. The $25,000 cash received in good faith for the matching funds contribution is a CONDITIONAL contribution. As such, it cannot be recorded as a contribution until such time as the donor-imposed condition is met. Since the condition was not met, this contribution does not qualify as a reportable donation. Notice also that the funds were designated for use in the 20x7 capital campaign during 20x7. Since no matching funds were received during 20x7, it is likely that the conditional donation would have to be returned to the donor.

3. Finally, it is important that you understand that contributions are reported as "revenue from contributions" on the statement of activities for the period in which the contribution is promised -- regardless of when the related funds are actually received or expended. Thus, the $37,000 for the bus was NOT included as a temporarily restricted contribution for 20x7 in Item 4 above because that was a 20x6 contribution. It would, therefore, have been included as a temporarily restricted net asset contribution on the 20x6 statement of activities.

That is also the case for the $22,000 20x6 unrestricted cash contribution collected in 20x7, as well as the $10,000 20x6 restricted use (community college scholarships) cash contribution collected in 20x7.

5. /L/ The debt security endowment was the only permanently restricted 20x7 contribution. The contribution is valued at its fair market value on the date of receipt -- in this case, $88,000.

6. /D/ The only revenues properly categorized as fees are the $5,000 of admission fees relating to the music festival. The federal youth training fee is a grant contribution, in spite of the term "fee" used in its description.

7. /E/ The investment income from debt securities is the $9,000 interest earned LESS the $1,000 reduction in fair value between time of receipt of the instrument and the end of the year. Note that this amount would be reported on the 20x7 statement of activities as temporarily restricted as to use.

8. /O/ Program expenses are those expenses that were made with respect to the program activities of the organization. They do not include any general and administrative or fund-raising expenses. The total of $99,000 is made up of the following items:

Fair market value of donated
books distributed to children   $8,000

Salary paid to instructors in
federal youth training
program                         26,000

Salary paid to director of
community services              50,000

75% of rental space cost allocated to community activities                    15,000

9. /B/ The only fund-raising expenses identified in the fact pattern are the $2,000 for pledge cards and the $4,000 relating to the music festival. Since the question specifically excludes special events, only the $2,000 applies.

10. /A/ The income on long-term investments is temporarily restricted for use for community services. None of it, therefore, is unrestricted.

11. /A/ Although there were indeed contributed services, they do not satisfy the criteria necessary for recognition as contributed support. They were not provided by professionals in the area of service designated, they were simply provided by a group of "concerned citizens." Furthermore, the services do not appear to be of a professional nature such that they would have been required to be purchased from qualified professionals in the absence of their being donated.

12. /O/ NFP organizations follow the provisions of ASC Topic 230 when compiling the Statement of Cash Flows. Unrestricted promises collected are classified as operating cash flows.

13. /O/ Although the good faith advance is a conditional contribution and will likely have to be returned because no matching funds were received during the period, the cash flow from receipt of the advance must be acknowledged in the statement of cash flows. It would be classified as an operating flow because its underlying nature relates to operations -- i.e. contributions.

14. /I/ The purchase of a bus is a cash flow relating to an investing activity.

15. /F/ Principal payment on a short-term bank loan is a financing outflow.

16. /I/ Purchase of equity securities is an investing cash outflow.

17. /O/ Dividend income is classified as an operating cash inflow.

18. /O/ Note that interest payments are classified as operating outflows, not financing outflows.

19. /O/ Interest earned is classified as an operating cash inflow, not an investing activity.